History of Pope Boniface VIII and His Times

STATUE OF BONIFACE VIII, IN THE CATHEDRAL, FLORENCE.

HISTORY

OF

POPE BONIFACE VIII

AND HIS TIMES

WITH

NOTES AND DOCUMENTARY EVIDENCE

IN SIX BOOKS

By
DON LOUIS TOSTI
BENEDICTINE MONK OF MONTE CASSINO

TRANSLATED FROM THE ITALIAN
BY RT. REV. MGR. EUGENE J. DONNELLY, V.F.
PASTOR OF ST. MICHAEL'S CHURCH, FLUSHING, L. I, N. Y.

"Entering Alagna, lo the fleur-de-lis,
And in his Vicar Christ a captive led!
I see him mocked a second time;—again
The vinegar and gall produced I see,
And Christ himself 'twixt robbers slain."
DANTE, Purgat., canto XX.

NEW YORK
CHRISTIAN PRESS ASSOCIATION
PUBLISHING COMPANY

CONTENTS.

	PAGE
DEDICATION.	
TRANSLATOR'S PREFACE	7
BOOK I	15
BOOK II	99
BOOK III	151
BOOK IV	216
BOOK V	266
BOOK VI	362

NOTES AND DOCUMENTS.

Brief of Pope Alexander IV in favor of Benedict Gaetani (*Extract from the archives of the church of Todi*)	455
Decree of the Canons of Todi in favor of Benedict Gaetani	455
Note relative to the duel between Peter of Aragon and Charles of Anjou against the insinuations of Potter	456
Note relative to the Master of the Court (*Dominus Curiae*) a title given to Benedict Gaetani by Ptolemy of Lucca	460
Concerning the abdication of Celestine V	463
Profession of faith of Benedict Gaetani before his elevation to the Papacy	465
Encyclical of Boniface with regard to his Pontificate	466
Letter of Boniface to Philip the Fair	469
Imprisonment and death of Peter Celestine	469
His renunciation of the Papacy	470
His return to his cell on Mt. Morone	471
The search after him	472
His flight across the sea	473
His capture and confinement in the castle of Fumone	474
His death and miracles thereat	476
Letter of Boniface to the Sicilians urging them to return to submission to the Church	476
Another letter to Frederick of Aragon to prevail upon him to leave Sicily	477
Letter of Boniface to the provincial of the Friars Minor with regard to the conversion of Guy of Montefeltro	479
Constitution on the Ecclesiastical immunities; the bull "*Clericis Laicos.*"	480
Letter of Boniface to Philip the Fair	481
Division of the fiefs among the Colonnas (*From the archives of Constable Colonna in Patrini, Mon. 19.*)	486

CONTENTS.

	PAGE
Act appointing James Colonna absolute administrator of the property of the Colonnas (*From the Barberini archives in Patrini Mon 21*)	489
Proceedings against the Colonnas	490
The Colonna libel against Boniface	493
Sentence of Boniface against the Colonnas	496
Brief of Boniface entrusting the direction of the war against the Colonnas to Landolph Colonna	500
Reply of Boniface to the Roman people	500
Two sermons of Boniface XIII, delivered at Orvieto, in presence of the Cardinals, on the occasion of the canonization of Louis IX, king of France	502
Arbitral decision of Boniface in the proceedings pending, between Edward of England and Philip the Fair	508
The evil counsel of Guy of Montefeltro	511
Bull instituting the Jubilee	521
Exclusion of the Sicilians and the Colonnas from the indulgence of the Jubilee	522
The offerings of the Jubilee	523
Letter of Boniface to Charles II reproving him for his impudence	527
Letter of Boniface to Cardinal Acquasparta charging him to pacify Florence	528
Letter to the French clergy relative to the appeal of Charles of Valois	528
Letter to Cardinal Acquasparta, Legate to restrain Charles of Valois	530
Letter of Boniface to Philip the Fair regarding the Archbishopric of Narbonne and the county of Maguelonne	531
Letter to Philip the Fair, annexed to the Bull, "*Ausculta*"	533
On the works of Egidius Colonna	535
Letter to the clergy of France, annexed to the Bull, "*Unam Sanctam,*"	536
An observation on the constitution "*Unam Sanctam,*" and on the book of Dante, De Monarchia	539
A letter to Albert, king of the Romans	540
Constitution of Boniface regarding his conflict with Philip the Fair	541
The piety of Boniface	542
Bull of Benedict XI, against the persecutors of Boniface	544
The infamous erasures in the register of the letter of Boniface	545

DEDICATION.

To thee, Dante Alighieri,
We consecrate these books,
Which recall to a new life
The memory of Boniface the Eighth.
The political sorrows which troubled thee,
Do not dare to profane thy noble heart;
And even when the anger of thy mind
Suggested the strangest conceptions
Thou remaindest an Italian.
So in the presence of Boniface
Whom thou considerest an enemy,
And whom thou loadest with eternal infamy
As is eternal the poetry thou madest,
Respectfully bow thy head;
And venerate the Vicar of Jesus Christ.
Bear to-day,
That to thy soul freed from anger
History may present herself
And speak to thee of a man
Whom thou wouldst raise to the heavens
If the destinies of thy Florence
Had been less tempestuous.
More on the strength of his virtue
Than on these pages,
He rises so high
As to place himself without blemish before thee.
He pardons thee.
And on the volume thou hast written,
A last refuge
Of Italian grandeur
Let them lie
Reconciled with him,
The sovereign keys
As a proof of this union
Which alone can render fruitful the hopes
Of mother country.

TRANSLATOR'S PREFACE.

A BACKWARD glance through the history of the Middle Ages may show us not a few majestic figures among the popes, but none so striking and remarkable as that of Boniface VIII. Surrounded by stern and simple times he appeals to us with peculiar directness because of the almost universal and lasting denunciation of historians, both of his own and later times. The history of the Church during these times is wholly a history of the struggle of the Papacy against the supremacy of the Imperial power. Some popes more than others are distinguished for the bold resistance they showed to this unjust assumption, and strove to maintain the rights of the Church, among whom are to be particularly mentioned Alexander III, Gregory VII, Innocent III, and Boniface VIII.

Pope Boniface VIII deserves to be called the last pope of the Middle Ages. It was during his Pontificate that the temporal power of the Holy See was, for the first time, attacked by France, and the prestige of the Papacy was subjected to the most violent outrages. He was a great medieval pope. His figure can be justly compared with that of Innocent III, or Gregory IX. Like them he solemnly affirmed the pontifical authority; like them he fought princes with a stubbornness which alone equalled the consciousness he had of his own rights. By his sumptuous ceremonies, by his striking and eloquent Bulls, he manifested to the world the grandeur and power of the Papacy. The Pontificate of Boniface VIII is the beginning of a transition period; it exhibits the sinking of the papal power and the rising of the secular state-idea hostile to the Church. The subordination of the secular under the spiritual order was denied. The See of Peter was shaken but not destroyed.

But he is the last pope of the Middle Ages, because in the

combat which he sustained against the enemies of his temporal power, he was, in the main, vanquished. He disappeared at the dawn of the fourteenth century, and as is well known this period marked the decline of the Middle Ages. The old Christian republic into which the European states had resolved themselves, had disappeared. Nationalities began to assume form; heresies succeeded in implanting themselves, in living, in prospering, for a time. After the sojourn of the Popes at Avignon, which was a kind of a gilded captivity, the Great Schism began to divide Christianity into two or even three parties who engaged in long and bitter struggles. The faithful were unable to distinguish who was the true pope; even the saints themselves were beguiled; Councils did nothing else but increase the evil of the situation, and on all sides men of courage were bewailing the misfortunes of the Church. At the same time frightful wars harassed the people and epidemics devastated the half of Europe. Boniface VIII had long been dead before these disasters appeared, but he preceded them immediately. His end so sad and gloomy after the outrage of Anagni seemed to forebode that evils without number would be visited on the Church; and it was no vain foreboding. This is the reason why we have said that he was the last pope truly medieval. His grand figure in the last days of the Middle Ages blazons forth, and his fall precipitates that of this stormy epoch.

One can easily understand how the history of such a pope has been the subject of many impassioned and biased works. French writers had studied the reasons which led to the differences between Boniface and Philip the Fair, and from the first, they are violently hostile to the Pope. One can be convinced of this by reading the work published by Dupuy in 1655. Other writers are milder and less bitter in tone, but they make no effort to conceal their bias.

The chief reproaches that are brought against Boniface VIII relate to the abdication of Celestine V; his own election to the Papacy; the imprisonment of Celestine V; the quarrel that arose between him and the Colonna family, and Philip the Fair. But all these charges will be met and explained to the reader during his perusal of this history. Moreover the moral portraits of Boniface and Philip the Fair being traced, there is no doubt that approaching them nearer in order to observe their conduct in the famous quarrel, the truth will be seen more plainly and more easily.

Like Gregory VII, who was the foremost man in the pontificates of his several predecessors, on whom they relied for support, and who strongly defended the rights of the Church, so Benedict Gaetani (Boniface VIII), was the great factor and most celebrated personage in the administration of the five preceding popes; who was sent on the most difficult embassies, and was called upon to manage affairs of great moment and settle the difficulties between the Church and princes. The knowledge of all the evils which agitated the Church within his own memory, together with others which for a long time previously beset her, served as generating facts which gave form and character to the one thought which entered deeply into his mind, namely the Church reduced to servitude not by secret enemies, but by those who called themselves her children and her vassals, and forced to work in this humiliating condition. Under such circumstances a man like Boniface, on whom nature had lavished her choicest gifts, and who was equally skilled in canon and civil law; whose talents and accomplishments fitted him to be no less a secular prince than the Head of the Church; whose strong sense and firmness of character enabled him to fully comprehend his mission and his office, and to go straight through with whatever business he had in hand, without turning to the right or to the left; who surpassed all his predecessors in talent for affairs, experience of practical life, and who was still in the full tide and vigor of manhood, must, when calling upon the memories of Gregory VII and Innocent III, have resolved to follow their example in pursuing a well-defined policy, and assuming a bold and determined attitude. The character of the first decrees issued by him, placed him as a churchman beside Innocent III. Although the views entertained by Boniface regarding the relations of Church and State, were not precisely those put forward by his great predecessors, Gregory and Innocent, they differed from them only because the altered circumstances of his age called for a corresponding change of ecclesiastical policy.

Boniface during all his Pontificate strove to maintain the rights of the Church and of the Holy See as he had received them from his predecessors. He aimed at nothing else but to preserve intact these same rights of the Church, not only in the sanctuary, but also in the heart of civil society itself, over the temporal destinies of which he could no more cease to preside, than the soul over the purely material functions of the body. Philip the Fair was determined to thwart him, and to exercise his rule with absolute independency from any spiritual control.

The resistance with which he opposed all manner of injustice during his lifetime, opened a way after his death to resentment, which furiously assailed his memory and oppressed it. The tendency of the writers of the time being in favor of either Guelph or Ghibelline, they portrayed the actions of this Pope to suit their own views, and just as rumor expressed them. Philip the Fair in France, the Colonnas in Italy, the proud Roman Patriciate, and all those who had experienced the strong temperament of Boniface in anger, cast the stone of vituperation upon his sepulchre, in addition to a cry of execration and vengeance. Care must be taken so that his character must not be judged by what French writers say. His character and career ought in all fairness to be judged by a contemporary instead of a modern standard of ethics and ideas. To judge him impartially one should transport himself to the age in which he lived, and take into account the then political institutions, and the principles of legislation and government. Both those of his own and those of later times, wrote under the guidance of unreasonable prejudices, because they knew only French facts, or were under the impression of some momentary quarrel with the Holy See.

The memory of Boniface has been assailed by Dante, who puts him in a poetical hell, but his opinion is vilely prejudiced on account of political reasons, and he speaks with the usual license of a poet, and not with the truthful spirit of a historian. But after the outrage at Anagni he relented at its contemplation, and forgot his political feeling to give vent to his indignation at the insult offered to Christ's Vicar in the following verses:

> " Entering Alagna, lo the fleur-de-lis,
> And in his vicar, Christ a captive led!
> I see him mocked a second time;—again
> The vinegar and gall produced I see;
> And Christ himself 'twixt robbers slain."

Petrarch his fellow poet and contemporary calls Boniface (*meraviglia del mondo*) the marvel of the world. It has been the sad fate of Boniface VIII to have made many enemies. Most Protestant authors have numbered him among the wicked popes.

But he has found some apologists and defenders, and among them the first place is to be given to the celebrated Benedictine of Monte Cassino, Dom Louis Tosti. This historian is among the foremost of Italy whose various works have been favorably received everywhere, and have made him renowned for splendid historical attainments. His work: "The Life and Times of Boniface VIII," which we present to the public in an English dress, is an admirable and effective defence of that Pope. In it he breathes the true spirit of a historian; he neither apologizes, nor does he advance a proof, without producing documentary evidence from the most approved sources. In the compilation of this work Tosti had access to many unpublished documents in the Vatican Archives, and to have drawn from them much information of the greatest value. This book which we present to the English reading public, is not a controversial work. It has not been written, nor translated with the view of reviving doctrines which, confessedly, exercised a salutary sway in the Middle Ages, but of which no one dreams of seeing them exercised in the actual state of the world, at this hour, when the Church, very far from claiming an interference in the temporal affairs of states, prefers rather to preserve her incontestable spiritual rights.

To establish in its day truth obscured by passions; to render to virtue its honor, and to avenge the opprobrium of six centuries; to inflict on crime triumphant the reprobation it deserves; to serve also the designs of divine Providence, which does not defer always the cause of justice to the future life, such is the noble purpose which Dom Tosti had in view, and which we also maintain in our work of translation. "The History of Boniface VIII and his Times," is then solely a work of historical reparation, a satisfaction due morality and society.

If, profiting by the generous efforts of others before him to restore the memory of a pontiff persecuted and outraged during his life, and calumniated and execrated after his death, the illustrious Benedictine has succeeded in defending it in a most complete manner, yet he has not pretended to have said the last word in this solemn discussion. But by furnishing some important points of procedure, he has contributed to the triumph of his client, of his hero; and this service, we confidently believe, will win for him the sympathy not only of Catholics, but also of all those honest souls, steadfastly faithful to the sacred principles of equity.

Boniface was a man of great and remarkable qualities. In his day, before his ordination, he was known far and wide for his knowledge of civil law, and his fame as a lawyer has been preserved and handed down to the present day by a collection of laws bearing the title: "The Gaetani Code of Laws." He became so well-versed in canon law that he was considered the first canonist of his age, and his reputation for learning soon became widespread. He was an admirer of the fine arts, and a strong and liberal protector and patron of artists. He embellished his beloved town of Anagni, where he fixed his summer residence, and restored its cathedral, in memory of which the people placed his statue in a niche of the facade, which exists at the present time. He completed and opened to divine worship that beautiful Gothic cathedral of Orvieto. In Rome he rebuilt the church of St. Lawrence in Panisperna. He invited the celebrated Giotto to Rome, and engaged him to decorate the churches of St. Peter, and St. John Lateran, and in the latter there is still to be seen the portrait of Boniface drawn by that artist. His literary acquirements no one disputes. The Sixth Book of the Decretals will attest them as long as God's undying Church shall last. He elevated to the honors of the altar Louis IX, the grandfather of Philip the Fair. He increased the solemnity of the feasts of the four evangelists; and raised the feasts of the four Latin Doctors, Augustine, Ambrose, Jerome and Gregory, a degree higher. He composed the hymn "*Ave Virgo Gloriosa,*" and the prayer: "Deus, qui pro redemptione mundi;" and he left five orations on the canonization of St. Louis, the purity and elegance of whose Latin is still much admired. General science owes to him the foundation of the university of the Sapienza at Rome, as well as the university at Fermo. Religion owes to him the consoling institution of the Jubilee, the most beautiful conception of his Pontificate.

Cardinal Wiseman who has written an able defence of this Pope says: "Accustomed as we have been to hear and read so much to the disadvantage of Boniface VIII, we naturally required some cause, however slight, to turn our attention towards a particular examination of such grievous charges. The pencil of Giotto must claim the merits, such as it is. The portrait of Boniface by him in the Lateran Basilica, so different in character from the representations of modern history, awakened in our minds a peculiar interest regarding him, and led us to the examination of several popular assertions, affecting his moral and ecclesiastical conduct. He soon appeared to us in a new light; as a pontiff who began his reign with most glorious promise, and closed it amid sad calamities; who devoted, through it all, the energies of a great mind, cultivated by profound learning, and matured by long experience in the most difficult ecclesiastical affairs, to the attainment of a truly noble end; and who, throughout his career, displayed many great virtues, could plead in extenuation of his faults, the convulsed state of public affairs, the rudeness of his times, and the faithless, violent character of many among those with whom he had to deal. These circumstances, working upon a mind naturally upright and inflexible, led to a sternness of manner and severity of conduct, which, when viewed through the feelings of modern times, may appear extreme, and almost unjustifiable. But after studying the conduct of this great Pope, after searching through the pages of his most hostile historians, we are satisfied that this is the only point upon which a plausible charge can be brought against him; a charge which has been much exaggerated, and which the considerations just enumerated must sufficiently repel, or in a great part extenuate." The same author makes one or two other remarks: "Although the character of Boniface was certainly stern and inflexible, there is not a sign of it having been cruel or revengeful. Throughout the whole of his history, not an instance can be found of his having punished an enemy with death. When he was returning to Rome, after his liberation, in a triumph never before witnessed, Cardinal Stephanesius tells us, that his principal enemy Nogaret, or Sciarra Colonna, was seized by the people and brought before him, that he might deal with him as he pleased; he freely pardoned him and let him go. So, likewise, when Fra. Jacopone fell into his hands, he dealt leniently with him, and confined him, where others would have treated the offence as capital. These examples of forgiveness and gentleness, ought surely to have due weight in estimating the Pope's character."

And so we send forth this work to the English reading public, that they might gain a right idea of his character as well hoping that it may be able to remove the mass of error and calumny that has accumulated around the name of Boniface VIII, for the past six centuries, and likewise remove the obloquy which still rests on his memory. If this end be attained the labor of translation will be rewarded, and we shall be amply repaid for having undertaken it. May justice and truth prevail regarding this great, learned and magnanimous Pope, and may he have the place he merits among the Sovereign Pontiffs, which is among the highest and the greatest.

EUGENE J. DONNELLY.

October 26th, 1910.

BOOK FIRST.

SUMMARY.

1217 to 1295.

Classification of human events from the fall of the Roman Empire to our own times.—The Pontificate of Boniface is a generating fact.—How he personified the separation of the priesthood from the Empire.—Reflections on the political ministration of the Papacy.—How the civil Pontificate will always live, although the exercise of it ceased after Boniface—Charles of Anjou and the Roman Pontiffs—Mistakes which the latter made.—The trouble they prepared for their successors.—The Sicilian Vespers.—The birth and education of Benedict Gaetani.—His first employments in the Church.—His first embassy to Rudolph, at war with Charles, for the possession of Provence.—He is created Cardinal.—Another embassy to restrain Charles from fighting a duel with Peter of Aragon—Indiscretions of Martin IV.—Naples and Sicily under Pope Honorius.—Dionysius, king of Portugal, troublesome to the Church.—Cardinal Gaetani is sent with other cardinals to pass sentence on him—He goes to France in the quality of legate on affairs relating to the Holy Land, and becomes acquainted with Philip the Fair.—He makes every effort for peace, and writes the treaty of Tarascon.—Conclave held after the death of Nicholas III.—Divisions and delays of the Cardinals.—Charles the Lame intrudes himself among them and Cardinal Gaetani ejects him—Peter Morone elected Pope—A description of him.—He accepts the Papacy.—He falls altogether under the power of Charles and perverse men—He is crowned.—Gaetani is the last one to repair to Aquila—In what condition he found things, and how he came to be Lord of the Curia.—Peter Celestine exasperates the Cardinals.—They begin to advise him to resign.—He is disposed to do so.—He takes counsel with Cardinal Gaetani.—Artifices of Charles II.—Abdication of St. Celestine.—Dispositions of the Cardinal electors—Gaetani' elected Pope.—Calumnies regarding his election.—First measures of Boniface which disturb the beginning of his Pontificate—He repairs to Rome.—An observation—Ceremonies of the cornonation of the new Pope.—Encyclical of Boniface.—Letter to King Philip the Fair.

IT was with much agitation of mind that we proposed to narrate the history of Boniface VIII, for the reason that his name, in many books, groans under the weight of the greatest abuse and slander. We shall not now speak of the reasons for the almost universal and lasting denunciations of historians (both of his own and later times), nor of their justice, nor their iniquity; these causes are very clearly revealed from the facts themselves without any effort on the part of the narrator. To prepare the mind of the reader, however, we must make known the motives which inspired us with courage to publish anew the true facts of the history of that Pontiff.

To form a judgment on past events, and to discover the evidence of their moral right, it does not suffice to examine them severely and intelligently; the true science of history consists in choosing from among them those which, in the order of human events, start up as beginnings and fertile causes of great changes. Upon these as on a high elevation the historian places himself in order to view and follow the successive development of subordinate events which lie hidden, and 'which come forth when circumstances have reached their maturity. The events which we call generators, are the great social revolutions, always preceded by secret causes which prepared the way for them, and always followed by consequences which reveal their power. When a fact of this nature strikes the mind of a philosopher, it there awakens a struggle, more or less prolonged, of two contrary ideas in the breasts of the people, and the victory of one of them over the other. The fact that expresses the triumph of the victorious idea, is precisely that which is called a revolt, because it allures the vanquished idea and causes it to pass under its sway.

To write a complete history of the human family, it will suffice then to discern these generating facts; because from a study of them every other fact will be revealed, being made clear by the light from the generating fact. Hence, turning our attention to events which form the history of society from the fall of the Latin Empire to our own times, we find three events which merit the name of revolutions; namely, the terrible invasion of the Barbarians into Europe; the quarrel of Philip the Fair with the Holy See; and the revolution at the end of the eighteenth century, commonly called the French Revolution.

A government without rule and restraint, which establishes itself on the ruins of the virtue of a people, is of itself alone a sufficient preparation, and as well a necessary cause of revolution, internal or external, as the force may be which accelerates the turbulent fact; and the struggle is then between right and force, order or disorder. From Augustus to Augustulus this cause unfolded itself, and sapped the foundation of the edifice of the ancient civilization, which crumbled away when an external force, the Barbarians, ruined the Roman Empire. The idea of disorder and tyranny having triumphed invisibly, on its ruins and amidst the horrors of a boisterous cruelty they led Pagan Rome, a slave, to the feet of Christian Rome, and made her thus submissive to the idea of justice and order. They could not personify that idea, because they were barbarians; therefore, triumphant, but wandering, they walked the earth, but could not vivify it. This task was undertaken by the Roman Papacy; and the day on which Pope Leo placed the imperial crown on the head of Charlemagne, it seems to us the great revolution was accomplished. Right administered by the pontifical hand ruled both princes and people; and as it is the life of human society, the Popes penetrated deeply into this society; they even took possession of the heart, to revive the sources of its life, and equally subservient to them they held the ruler and the ruled. This was the infancy of the rising generations, and it was in peace. But, advancing in social life, the princes were the first to be enamored of ancient pagan Rome, which in its cold but still dangerous ruins concealed the idea of the monarchy of Augustus. They declared openly for it, they cleansed it from the obscenities of a Tiberius and a Nero, they marked its brow with the cross of Christ, they made it sit with them on their thrones, and they began to antagonize the Papacy, to drive it out not only from civil society, but to consign it again to the catacombs.

The Emperors of the house of Hohenstaufen and the Popes of their times, were the expression of the great struggle between the Church and the Empire, which was to prepare another revolution, that is to say, the victory of either one of the two powers over the other. As long as the Empire was personified by men whose strength of mind equalled the greatness of the idea they represented, the power of the Church, finding in her pontiffs a strong and solid prop, held good and survived. But, on the death of Frederick II, the idea of the pagan monarchy was enfeebled by reason of its division among many crowned heads, and the Pontificate counting on a complete victory, moderated that vigor that had been displayed by Innocent III, Gregory IX, and Innocent IV.

The pontifical energy revived however at the excesses of King Philip, and it confronted him with the breast of Boniface VIII. All the kingdoms were silent spectators of the struggle for the principles which these men represented. And when they saw the Pope imprisoned, struck, fall into the grave, and saw the stone of vituperation placed upon this grave by a Christian king, they realized that a revolution was now completed, the separation of the Priesthood from the Empire.

When the Church was set aside, the right which the popes had visibly exercised over the head of kings was replaced by an invisible right which the princes invoked, and by virtue of which they ventured to reign; this right the people did not see and to it they could not appeal. In vain did the kings have recourse to the theories of those learned in law, to render this right perceptible; how could lawyers inspire men with as much respect as the Pontiffs? The people often with both hands closed the volume of a right which the will of another man could not sanctify in their eyes; then commenced the fierce struggle of interests between the people and the kings, or the fight for liberty and for power, for the people in their ignorance did not understand how the power can reside in a man. This inability was formerly supplied by Faith, and with this there was nothing easier to comprehend than the power in the Pope, the representative of Jesus Christ. Now as France had accomplished the revolution which separated the Priesthood from the Empire, she achieved also the end of the struggle between monarchy and democracy. To France belonged this mission; for in her impetuosity to separate herself from the sacerdotal principle, not finding in the monarchy the guarantees of the Church, she must necessarily tend to clash indirectly with the principle of democracy. Therefore all modern history springs from these three revolutions, the source and origin of every other event, from the barbarians victorious over the Latin Empire; from the priesthood excluded throughout France from the heart of civil society; and from the monarchy, overthrown by democracy in France.

From which it appears, that in every revolution, the men who represent the conquered or the conquering principle should have the spirit so strongly tempered as to sustain the terrible conflict in which they are engaged. If they be feeble, there will be no struggle, and if there be no struggle, there will not be a revolution. If then they represent the conquered principle, they have a right not only to be honored by posterity for their courage, but also to be venerated by reason of the pains of their martyrdom. It is true that to this double dignity only those can aspire, who through sufficient personal valor, or by reason of circumstances, so closely allied themselves to their great and dangerous principle, that their ruin entails that of their principle, and soon the struggle disappears to give place to the easy and successive conquests of the victor. Now, of the three aforesaid revolutions that alone in which the Priesthood was excluded from the State, seems to offer the wonderful man of whom we speak. In that of the barbarbians, pagan Rome did not have a respresentative who identified himself with the idea and represented it, and so the struggle was rather material than moral. In the French Revolution Louis XVI divided with all the crowned heads the hazardous charge, and although materially he alone might be in the hands of the democracy, morally he was only a member of the great monarchical body, and the king being dead, it cannot be said that the principle was dead, but living.

Boniface alone by the loftiness of his courage, as well as by reason of his office as head of the Church, in which the monarchy is universal, so closely identified himself with the principle of the civil priesthood, that it died with him. That is what we shall show when at the end of this history we shall have related the great revolution in which the conquered idea was so magnanimously represented by this Pontiff. Having thus spoken of the moral and political conditions in which Boniface is necessarily placed, when we call upon him to render to the men of our own times an account of his administration, we have perhaps aroused great anxiety in the soul of those who think (and

we are of that number) that the civil ministry of the
Roman Pontificate still continues. We have said, in fact,
that Boniface carried this ministry with him to the tomb;
it would seem then, that since that time the successors of
St. Peter have found on his chair only the keys to close
and open heaven, and no longer the sceptre of that power,
objective in Christianity, subjective in the Papacy, which
secures everything by the reconciliation of the contrary
elements in the human family. Yet it is not so. The objective idea never dies, it is eternal like God. The Papacy
can lose the exercise of civil power, which depends upon
the mutability of human things, but in itself this power is
immutable; it will last as long as the Church, always ready
to resume its influence over civil society, the moment
Providence commands it or the misery of humanity arouses
this beneficent power to action.

In the human individual, life is sustained by reason tempering the spiritual and corporal forces; so the race is
kept alive by the reconciliation of power and liberty derived from the supreme reason, which is God. This supreme reason presides over the opposing factions, and
while it unmoved is a spectator of the combat, at times
it intervenes, and balancing their forces, preserves them
from death and makes them live. This supreme conciliating reason is determined by the Roman Pontificate (we
speak to Catholics), and through it it is known, and scatters its benefits among men. And just as human reason
in the individual, and the supreme in the universe permit
evil, without losing anything of their power so the authority of the pontificate, the voice, as we have said, of this
sovereign reason which conciliates the opposing interests,
is not changed in nature because of accidental circumstances which may arrest the course of its subjective
power. We may remark here, that an arbiter who is
charged with the duty of conciliating two adversaries,
must be free from their faults; for by identifying himself
with one of them by these faults, and for that reason
repelling the other, he would become unfit for his office
of conciliator. All human history is but the development
of this struggle of opposing elements viewed by the supreme reason, and the revolutions are the victories which
the opponents gain the one over the other.

Boniface personified the supreme pontificate in the beginning of the 14th century. Behind him lay the infancy of human society, or the Middle Ages; before him this same society full-grown, or the Renaissance. It has been said of a great man that he was seated as arbiter between two centuries; greater than he, Boniface took the position of arbiter between two vast epochs. He combated in the Middle Ages the tyránny of princes, and in the Renaissance the indocility of the people, who emboldened by youth, sought to be freed from a guardianship which they considered useless, unbecoming and hurtful to their own liberty, and besieged the papal throne with the demand, like the prodigal son in the Gospel: " Give me the portion of substance that falleth to me." A youthful error this it is true, yet one which wounded sorely the fatherly affection of the Papacy, and which recoiled heavily on the head of the proud guilty ones. In Boniface the Papacy vexed in front by the bold bearing of the Renaissance, harrassed behind by a force unfriendly to it and to the people, saw its guardianship cease. It mourned not for itself, but for the youthful and over-confident humanity, and it asked pardon for it from Christ, as for him who knows not what he does. Henceforth the time of guardianship had passed; and the people became impatient to measure their strength with power. But in the tomb of Boniface, where the pontifical guardianship lay buried, dwells unchangeable the right of its conciliating power. Men, in fact, can refuse it recognition but not destroy it; and in the fatigue of the struggle, in the sterility of the means employed by both parties to come to an agreement, the consciousness of this holy power will ever live and rule, the preserver of contending elements which she conciliates, in justice.

It is clear to all how Pope Boniface VIII, viewed in the exercise of this sublime ministry, becomes the subject of a most important history. At the first glance all the faults with which he was reproached, and upon which alone he has been judged, become diminished and disappear. So instead of beginning by replying to the accusations of simony, of excessive and gross ambition which were brought against him, we shall conduct the reader to him by another way, in order to have the reader study him in the very sanctuary of this providential reason, into which those never penetrate who, arresting their view on the mere surface of human events, obtain but an incomplete knowledge upon which they base their invectives and their maledictions.

To rightly estimate the character of the Pontiff, whose life we are about to relate, it is necessary for us to glance rapidly over certain events which took place before his time and which influenced his education. For no one can doubt that though we owe to nature the endowment of our character, the circumstances of the times contribute much to form it. That was a wise and salutary move on the part of the Roman pontiffs, to keep at a distance from their see the imperial power, in order to give more space to that of the Church which strives, without ceasing, to extend itself to the uttermost limits of the earth.

Alexander III made the Lombard republics his advanced ramparts, the kingdom of Naples and Sicily, which Innocent III preserved with so much care for his ward, Frederick II, was to serve as the last bulwark and refuge in time of danger. But this double combination, an inspiration of deep wisdom, failed of its intent. In fact the republics, after having used their strength against the foreigner Barbarossa, turned it against one another, and prepared the way for the domination of many masters; on his part, Frederick II, from a king having become emperor, annexed the kingdom of Sicily to the empire. The remedy then increased the evil which the Popes had hoped to avert; for the Emperor who formerly had to fear the Lombards or the Normans in Sicily, now settled himself there as in his own home, and from there, as from a citadel, thundered against Rome. There was no more waiting for the German armies to cross the Alps; they were camping at the gates of Rome, and the Pope, who, up to that time, had been apprised of the impieties of the imperial power only by letter or legate, saw them with his own eyes. Innocent had intended to make Frederick only a vassal king of the Holy See; but Frederick proclaimed himself emperor as if he had been an independent sovereign. So this proximity served to add prominence to the struggle between the Priesthood and the Empire, and to increase the perils of the Papacy.

Frederick would perhaps have carried into effect the terrible imperial idea, and would have himself reduced the rights of the Church to that sad state into which they were afterwards precipitated by the work of Philip the Fair of France, if he had tempered the roughness of his German nature with the cunning and dissimulation which he perceived in the southern countries where he was educated, and which he made use of more than once in dealing with the Roman pontiffs. But he broke out against the Church after the manner of Nero, and showed no respect for the religious convictions, which at that time were the most solemn expression of the religion itself. These faults became more conspicuous when contrasted with the virtues of St. Louis, king of France. Besides, the other princes, not wishing to assume the rôle of vassals, became alarmed at the doctrine fabricated by the jurists of Frederick Barbarossa, which aimed at nothing less than the resurrection of the empire of Augustus in the German emperors and to establish in their favor a universal monarchy. This is the reason why in the first council of Lyons, Thaddeus of Suessia, the defender of Frederick, was received so coldly by the assembly, and the sentence of excommunication and the deposition hurled against the emperor by Innocent IV. was received without objection by the other kings.

The formidable imperial power so baneful to the Church can be said to have died with Frederick, and yet that which seemed to point to a lasting victory for the Church prepared its overthrow. The inconstant loyalty of the Neapolitans and the rivalries which sprang up among the sons of Frederick relieved the minds of the popes; the easy victories over Manfred; and the increasing moral decadence of the imperial dignity after the death of this emperor, made the popes descend from lofty views which they had displayed in their ministry and to which the greatness and dignity of the enemy whom they fought had raised them. Therefore the war which they carried on, in the kingdom of Naples, against the last remnant of the house of Suabia, excluded from the throne by the sentence of the Council of Lyons, and the results of this war, can be considered as a new period of facts which begins with the death of Frederick.

The last will of this emperor and the sovereign dominion

of the Pope over this country were the subject of the discord. Although it is true the pontiffs defended there with the rights and patrimony of the Church their own liberty, yet we must admit that the contest had diminished and did not assume the proportions of the gigantic and heroic combats of Alexander III and Gregory IX. Nevertheless it is to be equally maintained that the popes, engaged in the affairs of the narrow space of the kingdom of Naples and Sicily, exercised an influence over all the thrones of Europe by making sparkle the royal crown which they held in their hands, and by looking about to find a prince worthy to wear it. The events which were taking place in the kingdom of Naples were as the center whence the movement started which put the princes in communication with one another and with the Church. If Naples and Sicily had been suited for a republican form of government; if for a long time the people had not been taught to live under monarchical rule by the laws, by the civil institutions, and by the manifest splendor of those who up to that time had worn the crown, perhaps the popes might have preserved a supreme sovereignty over that kingdom; a conciliatory protectorate, or immediate government by some one appointed by them, could have cast in the shade those quarrels always so dangerous to which hereditary pretentions are wont to give rise. But even though they had desired it, they could not have accomplished it for the aforesaid reasons; and they had to intrust to others the sovereignty which they could not without difficulty preserve among an excited people, who were aroused at first by the liberty of choice among the parties, and later on by the necessity of defending their own rights.

Charles of Anjou, summoned by the Pope, came to rule over Naples and Sicily. He was a prince poor in worldly goods, but of boundless ambition. Seated on an unexpected throne, he should have made for himself an inviolable law of respecting the rights of the Church and those of the people the direction of whom she had confided to him. He proposed to violate both, because they were incompatible with his desire of acquiring unbridled power. He made open war against the Sicilians; but against the Church the adversity of circumstances, and not moderation of spirit bound him to secret attacks. He had always to fight in Peter of Aragon and the Sicilian people, two powerful adversaries who kept him manifesting an apparent respect for Rome. Rome and justice were powerless to resist him, and he changed his dominion into a tyranny. Charles overthrowing the sacred rampart of this double authority, is the entire history that educated the mind of Benedict Gaetani, and prepared the pontificate of Boniface VIII.

To us who judge the causes by the effects, that plan of the Popes in calling a foreign prince to rule over the southern part of Italy, certainly does not appear salutary or wise. It resulted in nothing else, but furnishing the French against their will with means to increase the evils which the Germans had already brought upon the unfortunate people of Sicily. There is no doubt that the Papacy needed an armed and powerful defender; but Alexander III had found how to clothe the papal power with a breastplate of iron, by making himself the soul of the Lombard League, preferring rather to engage as defenders the people whose liberty he had protected rather than the princes to whom he had given sovereignties.

When the last scion of the house of the Hohenstaufens, the young Conradin, drawn into the kingdom of Naples by a sort of fatality, had lost his life at the hands of the Angevine butcher, Charles aspired to a power which surpassed exceedingly the limits marked out by Clement IV. The favor of the Roman See, and the condition of his kingdom, furnished him, more than any other prince of his time, with the means of gratifying his desire. Northern and Central Italy by reason of the sudden overthrow of the Ghibellines, offered him in the triumph of the Guelphs, at the head of which he could have placed himself as the champion of the Church, an arm by which to secure for himself an Italian principality. The sea which surrounds Sicily and so benignly bathes the vast coast of the Neapolitan country, offered him the occasion of increasing his power by a naval force, and of extending his conquests, under the pretext of a crusade, along the coasts of Africa towards the weak Byzantium and the regions of the Levant. In 1267 by a promise of aid to Baldwin II, Emperor of Constantinople, he obtained from him the principality of Achaia and all the country which the Latins still occupied. Coveting with an insatiable gaze the very throne of Constantine, he gave his daughter Beatrice in marriage to Philip the only son of Baldwin. So thanks to these matrimonial alliances, bargains familiar to princes, he had established a remote right to the throne, which made Michael Paleologus fear. If the opportunity was great, the knowledge of it and the will to use it were no less important. He knew it, and embraced it, whilst the popes believed him modestly engaged in studying his diploma of investiture. However when in May 1265, Charles entered Rome, and haughtily lodged himself with his knights in the papal palace of the Lateran without the permission of Clement, it was very evident that his eyes dazzled by the crown about to descend on his head, saw no longer the hand which bestowed it. Clement protested forcibly against this want of respect;[1] but his mind did not penetrate the depth of this audacious proceeding.

But what contributed to raise Charles the sooner to that height of power which he reached, was the vacancy in the Roman See which lasted two years and six months. Our readers would do well to remark here that after the arrival of the Count of Anjou, these prolonged vacancies became very frequent. In virtue of his office as senator of Rome, he exercised the sovereignty in that city and over all the patrimony of the Church; moreover he concentrated in himself all the indirect power of the popes over the Italian cities. Never have factions greater need of a chief than in time of prosperity and victory. Now the Guelphs not finding any longer in the See of St. Peter their natural head, all turned to Charles as their assured protector. So great was the confidence of Charles that in the diet of Cremona, which he had held by the Guelphs of Lombardy, and presided over by his envoys, he humbly requested them to name him their chief, which word did not sound like lord. The principal towns of Lombardy and Piedmont acceded to his wishes; but the people of Monferrato openly refused and said; "that they would receive Charles as a Friend, but as a lord never." The ready compliance of so many cities proceeded from the extinction of that noble consciousness of their own liberty which had been so exalted during the wars against Barbarossa; then too, the

---

[1] Raynaldus. Annal. Eccl. Epistola ad Carolum 1265-12.

long prosperity of the Ghibelline party in permitting Ezelino da Romano, Albert Pallavacini, and Buoso da Doara to exercise sovereignty over them, had already accustomed their minds to the idea of servitude. Democracy died with the League, aristocracy was consolidated under Frederick II, and from aristocracy to a monarchy was an easy passage which Charles tried.

He did not have to negotiate much with Tuscany; appointed by the Pope imperial vicar of this country, by virtue of this title he obtained for ten years his sovereignty over Florence. This was the reason of the change which this city underwent in its governmental constitution, after the expulsion of the Ghibellines. It increased the number of the advisory counsels, curtailing thereby the power of the noblemen of the city; it augmented the power of the people, and, by the over difficult distribution of this power, it enkindled in their breasts the fire of lamentable rivalries, the cause of cruel broils between the nobles and the populace. These dissensions could have opened to Charles a way to sovereignty over the ruins of the republic; but the opportunity escaped him, and all the effect of these deadly discords was to destroy the Guelph party by dividing it into the Whites and the Blacks, and as a consequence to deprive the Roman Pontiff of his greatest support, and to remotely prepare the decline of the Florentine the elevation of the Guelphs, in order that he as the head had for their object the suppression of the Ghibellines, and republic. The efforts then of Charles throughout Italy of the latter might rule over all Italy. But it was not for this purpose that the popes had called him.

Finally Theobald Visconti became Pope under the name of Gregory X. He was a holy man, and he would have more willingly passed his days as a crusader in the Holy Land, than in the Apostolic See. He saw at first in the ambition of Charles no other inconvenience than the endless duration of the war on account of exasperating the Ghibellines; but when he wished to remedy affairs, he found this prince a very wicked son of Holy Church. In fact when Gregory was in Florence to effect a peace between the Guelphs and Ghibellines, the marshal of the king threatened with death and drove back the pontifical legates who were obliged to depart, leaving matters in the same condition as they were and Florence under an interdict.

This Pope had dearest to his heart the conquest of the Holy Land, and as a consequence the reunion of the schismatic Greeks to the Latin Church. To the attainment of this he directed all his energies. During the whole of his pontificate Gregory cherished the project of a new crusade, and in order to bring it and the reunion of the Greek Church to the Latin more prominently before the people of Christendom, he convoked the fourteenth œcumenical council, the second of Lyons. Though Charles did not interfere with the project directly, he began to obstruct it indirectly by his ambitious designs. The peace and good will which the Pope ordered his legates to preach in all the Italian cities, and the most ardent desire he had of numbering among his flock the schismatic Michael Paleologus, were displeasing to the Angevine. He did not wish peace, because it deprived him of the exaltation of the triumphant Guelphs which was useful to him; and by no means did he wish the conversion of the Greek prince. If Michael returned to the bosom of the Church, Charles could not, without ceasing to be a devoted son of the Church, wage that war against him which he meditated in order to usurp the throne of Byzantium. Paleologus, endowed with that shrewdness which distinguishes his country-men, perceived this consequence, and was forced to reenter the fold of Christ, and to shelter himself behind the chair of St. Peter, making use of it as a rampart against the power of Charles. In the fourth session of the Council of Lyons Gregory shed tears of joy and consolation over the conversion of the Greeks; and we can believe that Charles shed tears of grief and madness. Every one knows how quickly this apparent conversion was effected, and how in the fifteenth century, the successors of Paleologus, made use of this same cunning when they were threatened no longer by the Christians, but by the Turks.

This Pope in the innocence of his design, caused king Charles another vexation, the consequences of which he was ignorant, and it was the friendly relations he established with Rudolph of Hapsburg, created by the electors king of the Romans. Requested by the ambassadors to confirm this election Gregory, after having received from

Rudolph the oath of obedience and fidelity to the Roman See, not only confirmed him as king, but even wrote most eagerly in his behalf to many princes and even to Charles in order to establish friendly relations towards him. Moreover he notified Rudolph by letter to hold himself in readiness to receive the imperial crown; and to repair as soon as possible to the place he would designate, where they would meet and confer. In fact the Pope and Rudolph met at Lausanne, and warmly embraced each other. Rudolph swore again to preserve all the property of the Church, to defend all her rights especially those which she held over Sicily, and to go as a crusader to the Holy Land. The Emperor drew nigh to the Pope, but not the Empire to the Church. However these friendly feelings went to the heart of Charles. He was unwilling to have any one else divide with him the pious office of defender of the Holy See, and he did not care to see the imperial power in Italy for the reason that it would frustrate his designs. Nor did he reason wrongly. For the subdued Ghibellines turned to Rudolph, as to a support by which to revive their hopes. They rushed to him, and recalled to his mind the old theories of the rights of the German Empire over poor Italy. We do not know whether in the interview at Lausanne Gregory openly manifested to the Emperor elect his displeasure at the actions of Charles, nor whether he encouraged him to fill his office in the affairs of Naples and Sicily; but it is certain that the oath taken to defend particularly the rights of the Church over Sicily must have been engendered from a conversation over the insolence of Charles of Anjou. In a word a great rivalry ensued between Charles and Rudolph, which would have been a weapon in the hand of a more able pontiff to humble the over-proud Charles.

The pious and peaceful Gregory being dead, fortune continued to smile on the ambitious projects of Charles, and the Pontiffs Innocent V, Adrian V, and John XXI, who succeeded Gregory, placed no obstacles in his way. Under the latter he even saw added to the crown of Sicily that of Jerusalem, bestowed upon him by Maria Elizabeth, daughter of Behemond IV, prince of Antioch. Sanuto relates that the greater part of the papal curia assisted at the act of donation to which many cardinals subscribed their names.[2] And this was not an empty title, for he soon took possession of Ptolomaïs, through Count Roger of St. Severino aided by the Knights Templar.

In the meanwhile the more he advanced in power, the more he oppressed the realm entrusted to him by the Church to rule. His victory over Conradin summoned by the despair of the inhabitants, made him bolder, and changed his rule into a unbridled tyranny. Such was his conduct from the beginning of his reign and we do not perceive that any pope made an effort to restrain him. Yet the popes should have opened their eyes to this French predominance, not only through pity for the oppressed people but also because the latter in their fury to relieve themselves of the yoke, could involve in one and the same ruin as did really happen the rights of the vassal prince, and those of the sovereign Church. In fine the compacts swore to by Charles at the time of receiving the investiture of the kingdom from Clement were formally violated.

The clever Cardinal Orsini, under the name of Nicholas III ascended the papal throne. Less pious than Gregory X, he did not occupy his mind so much with the affairs of the Holy Land, as with those which encompassed him at home; and so he set out to clip the wings of Charles. Among the conditions to which the latter had sworn were those of not meddling in the government of Tuscany and of Lombardy,[3] and of not accepting any office as ruler or governor in the states of the Church. The first condition he shamefully violated; from the obligation of the other he was freed by Clement himself, who was still in such fear of the house of Suabia that in order to have Charles near him, he created him a senator of Rome. Pope Nicholas wanted to enforce on Charles the observance of these two clauses; and being a man skilled in affairs he so worked on the minds of Rudolph, king of the Romans, and of Charles, that while he was ardently arranging peace between them, and striving to unite them also by the bond of relationship, he made use of the German prince to hold Charles in awe. A war in Italy between them would have

---

[2] Lib 13. C. 15. Par. 12.

[3] "Vel intromittatis vos ullo modo de regimine ipsius imperii, vel regni Romanorum, seu Theutoniae, aut Lombardiae, seu Tusciae vel majoris partis carum."

been injurious to the Church. A victory for Rudolph would revive the fear of the imperial power, and the triumph of the Ghibellines; his defeat would give Charles unlimited power. Peace, on the contrary, by holding the two princes in mutual regard, gave an occasion to the Pope to continue the pious work of Gregory X, namely the conciliation of the factions. In fact, fearing that Nicholas III would proceed too far in his friendship for the king of the Romans, who through desire for the imperial crown was most deferential toward the popes, Charles submitted with wonderful docility to the injunction that was laid upon him to resign his office of vicar of Tuscany and senator of Rome. It seems that Nicholas III was slow to credit such docility, for Giordano relates[4] that he sent a cardinal to observe what impression this sacrifice made on the mind of the king. Now Charles perfectly dissembled his interior displeasure by according the pontifical messenger a most honorable reception and by addressing him in terms most affectionate and well-chosen. So Nicholas, having heard this, remarked that Charles received his goodness of soul from the house of France, his sagacity from Spain, his mother being Blanche of Spain, and his discretion in words from his frequent intercourse with the Roman Curia. This action of Charles, and this appreciation of Nicholas strikingly reveal the character of the two men and show that they understood each other. Charles being degraded, Nicholas sent the German out of Italy. Yet the imperial agents were known to exact still the oath of allegiance from the towns comprised in the territory of the Church. Nicholas warned Rudolph that according to the imperial patents of his predecessors in favor of the papal see this patrimony extended from Rodicofani to Ceprano, and that the Romagna, the Marches of Ancona, the Five Cities, and all the other land contained in that tract of territory, were all ecclesiastical and not German

[4] "Rex Carolus privatur officio senatoris, et eodem anno vicaria Tusciae per eundem (Nicolaum) . . . Papa misit unum cardinalem, qui patientiam regis tentaret super praedictis sibi ablatis: et audito, quod cardinalem honorifice recepisset, et modeste respondisset, ait: felicitatem Carolus habet a Domo Franciae, ingenii perspicacitatem a regno Hispaniae, discretionem verborum a frequentatione Romanae Curiae" Raynaldus 1278,69.

property. As a result of the documents subscribed to by the Emperor and the Pope, that which was an ancient right became a fact,[5] and the Church enjoys all the territory she possesses to-day.

After Charles had been pushed back in the confines of his realm, the ecclesiastical patrimony was now clear of foreigners, many cities were pacified by the efforts of Cardinal Latino, and thus the Chair of St. Peter felt itself secure in its own territory and the Pope who occupied it thought of gathering from the accrued advantages salutary fruit for all Italy. If Ptolemy of Lucca, Giordano and Platina can be believed, Nicholas and Rudolph meditated a design fraught with most serious consequences to the future destinies of Italy and all Europe. The Pope had conceived the project of dividing the Roman Empire into four great sovereignties: that of Germany for Rudolph and his descendants in hereditary succession; that of Dauphiny and a part of ancient Burgundy for Clementia, daughter of Rudolph, and wife of Charles Martel, grandson of the king of Sicily and their descendants; Italy was to be divided into two kingdoms, that of Tuscany and Lombardy, which were to be given respectively to the two nephews of the Pope, the princes Orsini. We believe it quite possible that such a thought entered the mind of the Pope. Affairs in Italy were in such a condition, and the mutual interests of Nicholas and Rudolph would thus have been so well consulted that it is easy to believe that both would have agreed to this project. By making a division into four monarchies, namely, Sicily, the States of the Church, Tuscany, and Lombardy, Italy would be spared the anguish of her republics, and this multitude of Lords who raised themselves upon their ruins; her inhabitants would present ranks at once closer and more united against the encroachments of foreign monarchies; in fine they would have less to fear from the imperial domination so divided. The sudden death of Nicholas frustrated the vast design.

After the death of Nicholas, Charles took new courage. Knowing how little he might expect from a pope, shrewd and watchful, he wished to create one who would do his pleasure. A son and vassal of Holy Church, he made bold

[5] Raynaldus 1278, 47 et seqq.

to intrude himself among the cardinals in conclave at Viterbo. He cast into prison three cardinals who opposed his designs, and kept them there on a diet of bread and water, until in sheer desperation they agreed with the other Italian cardinals and voted for a Frenchman as pope, Cardinal Simon de Brie, who took the name of Martin IV.[6] Charles could not have found another man more devoted to his interests. At one stroke all the work of the popes from Gregory X to Nicholas was undone. Charles was again created a senator of Rome, and the government of all pontifical towns was entrusted to Frenchmen, creatures of this prince. Paleologus, against whom Charles vigorously pushed forward preparations for war, was excommunicated.

No longer were legates seen piously occupied, as had been Cardinal Latino, in traveling through Italy to reconcile the Guelphs and the Ghibellines, but in their stead sinister messengers charged with the destruction of the latter. The rude repulse of the ambassadors of the Lambertazzi, the first of the Ghibellines of the Romagna to present themselves before Pope Martin at Orvieto suing for peace, was a cruel action; and equally harsh were those censures angrily hurled against Forli, whither the Ghibellines had retreated. However, those French agents such as John of Pà, Count of Romagna, found a most powerful obstacle in that eminent warrior, the support of the Ghibellines, Guy of Montefeltro, who often taught these strangers to be a trifle more self-restrained in the land of others. Unfortunately, the Italians combined with these strangers, because they were Guelphs.

In the meantime unhappy Sicily was in agony. Charles was no longer under any restraint; he was king and pope at the one time, and the hour was at hand when the excesses of an unrestrained tyranny drove the people to have recourse to the most frightful means to end it. Power, and might pressed heavily upon them, but buoyant minds were meditating a design to free them. Among the sufferers was John of Procida, whom we consider unique in the history of those who by one stroke have broken the chains of an oppressed people. To form domestic conspiracies, to complete them by a thrust of the dagger, is not a rare

* Record. Malasp —John Villani.

thing, and the number is great of those who have hurled a prince from his throne by a daring blow; but they could not prevent a renewal of the tyranny, either in a new prince who ascended the vacant throne, or in the frenzy of a disordered democracy. But to lay the wires of an immense plot which is at once to restore those rights which a despairing people had lost; to know and employ the chiefs to whose hands he must entrust the wires of this vast network; to remain, despite impatient yearnings, calm and immovable within the limits of prudence and justice so as not to miss his end; to prepare for a people flushed with victory new laws of government in the shadow of which it could take breath and establish itself; in a word, side by side with the tyranny which oppressed it, during a long period to make the power of regeneration march in secret and bring about its triumph, this was the gigantic labor performed by John of Procida to change the lot of Sicily, and which entitles him to be regarded as a genius truly extraordinary. He sounded the dispositions of Paleologus, dismayed at the warlike preparations of Charles, and from him received much gold. He revived in Peter of Aragon the right of sovereignty over Sicily which he claimed by reason of his marriage with Constance, the daughter of Manfred, the last of the Hohenstaufens, and from him he received a large quota of soldiers. If certain historians are to be believed, it was he who suggested to Nicholas III the grand design of division, and the wrath of a people, downtrodden and exasperated, would be joined to the indignation which the impieties of Charles caused the Pontiff. It is also said that Nicholas flattered John of Procida, and expected Sicily to give the blow which the arm of a pontiff could not strike. If we do not reject absolutely the current rumor, we can by no means admit as certain on mere hearsay this appalling solidarity; but we reject chiefly the reason assigned for it by later writers namely, the insolent refusal by Charles to unite the family of Anjou with that of the Orsini.

That Nicholas, jealous and proud of the glory of his family, had sought a royal alliance for it, which the Frenchman haughtily opposed, we may believe; but that this pope, out of revenge for this insulting refusal, had entered into the conspiracy of John of Procida, nothing is more improbable. To deliver Sicily from the yoke of Charles, consecrated by papal investiture, was an act heroic in its purpose, which a miserable family pride could not have dictated. The death of Nicholas surely must have been very distressing to John of Procida, but it did not compromise the success of the enterprise. The Sicilians found a compensation for this loss in their desperation, which was extreme when they saw that Martin instead of tightening the reins on Charles, only slackened them the more. However, the Pope was not ignorant of the armaments prepared by Peter of Aragon, and suspected the end that the husband of Constance had in view; yet fascinated as he was to the interests of Charles, he remained inactive and took no notice of the clouds which were gathering both within and without Sicily.

At length the famous Sicilian Vespers were sounded, and there was won by the sword that justice which had been implored in vain from the Pope; a diabolical revenge for a tyranny still more diabolical. The Sicilians arose to a man to drive out the detested Angevine, but they respected the Church. In fact the inhabitants of Palermo, convened in an assembly, gave proof of moderation and of a feeling altogether Roman when they took the resolution to govern themselves in common under the protection of the Church,[7] and all this in presence of a tumultuous people still disgusting from French blood; all this notwithstanding the thirst for revenge which devoured them, and in the midst of the anxiety which their hearts experience on recovering liberty bought by so much daring. They separated the lost rights of Charles from those of the Church; and far from confounding her with this wicked prince, they requested her to ratify in some way an act to which a sense of natural justice had borne them, but one which the meekness of her head could not allow her to undertake herself. Most excellent dispositions! Any pope other than Martin would have favored them, sparing thereby his successors the embarrassment of many affairs difficult to judge. After the bloody Sicilian Vespers Martin clung more closely to Charles, and this king blinded him to the extent of drawing him in his train into those perfidious ways into which his pride precipitated

[7] Barth de Neocastro C. 14—Nicol Special. C. I. C. 4.

him, and in which he lost the kingdom of Sicily. All the island was aroused and united itself in an admirable republican federation under the standard of the Holy Keys. The heroic defence of Messina, before which the anger of Charles spent itself, demonstrated to the entire world that the arms of these people were deserving of success. The messengers from Palermo presented themselves before Martin; they asked forgiveness for the means they had employed in securing their freedom, and they implored the protection of Holy Church; but their petition being answered in a harsh and unbecoming manner, they returned home, and took up arms not only against Charles, but also against the Church. And thus through the fault of this pope confounding the rights of St. Peter with that of Charles of Anjou, future popes found themselves burdened with the odious task of fighting a high-minded people to sustain an unworthy prince, because they could not recover otherwise the right of sovereignty which the Church possessed over Sicily.

All these things were witnessed by a certain man, Benedict Gaetani by name. He was already a member of the Papal Curia, and called to take part in the administration of the momentous measures of the times. Wherefore one thought entered deeply into his mind, and instructed it by facts that gave form and character to every other thought; this thought was inspired by the spectacle of the Church reduced to servitude not by secret enemies, but by those who called themselves her children and her vassals, the Church obliged to act despite appearances the most odious which could be understood only by calm and far-removed discerners of the events that went before.

Anagni, a most ancient city, once the chief seat of the Hernici, is situated in that part of Italy that is called the Campagna. It has a charming location on the summit of a hill at the foot of the Apennines which extend towards Rome, and embrace, with the mountains of Piperno and of Sezze, facing the sea-coast of Terracina, the fertile Anagni valley. After the invasion of the barbarians it was the most renowned city in this Cistiberine part of the Papal States which bordered on the kingdom of Naples. At the time in which the events of our history were happening it had already been the birthplace of three pontiffs, Innocent III, Gregory IX, and Alexander IV, and they contributed to its splendor. It was also the seat of very illustrious families, namely the Ceccani, the Tusculani, the Frangipani, the Collemedio, Annibaldeschi, and greatest of all the families of the Counts of Segni and the Gaetani.[8] Whence the latter had come to Anagni, whether they were the same family as the Gaetani of Gaeta, to which Gelasius II belonged, we do not know; and as the reader cares to learn only of the deeds of Boniface, we shall not impose on him a treatise on the origin and descent of the family. In the thirteenth century Loffredo Gaetani, son of Matthias, had been a captain in the army of King Manfred; he married one of the Conti family, niece of Alexander IV,[9] by whom he had many children, among them Benedict, the subject of this history. We do not know in what year he was born, but it is certain that his birth took place in the thirteenth century about the second or third decade. Osius and Rossi aver that he lived 86 years, basing their opinions upon the fact that in the year 1255 he accompanied the legate Cardinal Fiesco as secretary.[10] Before this time, in Rome, he exercised the office of an advocate. Now supposing that he exercised this office and accompanied the legate in mature age that is to say, at thirty or forty years, it is then clear that he must have been born in the second or third decade of the century. From his childhood he inspired his parents with great hopes by the keenness of his dawning intellect and by his fiery soul, a possession common to all the Italians of those times, who under a rough exterior possessed hearts capable of performing noble deeds. Great-souled fathers, of a now degenerate race, then begot great-souled sons. To be instructed in piety and learning he was sent to a monastery of the Friars Minor at Velletri, and was entrusted to the care of Friar Leonard Patrasso, his uncle.[11] Benedict Gaetani always remembered these first years of his life and showed his gratitude both towards the Friars, by heaping favors upon them and by appointing in 1300 a cardinal from their order, which he greatly favored, and

---

[8] Cayro. History of the city of Anagni, p. 65.
[9] Charles de Lellis. Fam. Gaetani. [10] Rubeus. Life of Boniface VIII.
[11] Teuli. History of Velletri. Book 2., chap 5.

also towards Velletri itself, of which, when Pontiff, he accepted the office of Governor.[12]

In his day Gaetani was known far and wide for his knowledge of law, and it is surprising that the writers of his day did not hand down to posterity the name of the university in which he studied. Du Boulay places him among the most illustrious doctors of Paris, stating that he passed a long time in the University of that city.[13] This opinion is confirmed by the long stay made in Paris by Gaetani, who in a certain Bull says that he had been a Canon of the Church of Paris; and from his own words it clearly appears that he not only enjoyed the fruits of that Canonry, but also exercised the office personally.[14]

He became so well versed in law, especially ecclesiastical, that his reputation for learning soon became widespread. This reputation obtained for him many and rich prebends in various churches. He was a canon at Anagni; and although the canons of Todi could not by law receive any one in their chapter unless he was in Holy Orders, yet they granted the request of Peter Gaetani, who asked that his nephew Benedict, as yet a layman, be received by them as canon, on account of his virtues and great erudition. Even the canons of Lyons had him for a fellow member.[15] The lustre of his birth, and more especially his reputation for learning soon opened the way to ecclesiastical preferments. He was raised to the office of Notary Apostolic,[16] whose duty in the early ages of the Church was to write and preserve the acts of the martyrs, and in later ages the Bulls, the decrees of the pontiffs, and the canons of the Councils. Gaetani also exercised the office of Consistorial

[12] Borgia. History of the Church and City of Velletri B. IV., p. 295.
[13] Du Boulay. Hist. Universitatis Paris. Catal. III. Tom. 2., p. 676.
[14] " . . . . Quod ejusdem Ecclesiae copiosa benignitas nos olim dum in "minoribus ageremus, de ipsius honorabili gremio existentes fovit ac tractavit ut filium, maternis fovet et lactavit uberibus." Du Boulay.
[15] In the Bull by which he bestows on Gaetani the Deaconry of St. Nicholas-in-chains, Pope Martin IV enumerates all these prebends: " . . . ut ecclesias S. Nicolai in carcere Tulliano de Urbe, et de Barro in Ligonensi, et de Piliaco, archidiaconatum in Carnotensi, ac ecclesiaim de Thoucester, canonicatus quoque ac praebendas in Ligonensi, Carnotensi, Parisiensi, Anagnina, Tuderina, S Audomari Morinensi, as in Basilica S. Petri de Urbe retinere possit."
[16] Bull of Clement V. Rubeus. Life of Boniface VIII, p. 3.

Advocate an office no less elevated than the first named, inasmuch as the Consistorial Advocate, created for the first time by Pope St. Gregory the Great,[17] were deputed to plead the causes of the churches and of the poor. What an amount of knowledge and strength of character were required in the exercise of this office,[18] we can readily gather from the words of the pope who placed them in office, and also from one of the constitutions of Pope Martin IV, who wished these Advocates to be the very personification of wisdom and honesty.—

We ought to record that Gaetani performed his duty well in all these offices, and this convinced the popes that he had a talent and mind fitted for greater things, and capable of taking part in the management of the difficult issues between the Church and princes. There was a very important task namely of resisting Manfred who was furiously roaming over the kingdom of Naples, waging war against that part of it belonging to the pope, and making himself master of it by force of arms. Pope Alexander IV had not the means to resist him, nor could he trust the inconstant Neapolitans. He thought of inviting a foreign prince, and of investing him with the realm, and thus close the gate to any one whomsoever of the Suabian line. He dispatched Cardinal Ottobono de Fiesco, who was afterwards Adrian V, as legate to Henry, King of England, that he might offer in fief the kingdom of Sicily to Edmund his son. Benedict Gaetani went with Fiesco on this legation, which failed to achieve the desired effect; yet in the compacts sworn to by the king for his son, the Pope had a solemn testimony of how by public official act the direct and supreme dominion of the Church over the kingdom of Sicily had been recognized. Among these compacts sworn to by the English king was this one, that Edmund, being king of Sicily, could not aspire to the imperial crown; and if by any chance he took the title of emperor, he would lose the royal crown. A wise provision this, suggested by the still recent memory of Frederick II, the vast extent of whose domain occasioned untold vexation to the Church.

It was after the return of Gaetani from England with

[17] Vid. Piazza. Opera Pie di Rom., cap. 27, page 288.
[18] St. Gregory. Book 4, Index 13, cap. 69.

Cardinal Fiesco, that Peter, his uncle, entreated the Canons of Todi (1260), to admit him as one of their members. These canons, as we stated before, did not have it in their power to receive one who was not in major Orders, and such was Benedict Gaetani. But wishing to gratify the uncle and to honor the nephew, he obtained from Pope Alexander IV a Bull granting the necessary dispensation in order to favor Benedict,[19] and they accordingly received him as one of their number.[20] In consequence Gaetani kept Todi ever in fond remembrance when he became pope, and entertained a singular affection for it. He presented to the Cathedral of Todi the armorial ensign representing the Saviour with the Apostles Peter and Paul, and the red banner with a white cross and the papal keys; he ordered the façade to be built and two bells to be cast, one of which was called Boniface; he desired moreover the Canons of Todi to come to Rome every year to receive Communion on Holy Thursday. He also bestowed benefits on the city, by releasing it from the patrimony of St. Peter, and declared the territory of Petignano to be subject to it and not to Orvieto any longer. In return for all these favors there is celebrated to this day in the Cathedral of Todi an annual mass for the repose of his soul.[21]

In the prologue of this history we remarked how jealously Rudolph, King of the Romans, and Charles of Anjou, King of Sicily, regarded each other, and how skilfully Pope Nicholas III restrained them, directing their plans not without the advantage of the spiritual and temporal rights of the Papal Chair. But it happened that a great incentive for war between these princes was afforded by Provence. Raymond di Beranger of the house of the Counts of Barcelona, the last Count of that house, had died without male issue. Of the four daughters which Beatrice of Savoy bore to Raymond, all were married, three becoming queens; Margaret wedded St. Louis of France; Eleanor espoused Henry, King of England; Sanchia became the wife of Richard of Cornwall, elected King of the Romans; while Beatrice married Charles of Anjou. In the year 1261 the wife of Richard died, and in 1267 that of Charles. Eleanor and Margaret were still

---

[19] See Docum A.   [20] See Docum. B.
[21] From the Archives of the Church of Todi.

living when Charles took absolute possession of Provence, and exacted the oath of fealty from the entire province. The surviving queens protested, demanding that the territory of Provence be divided into four parts, so as to preserve their own and their children's rights. Margaret was the loudest in her protestations; and expecting little or no aid from King Philip, her son, she had recourse to her nephew, Edward I, and to Rudolph, King of the Romans. Her appeal to the latter bore most fruit. In return for his investing her with that part of Provence and Forcalquier which she claimed, she recognized the sovereignty of Rudolph over the ancient kingdom of Arles. This compact was pleasing to Rudolph, and more pleasing still was the favorable opportunity for breaking peaceful relations with Charles, who lorded over Italy in his place. The Angevine had been weakened by the loss of the vicariate of Tuscany, this having been taken from him by Pope Nicholas III who thus stripped him of a great part of his sovereignty in Italian affairs; yet seeing himself face to face with Rudolph, who was aroused against him by Margaret, his sister-in-law, Charles, resolved to resist him, so as not to lose his present possession of Provence. In the beginning of the year 1279 he dispatched his eldest son Charles, Prince of Salerno, surnamed the Lame, to Provence, to recall and accentuate by his presence the fact of his possession. The royal son visited the province and repairing to the court of his uncle, Philip of France, he was accorded a most splendid reception. This reception convinced Margaret of the dispositions of the King of France, her son; he would prefer to see his uncle independent lord of Provence, than see his mother vassal of the Hapsburg prince. This circumstance encouraged Charles to take a firm stand against Rudolph.

If Charles and Rudolph flew to arms, Pope Nicholas foresaw the ruin of that peace which he had established with so much care, and that the war of Provence would soon extend to Italy. A just disposition of their rights would appease them. He turned his eyes to Benedict Gaetani, and considered him fitted to accomplish the difficult task in company with Cardinal Matthew Acquasparta. To be considered worthy of this mission, Gaetani must have previously given sufficient proofs of consummate diplomacy and his devotion to the Pontiff. This was the first time that he had an opportunity to study the bend of the princes of his time. Nicholas bishop of Tripoli had preceded these two legates in Germany and had the matter well under way; it was happily concluded by Cardinals Acquasparta and Gaetani. Thanks to their care, Charles and Rudolph came to terms. The latter retained the sovereignty over Provence and Forcalquier, the former was left in undisturbed possession of it, receiving feudal investiture from Rudolph. The investiture of the fourth part of Provence which had been given to Margaret was revoked. Mutual promises of peace between the two kings ratified the treaty. Letters from the Pope appeased the troubled mind of the disappointed queen.

The two princes concluded the treaty by separate documents drawn up by the legates.[22] As Gaetani took part in this work, it is well to observe how clearly are reflected the profound sentiments of peace and justice which animated him and which were to make him so zealous a defender of these two virtues during his pontificate. As a means of closing the way to any dispute whatsoever we read in the document of Charles: " If by any misfortune, " which may God forbid, there should arise any dispute " between us and the King of the Romans, the one will " not declare war against the other; neither by himself " nor by others will he molest the vassals of the other . . . " . . . but we will have recourse to the Roman Pontiff; " and we and the said King of Romans will abide by the " decision of the Pontiff given in the matter of our dispute, " whenever we cannot by ourselves find a means of agree- " ment. Besides these conditions which are to be rigor- " ously observed, we absolutely and freely determine by " this document to subject ourselves to the Roman Pontiff " both as regards spiritual and temporal matters. We " have come to the express agreement that in reserving to " the Roman Pontiff now and hereafter the full and entire " right to interpret the clauses herein contained and to " make known their meaning, we find ourselves in an " especial manner to receive this interpretation and declaration." . . . . . .

When Gaetani had returned from this legation, Nicholas

[22] Raynaldus, 1280. 2. 3. 4.

III planned to reward him for his services, and accordingly he appointed him a cardinal priest of the title of St. Sylvester and Martin-ai-Monti.[23] To this dignity Martin IV afterwards added the Deaconry of St. Nicholas-in-Carcere, permitting him to retain at the same time the prebends he enjoyed in many churches.[24] Martin sought thus to make use of the knowledge of Gaetani, in calling upon him to take part in the difficult administration of papal affairs. Unfortunately, by lingering in the clutches of Charles, he put the cardinal to the necessity of using his talents more in repairing the disasters than in increasing the prosperity of the Apostolic See.

After the sad Sicilian Vespers, it seemed that the astonished eyes of all Europe were fixed on that blood-bathed island. Charles and Pope Martin in league used all their endeavors to lead it back to its former subjection, the one by investing it with armed men, the other by terrifying it with threatening Bulls and by shrewdly working upon their minds through the friendly overtures of a legate, Cardinal Parma. The arms of Charles for a time prevailed, but never the bulls nor the legates. All the anger of Sicily was pent up in the breasts of the inhabitants of Messina, who, strongly entrenched in their city, held out successfully against Charles. Whilst the fighting was going on there, the Sicilians, rebuffed by Martin, a pope who was too much of a Frenchman, irrevocably entrusted to Peter of Aragon the supreme direction of their affairs. This Spanish prince reanimated the desperate courage of this freed people by furnishing them with troops. Thus taking shelter under the good services of a king, Sicily became day by day more formidable to the French, and the fortunes of war were equally balanced on both sides. The strife was no longer between an old king skilful in the art of controlling a people by his will, and a people, who, when the first intoxication of liberty gained with so much eclat

---

[23] Ciacconi Vita Pont.

[24] "Ut Ecclesias Sti. Nicolai in carcere Tulliano, de Urbe et Barro in Lingonensi et de Piliaco, archidiaconatum in Carnotensi ac ecclesiam de Thouchester, Canonicatus quoque ac Praebendas in Lingonensi, Carnotensi, Lugdunensi, Parisiensi, Anagnina, Tudertina, Sti Audomari, Morinensi ac in Basilica Sti. Petri de Urbe retineri posset." Bull. Martin IV apud Rubeum Vita Boniface, p. 3.

had subsided, would readily allow itself to be enslaved again; but a king was matched against a king of the stamp and character of Peter of Aragon. This latter summoned to Sicily, Constance, his wife, and James, his eldest son. Although victorious and powerful by reason of the Sicilians' renewal of the rights which his wife Constance of the Suabian House had given over this realm, yet inasmuch as he was in pecuniary straits, he sought an opportunity in which by stratagem he might overcome Charles. The Frenchman that Charles was, and the impetuosity which his advanced age did not lessen, soon afforded the opportunity. Descending from the height of his throne to the station of a private individual he challenged Peter to a single combat, and agreed to leave to the issue of this combat, the settlement of the right of sovereignty over Sicily. Peter accepted the challenge, and chose as the place of combat the plains of Bordeaux, in Gascony, neutral territory that belonged to Edward of England. The writers of the time, according as they were Guelphs or Ghibellines, attribute to the cunning of Charles or Peter, this expedient whereby to put the other at a distance from Sicily. Having settled the place of encounter, they agreed to meet there on the first day of June, 1283; Edward of England was to be referee, or in his stead the governor of the territory. One hundred knights were to accompany each prince, and prove with him their right by skill in arms. The two kings swore on the Gospel to stand by the agreement, and forty barons took the oath for them. The one who failed to keep his promise, would be covered forever with infamy and would lose both the name and honor of king.

The Papal Curia disturbed by the Sicilian movement beheld with astonishment and sorrow the ill-advised determination of Charles to engage in a duel with Peter. To entrust one's life to the issue of a single combat was wicked, unbecoming to a royal personage, and hazardous to the Church. The absence of Charles would confirm the Sicilians in their independence, facilitate the conquest already commenced in Calabria, and if the Frenchman was defeated, all was lost in Sicily for the Pope. Pope Martin was firm as ever in his sad mistake of identifying the rights of Charles with those of the Church, and thus he dishonored the Church which he made responsible for the

tyranny of the Angevine. Perhaps equally solicitous for the rights of Charles and of St. Peter, he determined to oppose the project and wished to prevent Charles from the plebeian combat. He appointed Gaetani as legate to restrain the enraged Frenchman, and made him bearer of a letter full of salutary advice, disclosing the evils that would result were he to persevere in his intentions, and declaring the oath he had taken to be of no force, for the reason that an unlawful act is not binding on anyone. He concluded with these words: " Moreover, because of
" the singular solicitude and love we have for your person,
" we wish to provide for the event of failing to persuade
" you, in which case it would be necessary that some one
" confirm by spoken word what we would fain have already
" convinced you by writing. Wherefore with the advice of
" our brethren we send to you our beloved son Benedict
" Gaetani, Cardinal Deacon of the title of St. Nicholas-in-
" Chains, in our opinion a man of profound wisdom, faith-
" ful, shrewd, resourceful, prudent, a warm supporter of
" your glory and of your royal dignity. Since the Church
" is unable and unwilling to permit the course to which
" you are committing yourself, he will more clearly make
" known to you our mind, and with the greatest prudence
" he will reveal the vast and innumerable dangers, which
" your absence from the kingdom of Sicily in these days
" cannot but entail, dangers real and not imaginary. He
" will not neglect to tell you of what rashness you are ac-
" cused, in order to determine you to obey without delay
" and without contradiction our prayers and our advice
" and to settle your mind on the order we have given.[25]

There is no doubt that the more the Pope longed for it, with greater ardor did Gaetani strive to bring Charles to his senses; but all in vain, for the obstinate prince was determined on fighting the duel. It was well for him that the duel was not fought; because the crafty Peter either did not come, or came in a manner so as not to be seen by Charles, who remained with his knights vainly awaiting his arrival. Then it was Gaetani learned that when the Pope raised his voice even in wise counsels to the princes of those times for their own interests, it had no effect on their will: he could conclude that the Papacy speaking to

[25] See document C.

them in the name of justice would meet with only pride and arrogance. He learned this truth beforehand; the time to test it was near at hand.

Pope Martin himself was also lacking in prudence, for his duty was to defend the rights of the Church in Sicily without ever making himself a minister of the anger of Charles. He not only declared Peter a usurper of the Sicilian kingdom, but deprived him of the kingdoms of Aragon, Valencia and Catalonia, with which he invested Charles of Valois, the second son of Philip the Bold of France, who was to hold them in Fief for the Holy See. This only fanned the war flame which burst into a blaze between Peter and Charles of Valois, the reason of which was that the former desired to preserve what was his own, and the latter to maintain the title of king which he held by appointment from the Pope. Some French soldiers summoned to Italy strengthened the Guelph party, and enabled it to rule the Ghibellines with rod of iron. These measures were a cause of most grievous injury to the Church and to Charles himself, for they aroused anew in the hearts of the Sicilians the spirit of revenge and gave them the courage of despair; moreover they shook even the loyalty of the Neapolitans. In fact the Sicilians, led by that most skilful naval commander Roger of Loria, after a fierce battle near Malta, dispersed a fleet of twenty galleys, which Charles had dispatched from Provence.[26] Moreover in the very waters of Naples they utterly defeated the navy of Charles the Lame, and captured him with all his barons.[27] In the city of Naples the people then began to cry out: " Death to King Charles, long live Roger of Loria." However the freedom of Sicily which escaped altogether from the hands of Charles, the surrender forced or voluntary of many cities of Calabria and the Basilicata, and the captivity of his son, all these misfortunes dealt a death blow to the heart of that prince whose every ambitious purpose up to that time had been favored by fortune. He died the seventh of January 1285, leaving a war to his son, misfortune to his people, and to the popes the obligation of regaining Sicily for the Church, among thorny embarrassments occasioned by

---

[26] Nic. Special Hist. Sic. lib. 1 c 26 S. R. I. T. 9.   [27] Ibidem.

dynastic interests too little sacred. In the same year there followed Charles to the grave Pope Martin, Philip the Bold of France, and Peter of Aragon; the former two were succeeded respectively by Honorius IV and Philip the Fair, while Peter's eldest son Alphonsus ascended the throne of Aragon, and James, the second-born that of Sicily. Naples was reserved for Charles the Lame.

Honorius of the Roman family of Savelli ascended the Papal throne, confronted by many difficulties in which the French Pope Martin had involved the Papacy. Every means which the supreme priesthood in those times offered him, he determined to employ, to drive James from Sicily, and to place Charles of Valois on the throne of Aragon, that is to say, by hurling censures, and by laying tithes on the churches. But affairs turned out unfortunately both in Spain, whence Philip of France was forced to withdraw and in Sicily where James was solemnly crowned king, although he had been excommunicated together with his mother Constance. In his trouble the pontiff turned his attention to the kingdom of Naples whose affairs were administered by the Count of Artois and his own legate Gerard of Parma. To appease the minds of the Neapolitans, embittered by the wrongs inflicted on them by the House of Anjou, he wrote an excellent constitution of government entitled: "Pacts of Pope Honorius." To this document Benedict Gaetani signed his name together with thirteen other cardinals.

In the meanwhile Charles II, having escaped from the fury of the Sicilians who wished to kill him to revenge the deaths of Manfred and Conradin, languished in prison in Catalonia. In him were placed the rights of the Church over Sicily, because these had become involved with those of the family of Anjou; hence the pontiffs forced to exert themselves for his liberation, could not effect this without some sacrifice of their own interests. There did not appear any prospect of spontaneous agreement between him and his conquerors, for the war against Aragon, suspended by the death of Philip III, had been resumed by Philip IV, the Fair, an ally of his maternal uncle, James, king of Majorca. Alphonsus was too stubborn to heed censures, still less the peaceful propositions of the Pope, especially since the war in Aragon was going favorably to him, and in Sicily he had nothing to fear so long as the terrible Roger of Loria lived to command his fleet. The youthful prince Philip grieved less over the imprisonment of Charles, as he did not aspire to extend his sovereignty in Spain. Only Edward of England, bound by the nearest ties of relationship to these princes and older than they, was moved by the heartrending letters of the children of Charles,[28] and prepared to negotiate for his release. He calls to a council in Bordeaux the ambassadors of France, of Aragon, of Naples, of Sicily and of Castile. In this council he suggested, in order to obtain the release of Charles, that Sicily and the territory in Calabria which they had conquered, be ceded to Aragon; and besides that the Count of Artois should renounce his claims to the throne of Aragon. Some details of less importance accompanied these main clauses of the treaty. Charles longed for his release; Alphonsus, although victor, desired peace on account of the weariness displayed by his people and the apprehensions caused him by Sanchez of Castile. Philip was silent on the conditions, but Honorius strongly opposed them.

Imagining these propositions to be a treaty concluded and signed by Charles, the Pope wrote energetically to him in order to annul the treaty. He was unwilling and rightly so, that the sovereignty of the Church over Sicily should be bartered for the liberation of Charles. Being a vassal of St. Peter, Charles of his own free will could not relinquish that kingdom without the Pope intervening as the principal party in the transaction. The war against Aragon was resumed; that against Sicily became more fierce, and again in the waters of Naples the admiral Roger of Loria conquered and dispersed the French fleet, crowning this victory by recovering the city of Augusta. Worn out in their fruitless efforts to adjust the affairs of indomitable Sicily, the popes of those times ended their days, and so in the like manner Honorius died. During the ten months that the papal chair remained vacant, Edward renewed his efforts for the release of Charles, and this was finally accomplished by the treaty of Oleron by which Charles obtained his freedom. But Philip the Fair who had held himself aloof from these agreements, no

[28] Rymer, 7, 2, p. 317.

STATUE OF BONIFACE VIII, SET IN THE FACADE OF THE CATHEDRAL OF ANAGNI.

sooner saw his uncle liberated, and Alphonsus suing at Rome for peace through his legates, than he prosecuted vigorously the war that James, king of Majorca, waged for him against Aragon.[29]

The successor of Honorius, Nicholas IV, whose moderation made him supposed to be favorable to the Ghibelline party, ascended the papal throne at a time in which the entire religious edifice of the Middle Ages was crumbling day by day. The hope of the liberation of the Holy Land, the attainment of which was longed for by so many generations, being abandoned by the Christian princes, perished on the fallen walls of Ptolemais (Acre). The priestly influence, violently expelled from the heart of civil society, could not, on reentering its sanctuary, defend the threshold against the tyranny of the princes who followed her there. In fine the Church even of Rome had been injured in its temporal sovereignty by the loss of Sicily, which the sovereigns negotiating peace placed in the scale of the agreements as a thing not sacred. Hence, no more were seen before the successor of St. Peter, monarchs respectfully bowing their heads, but bold and haughty jurists. Of these three evils which affected the heart of the Roman Pontiff, the usurpation of ecclesiastical rights by princes, in virtue of a right created by lawyers, was the most terrible. Nicholas felt all the bitterness of it, and with him all those whose advanced age permitted to recall the reign of Innocent III, or who, by the maturity of their judgment and learning foresaw the evil consequences of this abuse. We think that for this double reason Cardinal Gaetani was not the one least distressed; for we find him working to repair these evils in his third legation.

All the princes more or less openly made war on the Church, violating in her possession and sacred persons her rights and her liberty. But Dionysius, King of Portugal, showed himself more quarrelsome than others. Alphonsus had been a covetous man himself and passionate, but at his death had deplored the injury he had caused to the Church. His son Dionysius inherited more the malice than the repentance of his father. Clement IV, Gregory X, and John XXI had failed in their admonitions to his father and in the censures with which they had struck

[29] Surita Ann. L. 4 c. 110, 111.

him; alike unfortunate, Nicholas beheld the injustices of the son without hope of correcting them. Dionysius had married St. Elizabeth, daughter of Peter of Aragon, and the sanctity of his wife should have chastened him and moderated his desires; but unfortunately, the great ones of earth were already becoming acquainted with that compensation system which teaches that without danger to the soul a man can unite good works with the usurpation of ecclesiastical rights. Dionysius was disturbed in mind by the anathema hurled against him by the Pope on account of his sins, but he was not turned from his course of action; the people on all sides began to make a clamor, but he pretended not to notice it. At length he was brought to his senses, and he agreed to submit to the judgment of the Pontiff his disputes with the hierarchy of his realm.

The royal and ecclesiastical procurators arrived in Rome. The king was represented by Martin, chorister of the cathedral church of Talavaras, and John, canon of Coimbra; the archbishop of Braga, the bishops of Coimbra and of Lamea, had charge of the interests of the Portuguese Church. The Pope named a commission to hear and pass judgment on the affair. It was made up of three cardinals, Latino, Bishop of Ostia, Peter, Cardinal of St. Mark, and Benedict Gaetani: a venerable tribunal, in which virtue and talent combined, offered justice the surest guarantees, because the first two excelled in sanctity, and the third in knowledge of the law. The Portuguese prelates complained of the oppression of the churches and the clergy of the kingdom, which left no vestige of ecclesiastical liberty;[30] their complaints were recounted in forty articles. The judges decided and the parties submitted to the judgment; it repealed the laws of Alphonsus and Dionysus; freed the churches and clergy from laical impieties, and pronounced penalties against the offenders. We find that after the heads of accusation upon which the judgment of the cardinals bore, all the favor that the royal procurators obtained was the declaration of the innocence of their king in the past, and a promise of faithful observance of the compacts in the future; for each article is constantly followed by formula: " Up to this

[30] Raynaldus, year 1289, no. 17.

time the king has not done this," and in "his name we promise that he will not do it."[31] However the treaty was ratified by public acts and by the papal authority, which deputed the Prior of the Friar Preachers of Lisbon to receive the oath of the king and absolve him from censures.[32]

The affairs of Portugal being settled, Benedict Gaetani was entrusted with another mission, in the performance of which he was to acquire a great knowledge of the men and things of his time. He was ordered by Nicholas to go as legate to France, where the affairs that particularly occupied the mind of the Pontiff took a disastrous turn, and became more and more entangled. Hopes regarding the Holy Land were on the wane; Tripoli had fallen, and Ptolomais (Acre) alone remained standing, but to become the prey of the immense army of Kalaun Elalfi, Sultan of Egypt, who was now besieging it. Nicholas alone felt truly grieved over the desperate straits to which the faithful in the Holy Land were reduced; the other princes were glad because they found occasion to gorge themselves with sacred tithes, under the pretext of a prospective crusade. The clergy could not always remain impassible to this iniquitous collection; but if they resisted, they would be at variance with royal ministers, and they would be losers. That which avarice coveted, tyranny extorted. To remedy these scandalous abuses, it was necessary to urge the princes to a crusade and make war on the Sultan, or oblige them to restore the tithes, and at last establish peace among themselves. Philip was more insolent than others to the churches; and as he exhausted the treasury with more avidity than the rest, so he was more vigorously opposed to peace; because he coveted Aragon, he had no intention of tiring himself by a war which others would make for him. Gaetani and Gerard of Parma entered France, bearing letters of credit the most flattering and the most honorable. The Pope expressed himself thus:—
" Full of consideration for your persons, of whose great
" merits, many virtues, and tried honesty we are not
" ignorant; knowing that we love peace and amity; that
" the honor and elevation of the two kings, Charles the
" Lame and Alphonsus of Aragon, are dear to your heart;

---

[31] Quod rex non fecit hactenus haec, et promittunt ejus nomine quod non faciet in futurum.   [32] Raynaldus, year 1289, no. 17.

"wishing to show all our affectionate solicitude for the
"conclusion of this treaty, we order you, by these apostolic
"letters, to accept with good grace, on account of respect
"for God, the burden we impose upon you of entering this
"country (France). We regret very much separating
"ourselves from you whose presence is so valuable to us.
"Exert yourself to treat this affair, and all that which is
"attached to it, in the manner that your wisdom and
"prudence will judge most useful for the peace of the
"world, for the glory of God and the Apostolic See, and for
"the interests of the Holy Land, which holds the first
place in our thoughts."— We do not often find expressed in letters of this kind the disquietude felt by the pontiff because of the enforced absence of any legate. It shows that Gaetani was the very soul of the affairs at the papal court. We find him and Cardinal Gerard sent on the greatest and most intricate missions of those times. They undertook to negotiate two grave affairs: the one of establishing peace between the Christian princes fighting for the usurped Sicily and the disputed Aragon; and the other to obtain aid for the Holy Land.[33]

(1290) Hardly had they arrived in Paris, when they called together all the prelates of the kingdom to the church of St. Genevieve, and there held a synod.[34] They turned to the consideration of the complaints of the churches oppressed by the royal ministers, especially those of Poitiers, of Chartres, and of Lyons, as the Pope had indicated to Philip in the letter in which he recommended to him the legates.[35] There was question next of taking from the king all the tithes collected for the Holy Land by his father, Philip the Bold, and which had not been used for their sacred purpose. Nor was there any hope that they would be spent by Philip the Fair, for the crusade for which he had no inclination. This council was probably unfruitful since it was concerned in wresting money from the hands of Philip. Entering a little further within the court, the legates tried to calm the mind of Philip against Edward, King of England. They tried to stifle the quarrel, which burst forth as violently and for so long a period. Neither in this did they succeed in their

[33] Raynaldus, 1290, no. 17.   [34] Vide Council. Collec. an. 1290.
[35] Raynaldus, 1290, no. 19.

intent.³⁶ Gaetani sounded Philip and found him bitter and savage; he never forgot it.

The legates now came to the subject of the peace. The treaty of Oleron had released Charles the Lame from prison, but it did not guarantee the rights of the Church over Sicily. This prince had been compelled to cede to James, Sicily and Reggio, a city of Calabria, to induce Charles of Valois to renounce his claims on Aragon; to engage the pontiffs to confirm the terms of the agreement, and to remove the many censures against the family of Aragon; besides fifty thousand marks of gold and silver were to be paid by him to Alphonsus, and another twenty thousand was to be guaranteed by Edward of England. A space of three years was allowed for the fulfilment of the promises, after which time, in case of failure, Charles was to betake himself on foot as a prisoner to the Aragonese.

In the meanwhile as a pledge of the given promise, Charles was to deliver up to Alphonsus his three sons Louis, Robert and John, and fully sixty of the people of Provence.³⁷ As soon as Charles had made known to Pope Nicholas, in the interview they had at Rieti the conditions on which he had procured his liberty, he was severely reprimanded. The Pope declared them unjust and unlawful, because they were agreed to without his consent and because they violated the rights of the Church over Sicily.³⁸ According to this decision it followed that Charles should again place himself in the hands of Alphonsus. But Nicholas freed him; he released him from his oath, for the reason that Charles had not the power to cede the kingdom of Sicily which was not his to give, but belonged to the Church; and because having been made prisoner in an unjust war he was in no way bound to resume his chains.³⁹ To ratify his words, the Pontiff solemnly crowned Charles King of Sicily. Yet Charles was uneasy in conscience. At the end of the three years, the conditions which he had signed were still unfulfilled, and so whilst Aragon was

---

[36] "Qui super negotiis nihil facere potuerunt" Giordano, M. S. Vatie. apud Raynaldus 18

[37] Rymer. Tom 2, p. 342.   [38] Villani. lib. 7. cap. 130.

[39] These reasons were explained in the letter: "Si graves," directed to Alphonsus, 15 March, 1288.

invested by James of Majorca on the one side, and on the other by Sancho of Castile, and the minds of all were occupied with the war, he seized the opportunity and presented himself at the frontier of the realm, between the hills of Pannisar and Jonquire, offering himself (to whom we do not know) as a prisoner of Alphonsus. No one was willing to receive because no one understood this offer. But in the meanwhile a notary drew up an official document stating that Charles unarmed, with a small number of retainers, had come to the confines of Aragon, and that Alphonsus had not put in his appearance to claim him again as prisoner and restore the hostages:—in a word, it was a repetition of the comedy which Peter, the father of Alphonsus, had probably played on the father of Charles in the famous duel of Bordeaux which was never fought. Thus Charles, through the Papal absolutions and his own cunning, from a debtor became a creditor, and regarded himself legitimately authorized to enter into war with the Aragonese King. But the latter, who was victorious, menaced France; whereby Philip, yielding to the entreaty of Charles, was obliged to suspend the war against Aragon, and to establish an armistice until the first day of November of the next year. During this time a definite peace could be arranged in an assembly to be convened at Tarascon, the Papal legates and those of Edward being mediators.[40]

(1291) Such was the state of affairs, when Gaetani and Gerard of Parma arrived at Tarascon to negotiate peace. It was a numerous assembly. There were fully twelve ambassadors from Aragon, for it was desired that the clergy, the barons, the nobles and the citizens of the realm be represented in that assembly. Charles II was present in person; four ambassadors of Edward came with the title of mediators, but Philip sent no representative. All were in favor of peace; but it was difficult to agree on the terms, because the conditions exacted by Rome caused the treaty of Oleron to be rejected, seemed too onerous to Alphonsus; and even though he had accepted them, Charles of Valois would have been dissatisfied and deprived of his rights over Aragon. Therefore the regrets of the losers were to be tempered by the substitution of some new acquisition.

[40] Mariana XIV, 13-633.

This was altogether the work of the Papal legates and chiefly of Benedict Gaetani, who during his pontificate showed so much equity in such matters, when submitted to his judgment. In the treaty that was drawn up it was agreed: that Alphonsus should surrender all claim to Sicily, refusing every aid to his brother James who held it, and that he should recall all the Aragonese and Catalonian soldiers from that island; that he should go as a crusader to Palestine; that he should pay into the treasury of the Church every year thirty ounces of gold, a tribute to which his great-grandfather was bound; that he should be allowed to remain in peaceful and lawful possession of the kingdom of Aragon, and should be acknowledged as king; that he should be dispensed, at least for some time, from the obligation of restoring to the King of Majorca, the Balearic Islands; that he should be restored to the favor of the Church, and be pardoned for past trangressions; that he should return to Charles, his sons and the Provence barons, whom he held as hostages; that Sicily was to be given to the conquest of the King of Naples; but that in return Charles should cede to the Count of Valois the provinces of Anjou and Main, to make up for the loss of his rights over Aragon, and that he should give him in marriage, his daughter Margaret. All parties being perfectly contented, the treaty was signed on the 19th of February, 1291. However the hope of peace was not realized. Alphonsus died, still young, in June of the same year,[41] and Philip was unwilling to ratify the treaty.

Having returned from his mission to France, we do not find that Gaetani was employed in any particular affair, although certainly he must not have been idle in the Papal Curia at a time in which the Church was suffering many and most grievous misfortunes. Perhaps he was still on his way returning from Spain, when in May all Christian domination in the Holy Land ended with the fall of Ptolemais (Acre). Sixty thousand Christians having perished by the sword, by fire, and by drowning around its walls, sadly announced that the sincere faith of the Christians, that generous mover of hearts in the council of Clermont, expired in the hearts of the princes, and in the breasts of the people. Urban II had opened and Nicholas

[41] Mariana, L 14, c 14.

IV had closed the grand period of the Crusades. And just as the former left in the papal chair an ardent hope as an inheritance to his successors, the latter left sorrows, which could not be assuaged by the vain and fleeting hopes, which, at the most, nourished weak efforts, but did not satisfy the desires. Thus Nicholas for another year dragged along his life in misery, convoking provincial councils in order to repair the disasters in the Holy Land; urging princes to prepare a crusade; striving to convert the kings of Armenia to the faith and propose to them the conquest of Palestine; and hurling anathemas against Sicily, which had stubbornly chosen as King Frederick, the son of James, who had gone himself to reign in Aragon.

The grave being closed over the remains of Nicholas, the Papacy in a sad and pitiable state remained in the hands of twelve cardinals, among whom was Gaetani. Six were Romans, four from another part of Italy, and two were French. Cardinal Latino of Ostia was the most renowed for piety, Cardinal Gaetani for wisdom and learning, while Cardinal James Colonna, and Matthew Rosso of the Orsini rivalled one another in power. The obsequies over the dead Pope being ended, they met in conclave in the palace built by Nicholas IV, near the basilica of St. Mary Major. Memorable conclave! The usual prayers were recited, and the Cardinal of Ostia exhorted them to concord. Stephaneschi, who later became Cardinal of St. George in Velabro, has transmitted to us in verse the words of the pious Cardinal of Ostia; and touching upon the many misfortunes that were to be repaired on account of the ruined state of the affairs of the Christians in Syria, and the usurpation of Sicily, he ended with this Roman thought: "And we who "distribute realms, are ourselves beset on every side."[42] But scarcely had the twelve cardinals entered upon serious deliberation, when there arose a great division among them. Their minds were fluctuating, and their bodies were restless. They changed their place of meeting, and proceeded to the palace of Pope Honorius IV at the church of St. Sabina, and afterwards they went to the church of St. Mary of the Minerva.

[42] Jacob. S. Georg. Vit. S. Voel. L. X. c. 1: "Et nobis qui regna damus, nos undique turbant!"——

Cardinals Orsini and Colonna were contending, and each one drew to himself a part of the electors. The former desired a pope who would be friendly to Charles II, the latter opposed such an election.[43] On which side Cardinal Gaetani arrayed himself we do not know, but it is certain that he was neither the author nor fomenter of discord; rather according to the testimony of Platina,[44] in the severest terms he urged the discordant parties to come to a happy agreement by electing a pope. But if we be allowed to make a conjecture from the friendship which bound him at that time to Colonna, by the means of whom he became Pope, we may affirm that he supported the Colonna side.

That roving conclave held a session for almost three months, and nothing resulted from it. In the meantime the summer was advanced, the heat was noisome, and many fell ill. The French Cardinal Cholet dying on the 2nd of August, diminished the number of the electors, who, being frightened, desisted from the fruitless deliberations. Gerald of Parma, Matthew Acquasparta, Peter of St. Mark, and the Frenchman Hugh of St. Sabina betook themselves to Rieti; Matthew Orsini, James and Peter Colonna, and the bishop of Tusculum remained in Rome; Benedict Gaetani repaired alone to Anagni. He was worn out by a long and obstinate illness, which came nigh causing his death.[45] In October they assembled again in the Church of St. Mary of the Minerva more disunited than before.

(1293) The year 1292 elapsed, and as yet no hope appeared. In the meantime those quarrels of the nobility fomented by Colonna and Orsini in the conclave, on account of which each of them was stubborn in his opinion concerning a new pontiff, were deplorably manifested in the election of a new senator. One must be elected; but the Orsini and Colonna families each desired that this office should be accorded to their own respective families, and as a result they divided the people of Rome into two bloodthirsty factions, which, fighting furiously for six months, stained the city with blood and rapine. Finally for the sake of peace it was deemed necessary to elect two senators,

[43] John Villani, lib. 7, c. 150. [44] Story of the lives of the Pontiffs.
[45] James St George in Preface.

one from the Orsini and one from the Colonna families. These exterior disturbances which arrested the attention of the proud patricians, were also the cause of division among the Cardinals, who, as St. Antonius observes,[46] seemed to attend to their own interests and not those of Christ in the matter of that election.

Summer returned, and they also returned to disagree. The Roman Cardinals with Acquasparta and Gerald went to Rieti; three others remained in Rome. Gaetani alone retired to Viterbo. This solitude chosen by Gaetani clearly shows, that abhorring the scandalous delays which prolonged the widowhood and the perils of the Church, he kept aloof from the base and wearisome intrigues of the various parties. But a threatened schism suddenly reassembled them at Perugia. The two Cardinals, Colonna and John bishop of Frascati, agreeing in sentiment, believed that, because they were dwelling in Rome, they alone could elect a pope; and signified to those absent that they should come if they wished to select one with them. All were aroused by this procedure; they assembled in Perugia, but their minds were not changed. Then filled with a noble indignation Gaetani began to lash their unfeeling hearts most severely, because they had resolved to choose a pope in such a manner. We may be sure that the sharp but most just rebuke had an effect on the obstinate electors.

It was towards the end of winter that Charles, the Lame, on his way from France, came to Perugia to meet his son Charles Martel, titular king of Hungary. The Cardinals had prepared extravagant honors for him. Two of them, Napoleon Orsini, and Peter Colonna, with a numerous escort went out of the city to meet him; and the others received him at the doors of the Church, and made him sit down among them in the conclave. Nay more, the first seat was given to Charles, King of Naples, placing him between the first two Cardinal Bishops; the second seat was given to his son between the first two Cardinal Deacons. An unbecoming session and full of danger. They were bound by the chains of discord, and they had desired to be bound also by those of a prince. Charles made a speech to the cardinals, exhorting them to elect a pope quickly; Cardinal Latino replied for them. All these pro-

[46] P. B tit. 20, c. 7.

ceedings Gaetani beheld and heard with great displeasure, and indignation. For a princely layman to be seated in the first place among the papal electors in the sacred councils was an intrusion into affairs which the Church holds most dear and which she would not allow a profane hand to touch; and the presence of a king among prelates, already weakened by dissensions, was a lessening of their liberty. Nor is it to be believed that that speech of the king advising a quick election was prompted by love for the Church and religion. He desired to see a pope elected, yet he wanted one according to his own liking and who would further his own interests and this action was not a suppression of discord but rather a fomenter of it, and an impertinence. In fact he was sharply rebuked by Gaetani, who himself in a violent manner had tried to compel the electors to bring the affair to a termination.[47] We know not whether it was from these rebukes, or from others which Gaetani gave him for his impertinent intrusion, arose those sharp words which passed between Gaetani and the King.[48] Muratori supposes, and we venture to hold the same, that the cause of the breach of friendly relations between these two personages was, that the noble-souled Cardinal had frankly told the King that it did not belong to him to designate the time for the election of the pope. But why then had the eminent annalist assigned pride as the cause of the action of Gaetani? That act of his, suppressing the importunities of a prince in the affairs of the Church, was most praiseworthy; we do not find that it had its origin in pride, but rather in the consciousness of his own office, which was that of a cardinal, during the vacancy of the Apostolic See, to defend the liberty of the Church.[49] Charles the Lame, went away displeased, and was taught a lesson by Gaetani.

(1294) But the cursed discord did not disappear. Finally twenty-seven months after the death of Nicholas, it

---

[47] Platina.
[48] Gordan. M. S Vatican. Raynaldus. "Dura Quoque verba, (Carolus) cum domino Benedicto Cajetano habuit, nihil tamen profecit." Ptol. Luc. Hist. Eccl. cap. 29. "Dura verba habuit cum Domino Benedicto Cajetano. Non proficiens antem, venit in Regnum." Idem Annal. S. R. I. T. 21, 1300 . . " quod Regem Carolum Perusiis multum exasperasset."
[49] Muratori Annals.

happened, that a very young brother of Cardinal Matthew Orsini died, and the Cardinal of Tusculum, John Boccamazza discoursing with his colleagues injected into their minds mournful thoughts that are always productive of good. And perceiving that these discourses had penetrated their guilty consciences: "Why," said he, "do we not immediately choose a head for the Church? What is the "reason of this discord which divides us?"—"Oh! we "wretches!" then broke forth Cardinal Latino Mala-"branca all dismayed, (he whom some authors declare is "the author of that prophetic and solemn poem, the Dies "Irae),[50] how terrible is the anger of the Lord, which is "raging over our heads, and which before four months will "strike us, as has been revealed to a holy man!" "What, "Cardinal," interrupting him, said Gaetani with a smile, "Is this perhaps one of the visions of Peter of Mt. Mor-"rone?"—"One of his exactly," replied Latino, "and I "have a letter in which he tells me that he has received a "command from God to warn you of these threats." That sufficed to fix the thoughts and conversation of all on that famous hermit. Then they began to converse about his austerities, his miracles and his virtues; and someone even proposed him for supreme pontiff. Cardinal Latino, who was most devoted to the Saint of Mt. Morrone, took up the proposition, and without any further delay strengthened it by giving him his vote. At once they were all filled with the thought of the wonderful sanctity of the hermit, and for that reason alone judged him worthy of the Papal Chair. They united in giving their suffrage to Peter Morrone, and Cardinal Latino, as senior deacon of the conclave, received the power to select him in the name of all. Gaetani was among these, yet it does not seem, judging from his delay in repairing to Aquila to do homage to the new Pope, that in the interior of his soul he approved of the choice. He above all others knew the immense weight of the Roman Pontificate, and could judge whether the shoulders of a holy, but inexperienced, hermit were able to support it.

The Pontiff elect was a man of most austere life, who, shut up in a narrow cell among the rocks of the high mountain of Majella near Sulmona, seemed to be no longer a

---

[50] See Cardella, History of the Cardinals, T. 2, cap. II.

thing of this earth, so much had he been separated from men. It is the common opinion that he was born at Isernia, a city of the county of Molise in the kingdom of Naples, his parents being Anglerius and Mary. While still very young he was filled with a great love for solitude, and he longed to imitate the ancient dwellers of the desert of Thebaïs. At first he became a monk of St. Benedict, and afterwards without becoming acquainted with men and the things of this earth, he repaired to Majella, and there practised all manner of austerities. His holiness of life, the wonder which his extraordinary austerities excited, and the report of the miracles worked by him attracted many around him, who wished to imitate his life and example; and in a short time from being a poor lonely hermit he found himself the head and founder of a congregation of religious who afterwards from the name he took in the Papacy were called Celestines. He repaired to Lyons, where the council was being held, to have his congregation and rule approved by Gregory IX. Immediately out of compassion for the rigors of these penitents, people responded with loyal offerings. Grants of land were given them; suddenly churches and monasteries arose, which in their splendor made them forget the poverty of the beginnings of the congregation. During the lifetime of the Saint, they even acquired a monastery in Rome near St. Peter's. From the monks who lived there, Cardinal Latino learned the merits of their founder, to whom he displayed great love and devotion, giving expression to it by an annual gift of alms. Although the order founded by him had prospered, leaving the government and direction of it to others, he thought of nothing else but of attending to his own soul; and so to be alone he retired to the rocks of Morrone, a part of Majella, and from which he took his name.

The holy hermit Peter was more than seventy-two years old, and doubtlessly he presented the appearance of one bordering on the grave, when at the end of a day in July the deputies of the conclave arrived in Sulmona, to bear to him the honor of the pontifical tiara. They were the Archbishop of Lyons, the bishop of Orvieto and the bishop of Porto, together with two Apostolic Notaries. At the break of day they set out to ascend the mountain; and while wet with perspiration and out of breath they were ascending by a little narrow path, they see coming near to them and overtaking them Cardinal Peter Colonna, who to make himself the first bearer of a so joyful message, had come quickly from Perugia. They arrived at a small enclosure surrounded by a wall, the opening to which was a small gate, and further on there was a little cell which a wall divided into two very narrow rooms. On the outside wall there was a window, that would not admit the head of an observer, because it had been provided with iron bars, at which the Saint placed himself in his infrequent conversations with visitors.

Before this window presented themselves the bearers of such great news. In the little cell they saw a very old man, clothed in rough skins, and disconcerted by the sight of them. His beard was white and shaggy; his cheeks furrowed, and his entire person enfeebled by long fasts. From out the pallor of his countenance two black eyes, suffused with tears, spoke of the sweetness of the soul enamored of its God. Although in such squalor, the hermit and the cell emitted the very air of Paradise. At such a sight struck dumb and filled with holy admiration, the prelates uncovered their heads, and falling down reverently kissed the ground; the holy hermit did the same. The Archbishop of Lyons was the first to break the silence, explaining to Peter how he had been chosen Supreme Pontiff. He likened the Church to a ship tossed to and fro at the mercy of the wind and waves, awaiting him to unfurl the sails, grasp the helm and guide it to the port of safety. And thus speaking, he displayed to the eyes of the bewildered hermit the sealed papers, which contained the important decree.

Overwhelmed by the greatness of the office, and the honor which they desired to bestow on him, the poor hermit knew not what to do. Before giving an answer he would first interrogate God in prayer, and they should pray with him. He then received through the window the wonderful document, and retired.[51] Prostrating himself

---

[51] The original of this decree, bearing the seals in red wax of the eleven cardinals, was preserved in the Abbey of the Holy Spirit at Sulmona. Afterwards by the order of Clement VIII it was placed in the Vatican archives, after having passed successively through the hands of Cardinals Facchinetto, Bellarmine and Baronius—Vide Suppl Life of St. Peter Celestine, by Lelii Marini, ch 8, apud Boll. Maii T. 4.

he prayed to know the will of God. Shortly afterwards he returned to the messengers, telling them that he would accept the office of supreme pontiff. Hardly had he finished speaking, when they cast themselves at his feet and kissed them, notwithstanding they were covered with poor and coarse shoes.

As soon as the news of this election had spread, an incredible number of people flocked to see him, and to receive the blessing of the invisible hermit, so unexpectedly raised to such a high dignity. Charles II, the Lame, with his son Charles Martel, came with alacrity to see him, not only to receive his blessing, but also to enter into his good graces, and direct and rule him. The success of his plan was not difficult. Peter had no decision of character, because he was old and enfeebled by penances and his mind was ill-adapted to perceive the cunning of the children of Adam. He had no knowledge of mankind, because from his youth he had fled from society; his mind was not cultivated by study, being satisfied only with that joy of heart which he felt in his contemplations of God: and thus devoid of human resources, he could not deliver himself from the impositions of the royalty and the common people. Charles II troubled him, and the advocates of the Curia harassed him. Ignorant of the laws, he summoned laymen and jurists to his support,[52] who knowing and adopting the best means of ingratiating themselves in the needful soul of the new Pontiff, settled there. To establish themselves firmly in that position they displayed certain deferences to the cardinals and clerics, insomuch that Peter, contrary to custom, chose a layman as secretary.[53] To Charles and the advocates of the Curia were added twelve Celes-

[52] " Jacob. S. Georg. . . . " laicaeque manus subrepere passim.
Consiliis tentant divi in precordia Patris
Ecclesiae. Nam gnarus opes et jurgia mundi
Temnere, pomposam Juris vitaverat artem.
. . . . quo factum est, ut sibi magni
Crederet hic Laicos, quos Juris in arte peritos
Prudentesque ratus . . . .
. . . . dum metuit Peter almus fraudibus arctum
Ingenium vinci Procerum, dubiique sodales
Redduntur Fratres, proprium ne forte Senatus
Campellat mutare gradum."
[53] Ibid. " . . . deerat fiducia Cleri."

tine monks, pious men, but rough and uncultured,[54] who hedged him in, who influenced him, and who would never let him leave them. Thus did the holy old man all at once remain confined in the clutches of Charles, in the cunning of the greedy employees of the Curia, and in the small and indiscreet ambitious projects of his monks. So that he did not act, and did not undertake anything unless at the instance of Charles, and by the advice of those around him of whom we have spoken. In the meanwhile the Cardinal electors still remained in Perugia expecting the Pope elect to come to meet them as they had besought him to do, in a letter which was attached to the decree of election. But instead of seeing the Pope, they received a letter from him, in which he announced that he was not able to travel so far. Accustomed to the snows of the Abruzzi mountains, he could not bear the summer heat; being a very old man he had not sufficient strength for the journey, and hence they should rather come to him. The Fathers perceived which way the wind of Mt. Morrone blew, since it is supposed that they already knew how affairs were directed. But they would not yield. They urged their request; he should come on a litter; he should leave the kingdom, or in other words, remove himself from the influence of Charles. He was unwilling, because Charles was unwilling.[55] The hesitation and delay of the Cardinals in coming were not displeasing to Charles. Time with him was precious, and he used it admirably. According to Stepheneschi he persuaded the holy Pope to repair to the growing city of Aquila to receive the pontifical insignia,[56] and to begin immediately to appoint new Cardinals in the choice of whom the impertinent prince would show his power. Peter entered Aquila triumphantly, but mounted on a mule, the two kings on foot holding the bridle. Opinions vary concerning that spectacle. Some praised Peter, calling to mind Christ entering Jerusalem; while others would rather have seen that humility less displayed.

The cardinals departed from Perugia startled by this intelligence. Their saddened minds perceived the misfortunes which in the future would befall the Church under

[54] Ibid. " . . non culta satis, sed rustica turba."
[55] Ptol. Luc C. 30 "ad instantiam Regis venire recusat."
[56] Ptolomy Eccl. History C. 29. "Ad instantiam Regis, et suorum."

the weak rule of the Saint. We know not whether they felt regret for having raised him to such a high office, but it is certain that Ptolemy of Lucca, a contemporary writer, and an eye-witness of the things he relates, assures us that Cardinal Latino Malabranca, on the day that he died in Perugia, the 10th of August, bore on his soul to eternity the weight of that election,[57] to which afterwards all the other cardinals had agreed. Their manner of going separately to Aquila, proved their little satisfaction;[58] and they went more to ward off dangers, than to honor Celestine.[59] The latter in the presence of a large concourse of people received the papal insignia from the hands of Napoleon Orsini, who had come from Perugia with Cardinal Hugh of St. Sabina. The new Pope took the name of Celestine V.

Benedict Gaetani was the only one who still lingered in Perugia. We know not with what ardor he acquiesced in the election of the holy hermit, but we are certain that he more than the others beheld and foresaw its sad consequences for the Church. He heard certain rumors of the infamous actions and iniquitous practices of the ministers. The employees of the Curia were reaping a harvest in the Papal Court, abusing the holy seal, by dispensing benefices recklessly and with such a great cupidity for gain, that often the same gift of prebend was found to be given to many. They had the parchments already stamped with the papal seal, so as to be prepared to write that which would better satisfy their thirst for gold. The saintly Pope neither saw nor heard of these transactions. Charles ruled, and swayed the mind of Celestine according to his own pleasure, and held him, as it were, a prisoner. In fact he was a puppet in his hands. Gaetani heard, and delayed to go and pay his respects to the Pope, tempering his mind through these deplorable facts by feelings of noble indignation, which were to break forth in his own pontificate. It was said that Gaetani refrained from going to Aquila, in order not to meet Charles, whom he had re-

---

[57] Ptolemy Eccl. History, c. 30, "in quo totum pondus incumbebat super electrione Caelestini." [58] Ptol. Eccl. Hist., c. 31. "aliqui procedunt ad Papam, aliqui subsequuntur versus Aquilam" [59] James St. Georg., c. 175. ". . . celerant ad tanta pericula cursum."

buked and wounded deeply in the conclave at Perugia.[60] But finally with the desire of repairing so much disorder by his judgment and good sense, and not to appear disrespectful to the Pontiff, he went to Aquila.

When he arrived there he found that the reports were not exaggerated but true. His heart was filled with grief because of the degradation to which the Papacy had been subjected. This feeling arose not only from holiness of heart, but also from strength and nobility of soul, chiefly because the outrage on the Apostolic See was committed by the enemy Charles, and by a handful of rascally advocates of the Curia. However for the honor of the Church he set about to take into his own hands the reins of government, which were held so loosely by the hands of Celestine. So great was the authority which his high ability, his skill in management of affairs, and his knowledge of the canons gave him, that he became most powerful, and as it were the master of the Papal Curia. Ptolemy of Lucca, relating how well Gaetani knew how to conduct his own affairs, insinuates that he possessed himself of power, more for his own private interests, than for the good of the Church. Yet it must be remembered that this kind of preponderance or dominion of Gaetani was in the Papal Curia, and not over the Papal Curia. This Curia could then be divided into two parts, one composed of Charles, the advocates of the Court, the Celestine Monks, and of John of Castrocielo, a Cassinese monk, Archbishop of Benevento, who had known how to enter into the good graces of the Pope, by taking off his dark habit, and putting on the gray color of the Celestine monks;[61] and of some French cardinals. The other part was composed of all the cardinals who raged against Charles and deplored the weakness of the Pope. Gaetani could not be the master of both these parties, opposed as they were to each other, but it might be said that he was rather the leader of that party which opposed the artifices of Charles the Lame, with whom he was in such bad favor. This domination was founded in the dependence they had on him, as

[60] Ptolemy Eccl. History, chapter 31. "et dubitabatur quia non veniret, quia Regem verbis offenderat in Perusio."

[61] Jac S. Georg., c. 77-275. . . . Monachi dimissis vestibus atris, Praesulis induitur habitum, pertingere sperans Irrubare caput.

a man of singular ability above all the other cardinals. In fact even after his arrival things were going from bad to worse, as it appears from that desire of the Pope to change into Celestines all the monks of St. Benedict, and to put the monastery of Monte Cassino into a scandalous confusion by stripping the monks of the dark habit; and especially that creation of new cardinals, all the work of Charles. The fact of Gaetani not having taken part in that affair shows that he and the king continued to view each other askance. In the ember days of September Celestine created twelve cardinals, seven of whom were French, and five Italians all creatures of Charles. And this is how the deed was done. Charles and Hugh Sequin, Bishop of Ostia, designated a long time ahead those who were to be made cardinals, and their names were given to the simple-minded Pope, who in all things did the pleasure of Charles, and these names were kept concealed from all the other cardinals. Only Hugh Sequin was taken into the secret, as we have said, and two Roman cardinals, who it is almost certain were the two Orsini, because in the conclave they were ardent partisans of Charles. It cannot be supposed that Gaetani was one of these, because it was customary for Stephaneschi to call only those Romans, who were natives of Rome. In fact among the twelve elected was John Gaetani of Anagni and he declares that not one of them was a Roman.[62] Nothing of the secret was allowed to leak out. On Friday the vigil of their creation the names of the elect were made known to the cardinals, who were deeply wounded by this proceeding, and with reason, because the Pope should have consulted them rather than Charles. Thus that mastery over the Papal Curia which Ptolemy of Lucca affirms, does not appear from the fact so important as a notable increase in the college of the Cardinals; so it remains evident that up to the 18th of September Gaetani was certainly not among the friends of Charles.[63]

It is true that Charles feared him, and he had good reason to fear him from Perugia, and hence in order to prevent a storm which he would have raised among the other

[62] See Note D.
[63] Id. ib . . . nullum, queem subdita sedi Immediata porit tellus, ex ordine Patrum Murro dedit. . . .

cardinals because of the royal selection of cardinals, to appease him and gain his favor, he caused John Gaetani, a nephew of Benedict, to be made a cardinal. But the slavery into which the Church was reduced by Charles would not allow the minds of Gaetani and the other cardinals to be appeased, so greatly distressed and desperate were they by reason of the bad government of Celestine. Affairs reached a climax when, the season now having become cooler, believing that the Pope should repair to Rome, they beheld him most tenacious of his decision to follow the advice of Charles and go instead to Naples.[64] The artifices of Charles the Lame, were shameful and barefaced, but the Saint did not perceive all the evil that they contained. They were exasperated also by the revival and renewal which Celestine made of the constitution of Gregory X concerning the holding and the regulation of a conclave.

This constitution ordains that, ten days having elapsed from the death of the Pontiff, the cardinals without waiting for the absentees are to assemble in a place strictly and securely locked. Neither by letter nor by word of mouth nor by any other sign are those in conclave to hold intercourse with an outsider, under pain of anathema to the transgressor. They are to remain there until they have chosen a successor. Should, however, more than three days elapse before a choice is made, for the next five days their fare shall consist of one dish, after which it is reduced to bread and water and wine, which shall be their only nourishment until their work is done. The revival and renewal of the Gregorian Bull wounded deeply the electors, so undisciplined had they been in the late conclave and so agitated. This decree was followed by another, releasing Charles from the oath required of him by the cardinals, not to detain them and confine them in his kingdom, in the event of choosing the new Pope after the death of Celestine. So that Charles the Lame, by this Bull and by the opportune release from his oath, was promising himself to hold in his own hands the imprisoned cardinals choosing the new Pope, or in other words, to create him himself. But we shall see later how these pre-conceived hopes van-

[64] Jac S Georg. . "Subductus Carolo coetuque sequente Parthenopen deflexit iter.

ished in smoke. Finally their minds surcharged with indignation broke out in open and forcible clamors at the sight of John of Castrocielo, Benedictine Archbishop of Benevento, being suddenly made a cardinal by Celestine without even the ceremonies of creation. For one evening after supper, no sooner was it said, than he transformed him into a cardinal. The exasperated prelates gave expression to downright disapproval and to such vehement denunciation that John was forced to lay aside the irregularly received dignity, and Celestine had to confer it with the usual ceremonies of installation. So raising around the Saint, if not a reverent, at least a not unjust tempest, they followed him to Naples.[65]

The cardinals in their displeasure and indignation at the actions of Celestine, because they openly despaired of any amelioration, had commenced from the time they were in Aquila to broach and whisper words of abdication. In spite of the efforts which Charles might make to dissuade the Saint from the untoward temptation, undoubtedly the thought entered the mind of the good Pontiff. In fact in that revived constitution of Gregory X, he speaks not only of the case of death, but also of renunciation, a sign that the latter was already fixed in his heart. So the more things went wrong, the more openly did some of the cardinals act, and they began to urge the Saint to resign the Papacy, telling him openly, that so long as he remained Pontiff, the affairs of the Roman Church would be imperilled and be ever in confusion.[66] It would not be unlikely to suppose that Gaetani was one of those who urged him to resign. Those incentives to resign, and the charging him with the evils of the Church threw the mind of the Saint into great consternation; and since he had not coveted the unexpected honors of the Papacy, nor after assuming them was he elated, he became strongly apprehensive of the dangers of his soul.

Advent approached. He had always sanctified this season by extraordinary austerity, and he did not wish as

---

[65] Jac. S. Georg., cap. 11.
[66] Ptolemy of Lucca. Eccl History, c. 32. "Multum stimulatur ab aliquibus Cardinalibus quod Papatum cedat, quia Ecclesia Romana sub ipso periclitabatur, et sub eo confundebatur."

Pope to intermit the pious custom. He had caused to be built in the papal palace a miserable little wooden cell, which reminded him of the one on Mt. Morrone, and in this he shut himself up; and he left in the hands of three cardinals the chief management of affairs, and all care of government, retaining for himself only the thought of his soul and of God. We do not know who these delegates were. The Bull of this deputation had been already written, when having returned to Rome Orsini withheld him from its publication, so that it might not be said that the Church was governed not by one, but by three Popes. The reader may imagine how these three cardinals raged against Orsini. These dissensions disturbed the mind of Celestine continually, and he was convinced that they happened through his own fault.

These troubles of mind had increased in the solitude in which he placed himself. Bright visions of the once happy life he had on Mt. Morrone, unintimidated by papal pomp, were confidently presented to his mind, and infused into his soul pleasures and sweetnesses that worldly honors do not confer. Then he longed most eagerly for the lonely rock of Morrone, and his heart was frightened by the fear of hell into which he might fall headlong for the evils he was known to have brought upon the Church by his shortcomings. And in this longing for the past, in grief for the present, and in fear for the future, he went for spiritual advice to Fra Jacopone of Todi, of whom we shall speak later, who although not ordained, was yet pious and strong in the pursuit of evangelical perfection. He was one of the Franciscan friars who were the dearly-beloved of Celestine, on account of the singular severity of the life they led. The Friar admonished him: that he should take care; that the Papacy was for him a terrible experiment, in which his sanctity would be tested; that he was a spectacle for the eyes of all; that he should consider the Roman Curia as a furnace in which gold is tried and separated from the dross; a great unhappiness to lose God for that; that he should have been averse to placing around his neck a yoke, the acceptance of which could hurl him to eternal perdition; finally that he should flee the frauds and deceits of the advocates of the Curia, and of the flatterers intent solely on their own gain. He should look to himself.[67]

No one can express the consternation which these admonitions of Jacopone produced in the mind of the holy old man. His conscience smote him for the bad condition of affairs; he feared the divine punishment; he wished to cast far away the enormous burden of the pontificate. In the midst of his sighs he cried out from the depth of his anguished heart: " Oh, miserable—me! Oh, wretch that I " am! They tell me that I have command over souls, and " why is it that I have no power over my own, and assure " its salvation? And what is this the Lord has done? " Has He perhaps placed me so high, in order to hurl me " down further in the depths below? Every day I have a " complaint, a murmur against me. I see the cardinals " jarring, and quarrelling among themselves. . . . What " shall I do? . . . Is it not better for me to break the " chains which bind me to this most fatal throne, and to " leave it to one who may know how to sit on it, and let " me then take myself after such a storm to the port of my " little cell."——

Whilst he was revolving these thoughts in his mind, he took by chance in his hand a certain little book containing a compendium of the ecclesiastical canons, to which he was wont to have recourse for advice during his life as a hermit; and turning over the pages, his eyes rested on one, which told how a cleric can resign a dignity or benefice for a just reason with the consent of his superior. This canon seemed to be his liberator, and he gave the entire consideration of his mind to it; but there being no one superior to him, into whose hands he could resign the Papacy, this fact threw him into a state of great uncertainty. He wished to issue from it. He went for counsel and advice to him, who among all the cardinals, was the most renowned for sound judgment and learning, Benedict Gaetani. This man entered the small, dark cell, being called to pass judgment on a matter, which was to remove the papal tiara from the head of Celestine to his own. And having heard the question, he replied in a manner which concealed his interior delight,[68] that he could resign, when-

---

[67] Book 1, Satire XV.—See Bollandists, May T. V., p 523.
[68] " Ille tamen cautus mentem simulare." Jac. S. Georg, c. 111.

ever there was a sufficient reason to do so; and alleged the example of another pope who had also resigned. The Saint answered that a sufficient reason was not wanting. And that was all that transpired between them.[69] But the mind of Celestine was not satisfied by that advice; and so he summoned another counsellor. He gave the same opinion. And as yet not contented, he interrogated some other of the cardinals.

These consultations of the Saint could not be kept so secret, as to be withheld from the knowledge of those who certainly did not care to see him retire from the Papacy. These were especially those froward Celestine monks, whom Stephaneschi insists upon calling rough and uncouth men. They wondered greatly at this novelty and they sent a pressing remonstrance to the Saint, representing, how, if he laid aside the pontifical dignity, they would be exposed to all manner of insults; and his beloved congregation would die at its birth. They did not rely alone on their own remonstrances. They raised a pious tumult among the people of Naples, accustomed to such excitement, who with irreverent importunity having broken through the outer doors of the papal palace, forced an entrance into the cell of the Saint. There some of the chief men conjured him in the name of God to dismiss from his mind the idea of resigning, which would deprive all the kingdom of so great an honor. Celestine met their remonstrances with a suitable reply, which disguised the unalterability of his purpose.

Having weathered this storm, the Saint set about immediately to put into effect that which he had for a long time contemplated. The cardinals being called together, he humbly declared his inability to bear any longer the burden of the supreme pontificate, and asked them publicly for their advice. The cardinals replied, that he should allow his desire to mature; that he should shun his evil advisers; and that he should order public prayers in order to know the will of God in an affair of so great importance.

These public prayers, which the cardinals recommended, served as a favorable occasion for Charles to delay the execution of the designs of Celestine. He summoned apart the clergy of Naples, who if they did not regard Celestine

---

[69] The same author.

in the same light as Charles, yet considered him a Neapolitan Pope, and loved and revered him as a saint. Then he arranged a procession in which all the priests and friars marched, and together with these as many bishops as he could collect, and they proceeded to the castle in which Celestine dwelt. Friar Ptolemy of Lucca, who was present, mentions no cardinal among them. As soon as these suppliants had arrived at the door of the palace, according to custom, they began in a loud voice to entreat Celestine to impart to them the papal benediction. Not to show irreverence to a sacred ceremony, Celestine came to a window in company with three bishops and gave the blessing. Then a certain bishop, an agent of the King, besought the Pope to listen to them; and as soon as silence reigned, in a loud voice that was heard by all those in the procession, he cried out: " That they did not want him to resign; that he should remain for the glory of the kingdom." Then one of the aforesaid three bishops from above replied for the Pope. " That they should quiet their fears; that he would not " resign as long as there did not appear a reason contrary " to his conscience, which directed him." The royal messenger was satisfied; and as a sign of their joy in the loudest tones they began to sing the Te Deum, and the joyful procession marched back to the Cathedral.[70]

But Celestine was frightened by the fear of losing his soul in the Papacy, and seeing the way open by the advice of Gaetani and other cardinals, he did not allow himself to be overcome either by the procession, or by the cry the King made by the mouth of the bishop. For almost eight days he spoke not a word of his resignation, in order to stifle his feelings, and not be molested. During that time going again to Gaetani, he was instructed by him in all he would have to do, as he desired to perform the act of abdication so that the canonical form would not be wanting, and he made him draw up the act of the great resignation.[71] After this was performed, on the 13th of December the feast of St. Lucy, he summoned the cardinals in consistory. And being clothed in the red cloak, and all the other insignia which the Pope wears in the solemn ceremonies, Celestine entered the assembly, and seated

[70] Ptolemy of Lucca. Eccl History, c. 32.
[71] Anonymous. Life of St. Celestine. MS. Vatic. Arm. XII.

himself. Under the cloak he carried the act of resignation. The cardinals knew of his intended resignation, but they did not know when it would take place. He commanded them to remain quiet, and not dare say a word; then unfolding it, in a clear voice he read the famous act: "I, "Celestine, moved by legitimate reasons, that is to say, for "the sake of humility, of a perfect life, and for ease of "conscience; on account of weakness of body, of want of "knowledge, of grief occasioned to the people, and in order "to regain the peace of my former state of life, with all "my soul, and freely I surrender the Papacy, and I ex- "pressly resign the chair, the dignity, the burden and the "honor, giving from this instant full and free power to "the College of Cardinals to choose and provide, but only "in a canonical way, a new pastor for the universal Church." During the reading of this the cardinals, deeply moved by the great humility of the Saint, could not restrain their tears. Fearing that the mere assent of the College of Cardinals to his resignation might not be sufficient for the validity of the act, at the instance of Matthew Orsini, the oldest of the Cardinal deacons, he published a special constitution covering the ground, in which he declared a Pope might abdicate, and that the College of Cardinals was competent to receive the act of abdication. This was embodied in the Sixth of the Decretals. This being settled, Celestine divested himself in their presence of all the papal insignia, and having resumed the hairy garment he wore on Mt. Morrone, he departed from the consistory. The cardinals accompanied him, and with many tears recommended to his prayers the Church deprived of a pastor. Thus did Pope Celestine V, after five months and nine days, leave the papal chair, not thrust down, not induced, not deceived, at least by Gaetani. Some writers detract from the greatness of that act, and bestow on it a vile character. Among these is the irascible Dante, who in the departure of Celestine from the Papacy rabidly deplores the entrance into it of the detested Boniface. But as the possibility of such a resignation having arisen solely from the timidity of the renouncer did not enter their minds, they must then, either by conjecture, or by an evil interpretation of circumstances, or from a prejudiced opinion of the natural dispo-

sition of Benedict Gaetani, attribute it also to his artifices.
And let the reader know that the story of these artifices
began after his elevation to the Papacy; and if Gaetani
had never become Pope, there would have been no mention
of these artifices impelling the simple old saint Celestine
to resign. Other writers extol to the heavens the abdication, as the act of an angel and not of a man, claiming,
that the act of discarding the insignia of St. Peter through
fear of sin, is such a great spiritual disposition of soul,
that does not generally fall to the lot of the sons of Adam.
Among these is the moderate Petrarch.[72] But the true
estimate of him was that given by Clement V in the Bull
in which he raised Peter Celestine to the honors of the
altar. Of him he says: " A man of stupendous simplicity,
" and unskilled in matters concerning the administration
" of the universal Church (for from his boyhood to old age
" he had not applied himself to worldly affairs, but only
" to those divine), prudently viewing himself with the
" closest attention, he freely and entirely resigned the
" honors and burden of the Papacy, in order that no evil
" would be occasioned to the Universal Church by his gov-
" ernment of it; and because being freed from the disturb-
" ing cares of Martha, he could with Mary stand at the
" feet of Jesus in the peace and happiness of contempla-
" tion." [73]

The ten days having elapsed from the abdication of
Celestine, the cardinals, according to the approved Constitution of Pope Gregory X, met in conclave. In all there
were twenty-two. Eight were French, Hugh Billom,
Bishop of Ostia; Bernard de Got; Simon of Beaulieu; John
Lemoine; William Ferrier; Nicholas Nonancourt, Robert,
formerly abbot of Citeaux; and Simon, who had been a
monk of Cluny. All these with the exception of Hugh,
were created by Celestine, and hence desired by Charles of
Naples. Thomas of Teramo, and Peter of Aquila were
Celestine monks; Landolf Brancaccio and William Longo,
State Chancellor of the King, and Benedict Gaetani,
Junior, were also creatures of Charles. Of these if we except Gaetani, who by reason of blood relationship, would

[72] Life of the hermit. Book 2, chap. 18, page 266, V. 1. Basilea edition, by Sebastian Henripetri 1520.
[73] Bull of Canonization of St. Peter Celestine.

naturally favor the election of his uncle, certainly not one of the others would care to see him chosen. The fact of the Saint calling on Gaetani for counsel, and the weight which his opinion and advice must have had on his mind on account of his reputation for learning, should have closed the minds of those devoted to Celestine against every thought of creating Benedict Pope. On the contrary the other cardinals, namely, Gerard of Parma; John Boccamozzo; Matthew of Acquasparta in Umbria; Peter Peregrosso of Milan; Matthew Rosso Orsini; James Colonna; Napoleon Orsini; Peter Colonna, all Italians and five of them Romans, deplored so exceedingly such a large number of Frenchmen admitted to their College and the dangerous removal of the Papal See to Naples, that they would certainly favor the election as Pontiff of one of their colleagues, who would be at least an Italian, and who would have the courage to tear himself away from the influence of Charles the Lame, and straightway bring back the court to Rome.

Charles was not a cardinal, but under Celestine he had cardinals created, and for that reason although he did not have a vote in the election of the pontiff, he could have, and did have in fact, the desire of the choice of a person who would favor his interests. The kings of France have shown later how agreeable it was to have in their house (we refer to the captivity of Avignon) the Roman Pontiff; but Charles the Lame had already experienced and for that reason let not the reader ask what cardinal he wished to see elected. Of course it would be a Frenchman. An Italian he would not have, much less a Roman. For besides being pained by the loss of liberty and dignity which was inflicted on the Papal See by that exile in a prince's house, their love of country was wounded by being deprived of that honor. Moreover more in those times to have a Pope of a vigorous disposition was not the most ardent desire of any crowned head. Hence Stephaneschi, who was at that time a member of the Papal Curia, and an eye-witness of events, informs us that Charles nourished a secret hope, which by the mercy of God remained in embryo. To whom the royal suffrage was given, we know not; and to surmise would be to give full play to the imagination.

With these feelings the twenty-two cardinals shut themselves up in conclave in the royal castle, being menaced in their liberty, inasmuchas Charles had even intruded himself there.[74] Each one had his own views, but all were dominated by a force that emanated from the conditions in which the Church found itself after the brief rule of Celestine, and which was impelling them to disregard their own interests, for the safety and relief of the Holy Church of God. A mysterious force which not all would recognize in assemblies for the election of a Supreme Pontiff; because wholly absorbed in the human weaknesses which can manifest themselves in that sort of assemblies, they will not consider that in the midst of so much humanity the will and power of God may rule. Party spirit and every other imperfection also can be discovered in these meetings, the cardinals not ceasing to be human, even if they are in conclave; but the final result is wholly the work of God who uses for a good purpose this human nature of ours, miserable though it may ever be. Therefore in case the minds of the electors had become dissipated by private desires, one fact would unite them forthwith, namely, the renunciation of Celestine, for which it was necessary to elect as a Pope a man able to resist the possibility of a threatened schism, and firmly to set out at once for that city which alone is the seat of the Papal power. Nay, judging from the very short time they had been in conclave, it can be truly said, that already before entering they had fixed their minds on Gaetani. Their assembling served for no other purpose but to make known their minds; for scarcely had a day of the conclave been passed, the holy sacrifice having been offered, and the usual prayers were said, when by an overwhelming vote Benedict Gaetani, then Cardinal priest of the title of Sts. Sylvester and Martin, was elected Pope.[75] Reading the account of John Villani,[76] in which he states that Gaetani made use of bare-

[74] Ptol Luc. Hist. Ecc., c. 34 [75] Jas. St Georg The election of Boniface VIII B. I.

[76] Villani S. R I. T. 13, page 347. Book 8, c 6. "In the year 1294, Cardinal Benedict Gaetani, having by his address and sagacity induced Celestine to resign the Papacy, as we have mentioned in the preceding chapter, followed up his undertaking and worked on the minds of the cardinals, and the courier of King Charles, who held the friendship of many cardinals, especially the twelve created by Celestine. Being in the country of Charles he went to him one night incognito with a small retinue

faced artifices to enlist King Charles in his favor, and that he did obtain his assistance in his endeavors to gain possession of the much-desired Keys, the reader will wonder at the source and truth of our account. But, thank God, we are living to-day in times in which our minds, being freed from the preponderant influence of the opinions of others, advance more freely in the search for truth and possess innumerable means of arriving at it. Very many writers, following the opinions of Villani and Dante, and without any further inquiry have charged Gaetani with the foul crime of simony.

Villana arrived in Rome during the year of the Jubilee, that is six years after the election of Boniface, and in that year he wrote his history. He had not witnessed the resignation of Celestine and the election of Boniface. So he gathered his information of the events from hearsay, as it passed from mouth to mouth. Now we who live in a more civilized age know by experience, how and to what extent great events still recent, and not matured for history, may become distorted in character and in circumstances, especially if human passions be aroused by them. Hence imagine how many opinions existed disputing these two facts, the renunciation of Celestine and the election of Boniface, in that obscure XIIIth century, in which owing to the want of printing and the lack of intercourse among people, they were permitted to intrude themselves with a tyranny and an arrogance which proceeded from the factional fights of families and kings.

When Villani was stopping at Rome, the anger of the Colonnas was at fever heat, and it was precisely this family that spread the famous libel relative to the election of Boniface, which it said was invalid because of the invalidity of the abdication of Celestine. Anyone who knows

and said to him: "King Charles thy Pope Celestine was willing and able to serve thee, only he knew not how; as for me if you induce your friends the cardinals to elect me Pope, I shall know, and shall be willing, and shall be able to set before thee all the power of the Church." Then the King trusting him promised it; he ordered his twelve cardinals to give him their vote, Matthew Rosso and James Colonna, who were the leaders of seven Cardinals perceived what was transpiring, and forthwith gave him their votes, Matthew being the first to vote for him. In this manner he was elected Pope in the city of Naples on the vigil of Christmas in the same year.——"

what was the temper of the Roman people at that time, and especially under a Pope vigorous and firm as Boniface was, will readily understand how greedy it would be to seize and propagate forthwith false accounts.

All admit that Gaetani had a soul so noble and lofty, that it went, so to speak, beyond the limits of virtue, and almost degenerated into pride; that in the conclave of Perugia he made Charles feel it severely, and that afterwards these two personages were not in accord at all regarding the renunciation of Celestine, because Gaetani aided him to relinquish the Apostolic See, while on the contrary Charles tried to make him retain it. No one who has the least bit of sense can believe that at the time of the aforesaid procession arranged by Charles, according to Ptolemy of Lucca, at a time when the King and Gaetani were clashing most violently, the one could promise the tiara and the other could bow the head before the Prince and promise favors. Nor was Charles such a simpleton as to prefer the promises of Gaetani to the profitable and actual simplicity of Celestine; nor so foolish as to treat with Gaetani of his promotion to the Papacy, and at the same time impede the departure of Celestine from it. If therefore the disputed renunciation and during the time the dispute was going on, Gaetani could not have come to the shameful agreements with the King, when shall we find them conferring and trafficking regarding the place belonging to the Son of God? Is it perhaps when the Pope was seen changed into a poor hermit, and Charles was foiled in his efforts? We grant that the reason of time may warrant such an assumption, but not the character of the persons. For although ten days may have elapsed from the resignation of Celestine to the holding of the conclave, a most opportune time for the nightly colloquies of Gaetani with King Charles, we cannot imagine how these two persons, angry and full of threats as they were, could come to such friendly conferences so suddenly. We know that the ambition of both could have calmed on a sudden their angry minds, for their mutual advantage; but this shows us precisely the impossibility of the dishonest agreement, since the advantages were not equal in the eyes of Charles and Gaetani.

According to the account of Villani, we are to believe

that Gaetani by night accosted Charles, and promised to favor him more than Celestine had done, if he would aid him to ascend the vacant chair, and that Charles with a cheerful mind granted his request. Charles promised a certain and immediate benefit, and Gaetani a future and uncertain favor. Very unequal promises. And then what was the favor? The Dominican friar, Alphonsus Ciacconius [77] affirms, though Villani says nothing of it, that the favor was the recovery of Sicily. But the recovery of Sicily would not have been an extraordinary benefit. All his predecessors in the Papacy had worked strenuously to wrest it from the King of Aragon, and place it under the authority of Charles, as they demanded the rights of the Church be identified with those of the house of Anjou; and so to the attainment of this the efforts of Gaetani would be used, as it happened, even without promising it to Charles. Charles was promising much, and Gaetani little or nothing. Are we then to believe that this Gaetani, the most renowned among the cardinals for judgment and learning, the lord of the Papal Court, who did not flinch before the report which, thanks to the infamous artifices of the Colonnas and the French, accused him of intruding himself into the Papacy; who did not flinch in the presence of that terrible and brutal Philip the Fair; who did not flinch at Anagni before the daggers of Sciarra Colonna, and that French ruffian Nogaret, are we to believe, we repeat, that he flinched in presence of Charles the Lame, over whom he had lately triumphed by the renunciation of Celestine?

And even supposing that the excessive ambition of Gaetani would at this point have unnerved his courage, who will believe that Charles most cunning that he was, would have relied on the promises of Gaetani who also was considered to be a most crafty man? Who will believe that Charles with a college of French Cardinals most docile to him by reason of a common fatherland, wishing to have a Pope altogether according to his liking, would have leaned towards Gaetani, Roman to the core, the bitterness of whose mind he had already tasted? Shall we say that perhaps the reputation for judgment and skill in administration enamored Charles of Gaetani, and satisfied

[77] Vitae Pontif. Rom.

him with the certainty of favors greater than those which resulted from the incapacity of Celestine? But to such a conclusion Charles could not come, for he would know, that if ambition rendered Gaetani a friend and a promiser of favors, this ambition being satisfied, he would return to his first disposition, and even more severe and more inexorable, as it were, through shame for having prostituted his magnanimity; and then his judgment and skill in the management of affairs would become very sharp weapons with which to wound the King.

We would not have entered into this discussion if all the writers, eye-witnesses of the events, or at least some of them had mentioned the evil artifices used by Gaetani to bcome Pope; but finding the recital in only later writers like Villani, or rabid ones like Dante, we have desired to measure these words with them less out of love for Boniface VIII than for the love of truth. In fact Ptolemy of Lucca who was in Naples when the election of Gaetani took place says absolutely nothing of simoniacal practices.[78] James Stephaneschi, Cardinal of the title of St. George in Velabro, who not only resided in Naples in those times, but also was a member of the Papal Curia, having been created by Celestine a Canon of St. Peter's, and Auditor of the Rota,[79] is altogether silent on the compacts with Charles. But if we believe that he, out of love for Gaetani, by whom afterwards he was created Cardinal, had kept silent concerning his simony, we must admit, that if this was so, he ought not to have mentioned the deception of Charles, but have passed over in silence this account as likewise the story of the nocturnal conference related by Villani. But on the contrary Stephaneschi without any artifice of words, bluntly relates, that Gaetani being elected Pope, Charles saw his hopes perish, thanks be to God; and

[78] "Post cessionem autem ad modicum tempus juxta formam decreti ad electionem alterius procedunt, praesente Rege Carolo Neapoli, et in vigilia Nativitatis Dominicae in Dominum Benedictum Gaytani vota sua dirigunt, et in Summum Pontificem assument, et Bonifacius VIII vocatus est." Eccl. History, c. 34 . . . "Dictus Caelestinus Papatui cedit, et sua resignatio a Cardinalibus acceptatur. Tunc ad electionem procedunt, et Dominum Benedictum eligunt, Vocatusque est Bonifacius octavus, et hoc totum Neapoli est factum, et presente Rege."—Idem Annales year 1294. —S. R. I. Tom XI, pages 1300, 1301.

[79] See Cardella, History of the Cardinals, T. 2.

adds a warning that no one should violate the liberty of Mother Church in the selection of her spouse; an evident proof that Charles was present to turn away the votes from Gaetani.[80] Therefore far from their having come to any compact between them, the Pope elect and the King were at war with each other, and the latter would most rather have preferred as Pope, any other Cardinal than Gaetani. So by combining the testimony of contemporaries with the arguments of criticism founded on prior facts, on the circumstances of the time, and on the character of the persons, we know not what foundation of truth there remains to the account of Villani and the poetic fantasies of Dante. Finally the ultimate confirmation of our statement is that in the famous libel composed by the furious Colonnas, with which they strove to show the invalid election of Gaetani, we do not find that the sin of simony, but that the invalid abdication of Celestine laid the foundation of his intrusion into the Papacy. The Colonnas at that time knew what they were doing; and as members of the conclave, they were not ignorant, if there were such, of the simonical practices of Gaetani. The sin of simony alone was sufficient to wrest from the hands of Boniface the basely bought Keys of St. Peter.[81]

[80] James, Cardinal of St. George. The coronation of Boniface, Book I, c. 1, 2.

" . Nam plurima nomina Fratrum
In te conveniunt (alii licet altera fassi)
O Cardo Benedicte sacer, Levitaque quondam,
Eligeris: nam digna quidem concordia vocum
Accessit .. . .
... . .. Caroli spes cepta precando
Defecit, miserante Deo. Sunt ista relatu
Digna, quod et Patri, necnon sibi praestita noscens
Munera ab Ecclesia, vultus avertit et ora.
Nec Matrem violare licet, quin libera possit
Desponsare viro. Caveant quicumque sinistris
Fraudibus injectant oculos, ac ipsa Potentum
Formide! subjecta manus: sic gloria praestat."

[81] We have found in the Vatican Library a MS. of the Urbinate signed no. 1275, the title of which is: "The life customs and events in the Pontificate of Boniface VIII" The anonymous author says in the preface: "The most essential part in the life of Boniface will be that which I have drawn from many notices, and from an old book of the years 899, 1323 and 1294." The last years very strongly support our statement.

Now to return to our narrative. As soon as Gaetani realized that he was elected Pope, he felt his soul oppressed by the greatness of the office, and he could not refrain from weeping. Having grown old in the Roman Court he knew what a Supreme Pontiff should be; he understood the times, and he was not ignorant how cruelly care would gnaw under the purple. He accepted the burden which Heaven imposed on him, and took the name of Boniface, the eighth Pope to bear that name. He seemed to have a presentiment of a stormy future, and wishing God to witness the dispositions of his heart that He might come to his aid, he took, as was the custom of Pontiffs, as a motto for his seal these words of the Psalm: " Deus in adjuorium meum intende "—" Incline unto my aid, O God!"[82]

Being raised to the highest place, the Church seemed to him torn and shattered by the weak administration of Celestine, or rather by the frauds of those, who taking advantage of his ignorance and inexperience, had made the holy Hermit open his heart to grant all manner of concessions, and had wantonly gathered the fruits of them. In a discourse delivered to the cardinals, Boniface referred to the evils brought upon the Church, and to repair them he revoked all the favors and concessions which had been granted by his predecessor, " not in the fullness of his power, but in the fullness of his simplicity," as James of Voragine remarks[83] This measure seemed to Giordano[84]

The author narrating the exaltation of Boniface to the Papacy, far from even hinting that he owed the place to the work and favor of Charles, clearly says that Charles did not want him as Pope, since "the King of Naples, knowing him to be a covetous, avaricious, venomous man and a traitor, (although he was learned and fit to manage the Papacy), never wished to have him nominated "—The writer throws off all restraint in maligning Boniface.

[82] Ciacconius. Lives of the Popes. [83] Chronicles, Genu. S. R. I. T. IX.

[84] Giordanus Vatican M S. 1960—" Sed ex hoc factus est fastosus et arrogans, omnium comtemptivus: unde factus Pontifex praedecessorum suorum Nicholai et Caelestini gratias revocavit " Raynaldus, year 1294, no. 23. Stephaneschi does not mention Nicholas; there was no reason to revoke his concessions.

[84] " Ad perpetuam rei memoriam. Caelestinus Papa V. seductus instantia et ambitione plurimorum, concessit varia minus digna et inordinata et insolita. Quapropter ipse recognoscens suam insufficientiam et periculam pati ex hoc universam Ecclesiam, renuntiavit Papaptui; et humiliter postulavit, et voluit, ut quae per ipsum improvida facta fuerunt,

to be the effect of a bold and contemptuous mind; but with regard to those forged Bulls, which were Papal only in name, as Celestine himself ignored them, we do not know why it did not spring from a mind solicitous for the welfare of the Church, rather than from the low voice of a childish pride.—Most certainly this was the first act which revealed the strong temper of mind of the new Pope.[85]

On his first ascending the Papal Chair to scatter discontentment amongst such a great number who were enjoying the favors of Celestine, and of which they saw themselves deprived at one stroke, was a striking proof of the firm determination of Boniface to observe justice in spite of every obstacle. Those good Celestine monks, whom the people revered as saints, lamented the resignation of their founder; that crowd of wicked agents of the Curia bewailed the good times of Celestine. To these malcontents were added all who were deprived suddenly of their benefices, and other favors so wickedly acquired, and all these joined sides to increase the complaints and hatred for Boniface. Hence the reader may see that on the first appearance of Boniface to the world as Supreme Pontiff, he did not even enjoy that indulgence of a general judgment which is wont to be accorded princes of a new regime. But hatred and revenge furiously gathering about him, disturbed the beginnings of his Pontificate, and engrossing minds, rendered them slow to believe the good that he did, and over credulous of the evil.

Hardly having been proclaimed Pope, Boniface, though advanced in years and in spite of the vigors of winter, did not endure any longer his separation from the Roman See. He knew from experience what a prolific source of calamities the exile of a Pope would be to the Church, and with what chains that pious imprisonment in the palaces of laymen would bind his will. So brooking no delays, he departed from Naples, though before leaving he exhorted the Neapolitans to remain faithful, and Charles to exercise a benign rule over his people, wearied and worn out by wars.

futurus ejus successor provide revocaret. Et postquam fuimus ad apicem Apostolatus assumpti, nobis, dum adhuc essemus Neapoli, preces fudit, revocare quae ipse fecerat curaremus " Register of Boniface M. S. Vatican. an 1 n 75. [86] James Card. of St. George. The coronation of Boniface VIII, Book 1, c 1.

Arrived in Capua, he took the way to St. Germano, and went to pay a visit to the monastery of Monte Cassino, which perhaps was still in disorder on account of the forced reforms of the Celestines; and then following the way to Ceprano he descended into the fertile valley of Anagni. All the city, which was his birth-place, out of reverence for him as Pontiff, and out of domestic love, turned out to meet him. Splendid honors were accorded him by companies of noble knights, and many people bearing in their hands palm-branches, and singing and dancing as on a feast day. Among those who came to meet him there was a large number of Roman Patricians who had been deputed to offer to him the dignity of Senator. This offer so greatly increased the desire for Rome, that he could not remain in domestic joys and so he continued on his way. Stephaneschi remarks, that neither the rigors of winter, nor the fatigues of the journey caused him any inconvenience so happy was his soul on recovering liberty.[86] Finally he appeared before the eternal city, which lies immense and silent in a desert country. About three years had passed since the city had been deprived of the person of the Pontiff; and the deprivation was a loss of that soul which gave it life, since the ruling spirit of the Cæsars had left it like a dead body buried under the ruins of its greatness. So the approach of Boniface filled all Rome with incredible rejoicing; a splendid welcome was accorded him by the military and the clergy, who went out to meet him with every sort of pompous offices. Boniface on first arriving repaired to the Lateran Basilica to pray, and afterwards he took up his abode in the Vatican palace.[87] Thus have we conducted this Pontiff to Rome, clearing the way of the ugly sin of simony, leaving behind his aforesaid enemies astonished by his wonderful elevation to the Papal throne, but ready to break forth, and combine with subsequent enemies, powerless to suppress the truth, but yet too powerful by reason of the times to disturb history, its august agent.

Wishing to speak somewhat in detail of the ceremonies and vestments used by the Popes at their solemn coronation in the time of which we speak, it is necessary that we

---

[86] "Nec labor aut algor fessus sumptusve gravare: Tanta quies animis, libertas reddita cum sit" [87] James Cardinal of St. George. Ib.

should anticipate by an observation, the uneasiness and scandal which may arise in the mind of the reader from seeing the successor of the Fisherman crowned better than emperor, all glittering with gold and precious stones, and after the manner of a king. In this observation we would not spend the time, if we did not know how much the minds of some may be disturbed by this magnificence and splendor of ceremonies of the Vicar of Him who had not whereon to lay His head.

When Christ came on earth to confirm the law of nature in the heart of men, and to establish the more perfect law of the Gospel, the gates of hell commenced against the Church a war, which will last as long as the world, and will conduce to nothing but triumphs for the Church. The Emperors of Rome were its ministers and satellites and in their cruel skill many were the torments and the tortures they inflicted in order to eradicate and destroy the Church of Christ. But persecuted and not conquered, in the dark shades of the Catacombs and in the deserts, the Church fed the faithful with the bread of the word of God, and pointed out the way to Heaven by the poverty even of her exterior worship. And this sufficed for men just out of the school of the Apostles, and little in need of sensible aid to elevate the spirit. Hence those poor unadorned robes which Linus, Cletus, and Soter wore, were sufficient for the Pontifical dignity, because the hour had not as yet come, in which the Church strengthened by the blood of the martyrs, was to change the whole aspect of civil society, and direct it not only to its last end, Heaven, but also to that of human prosperity by the preservation of order. Facts have proved that such has been and ought to be the double office of the Church. When the anger of the Cæsars had been appeased, and the valor of the first Christians had grown weak, the Church had to add to the forms of external worship, because it had become urgent upon her to speak to and convince the senses, which began little by little to prevail over the spirit. Churches arose, and were enriched for the nourishment of religion; and the Church here below in the outward spendor of her forms, became an image of that Church triumphant under whose feet are silent the storms of this world. That is why the rough robes of the first Pontiffs were transformed into others of a silken texture, which did not adorn the shoulders of the Vicar of the Son of Man, but those of the Vicar of Christ the conqueror of death.

Religion had been up to that time cloistered in the sanctuary, as it were, in order to complete the work of human civilization by heavenly discourses, but now she issued forth as a queen to the civil conquest, dragging after her, conquered and bound, anarchy and tyranny, and imprinting on the foreheads of the successors of Augustus the sign of the cross. So when the Church placed herself at the head of the people bearing in hand the standard of the cross, all the princes and emperors she met on the way, far from opposing her glorious march to true civilization, amazed but reverent bent their knee, and together with the people they formed but one family, as one was the standard, which sanctified every command and suggestion. This is the reason why the Popes saw themselves instantly borne from the depths of the Catacombs to the height of a throne, which has for its footstool the thrones of the emperors. And this is the reason why religion having become the mistress of the world and resplendent by the outward forms of worship, her Popes should wear a crown, be clothed in purple, and adorn the person with precious stones. And by reason of these brilliant insignia of universal authority, the people were accustomed to revere the Pope not only as the Vicar of Christ, but also as the preserver and champion of civil justice. And from that time the voice of the Pontiff was so powerful as to make itself heard to the confines of the world those words of the Royal Psalmist says: "*Be ye wise, ye judges of the earth.*"

It was a Sunday, the fifth of January. At the break of day Boniface with all the College of Cardinals, bishops and all the other clergy, repaired to the Vatican Basilica for the solemn ceremony of the Papal consecration and coronation. As soon as he arrived in the Basilica, taking off the robes that he wore, he put on the white alb, binding it at the waist with a cincture; then a purple stole, and a dalmatic with sleeves, such as is worn by a deacon, and a mantle, or long trailing cope, which two ministers held up at the sides, and which was retained in place on the breast by a gold clasp, in the centre of which glistened a beautiful carbuncle surrounded by precious stones. On his head was placed a mitre with two points, signifying the old and the new law, covered with gems, which had two pendants falling on the shoulders. He covered his hands with gloves or chirothecas, and on his finger he wore a ring of priceless value. When the Pontiff was surrounded by the cardinals and the bishops, all vested in white, the archdeacon organized the procession that conducted the Pontiff to the altar of St. Peter; as he proceeded slowly, he held his hand raised imparting continuously his blessing to the people. Having arrived at the choir three cardinal priests approached to revest him with the chasuble, and kissed his breast with great reverence, he himself receiving them with that sign of peace. Afterwards he seated himself on a faldstool, placed between the altar and the pontifical throne. Then the suburban bishops of Albano, of Porto, and of Ostia presented themselves before him, and successively offered prayers, which we here produce, and which seem to us remarkable and filled with the spirit of God. The Bishop of Albano prayed first: " O God, who does not " despise any one who devoutly invokes Thee, we beseech " Thee to listen to our prayers and bestow the abundance " of Thy heavenly benedictions on this Thy servant Boni- " face, whom the common suffrage of Thy people has raised " to the Apostolic Throne in order that he may know that " it is by Thy grace and favor that he has obtained this " high dignity."—The Bishop of Porto then prayed: " Omnipotent and Eternal God, answer, according to " Thy great mercy, our prayers, and fill with the grace of " the Holy Spirit this thy servant Boniface, that he, who " by the ministry of our service has been constituted the " head of the Church, may be strengthened with the firm- " ness of Thy power."—And finally the Bishop of Ostia prayed: " O God, who hast desired that Thy Apostle " Peter should be endowed with the Primacy in preference " to any one of the other Apostles, and had entrusted to " him the burden of the whole Christian world, we beseech " Thee to be propitious to this Thy servant Boniface, whom " we have raised against his will to the throne of the Prince " of the Apostles, that inasmuch as he is made greater by " such dignity, so may he treasure up merits of virtue, and " thus through thy aid worthily carry the weight of the

" Universal Church and receive from Thee, who art happi-
" ness itself, the merited reward."——

Boniface advanced with great solemnity to the altar of St. Peter. This was of sculptured marble, at the sides of which arose four columns of porphyry, supporting a canopy of silver, blackened by time, as a precious covering for the bones of the Apostles, which reposed beneath.[88] We believe, following the authority of Page,[89] that when Boniface arrived at the altar of St. Peter, before being consecrated (since he was not bishop) he made that profession of faith, which we find among the facts added to Ciacconius by Augustine Oldoini,[90] and which we herewith translate: "In the name of the Holy and undivided
" Trinity, in the year of the Incarnation of Our Lord, 1294,
" the eighth Indiction, I, Benedict Gaetani, Cardinal
" Priest, and chosen by the grace of God to be the humble
" minister of this Holy Apostolic See, promise to thee
" Blessed Peter, prince of the Apostles, to whom Jesus
" Christ Creator and Redeemer of the world, entrusted
" the keys of the heavenly kingdom to bind and loose in
" heaven and on earth, saying: Whatsoever thou shalt bind
" on earth, it shall be bound in heaven, and whatsoever
" thou shalt loose on earth, it shall be loosed in heaven;
" and I promise to thy Holy Church, which with thy as-
" sistance I this day undertake to rule, that during this
" miserable life I shall not abandon it, I shall not deny
" it, I shall never disown it; nor for any reason or occasion
" of danger or of fear shall I abandon it or separate myself
" from it; but even unto death and at the price of my blood
" I shall strain every nerve to preserve the integrity of the

---

[88] James Cardinal of St. George. Coronation of Boniface VIII, chap. 2.

[89] Brev. Gest. B. R. P. P. in the life of Boniface VIII, n. 10.

[90] Tom. 2 Col. 311—Abraham Bzovio and Raynaldus relate this, (appendia to vol. 3) from the Vatican MS. of Cardinal Nicholas of Aragon. Wading and Page declare this formula of profession of faith to be apocryphal, because in some parts the account of Raynaldus differs from that of Page. But the variances are not such as to make us believe it apocryphal, as Mansi observes. We know no reason for Ciacconius maintaining that Boniface was the first to make a profession of faith before becoming Pope. Baronius relates that the Popes of the ninth century did so (year 869, sec. 59), which we find in the MS of Anthony Agostini; besides it is spoken of in the Diurnal of the Roman Pontiffs (sec. 33 and 35), which Garner mentions.

"true Faith, which I have found in thy Holy Church, "Christ its author transmitting it through thee, and the "blessed Apostle Paul, and by thy successors handed it "down to me who am nothing."—And so he goes on promising to be the preserver and defender of all the dogmas approved by the eight Ecumenical Councils, the papal decrees and constitutions, being aided by the advice of the cardinals. And he concludes: " I have then with my own "hand subscribed to this profession of faith, which I have "had written by the notary and secretary of the Holy "Roman Church, and I sincerely offer it to thee, O Blessed "Apostle Peter, with a right intention and devout con- "science over thy holy body and before thy altar." [91]

Then he began the pontifical Mass, and having finished the Introit he sat on the faldstool, and the prelates and priests came forward to kiss his feet; then having gone to the altar of St. Peter he received from the two oldest Cardinal Deacons the white pallium with its black crosses. Then one of them who placed it around the neck of the Pope, pronounced these words: " Receive the pallium, "which signifies the fullness of the pontifical office, for the "honor of the omnipotent God, of the Glorious Virgin and "Mother of God, Mary, of Blessed Peter and Paul, and of the Holy Roman Church."—After the pallium was fastened with three gold pins, the Pope arose, incensed the altar and seated himself on his throne. The Cardinals advanced to kiss his foot and cheek; which homage being finished, the oldest of the cardinal deacons with rod in hand, arranged all the assistants in two files, and in a loud voice said: " Graciously hear us, O Christ." At once the judges and secretaries exclaimed:—" Long live our Lord Boniface, created by God Supreme Pontiff, an universal Pope."—The Pope invoked the Saviour of the world thrice, the Blessed Virgin twice, and a few of the saints from the Litany once; the others answered: " O Lord, aid him." This ceremony was called the " Eulogy " of the Pontiff. With the usual ceremonies he was anointed and consecrated Bishop and Pope. Then having seated himself on his throne before the door of the Basilica of St. Peter, in the presence of an immense concourse of people, the oldest of the cardinal deacons, having removed the

[91] See Document F.

INTERIOR OF ST. JOHN LATERAN, THE MOTHER AND MISTRESS OF ALL CHURCHES.

mitre, solemnly placed the tiara on his head, saying: "Receive the tiara, in order to know, that thou art the Father "of Princes and of kings, the ruler of the earth, Vicar on "earth of Our Saviour Jesus Christ, to whom glory and honor forever and ever."—This tiara resembled a Phrygian biretta, with a simple crown at the base, a sign of royal power, which Constantine allowed Pope Sylvester to wear, as Stephaneschi asserts.[92] Boniface desired to increase this by adding a second crown, as Papebroche relates,[93] to signify the double power, spiritual and temporal of the Pope.[94] On the head of Boniface was placed the tiara with two crowns, the texture of which was formed of peacock feathers, and at the top was set an immense carbuncle, below which there were set round by turns flaming rubies and all other kinds of most precious stones, with which it had been lately adorned by order of Boniface.

The solemn cavalcade to the church of St. John Lateran followed the ceremony of the coronation. The Pope rode a white steed, whose back was covered with a purple cloth, the head and breast being bare. The horses which the cardinals and prelates rode were covered with white material, and those of the subdeacons, chaplains and clerks were bare. As soon as all were ready to start, the eldest of the deacons arranged the cavalcade in this manner: at the head of all went the Papal horse richly caparisoned, and led by the bridle; afterwards came a subdeacon carrying a cross, a custom established by St. Sylvester, as Fivisani states.[95] Then twelve standard bearers with scarlet banners, and two others carrying a cherub at the point of a lance. Then followed two naval prefects (an office which no longer exists) vested in copes, the clerks, the advocates, the judges, the singers, the deacons of the Epistle and

[92] Chap. 7. [93] In conatu Chron. ec ad S. Sylvester n. 5, page 128.
[94] Pope Innocent III would have mitre and tiara mean the same, saying in his sermon on St. Sylvester: "R. Pontifex in signum imperii utitur Regno, et in signum Pontificii utitur Mitra." And more solemnly elsewhere: "Ecclesia in signum temporalium dedit mihi Coronam; in signum spiritualium contulit mihi Mitram pro Sacerdotio, Coronam pro Regno: illius me constituens Vicarium, qui habet in vestimento et in femore scriptum.—Rex regum et dominus dominantium —(Burio Notices Rom. Pontiffs, page 579). See also Fioravanti. Denarii Summorum Pontificum pages 56 and 57, letter N. S.
[95] De ritu S. Crucis Pontifici praeferendae commentarium Rom. 1592 in 4.

Greek Gospel, the country abbots, the bishops, the archbishops, the city abbots, the patriarchs, the cardinals, the cardinal deacons, the cardinal priests, and finally the Pope on a white horse, attended by a subdeacon who held an umbrella over his head. For a short distance King Charles the Lame, and Charles, king elect of Hungary, held the bridle of the Pontifical horse, and they were relieved by two nobles. No one is to wonder at this part of the ceremony, and judge it a little unbecoming to royal dignity, when we consider that these kings attended and performed this humble act both as vassals of the Church, and followers of the Vicar of Christ.—

The cavalcade being thus formed, marched along the street called Papal, to the church of St. John Lateran, and along the route in certain places some member of the Pope's family threw money among the people. Upon arriving at the portico of the Lateran, the Pope was met by the canons of that Basilica, and having taken off the Tiara, he seated himself on the prophyry chair, called the "Stercoraria." Hardly was he seated, when some of the cardinals came forward and paying him all kinds of honors, raised him up; and he, standing took three handfuls of money and cast them among the people, saying: "Gold and silver I have not, behold what I have." So in the midst of all those honors, emblematic of the Papal dignity, by sitting on a chair of lowly name, and by scattering a little money, he signified the humility and poverty of human nature, which was not transformed by such a stupendous elevation of state.

Having left this seat, he was escorted by the cardinals to the altar of the Basilica, where loud voices were heard proclaiming him Pope: "St. Peter has chosen Boniface." At the altar he prayed and blessed the people, and repaired to a raised marble seat and extended his foot to be kissed by the Lateran canons. Afterwards he was conducted to the palace of Pope Zachary, at the entrance of which he seated himself on a faldstool, and listened to an address of praise, as was previously done at the Vatican. He then went to the Church of St. Sylvester, and also lingered at the entrance, where there were two porphyry seats; he seated himself in the one that was on the right, and the head canon of the Lateran handed him a crosier as a sign of jurisdiction, as well as the keys of the Basilica and the Palace; holding these insignia in his hands he sat down in the chair on the left, and returned them to the one who had presented them. The head canon placed around the Pontiff a red silk cincture, from which hung a purple burse containing twelve precious stones, the moss agate seals. And thus arrayed, the Pope extended his foot to be kissed by the officials of the palace, and with three throws he cast ten pennies of Provence among them saying: "*Dispersit, dedit pauperibus; justitia ejus manet in saeculum saeculi,*" "He hath distributed, he hath given to the poor; his justice remaineth forever and ever."— Afterwards he visited the chapel of St. Lawrence, and having taken off the pallium and the other vestments, clothed with the Pontifical cloak he retired to his apartments for the solemn banquet.

We are not sure whether the Cardinal of St. George was carried away by the force of imagination in describing in verse the hall where the papal banquet was held. But we may credit all he says, basing our belief on the greatness and magnificence of the soul of Boniface. The hall was resplendent with gold; the walls were decorated with the richest ornaments; jewelled drinking cups and precious dishes covered the bedecked tables; and a very large number of nobles by their richness of dress added to the splendor of the scene. The Pope sat at a separate table, which was raised above the others, and had a richer display of ornaments; before him stood the Cardinal Bishop of Ostia with two Cardinal Deacons holding a towel while he poured water for the Pope to wash his hands. The Pope invoked the blessing, seated himself at his own particular table, which was at the head of two long rows of other tables. At those on the right the Cardinal Bishops and Priests were sitting; at those on the left the Cardinal Deacons, and on each side the prelates, barons and other lords were arranged. The Pope was attired in mitre and pontifical robes; before him were the most illustrious nobles, and Kings Charles the Lame, and Charles of Hungary, in royal garments and wearing crowns, attentive to the commands of Boniface, like knights-esquire. The two princes remained in this obsequious attitude until the end of the first course, and then they retired to occupy seats at the first table between the Cardinal Bishops and Cardinal Deacons. When the feasting was over, the Pope was conducted to his apartments, and thus the ceremony of the solemn coronation was brought to an end. If Wadding is to be believed, these feasts were disturbed by sad accidents. On the arrival of Boniface at the Lateran Basilica, the day was turned into night by the darkest storm clouds, which burst into a raging tempest, and which extinguishing the torches and lamps, seemed as if it would prohibit an entrance into the Basilica to the Pope who was approaching. Besides as Boniface was leaving the Basilica, an altercation arose among the people, the greatest confusion followed, and more than forty of the Papal retinue were killed. If these facts are true, we do not doubt that those sad disorders of the elements and of men were precursors of those more terrible disturbances, which would later on agitate the chair of the imperturbable Pontiff.

As soon as Boniface was seated in the Apostolic Chair, he wished to announce to the Universal Church his assumption of the Papacy. The Bull which he addressed to the Archbishop of Sens and his suffragans, is a splendid monument of the eloquence, which breathes the very spirit of God, and which never became degenerate notwithstanding the great and lasting domination of the barbarians inflicted on our country. And since the entire soul of Boniface appears in the writing, we shall produce it in the vernacular, though we shall not be able to equal the excellence of the original text,[96] which may be found among the documents at the end of this work. " That God wonderful and
" glorious in his works, who, being most bountiful of
" mercy, exercises his compassion in this world full of
" trials and dissensions, is no less propitious in favoring
" opportunely his Church, which he the maker of all things
" has founded, and has built with a deep and firm founda-
" tion on the immovable rock of Faith. As her watchful
" custodian, he is ever at her side, never sleeping, nor slow
" in hastening to her in her needs. He is indeed her paci-
" fier in disturbances, her relief in tribulations, and her
" succor in necessities. And therefore his boundless com-
" passion is chiefly exercised in her favor, when, in a dark
" hour, the storm clouds of this world rise up against her.

*See Document B.

"Hence she is fearless in the midst of anguish and afflic-
"tions, gathering strength in persecution, for she is in-
"vigorated in the presence of evils. For fortified by divine
"aid, she is not to be intimidated by the sound of threats,
"nor overcome by the assault of adversities, but more se-
"cure in terrors, more constant in misfortune, trampled
"upon she prevails, suffering she triumphs. This is pre-
"cisely the Ark, which by the swelling of the waters is
"raised aloft, and having passed over the summits of the
"mountains, sails safe and free beating down the waves
"of the mighty flood. This is surely that vessel, which
"amid contrary winds is tossed about by the furious mo-
"tions of a raging sea; yet firm and staunch it is not
"shattered by the surging billows, nor engulfed by the
"stormy anger of the sea; but weathering the risen temp-
"est, and riding the proudly foaming billows, she triumph-
"antly pursues her course. The sails of right intention
"being unfurled on the living tree of the saving Cross
"ever looking towards Heaven, intrepidly she passes over
"the stormy sea of this world; because she has with her a
"watchful pilot the master of the seas. Wherefore under
"his rule and safe direction, and the inspiration of the
"Holy Ghost, the clouds of adversity being dispersed,
"victoriously she pursues her course towards the port of
"the heavenly country, to which she is conducted by a
"supernatural hand. And although the Church was op-
"pressed and disturbed by innumerable misfortunes that
"which opens the deepest and most painful wound in her
"heart, is to be bereft of a good and provident pastor. . .
"In truth the Roman Church deprived of its head by
"free and spontaneous resignation that our beloved son
"and brother Peter Morrone, lately the Roman Pontiff,
"has made for certain reasonable and legitimate causes,
"in presence of our venerable brethren the bishops, and
"our beloved sons the Cardinal-priests and deacons,
"among whom we were numbered, on the feast day of St.
"Lucy, Virgin and Martyr lately passed, this resignation
"being received by the aforesaid cardinals, since from the
"acts of the first Pontiffs, and by a constitution he de-
"clared openly that the thing could be done lawfully, and
"the express consent of the same cardinals was added for
"the legitimacy of the act; the cardinals considering most

"attentively what great evils and manifold calamities "would follow from a long vacancy in the Church, and "besides wishing most ardently to obviate these dangers "by immediate and efficacious remedies, on Thursday, the "23rd of December, after the holy sacrifice was solemnly "offered in honor of the Holy Spirit, and the usual hymn "was devoutly sung, shut themselves up in conclave in a "certain room of the new Castle situated near Naples, "where the same brother Peter, was residing with his "family, in order that by the mutual and opportune ex- "change of sentiments, the Holy Ghost cooperating, they "could the sooner provide for the want of the Church. On "Friday the day following the aforesaid cardinals, hav- "ing raised their thoughts in prayer to the Lord, who "looks with favor on holy desires, proceeded to the elec- "tion by way of votes in order to avoid the above men- "tioned evils. Finally the divine clemency having pitied "the Church, and not wishing to subject it to the dangers "of a longer vacancy, the cardinals cast their eyes (at "that time a Cardinal-Priest of the title of St. Martin) "and although there were many among them more fitted "and more worthy, they canonically selected us as the "Supreme Pontiff, placing on our shoulders a burden so "very weighty. But after deep and careful meditation "considering the difficulties of the pastoral office, the "anxieties and continual trials, and the excellence of the "Apostolic dignity, which just as it elevates one by the "title of the highest honor, so it humbles one by the great- "ness of the burden; moreover being mindful of our many "imperfections, we strongly feared and hesitated, and a "great stupor stunned our mind. . . . . However "lest perhaps we might be thought to impede the work of "divine Providence, or not wishing to conform our will "to his pleasure; and besides being unwilling to change "the unanimity of the electors into disunion by our dis- "sent, we submitted to their pleasure by taking on our "weak shoulders the yoke they wish us to carry, not that "we confide in the strength of our own integrity, but be- "cause we hope for clemency from Him who never aban- "dons those who confide in Him; for He is ever propitious "to them by suitable helps, and from his most high throne "in Heaven mercifully guards and defends the Church

" his spouse, and ceases not to exalt it by abundant gifts
" of compassion.

" Therefore truly in need of your prayers and those of
" others on account of our shortcomings, with solicitude
" we exhort you, and confidently ask you, that by diligent
" intercession you will aid us before the Eternal King,
" recommending our lowliness by devout supplication, so
" that He may condescend to multiply the gifts of his
" grace to us, and pour forth an abundant shower of his
" heavenly blessings, in order that, devoutly directing our
" actions to Him, we may rightly rule his Church, which
" He has been pleased to commit to us, and that we may
" take due care of the universal flock, which is committed
" to our vigilance. We then shall bear strongly in mind
" to assist your Churches benignly, and promote their in-
" terests by suitable favors." Given in the Lateran on the 9th Kalends of February, the first year of our Pontificate.

We have not found in the well-preserved register of the letters of this Pontiff, which is in the secret archives of the Vatican, any letter directed to Princes, informing them of his elevation to the Papacy. Only one is found, which is second on the register, and it is written to the King of France, Philip the Fair, on this subject,[97] which full of salutary instructions, is a clear manifestation of that love which Boniface bore to Philip, with whom he had been acquainted from the time he had been sent as a legate into France by Nicholas IV. Which fact recalling with brotherly affection, he promises that it would be taken as a sign of future pontifical favors. And continuing with candor and with a majesty truly Roman, he wrote:
" We beseech and urgently exhort your royal Highness,
" and we entreat you in the Lord Jesus Christ, that con-
" sidering attentively how the honor of the King loves
" justice, you observe scrupulously the limits of this virtue,
" and that you study to love it sincerely, not abandoning
" equity, nor omitting clemency, in order that the immense
" number of people subject to you may rest in the bosom
" of sweet peace, and repose in a rich quiet leisure. More-
" over favor with royal kindness, and exert yourself to
" defend valiantly and protect in the fullness of her liberty
" and her rights, your Holy Mother, the Church, and her

[97] See Document H.

" prelates, the true ministers of our Saviour, and the other
" ecclesiastical personages consecrated to her service, or
" rather in them honor the King and Master of Heaven,
" through whom thou rulest and art ruled; that acting and
" behaving towards them, like a blessed and favored son,
" you may not only be a worthy imitator of your ancestors,
" who during life showed the greatest reverence and re-
" spect to that same Church, but that you may even sur-
" pass them for the praise and glory of God, and for the
" furtherance of the glory of your own honor and name.
" Placing then in us a firm hope and confidence, as in a
" kind and sincere father, who bears towards you a cordial
" love, and who will not cease to love you, do not hesitate
" to have recourse to us in your own pressing affairs, and
" those of your kingdom. For on the day that we shall be
" entreated by your royal person, willingly, and as far
" as we can with God's help, we shall satisfy your royal
" desires, intending always not only to preserve carefully
" your prosperity and that of your kingdom, but also to
" promote and increase it by the gift of great favors."

Such was the kind feeling which Boniface bore towards Philip IV, surnamed the Fair, when he came to rule the Christian Church; that Philip, we say, who soon we shall see impelled by an innate pride, by court intrigues and jealousies of state, so that he waged a brutal war against him, hurled him into his grave, and with incredible rage was cruel to his memory, not hesitating to disgrace himself by fabricating calumnies against that magnanimous successor of St. Peter. Angry passions which swayed the minds of those of his times, bitter and unamenable to reason, will not suffice to conquer the power of history, which as a queen in the midst of the ages, dispenses praise and blame with an iron hand.

BOOK SECOND.

SUMMARY.

1295—1296.

The mission of Boniface in the Papacy.—The Guelphs and the Ghibellines; the former allied to the Papacy, and the latter to the Empire.—The character of these parties.—It becomes difficult for the Popes to govern the degenerate Guelphs.—Some cardinals and the Roman nobility increase the difficulties.—The aid which the Friars brought to the Papacy, and their faults.—Boniface unprovided with means resists the Ghibellines, and what enemies he encounters.—He repairs to Anagni, and is hospitably entertained by the Colonnas at Zagarolo—How and why the former Pope Celestine disturbed the repose of Boniface—The flight of Celestine.—The Camerlengo of the Pope is dispatched after him.—He flies and wanders along the sea-shore at Viesta.—He is intercepted and conducted to Boniface.—How Boniface received him, and why he shut him up in the castle of Fumone.—Opinions formed by people concerning this imprisonment.—Death of Celestine—The frenzy of fanatics at the condition of his skull.—Boniface undertakes to be peacemaker among princes; and revives the rights of the Church over the kingdom of Naples.—How he hoped to bring about peace—He draws up at Anagni a treaty of peace between Aragon, France, and Naples.—He dispatches a legate to Catalonia to attend to it, and the instructions he gives him.—He follows him by letters, and clears the way of obstacles.—He invites Frederick to an interview—Frederick before proceeding consults the Sicilians, who by letters advise him not to take the step.—His meeting with Boniface.—What things Boniface promises him, if he will leave Sicily.—Charles II being absent, how Boniface provides for the government of Naples.—He undertakes to pacify northern Italy—Genoa and Venice.—He wishes to disarm these two unfriendly republics, but the Genoese frustrate his designs.—Florence always Guelph in her principles, is torn by internal dissensions.—Boniface delivers her from a foreign governor.—How the factions agitate Romagna, Umbria and the Marches, and what the effect of the papal power over these provinces.—Guy of Montefeltro and his deeds.—Boniface cares for the government of Romagna, and returns to Guy the possession of his estates—The fire of war cannot be extinguished there.—He dispatches William Durant.—Who was this man.—Philip, the Fair.—A description of him.—How France feebly opposes him in his tyranny, and how the jurists aid him.—He finds the Pontiffs to be an obstacle.—He dishonors himself by criminal and base robberies.—A description of Edward of England.—He is at war against Philip.—Both fortify themselves by alliances, which disturb the greater part of Europe.—Why Boniface interposes as a peacemaker between them.—He dispatches legates to bring them to an agreement.—They obtain a truce, but it is soon ended by the French resuming hostilities.—Letters of Boniface to Edward.—Other legates are sent to Adolph, King of the Romans, and the words by which Boniface addresses him.—Sad effects of the war.—Philip the Fair debases the public money.—Religious conditions of Denmark; the encroachments of the King restrained by the bishops.—The kings persevering in their tyranny, the bishops resist them.—Eric VI of Denmark, imprisons the Archbishop, and the Provost Lunden.—With what hypocrisy he justifies his violent tyranny.—Escape of the prisoners, the prudent but vigorous remonstrances of Boniface to the Danish King.—Sicilian envoys to James, King of Aragon.—Their grief and that of all Sicily at seeing themselves abandoned by him.—Frederick is proclaimed king.—Boniface sends Calamandrano to Sicily to establish peace.—His overtures are furiously rejected by the inhabitants of Messina.—But Roger of Loria is detached from Frederick.—Boniface creates new cardinals.—He raises the feasts of the Evangelists and the four Latin Doctors, Augustine, Ambrose, Jerome and Gregory.

THE thirteenth century was just ending when Boniface assumed the government of the Roman Church. In the difficult administration he had been preceded by two great popes, Gregory VII and Innocent III, who although they had used their every endeavor to reestablish the Church of God after the disastrous times of the Barbarians, yet they had not been able to perpetuate in a way that foresight of theirs which would render impossible the return or rather the continuation of the causes which promoted clerical disorders, and imperiled the liberty of the Church. Gregory had brought back the clergy to a consciousness of their high dignity, lifting them out of the mire of human defilement; Innocent placed the Church on a high throne from which she commanded the entire world. We have said, in the beginning, that after Innocent up to the epoch of which we are narrating the history, the work of these pontiffs had been without ceasing threatened; and in such a state, when Boniface ascended the throne, did he find the Church which he swore to preserve free and uncontaminated. The corruption of morals up to that time had been engendered by ignorance, or blindness of mind; the servitude was that imposed by the German Empire. Knowledge being propagated in the numerous universities founded throughout Europe, and the imperial colossus having fallen, it seemed that the times would become better. But the tyrants had multiplied on the ruins of that empire; and whilst minds wearied themselves in the search after the True in the dry fields of law and theology, hearts were beating strongly by reason of civil strifes; and in the clash of factions human cupidity was aroused, and raged furiously when charity for fellow creatures was driven out. So while the electors of Germany with the imperial crown in their hands did not know to whom to offer it after the extinction of the powerful house of Suabia; awhile Bologna, Padua, Naples, Paris, and Cologne, were admiring people of wisdom within their walls, the Church was bemoaning a new servitude that was imposed on her, she was feeling ashamed on account of the disorderly actions of many of her ministers.

The struggles between the orders of civil society had succeeded the rivalries of the great families, and if those gigantic catastrophes visited on entire peoples no longer occurred, nevertheless men were led to more lasting lamentation on account of the rabidness of the factions which are the results, either of elevation to rank, or descent from the same. The princes were contending among themselves, because invested with power, they weighed their rights in the scales of justice; the people forced by necessity, bearing still the bloody traces of foreign incursions were stimulated to reestablish themselves and arrive at the difficult adjustment of their own rights. The Roman Pontiff could still raise himself as the arbiter of justice above kings and the people, but the close contact of the Guelphs and Ghibelline parties to his chair was a great danger; so he was seen now and then to waver and to be wanting in that imperturbable firmness so necessary for such an office. For this reason Boniface supreme head of the Church, should first be considered in the center of the Guelph and Ghibelline factions, from which emanate all his relations with the Church, with Italy, and with the world.

The two factions of the Guelphs and Ghibellines in Italy seemed two branches productive only of bad fruit, and by which was wasted all the strength of the old Latin blood that was needed to nourish the trunk of that nation and give it new life. Foreign in its origin, God had prepared for the people of Italy a family life. The Barbarians, the Italians and the Greeks measured swords to determine for the future which one would hold sway over the Italian territory. The Papacy could speak words of peace to all of them, because its dominion was not of the earth. It did in fact speak to them when it withstood not the men individually but the errors they personified. It told the Barbarians that savage force was not the reason of God; it told the Italians that their own country appealed to them to live fraternally in the courts of the Lord; it assured the Greeks that the imperial was not the will of God. The Barbarian became Italian the Italian became papal, the Greek retired from the shores of Apulia and Calabria; because God did not wish even a small corner of Italy to divide with the latter the punishment which was to make them pass from the corrupted theological disputes of the courts of the Constances, of the Zenos and of the Heraclii into the mire of Islamism.

The German emperors came unexpectedly on the scene, and their power and the splendor of the imperial monarchy engaged the attention of many, and revived in them the memory of the ancient Latin empire. So were men divided, who all of one accord looked upon the Roman Papacy as a nucleus of a civil reorganization. Some turned hopefully to Rome, others to Germany. The former less refined in mind, but more generous of heart, being jealous of liberty consecrated it by entrusting it to the Vicar of Christ; the latter more active minded in order to profit by ancient memories, being anxious for greatness, sold their liberty. Strange names, bloody ones of foreign factions, were applied to the Papal and imperial partisans. Guelphs the one, and Ghibellines the other, were the names by which they were known.

In every action there is a principal which individualises it, and it is always either really or apparently good. A paternal and defensive dominion the Guelphs sought from the Papacy, the Ghibellines a splendid and a powerful one from the Empire. But if the former did not violate justice, the latter scorned it by inviting a most powerful foreigner into their weak country. The diversity of language and of customs, the seas which separate, and the mountains which enclose, are the boundaries set by Heaven for indicating the individuality of nations, and how each may sit protected at the feet of that justice which dispenses to each its own. Hence that overflow from beyond the Alps of foreign races summoned for the wedding of Italy to the dangerous imperial monarchy was a violation of the laws of Providence, a sacrilege against justice, and a ravishment of the mother country.

Therefore the Papacy was called, and by reason of its mission, found itself at the head of the Guelph faction, together with all the clergy; so that it seemed that the adhesion of the Guelphs to Rome was an answer to that appeal for order which was made by the Vatican to all Italy in the times of the Barbarians. So long as they did not break faith with the Pontiffs, and nobly struggled for justice and for the freedom of their country and the Church, they were a wonder to the world; it was not in the defiles of the mountains, but on the open field of Legnano that the Lombards stood united and immovable in face of all Germany, and were victorious. But this victory vitiated the minds of the victors, and whilst Alexander III blessed their victory, misunderstandings arose among themselves. Principle was no longer regarded, but men hated one another; and all were badly misled. Guelphism (we mean the idea and not simply the name) had only one period, in which it was truly represented in all the purity of its idea by the Pope and by the Lombard League. From that time deplorable indeed were the reasons why an Italian was a Guelph or Ghibelline. Jealousy between the nobility and populace, and municipal emulation possessed their minds and hearts rather than the grand Papal idea; and whilst the Guelphs were smiting their adversaries with their hands, they gazed with threatening eyes and hearts upon the people or city against which they were more directly waging war.

The original object being lost sight of, minds fluctuated, fraternal blood was spilled, and the Italians with their own hands were shaping a future, the worthy recompense of so many fratricides. Men there were of lofty minds, like Dante, who in Guelphism had placed the highest hopes of good; but being confused and plunged in civil discords, they could not sacrifice the present necessities for a principle, which through human perversity resulted in a barren Utopia. The character of the factions being changed, the Popes could no longer direct that of the Guelphs. They changed their tactics and called the French into Italy. In this they made a grievous mistake, although their error was a necessary consequence of that of the people. But they suffered punishment for it in the multiplication of duties which they were obliged to fulfil; namely, to put an obstacle in the way of the mercenaries who were overrunning the Empire, to resist the Ghibellines, and to combat vigorously the vice that was gnawing the vitals of Guelphism. So that the work of Alexander III was a solemn creation, prolific of incredible hopes; that of Boniface was a work of ardent reparation, in which the flowers of hope had faded. The former acted with the strength of a vivifying thought; the latter with the force that symbolized the sword of justice.

The Guelph was the Papal party, and hence no one must wonder if the clergy enrolled themselves in it with such fervor. Nay more, as every principle which a body of men personifies must needs strengthen and sustain itself on the altar of martyrdom, the bitterness and honor of martyrdom belonged altogether to the clergy, especially under Frederick II. But being as they were men, and most tenacious of the idea of a necessary adhesion of the Guelphs to the Church, in the general contamination of the holy idea, they prevaricated with the others, and the clerical dignity was stained with civil cruelties. They should have surrounded and protected the Papacy like a wall, and obedient ministers to its commands should have hastened to its aid, and by sanctity of life and meekness of conduct they should have calmed the angry minds, should have contained themselves in victory, and should have elevated themselves to the height of the object to which they aspired. But unfortunately they were more Italian than clerics, and divisions arose among them. Of all the clergy that of Rome was the most bare-faced in this fault, and the most injurious to the Guelphs and the Papacy. They might be called the ecclesiastical aristocracy, on account of their immediate service close to the Papal Chair. But what contributed to plunge them into the general corruption was the poison that was injected into them by the corrupt nobility of those times, to whom the highest ecclesiastical preferments had been shamefully enfeoffed. It appears that the Orsinis, the Colonnas, and the Savellis had an acquired right to the dignities and the highest offices in the Church, and for that reason many cardinals and prelates participated in the vices of those families which composed the Roman Patriciate. A calamitous patriciate which grafted the ferocity of the Barbarians to ancient pride. Like a parasite plant, it afflicted the Roman See by robbing the people of the nourishment of civil virtues, and by depriving the prince of the sinews of government. The pontifical tiara with which, so to speak, their families in succession were honored, rendered it still more arrogant, and increased the boldness of action. The frequent vacancies of the throne habituated it to the impieties of anarchy. When restrained, it grumbled, when unrestrained, it was terrible. These patrician families were never truly either Guelphs or Ghibellines; but they used these names to express not the nobility of a principle, but the feuds of their vile ambition. Rivals among themselves, they attacked one another in order to supplant one another in turn; and the prelates who were members of these families brought into the papal court, and into the offices they held, all the passions of their house, and deprived the Papacy of that dignity and power which it needed in order to purify Guelphism of the vices which were corrupting it.

The institution of the Franciscan and Dominican orders was a powerful and salutary remedy for all the evils engendered by the bad citizens and clerics in the heat of those party strifes. The Friars Minor and the Preachers, inasmuch as they were not contemplative and not cloistered, but out in the very heart of cities which were in a ferment of domestic broils, were tried champions of Guelphism. To both clerics and people they seemed marvellous, and as it were, heavenly beings by reason of their poverty of life and austerity of manner, and so they could preach to both, holiness and peace. Oftentimes when the swords were raised in combat, they were lowered at the appearance of a friar; and those feelings of hatred and revenge, which the influence of charity and reason could not stifle, were subdued entirely by their words. They were accessible to the people by reason of their poor habit and food; and they were sought after by the nobles, who in the weariness of their sins, by relieving their poverty with a liberal gift of alms, they wished to make them the mediators of their eternal salvation. Many famous for misdeeds, when dying, eagerly longed for the rough habit of the Friars Minor.

The Popes found in these religious an expedient which the secular clergy no longer offered. Often a friar was a Papal messenger to princes, and to peoples; they were raised to the episcopate, and to the honors of the cardinalate. Exempt from episcopal jurisdiction, they were subject only to the Roman See, and they received immediately from it the faculty to preach and administer the sacraments. They were a sacred militia, which free from worldly cares, numerous and strongly united, went forth at the beck of the Rome Pontiff; and like a balm spread itself in the body of the clergy to preserve it from corruption. But alas! this remedy became such as to lose its power. Their contact with the people lessened the old reverence the latter had for them; the laxity of some of them in the observance of their austere precepts, and their haughty disobedience to the Popes fostered schisms among them; and the privileges accorded them aroused the jealousies of the bishops. The heresy of the Fraticelli (the Little Brothers), the result of a disordered zeal; and the bold and wild theories of William of St. Amour embraced by many, wounded grievously the Order of St. Francis; and it never regained all that civil mission which it received from the Roman See at its institution.

Wherefore as soon as Boniface was seated in the chair of St. Peter, he found things in desperate straits. He must oppose Ghibellinism already fallen from a certain nobility of principle, which consisted in the delusive hope of reviving the Roman Empire, and which was only holding on to existence from the result of that principle, namely the unjust exclusion of the Papacy from the bosom of civil society; he must prop up Guelphism and purify it, and he must check the excesses of the Roman nobility. And it seems to us that the three enemies that he encountered in this triple undertaking were Philip the Fair, Dante, and the Colonnas. By all he was oppressed but not conquered.

Philip the Fair smote him with the force of the civil law; the Colonnas with the law of the Church; and Dante with that of opinion.—As soon as the coronation was finished and the first months of his pontificate had passed, the air of the city grew so bad in the beginning of summer that Boniface left Rome and set out for Anagni. At that time the Colonnas had no doubt of his legitimate election to the Papacy; and moreover they considered themselves his most devoted friends. In fact, inasmuch as the road to Anagni touched the territory of Zagarolo, a fief of the Colonnas, these princes offered the Pope hospitality in their own house. All the Colonnas were round about him waiting on him with all attention and reverence, and so affectionately that it did not seem that they were entertaining a Gaetani, but one of their own family. Boniface, as we shall see, remembered this friendly reception.[1]

St. Peter Morrone was the first to disturb the mind of the new Pope. Boniface feared nothing from him personally; nor did he think that the fire of human ambition burned under the sackcloth of the hermit, who so willingly had laid aside the papal crown. But his sleep was disturbed by the machinations of those who, displeased at the resignation of the Saint, could have urged him to reascend the chair of St. Peter using the same line of arguments which had induced him to resign. In a hypercritical manner they could present themselves to Peter and declare to him that his resignation was null and void; and for that reason Boniface was not a legitimate Pope; the Church of God by his fault was not united in a holy marriage with her legitimate spouse, but chained by the wiles of a wicked lover; and it is certain that the Hermit not from a spirit of pride, but from the fear of losing his soul, could have been induced to raise his weak arms to reassume the relinquished keys, and there would not have been wanting those who would have aided him in the accomplishment of this undertaking. Wherefore Boniface wished to have him brought to himself in Rome, or to some other part of his territory, in order to remove him from the evil and malicious machinations of his monks, and of the people,

---

[1] See the Bull: "Praet. temporum." Raynaldus year 1297; no 27.

who were always recounting the repeated miracles wrought by Celestine.[2]

Angelarius, Abbot of Monte Casino, had been deputed by Boniface to find him, and bring him to Rome. But in the meanwhile the Saint suddenly disappeared. He went to St. Germanus, and for the night he was hospitably received in the abbatial palace. Here he revealed to a certain priest the reason of his flight, beseeching him to keep it secret, and from the same he procured a horse, and every assistance whereby he could arrive secretly at his cell of the Holy Spirit. When he arrived at Sulmona there was a great festival, and the people met him and welcomed him as a wonder worker. He desired only to bury himself again in his cell on Mt. Morrone. But Boniface, as soon as he learned from the Abbot of Monte Casino of Celestine's escape, became greatly apprehensive of the danger of a schism, which the aforesaid rendered probable, and he forthwith dispatched Theodoric of Orvieto, his Chamberlain, to Sulmona, in order to explore the neighborhood in search for Celestine. Theodoric went and found him in his cell enjoying a holy peace, and he was already returning, when other messengers from the Pope came hastening with other instructions relative to Celestine. But it was too late. For the latter for the second time had taken flight. After wandering for two months he finally arrived in Apulia, where in a wild forest he rested and hid himself. In the meanwhile the news of his flight was spreading, and the people were on the alert to see the man remarkable for miracles, and for his renunciation of the Papacy; and in every place through which the fugitive passed, the cry was immediately raised: "Here is the Saint, here is Brother Peter Morrone." Celestine was fleeing not through fear of the Pope, who, as a prudent measure, wished to keep him close to him, but because longing for solitude, and compelled to live in the Papal Court, he was deprived of the benefit of his abdication. His followers had chartered a vessel for him, because he wished to go beyond the sea; but a storm of long duration having prevented his departure, he was finally intercepted a few

---

[2] James Card. of St. George. In the poem of St. Celestine. Preface of Bull, page 440, no 13.

miles from Viesta, and was retained in that town until the wishes of Boniface in his regard could be learned.

We do not believe that they waited long to hear them. Charles of Naples, profoundly inclined before the power of Boniface, was also himself by means of his ministers on the track of the holy hermit, to intercept him. The memory of the happy times of Pope Celestine could not have been embittered in him by a sadder duty. William Stendard, the constable of the kingdom, was charged to conduct the Saint well escorted to the boundary of the kingdom, and he consigned him to the Chamberlain of the Pope, who in the middle of June, 1296, presented him to Boniface at that time residing in Anagni.[3] The latter well knew the danger that beset the Church by leaving Celestine under the influence of his monks and of a people captivated with wonder by the miracles which were related of him. In fact they had already urged him to reascend the Papal Chair;[4] which design obtained the support of many who could not persuade themselves that Boniface was the true Pope, holding the abdication of his predecessor as invalid. However Boniface resolved to proceed cautiously in the matter of the treatment of a saint, as it was easy to wound the piety of the people. Whereupon having accorded a kindly welcome to Celestine, and having given him a room in his own palace, he summoned the cardinals in consistory in order to obtain their opinion on what was best to be done in the matter.[5] Some thought that without any danger, the Saint could be allowed to go free to his cell on Mt. Morrone; others advised, that he should be guarded with great care, in order that his simplicity might not be abused to the detriment of the Church. Boniface adopted the latter proposal, and had him shut up in the Castle of Fumone, in Campania, where to satisfy the desire of the Saint, he ordered a cell similar to the one on Mt. Morrone, to be constructed for his habitation.[6] Visits to the recluse were forbidden to every one; two monks of his own order, were the only ones exempted from this mandate, at the re-

[3] Lelius Marini. Life of St. Peter Celestine. apud Boll. chaps X and XI.
[4] Ibid chap. XI. [5] Petri Alliaci. Life of St. Peter Celestine.
[6] "Cellam igitur optanti, in castro Fumonis firmo cellam, qualem "verosimiliter Sanctus ipse designarat, ad formam ejus, quam in Murrone "habuerat, fieri jussit." Ibid. no 118.

quest of Celestine. It is related, that not being able to bear the narrow confinement of the prison they soon began to grow ill, and were obliged to depart while others took their places in turns. Peter Alliacus states that Boniface placed a guard of six soldiers about Celestine, and about thirty other men whom he calls satellites.[7]

Let the reader now imagine how the imprisonment of a man already venerated as a Saint and a wonder-worker, was discussed by the people, by the Celestine monks, and by those to whom the elevation of Gaetani was displeasing, on seeing removed from their influence their only counterpoise to the power of Boniface. The narrowness of the cell in the castle of Fumone, and the austere penances practiced by Celestine, which on Mt. Morrone had won for him the name and veneration of a saint, now in the castle of Fumone begot for Boniface the name of a tyrant, and for Celestine the honors of martyrdom. The armed men placed on guard about the castle, and the resolution to allow no one to visit the prison were adjudged acts of the most cruel jealousy of authority, and an unnecessary precaution for the quietude of the Church. To the people there did not appear any danger of a schism, but they saw only an innocent man of God shut up in the famous castle. Therefore the blackest calumny against Boniface was spread; and woe to any one when such a thing is founded on a real or apparent violation of the religious convictions of a people, and such a people as was that of the thirteenth century. The blame which was heaped upon the head of Boniface became something supernatural, a power in the hands of his enemies, and only to be removed by the later judgment of historians.

Celestine lived nine months in the castle of Fumone. In the month of May there appeared on his right side a virulent tumor, which baffling all skill, brought on death on the 19th of the same month, in the 70th year of his age.[8] Boniface, as soon as he heard of his death, sent immediately to Fumone Cardinal Thomas of St. Cecilia, and his Chamberlain, who had the obsequies of the Saint held in the church of St. Anthony of Ferentino, to which flocked a great number of the clergy and prelates of the province

[7] Peter Alliacus. Life of St. Celestine, c 3, n. 17 apud Boll.
[8] Lelli Marini sup. Vit. Celest. cap. 11, no. 121.

of Campania. Besides in the Vatican Basilica he honored the dead man with solemn obsequies. The body of the Saint rested in the church of St. Anthony until the year 1327, when it was transferred to Aquila and buried in the church of Collemaggio.

At this time his followers gave loose rein to their unprincipled and depraved imaginations. A nail having pierced the skull of the Saint, they spread the report that Boniface had shortened his life by ordering a nail to be driven in his head. The nail was found (who had found it we know not); and blood was still seen on the point of it. They inserted it into the little hole, and as it fitted wonderfully, the proof was established that this had been the instrument of his death. From that time this nail was preserved as a relic; and in the church of St. Mary of Majella they depicted in a certain fresco the martyrdom of St. Peter Celestine, representing a nail being driven into his head by the order of Boniface, which fact they declared by an inscription at the bottom. To remove all doubt of his martyrdom they placed palms on his tomb, and all those who beheld them knew from those symbols that among the persecutors of the Church there was a Supreme Pontiff, Boniface VIII.

Boniface, as soon as he had taken in his hands the Church government, thought of securing a true and firm peace, for at this time affairs were in a precarious condition on account of the state of feelings among the princes, and worse things were threatened for the future. But peace must not be secured with injury to the rights of the Church. He began to refresh his memory with a knowledge of the rights, which he as head of the Church had over the kingdom of Naples. Charles I of Anjou had sworn fealty to Clement IV and to John XXI. Charles the Lame had renewed to Nicholas IV the promises which his father had made, and in a solemn act declared the homage which the king of Sicily was bound forever to pay, alleging the most ample promises of Charles I.[9] Boniface requested Charles II to renew them, renewing at the same time the Bull of Nicholas IV;[10] and he confirmed the right by deed, absolving Charles from every censure he may have incurred by not having paid tribute to St.

[9] Raynaldus, year 1289. [10] Raynaldus, year 1295.

Peter.[11] The treaty of Tarascon drawn up by himself, when he went as legate with Gerard of Parma to negotiate peace, and subscribed to at Brignolle the 19th of February 1291, became worthless by the death of Alphonsus of Aragon, who died suddenly, on the 19th of June of the same year. James had proceeded swiftly to Spain, and had seized the crown of Aragon in the city of Saragossa in October; Frederick, his brother, took charge of the government of Sicily, as his vicar; Philip of France finding in the death of Alphonsus a just reason for not ratifying the treaty, pretended to invade Aragon, only for the sake of wresting from the French clergy ten years of tithes;[12] the Sicilians gladly rallied around Frederick; and Nicholas IV, the Pope at that time, again despaired of the desired peace. But since the condition of James on the throne of Aragon were similar to those of Alphonsus, namely, with a people tired of bearing, besides the weight of pontifical censures, that of war; with an exhausted treasury, and with the danger of losing Aragon to preserve Sicily, he was inclined to peace, and desired to renew the broken treaty. In fact Pope Celestine now hoped to obtain the happiest results by peace; he proposed another treaty similar to that of Tarascon, but none was concluded.[13]

When the report was spread that Boniface had been raised to the Papacy, negotiations were quickly renewed, and the ambassadors of France and Aragon met to deliberate again.[14] In the meanwhile Frederick himself made advances to Rome, in order perhaps to discover in what way the wind was blowing for him. He sent as legates to Boniface, Manfred Lancia and Roger Geremia who were cordially welcomed and given the most flattering promises. The Pope's hopes for peace grew stronger; in fact, Frederick not being as yet a king, but only the vicar of James, the task of driving him out of Sicily seemed easy. For that reason Boniface and Charles II undertook to coerce James, thinking that having forced him to leave Sicily, there would be no obstacle in the way of restoring it to the subjection of the Church; but they did not reflect that the Sicilian people also had a will in the matter, which

[11] Raynaldus, year 1294, epis 118. [12] Raynaldus, year 1291, 56.
[13] Luning, T. 2, n. 63.—Raynaldus, 1294, 15.
[14] Surita, Annl. Arag. Lib. V, c 9.

although excluded from the treaties was nevertheless powerful, because supported by force. Therefore the Papal legate urged James to restore Sicily to the Church; and the royal representative Bartholomew of Capua urged on Charles of Valois to war against Aragon, that he might secure the Papal privilege which gave him the crown. The discontent among his people, the war in Sicily and the threats of the French prince persuaded him to negotiate peace.[15]

He summoned a parliament of barons; he declared to them how the papal censures annoyed him; that he desired peace, and to confirm it he was willing to send legates to the Pope. Four ambassadors went to seek Boniface at Anagni. In full consistory they stated the reason of the embassy, and such was the kind welcome extended to them that it was clear that the Pope desired nothing more than harmony among Christian princes after such lasting dissensions. The matters to be treated were presented. Besides the Aragonese there were assembled also ambassadors from France, the Bishop of Orleans, the abbot of St. Germain des Prés, Charles of Valois, and Bartholomew of Capua as the representative of Charles II. Boniface presided; and most skilful as he was in negotiations he conducted the proceeding so well, that on the 5th of June he happily disposed the minds of all to agree to the following articles, namely: that Charles of Naples should give his daughter Blanche in marriage to James, with a dowry of twenty-five thousand marks in silver; that James should restore Sicily to him and as much as he had acquired there by conquest; the reluctant Sicilians should be coerced by force; that he should release the hostages, Robert, Raymond, and John, the sons of Charles, with the other nobles and the knights of Provence; that he should pardon the partisans of the house of Anjou; that Charles of Valois should renounce the right over the kingdoms of Aragon and Valencia and over the province of Barcelona, which he had acquired by Papal investiture; mutual pardons and restoration of goods and property were to be granted to all those who had followed the fortunes of the Aragonian and Angevine parties; the Pope himself was

[15] Giann. Stor. Civ. T. III, p. 116.

to release Aragon from all censures, and bless it anew.[16] And whereas in every treaty the general articles to which all agree, are openly declared, the particular ones however are kept secret, and are reserved to be arranged privately, in order not to injure the main issue, in this treaty some secret articles were cared for by Boniface. Secretly he appeased the mind of James, by promising to invest him with Sardinia and Corsica; James on the other hand appeased Philip of France by promising him naval aid against Edward of England.[17] As to Charles, the better to feel sure of the king of Aragon, he asked his daughter Yolanda from him for his son Robert, promising in return to pay twenty-five thousand silver marks, which sum he did not possess, but which Boniface furnished in the form of a loan; the latter was obliged, by reason of this, to levy tithes on the churches of Italy.[18]

On the 21st of June Boniface solemnly ratified the treaty, which he declared in a Bull, to which seventeen cardinals affixed their names and which he concluded by affirming that James was invested by a ring with the kingdom of Aragon and Valencia; that the Cardinal of St. Clement was designated to go as legate to the countries beyond the mountains for the execution of the treaty.[19] Peace was proclaimed on the feast of St. John the Baptist, the Pope having granted the dispensation of consanguinity existing between James and Blanche, the daughter of Charles, so that a marriage might confirm the peace; and punishment was threatened against the violators of the peace. On the 27th of the same month, Boniface communicated the same to Frederick in Sicily.[20]

To draw up a treaty of peace, and to dispose the minds to agree to the proposed conditions, is not always difficult; but the fulfilment of an agreement has always been a most difficult task. To provide for this Boniface deputed William Ferrer, Cardinal of the title of St. Clement, who before the 21st of June set out from Anagni, where the Pope was then residing, for Catalonia, bringing with him

[16] Mariana. De Reb. Hisp. lib. 14, c. 17—Epis. Bonif. lib. 1, epist 184 apud Raynaldum. [17] Surita Annal d'Arag lib. 5, c. 10.
[18] Rayn. 1295, 24. [19] Raynaldus, year 1293, lib. I, 184, n. 2.
[20] Raynaldus, 1295, lib. Epist. 99.

Blanche, the affianced of James.[21] Boniface gave his legate all manner of instructions, and did not leave him an instant, being always at his side with letters. It was the constant custom of the Roman Pontiffs never to withdraw themselves from the immediate direction of affairs; for which reason they have left us those stupendous monuments of their wisdom and integrity of purpose, in the Registers, which if fortunately they were published in one complete collection, far from obscuring the brilliant idea of the Roman pontificate, they would on the contrary render it more luminous, and more worthy of reverence even in the eyes of those who revile it. Therefore hardly was the legate gone, than Boniface was following him with letters which bear witness of his prudence and discretion. He foresaw the many obstacles that the princes would place in the way to an agreement of the articles of the treaty, some of which it had been impossible to remove by word of mouth to Cardinal William, and so on the 30th of June he wrote him from Anagni a letter, in which among other things were read: " That if the explanation " of that treaty became involved with some other things, " and place the mind in a state of uncertainty, he should " fix his eyes on the crucifix, and conform his conscience to " it; that whenever anything arose unforeseen by him, he " should behave in such a concilatory and humane man-" ner, that tempering severity with mildness, the minds of " all might be won over to justice by the sweetest ways."

The Legate, being sent on his good way, was not left alone, but was followed by the most fervent desires of peace, and directions for difficulties which could not be solved in drawing up the treaty, since the Legates declared that they did not have the power of deciding for their lords. One of these difficulties was the possession of the valley of Arany which formerly was held by the prince of Aragon, but now was in the possession of the King of France, who did not wish to see it included among those states, the right over which had been reacquired by King James. The other was the possession of the islands of Majorca and Minorca, which James would not restore to his uncle, also called James, who in the war between Valois and Aragon had been despoiled of them by the Aragonians,

[21] Epistolae, Bonifac. ad Fredericum apud Rayn., 34.

because he followed the French party. Boniface, to whom the attainment of peace was uppermost in mind, earnestly strove to persuade Philip of France [22] from stirring up the minds again over the question of that valley of Arany; that he would leave it to the judgment of the Legate, until it was ascertained at what time it had come under his authority, whether before or during the war between France and Aragon; if before he should retain it; if in time of the war he should restore it, as subject to the avowed agreements to restore everything taken from James. The King of Aragon was urged to surrender the islands of Majorca and Minorca on certain conditions, the arbiter of which must be the Legate. Matters went according to the mind of Boniface, and peace was established.

It did not seem impossible to bind France and Aragon to the peace, both because of the weakness of James in the face of a multitude of enemies, and because of the desire of Charles the Lame, a Frenchman, to recover the fair province of Sicily. But the great difficulty was to persuade Frederick to surrender to another the authority over Sicily, which he was already ruling as the vicar of his brother James. This difficulty was increased a hundredfold on account of the intense hatred of the Sicilians for the French, whose blood shed in the unhappy Vespers was still warm; and the feelings of a people emboldened by a recent victory are not easily controlled by any one. As the report of the treaty had spread, Frederick, aroused by the chagrin of losing Sicily and urged on by the Sicilians, had already begun to protest against the treaty.[23] However Boniface did not despair of bringing his designs to a successful issue, although it would be a desperate work to reconcile the interests of the Church in Sicily with the contentment of the Sicilians. He must speak kindly to the legates of Frederick whom he should welcome heartily; afterwards he should win over by the softest persuasion Frederick himself, John of Procida, and Roger of Loria, the supreme directors of the sentiments of the Sicilians, the one the leader of civil, the other of military affairs, and with what result every one knows. And whereas it

[22] Raynaldus 26. Epist. 208.
[23] Epist. Bonif. ad Fred. in Chron. Anony Sicu. cap 53.

would be a loss of time and labor to express in a letter the arguments of persuasion, he considered it better to invite the aforesaid to a friendly interview. He dispatched Bernard of Camerino, his chaplain, who brought the most affectionate letter to Frederick,[24] such as a father would write to his son, enlarging on the compassion of Mother Church, and how she is ever inclined to welcome to her bosom, whoever having strayed away will return to her in the sincerity of his soul. The Pope affixed to the letters a safe-conduct for Frederick and the others invited to the interview. As soon as Frederick had received the Papal Legate and had read the letter, although he knew the object of the desired interview was his departure from Sicily, he yielded to the exhortation of Boniface, by observing how the other affairs of James included in the treaty of peace had been so adjusted by Boniface that they would not suffer damage or injury; and he did not doubt that urged to leave Sicily, he would be recompensed by the gift of another seigniory. However, he wished to know the sentiments of the Sicilians concerning his journey to the Pope, and he addressed to the University of Palermo a letter, to which he attached a copy of the letter of Boniface to him. The people of Palermo answered the letter of Frederick by another, the bearers of which were Nicholas of Mayda, Philip of Carastono, judges, and Peter Philosopher, which ambassadors of the commune should add strength to the letter. In this letter there were most fiery words to deter Frederick from going to the Papal interview: " He should remember," they said, " the bad feeling borne towards his ancestor Peter by the " Roman Pontiffs, and with what fury they had carried " on war against themselves, for no other reason than to " thrust the sword into his vitals for his final ruin; he " should remember how much human blood they had shed " in Catalonia taking sides with Philip of France, unmind- " ful of the charity of the Founder of the Church, who " desired neither bloodshed nor war. . . . . Con- " sidering then the manly constancy with which his father " Peter and his brother James maintained possession of " the island, they wondered how he, as it were, degener- " ating from his elders, would desist from his generous

[24] Chron. Sic. Anony. cap. 53.

" purpose of protecting unfortunate Sicily; how he would
" depress on a sudden their raised spirits, and how he
" would go to repose in the arms of the Pope in an artful
" interview. He should not be frightened by the noise of
" those words which the shrewd Pope threw out to him, in
" order to deprive him of courage for his noble designs.
" The work he had undertaken, which his elders had
" happily effected, would not displease God but be grate-
" ful to him; that it was the hand of God which up to that
" day had fought for Sicily, battling against an immense
" multitude of proud enemies; that it was the valor of
" God by which one against a thousand fought victoriously.
" Not to fight against, but for God, who take arms for
" his own prince and for the people who have entrusted to
" the hands of this prince their every hope and dearest
" destiny. Therefore prostrate at his feet they besought
" him not to go with the chief men of the island to that
" sinister interview, which would be productive of sad
" consequences both to him and to them; finally that he
" should think of taking in his own hands the government
" and protection of Sicily, and they would be most ready
" to sacrifice for him their lives and goods."

This persistent opposition went to the heart of Frederick, who, born a king, more than others felt the sweetness of command, and the fear of the loss of it; yet at the authoritative voice of the Pontiff he decided to go. And having taken with him as companions John of Procida and Roger of Loria, he sailed with a good fleet for Terracina, where he disembarked; and with a noble retinue he rode as far as Velletri. Boniface was awaiting his arrival in the open country, and as soon as he saw himself in the presence of Frederick, a boy of tender years, altogether encased in a heavy armor, he caressed him with both hands, and kissed him on the brow; then in wonder he said to him: "So soon, O noble youth, are you accustomed to arms?"—And fixing his gaze on the terrible Roger of Loria: "Are you that terrible enemy of the Church, who has massacred so many people?" And he quickly replied: "Your predecessors were the cause."[25]—Then he took the young prince aside, and in the kindest of manners he tried to persuade him to leave Sicily; and to compensate him

[25] Franc. Maurolyci. Sicancicae Hist. 1, 4, apud Burmani.

for the loss he proposed a marriage for him with Catherine, daughter of Philip, and niece of Baldwin II, titular Emperor of Constantinople, and also niece of Charles the Lame, which marriage would obtain for him the right to ascend the throne of the Grecian Empire; he promised besides to furnish him with abundant means to carry on the war against Paleologus who had taken it from Philip. The youthful prince apart from Roger and John of Procida replied that he would consent to the nuptials, if the Sicilians would also consent;[26] and with this he parted with the Pontiff.

The intention of Boniface in this matter was not to beguile the youth; because as Pope he could not bear without sorrow that the Sicilians unmindful of the dominion of the Church over their islands should transfer it to Frederick; and from the marriage, which he encouraged Frederick to contract, there was no little benefit to be derived for the Church. The reunion of the Greek and Latin Churches, the conquest of the Holy Land, the foremost desires of the Roman Pontificate, would have a firm basis in a Catholic prince seated on the throne of Constantinople. Hence in the month of June of this year he sent John, Abbot of St. Germain des Prés to Catherine with letters expressing to her, how for her own good, and that of the Church, she should select as husband Frederick of Aragon; and how it should be sworn to by the latter and her grandfather Charles II, to conclude the affair by the end of September; that John the Abbot would come to conduct her to him honorably, and at her earliest convenience.[27] Moreover he addressed letters likewise to Philip of France, admonishing him to exert himself to induce Catherine to consent to this marriage. But the expulsion of Andronicus from the throne of Byzantium was a difficult undertaking and not near at hand, and he could not easily obtain the consent of Catherine to a marriage of such little benefit. She replied, that the noble blood of Frederick was pleasing to her, but she did not care to marry a prince without a state.

In the meanwhile the kingdom of Naples was without a ruler. Charles was still in France for the conclusion of the aforesaid peace, and Charles his eldest son, titular king of Hungary, had died in the June of this year. Boni-

[26] Mauroly. Sic. Hist. lib. IV, 199.   [27] Epist. 174 an. 1. apud Rayn. 29.

face quickly provided for the administration of the kingdom as an affair of the Pontiffs, entrusting it to Philip, duke of Taranto, another son of Charles, and Landolph, Cardinal-Deacon of St. Angelo. But the Neapolitans felt aggrieved because Queen Margaret had been excluded from the management of the public affairs, and thy besought the Pontiff to place them under her direction. Boniface yielded to these desires, glad to show the supreme dominion he had over the kingdom, being able to change rulers at his own will, and in a most affable letter he appointed Margaret to fill the place of her absent husband. In that letter, having deplored the death of her son Charles, and having told how, by that supreme power which came to him from on high, he had entrusted to Philip and the Legate the direction of affairs, he substituted her in their place, prohibiting her from alienating any immoveable property of the state, to which prohibition he did not doubt, that also her husband Charles would conform with good graces himself; and finally he was sure that she would rule the kingdom with such prudence and strength of mind as to merit afterwards the reward of Heaven and praise of men. Here then is an instance of how that dominion of Rome over a state bridled the excesses of princes and secured the rights of the people. And no one better than Boniface could have exercised this salutary dominion, if his disposition of mind had not been deemed excessive pride in those stormy times.

Although the affairs of Sicily had occupied much of the Pontiff's attention yet they did not possess it so entirely, as to prevent him from directing the whole world towards the attainment of his great desire of universal peace. Whilst he was still hoping to pacify Sicily, before Frederick would make himself king, he turned his attention to northern Italy, where affairs were in a much disturbed condition owing to the brutal fury of the Guelph and Ghibelline factions; the nobles and the populace, state against state, city against city were rending themselves in fierce wars. But in a particular manner he exercised his care over the most powerful cities, with the hope that peace once established they would by reason of their wealth and grandeur be able to show, in the peaceful and good government of their republics, an example of civilization to the hundred desolate and warring cities of the peninsula. These were Venice and Genoa. The former was already powerful in the XIIIth century by reason of the riches which accrued to it from its maritime commerce, also by reason of the fortunate conquests in Dalmatia, of many islands in the Adriatic, and of the Grecian Archipelago, and more especially by reason of the internal constitution, which precisely in this age took the firm abiding form of that Queen of the Seas. The other rich also like Venice by reason of commerce, but less powerful since the conquests had been made by her private citizens, and by them retained, rather than by the city; and besides its government was not so strongly constituted as to permit it to hold in duty, both the populace and the nobles. Hence while Venice like an immovable rock in the sea opposed its exterior sides to the fury of factions, Genoa was ever agitated by internal strifes. Venice was always free, Genoa was often the slave of foreigners.

Through jealousy of trade Genoa at first vented its hatred against Pisa, and afterwards against Venice. This was always displeasing to the Popes, who desired to make use of these powerful republics for the overthrow of the infidels in the East. Almost two years had passed during which the Venetians and Genoese were furiously waging war against each other, when Boniface endeavored to soften their anger and reconcile the adversaries. Moreover he wished for peace in order to redeem the fallen fortunes of the Holy Land. But the desperate straits of the latter were well known to Boniface, and his apparent desire concealed his real desire, which was to divert the minds from intestine feuds and turn them in view of the common good, to the destruction of the Turkish power. He admonished the Venetians and Genoese by letter[28] to suspend hostilities until the feast of St. John the Baptist of the current year, during which time the ambassadors of both republics would meet in his presence to agree on a lasting peace. The legates assembled; but the Genoese came in bad faith. For while they rejected every proposed measure of agreement, justifying themselves under the plea that from their state they had not received the right to negotiate, in Genoa they were preparing a mighty

[28] Lib. I an 1 Epist. 117 apud Raynaldum.

fleet to assail the Venetians while engaged in the treaty of peace. The Pope, not wishing that the docility of the Venetians to his paternal instructions be detrimental to their republic, released them from the obligation of maintaining the truce, which the Genoese faithlessly observed,[29] and encouraged them to defend themselves. But that which the Venetians could have done against the Genoese was done by cruel discord. For in that very fleet there was kindled the fire of the factions, the leaders of the Guelph being the Grimaldi, and of the Ghibelline the Dorias and the Spinolas. They turned their swords against each other and many fell in the strife, and returning to Genoa they did not desist from blood and fire, until the Guelphs overcome by the Ghibellines were driven into exile. It was from this time according to Villani, that the decline of the Genoese republic began, as if in punishment for that fratricidal madness and for their contempt of the paternal authority of Boniface.

In the beginning of this book we discussed the subject of Guelphism and Ghibellinism, and why and how the Popes held themselves as the chiefs of the Guelph party; and we believe no Pope exerted himself so strongly to defend it and to combat the opposite party, as Boniface. Before he was Pope he was a Ghibelline, because his family followed that party,[30] and when he became Cardinal he did not renounce being Ghibelline both because of family affection, and because of the great contempt he had for the Angevines. When he became Pope, he transformed himself into a Guelph by reason of the office which he held. The city in which above others the fierce and rabid spirit of these factions was displayed was Florence; and for that reason from the triumph, or discomfiture of one of these in Florence, the civil changes in many other Italian cities proceeded. In the thirteenth century this city advanced much in richness, in splendor of buildings, and in number of people; but precisely in this same thirteenth century (1215) the cursed feuds began among the citizens, who divided themselves into Guelphs and Ghibellines on occasion of the murder of Buondelmonte; and in 1250 the office of first captain of the people was created with twelve

[29] Epist. 13 apud Raynaldum 38.
[30] Villani . . . . di sua Nazione Ghibellina.

elders, so much did the power to rule increase during the
wars against Pisa, Siena, and other powerful cities. The
Florentines were Guelphs by nature, and seeing their
country prosper under republican institutions, they had
no love for the Ghibellines who desired a foreign emperor
as chief. Yet for all that, dissensions existed among them,
owing to the enmities of the Uberti with the Amodei, so
that the Ghibellines having triumphed over the Guelphs
who at Montaperto, had formed the project, happily defeated by Farinato Uberti, to destroy Florence, as the only
possible way of making it Ghibelline. Just as this transient triumph was obtained through the aid of Manfred,
so through Charles of Anjou, the Guelphs not only received life, but firmly established themselves in Florence
and secured the entire government of the city; and under
the Guelphs the government exercised by the Priori of
arts, became entirely democratic (1285). The victories
gained by the Florentines over Pisa and Arezzo, Ghibelline cities, the internal prosperity of the city in commerce
and in the arts, should have induced the Florentines to
aim at the most holy object, which the mind of the Roman
Pontificate contemplated for Italy. They had always
found the Pontiffs favorable in their defence of Guelphism,
but always opposed when under the pretext of party
opinion, the citizens measured swords with one another,
and internal dissensions were enkindled. The Popes,
always Guelphs in their relations with Florence, were
peacemakers always whenever they did not fight for principle, but for individuals. In fact in the year 1273, the
Ghibellines reentered Florence only through a peaceful
agreement effected by Gregory X. This Pope, and others
with him, looked for peace and justice in Guelphism,
solely because they could obtain neither the one nor the
other in Italy whilst the Ghibellines ruled. Florence did
not lend itself to this most honorable design and far from
profiting by the power which came to her by her victories,
she turned it to her detriment. The nobles and the people
began to quarrel, and each party enrolled itself under the
Guelph or Ghibelline standard. In 1294 after the expulsion of the daring Giano della Bella and the overthrow
of the citizen party, a very great evil threatened Florence,
and perhaps all Tuscany, namely the arrival of foreigners

who would have nourished the furious dissensions, weakened the parties, and obtained dominion over those Italian peoples. Things were in such disorder, that the nobles, in order to regulate the public affairs, summoned John Da Caviglione, of the house of Burgundy, to make him the governor of their city. He came with well-nigh five hundred Burgundian and German knights, not only to assume the office of governor, but also that of imperial Vicar of all Tuscany, which he had received from Albert, Duke of Austria.[31] This Vicarship was displeasing to the Florentine nobles, for having made use of him and his people for the overthrow of the partisans of Giano della Bella, they did not wish to be burdened further with him as their chief magistrate, and refused to pay the salaries of his five hundred knights. The foreigner became angry, and having set out for Arezzo, he induced that city to take arms with him against Florence, the Guelph. This foreign scourge could render incurable the domestic wôunds; and this was the moment when the authority of the Pontiff was needed. Boniface met the danger at the earnest entreaty of the Florentines, who feared not only the people of Arezzo aided by Caviglione, but more especially these formidable words of right and Empire. The Pope induced the Florentines to pay twenty thousand florins to the Burgundian, who then departed peacefully, and thereby delivered Tuscany from grave dangers.[32]

The care displayed by Boniface in quelling the dissensions and restoring peace in other states was not less ardent in the states of the Church, which were horribly convulsed, by reason of the Guelph and Ghibelline factions. It is well known how fiercely were rent the cities in the Romagna, Umbria, and the Marches, when the other cities of Italy became republics. Although these provinces, after the famous battles of the Papacy with the house of Hohenstaufen, had remained subject to the Church, yet there was manifested in them a vice which was consuming a vast part of Italy, we mean the want of a bond which united the dominant to the subdued parties. Cardinal legates went to preside over these provinces, but this was the appearance, not the reality and power of government. The cities were governed in common, and

[31] Villani C. X. S R. J.   [32] Dino Com. S. R. T. V. 9.479. D. E.

the authority entrusted now to the people, now to the nobles tended toward ruin; because it was not sanctified by right; and abominable, because it was always dishonored by the blood of the citizens. In these furious brawls the Ghibelline Lambertazzi and the Guelph Geremei were engaged a long while in Bologna; the Polenti and the lords of Bagnacavallo in Ravenna; the Mendoli and the Brizi in Imola; the Manfreds and the Accarisi in Faenza; the Ciambacari and the Amodei in Rimini; the Galbolia and the Ordelaffi in Forli; the Righizzi and the people in Cesena. The Ghibellines tended to a monarchy or aristocratic constitution, and for that reason were easily subservient to the Empire; whereas the Guelphs, democratic in principles, found odious the restraint of the Empire, and accordingly they were more attached to the Church. The people being so divided the Pope had no control of them. At one time he was called upon to sit as arbiter to confirm the authority of one of the factions; at another time to solicit aid both of money and men for the Guelph party, not by reason of command, but by the will of the men who revered him as the head of the party, and not as the lord of the state. See to what narrow limits the Papal jurisdiction had been reduced in those cities. This had been further curtailed by the Counts of Romagna, the representatives of the imperial right. At the Council of Lyons Gregory X took pains to declare and confirm the rights of the Church in relation to the Empire, and to determine the limits of the temporal sovereignty of the Popes, which had been overthrown and rendered almost invisible by the reasons just given. In that universal assembly Radicofani and Ceprano were acknowledged the extreme limits of the Pontifical States, and these comprised the Exarchate of Ravenna, the Five Cities, the Marches of Ancona, the duchy of Spoleto, the county of Bertinoro, and the lands donated by the Countess Matilda. From that time there were seen no more in Italy those importunate Imperial Vicars and those Counts of Romagna. The Fathers of the Council of Lyons confirmed the right, but the fact, respected indeed by the Empire, was always enfeebled by the Ghibelline party.

The Popes were eager for a democracy confirmed by their theocracy, the Ghibellines however desired the sway

of a foreign emperor. Although the former had prospered
by the power of Charles, yet there were not wanting brave
and valorous men in the opposite party, who constantly
maintained a lively war. Uguccione della Faggiuola and
Guy of Montefeltro, terrible warriors belonging to the
Ghibelline party, arose to great celebrity. Guy especially
had always done very grave damage to the Pontiffs, roaming about Romagna with great bravery whenever called
upon to give battle to the opposing party. His blood was
truly Ghibelline, as his family had risen to a flourishing
condition through imperial favors. His grandfather Buon-
conto, son of Monfeltrino, received from Frederick II in
fief the sovereignty of Urbino, being already Count of
Montefeltro; and his father Monfeltrino II kept that state
which he left to Guy his eldest son in 1255. Guy surpassed
his ancestors in his ardent devotion to the Empire and in
military valor. Intrepid in war, he was too blood-thirsty;
a mark for papal censures he never seemed disturbed by
them. When the people of Forli, whose commander he
was were defeated he bowed his head in submission to the
wrathful Martin, he delivered up to him his two sons as
hostages, and underwent exile in Piedmont.[33] But returning to war when called by the Ghibelline Pisans, more terribly than ever did he afflict the Guelphs, until the
Pisans,[34] against his will, made peace with the Florentines.
Then he threw himself at the feet of Pope Celestine, we
know not whether penitent for his deeds against the
Church, or weary of his military life, asking pardon for
having brought on the rebellions of Cesena and Forli, and
many other evils occasioned to the Church; and he obtained it from the good Pontiff.[35] The proud spirit of
Guy was humbled, but the Romagna was far from being
peaceful, and when Boniface ascended the throne of Peter,
filled with a strong desire of peace as he was, he wished
immediately to provide for the good government of that
province; for the Count of Romagna, Robert de Corney,
who was governor of Romagna under Celestine, more
through appointment of Charles than of the Pope, had
embittered instead of appeasing the minds, insomuch so

[33] Giacch. Malasp. c. 227 228 —Villani, I. U c. 107.
[34] Villani. L. 8. c. 2.   [35] Epist. Bonif. apud Raynaldus 1294 n. 15.

that the province was altogether in revolt.[36] Boniface dismissed him from office, and appointed in his stead Peter, Archbishop of Monreale. In the meanwhile fearing that the restless Guy of Montefeltro, received in favor by Celestine, but not placed in possession of his sovereignties, might break the proposals of peace, he wished to gratify him, and keep him as a friend. On the 25th of May Guy was seen to enter Forli in the company of a papal legate, and to receive from the same the possession of all his goods and states. The restoration of Guy removed the danger that he would be hurtful to the Guelph party; but it did not bring peace.[37] The Archbishop of Monreale did little to establish peace in the province and did many imprudent things. He removed from command in Faenza Manghinardo of Sussiana; he undertook to demolish in Ravenna the palaces of Guy of Polenta, and of his son Lambert, and enkindled a terrible war in Faenza between the counts of Cunio and the Manfreds on the one side, and on the other Manghinardo, the Rauli and the Accarisi, who were defeated and expelled from the city.

Finally Boniface turned to William Durant, born in France at Puy-Nisson in 1237. He had as teachers Henry of Sousa and Bernard of Parma, men very renowned in those times for knowledge of law and skill in affairs. He was the author of the work entitled: "Speculum Juris," which Baldo, and Paul de Castro praised highly, and for which he received the title of "Speculator." Popes Clement IV, Gregory X, Nicholas III, Martin IV, and Honorius IV, appointed him to difficult and honorable offices in which he conducted affairs so skilfully, that he received another surname of "Father of the Practical." He went as Papal Legate to the Council of Lyons, and was made Bishop of Mende by Honorius IV. In the fourth year of his episcopate he was summoned to Italy by Boniface, who made him Marquis of the March of Ancona, and Count of Romagna, which office he once held under Honorius. His honesty and skill inspired the Pope with the hope of great things from him. But in the annals of Forli we find no record of anything done by Durant to establish peace in the provinces which he was called to govern, except cavalcades and some parleying which bore no fruit. It is true

[36] Ann. Caesen. S R. I. c p. 1110. [37] Chron. Foroliv. S. R. I. T. 22.

he did not remain long in that office, for he died on the 1st., of November of the following year 1296, and was buried in the church of St. Maria sopra Minerva in Rome, where his tomb is seen to this day.

Boniface had his eyes fixed attentively on the kingdom of France, and on him who ruled it, Philip IV, surnamed the Fair. The German Empire no longer caused fear; but France occasioned some apprehension to the Papal mind. And since in those times a people had nothing to distinguish it from its king, for its rights, its will, and its very existence were included in that of the prince, Boniface in thinking of France, could not but fix his mind on Philip who governed it. He was born in the year 1268, and his father Philip III having died on the 5th., of October 1285, he was only seventeen years of age when he ascended the throne of France. On the sixth day of January 1286 Peter Barbet, Archbishop of Rheims, anointed him king in that city; and Pope Honorius IV congratulated him in a Bull containing many special favors and indulgences for those praying for the happy commencement of his reign. As the laws of the kingdom declared that the king attains his majority at thirteen years of age, he was accordingly free from all tutelage, and he took the reins of government into his own hands. Of immature age, alone on the throne, and not steadied by the advice of another, he cast his eyes upon his subject people, and he saw them bowed before him, his youthful mind was immediately intoxicated with the idea of supreme dominion. His mind devoid of the science of government, and his heart spoiled by the flattery of courtiers, his will alone was the rule of governing and the law for the subjects. He took as wife Joanna of Navarre who brought him as a dowry this other realm, the counties of Champagne and Brie which had belonged to her father, Henry of Navarre, and the county of Brigorre, which from Simon of Montfort had descended to Theobald II, king of Navarre, the material uncle of Joanna. The increased territory inspired Philip with thirst for more; rendered him jealous of power, and inordinate in the use of it. As his grandfather was surnamed the Saint, and rightly; and his father the Bold, wrongly; he was called the Fair, on account of physical beauty. The beauty of his soul was marred by an insatiable lust for gold and in order to satisfy it, he never knew what justice was. He plundered the people, he robbed the churches. In the distresses of the people he was never compassionate; and he was a barefaced violator of the rights of the Church. France was reduced to such a condition, that far from correcting the vices of her king, she encouraged them. The feudal lords once formidable to the king, not only were subdued, but they did not offer any longer even a semblance of power to restrain the monarchy. After Louis IX had humbled them, they laid aside their rusty coat of mail and clothed themselves in the soft Italian and Flemish cloths; from warriors they degenerated into courtiers. The rest of the people were slaves. Authority in France was never so strictly confined in the will of the king, as at this time. In despotism and in rapine Philip had worthy and obedient ministers. In the former they were the jurisconsults, and in the latter two Italians, Biccio and Musciatto, sons of Guy de Franzesi. The lawyers built a bulwark of law, upon which they battled against the enemies of despotism, with that strength which arises in a body of men conscious of their own individual power in the state, and the support which it brings to the kingdom. And as a citadel of refuge they instituted the parliament in which injustice was clad in healthfulness of forms. Being thus fortified, Philip found no obstacles to his profligacy. Among the orders of the State that of the clergy was the only one that annoyed him. These were bound together by laws which were not the civil laws; they possessed rights which were not engraven in the human codices, and for that reason invulnerable by human power; they held a patrimony consecrated by religion to God; they had as their head the Roman Pontiff. Philip coveted their rights and possessions, and he was jealous of the Papal power. A Christian he was and his conscience might reproach him for his inordinate concupiscence of divine things; but his jurisconsults caused so much splendor to shine from the crown, that his sight was dazzled, and Philip saw no other God but this. And if any struggle was to be foreseen, this assuredly was no other but one with the Pope.

Boniface knew the character of Philip, since although immature in years, he had already shown himself ripe for oppression by an act of awful villainy which in Italy, even more than elsewhere, gave him a vile reputation. The Italians at this time were very active in commerce. Many of them carried it on in France, and as they were almost alone in trading they were very rich. On the night of May 1st, 1291, Philip arrested them unexpectedly at the instance of his ministers and cast all of them into dark prisons. After some time they learned that they were thus punished for the sin of usury, and that to make them confess it they would be subject to cruel torture. These unfortunates purchased their life and liberty with their riches; and the judges who were to have condemned them collected the money and brought it to Philip. The two Florentines Franzesi advised this robbery; and the jurisconsults palliated and justified it, not being ashamed of their ruffianism.[38]

In order that we may know how the relations between Boniface and Philip began to be strained, it will be necessary for us to say something about Edward of England, for the reason that from the enmity engendered between him and Philip followed the like feelings between Philip and Boniface.

Edward, the first of his name, son of Henry III, was fifty-six years old when Boniface assumed the Pontificate. In person he was tall, hence nicknamed, "Longshanks," but well proportioned; the length of his arms gave additional force to his stroke; and when he was once placed on his saddle, no struggle of his horse, no shock of the enemy could dislodge him from his seat. In temper he was warm and irascible, impatient of injury, and reckless of danger: but his anger might be disarmed by submission, and his temerity seemed to be justified by success. He was not hard-hearted; at least not without affection for his own family. He was in Sicily when he received the first news of his father's death; the tears which he shed on that occasion, though they excited the surprise of Charles of Anjou, bore honorable testimony to the goodness of his heart. Inasmuch as he alone had hastened to the declining fortunes of the Holy Land, and had arrested for a time the fall of Ptolemais, his name was dear to Christians and to Rome. He was considered as the champion of Christendom, the martyr of the cross. Returning from the East his

[38] Villani, book 7, ch. 146.

journey through Italy was a triumphal procession; at every city the magistrates, clergy and people, came out to receive him; and the Milanese forced on his acceptance valuable presents of horses and scarlet cloth. In ambition he did not yield to any of his predecessors; but his ambition aimed at a very different object. They had exhausted their strength in attempting conquests on the continent which might be wrested from them at any time by a fortunate neighbor; he aspired to unite in himself the sovereignty of the whole island of Great Britain. For that reason he set about to subjugate Wales and Scotland, and incorporate them with England. The many wars in which he was engaged necessarily involved him in extraordinary expenses, and to supply his wants he taxed the churches exceedingly. But the barons and bishops of England being fortified by the Magna Charta opposed his wishes vehemently, and used force to check him. Edward not only was restrained, but was even placed in great danger by reason of the taxes.

From 1284 to the time whereof we speak, Edward had conquered by force of arms all the country of Wales, and was proceeding gradually to obtain sovereignty over Scotland, having in 1293 received the oath of vassalage from Baliol, to whom by his selection had been given the crown of that kingdom. These successes violently excited the jealousy of Philip the Fair, but Edward gave him no cause to reprove him. As duke of Aquitaine, which he held in fief from France, among his first acts on ascending the English throne, he swore fealty to Philip. Edward found this yoke heavy, but did not shake it off; Philip however could not bear the thought of his conquests. These two princes began to be involved on occasion of a private dispute. In 1293 two sailors an Englishman and a Norman quarrelled and fought, and the Norman died from his wounds. This was the spark that kindled the fire of war first between the French and the English, and afterwards the sovereigns. In 1293 offences and retaliation were so frequent and warm that the navies of each country took part in the quarrel without the customary formal declaration of war. Fortune or valor favored the English, and the French were badly beaten. Edward considering the fray private and not ordered by him, refused to accept the part of the booty which was coming to him from the battle.[39] He did not desire war; but these precautions were not sufficient to prevent Philip from going to a meeting crowded with his jurisconsults, the omnipotent creators of law, who sanctioned Philip's secret design of driving Edward from the French continent.

In that disorderly war it was asserted that the people of Bayonne, the subjects of Edward, had attempted to surprise the port of Rochelle. Philip as the direct lord of Aquitaine ordered Edward's lieutenant to lodge the accused in a French prison. He neglected the requisition; and for that reason the officials of Philip wished to expel from that region the disobedient vassals, but they were driven back by arms. Then in consequence Philip sent a peremptory summons to Edward, as his vassal, ordering him to appear within twenty days, before his parliament, and answer for these offences against his sovereign. The English prince who saw the real object of Philip, endeavored to appease his resentment. He offered compensation to the French sufferers, and to make restitution for injury and loss; and when this was refused, proposed to refer the dispute to an arbitrator of their choice who might be the Pope, whose office it was to preserve concord among princes.

The offers he renewed through his brother Edmund, whom he dispatched as ambassador to France. But Edmund was a man of simplicity, and was no match for Philip and his lawyers. Philip's sole object, he was told, was to guard his honor, and to do this a promise was given that, if Gascony was surrendered to him for forty days in 1294, it should be at the expiration of that period faithfully restored. A secret treaty to that effect was concluded. It was signed by the consort of Philip; Edward signified his consent; and the French monarch, in the presence of several witnesses, promised to observe it on the word of a king. The citation against Edward was now withdrawn. At the expiration of forty days Edmund reminded Philip of his promise; but was requested to forbear till certain lords of the council would have departed from Paris. Some days after he repeated his demand, and received a positive refusal. Philip took his seat in his

[39] Walsingham 60–481.

court, rejected the arguments of Edward's advocates, and although the citation had been withdrawn, condemned him as contumacious, and pronounced judgment against him by default of appearance.[40] Friendship between the two princes was broken. Edward, by the advice of a great council, appealed to arms to enforce his rights.

In the coming war, each one of the opponents resolved to strengthen his side by alliances with other princes. Philip won over to his side Eric, king of Norway, enemy of Edward, who had excluded him from the throne of Scotland; Rudolph, the deposed king of the Romans who hoped to supplant his rival Adolphus of Nassau; Hugh of Longivy; James of Chatillon, lord of Leuse and of Condé; Florence, count of Holland; Otto IV, count of Burgundy; and finally some cities of Castile, and the communes of Fontarabia, and St. Sebastian. Edward called to his aid Adolphus of Nassau, king of the Romans whom Philip deprived of the territory of Arles and Burgundy; and Philip of Richmond, duke of Brittany. But more vigorous action devolved on them both reciprocally, in stirring up powerful enemies as it were in their own houses. Philip concluded an alliance offensive and defensive with John Baliol, king of Scotland, on whom Edward had imposed a heavy yoke, and they promised one another to move their forces against Edward if he should invade France or Scotland.[41] Edward from 1294 had concluded a treaty with Guy of Dampiere, Count of Flanders, and vassal of France, wherein the latter promised in marriage his daughter Philippa with a very rich dowry. But Philip the Fair by charming pretenses knew how to entice Guy and the affianced one to Paris, whom he wickedly imprisoned in the tower of Louvre. Guy found a way of escape, but his unfortunate daughter remained a prisoner until she died, as he said, of poison.[42] These acts of violence bound together more closely the Flemish count and Edward, and inspired the former with fury with which he later on waged war against Philip.

Whilst these princes were acting in this hostile manner, Boniface, who was at this time in Anagni, was entertaining strong hopes of peace. As he desired sincerely peace,

[40] Rym. ii 619-622. [41] Rymer. Tom. II, p. 695.
[42] Villani. VIII 19—Chron. Nangii 1294.—Walsing 29.

he made use of all the privileges of his office, as father of the faithful and peacemaker, to effect a peace between Philip and Edward. Claude Fleury observes that precisely the action of Boniface in this affair was ill-timed, in that he wished to intrude himself in other affairs, and make himself master of them.[43] But if the good confessor of Louis XIV, to the knowledge of jurisprudence which he eminently possessed, had added a little of that which is called the philosophy of history, he would have easily understood that the Roman Pontiff in the time of Boniface, by common consent of the people, was the acknowledged arbiter in grave controversies, which opinion did not prevail any more in his time. In fact Edward of his own free will suggested to Philip to submit their case to the decision of Boniface, because it was his duty to preserve peace among the faithful.

Therefore in order to soothe their angry feelings Boniface entered as mediator between Edward and Philip, and their followers, that if blood of the people might not be shed nor the revenue of the churches appropriated to carry on the war. It is true however that in all this affair of the peace he always leaned to the side of Philip the Fair, and the issue resulted in his favor. In February 1295 he dispatched as legates to England and France, Cardinal Bernard, bishop of Albano, and Cardinal Simon, bishop of Palestrina, to urge these kings to lay down their arms. They were ordered to serve those unholy alliances; to absolve the parties from the oath that bound them; to remove all obstacles in the way of peace; and they had full power to threaten them with censures, closing at the same time any way of appeal.[44]

In May 1295 the legates arrived in Paris;[45] and from there in July they set out for London. Edward received them with all honor and respect, and summoned a great parliament at Westminster. In this parliament the legates explained the reasons of their embassy, and Edmund, the brother of the king, and John Lacy made known the reasons of their war with France, which at present was suspended. The papal projects for peace, although pleasing to Edward, could not be accepted by him without the

[43] Lib. 89. num. 42.   [44] Raynaldus, 1295, 41 Epi. 2. Lib. 1.
[45] Chr. Guill. Nangii apud Achery, T. 3. 1295.

consent of Adolphus, King of the Romans, who was in league with him. He agreed, as God willed, to a cessation of hostilities until November.[46] But alas! in the midst of these hopes, suddenly the French made a descent on Dover and brought it to ruin; as soon as the news of this reached Edward, not only did he break the truce, but his anger and indignation was increased.—

In the meanwhile Boniface accompanied from afar his legates by letters so as to give strength and support to their proceedings. One dated the 28th of May, 1295, from Velletri, he addressed to Edward, which may have arrived while the parliament of Westminster was in session. In this letter he exhorted him to dismiss the thought of war, as those feats of arms which he practised were a work unsuited to his years, verging as he was on old age, and the body advanced in years being unable to endure them. Had he forgotten, that he was bound by now to the supreme King, for the rescue of the Holy Land? Was he not mindful of the injury he would do to his eternal salvation, by turning the forces against his fellow Christians, which he should rather turn against the infidels? Did he not consider the contest unbecoming a king, and an occasion of joy to the enemies of the Cross? He besought him through the Lord Jesus Christ, through reverence for the Apostolic See, and for the good of his soul to make peace with Philip.[47] For the attainment of the same peace Boniface sent as legates to Adolphus, King of the Romans, the Archbishop of Reggio and the Bishop of Siena. Adolphus trusting in Edward hoped to gain many advantages by the war; but his rival Albert who wished to deprive him of the crown, kept him uneasy, and rendered necessary the good-will of the Pope. Wherefore he had already sent his messengers to make profession of his devotion to the Roman Church, but they made no mention of peace. Boniface returned him thanks for his devotion, and signified to him his good-will. He exhorted him not to have his actions at variance with his words; he desired peace between him and Philip, and to accomplish it he sends him as legates the two aforesaid prelates.[48] In another letter, reminding him of his unstable sovereignty,

[46] Rymer. Tom. II Pag. 685. [47] Chron Vill. Nangii;—Matth. Westm. 4—Knyghton de Ev. Angli. lib III, page 2503. [48] Raynaldus 1295 Epi 171.

he began in a certain way to complain, because at his solemn elevation to the Papacy, he did not see the usual ambassadors of the King of the Romans: "Are these, my son, the laudable beginnings of your greatness? Are these "the invitations and the encouragement you give the Ro- "man Church to aid you in your needs? In fact consid- "ering yourself elected, and as it were called by God to "strive for the peace and tranquillity of all Christendom, "in the very beginning you prepare yourself with all your "strength, and gird on your armor with all skill, to involve "the world in troubles, to stir up strife among Christian "princes, and you use your efforts not without great detri- "ment to your honor. Is it perhaps becoming to you, so "great and powerful a prince, to be enticed to take up "arms, like a common soldier, by the attraction of some "stipend?[49] As a lover of your honor, reputation and "advancement I put before you these things."—

And in order that his words might be supported by a more effectual argument, after having by letter exhorted the bishops of Germany to receive his legates honorably, and to consider as valid any censures which they might impose upon the contumacious; and after having tried to move the mind of Adolphus by means of a certain Diterius, a Dominican Friar, of great authority with the king on account of his piety,[50] he then began to write to the Archbishop of Mainz, that in case Adolphus would not desist from the war, he should refuse him aid and subsidies. This was taking all power from the king. For when he ascended the throne he found that the princes of the Empire, during the interregnum, had usurped many monetary rights which belonged to the sovereign, and the benefits pertaining to the German crown; and therefore, the income from his paternal states being meagre, it was only from the prince electors, and the vassals that he could obtain support in money.

Laudable was that work which Boniface set out to perform, to restrain the warlike intentions of these two

[49] And it was true. "Romanorum Rex Adulfus Regi Angliae Eduardo pecunia contra Regem Franciae confederatus . . . ." William Nangii Chron. 1294.—"Rex Angliae misit Regi Romanorum XXX millia Marcorum, ut retulit qui vidit . . . . ." Chron. Colmariense, par. 2.

[50] Raynaldus year 1295-46.

princes for the good of their people and of the Church. The war could not be carried on without money, and to obtain it Edward as well as Philip levied many and heavy taxes on both the laity and the clergy; so that the former were impoverished, and the latter complained of the violation of their sacred immunities. Precisely in the very month of May that the Papal legates had arrived in Paris for the sake of making peace, Philip disgraced his royal dignity, and outraged in the most vile manner the sacred rights of his people by that cursed war. He caused to be published throughout the kingdom the following scandalous edict. " The pecuniary distress into which the affairs " of the kingdom were placed, made it incumbent on him " to coin a money, which would perhaps be wanting in " weight and value; and he bound himself and his wife " Joanna of Navarre, to make good the loss that anyone " would suffer thereby."—This fair promise prevented the stupefied French people from crying out immediately, but afterwards they did protest and complain when the King absolved himself from making restitution.[51]

But whilst the heart of Boniface was grieving over his fruitless efforts with the English and French princes, another Northern prince, laid his hands rudely, not only on goods but also on persons consecrated to God. This prince was Eric IV, king of Denmark. But before speaking of his violence towards the Archbishop of Lund, in order to understand it better, it will be necessary for us to go back a little. After the death of Pope Innocent III, the clerical immunities and the ecclesiastical patrimonies began to be affected greatly, and the secular power with little moderation violated them, in the more civilized countries through the pretext of avenged rights, in the less civilized through impetuosity of power. Among the latter were the kings of Denmark, a kingdom which comprised the great peninsula of Jutland, and other islands. Although the light of the Gospel was brought to it in 826 by St. Anscherius, a Benedictine monk from the monastery of Corby in France, yet the Danes persevered in piracy, which they practised especially to the detriment of France.[52]

[51] Ordin, of the kings of France T. I, p. 325 . . . . "Daus la quelle il manquera peut etre quelque chose du poids ou du titre."

[52] Art de Verif. les dates.

Piracy having ceased, their rough habits endured, and in Danish history there are ever to be deplored cruel wars, the murders of kings, rebellions of the peoples; in a word, little soundness of justice, much uncontrollable power and savage force. There is no doubt that even the clerics were not all free from the vices of that people, but it is certain that reverence for God and his ministers was a shield often too weak to withstand the attacks of the inordinate power of the Danish princes. We find that from the year 1257, the bishops were subjected to vexations by the violence of the secular power, and resolved to fortify themselves against it by decrees enacted in a national council. They came together, and in a synod enacted four decrees, which are found among the epistles of Alexander IV,[53] published by Raynaldus and Mansi,[54] the preface of which is the declaration of the reasons for this sacred assembly, and which it may be well here to produce. " The Danish Church being exposed to such grievous perse-
" cutions from tyrants, who do not even hesitate before
" the eyes of the King to inflict injuries and threats on
" the persons of the bishops, who present themselves as a
" wall of defence to the house of God; which threats are
" rightly to be feared, since the clergy are deprived of all
" protection of the secular power, who and the tyrants free
" in audacity, and unrestrained by royal fear, can proceed
" to worst excesses, hence the Church has enacted by the
" authority of the present Council. . . . ." The decrees then follow, which full of Apostolic liberty of judgment, serve as a wall to protect the episcopal immunities against the tyranny even of the king. They decreed to interdict the divine offices throughout Denmark, if a bishop were imprisoned, struck, or maltreated by the order, consent, or approval of the king. If these evils were visited on a bishop by a foreign potentate, under the suspicion of being abetted by the king, or some noble of the kingdom, the diocese of the prelate maltreated will remain interdicted. The kingdom will be interdicted, if the king, after being admonished by two bishops or clerics, stubbornly refuses to repair the injury within the space of six months. Solemn excommunication was hurled

[53] Lib. 3. Epist. 674.
[54] Coll. Max. Concil. Tom. 23, colum. 945 for year 1257.

against any priest or chaplain celebrating the divine offices in time of interdict, either in public, or in the presence of any one of these potentates.

From the remedies applied for their removal the evils become known, which far from diminishing, only increase, since the Danish kings could not be persuaded that God rules over the churches by His ministers. The blows were always directed against the Archbishop of Lund, the principal See of Denmark. One year after the aforesaid synod, Christopher I cast into prison James Erlander, Archbishop of Lund. We come now to the time of Eric Menved, and new disputes with John Grandt, Archbishop of Lund. The reason of the dispute was the assumption of his see by Grandt before being confirmed in it by the approval of the king. He repaired to Rome to confer with the Pope on the wants of his see, and on his return in 1292 he held a synod of his suffragans at Roschild to guarantee the liberty of the bishops wickedly attacked by Eric.[55] That which should have instructed the prince in wisdom and prudence aggravated him, and deceived by that pestilential plague which ever besieges thrones, we mean the flatterers,[56] he became exceedingly violent. A certain Rannon Jonah, the majordomo of Eric's father, Eric Glipping, had been cast into prison, being accused of the conspiracy against his lord Eric, who was killed while asleep by the blow of a club in the village of Finorap, near Wilburg, in 1286. Under torture he confessed the crime, and he paid the penalty with his life. The deceased Ranon was a nephew of the Archbishop of Lund. This relationship served as a good pretext for considering the prelate guilty, and for judging him accordingly. He ordered his brother Christopher to imprison the Archbishop and James Langius, provost of the diocese of Lund; and to justify the sacrilege, he spread the report that the Archbishop had been an accomplice in the murder of his father

---

[55] Joh. Isac. Pontanus Rerum Damicar. Hist. Edict. Amstelodami 1631 in fol. lib. VII, pag. 378.

[56] . . . . Serenitas regia pravis, ut creditur, stimulata sussuris, et mendacibus provocata suasibus perversorum, qui mala malis adjicere satagunt! (Epist 358 ad Reg. Danic. Bonifac VIII.) And I believe he also alluded to the mother of Eric IV who was regent during the tender years of Eric.

Eric Glipping, because he was a blood relation of the arch-conspirator in the crime; and besides he had assumed the See of Lund against his will. After nine years the Danish King took notice of the complicity of the Archbishop. His innocent relationship with the conspirator was a crime, and the exercise of ecclesiastical freedom was a fault. But no, the prelate was guilty only of a noble resistance to the tyranny of an arrogant prince. In fact, in order to conceal the true reason of that imprisonment, feigning devotion to the Church, the King issued certain royal decrees in which he declared, that he undertook the defence of the church of Lund deprived of a pastor; that he is the vindicator of the rights and liberties of the same. . . . . . "We will not allow," said he "holy Mother " Church, or the clergy of this diocese, now deprived of its " pastor, to be oppressed and harassed in their property, " rights and liberty by the violent attacks of certain " tyrants; as we are specially obliged by the office we hold " to provide carefully for their peace and quiet." He wished to expel tyrants, and yet making himself Pope, he was a wolf in the fold." [57]

Therefore to the greatest injury and scandal of the Church of Lund, the Archbishop and Provost languished in prison for some weeks, and there did not seem to be any hope of release. Finally, the Provost escaped from prison, in a way known only to God, and went straight to Rome, and poured out his complaints to the Papal Court, for he had left Denmark involved in a terrible civil war. Boniface listened attentively, as he should to the complaints of the fugitive Provost, and that the recital of such great violations of ecclesiastical immunities went to his heart, is not to be doubted. Yet he restrained his just indignation, and did not proceed with severity against Eric, before everything had been made clear. He sent as legate, Isarno, Archpriest of Carcassone, who was to execute that which he had expressed in a letter to the Danish King. Boniface began by lamenting the evils which encompassed Denmark and says: [58] " His heart was pierced " to hear how the kingdom is torn by discords, the " whole nation being in revolt; the salvation of souls being

---

[57] Pontan. Dan. Hist. Lib. VII, p. 380. [58] Spis. 358, Raynaldus 50.

" neglected, as all thought of piety had vanished; and for
" that reason the way was wide open for wicked deeds,
" for the performance of horrible and nefarious designs,
" for the stirring up of litigations, and for inciting
" hatreds. All this was owing to the sacrilegious oppres-
" sion and imprisonment of his brother John, Primate of
" Lund, with an affront so great to the Divine Majesty,
" with contempt for the Apostolic See, and injury to ec-
" clesiastical liberty; he besought him through Christ our
" Lord, and commanded him to release the Archbishop,
" and not hinder him from coming to Rome, as his im-
" prisonment was a most grievous offence to the King of
" Glory, who kept him on his throne; a disturbance in the
" Church, and a scandal to the faithful. Finally he would
" send him legatees well instructed in the affair, to make
" themselves understand it more clearly, and who would
" make wholesome and energetic provisions for peace in
" the kingdom."

The Archbishop did not await from the king the privilege of repairing speedily to Rome, but through the pious artifice of his bearer of food, who had concealed, in a large loaf of bread which he carried to him, a file and a silken ladder, he possessed at length the means of escape from prison. The reader can readily imagine how quickly he set out for Rome, and how strongly he complained of the persecutions he had undergone.

The bright hopes which Boniface entertained as a result of the interview with Frederick at Velletri vanished. The Sicilians abhorred the French yoke, and Frederick himself heard the voice of ambition which called him to the throne. The legates dispatched by Boniface could nowhere find a hearing, as every one in Sicily was wholly engaged in certain reports about James of Aragon, who faithful to the promises of peace, set about to fulfil them to their great despair. It was said that he had surrendered his rights over Sicily to Charles of Naples. Then Constance, the mother of Frederick, having summoned a parliament of the chief men of the island, resolved to send legates to James to learn the truth of these reports and to dissuade him from ceding his rights. These who were sent were Catalio Rusto, Sartorio Bisala, and Hugh Calac. They represented not only Constance, but all

Sicily.[59] When they arrived at Barbera in Catalonia on the 29th of October,[60] they found things just as they had been reported in Sicily; they were even witnesses of how solemnly peace was proclaimed between Charles and James; and they saw Blanche led as a spouse to him by the two legates of Boniface, as William Cardinal of St. Clement, whom the Pope had designated to accompany the betrothed, had died on the way. Great was the grief which seized the Sicilian ambassadors; and going before James, in the most forcible and eloquent manner they strove to dissuade him from his purpose, because his renunciation of Sicily would cast them headlong into the arms of the detested French. But although James was affected by their words, he remained faithful to the promised peace, and with kind words he dismissed the legates. Driven to desperation, they burst into tears and wailings, tearing their garments in token of their unmeasured grief; and in presence of the entire court of Aragon they solemnly declared that they would consider themselves absolved from all allegiance to James, and free to create any king they pleased. They did not wish to depart before James had given them in writing his renunciation, less as a document of the fact, than a marvel for posterity. For they could not understand how James, called by them to rule over Sicily, now could so cruelly abandon them to their enemies. And with this document they departed. On the journey they showed their anguish in other ways. They put on long trailing garments of mourning, and they painted black the masts and the sails of the ship on which they sailed, that it might be apparent to every one that they were the bearers of sad news.[61]

The Sicilians, assured of the truth of the concluded peace, and the surrender of James of Aragon of his rights over Sicily into the hands of the Pontiff, the direct lord of that island, as appears from the chronicles of the time, expressed their surprise and complaints. But there is reason to believe that the fact was agreeable to them; for being absolved from all allegiance to Rome and to Charles

[59] Franc. Maurolyci. Sicu Hist. lib. IV F apud Burm; Fazzelli De rebus Sicul. lib. XI cap. 3 ibi.   [60] Nic. Speciale Chron. Sicil. c. 52.
[61] Lucii Marinei Siculi de rebus Hispaniae lib. XI, apud Andream Scottum, Frankfort 1630.

by their volition, and from James by his renunciation, they felt themselves free both in body and mind to establish a form of government, which born of the people would create a standard of justice between the people and the prince, as a regulator for the monarchy and an assurance of the prosperity of the subjects. The proposition was not displeasing to Frederick, since to an ardent and ambitious youth the viceroyalty meant little whereas the crown meant very much, even if offered by a people rebellious to the Holy See. Therefore a parliament was held in Palermo, where, as yet timid, because of the uncertainty of the universal choice, the Sicilian raised the cry of Frederick as lord and not as king of the island. More solemn was the assembly of Catania which met in the Church of St. Agatha, where not only the syndics, but also the chief men of the kingdom united in consultation, with one voice proclaimed Frederick king.[62] Roger Loria, and Vinciguerra Palizzi, fiery orators, harrangued them. They would recognize in the people the right of selecting the king, and to justify the act, they did not disavow the right of Rome, affirming that James could resign his own right over Sicily into the hands of the Church, but that he could not despoil Frederick. In fact James did not resign the crown into the hands of the Sicilians, but into those of Charles; and in compensation he received from the French king the provinces of Anjou and Forcalquer.[63] To appear more reasonable they should have protested more frankly, and have said that, not wishing to have the sovereignty of Rome represented by Charles they had the right to elect a king.

As soon as Boniface had heard of the acts of the parliament of Palermo, he began to despair of bringing the Sicilians back to the obedience of the Church by mild and peaceful measures. However, though he could have made war, aided by the French and the Aragonians, yet he suspended hostilities and resorted to peaceful ways. The last efforts, which were also to prove vain, for the reason that a people lately out of servitude, and confident of its own strength and valor, will not allow itself to be led. The open wounds inflicted by the first Charles were still bleeding, and the intoxication over the French

[62] Nich. Special. lib. 2 cap. 23—Fazzel. lib. IX c. 2. [63] See Document K.

Vespers was still clouding their minds. It is true that the Sicilians suffered under the French, and their anger and abhorrence of their government were just, yet it was also true that under Boniface the same rascality would not be practised with impunity. He was just and powerful. On a former occasion complaints hardly listened to in the papal court preceded and engendered that terrible revenge, and now robbed the Sicilians of all confidence in Boniface. The Pontiff knew this, and in order to disabuse their minds of all fear of a foreign tyrant, he proposed to them by his legate Boniface Calamandrano, Grand Master of the Knights of St. John, the most just conditions, telling them: "That by the treaty of peace "with James, Sicily was returned to the full control of "the Church; that he, Pope, as father of the family and "lord, wished to provide for their safety; that a people without a ruler could not subsist; that they might select "from the college of Cardinals one whom they might "think was most fit to rule over them; and that he would "consent to their choice." No Frenchman, nor any stranger whosoever was in question. Boniface wished the Sicilians to be under Italian rule. It was better to hold the reins in his own hands than transfer them to Charles; nor could the latter complain of Boniface, who owing to the intolerance of Sicily, which was shaking off the Papal yoke, as direct lord could provide measures against it, much better than the French lord, who was a vassal. And Boniface reasoned correctly. For already there entered deeply into his mind the bad faith of James contained in saying to the Sicilian legates, that he left them free to choose the king; and also that Frederick was a knight and knew what to do. And it was better for the Sicilians to obey the Pope, an Italian, than an Aragonian. For if the Sicilians had been cooler headed, they could have expelled Charles, breaking the bond which united Rome with Anjou; and in expelling the French they would have had a helper, and not an enemy in Boniface. The events which happened later between the Pope and Philip the Fair, would have confirmed Boniface as an ally; but they would have no one but Frederick.

In the strongest manner, but with weak reasons, Boniface again tried to persuade Frederick to leave Sicily.

He returned again to the project of a marriage with Catherine, the titular Empress of Constantinople.[64] But Frederick preferred rather to retain Sicily than undergo the risk of an uncertain conquest; nor did Catherine wish to be married to Frederick, a king without a kingdom. Yet Boniface was using this argument, enforcing it with promises of aid to raise Frederick on the throne of Constantinople. But Frederick would not leave nor would Constance, his mother, accede to the wishes of the Pope.

The promises assured in the letters were made known to the people of Messina by Calamandrano in a public conference; and then he unfolded certain parchments all white, and provided with the papal seals, saying that their every desire, immunity, freedom and every other thing good for their government could be written in these, because the Pope would hold them as granted and sacredly valid. But their minds were unalterably intent on Frederick, and were trained not to confide in the Roman Court. They considered those promises as treacherous, and they rejected them, replying:—"That they had already created Frederick king, and the coronation only was wanting, which would soon take place." And Vinciguerra Palizzi, and Roger of Loria electrified the crowd with the eloquence of tribunes. At the same moment Peter Anselone broke through the ranks with naked sword in hand, and flourishing it in the face of the legate, who still held the parchments unrolled, assailed him with these words: "The Sicilians do not purchase peace with paper, but with the sword. That he should quickly leave the country under penalty of death." The Grand Master departed immediately, not wishing, as Speciale relates to suffer martyrdom.[65]

However, although the embassy had failed in persuading the minds of the Sicilians, yet the effort of the Grand Master to deprive them of a most powerful support, namely that valiant naval commander, Roger of Loria, was not unsuccessful. While the Sicilians were laboring to free themselves from the papal jurisdiction, Roger, by his skill and power made himself master of two islands lying along the African coast, and directly comprised in the

[64] Ep. Raynaldus, an 2 n. 8.
[65] Nic. Speciale, cap. 14, lib. 2—Fazzello, cap. 2.

sovereignty of Tunis. He had the intention of keeping them for himself and his descendants, and make himself a lord. Yet he feared, that the king of Sicily might covet them, and deprive him of them. Happily he had recourse secretly to the Pope. He besought him to use his authority to confirm him in the possession of that territory, and promised in return to raise in those islands churches and altars to Christ. There could not have come to Boniface a more favorable opportunity for detaching this valiant captain from the friendship of Frederick. He intrusted to Calamandrano a letter directed to Roger, in which he expressed his satisfaction over the conquest, and the hope that it might open the way to the light of the Gospel for that infidel nation. Willingly with the fulness of Apostolical authority he grants to him and his descendants the possession of the two islands with full jurisdiction; he might hold them as a fief of the Roman Church, for which he would pay yearly to the Roman Curia the sum of fifty ounces of gold; that from Calamandrano he would receive the investiture of the fief, and to the same he would swear fidelity to the Roman Church. The letter of Boniface attained its end, for Roger thereupon entered the service of Charles of Naples.

On the ember days in December of the first year of his pontificate, Baniface created six cardinals. It is true, that the mind does not always rise to the high dignity of the office, especially when it feels itself bound by the sweet ties of blood relationship. But the fault grows less, if in the bestowal of sacred dignities merit is united with relationship; and this is precisely what we must maintain in regard to Boniface. Among the six honored with the cardinals we find two of the Gaetani family, and one Count of Segni, a cousin of the Pope. But they as well as the others were remarkable for gifts of mind and heart. James Thomas Gaetani of Anagni, his nephew, a sister's son, was a Friar Minor, and Bishop of Alatri.[66] He was created Cardinal of the title of St. Clement, and previously exercised the office of legate on many occasions, which in those times were entrusted only to those most skilful in the management of affairs. He showed his great love for art by embellishing the church of his title

[66] Wadding. Annal. Minor. Tom 5 page 335.

with most beautiful mosaics.[67] Andrew, of the Counts of Segni, great-grand-nephew of Alexander IV, was possessed of such sincere and profound humility, that when the honors of the cardinalate were offered to him he refused them, so that Conteloro could not find his name in the series of cardinals.[68] Finally Francis Gaetani, his nephew, was skilled in the science of law, and of great goodness of life, one who, it is said, assisted in the compilation of the Sixth of the Decretals, and whom we shall find boldly and courageously defending the innocence of his dead uncle. Honoratus Gaetani, of the ancient Counts of Fondi, kept his memory green by a slab which he placed in the portico of the church of St. Mary in Cosmedin, from which Francis had taken his title.[69]

The other cardinals created by Boniface in this first year of his pontificate were Francis Napoleon Orsini, Peter Valeriano Duraguerra da Piperno, and James Gaetani Stephaneschi; they were of equal merit and virtue with the first named.[70] To this Stephaneschi, whom some have erroneously called a relative of Boniface, we are indebted for memoirs in verse that he had left us of his epoch and for many works with which he charged Giotto, the father of Renaissance painting. By his order Giotto decorated the church of St. George in Velabro,[71] from which he took his title as Cardinal; and having written the life of St. George, he had the same painter beautifully illuminate his book. A precious jewel, which is still preserved in the archives of the Canons of St. Peter. Vasari makes no mention of these works of Giotto.

James was of the family of Stephaneschi and was born in the Trastevere quarter of Rome.[72] He wrote three

[67] Oldin. Add. ad Ciaccon. T. 2. Page 323.
[68] Cardella. History of the Cardinals. Tom. 2. page 5—Wadding ibid
[69] Idem. [70] Idem. [71] Ferriggio. Notti Vatic. p. 163.
[72] This is how he speaks of his birth and his works in certain verses With which he prefaces his work on the life of St. Peter Celestine:

"Urbs mihi principium generis: Jacobus mihi nomen
Cajetanus erat; fluvii trans Tiberis amnem
Stephanidem de stirpe satus producor ab Ursa.
Murronem cecini repetentem claustra Monarcham,
Insertumque polo; Bonifacius utque triumphet
Urbe sacra diadema ferens, quo Cardine fultus

poems on the life of St. Peter Celestine, his canonization, and on the coronation of Boniface VIII. He had great devotion to Saint Celestine, which prompted him to write these verses, which he dedicated to the Abbot and the monastery of the Holy Spirit of the Celestine order near Sulmona. As we read in his letter of dedication, he did not wish his manuscript to be corrected by a strange hand, promising, that when he had time he would himself purge it of all faults; and he desired that it should be perpetually preserved in that monastery. These verses are preceded by a summary of the subjects treated in the poem, and followed by the office of the Saint which he had also composed. Although he called the manuscript sent to the Celestines of the Holy Spirit the original, yet we can not bring ourselves to believe that it was the autograph but a copy; for we find the characters so greatly marred by faults, that it is impossible in many places to understand the sense. The same injury was done to all the other writings of Stephaneschi. Daniel Papebroch published these three poems in the grand collection of the Bollandists, having had at hand the manuscript of the monastery of the Holy Spirit, and another of the Vatican. Muratori reproduced them in the Lives of the Pontiffs,[73] but he did not correct the verses of Stephaneschi, nor make the sense clear. We are sure these two worthy men could have improved these editions, if they had in their possession a third manuscript which Labbe calls the Naudean, and which he places among the manuscripts of Paris.[74]

Stephaneschi also wrote a prose work on the jubilee of Boniface VIII, followed by two short poems, which Julius Rosea first published and annotated; it afterwards was reprinted by the Doctors of Cologne in the grand collection of the Fathers,[75] both in the Cologne edition and that of Lyons.[76] Among the Roman "Ordo," published by Mabillon,[77] he places a treatise on the ceremonies of the Roman Church divided into one hundred and eighteen

    Hunc panxi, Coloque patrem metroque
    Centeno, fudique prosa. Deus hinc tibi Laus est."
    Vide. Bollandists. Maji Tom. V, p. 436.—

[73] S. R. I. tom. 3.   [74] Catalog. Biblio, M. S. S. p. 236.
[75] Tome XIII.   [76] Tom. XXV.   [77] Musei Italici T. 2, Ordo XIV, p. 241.

chapters, and with a reasonable foundation he attributes the work to James Gaetani Stephaneschi, and does not hesitate to place his name as the author on the title page.

The three poems on the life and canonization of St. Peter Celestine, and on the coronation of Boniface VIII, are precious documents which relate the history of those events of which Stephaneschi was an eye-witness. In them there is great liberty of detail, especially in matters relating to Peter Celestine. For although Stephaneschi shows himself most devoted to him, yet when he touches on the evil which accrued to the Church from his inexperience, he speaks very openly. Owing to the difficulty of the metre, and to the errors of those handling them, there is much obscurity in his verses; but we are surprised that it does not disappear in prose writings; as a result the treatise on the Jubilee in many places is rather an enigma than a narrative.

James Stephaneschi died at a very old age in Avignon in the year 1341. His body was brought to Rome where it was interred in the Vatican Basilica in the chapel of Sts. George and Lawrence which he had built.

Boniface intended also in the first year of his pontificate to increase the divine worship. Head of the religion of Jesus Christ, and possessed of a spirit so noble as to comprehend fully what religion is, the only fructifier of human genius and the mother of every holy affection; so, being placed so high he could not remove from his mind those most distinguished souls who made their minds and their eloquence a foundation as it were of the Church. Worship was given in the Church to the Apostles, the Evangelists and to the four Doctors, Ambrose, Augustine, Jerome and Gregory the Great, but Boniface wished to increase this with particular honors. For it did not seem ever sufficient, the honor the faithful could pay to the Apostles, the first preachers of the divine word which renewed the face of the earth, to the Evangelists the first writers of it, and to those Fathers the great priests of the divine traditions. Seated on the chair of Peter he felt beneath him a certain immovability, which was not owing to human vigor and strength, for he knew that the Apostles and Fathers were the holy foundations, and the supports of the divine edifice. Wherefore he published a decree to all the faithful, directed to the Archbishop of Rheims and his suffragans, in which he ordered to be celebrated with the most solemn rites the feasts of the Holy Apostles, the Evangelists, and the four greatest Doctors, Ambrose, Augustine, Jerome, and Gregory the Great, two of whom were Italians. How beautiful are his words: " The splendid and salutary teachings of these "most illustrious Doctors have illustrated the Church, "have adorned it with virtue, and have formed the man- "ners of her children. Moreover by them, as luminous and shining lights on candelabra in the house of the Lord, "the darkness of error having been dissipated, and entire "body of the Church sparkles like the morning star. "Moreover their rich eloquence, watered by a spring of heavenly grace, discloses the mysteries of the Holy Scrip- "tures, loosens the knots, dispels obscurities, and solves "the doubts. And by their profound and magnificent dis- "courses the grand edifice of the Church is resplendent "as with glowing gems, and by the singular charm of "their words she is exalted and shines with new glory." [78]

[78] " Horum quippe Doctorum Praelucida et salutaria documenta praedictam illustrarunt Ecclesiam, decorarunt virtutibus, et moribus informarunt. Per ipsos praeterea, quasi luminosas ardentesque luncernas super candelabrum, in domo Domini positas errorum tenebris profligatis, totius corporis Ecclesiae tanquam sydus irradiat matutinum; eorum etiam foecunda facundia coelestis irrigui gratia influente, scripturarum enigmata reserat, decoris eorum sermonibus ampla ipsius Ecclesiae fabriea velut gemmis solvit nodos, obscura dilucidat dubiaque declarat. Profoundis quoque ac vernantibus rutilat." Rayn. 1295-55.

BOOK THIRD.

SUMMARY.

1296-1297.

The coronation of Frederick in Palermo.—Boniface excommunicates him.—And creates James of Aragon Gonfalonier of Holy Church to combat him —The commotions in Sicily influence those in the Romagna —Boniface wishes to pacify the latter.—He aids Guy of Montefeltro to become a Friar.—At the same time Louis, son of Charles the Lame, becomes a Friar also.—Pisa entrusts her government to Boniface —He becomes the mediator between Genoa and Venice.—He writes to the legates in England, to Philip, and to Adolph.—Haughty reply of Philip.—Affairs of the church of Pamiers.—Boniface makes the city a Bishopric, and founds an academy there.—The layman grieve the Church.—The famous constitution "Clericis Laicos."—It was neither new nor abusive —Philip rages and publishes an impertinent edict.—The paternal Bull with which Boniface opposes it.—The constitution is received in England, firmness of the English clergy.—The Fraticelli, and their origin.—Causes of their strifes with the Popes and especially with Boniface —Jacopone da Todi.—Sicily; and the methods adopted by James to make Frederick leave —Treaty which James made with Boniface —The Roman Patricians —The Colonnas and their family.—How they became enemies of Boniface.—The Brigandage of Sciarra Colonna.—Rebellion of the Colonnas; and threats of Boniface —They spread the famous libel against him.—Its effect.—The Bull "Lapis abscissus" is hurled against them.—They reply with new insolence —Arms are taken up —Messages of the Roman people to Boniface, and his reply —Crusade against the Colonnas.—Boniface clothes the cardinals in purple.—He canonizes Louis IX of France.

WHEN the Sicilians had violently expelled Calamandro, the papal envoy, it closed the way to all agreement, and by destroying the hopes of Boniface those of all Sicily were revived. The whole island was agitated as on a feast day, and in the transports of a liberty which made them forgetful of the wounds of the French tyranny, they raised to the throne the young Frederick, darling son of the beautiful Constance. They had seen how a sceptre was obtained by conquest or by inheritance, how it was placed in the hand of a prince by Papal investiture, but as yet they did not know what it was to take a crown themselves and place it on the head of a king of their own creation. On the 25th of March they had experience of this; and accordingly the religious and civil ceremonies were carried out with incredible pomp. Frederick was anointed and crowned king in the cathedral of Palermo He afterwards rode through the city holding a globe and sceptre in his hands. It seemed that no other prince ascended the throne with a greater desire of the people than he. Favors and civil ordinances followed the fetes. The former were most beautiful, because they were distributed by a new prince; the latter were wise, because they were sanctioned by the people who raised him to the height of the throne.[1] The division of the power between the king and an annual parliament in which all the orders of the kingdom were represented was agreeable to the people, who submitted willingly to the laws. Charles II and the Pope had much to fear from this king, who safe in the possession of Sicily might cast yearning eyes on the Neapolitan territory, and might hope to bring it under his authority less by force of arms, than by the allurement of a new government. Frederick set out immediately for Reggio and was threatening Calabria.

It seems that the brandishing of the sword in the face of the ambassador, the bearer of peaceful proposals; the pointing of it at his loins, and his rude expulsion, had always been considered, and for that reason, even in the XIII century, a crime against the rights of nations. For which reason Boniface, seeing that all hopes of peace had vanished, resolved upon adopting severe measures. In this he was urged on by the actions of Frederick with the Ghibellines of Tuscany, of Lombardy, and certain of his envoys who were secretly roaming through the kingdom of Naples exciting the people to rebellion, and to oppose these he dispatched Cardinal Landolph to Naples.[2] So on Ascension day he wrote and proclaimed in the Basilica of St. Peter a solemn admonition against Frederick. After calling attention to the censures hurled against Peter of Aragon, and his abettors in Sicily by Popes

---
[1] Nic. Special lib. 3, c. 1—Anonym. Chron. Sie. e. 54.
[2] Raynaldus. ad annum 1296, n. 20.

Martin, Honorius, and Nicholas, the treaties made with James, and the insolent expulsion of his legate, he condemns the coronation of Frederick, and his hostile intrigues with the enemies of the Church; he annuls the acts of the new government; he commands him to lay aside the sceptre, and immediately to refrain from exercising the office of king; he fixes as a peremptory limit the octave of the feast of the Apostles, which having expired, Frederick and the Sicilians, if contumacious, will incur solemn excommunication; he forbids anybody to league with them;[3] and deprives them of every privilege and right granted to them by the Holy See. The admonitions were of no avail. Boniface on the feast of the Dedication of the Vatican Basilica hurled against Sicily the threatened censures.[4]

(1297) Force of arms was necessary, because the Sicilians felt no remorse; they even set about vigorously to make war on the Neapolitan territory. Frederick was leader of the army, and Roger of Loria of the navy. Success attended them. Squillace was taken by force, Catanzari surrendered conditionally, and Cotrone and other places being captured were plundered.[5] Boniface, before the oronation of Frederick, had already turned to king James by letters of the 20th of January, sending as legate to him, Leonard, a Franciscan Friar, to remind him of the benefits he had received from the Roman See, of his duty to assist her, and invited him to come immediately to Rome. And sixteen days having scarcely elapsed on the 5th of February, he addressed another letter to James,[6] creating him standard-bearer of Holy Church, and sovereign defender of the same Church against her enemies. The letter begins " Redemptor Mundi," and mentions the conditions on which the Pope confers the high office on the king of Aragon. And whereas the chief enemies were the Turks, who were overrunning the Holy Land. the king was particularly appointed against these. There is no mention of the Sicilians, because up to February the coronation of Frederick had not taken place, but it is to be understood that it was against them that James was to set about to put his fleet on a war footing well provided with

[3] Rayn. 1294. 14. lib. 2 epist. 37.   [4] Rayn. 15. lib. 2 epist. 100.
[5] Nic. Spec. lib. IX cap. 3.   [6] Rayn. ad annum 1294, 19.

arms and men and military stores sufficient for fully sixty galleys, the Church was to pay as much money as was sufficient for the armament and maintenence of the vessels: the supreme commander was to be James, who at the beck of the Pope was to be ready to move against the Turks, or any other enemies and rebels of the Church; the spoils taken from the enemy were to be divided into two parts, one to be given to the King, and the other to remain in the custody of the Pope for the benefit of the Holy Land; the territory to be conquered, if it previously belonged to a Catholic prince, was to be restored to him, but if to an infidel it was to remain in custody of the Church until the Pope disposed of it; the tithes of Aragon for three years were to be given to the King if he responded to the call to wage war for the Holy See; and his states during his absence in the service of the same, were to remain under the protection of St. Peter. These were the chief conditions under which Boniface appointed James to the office of Standard-bearer of the Holy Church. He followed this up with a letter dated the 5th of February, in which he urges him strongly to come. But James did not come for a year after. In the meanwhile Boniface was doubting of his faith. Then he urged Charles to the defence; he was willing, but powerless owing to the lack of money, as he had spent so much in purchasing peace from James. But Boniface came to his assistance manfully. He filled his treasury with five thousand ounces of gold,[7] and as he was about to wage war against the enemies of the Church, he granted him the privilege of collecting subsidies from the sacred patrimonies without the papal permission.[8] He commanded the bishop of Marseilles to aid Charles by the ecclesiastical tithes to form a navy.

These commotions in Sicily were incentives to the dissensions prevailing in the Italian mainland. The cities and people were divided into Guelphs and Ghibellines, and the rise or decline of the French royalists in Italy was a grave cause of agitation, as the house of Anjou was at that time the heart and support of Guelphism, since the Popes, either because of their love for France, or because of laxity of spirit, allowed the control of the Guelph party to

[7] Lib. 2 ep. 18 Rayn. 15.   [8] Rayn. lib. 2 epist. 576.

pass from their hands. As we have seen before, William Durant was Count of Romagna, being appointed governor of that province and of the Marches by Boniface. And when in the year previous he undertook the government of those regions, Azzo VIII, Marquis of Este, through ambitious motives enkindled more intensely the fire of dissension between the opposing factions. This proud lord wanted to make himself master of Parma, which in December had been the theatre of intestine strifes. He welcomed the return of the banished Sanvitale, that he might have an occasion for invading their native country. Parma resisted him, aided by Milan, Bologna, and the lord of Piacenza, Albert Scotto. In this year as the Parmesans and the Bolognese were fortifying themselves, having as allies the people of Brescia, and the exiles of Reggio and Modena,[9] so Azzo VIII turns for assistance to the Ghibellines of the Romagna. He gathered about him the most powerful Ghibellines in these provinces. Maghinardo da Susiana with the men from Faenza; Scarpetta Ordelaffi, with these from Forli and Cesena; and the famous Uguccione of Faggiuola with all the Ghibellines banished from Bologna, Rimini, Ravenna, and other cities. These men assembled in council with Este at Argenta, and decided to take Imola from Bologna.[10] As soon as Durant, Count of Romagna, heard of that intention he called the Bolognese to arms; but having encountered on the banks of the river Santerno the hostile Ghibellines under the leadership of Azzo, the latter were victorious and took possession of Imola.[11] In April of the same year, William Durant, as a punishment for their going in league with the Ghibelline Azzo of Ferrara, deprived the cities of Cesena, Forli, Faenza and Imola, of all their privileges, honors and dignities. A weak and senseless revenge which did not indeed calm, but rather embittered their feelings the more.

Pope Boniface tried another way to put an end to these tragic scandals. He would obtain peace without resorting to war. He would have each one state his case to a judge, whose decision would take the place of victorious battles and stifled revenge. Anyone who studies those

[9] Chron. Parmen. S. R. I. tom. 9.   [10] Chron. Esten. ib.
[11] Mat. de Griff. Annal. Bonon. T. 18 S. R. I.—Chr. Foroliv. T. 22.

times, and preceives that confidence was wanting everywhere, will admit, that Boniface, on account of his wisdom and by reason of the office of Pontiff which he exercised, and because he alone was revered and respected, was the only one capable to preside as judge over these stormy suits. The sequence of this history will prove this better. Therefore with a peaceful pacifying intention, whilst affairs, as we have said, were in a badly disturbed state in the territory between Rimini and Parma, he appointed as peacemaker the bishop of Pavia and wrote letters to Guy of Montefeltro the most influential man in the Ghibelline party, urging him to appear with other nobles before the Papal curia, that they might come to a friendly understanding in those things which caused such dissensions between the two parties.[12]

Guy had previously submitted to Celestine and Boniface that he might be absolved from censures, and now tired of the adventures of war, weakened by old age, he was engaged with the thought of death, and wished to make a solemn expiation of his sins. Guy betook himself to Boniface: instead of treating of the affairs for which he was summoned, he confessed to him that he came for no other purpose but that of his soul; that he heard a voice deep in his heart which was calling on him to become either a knight in some military order or a Franciscan Friar; and he, that terrible Ghibelline, humbly besought Boniface to give him spiritual direction. This scene was a beautiful subject for an artist's pencil. The Pope graciously complied with the desire of Guy and favored it, not only as the pious resolution of a converted sinner, but also as a means that would well contribute to bring about peace in his provinces. He replied, that he would assist him whether he wished to be a friar, or a knight. But afterwards on reflection, thinking that to hold that energy there would be needed well-tempered steel, he would advise him to choose the rough habit of St. Francis rather than the sword of a knight. Guy consenting, he wrote a

[12] Lib 2. Ep. I. ". . . . . . Ut te ac aliis nobilibus personis hujusmodi in curia nostra praesentibus, nos per te ac illos, de praedictarum partium conditionibus informati, tractare, ordinare, disponere, et providere possimus ea, quae ad vestrum et aliorum ipsarum partium bona, statum, tranquillitatem et pacem viderimus expedire."

BONIFACE VIII RECEIVING ST. LOUIS OF TOULOUSE, SON OF CHARLES MARTEL, KING OF NAPLES.

letter to the Minister of the Friars Minor of the province of Ancona, telling him that his noble and beloved son Guy, Count of Montefeltro, touched by the hand of God, and repentant of all the evil done to Mother Church, had expressed the desire of doing penance, and dying among the friars in holy service, his wife consenting, who would also take herself a vow of chastity. He then arranged that after taking their vows together, they would also make their solemn act of separation. Of movable property Guy would take some to reward his courtiers; of the immovable goods there would be assigned an annual stipend of one hundred lire of Ravenna for the support of his wife, who on account of old age was allowed to remain at home and not enter a convent; and what remained of his wealth, was to be entrusted to an honest person and kept in a safe place, until the Pope would provide as to its use.[13] Guy became a friar in the monastery of Ancona, and after two years of a most edifying life of prayer and good works, he rendered his soul unto God.[14] Such was the end of Guy, a man, to use the words of the chronicle of Asti, the most wise of men, brave, generous, most skilful in war, and who had not his equal in that he entered among the Franciscan friars.[15]

Another person of distinction in this same year also wished to become a Friar of St. Francis. If he was not famous for great deeds like Guy, he was illustrious by the splendor of his birth. This was Louis, son of Charles the Lame, who, as we have seen, had been a hostage in Catalonia with two other brothers. As he was returning with his father from Catalonia after peace was concluded with James, he expressed the wish to lead the life of a Friar Minor. Passing through Montpellier, he first made known his desire to the friars there. Bnt they refused to gratify him, fearing that if they received him and invested him in the holy habit they would incur the displeasure of his father. When he arrived in Italy he met his mother,

[13] Ep. Bon. Ministro prov. Ord. Min. Marchiae apud Wading T. X, p. 349.
[14] Epist. Bonif. apud Wading.
[15] Chron. Asten. cap. 23, S. R. I. T. XI col. 189. "Sapientissimus virorum fortis et largus, et callidissimus in bellando . . . . poenitentia ductus, humilis et contritus, de quo vere dici potest: *non est inientus similis illi. ordinem Fratrum Minorum intravit.*"

Mary of Hungary, with her other son, Charles Martel, and, as she had not seen him for a long time, with a heart full of joy and by the impulse of maternal love she threw her arms around his neck to embrace and kiss him. But the holy youth, most careful of his purity, turned his face away refusing to be kissed. Astonished at his conduct his mother asked: "What could there be sinful in that embrace?" With bowed head and his face suffused with blushes, he replied: " I know very well you are my mother, " but moreover you are a woman, whom a servant of God " is not allowed to kiss."—He was enrolled among the clerics, and raised to the subdiaconate at Rome; afterwards he was ordained deacon and priest at Naples in the Church of St. Lawrence Major. He dwelt in a suburban monastery with the Friars Minor, applying his mind to spiritual things and the acquisition of ecclesiastical sciences, until, the see of Toulouse having become vacant by the death of Hugh Mascerio, Boniface knowing Louis to be of mature judgment and sense, appointed him the Bishop of that see. The royal youth would not accept the office unless he was allowed to wear the habit of St. Francis. The privilege was granted, and he was consecrated bishop by Boniface, being at the most twenty years old.[16] St. Antoninus narrates his virtues while bishop, which were great and many,[17] though of short duration, as the holy young man died two years afterwards.

On April 17th, the Pope sent Peter Cardinal of St. Maria Nuova, with full authority to readjust affairs in the Italian provinces, and aid the efforts of the Bishop of Pavia, sent on the same errand in January.[18] These cares of Boniface, and the departure of Guy of Montefeltro, the commander of their armies, induced the Pisans, as the Guelph party was in the ascendancy, to place all their confidence in the Pope: a sure sign of the certainty they had of the honesty of his mind. And although inflicted with censures by him for the irreverent things done to the churches, yet they did not hesitate to entrust the government of their city to Boniface, proffering him four thousand livres of gold wherewith to pay the magistrates he might appoint. To an ambitious man and one covetous

[16] Wading Annal Minor, ad annum 1290 n IV. V. VI.
[17] Chron. 3, p. 585. 24, cap. 4.   [18] Lib. 2. Epist 43. Rayn. 1.

of the property of others, these offers would not have been made. Boniface absolved the Pisans from censures and accepted the care of governing their city. As his vicar in the government of Pisa, he appointed Elias,[19] Count of Val d'Elsa. He ordained that he should repair to the city and begin his office of governing it in September, which office he would hold for a year. His salary was to be four thousand livres. He was allowed to maintain with him four soldiers, as many judges, and twelve horses, of which at least six should be war horses. He urged him to use prudence, that he might be successful in governing. The provost of Venza accompanied the Count in order to absolve the Pisans from the interdict, and receive the five hundred marks in reparation for their office.

Venice was born a mature republic, and for that reason she had escaped those foolish party contests of the Guelphs and Ghibellines, a sure sign of civilization being in its infancy among people who practised them. But firmly established by reason of a strong republican constitution, it was Guelph in principle, and like every other Italian people jealous of its independence, was a deadly enemy of the Ghibellines. For which reason the eternal emulation with Genoa, which was cruelly torn by factions, enkindled the flames of war, which burst forth more or less violently according as the Ghibelline faction became more or less predominent. Now it happened on the 30th of December of the same year that the Grimaldi and Fieschi the leaders of the Guelph party were involved in an unfortunate civil contest with the Doria's and the Spinola's, the chieftains of the Ghibellines. With such fury did they fight, that forgetting they were in their own country, they laid it waste by fire and sword. The sanctity of the churches was not respected. For the Grimaldi having taken refuge and fortified themselves in the tower of the Church of St. Lawrence they were besieged by their opponents, and in the storming of it the roof took fire.[20] Moreover from Lombardy auxiliaries arrived who increased the flame of those scandalous contests, until having conquered and expelled the Guelph party on the 7th of February, Conrad Doria, and Conrad Spinola reigned supreme in Genoa. After

---

[19] Lib. 2, ep 11 Raynaldus 4.
[20] Georg. Stella Ann. Gen. cap. VIII S. R. I. t. 17.

these domestic strifes a war with Guelph Venice ensued; or rather, the damages done by Venice to the possessions of Genoa in the East, namely the burning of her ships, and the capture and sacking of the city of Caffa in the Crimea.[21] A detailed account of this is contained in the chronicles of Andrew Dandolo.[22] In the midst of these insane strifes Pope Boniface wished to interpose himself, and as we have seen in the previous year he made use of every effort to unite them in peace, but in vain. In this year he renewed his efforts for the same end. He wrote to the Genoese[23] and Venetians to send their legates to him that he might end the war between them and establish an alliance. In the severest terms he particularly commanded the Genoese, who in fact acted more scandalously than the Venetians, to respect a truce until Easter. But they would not listen to him.

We return to the quarrels between the Kings of France and England. Edward, constantly annoyed by the Welsh and kept on his guard by the Scotch, truly desired peace with Philip. He tried to obtain it somehow. In December, 1295, Margaret of Provence, widow of St. Louis, the grandmother of Philip, and his own aunt, had died. Under such circumstances it was utterly unbecoming for persons so closely related to be at war, and so Edward wrote to all the bishops of his kingdom that they might pray for the soul of his aunt, the Queen of France,[24] which merciful solicitude he fancied would persuade Philip to make peace with him. And so much did he flatter himself on the feasibility of the thing, that on the 1st of January he gave the fullest power to two legates of Boniface, to the Dukes of Brabant, to the Earl of Pembroke, to the Counts of Savoy, of Bar, and of Holland, and to fourteen of the Chief men if his kingdom, to negotiate at Cambrai a truce with Philip.[25] Philip turned a deaf ear to the peaceful proposals, and persevered in the slow but exterminating war in unhappy Gascony[26] with the worst results for Edward. But Edward was compensated well for whatever damage was done him by the victory he obtained

---

[21] Cont Dandol S R. I. 12, col. 406 [22] Ibidem. [23] Lib 2, epist. 38. 39, Raynaldus 5 [24] Chron. Nangii 1295—Rymer T. I. pag. 705.
[25] Rymer. Tom II, p. 702, 703
[26] Chron Guill Nangii, 1296—H de Knyghton lib. III. p. 1509.

under the walls of Dunbar over the Scotch. Forsaken by Philip, they lost their king Balliol, who was cast a prisoner into the tower of London, and their liberty, becoming from that time vassals of Edward.[27] He continued his conquest of Scotland, yet he did not cease through papal legates and the other deputies to negotiate a truce with Philip until Christmas, according to the wish of Boniface. The subjugation of Scotland displeased Boniface, because over that kingdom, as will be said, the Church believed she possessed some rights of dominion; he was also displeased at the little success of his legates. Moreover Guy, Count of Flanders, whose daughter, as we narrated, had been wickedly imprisoned by Philip while on her way to her husband, was asking for justice and aid against oppression by French arms.[29] In the strongest terms by letters Boniface exhorted his legates to obtain a truce, if not peace; to restrain the angry princes from shedding blood, and from exhausting the holy patrimonies. They should make known the views of the Pontiff, and his desire to cross the mountains to make peace among those at variance; that the college of Cardinals could not come, because many were advanced in years; that Italy being convulsed, and Sicily in a furious war against Charles, demanded his presence; and that they should counsel the princes to send representatives, and to be satisfied to submit to his judgment the reasons of their dissensions.[30] The admonitions to his legates he followed by a Bull dated the 13th of August,[31] which inflicted excommunication on any one who would violate the truce of two years.

He addressed also urgent letters to Edward, Philip and Adolph, in which he recommended them to leave in his hands the settlement of their disputes. "We pass the night lying awake," he wrote to Adolph, King of the Romans, "in order that between you and Edward King "of England and Philip of France, our most dear sons in "Christ, we may be able by a peace or truce, to prepare "and establish quiet and peace in Christendom, whereby "the faithful chieftains and their followers will not turn "against one another those swords which should be un-

[27] Nicol. Trivet Chr. p. 217—H de Knyghton lib. III. p. 1581.
[28] Rymer. Tom. II, p. 709-710-716   [29] Spond. anno 1296.
[30] Raynaldus 21,   [31] Idem 29-1296.

"sheathed against the enemies of the Cross and the Faith
"for the recovery of the Holy Land. Wherefore with
"most fervent admonitions, exhortations and prayers we
"beseech you by Christ's Precious Blood, not to wage war
"against Philip, King of France, and his kingdom; and
"incline your soul and submit to a peace or at least a long
"truce, during which you can effectually in our presence
"negotiate for peace with the representatives of your ad-
"versaries."[32] From a letter of Boniface to Philip[33] it
is evident that Edward and Adolph had sent representatives to the Roman Court to submit to the judgment of
the Pontiff their reasons. But Philip the Fair, when the
papal wishes concerning the truce, and the threatened
censures were disclosed to him, became enraged; he rejected them, and haughtily replied: "The kingdom was
"his own; in temporal affairs he recognized no superior,
"to no one on earth was he subject; and he was prepared
"to do the will of the Pope only in spiritual things." The
benign Bossuet extols to the skies this answer of Philip.
But he was too much attached to the greatness of Louis
XIV, to be able to view in the right light this apparent intrusion of Boniface into the affairs of France.[34] Without
entering into an examination of the indirect power which
the Pope could have in those times in the civil affairs of a
state which being Catholic was spiritually subject to him,
we can linger over the fact of the many misfortunes which
befel the people precisely because princes returned these
haughty answers to the Pontiffs.

Up to now one can easily believe that Boniface truly
loved Philip the Fair. The letters he sent him announc-
ing his elevation to the Pontificate; the strong pressure he
brought upon Edward and Adolph, that they should not
disturb him in the posession of Gascony and Burgundy;
the privilege bestowed on him, his wife and children, that
they could not be excommunicated by any one without the
express permission of the Holy See,[35] and his efforts to
maintain Charles, a Frenchman on the Sicilian throne,
were certainly unmistakable signs of his love and benevolence. But love should not blind the Pontiff to such a de-

[32] Raynaldus 1296–18. [33] Ibi. "crebris, rumoribus."
[34] See Bianchi, "The Indirect power of the Church", T. 2 Book 6 V, page 454. [35] Regesta Vaticana, Ep. 159.

gree as to make him overlook justice, especially when the defence of it is demanded for churches, and consecrated persons who had no other refuge but the see of St. Peter. Philip was entirely ignorant of this, because in the intoxication of power his intellect was clouded. The reader will observe that we now begin to touch upon the remote causes of the great quarrel between Philip and the Pope, which afterwards assumed gigantic proportion to the great scandal of the faithful. We begin with the affair of the church of Pamiers, in which the sparks of the great conflagration began to be lighted. Pamiers was a city in France,[36] in the county of Foix, its name formerly was Fredelac and afterwards Pamiers, from the castle of this name in the diocese of Toulouse. In the 8th century the Counts of Carcassonne built there the abbey of St. Antoninus, which was given as a dwelling to the Canons Regular of St. Augustine. Roger Bernard, Count of Foix, in 1149 or thereabouts, gave the city of Fredelac, with the castle of Pamiers to the Abbey. But as often happened in those barbarous times, and because the piety of the benefactors grew wearied, and that of the receivers of the gift grew cold in the midst of riches, robbery followed the pious offerings, and for that reason frequent wars were waged between the Counts of Foix and the Abbots of St. Antoninus[37] to the detriment of the latter, who lost possession of Pamiers; for we find that Bernard III in 1265 restored to it the Abbey, consoling thereby Amanieu d'Armagnac, Archbishop of Auch, his tutor.[38]

We believe that the Count made this restitution by order of St. Louis IX. Pope Clement IV had requested him to take the city of Pamiers under his protection for the honor of Holy Church, and to shield it from the violence of the Counts of Foix, by placing it under the guardianship of the Abbot of the monastery of St. Antoninus. St. Louis complied and he promised that at a stated time he would leave it under the full control of the aforesaid Abbot. Philip the Bold did the same. But the time had arrived when Pamiers should pass from the royal control to that of the Abbot, yet Philip the Fair would not sur-

[36] See Hadr. Valesii Notit Galliae ad vocem "Apamiae."—
[37] The great dictionary of Moreri & Pamiers.
[38] Gall Christ, D. Sainte Marth. Tom. I, col. 993, Eccl. Ansciensis.

render it. Nay, importuned by Roger Bernard III, Count of Foix, he wrote letters to the Seneschal of Carcasonne telling him to extend a strong hand to the Count and aid him in obtaining the mastery over Pamiers. This was a shameful violation of the rights of that church. The Count entered the city as an enemy, and extorted an oath of fealty from the officials of the Abbot. Inasmuch as this act was done at the instance of Philip, it was an usurpation of the sacred patrimony, contempt was shown for the provisions of Clement IV, and much scandal was given.

Down to our own days Boniface has been generally condemned by all historians as a man of irascible and disdainful temperament; but in his letters we find such control of temper, and such a mild declaration of rights, that considering his natural disposition of being proudly intolerant of every injustice, it seems to us marvellous. In fact, the dishonorable invasion of the sacred patrimony of the Abbey of St. Antoninus by Philip through the Count of Foix, he answered with a fatherly exhortation to repair the evil deed, restoring that which was seized to the Abbot, and remembering how his grandfather and father respected the rights of the Abbey, he should preserve and guard them. There were no threats, nor severity of language.[39] However Philip would not obey the Pontiff, nor would the Count, who was under the protection of the King. The Count threatened with censures became contumacious, and the censures passed into effect; Philip, because he was King, was not even threatened, and he persevered in his obstinacy. Then Boniface to make the church of Pamiers more venerable, erected it into a Bishopric, thereby hoping that if the personality of an Abbot was not sufficient to restrain the rapacity of the prince, the dignity of a Bishop might be able to do so. For this purpose he published the Bull "Romanus Pontifex" dated at Anagni, the 23rd of July, in which separating the city of Pamiers from the vast diocese of Toulouse he made it a new Episcopal See.[40] The secret motive of this ordinance was the present act of violence, but the ostensible

---

[39] Epist. ad Philip. Raynaldus 52.

[40] Bullarum, Diplom. amplis. Collect. Caroli Cocquelines Ed Romae 1741. T. III, p. 79—William Nangius. ad annum 1296.

reasons for it were the immense size of the diocese of Toulouse, which, owing to the difficulty and slowness of the Bishops in visiting the entire diocese, was a grievous detriment to souls. He designated as cathedral, the Church of St. Martin, where the body of St. Antoninus reposed. The Abbot Bernard Saisset he made the first bishop; he defined the limits of the new diocese, and assigned it a revenue. And in order that Pamiers as a city might correspond to the new honors granted it as a Bishopric, Boniface founded there an Academy.[41] These provisions however Philip believed to be infringements on his power, and were occasions of more burning hatred, which increased in violence more and more.

Strength and vigor to preserve the ecclesiastical immunities were necessary in these times, when conspiracy to plunder and outrage the rights of churches was almost universal. The care and anxiety for the goods of the Church were not wanting in Boniface. Ever watchful over all the churches, he saw the snares and evils which beset them; and there was no church no matter how, distant, nor violator of its rights, that ever escaped his notice. He wrote to the Archbishop of Arles, and the Bishop of Marseilles,[42] urging them to resist a certain law passed by the people of Marseilles, forbidding donations to be given to clerics not belonging to their city.[43] He excommunicated the Duke of Carinthia, the proud violator of the rights of the church of Trent.[44] He cited to judgment the magistrates of Lucania, for oppressing the Church; and summoned to Rome the Bishop because of his heedlessness of laical impertinence. The Pisans and Orvietans, guilty of the same fault, he loaded with censures.[45] He waged a terrible war against vice which is a pest in every civil community. Being told of the grievous usuries which had been practised by a certain man now deceased, he wrote to the Bishop of Metz, commanding

---

[41] Epist. 658. Raynaldus 53 —

[42] See, Reg. Vatic. M. S. an. 1 Epist ad Arch. Remensi. "Ut procedat contra injuriam allatam Ecclesiae Laudunensi." Epist. 355 Ad Philippem Regem, quod faciat justitiam eidem Ecclesiae Epist. 356. Eidem quod non molestet Episcopum Lingonensem. Epist. 546, etc.

[43] Epistola 223 Raynaldus 54.

[44] Epist. 151 Rayn. Ibi.   [45] Epist. 146-150. Tay. ibi.

him, as an example to others, to disinter the body of that wicked usurer and cast it out of the consecrated ground.[46] He knew well that the bosom of the Church should be closed against those who had shut their hearts to pity and justice. Moreover it appears that he labored strenously to exterminate this pestiferous race of man, for we find in a letter which he wrote to the Bishop of Autun that he imposed on him the obligation of expelling from his diocese all those guilty of usury.

The clerical administrators of the sacred patrimonies were in a dilemma. On the one side was the rapacity of princes, and on the other were the threats and prohibitions of the Popes. At first with the permission of the Bishop they could of their own will assist laymen reduced to dire straits; but there were censures for laymen compelling them to do so, though not for clerics donating the sacred patrimony; so that often not forced by fear, but with a desire to please the princes, it happened that they enriched the princes with the sacred gifts of the faithful to God on the altar. Boniface however erected defensive barriers around the goods of the Church, as Councils and former Popes had done. The permission to make these donations he reserved to the will of the Pope alone, and by censures he restrained the clerics from offering them, in the same manner as already the violent laymen had been restrained from seeking them.[47] For this reason he wrote and published that famous constitution "Clericis Laicos", which replete with the sacredness of the rights of the Church, sounded unpleasantly in the courts of princes, and was a scandal to the proud, just as the author himself of justice was and ever will be to the wicked. The constitution thus begins: "Antiquity shows us the "enmity of laymen against the clergy, and our experience "in the present time manifestly supports that teaching, "since without considering that they have no power over "the persons or property of ecclesiastics, the laity lay "imposts on the prelates and clergy, both regular and "secular; and we grieve to say, that some prelates and "other ecclesiastics, having more fear of the temporal "majesty than of the eternal, acquiesce in that abuse.

[46] Regest. M. S. Vatic. an I Ep. 508.
[47] Regest. M. S. Vatic. Anni II Epist. 59.

"That we may obviate this, we ordain that all the prelates
"and ecclesiastics, regular and secular, who pay to lay-
"men tithes or any other portion of their revenues, under
"the name of aid, subvention, or any other, without the
"authority of the Holy See, and the kings, princes and
"magistrates and all others who shall impose such
"burdens, or who shall give aid or consent thereto, shall
"incur excommunication, absolution from which is re-
"served to the Holy See, notwithstanding any privilege."—

In this Decretal, which Bossuet blindly calls an instigator of hatred,[48] many see the hidden spark of that fire of wrath that broke out between Philip and Boniface; and for that reason on the head of the latter rests the entire blame for the scandals which followed. But here it is necessary to explain clearly this affair, because not agreeing with the opinion of Bossuet and Fleury and all that set of lawyers (a race of men who by their subtlety adapted themselves to every kind of government, and for that reason willing tools of the profligacy of the people, and the best counsellors of oppression), if facts related were not cleansed from the foulness with which they were defiled by courtiers, we would be unfaithful to our office of historian.

Now first of all it is to be observed that Boniface did not fabricate by himself a new constitution, but rather reproduced and confirmed those solemn decrees, which Councils and former popes had published, in order to bind the hands of the laity attacking the property of the churches. The XIXth Canon of the third Council of Lateran smites with censures laymen who impose taxes on the goods of the churches ;and the XLIVth Canon of the fourth Council of Lateran, besides confirming these censures, further adds that subsidies even in case of necessity cannot be drawn from the churches without the permission of the Pope.[49] Pope Alexander IV renewed these censures particularly throughout France.[50] It cannot be said that the decretal of Alexander and the prohibition of Boniface were something new in France. For the learned

---

[48] Defen Declaration. Cler. Gallic. T. 1, p. 2, book 7 c. 23 pag. 286, col. 2, in fin.   [49] Sext. Decr. de Eccl. immuni. Cap. *Non minus,* and under the same title cap. Adversus.   [50] Ib. Lib 3, tit. 23, cap. 1.

Tomassinus [51] with the clearest proof declares that never had the kings of France in the excess of their power wrested anything from the clergy, without the permission of the Pope and in the case of supreme necessity. Therefore the present Constitution was not new, nor was it issued particularly against Philip; it was not untimely in those ages when the princes, and especially the French king, the shameful debaser of the coins, were unrestrainedly usurping ecclesiastical property; it was not importunate inasmuch as these canons had been generally received in the Christian kingdoms, and especially in France. And let the reader remember that the rights of the Church in those times were strong and vigorous, and not like to-day adjusted to the times by a Concordat which a discreet fear prefers to something worse; and for this reason to judge the facts of that age the reader must abstract from present conditions, and so will not wonder that Boniface in this Constitution made the thunder of censures resound in the ears of kings and Emperors.

Although in the said decretal there was nothing singular, or any departure from the usual forms with which the Popes always clothed their decrees, and there was not one syllable that pointed expressly to France, yet it raised the greatest storm in the court of Philip. A hornet's nest of courtier doctors gathered round the haughty prince, complaining hypocritically of Papal tyranny which they declared lay hidden in this decretal of Boniface. And they pretended they were busily striving to retain on his head the royal crown, of which, as they wickedly affirmed, the ambitious Pope wished to deprive him. Everyone knows how quickly the mind of a beguiled prince is prevailed upon when he is urged by flatterers to that to which he is inclined. Philip, haughty of spirit and touched to the quick, when he saw the abundant source of wealth from the patrimony of the churches was closed to him, flew into a passion, and published an edict forbidding both the laity and the clerics, his subjects, to send money out of the kingdom, even to the Holy See for pious reasons. He could pass laws relating to the goods of laymen, and also to those of the clerics, over whom, as vassals, he as prince

---

[51] Tomassinus De vet. et nov. Eccl. discipl in Benef. par. 3. lib. 1, cap. 43 n. 9. in fin.

could exercise his power; but tithes, the offerings, and private goods which the faithful had left to the churches for the good of their souls, he could not touch, nor even desire. In those times there did not exist those rights called " Regalia "; and the prince according to the canons, which were accepted by all, enjoyed no other privilege but that of guarding the vacant benefices, preserving their revenue for the successor, and (when the title was of royal patronage) choosing the person to fill the vacancy. Now the law forbidding the donation of money from the revenue of the churches, was an open violation of the canons which forbade laymen intruding themselves in the administration and the expenditure of the sacred revenues; and was a tyrannical destruction of ecclesiastical liberty. Nay more, this edict savored of downright robbery. Engaged in church service there were many French beneficiaries residing outside of the kingdom, and the annual stipend was held back from these, as they could not receive it on account of the royal edict. The first among these beneficiaries was the Pope himself, to whom from France came the offerings which the pious faithful gave for the recovery of the Holy Land, and also the revenues from the benefices which belonged to the Holy See. Therefore this edict was unjust and outrageous to the Pontiff.

Let us observe the conduct of Boniface, who was reputed to be a most proud man, and prone to anger. He certainly could not wish evil to the family of France, without endangering his own interests thereby; and the constancy with which he upheld the fortunes of Charles of Anjou in the kingdom of Naples, and the many things he did for the benefit of Philip, are certain arguments which go to prove, that like his predecessors, in the struggles of the Italian factions, he made use of the royal house of France as a prop for his throne. In fact so far removed from his thought was king Philip when he wrote the Constitution about ecclesiastical immunities, that at that very time he was revolving schemes to advance the interests of that king. On the same day the 18th of August, on which he published the Constitution, he wrote to Philip imploring him to send to Rome Charles of Valois, his brother, that they might consult together on important and secret matters. It was rumored, as Spondano [52] asserts, that the interview concerned the elevation of Charles as Roman Emperor, that he might lead the expedition for the relief of the Holy Land. Finally Boniface published the celebrated Bull "Ineffabilis" [53] as a reply to the insolent edict. This Bull was couched in terms of the noblest indulgence and most touching kindness. "The time is ill-suited," wrote the Pope, " to the provocation of a dispute with the " Vicar of Jesus Christ, since from the moment of our " accession we have not ceased to watch with heart-felt " earnestness over your interests, and endeavored to effect " an honorable reconciliation between France and Eng- " land. We have not decreed that ecclesiastics should not " contribute to the defense and wants of the kingdom, but " that our leave is necessary in such subsidies, in order to " put a stop to the unbearable exactions of your agents " over the clergy. In cases of need we would rather sell " the sacred vessels and crosses of the churches than ex- " pose to the least a kingdom such as France, always so dear and so devoted to the Holy See." These noble words were powerless with Philip; his pride would yield to no concession.

We do not find that the French clergy exulted over the publication of this constitution which defended their liberty against the preponderance of Philip, nor that they were distressed because of his impertinence to the Pontiff. In England, on the contrary, we find that both the one and the other sentiment were manifested by the clergy under the leadership of the brave Robert of Winchelsea, who had succeeded not only to the chair of the martyred St. Thomas à Becket, but also to that manly valor which prevails only in the sanctuary of Faith. He had received the constitution of which we speak; and he addressed a letter to Richard, Bishop of London, dated the 5th of January of this same year 1296, in which he transcribed the entire constitution " Clericis ", and the words of the two legates, Cardinals of Palestrina and Albano, commanding the same to be promulgated immediately.[54] Moreover in another letter

---

[52] Ad an 1296. n. 2.   [53] See Bull at end of the work
[54] Concil. Magnae Britanniae et. Hiberniae, Vol II, pag 224 . . . . patenter ac diligenter in omnibus exequamini, sue exequi faciatis, et ea

dated the 17th of February of this same year he began by stating that the ancient custom of the Church was to pronounce excommunication against the violators of her liberty, and he confirmed the same according to the recent constitution of Boniface. Less obstinate in wrong doing than Philip, Edward of England surpassed him in his brutality to the clergy. Having brought to a successful termination the war against John Baliol of Scotland, and being on the point of declaring war against Philip, he oppressed the churches with heavy exactions. He did not obey the constitution "Clericis Laicos", and began to object and fume more furiously than Philip. He demanded money from the clergy and was positively refused. The threats of Boniface deterred them. Then when the allotted time, which had been given to the clergy wherein they were to decide, had passed, and they still refused to comply with the request of Edward, in the most ruthless manner he sealed up the doors of the clerical granary. In return Robert, Archbishop of Canterbury, ordered that, as long as he had affixed the royal seals to their granaries, they should publish the constitution of Boniface in all the cathedral churches. And inasmuch as it was necessary to strengthen the minds in their just resolutions, and to display a strong and united resistance, he summoned a council of all his suffragans to meet in St. Paul's Church, London. The convocation met on "Laetare" Sunday. Edward became alarmed, and before they began their deliberation he wrote to the assembled prelates forbidding them under the severest threats to proceed to any measure prejudicial to the rights of the crown, or to pronounce any censure against persons employed in the king's service, or such as had already submitted to his will.[55] For eight days, discussion was held on the royal petition, when of one accord the recent ordinances of Boniface were upheld. There was no entertainment of the contrary opinion of

singula, quatenus ad vos pertinent, observetis ac faciatis inviolabıleta observari."

[55] Ibidem —" Nous defendons a vous touz et a chascun devous . . . . ne nul de vous nulz choses ne ordeins, ne facies, ne assente a nul ordenance a la dit assemble, qui puissont turner a prejudice ou a grievance de nous ou de nul nos ministrers, on de ceus, que sont a nostre peax, et a nostre foy, et a nostre pretection, ou de nos adherents, ou a nul d'eux,"

the clerical courtiers and curials, who unmindful of their high dignity and their sacred office, had been the counsellors and abettors of the king in his impious cupidity; when they departed their consciences were laden with these dry words of the Archbishop: " Let each one attend to the salvation of his soul." The decision of the Council was brought to the King by certain bishops and other messengers, and the knowledge of it made him furious. Hardly had he seen the bishops coming than he licensed his courtiers to unhorse them, and seize upon their horses. He forbade all lawyers to plead for the clergy before any tribunal whatsoever. He broke out into open war against them; and with a semblance of a real thief he commanded the ordained clergy either to cede to him a fifth part of their revenues, or pay the penalty for their contempt of the royal authority. And he spoke the truth, for with the exception of certain weak prelates who accorded to the demands of the king, the others remained resolute and all their real and personal property was confiscated. In order that the royal pleasure might go into immediate effect, the sacred property was put up at auction; thus the sacrilegious buyers might delay in taking possession of it. So much with regard to their property. Neither were the persons of the clergy secure. The King having allowed the soldiers to injure the clergy, the latter never dared to ride singly, but together in a great number.[56] But Robert, Archbishop of Canterbury, was an almost incredible example of Christian constancy. On him more than others the king vented his fury, and he more than others by an invincible fortitude withstood the anger of the powerful monarch. He was deprived of all his possessions, abandoned by his servants, driven from his home, and every friendly door closed against him by royal command; the illustrious prelate led a miserable life, begging a morsel of bread and a place to rest. He endured all this invincibly for the liberty of the Church. Would that there had been many similar prelates to support the arm of Boniface in his laborious administration of the Christian Church for their own good and that of the faithful.[57] And behold, a scandalous persecution in the English

[56] Henry Knighton. Can. Leveest. de Event. Angliae Lib 3 cap V. col. 2492.   [57] Westmonast. Flor. Hist anno 1296.

Church, the like of which would not have happened in pagan times. Now the reader can learn what sort of people Boniface had to deal with, and let him reflect if to the fetters of excommunication some other punishment could reasonably have been added. Afterwards as we shall relate, Edward repented of his evil deeds, but Philip never gave this consolation to the Church.

Even in Germany we find that the constitution which was offensive to Philip was reverently received and promulgated. In the collection of the councils of Germany compiled by John Frederick Schannat we read, that at the synod of Cambrai the Constitution of Boniface was ordered to be read in the vernacular four times a year to the people.[58]

These acts of open violence afflicted Boniface, and whilst his heart was grieved thereby, his care and anxiety for the internal order of the Church, and for the extinction of error, were not diminished. The actions of certain bad men did not escape his vigilance, who under the false garb of evangelical perfection were spreading themselves like a pestilence to poison weak and uncultured minds. In this century the Franciscan Order was a great help to the Roman See, and there is no doubt that in the stormy Pontificates of Gregory VII and Innocent III, it was a singular bulwark. It was yet in a flourishing condition, but just as in a healthy body sickly humors are engendered, so in this Order still young, wicked men were begotten and emanated from it. Corruption of heart and pride of spirit are the first causes of human folly and wickedness. The depravity of certain friars of St. Francis was the result of these. The Order had hardly existed for a century as yet, and already some of its members were descending from the height of perfect evangelical poverty. This fact aroused the zeal of certain friars, who holding tenaciously to the observance of the rule of their founder, began to separate themselves from the others as pure observers of it. The chief one among these was said to be Friar Peter John Oliva, concerning whom there is a differ-

[58] Item constitutionem SS. Patris Domini Bonifacii VIII. Eodem Modo praecipimus ab omnibus presbyteris, vel eorum vices gerentibus, saltem quater in anno in facie Ecclesiarum suarum in lingua materna nunciari et exponi. Tom. IV, p. 84.

ence of opinion. Some considered him a heretic, while others revered him as a Saint. He was born at Serignan in the diocese of Beziers, and entered the Franciscan Order at the age of twelve years. Thus having been early educated in the severe discipline of that order, he conceived the highest esteem for the rigid poverty of St. Francis; and since his fellow friars began to relax in the observance of this evangelical virtue, he took it upon himself to retain them in the ancient observance. Sharp-witted, and so well versed in the sacred science as to merit the degree of bachelor in the Paris University, he strongly censured by word and writing the departure from the rule of St. Francis in that matter which he considered the only ladder by which Heaven could be reached. As usual, some, though few, ardently followed him; whereas the other friars opposed him. Whether his impetuosity for reform led him into errors, or his opponents maliciously accused him of the same, we know not. Wading[59] cleanses him from all stain, and venerates him as St. Oliva; but Pope John XXII condemned his commentaries on the Book of the Apocalypse as baneful and teeming with heresies.[60] It is true that John, Canon of St. Victor, and Bernard Guido in the life of Pope John XXII agree in asserting that Oliva was the head of the Beguini.[61] St. Antoninus,[62] and Nicholas Eymerich[63] state the same. About the year 1278 he wrote the offensive commentary on the Apocalypse;[64] and therefore Oliva preceded other zealous Italian friars who caused a schism in the Seraphic Order through love of poverty, namely Conrad of Offida, Peter of Monticolo, Thomas of Treviso, Conrad of Spoleto, and Jacopone of

[59] Annal. Min. T. 2 ad annos 1282-1292-1297.

[60] John St. Victor, Vita Joan XXII apud Baluz Vitae Papar. Avenion. col 117.—Bernar. Guid. ap. Baluz ib. Col. 140. 167

[61] "Habuit autem ortum haec haeresis ex doctrina cujusdam fratris minoris, qui Petrus Joannis Biterrensis dicebatur, qui quandam postillam composuit super Apocalysim . . . . Joannes St. Victor ib.— Condemnavit quamdam pestiferam postillam fratris Petri Joannis de Serinhano dioecesis Biterrensis de ordine fratrum minorum . . . . . . a qua sumebat fomentum secta illa pestifera illorum, qui Beguini vulgariter, qui se fratres pauperes de tertio ordine S. Francisci communiter nominabant. . . . ." Bernard Guido ib.

[62] P. E. tit. 24, c. 9. q II.   [63] Direct Inquis. par. 2. quaest. 15.

[64] Oudin, Comment. de script. Eccl. Tom. III, sec. XIII. Col. 586.

Todi. It can be inferred that like Oliva in France, these latter in Italy, gave without meaning it, a beginning to the Fraticelli (the little friars). These friars laid aside the yoke of obedience imposed on them by their superiors; they separated from their brethren and went about preaching to the people a doctrine inspired by an evil mind and a heart without charity. It was rather the tares than the grain that they sowed.[65] The watchful eyes of the Pontiffs, fearing the worst, were on these wilful beings. St. Celestine was Pope at this time, and they both knew his weakness and understood how to profit by it. They sent two of their fellow friars Liberatus and Peter of Macerata to Celestine, beseeching him to allow them to live according to the rule of St. Francis in all its vigor, free from contradiction and free to choose any dwelling they saw fit. Celestine granted their request, and wished them to call themselves no longer Friars Minor, but Poor Hermits, or Celestine recluses. The bad fruits of these zealots were not slow in manifesting themselves. They transformed themselves into a sect at the head of which in Italy, were Peter of Macerata, and Peter of Fossombrone,[66] being called Fraticelli, Spiritual Friars, and also Beguardi, and Beguini. Their number was increased by the outcasts of monasteries, by malcontent and apostate friars, who were scandalized by the license given by Pontiffs to certain Franciscans, afterwards called Conventuals, to possess property. These sectaries begun by denying the right of the Pope to interpret the rule of St. Francis declaring the Pontifical power had ceased, and that the priesthood and the true Church were to be found only among themselves.[67] Poverty of life, a certain apparent austerity of morals so deceived many as to influence them to follow these fanatics; and even the women flocked to them. The subsequent actions of this abnormal assembly of friars and women are well told in the Constitution of Boniface, who no sooner learned of their deeds, than he visited on them all the force of the Papal authority. The Constitution declares that these headstrong men and women without any sacred mission, venture to forgive and retain sin; to hold

---

[65] Wading annal. ord. Min. anno 1317.
[66] Giordano MS. Vaticano n 1960; Baronio Sylva MS. p. 400. apud Raynaldum.   [67] S. Antoninus 3. par. tit. 24 cap. 9 q II.

daily and nightly conventicles to be instructed in those errors which afterwards they are to disseminate; to impose hands with the belief of communicating the Holy Spirit; that they are to show reverence to God alone; that they maintain the most efficacious prayers are those made whilst the body is in a state of nudity; that they condemn manual labor as a means of support; that it is lawful for women to indulge in betrothals with other women; and that men shamelessly naked may expose themselves to the gaze of women. Boniface declared them heretics, ordered the prelates to seek these wretches; and he wished also to revive in all their vigor against them those civil laws which the Emperor Frederick had proclaimed against heretics.[58]

We would not prolong the description of this impure sect, were it not that from their history much light is thrown on the motives of the dark portraits left us by the writers of this age of Pope Boniface, and why his name has been handed down to us loaded with petulant infamy. The heresies which harassed the Church in the thirteenth century, and which we may collate under that of the Albigenses, were founded on a certain mystical theology derived from the Manicheans, which the French first learned through their association with these heretics in their various crusades in the Holy Land. These baneful theories taken from the East, became visible in the West under those forms to which the temper of the public mind more inclined owing to the condition of the Roman Pontificate. In these times the Papacy, by its supremacy over the civil power and by its great wealth, was at the summit of its grandeur. Wherefore hatred for the political authority of the Church, love of most austere poverty, and obedience to God alone were preceded by the Petrobusian and Henrician[69] heretics, and into them was fused the sect of the Albigenses, a terrible and a much combated heresy. It is evident that these bodies of men wished to reform the Church, and under the name of reformers they disturbed both state and Church. In this respect they resembled the later reformers of Germany; but the times being dark, civilization youthful, and minds unrefined, they differed from them in that they indulged in filthy and brutal prac-

[58] Bull "Nuper ad audientiam". Bernin, sec XIII. cap. XVI p. 410.
[69] Bernini. History of heresy, sec. XII cap. 10 Tom. 3 p. 224.

tices.[70] So strongly were the minds of the Waldenses possessed of contempt for worldly things and love for poverty, that they even called themselves the Poor Men of Lyons and the Mortified. Princes and Popes with all their power and strength fought the Albigenses; and everyone knows what trouble they gave during the pontificate of Innocent III. But the fury of the just persecution, and the death of their protector, John Count of Toulouse, were the cause of their rapid spread in many parts of Europe, especially in Italy, namely Piedmont, Sicily, Apulia and even in Rome and its environs.[71] Gregory IX pursued them with great ardor, and even imprisoned some of them in Monte Casino.[72] As these heretics led by an evil spirit were proclaiming reform and were striving to effect the same in themselves by their cynical poverty and contempt for all earthly goods, so St. Francis led by the spirit God, as an antidote for the decline of the monastic orders, practised poverty which their riches forbade. The Friars Minor and the heretics at this epoch had one common object; the former tended to it by sanctity, the latter by rebellion. For which reason, if there was dissension in a body of the friars, those who caused the disorder and became wicked could necessarily border on heresy without leaving the community. And just as heretics are ever in bad repute, and as no monk though sharing their sentiments would wish to be contaminated by association with them, so it could happen that rebellious friars, persevering in their obstinacy could institute a new distinctive sect, different in name from those mentioned above but the same in nature. This is the reason why there is such disagreement among writers concerning the true founder of the sect of the Fraticelli, since it was not instituted by a man, but was founded on a fact. This fact was the dissensions created in the Franciscan Order by those over-zealous friars, who, scandalized because the primitive severity of rule was relaxed, rebelled against their legitimate superiors, and proud of being the true sons of St. Francis, they left their monasteries, apostatizing or instituting new societies. These exiles untractable to their superiors and to the Popes secured the protection of Pope Celestine V, as

---

[70] Benoist History of the Albigensian heresy Book I. [71] Benoist. History of the Waldensians. [72] Richard a St. Germain. Chron. year 1251.

we have seen, and already in 1296 there was in Palestrina a monastery of these Celestine Hermits, or Franciscans of strict observance, among whom was Friar Jacopone of Todi.[73] When Pope Boniface withdrew all the privileges of his predecessor and these hermits were suppressed, they began to bear resentment against Boniface, as we shall see when we shall speak of Jacopone. The other zealots among the friars devoted themselves to preaching dangerous and faulty doctrine, and to the formation of a sect, which was called the Fraticelli, (the Little Brothers), as it were the more humble friars; and the Brothers of the free Spirit, signifying that they were free to practise perfect poverty without any opposition; in Italy, France, Germany and Flanders they are known also by other names, which always indicated some virtue of St. Francis travestied and disfigured by them. In fact that shameful act of appearing naked, and declaring that the best prayers are those said while in that state, were a corrupt reminiscence, a parody of the action attributed to St. Francis, who through humility went out naked into the street to preach with Friar Juniper.[74] So although the Irish Franciscan Anthony Hickey, highly praised by Wading,[75] exerted himself strenuously to prove in a book entitled [76] "Nitela Franciscanae Religionis," that no Franciscan was the founder of the Fraticelli sect, yet we must admit that the revolt of these zealous, but unruly and disobedient friars, gave rise to this heresy.

Now the schism having arisen in the Franciscan Order, it begot two kinds of enemies for Boniface, the devotees, or Celestine Hermits, and the Fraticelli. The enmity of the first to Boniface was personal, because he compelled them to discontinue their singular and dangerous manner of living; and the enmity of the others was directed against the Papacy, because it pursued them vigorously, and declared them extinct.[77] The former, reputed as per-

---

[73] Marini. Memor. of Palestrina year 1294.   [74] Fioretti di S. Franc. (Flosculi)   [75] The writers of the Franciscan Order page 13, Roman edition, 1630.   [76] Lyons 1627. sumpt. Claude Landry.

[77] St. Antoninus Chron Par. 3 tit. 21 c 5, & I " Constituentes sibi Papam, vel potius Antichristum, Episcopos et sacerdotes, etc." And Sander, Hersey 180 declares them to say: "Nullum fuisse Pontificem vere Vicarium Christi, nisi eos qui paupertatem Christi imitati sunt. For that

fect friars by the people in general, had supreme sway over them; and the latter had the same power over the large number of their followers and abettors. Vile slanderers of Boniface, they found a reason for their slanders that doubt which was cast over the legitimacy of his elevation to the Papacy, on account of the peculiar abdication of Pope Celestine; and they succeeded marvellously in converting into a certainty that which was pending in the changeable minds of the people. And if Boniface had such formidable enemies, they were these insolent friars and those impure Fraticelli, who aroused public opinion against Boniface in the very beginning of his Pontificate, being urged on by the Ghibellines, in the same manner those seditions Colonnas incited against Boniface the higher classes of cities and courts, of whom we shall speak later. Therefore it is no wonder that the name of this Pope had been handed down to us loaded with such infamy, since he has not had time to triumph over the false opinions, and be presented in his true character.

From these details it appears to us that these imprudently zealous friars, who called themselves Celestine Hermits should be carefully distinguished from the heretical Fraticelli. We say this because we do not wish to bring disgrace on the blessed memory of Friar Jacopone, who was one of the former, and of whom it may be well for us to say something, inasmuch as he was one of the greatest and most powerful enemies of Boniface. Jacopo, or James, afterwards called Jacopone in derision, was born in the city of Todi, of the noble family Benedettoni. Well educated in the science of law, he adopted the profession of a lawyer, and being very skilful in legal proceedings, he became very famous, and was much sought after. In fact he enjoyed to the full the favors of fortune and the pleasures of this miserable world. He espoused a young lady, who by nobility of race and perfection of mind and body, was in herself of priceless worth; but to him also she was truly a treasure for the betterment of his soul. But although she was wont to appear outwardly

reason they declared themselves the only true poor of Christ, and five Fraticelli priests and thirteen Beguins created Pope a certain Friar from Province Dodecis.—Bernini, History of the Heresies of the XIII century, chapter XVI Tom. 3, page 409.

a woman of the world so as not to displease Jacopone who was all engrossed in worldly things, yet she bore in her bosom a heart entirely devoted to God. Now it happened one day that being invited by some ladies to go to an entertainment, to please her husband she consented; but secretly she resolved to avoid certain pitfalls, which are always to be feared by virtuous matrons under such circumstances. And lo! when the entertainment was at its height, the floor suddenly gave way and there was not one among that group of matrons who was not seriously injured and unconscious. At the sad news Jacopone hurried to the spot and found his wife. She was not dead; she still breathed. Hoping to revive her he began to loosen her clothing; she resisted with her hands, though she could not speak; she did not wish to be exposed to public view. Then raising her in his arms he bore her to a room near by, and removing the rich garments he found she wore underneath a rough hairshirt. This sight, together with the death of his beloved wife filled the afflicted mind of Jacopone with such a vivid realization of the transitory nature of all earthly things, that he almost lost his senses. Then comforted by the example of his holy wife, he gave himself wholly to God; and as formerly he had eagerly sought for bodily pleasures and for human applause, he now determined to chastise his body and to accept all contempt in order to stifle within him the lust for vainglory. So intent was his mind on this resolution, that dispossessing himself of his goods, he gave them to the poor and went on the streets feigning himself a fool for the love of Christ; for which he was mocked and derided by children, and from that time he was no longer called Jacopo (James) but Jacopone (silly James). At one time he appeared to the populace assembled for a public exhibition, nude to the waist, walking on all fours, with a bit in his mouth and a saddle on his back like a horse. On another occasion after besmearing his naked body with honey and then rolling in feathers so as to cover his entire body with them, he suddenly rushed in like a wild beast among a company of nobles celebrating the nuptials of his niece; they admiring his humility could not but believe he was a saint, and not a madman.[78] He entered the Order of St.

[78] Wading Annals of Friars Minor Vol. 3, pages 408, 409.

Francis, and to convince the friars that he was not really foolish, he wrote and delivered a treatise on contempt of the world, which proved that he was in his right mind. He suffered much from the friars and bore it all for the love of God. He had a fiery soul capable of great affection. His mind was acute, and his imagination lively. In a word he was a man who, if he had lived in the time of the Council of Clermont, could by himself have aroused a Crusade. Hence his poems are fervent though crude; his verses are harsh and irreverent, and his ascetical works are mystical and at times obscure. Hitherto Jacopone had been acknowledged a good friar and one of the founders of the Italian language, but from a close inspection of his writings, it seems to us that he was among that number of distinguished men who solemnly gave expression to our Catholic religion in those first movements of an age advancing in civilization. St. Thomas, preeminent for his angelic intellect; Dante for his creative power of imagination; Giotto and Blessed Angelico for their knowledge of the beautiful, who transcending the roughness of forms appeared more heavenly than earthly; and Jacopone for his warm language of the heart, had forcibly and simply outlined religion for future ages, and had shown it could be the mother of wonders, when the mind and its conceptions were vivified by our holy religion. Having spoken of Jacopone, we shall now return to the stormy times of Boniface.

A people who has just been delivered from a hateful subjection is always high-spirited and courageous; unity of sentiment adds strength, and the fear of the evil from which they escaped gives constancy. And such were the Sicilians; in the transports of a liberty they believed they had found, they desired, more than Frederick himself, the preservation of his crown, which to him too was so dear. Their army was very powerful, because like members closely united in the same body, prince and people had but one heart, but one arm, but one impulse to repel the common enemy; and besides they were skilfully led; Roger of Loria, the first captain of the age in the knowledge of the war was still in the service of Frederick. To oppose the Sicilians Charles II did not have a people who like them were aroused by hope or fear; Boniface having exhausted against the enemy the spiritual arms, which they despised, had no one else to depend on but James of Aragon. The affairs of Charles were in a bad condition, and the Pontiff was vainly pressing James to come to Italy. Annoyed by troubles in Murcia and Castile, and deterred by the perplexity of the situation in which he was placed, on the one hand by the offers of Boniface, and on the other by the great advantage it would be to Aragon to maintain Frederick on the throne of Sicily, James could not come to a decision. We do not say that some interior voice of relationship restrained him from waging war on Frederick, for this voice to a mind inured to the ever present desires of unrestrained ambition is like a gentle zephyr directed against a rock. However, although he did not appear in Italy, still secretly and by embassies he advised his brother to leave Sicily and the Sicilians to withdraw their support from him. From the beginning of the autumn of 1296 Friar Peter of Corbelles, a Dominican monk, was sent as legate by James to Frederick, bearing mild and harsh messages; namely urged the king to make peace with Mother Church, who had so exalted the house of Aragon by creating James the Standard Bearer and Admiral; to agree to an interview with his brother in the island of Ischia; to follow his advice, for if he remained obstinate, a sign from the Pope would suffice to declare war, and make it terribly effective against the enemies of the Holy See. The nobles who surrounded the young king looked dubiously upon the project of an interview with his brother, to which opinion Frederick also agreed. He dismissed the legate, and submitted the matter to a parliament which he summoned to meet in Piazza.[79]

Friar Peter had come openly as a messenger, others came with a secret mission to tempt the scornful mind of Roger of Loria and the maternal heart of Constance. Other private envoys had been sent to Frederick and to the principal cities of the Island, but they accomplished nothing; yet it was more than a victory to have disengaged Roger from Frederick and to have converted Constance to the side of Rome. In the parliament of Piazza as soon as the propositions of James were disclosed, they were

---

[79] Special. Book 3, chaps 12, 13, 14

rejected, and the departure of Frederick would not be entertained. The contrary opinion of Roger of Loria did nothing more than to conform them in their opinion, that he was already wholly devoted to Aragon.

The winter having passed in useless discussion, towards the end of March the expected James of Aragon finally arrived in Rome. He came full of hopes, as Boniface had enticed him by munificent promises. Boniface received him cordially; his welcome was a magnificent one. The arrival of the king in Rome brought also Charles II of Naples, and the good Constance, the last descendant of the House of Suabia, whose heart must have been divided, seeing herself situated between her two beloved sons bent upon waging a war against each other. There appeared also those two famous men, John of Procida and Roger of Loria. Having left the service of Frederick, they came to Rome to bow their proud heads to Boniface, who removed the censures they had incurred. Frederick also was invited but he refused to come. It was a great meeting of distinguished persons, and great was the matter they were called upon to discuss. Boniface rejoiced when he saw at his feet the father of the Sicilian revolution, and the terrible Roger of Loria who confirmed it by his valor. He beheld Constance who was mother, and he made use of her maternal influence to move the hearts of James and Frederick. He beheld the Aragonese and Angevine princes, and with all the strength of the Papal power he endeavored to urge and enjoin them to reconquer Sicily for the Church. He opened his mind to those assembled. The hatred between France and Aragon was of long standing. The Aragonese prince was the one who had received the crown of Sicily after the bloody Vespers. Boniface in the first place wished to reconcile James with Charles by a relationship by marriage. Jolanda, the sister of James, was given in marriage to Robert, the son of Charles. Royal nuptials, and equally magnificent royal feastings were celebrated in the Papal palace. Then they proceeded to more important affairs; and the Pontiff dealt generously with James by bestowing all manner of favors on him.

On the last day of December, 1296,[80] he had addressed

[80] Raynaldus year 1297 no. 2 and following.

to him letters expressing certain projects which he had formed in his favor and which were to go into effect in this year, James being present. It was a magnificent treaty, which Surita also relates,[81] by which James was to become king over other lands, and more closely united, and as it were, one with the Pontiff. This is the substance of it. The Popes claimed Corsica and Sardinia as belonging to them. This claim, however, was disputed in the year 1238, when Frederick II made his illegitimate son Enzio king of those islands, espousing him to Adelaide, the heiress of the two domains of Torre and Gallura. Rome protested vehemently, yet Sardinia was not detached from the Empire. But Rudolph, King of the Romans, in the year 1275, wishing to be anointed and crowned Emperor by Pope Gregory X, presented himself to him in the church of Lausanne,[82] and promised under a solemn oath to restore to the Church the Romagna and the exarchate of Ravenna, to defend her claim to Sicily, to respect her rights, to be most obedient to her, and finally he acknowledged in the same solemn manner her dominion not only over Sicily, but also over Sardinia and Corsica.[83] Therefore without difficulty Boniface could dispose of these islands in the present year, and he solemnly invested James and his descendants with the golden cup (*per cuppam auream*). The conditions on which the king bound himself to Rome were: that he was to pay homage to the Church as her vassal; to maintain in Italy at his own expense in the service of the Pope one hundred well equipped knights, each one having besides an armored horse at least two other animals to ride; five hundred foot soldiers well provided with arms, of whom a hundred at least should be archers, all to be either Catalans, or Aragonese; and their service was to last three months, counting the time from the day on which they set foot in Italy. And in case there would be need of a fleet instead of an army, he could require instead of the soldiers five

---

[81] Surita. An. Book 2. [82] Annals. Colmar. year 1275—Ptolemy of Lucca. Church History, book 13, chap 4.

[83] "Adjutores erimus ad retinendum et defendendum Ecclesiae Romanae Regnum Siciliae cum omnibus ad eam spectatibus, tum citra farum, quam ultra, necnon Corsicam et Sardiniam, ac caetera jura quae ad eam pertinere noscuntur." Raynaldus year 1275 no. 38.

galleys well equipped with men and ammunition; whether the force was to be a land or naval one, the king would be obliged to send it at once at a command from the Pope every year for a three-months service. He and his successors were to pay forever to the Pope an annual tribute of two thousand silver marks of good and honest money. He or any heir delaying or refusing to pay, the following punishment was without delay to be inflicted: the Prince would be excommunicated, then an interdict would be placed on the kingdom, and finally he would be deprived of his fief. Sardinia was never to be separated from Aragon; and if the king should become Emperor of Germany, it was to revert immediately to the Church. The king was to preserve the liberty and the immunities of the new kingdom; he was not to close the way of appeal to the Papal Curia; he was not to tax the churches; he was not to interfere in the election of bishops; upon the discovery of laws detrimental to the Church he was to annul them; he was not to think of taking any office in Rome, or in any territory whatsoever subject to the Roman See; he was to acknowledge always that Sardinia came to him in fief through the liberality of the Pope; and he was to understand that any doubt arising regarding his new possessions was to be solved exclusively by the Pope. Finally Boniface bound James by a solemn oath to observe the said conditions, and the king whoever he might be should renew them to each new Pontiff.

It was thus that Boniface enlarged the power of James, and stipulated that he was not to overstep the limits marked out. It was a wise provision to reserve the return of Sardinia to the Holy See in case the king should ever become Emperor. For the presence of an emperor, already powerful in Germany, would appear improper and as well full of dangers in an island close to Italy. Besides, by prohibiting James and his descendants, in their quality as kings of Sardinia, from holding any office whatsoever in Rome, and in the Roman territory, he closed the way to a repetition of those very recent ambitious projects of Charles I of Anjou, who was senator of Rome, the dangers and the sad effects of which were too well known to him. In a word, to use a comparison, he caparisoned the horse well, but he held the reins in his own hands to direct him. In fact the subsidies promised by James were certain, since he was to furnish them without conditions; and likewise certain were his obligations regarding Sicily; but the sovereignty over Sardinia was uncertain, not by right but in fact, for before enjoying it, he had to conquer the Pisans.[84] Boniface stipulated by another act that he could withhold the grant of Sardinia until the feast of All Saints.[85] It was clear by this that he wanted to assure himself that James acted sincerely, so that the crown of Sardinia would be suspended over his head. For if he would be a good servant of the Holy See, he was to have the crown, if not, the Pope was to withdraw it. And afterwards if James was victorious over Frederick, the Pope did not care to see Sicily fall again into his hands, for thereby a way would be open to James to negotiate, or to threaten, that the Pope must give up either Sicily or else Sardinia and Corsica. Boniface knew how to draw up a treaty, and how not to lose by it. In this treaty, as well as in the Bull by which he created James Gonfalonier and Admiral of the Holy See, the matter of the Holy Land was mentioned, so that the Pope might seem to have James in readiness only for the liberation of the Holy Sepulcher. Many, following the opinion of Surita,[86] perceive in this provision an artifice of Boniface to draw all attention to the East, whilst his whole mind and efforts were directed towards Sicily. But this was not a secret artifice; he worked openly against Sicily, and so he could not be accused of covert actions. It is true his eyes were turned towards the East, but owing to the unsettled condition of Sicily, his first wish was to obtain possession of that island, and afterwards to attack the Turks, which present and future undertakings he entrusted to James of Aragon, when he made him the champion of the Church. Therefore after all things were settled, each one departed to assume the respective offices to which they were assigned. James went to Catalonia to prepare the army; ranged under the standard of Charles, and contented with lands and the castle of Aci, which the Pope had given him in fief, Roger de Loria went to resume, in the waters of Naples, the sceptre of the

[84] Villani, Book 8, c. 18. [85] Raynaldus, n. 17.
[86] Surita, Annals, book 5, chap 35.

sea;[87] John of Procida, whose lands in the kingdom of Naples were restored to him, remained in Rome with the disconsolate Constance, who is said to have died there. Some others hold that five years later she died in Barcelona, and was buried there in the Franciscan church.

While Boniface was striving to overturn the throne of Frederick, the latter was busy in arousing enemies against him by hidden means. He knew how very powerful the Roman patriciate was, and how troublesome they were always to the Pontiffs. He remembered how turbulent and quarrelsome the Frangipanni were when Henry VIII attacked Rome. He remembered well how devoted the Frangipanni and the Colonnas were to Frederick II in fomenting intestine calamity of the Church. He knew how in times of great danger a mortal blow could be given a Prince by one of his own countrymen. Therefore he set about to ascertain how many of these Roman nobles he could lead over to his cause and urge to assail Boniface. The Gaetani, the Savelli, the Orsini, the Colonna, and other very powerful families, whose towers and castles in the neighborhood of Rome were always offensive and a menace to the Popes, were proud-minded, and ready for every feat of arms, whether in defence of themselves when summoned to justice by the Popes, or when the desire of fame impelled them to break the peace. These barons were avaricious of whatever benefit could be derived from a feudal possession in the Middle Ages. They had vassals who were engaged not in peaceful agricultural pursuits, but in those inglorious and barbarous tournaments. On their roving through the state they became the seducers of the people, whom they made serve as instruments for gaining power or possessions; and they were also hostile to the Popes. Every prince, who was an honest dispenser of justice, could in time of a foreign war shut himself up within the confines of his own state and there quietly and securely observe the course of events; but the Pope, exposed to complications from without, had moreover always reason to fear from those within. In fact this was the reason why Boniface dwelt for a time at Anagni, then at Orvieto, and then at Velletri; he was always on his guard against these powerful forces who could at any

[87] Special. Book 3, chap. 20-21-22.

time, like the wind, arouse the people against him. Among these powerful families, the Colonnas stood preeminent, for on account of the excessive favors heaped upon them by Nicholas IV, a Colonna, they were advanced to the highest offices of the state, and were supported by Peter and James Colonna, Cardinals of Holy Church. But that we may proceed with order to relate the occurrences that passed between Boniface and the Colonnas, it will be well to start from the beginning of the trouble.

In the year 1201 the leading members of the Colonna family were Giordano and Oddone, whom we shall call Oddone II, to distinguish him from others of the same name. They were perhaps sons of Oddone, lord of Palestrina, and they were masters of this place and also of Colonna, Zagarolo, Gallicano, and of the territory of St. Constance and St. John in Camporario, which were inhabited in those days.[88] Giordano had a son Peter, the other had a son called Oddone III. These sons being cousins and enjoying the inheritance conjointly, began to quarrel over their patrimony. In the year 1252,[89] the Prefect of Rome undertook to pacify them, assigning to each one his proper portion; but they were not satisfied, and shamefully renewed the quarrel. Finally a certain John, a Dominican Friar and a relative, was chosen arbiter, and sat in judgment and divided the lands. To Peter he awarded the territory of Gallicano, St. Cesarius, and Camporario; to Oddone that of Palestrina, Capranica, Colonna and other fiefs. This is taken from a document published by Patrini, which was found in the archives of the Constable Colonna. It is evident that the most powerful Colonnas were those of Palestrina, whose head was Oddone III, and it is the deeds of his descendants that shall be subject of our present narrative. Giordano, son of Oddone III, had five sons, the eldest of whom was James, now a Cardinal, the second John, the third Oddone, the fourth Matthew, and the fifth Landolph, and they were the possessors of rich lands, named Palestrina, Mount Capranica, Colonna, Zagarola, besides the half of the villa of Pietraporto, and the estate of Algido. In order to bring things to a peaceful solution these brothers

---

[88] Patrini. Mem Palestrina year 1201, page 132.
[89] Patrini. Mem. Palestrina year 1252, page 135.

by mutual consent appointed James, the Cardinal, administrator of their property in an attested instrument dated the 28th of April, 1252,[90] which Patrini found in the Barberini archives. In the period between 1292 and 1297 John Colonna, the second son, died, leaving his possessions to his six sons, Peter, a Cardinal, Stephen, John, James, nicknamed Sciarra, Oddone, and Agapitus. Now it happened that James the Cardinal, by the authority which his brothers had given him for the administration of the common inheritance, had made himself more than master of it, and uniting the interests of his nephews with those of his own, robbed his brothers of their property and reduced them almost to poverty.[91] Therefore this James, the wicked usurper, and his nephews, the sons of John, were the sole masters of the Colonna fiefs, and for that reason masters of Palestrina also, and were those whom we shall soon see who came to a strife with the present Pontiff.

One can clearly see how and why bad feelings were engendered between Boniface and the Colonnas; and we hardly know what to say about those very divergent opinions of various writers concerning the cause of this quarrel. We know however that a strong attachment to a party is most hostile to the truth of an historical narration. For if the truth be displeasing it is made obscure, it is so distorted that it becomes inaccurate; or it is allowed maliciously to wander in the maze of conjecture, in order that an opinion may be formed according to the writer's wish. Many historians have acted in this manner through malice and many others have blindly followed them in their description of the famous quarrel between Boniface and the Colonnas. Ferrettus of Vicenza, and Pipin, most ardent Ghibellines, whose opinion many others follow who glory in defaming a Pontiff, declare that Boniface fostered in his heart the strongest hatred against the Colonna family, because James and his nephew Peter Colonna, had not given him their votes in his election to the Papacy. On the contrary St. Antoninus [92] relates that the two Colonna Cardinals were the first to give Boniface their votes. This is the true opinion and it is supported

---

[90] See document at end of book.   [91] See document at end of book.
[92] Chronicles. Year 1295, par. 3, title 20.

by a fact. For if from that time an enmity had existed between Boniface and the two Colonnas, the former would not have put himself in the hands of his enemies, when after his election to the Papacy, on his way to Rome, he accepted the hospitality of James at Zagarolo, and James would not have cordially entertained him.[93] Nor is there any proof that a jealousy existed between the Gaetani and the Colonna family in those times, and afterwards tyrannically prosecuted by Boniface. There is no truth in the statement of Benvenuto of Imola, who commenting on the twenty-seventh canto of the Inferno, declares that the fire of hatred between the Colonnas and Boniface was enkindled by the snares that were laid to seduce the wife of James, Sciarra Colonna, by a nephew of Boniface. This villainy of a Gaetani, if there was any truth in it, would not have been passed over in silence by the infuriated Colonnas, at a time when they flooded all Europe with calumnies against Boniface and his family. Their silence on this point proves the falsity of the above statements.

But examining closely the documents of that time, it appears to us, that despite the expressed opinion that the first cause of these terrible differences originated with Boniface, yet from these records it is made clear that the first scandal arose from the Colonnas. And in fact although peaceful and even friendly relations had existed between Boniface and the two Colonna Cardinals, because of the influence they exercised on the other cardinals to elect him Pope, yet among the Colonnas themselves there was a silent war which did not break out in open violence owing to the weakness of one of the parties and the great strength of the other. We have seen how James Colonna, Cardinal of the title of St. Maria in Via Lata, in league with his five nephews, and abusing the confidence placed in him by his brothers, when they confided to him the administration of their patrimony, robbed them of that which he should have preserved, and reduced them to dire poverty. Now these family injustices could not be committed so secretly as to escape the knowledge of Boniface,

---

[93] "Et post electionem . . . . in castro tunc ipsorum (Columnensium) quod Zagarolum dicitur, et quod per dictum Jacobum tunc temporis tenebatur . . . . hospitati fuerimus confidenter. Bull, Raynaldus, year 1297, no. 39.

for the reason that the Colonna family was very prominent, and he was a severe upholder of justice. We know not whether the aggrieved brothers appealed to the Papal Court, but it is certain that the Pope interposed his paternal offices to end the tyranny of the Cardinal and their misery. He decreed that each one should receive his portion of the patrimony; that the administration of it by James should cease; and some assignment, over and above what was due, was to be made to the nephews, so as to dispose them to resign what they had usurped. These commands Boniface made to the Cardinal and his nephews in his presence, but instead of recognizing in these orders the love of justice or the infamy of their injustice, they by no means were disposed to surrender their plunder; and spiteful and furious with rage, they left the presence of the Pontiff, and never again did they see the face of Boniface.[94]

Among the nephews of the angry Cardinal James, there was another James, nicknamed Sciarra (Quarrelsome). He was a man brutal and passionate who perhaps more than others was enraged at seeing the goods of his uncles snatched from him. Breathing vengeance on the Pontiff, who had regulated the matter so justly, and not feeling ashamed, nobleman by birth as he was, to emulate the actions of the most barefaced robber, in company with satellites, who in those times were always at hand for the employ of these violent lords, he lay in wait to steal the rich treasure of the Pope as it was being brought from Anagni to Rome. It consisted of a large sum of gold and silver.[95] The attack was well-timed, for the Papal goods came into his possession and he brought them to his own house. This wicked deed,[96] the truth of which no one

---

[94] Raynaldus, year 1297, no. 26.   [95] Chronicles Foroliv.

[96] . . . . . . "quod Stefanus de Columna suum thesaurum fuerat depredatus; propter quod inter ipsum Bonifacium, et dictos Columnensos summa discordia extitit suscitata" Amalaricus S. R. I. T. 3, p. 435.—" In Rome there was the greatest division and war between Boniface VIII and the Colonnas, because the Colonnas had stolen a rich treasure from the Pope." Chronicles of Bologna S. R. I. T. 18, page 301.—" Eodem anno Columnenses Romani accesserunt et derubaverunt magnum thesaurum auri et argenti Domno Papae Bonifacio.—" Chronic. Estens. tim. 15, page 344—"Nobiles etim de Columna inimicos habebat, contra quos processit, quia Stephanus de Columna ipsius Papae fuerat proedatus thesaurum."—(George Stella, Annals of Genoa, Book 2, tom, 18, p. 1020.)

denies, was done not by a man reduced to desperate straits, nor one who pursued the ways of a highwayman, but by a noble and very rich lord unaccustomed to robbery. Hence revenge, which blinded and covered Colonna with such infamy, prompted him to commit this wicked deed. It is well to remark that the Pope made no mention of this grievous injury in the Bull, " Praeteritorum temporum," [97] where he complains of all the evil deeds of the Colonnas, as it were to show that he minded, not what was done to him privately, but the evil done to the Church.[98]

Wherefore having seen the bad disposition of the two Cardinals, James and his nephew Peter, and of the other nephews, and having been convinced by the robbery at Anagni that this was a family that it would be well not to leave unwatched at a time when through Rome envoys of Frederick of Sicily were roaming intent upon tempting the fidelity of his subjects, Boniface determined to watch them and provide against the consequences. He watched their movements attentively, and saw how well they received the messengers of Frederick, how they fraternized with them and how they favored them. He was unwilling to exasperate them by inflicting condign punishment, and so tried persuasion, entreaty and threats; but they followed their own will, and with the enemies of the Church plotted against her. James of Aragon was far away and was slow of action; Charles of Naples was powerless; the Ghibellines throughout Italy were in commotion as a consequence of the actions of the Sicilians and the machinations of Frederick; the Pontiff was threatened in Rome itself; then Boniface followed a course of action that any prudent man would in similar circumstances. He requested the Cardinals James and Peter Colonna to throw open the gates of Palestrina and Zagarolo, and allow the soldiers of the state to occupy the castles of those strongholds so as to keep out enemies of the Church. This was a very mild request, which any prince had a right to make in times of public danger. The two Cardinals outwardly pretended to accede to the request, but secretly they encouraged and assisted their nephews who answered the

---

[97] See Bull at end of book.
[98] John Villani, Book 8th, chap. 21—Ptolemy of Lucca, Short annals S. R. I. T. XI.—Chronicles Foroliv. S. R. T. Tom. 22.

Papal request with a downright refusal. The mild measures of Boniface having failed to bring the two Cardinals to a right way of acting, their perfidy obliged him to have recourse to severer measures. After mature deliberation he determined to punish them, but at the same time he resolved to go slowly, and wait for developments. He heard that the Colonnas were aroused to indescribable anger, and had vowed the most desperate vengeance on him; that the Cardinal Peter having laid aside all restraint, was eagerly engaged in circulating the invalidity of the abdication of Pope Celestine and hence the invalidity also of his own election to the Papacy. These were poisonous tares which could bring fruit of immense evil to the Church. He feared the sad consequences of a schism, knowing that, by the presence of the enemy Frederick of Sicily, the fury of the Ghibelline party, and the intolerance of the Princes of his rigorous defence of the liberty of the Church, the fuel was well disposed to receive the first sparks of a schism. Still he refrained from punishment. (Observe his moderation and forbearance.) On the fourth day of May he sent John of Palestrina, the major-domo, to Cardinal Peter, to tell him to come on the evening of this same day, to declare in presence of some Cardinals, if he believed him to be truly Pope. Peter perceived that this was evidently to draw him out in order the better to convict him, and he refused to obey.[99] Moreover considering himself unsafe, he departed from Rome with his uncle James and some of his brothers, full of threats and ready to perform wicked deeds. Now was the time to proceed to punishment; his office of Pope and prince demanded it. He held a consistory on the 4th, of May. He made known the faults of the Colonnas, their stubbornness and obduracy to all his admonitions and entreaties; and after taking counsel with the Cardinals, he passed sentence, to wit: that James Colonna, Cardinal of the title of St. Maria in Via Lata, and Peter, of the title of St. Eustachio, Cardinal-Deacons, would be deprived of the dignity of Cardinal, of the priestly office, and would incur solemn excommunication, if at the end of ten days they did not appear before the Papal See and submit to

[99] Histoire du diff. ent. Bonif. VIII et Philip. p. 33. Appendix tom. VIII.

its will; all their real and personal property in the Neapolitan kingdom as well as in the States of the Church would be seized; the descendants of John and Oddone nephews of the Cardinals as far as the fourth generation would be excluded from the priesthood; this same excommunication would be incurred by anyone taking sides with Cardinals James and Peter; and if any one, whether Cardinal or of any other dignity, dared to be their abettor of them in felony and schism, they would be deprived of their office and property; and those countries would be interdicted that would receive them.[100]

To some reader these punishments may seem exceedingly harsh, and he may suppose that calm reason in the mind of the Pope had been displaced by a hasty exuberance of anger. But in the course of this narrative we shall know better what was the true character of the Colonnas. Boniface already fully understood them. His object was not to humble the pride of a Cardinal only, but that of an entire family very powerful and insolent, on account of their great wealth and the strong castles they possessed at the very gates of Rome. Their actions under similar circumstances were still fresh in the memory of the public. It was only seventy years since the perilous felony of another Cardinal of the family, John Colonna, who received in Palestrina a garrison from a prince of Suabia, and had thereby caused much vexation to Pope Gregory IX. From that time, strongly attached as they were to the Ghibelline party, the Colonnas had not changed their spirit. And besides, that scandalous libel they spread among the faithful concerning the validity of the election of Boniface to the Papacy, showed a disposition on their part to plot against the Church.

Having learned of the terrible consistory, the Colonnas on the same day, the tenth of May, convoked a wicked council against the Pope in the Lunghezza, a territory belonging to the Conti family. John of Gallicano, an apostolic writer; Dominic Leonard of Palestrina, a notary; and two Friars Minor, Diodatus Rocci of Mt. Prenestino and Jacopone of Todi, took part in this council. For what reason the former two came to this conventicle, we know not, unless money may have enticed them. We are sur-

[100] Bull of Boniface. Raynaldus, year 1297, no. 27.

prised at Jacopone and the other Friar; but it is not an idle conjecture for us to say that because Boniface would not approve of that new order of Celestine Recluses, of which these friars were members, and to which they were much attached, they were prevailed upon to enter this schismatical company. So in this council the Colonnas, fuming with rage decided that Leonard, the notary, should draw up a document, in which he would declare that Cardinal Colonna had not wished to appear before Boniface through fear of violence; and to the request of the Master of the Camera, he replied that Boniface was not Pope, both because Celestine could not abdicate, and because his abdication had been wrung from him by artifice.[101] Oderic Raynaldus had in his possession this famous libel, which he found in the Avignon archives in the Vatican, and which he published in the appendix to the third volume of his Annals.[102] This document we shall briefly review. The first part contains the greetings of Cardinals James, of the St. Maria in Via Lata, and Peter, of the title of St. Eustachius, to all the readers of this public instrument. Then they begin by referring to Boniface. To the last words of his rescript they frankly reply by declaring that he is not the legitimate Pope. This fact they announce to the college of Cardinals, and they request them to remedy the evil, so that a false Pope, may not usurp the place of Christ, for the Church would thus suffer by an illicit and invalid administration of the Sacraments, which would take place through an illegitimate and false minister. They justify their attitude in the statement: " Many times " we have heard from persons of repute both laymen and

[101] It is well to remark here that the enemies of Boniface either inadvertently or maliciously disarranged the chronology of facts, and said that Boniface was the first to display harshness in the Bull: "Praeteritorum temporum." The Colonnas had already declared Boniface antipope, for which he sent to them his Master of Camera to ascertain the truth of this declaration. The envoy was sent on the 4th of May, and the Bull issued on the Tenth day of May, when after being summoned to appear, they refused, and fled from Rome. Then the Bull was published against them not as criminals, but as contumacious schismatics. They replied to the Bull by the famous Libel. The mind must follow closely the chronology, otherwise the facts change in appearance. In truth if the Bull "Praeteritorum temporum" may seem harsh against rebels, it is not so against schismatics.   [102] Year 1297, no. 34, vers. XI.

"ecclesiastics, a certain doubt with some foundation
"cast [103] upon the abdication made by Pope Celestine V
"of blessed memory, whether it was done legitimately and
"according to the canons. Now it seems most likely it was
"not, because that which is entrusted by God, or any other
"superior personage, cannot be taken away by any infe-
"rior person. And whereas the spiritual power which
"one cannot confer, cannot be removed by him; so the
"papal power conferred by God alone can be taken away
"by God alone. But if the abdication was valid, the papal
"power could be taken away by a man; therefore the ab-
"dication cannot be made.[104]

After syllogizing in this manner closely and carefully in thirteen articles they close the daring discussion by passing judgment on Boniface, declaring him deposed from the Papacy, and appealing to a future Council. The foundation of the argument was the work of both the enraged two Cardinals, but we believe that it was Jacopone who put it in this Aristotelian form. And it is easy to prove how and why the infuriated Colonna framed his argument against the validity of the election of Boniface. The ground of the reasonable doubt (*verosimiliter dubitari*), is to be found in the abdication of Celestine, which they contend could not be made. We do not believe it likely that a doubt entered the mind of anyone through any defect in the manner of election of Boniface, but through the unusual abdication of Celestine. A solemn renunciation of the Papacy was an unheard-of thing. It excited the greatest wonder and engaged the attention of many in those times. Some could not make themselves believe that the dignity almost divine of the Papacy, once assumed, could be relinquished. This difficulty was increased by the followers of Celestine; these monks were holy in the eyes of the people by reason of reform, and therefore of authority. Hence attention was fixed more on Celestine who had left the chair, than Boniface who sat in it. In fact before the Colonnas had engaged in this proud rebellion, we do not find that any one had questioned the validity of the election of Boniface to the Papacy. If any one did so, it was after the two Car-

---

[103] "Dubitari verosimiliter".
[104] See this document in full at the end of this book.—

dinals had drawn attention from Celestine to Boniface; and from the former's abdication, which they said could not be made, they asserted as illegitimate the elevation of the latter to the Roman Pontificate.

It is certain that the Colonna libel was productive of its desired effects. It disturbed weak minds by inspiring doubt; the enemies were delighted, pretending to have certainty. This is clear from the facts which we shall relate, and by the ardor displayed by the most learned canonists in refuting the libel. Peter of the Marches reduced to two heads the objections of the Colonnas, and ably refuted them.[105] John Andrew of Bologna, a famous lawyer, did likewise.[106] Egidius of Colonna, Archbishop of Bourges, with wonderful erudition, and with sound reason defended Boniface against the attacks of the Colonnas.[107] And when he came to the refutation of the false charge, which is contained in the twelfth and last article of the libel, namely that Boniface by artifice induced Celestine to abdication, casting aside every other argument, he appealed to the testimony of the living witnesses, who declared that Cardinal Gactani had urged Celestine to retain the Papacy, instead of renouncing it, alleging that his sanctity of life more than compensated for his ignorance of governing.[108] It may be well to remind the reader that at the time the Colonnas compiled the diabolical libel, Celestine had been dead already one year. Now if Boniface was not the true Pope because of the invalid abdication of Celestine, there could be no longer any doubt as to his claim to the Papacy after the death of his predecessor. And although Boniface might have been a false Pope up to June, 1296, when Celestine died, yet after that time he was true Pope by the consent of the Cardinals and all Christendom, who acknowledged him as such; which acknowledgments meant more than an election. Finally, these two Colonna Cardinals who were present and took part in the election, and who wished to dethrone Boniface, had no other proof for the defence of their position, than to

---

[105] De cause immediata Ecclesiasticae potestatis. Paris 1506.
[106] Lecture on the rules of 6th, book of the Decretals.
[107] De Renunciation Papae, and especially in chapter 23.
[108] . . . . "quia sufficiebat collegio quod nomen suae sanctitatis invocaretur super eos."

say that the abdication of Celestine was null. A poor and weak argument. Now what shall we say to them, and especially of Dante, who irreverently accused Boniface of simony, and of having bought the office of Pope? If there had been any truth to this sacrilegious bargain, the Colonnas would have made use of it as a two-edged sword to wound their adversary, and there would have been no need to weary themselves in forming syllogisms. The sin of simony was sufficient to deprive Boniface of the Keys of Peter which he iniquitously held in his power. In the famous Colonna libel there is no mention of simony.

After having compiled the libel the Colonnas were guilty of an act of most daring insolence, in that they had the base effrontery to affix a copy of the shameful writing not only to the door, but also to the high altar of St. Peter's church.[109] Everyone wondered at such audacity, but no one sanctioned the action of these schismatics. Boniface then took measures against them. On the feast of the Ascension, which in that year fell on the 23rd of May, as there was only one course to pursue, he confirmed the sentence passed upon the Colonnas in the Bull of May 10th, in another that he published which began "Lapis abscissus."[110] In this Bull speaking of that famous libel and the attaching a copy of it to the doors and altar of St. Peter's church, and of the contumacy in retaining the dignity of Cardinal and using the ring and red hat, he briefly mentions his right to the Papacy. He relates how suddenly and without foundation these doubts arose in their minds; how for three years they had been accustomed to obey and respect him as the true Pope; how they had participated with him in the holy mysteries; how they had been his ministers at the altar, his associates in consultation, in counsels, and in solemn definitions; that they had been, in a word, always with him never doubting his true dignity; how with the other Cardinals that had raised him to the Apostolic See, and had done this willingly and without fear, inasmuch as he could not excite fear before he was Pope; and that their good will was shown by the kind and warm reception accorded him at their home, and especially by James in Zagarolo, and all those other

[109] Bull of Boniface. Raynaldus, year 1297—Hist. du Diff. P. 34.
[110] See this Bull at the end of the book.

marks of homage and respect they had shown him as Pope. Then he confiscates all the possessions of James and Peter and the nephews; he banishes them from the state; he forbids any one to receive them, or hold relations with them; he renders them ineligible to public office, and strikes them with the major excommunication. This terrible constitution he placed among the Decretals,[111] as a perpetual reminder of their infamy. Spondano relates, and gives the source of his information,[112] how the College of Cardinals, moved to indignation by the infamous libel, published letters in which they refuted the false charges and certified to the legitimate authority of Boniface.

As the severity of the punishment increased, the minds of the Colonnas became more embittered, and they had recourse to violent measures. They assembled their forces in Palestrina, that Boniface might hear the sounds of arms. And as if that infamous libel did not suffice to give vent to their fury, they published other documents, in which they besmirched the name of Boniface. They accused him of being a monster of ambition, of avarice and of arrogance. They scattered these documents among the people and in the courts of princes. The latter especially read them with much avidity and fondly preserved them. Groaning under the power of the Pope, and impatient to break the yoke, they saw there an arsenal from which they could take arms at an opportune time. The place in which more than any other the news of these affronts was agreeably received was France, a kingdom which Philip ruled absolutely. On account of the Constitution "Clericis Laicos," he was still disdainful, and he felt his courage revive by the disputes which the Doctors of the Sorbonne were holding concerning the legitimacy of Boniface's claim to the Papacy. From the time of the abdication of Celestine, for reasons mentioned before the University was awakened to the fact, and struck by the novelty of it, wished to know for itself if it could be made, and hence if Boniface was really Pope. Certainly no restraint was placed on these Doctors in their debates. For these disputes were of that kind which make no noise, and are even necessary in Academies for practice and employment of

[111] Sixth Decretal, chapter Ad succidendos.
[112] Collect. Archiep. Auxitani Collegii Fuxensis Tolosani fol. 211.

time. The two Colonna Cardinals in the circulation of those libels could not forget the Sorbonne. In fact a letter dated the 15th of June was sent by them containing the aforesaid syllogisms, which if it was read at a meeting of the Doctors [113] must assuredly have occasioned a warm debate, and considering the fact that these academicians were always courtiers, one could unquestionably conclude, that they extolled to the skies this work of the Colonnas. And just as these writings brimful of canonical lore passed into the hands of Princes and Doctors, so as to arouse the more cultured minds, others of a different nature were circulated among the people. Jacopone wrote his verses in the vernacular, by means of which he crudely scored the Pope. In these verses there is much roughness of speech, which arose not only from the fact that the language was yet in its infancy, but also from a certain artifice of the Friar to make it penetrate deeply into the minds of the people. Thus this Celestine recluse who was scrupulous with regard to poverty, rushed headlong to enkindle the fire of schism. Who will ever be able to explain fully and well, the mysteries of that book which is called the human heart? Although Boniface had dealt the Colonnas mortal blows, yet his rest was disturbed by the fear of the Roman People, who, very fickle and controlled by the nobles, could be very troublesome to him. If Saintly Popes had feared and suffered much from the same source, Pope Boniface could not consider himself safe. So he retired to Orvieto. In that place he set about to make provision to subdue the pride of the schismatics with the sword. He enlisted soldiers and gave the command of them to Landolph Colonna, a cousin of the rebels. He joined to his force, Inghirano, Count of Bizenzo with the Florentine soldiers; as is evident from the letter sent by the Pope to Landolph from Orvieto on the 14th of September which Petrini published from the original in the archives of Castle San Angelo.

As soon as the news of these warlike preparations and of the intention of Boniface to fight had spread, the prospective war caused grave apprehensions to arise in the minds of the Romans. Pandolph Savelli, a man of civic virtue was a senator of Rome. This rupture of peaceful

[113] MS in Vatican Archives, Raynaldus.

relations was not pleasing to him. For by reason of the strength of the rebels, and the rigor of the Pope, Rome would have been plunged into the horrors of a civil war. He summoned the senate in council in the Capitol; and having debated the question, they resolved to send messengers to the Colonnas in Palestrina, to induce them to humble themselves, and submit to the Pontiff. It was done accordingly, and they made fair promises. Then envoys were sent to Boniface in Orvieto, bearing witness of the docility of the rebels, and entreating him to allay his anger by restoring to his favor these penitents, and to be willing to return without fear to Rome in the following spring. These things they represented by word of mouth and by letters, to which the cautious Pontiff immediately replied also by letters to the Senator Savelli and the Roman People. " Health and Apostolic Benediction to our be-
" loved son Pandolph Savelli, Senator, and to the Roman
" People who of all others are dearest to our heart. With
" paternal kindness we have received your numerous em-
" bassy, and we have listened attentively to what they
" have brought us by word and letters, namely, how the
" Colonnas being induced by messengers to yield to us,
" have promised to come to us, prepared to obey the com-
" mands of the Roman Church, and how we were entreated
" to pardon them. Holding the place of Him, Who has not
" made death, nor delights in the loss of the living; and
" Who, as often as His wandering children return to Him
" humble and penitent, pardons them; so whenever these
" schismatics and rebels will become repentant, and will
" confess their misdeeds, if they come to us personally
" without delay, and will surrender themselves and their
" castles into our hands, our heart will be open to receive
" them and treat them kindly, that the work of mercy will
" be agreeable to God, honorable to themselves and to the
" Church, and be handed down to posterity as a laudable
" example of clemency. We do not wish in the meantime
" to be led astray and be deceived by fair promises, and
" thus be delayed from proceeding against the rebels and
" their abettors. Most grateful for the request made to
" us to return to Rome in the spring time and to fix our
" dwelling there, let it be known that we love most to
" dwell there where the Apostolic See has been established,

" in which not only during life but also death we wish to
" remain; for we have built in the church of the Prince
" of the Apostles a chapel in which there is a tomb where
" our body will repose. We hold in suspense the question
" of our return until we see if the promises will be ful-
" filled.[114]

But the promises of the Colonnas were only a ruse, and an artifice to gain time. They did not go to meet the Pope, and they were guilty of worse actions. They welcomed to Palestrina, Francis Crescenzi and Nicholas Porri, the envoys of Frederick, the avowed enemies of Boniface, and entered into plots with them against the State. For this reason he published that terrible Bull, in which confirming the former punishments, he proclaimed a crusade against the Colonnas, as against contumacious schismatics and disturbers of the unity of the Church.[115] The inquisitors were ordered to pursue them and their followers; the people were called to arms, and indulgences were promised to those who would respond to this appeal. Matthew Colonna, Provost of the church of St. Omer in the diocese of Maurienne took the cross. The papal indulgences were published throughout Italy by the legate Cardinal Matthew of Acquasparta, who diligently encouraged the people to enter the crusade and subdue the Colonnas.

The deposition, excommunication and the war proclaimed against the two Cardinals of Holy Church were decreed by the Pope for a legitimate cause, yet Boniface felt that the magnitude of the punishment might lessen the esteem and reverence due from the people to the College of Cardinals, because they are the companions and counsellors of the Pope in the government of the Church, and eligible themselves to the Papacy. To remove the impression of abasement into which the College may have fallen after such thunderbolts of censures against two of their number, Boniface published a Constitution in which the severest penalties were threatened on those who molested or laid violent hands on a Cardinal. He specified the infamy of such irreverent beings: they would be deprived of their benefices if they possessed any, their goods would be confiscated, and their houses demolished. This

---

[114] See document at end of the Book. [115] Raynaldus, year 1297, no. 41.

constitution he placed later in the sixth Decretal.[116] Moreover to cleanse the venerable College from any foul stain with which the misdeeds of the Colonna Cardinals may have tainted it, he decreed that the Cardinals should appear dressed in purple like Kings. This privilege was formerly enjoyed only by Cardinal Legates "a Latere" to some princely courts,[117] as it were, to denote that he who deputed, not only wore, but also distributed those royal emblems.

1297.—Boniface with all his court was in Orvieto when he finished the process of the canonization of Louis IX, King of France, and grandfather of Philip the Fair. Louis had excited the wonder of all contemporaries by his self-restraint in the government of France in times when the people remained silent, and when religion was losing much of its force, by reason of its being involved in gross superstition. No one more than he had loved and practised justice towards his subjects. They found in his honesty and goodness of heart a guarantee, which is very rarely found in the very laws themselves. It was not thirst for power, but love for his subjects, that led him without desiring it, to weaken altogether the power of the feudal lords, and concentrate it in his own hands. In place of the feudal lords he substituted jurists who are the sole authors of all those laws which were enacted by Louis in relation to the Church. The Pragmatic Sanction, (which Frenchmen are wont to call the foundation of Gallican liberty), was published in March, 1268. It concerned the collation of benefices, and bore on the title page the name of Louis. It is a very short constitution, comprising only six articles,[118] but most fruitful of consequences which the lucubrations of jurists made them engender. To the princes and clergy of France it was a strong bulwark, forming a guarantee against what they called the usurpations of the Papal Curia. By this document the Pope in using his authority over churches, either for the punishment of the guilty, or to use the sacred patrimony, must first submit the affair to the judgment of the jurists, ever ready to despoil the Church to increase the power of the prince

---

[116] Tit. 9 de Poenis cap. Felicis Recordationis [117] See Pagi. Brevi. Pontiff Bonif. VIII, n. 34, 523. [118] Ordonn. des Rois de France, tom. 1, p. 97.

from whom they expected advancement. The piety of the Saint and the true love he bore the Church, together with the disturbed condition of the minds of the Pontiffs, were the reasons why no protest or complaints were made against this decree at Rome. But this seed sown by Louis IX, ripened under Philip the Bold, and under Philip the Fair bore fruit which Boniface was compelled to taste.

Still Boniface raised Louis IX to the honors of the altar. His memory had from day to day become more sanctified by miracles which the inquisitors after the strictest examination found to be genuine. Even if this had not been done, the faithful of that time could not have been restrained from venerating a man, in whose pure heart there was burned and spent itself the ardent fire of chivalry. His imprisonment at Damietta, and his slow lingering death calmly faced on a bed of ashes at Tunis, for the liberation of the Holy Land, were already a sufficient reason for the people to venerate him as a martyr. Under such circumstances the Pope could not refrain from ordering an inquiry to be made into the life and miracles of a king, who was an example not only of virtues, but also of devotion to the Holy See, and of most ardent zeal in those things in which the faithful were wont at that epoch to show their love and devotion to religion.

The Pontiffs had labored hard to gather sufficient evidence of the deeds of that Prince and of the miracles wrought in his name. Nicholas III before his death used to say that if two or three miracles could be proven, he would not hesitate to raise Louis to the honors of the altar, so strong and firm was his belief in his virtue. Under Martin IV, and Honorius three Cardinals were deputed to inquire into the matter, and they reported to Rome many miracles, which were closely examined and approved by the College of Cardinals. By Nicholas IV the matter was intrusted to three other Cardinals one of whom was Benedict Gaetani. A new investigation was made, and his life and miracles were again approved. Finally Boniface on the vigil of the feast of St. Lawrence and on the following day delivered two sermons to the Cardinals on the sanctity of Louis IX, and of his intention of proposing him to the veneration of the faithful. These two sermons known to very few were discovered in the library of the Canons of

St. Victor of Paris, and published by Duchesne.[119] The following strong words from his sermon fully express what was in his mind. "At first it is to be observed that "he who knows how to govern himself and his subjects, "the same is a true king. But he who knows not how to "govern himself and his subjects, truly can be said to be a "false king. He was certainly a true king, because he "governed himself and his subjects justly and holily. He "governed himself, because he subjected the flesh to the "spirit, and his passions to reason. Likewise he governed "his subjects well, for he preserved them in all justice and "equity. He also governed the churches well by defend- "ing the ecclesiastical liberties and rights. In our opinion "those who govern badly are not true kings."

In the other sermon he thus gravely explains with what caution the Holy See proceeded in the matter of the canonization of any one of the faithful who has piously departed this life. "Since," said he, "this act of enrollment among "the Saints by papal canonization is considered an act of "the highest importance in the Church militant, it is re- "served solely to the Roman Pontiff; that is why the Holy "See has wished to proceed with greatest prudence in that "of King Louis IX. Although his life had been so well "known, and although many miracles were wrought "through him; although the king, the barons and the prel- "ates entreated us often and earnestly to end this affair, "still the Holy See has wished that the private investiga- "tions that had been already made should be solemnly "prolonged for a longer period."

APPENDIX.

A PREPARATION FOR THE FOLLOWING BOOKS, AND TOUCHING ON THE BULL "CLERICIS."

WE have placed the Constitution "Clericis" of Boniface and his fatherly letter "*Ineffablis*" to Philip the Fair among the number of the documents at the end of this work. We hope that those who have read the first three books of this history, will not neglect to take cognizance

[119] Histor. Franc. Script. T. V. pg. 481. See Document at end of work.

of these two important documents. For as the remote cause of the quarrels between Boniface and Philip the Fair are contained in them, it would be impossible for those who ignore them to read with interest, or even understand well, what follows of this history. It is then to throw more light on the nature of the events, that we have judged it fitting to venture in this appendix upon a recital regarding this constitution and the admirable letter to Philip.

The taxes levied on the goods of the churches in cases of public necessity were always not only tolerated, but even were approved by the Church. Casting a glance over the times previous to those which are the subject of this history, we notice that these public necessities by common consent were the warlike expeditions to wrest the Holy Land from the hands of the infidels; the conquest of the Byzantine Empire, as the surest and shortest means of accomplishing the former design and the reunion of the Greek and Latin Churches; the wars waged by the Pontifical See against Frederick II, the avowed enemy of the Church; those waged against the Albigenses, and especially against the Counts of Toulouse their protectors; and finally those against Peter of Aragon, the invader of Sicily. Of these necessities, as is seen, only those of the holy wars concerned all the faithful directly; the others concerned them only indirectly, as when the Pope was in danger either with regard to his patrimony, his jurisdiction, or the preservation of some dogma, all the believers in his supremacy were called to his aid. The levying of the tithes on the sacred patrimonies in the case of public necessity which concerned the Christian republic was of right and of fact prescribed by the sovereign Pontiffs, both by the character of the subject which was sacred, and by the patrimonies which were equally sacred. But when public necessity affected the particular state of some prince, then inasmuch as the nature of the subject was not sacred, it pertained by right to the Pope and the clergy to consent to this tax, by reason of the sacredness of the goods it affected, although in the fact the prince, owing either to the urgency of the case, to tyranny, or to the weakness of the clergy, may have levied and seized it according to his pleasure. In fact it contained the whole history of the defence of the immunity of the ecclesiastical possessions courageously maintained by the Pontiffs against the power of kings, and the syllogisms of jurists. The justice or the injustice of a war undertaken by the king rendered just or unjust the demand of ecclesiastical subsidies; the exaction of them then without the consent of the clergy was always unjust. It is therefore clear that from the difficult appreciation of these reasons, and from the dangerous contact of the two powers there would arise a long train of dreadful quarrels.

The tithes for the holy wars in Palestine were at first furnished to the kings by voluntary gifts of the clergy, and as it were in the name of alms; but soon, according to the remark of that most sarcastic English monk, Matthew of Paris,[120] the pious need was converted into violence, and the shameful vice of rapacity was hidden under the mantle of alms. The clergy were so greatly alarmed that Peter of Blois, Archdeacon of Bath, cried out from his England to admonish the French bishops not to allow themselves to be robbed of their possession by the king asking money for the expedition to Palestine.[121] For he wrote to the bishop of Orleans: "Is it reasonable, that "those who fight for the Church should despoil the "Church? when they should on the contrary enrich her "with the spoils of the enemy, and with triumphal pres- "ents? Do these wretches and fools imagine that Jesus "Christ, sovereign justice, desires a sacrifice of iniquities "and sacrileges, and that spoils in such a manner gath- "ered can be of any service?"[122] Afterwards he concludes too severely by saying that the princes would exact no other thing from the pontiffs and the clergy but incessant prayers. But the Crusades were a necessity, and to

[120] Ad an. 1188: "Eodem tempore decima pars mobilium generalis concessa per Angliam, ut collecta ad subventionem Terrae Sanctae impenderetur, tam clerum quam populum exactione violenta perterruit, quae sub eleemosynae titus vitium rapacitatis inclusit." [121] Epist. 112.

[122] Quae ratio est, ut qui pro Ecclesia pugnant, Ecclesiam spolient? Quam inimicorum spoliis et donis triumphalibus ampliare debuerant? Putantne insipientes et miseri, quod Christus, qui summa justitia est, velit sibi de injuriis et sacrilegiis exhiberi sacrificium, aut sustineat commissa ex his spolia prosperari? Quid aliud a pontificibus vel a clero potest vel debet princeps exigere, quam ut incessanter fiat oratio ab Ecclesia ad Deum?

conduct them money was needed. The Lateran Council, held under Innocent III, 1215, therefore decreed that the Pope and the Cardinals should devote to them the tenth part of their benefices, and the clergy the twentieth. The First Council of Lyons, 1245, confirmed the canon of the Lateran Council by this decree: " Ex concilii communi " approbatione statuimus ut omnes omnino clerici vigesi- " mam, etc." The joint liability, and the establishment of the subsidies were determined by the needs of the kings and zeal of the clergy. The provincial councils, for example that of Avignon (1209), of Narbonne (1227), of Toulouse (1229), renewed the decrees of the general councils.

These tenth and twentieth parts were paid, but they were not always for wars in Palestine; and even when there was necessity, the kings were not always willing to go to the Holy Land, but that did not hinder them from collecting the usual subsidies, even after the complete extinction of the fire of the Crusades. This abuse compelled the Popes to place them under the obligation of undertaking the Crusade or of restoring what they had collected. Neither the one or the other would they do, both because the Holy Sepulchre was no longer so precious in their eyes that they would give up their lives for it, and because it seemed sweet to them to retain the fruits of their robberies, Nicholas IV in 1291 [123] wrote to Philip the Fair, and to Edward of England,[124] but Philip and Edward did not restore. In a word the princes abused the canons of the Council of Lyons; whenever they wanted to gain possession of some of the goods of the churches, they rushed to arms, they assumed the cross, they got in motion as if they were on the point of departing for the Holy Land, to which they did not even dream of going, and they exacted in this manner from the clergy the twentieth part which was fixed by the Council of Lyons.

This could not last always; in time the convenient pretext of the holy wars failed the kings, both because the people would not go any more to the Holy Land, and because the clergy, where they had been stupid, acquired wisdom in that expensive school. Summoned to pay, the monks especially made the greatest outcry. The chroni-

[123] Raynaldus ad an. 1291. 22. 56. 57.   [124] Raynaldus ad on. 1291.

cles of Matthew of Paris, and Matthew of Westminster resound with their complaints. At that time other ways to ask and to concede were employed, which we find were adopted for the first time by the bishops of the province of Tours in 1294, who granted tithes for two years to Philip for the defence of the kingdom and the churches: "*propter tuitionem regni et ecclesiarum.*" Thus a mutual agreement was made between the king and the clergy, by which the former bound himself to defend the rights of the Church, and the latter to aid him in the defence of the state. But this compact could not continued in peace; inasmuch as the Church would have to expect aid and the defence of her rights from the very one from whom she had to fear impieties and the invasion of her rights. So it clearly appears, that although the right of the immunity of the sacred patrimonies remained unchanged, yet the fact was often wavering, owing to the cessation of circumstances, as for example of the Crusades, of pirates and what not, which counselled moderation on the part of the clergy.

In England and in Spain the clergy showed themselves more tenacious of their rights, than those in France. The English feudal lords energetically resisted the king; they combined with the clergy, and the united resistance manifested to the king by the aristocracy and the clergy wrung from him the franchises for all the people held sacred in the Magna Charta. Requested to pay, the clergy never feared threats, they never yielded to caresses; the spirit of St. Thomas à Becket and St. Anselm seemed at that time to animate the episcopal body. When it became impossible for them to persist in their refusal, they always indemnified themselves for the subsidies which they granted by some new and explicit confirmation of their immunities. Edward I, engaged in a war with Philip the Fair, could not obtain the tithes from the clergy of the province of Canterbury, nor a fifth part of the revenues of the churches of the province of York, before his son promised in his name to confirm that part of the Charta which related to the immunity of ecclesiastical affairs.[125]

In Spain the taxes on the churches were more dangerous, but the firmness of the clergy was also greater. In

[125] Thomas Walsingham ad an. 1298.

that kingdom Crusades were not preached against infidels in a distant land, Crusades which were a necessity only through the impetuosity of the Christian faith. The infidel Moors were in the heart of the country, and the defence as well as the love of country made their expulsion a necessity. The princes of this kingdom demanded most abundant subsidies from the churches. They were not satisfied with a tenth or twentieth part, but they required a third. These third parts began to be collected for the first time in 1214 under Henry, King of Castile, who having succeeded his father Alphonsus at a tender age, gave unlimited authority to Alvarez his guardian, who placed the Church in a wretched condition by reason of these heavy exactions.[126] But solemnly excommunicated by the Dean of the church of Toledo, at that time vicar of the Archbishop of that city, not only did he restore what he had unjustly collected, but he even swore that he would cease his depredations. This first blow well given taught the clergy to do likewise. After the Council of Lyons was ended, Alphonsus of Castile, deluded by the hope of being Emperor of Germany, thought no more of the Moors. Gregory X, an ardent promoter of the Crusades, called him to his duty and granted him for six years the tithes of the churches of his kingdom, provided he would waive his claim to the empire, leave Rudolph of Hapsburg in peaceful possession, and renew the war against the Moors. This concession reinvested, it is true, as Mariana remarks,[127] the usurpations of the Spanish princes with a certain character of legality. However the clergy remained firm, as we have said, and the provincial councils in Spain [128] are a splendid proof of it

The movement of the Crusades was not so intense and so constant in any other country of Christendom as it was in France. For that reason the tithes for this necessity, called *Saladines,* were of earlier origin and more continuous than elsewhere. This is how they came to be imposed for the first time. In the middle of Lent a parliament was assembled in Paris, which was attended by all the barons, bishops, archbishops, and abbots of the kingdom, and an immense number of foot soldiers and knights, who as-

[126] Thomas Walsingham ad an. 1298. [127] Marian ann. "Hoc initium castellae regibus sacros templorum reditus decerpendi."— [128] L. 13 c. ult.

sumed the cross in order to go to fight in the Holy Land.[129] The King Philip Augustus showed himself disposed to set out for this reason, which was held to be of urgent necessity. With the consent of the clergy and the people it was decided that he could collect tithes from everybody, for that year only, and for the sake of the impending necessity: "*Omnibus et tantum anno propter instantem necessitatem.*" The details of these circumstances have been transmitted to us by Rigord, a monk of St. Denis, who was the historian and chaplain of Philip Augustus. The means seemed agreeable to Philip, who having tasted them, oppressed the churches unmercifully by unheard of exactions: "*Gravibus exactionibus vehementer oppressit et insolitis.*"[130] It is well to read in the chronicle of the religious which we have cited the pretexts by the aid of which the king tried to justify his usurpations, and with what unrestricted freedom the good monk wrote. Nevertheless the Prince realized his evil deeds; for he acknowledged the right of the immunity of the Church, and he by no means sought to weaken or destroy it. A proof of this we have in Rigord. Some moments before the battle of Bovine, Philip, who knew of all the extortions which Otho, Emperor of Germany, and John of England, in league against him, had been guilty of against the Church, began to pray, and Rigord, his chaplain, behind him heard him utter these words: "All our hope, all our confidence is in "God. King Otho and his army have been excommuni- "cated as enemies of the Church and as destroyers of her "possessions. The tears of the poor and the fruit of his "plunder of the churches and the clergy form the wages "of his soldiers. We are Christians in full communion "and peace with Holy Church. Although sinners, we do "the will of the Church of God and we defend according "to our power the liberty of the clergy." Then, according to the judgment of Philip, he who laid hands on the goods of the Church, and did not defend her liberty, was not a Christian.

The payment of the tithes was at first free and spontaneous in France; afterwards it was requested by the kings, and authorized by the Popes; and the requests of the former followed so frequently and so urgently, as well as

[129] Card. Aguir. Hispaniae.   [130] Duchesne. Script. Hist. Franc. T. 5.

the will of the latter, that it became an obligation for the clergy to pay on account of the urgent necessity; but their right to consent to or refuse this tax always remained intact. The wars against the Albigenses having been added to those of Palestine, under Louis VIII, the necessity of the tithes increased. A synod was convoked at Bourges, in which the legate of Gregory IX imposed this tax on the clergy for five years, in order to defray the expenses of the expeditions against these heretics. In order to persuade the clergy more easily, the king prevailed upon the legate to place himself at the head of the expedition, but the clergy would grant only a half of the tithes, and they objected to the use of that scandalous word, for which they substituted the word "subsidies," to close the way to the custom. The king died: the legate renewed the request, but the chapters of the provinces of Rheims, of Sens, of Tours, of Rouen, appealed to the Pope, because they did not want to see a gratuitous gift transformed into an obligation and a slavery: "*Attendentes quod hoc ipsum, quod* "*de libertate processerat, convertebatur in obligationem* "*et servitutem.*" The clergy complained then because they did not wish to be enslaved by a law; the kings, on their part insisted, because they wished to impose it. But although the right remained intact, yet the fact was strengthened, and these yearly exactions threatened to become a right. Louis IX ascended the throne; he was a saint, and we do not hear of him oppressing the churches; yet this constant ardor for the holy wars had exhausted the Church in France. Louis wanted some money for a crusade, and he asked it from the Pope; but the procurators of all the cathedrals of France, assembled at Paris, forwarded by letter their grievance to the Pontiff:[131] "Your Holiness knows, for the whole world is full of "them, the trouble and trials of the Universal Church, "and particularly of that of France, compelled to pay at "one time a tenth, again a twentieth, and at another a "hundredth part of its revenues, and to bear the weight

---

[131] "Novit vestra sanctissima paternitas, et in fines orbis terrae exivisse "quantis, perturbationibus et pressuris universalis Ecclesia, potissime "Gallicana sit turbata, nunc decimam, nunc duodecimam praestando, "nunc centesimam, nunc multarum aliarum exactionum gravamina sus- "tinando."

"of many other demands." Hence they protested, that by no other power than the Holy See did they hope to see their former liberty restored, and if help failed them, that pest of the tithes would be prolonged indefinitely: *"In "quibus nisi a sede apostolica plenam possit assequi liber- "tatem, pestis ista latissime se diffundet."* Duchene thus writes in the old chronicle of Neustria for the year 1254. The tithes imposed by a king, holy as Louis IX, were criticised even in England. Here are the words of sarcastic Matthew of Paris: "With the permission of the "Pope, he oppressed his kingdom in many ways, extorting "large sums of money under the pretext of making a "pilgrimage with great display, and he levied on the tenth "part revenues of all the churches of his kingdom." We do not believe that Louis oppressed the churches so heavily; but if there was reason for complaint under a saintly king it is easy to imagine how the churches fared under a king less pious.

The French kings had refused to go any more to the Holy Land, there were no heretics to be combated by arms, and consequently the old reasons for tithes ceased to exist. But since wars continually arose between Christian princes, there was constant need of money to maintain them, and kings presented themselves at the door of the churches, asking it for the defence of the kingdom: *"Ob "tuitionem regni."* Here was the difficulty; not to give was to provoke the anger of the king; to give was to betray the sacred immunities. The councils of the Lateran and Lyons ordered subsidies for the Holy Land, and not for other necessities. The warlike expeditions for the deliverance of the Holy Places, bore the evident character of justice and piety; but any other military expedition did not possess this mark without a decree to that effect. Moreover, in the first case the amount of aid to furnish to a prince on a crusade would be known, in the second case it would not be known, and hence the right would be undetermined. In the uncertainty the churches were oppressed by Philip the Fair, partly through the tyranny of the king, partly through the weakness on the part of the clergy. The clergy, thus oppressed, complained, but they did not resist like those in England. Boniface moved by these complaints published the constitution, "Clericis."

Now reflecting on these matters, can we say with Bossuet that it was unnecessary to publish that offensive constitution? The prohibition to the clergy to grant subsidies to the king without permission of the Pope was severe, and severe the punishment also, but the application of the law to Philip the Fair was most benign. So, although having suffered a little from this constitution which placed the sacred patrimonies out of his reach, and this pained him; yet he would not have published that disgraceful and unjust edict, if the flatterers, that torment of courts, had not gone about murmuring: " The prelates " and the ecclesiastical persons of your kingdom now can " no longer render you service nor give you the pecuniary " aid to which they are obliged by reason of their fiefs. " Now they can no longer make to their king the simple " gift of a horse or a cup." [132] When had Boniface thought of the goods which the clergy held in the character of feudatories? " Our constitution," said Boniface on the contrary, " does not admit of such malicious comments, " and the spirit which prompted it rejects the meaning " given to it by false commentators." [133] He declared that he did not forbid the concession of ecclesiastical subsidies to the king for the defence of his kingdom; but that he did not want it done without the special authorization of the Pope; and besides he was ready himself to dispose of the sacred vessels and the crosses, in order to cooperate in the defence of the kingdom of France. And finally here are the concessions which after all the clamors of Philip the Fair, Boniface granted him, in the affair of ecclesiastical subsidies, by another Bull entirely favorable to this prince, and explanatory of the constitution " Clerics."

1st. The intention of the pontiff was not to prohibit to the clergy the gratuitous gifts to the king or state in danger, provided there was no violence, but only exhortations and entreaties used to obtain them.

2nd. The clergy, possessors of ecclesiastical feudal property, remained obliged to fulfil their duty and to render homage due to the king.

3rd. In grave and sudden dangers of both king and state, the king could ask subsidies from the prelates, and

---

[132] See Document L. Ineffabilis.   [133] The same.

they could grant them, even without the permission of the Roman Pontiff.

4th. The judgment of the grievousness of the necessity, for the sake of which the clergy could be called upon, was left entirely to the conscience of the king, if he had reached his twentieth year, and to his ministers, if he was a minor.

The reader therefore will see that Philip, who considered himself grievously tormented by Boniface, was on the contrary most favored by him, and beyond other princes had the privilege of collecting subsidies, even without the permission of the Pontiff, in case of necessity. For this reason the disputes which arose later between the two men, cannot be ascribed to the fault of the Pontiff.

BOOK IV.

SUMMARY.

1297-1300.

The sovereign expression of the papal power.—It derived all its greatness from that of St. Peter —The Sixth Decretal —Dino da Mugello.—The Count of Flanders becomes an ally of Edward of England.—A formidable league against Philip the Fair.—He fights it and is aided by Boniface —Boniface is chosen arbiter by Philip and Edward.—His decision.—How it was received by the two Princes —Wallace disturbs Scotland —Scotch envoys to Boniface.—His letter to Edward.—Edward's reply and that of the English Parliament —Albert of Austria with the aid of Philip is elected King of the Romans.—Boniface will not confirm this election —The Armenians beg aid from Boniface against the Turks.—The Holy Wars —Boniface defends the Templars against the king of Cyprus —His moderation towards Philip —The usurpations of Philip in league with Albert —Sicily; and the acts of James against Frederick —Small gain do they bring to the Church.—Battle of Cape Orlando —Charles II, whom the Pope tries to restrain, undertakes an unfortunate expedition against Sicily.—Constitution of Boniface concerning corpses —He pursues the Fraticelli.—He favors the Friars Minor —He undertakes to subdue Palestrina.—The pretended counsel given him by Guy of Montefeltro —The Colonnas surrender at discretion.—The end of Palestrina.—Boniface approves the new order of St Anthony —The Greek Church.

WE have finally reached that stage of this history, when the mind of the reader has been raised by itself, as it were, to the height of that fact which has dominated all others, the subject of our narrative: we mean the development of the Papal power. And since we have said that this reached its extreme period during the lifetime of Boniface, a period, consequently, agitated and stormy like every living existence that ends; it is necessary for us to carefully turn our attention to it, in order to arrive at a knowledge of the scope of this narrative. But there is no need of much effort, since this fact is so forcibly characterized, that all the other facts which we shall narrate are founded on it, and dominating as it was, it becomes the one and only object of our study. In the moral order it is an invariable law, that the ending of a life is caused by the ending of its determining causes, which being consumed, so to speak, as they carry to the highest degree the power of existence, suddenly extinguish it.

The life of this absolute Pontifical power, considered in itself, had expression in canon law, which at once had produced a relative Pontifical power outside of itself in contact with the faithful. Now since this power under Boniface and through him, reached the highest point in its life, the Papacy of Boniface must have had a particular expression in canon law; and this portion of the canonical laws should above all others manifest a sensible vigor proportionate to the vital strength of that power. The volume of these laws was the Sixth of the Decretals.

The Papacy as a theocratic power assumed to rule the noblest part of the human individual, namely the intelligent spirit, in which there is liberty, that is to say, life through knowledge. Therefore every human knowledge not only clothed itself with the forms of that theocratic power, but also accepted it as an ideal. For which reason philosophy in the Middle Ages was only theology, art was theological, and the standard of right, preeminently the guiding spirit of the people was Papal. And since the first necessity is that of existence, which can not be without a determination, or right, it came to pass that men devoted themselves more closely to the study of this than any other science. The Universities of Bologna, Padua, and Paris in the thirteenth century were only assemblies of canonists; and Gregory IX, Innocent III, Honorius III, and Boniface VIII, addressed their collections of canons to the University of Bologna.

We shall not speak of the history of the Decretals, as it would be too great a digression; we wish to say however, that these were not the expression of arbitrary power of the Popes, but rather the consequence of that same Papacy which Christ had established in the Church. The preaching of the Gospel, to which the Apostles were deputed, had an immediate effect, namely the formation of the Church by unity of faith. The government of the Church, which also was entrusted to the Apostles, had not an immediate effect in its entire extension, proportionate to the efficacy of the power that was granted to the Apostles and the Episcopate. Preaching had for its object the existence of the Church, and the Church existed through the faith of those who composed it. The existence of the Church was absolute, and as regards its state of being it was unchangeable, unprogressive and actual as the faith which was its foundation. The object of its government was the formal existence of the Church in its relations with exterior objects, and as these relations are susceptible of development and of progress, so also the government should develop and progress. For this reason the ruling power of the Pope and of the entire episcopate could not manifest itself in the first age of the Church in the same manner as it did in succeeding ages. Preaching and the faith will always be the same; but the governing power will always vary according to the force of its progress; and will accompany the society of the faithful, which being human and visible, is visibly developed around the pivot of faith. Hence the scandal of the Jansenists and Regalists at seeing the Church, after the first ages, extend its power, and multiply its canons, is rather a sin against reason. Acknowledging the Church to be visible and directed by a visible power, they obstinately persisted in believing it despoiled of all power, or in other words in believing a contradiction.

Preach the Gospel, that is to say the faith to every creature, said Christ to the Apostles and their successors; but since this faith should be expressed perceptibly by works, by worship, and by the Sacraments, they could not complete their mission in a manner so as not to leave the exercise of it to their successors until the end of time. The visibility therefore of the Church is the soil on which the power of governing must indeterminately develop itself. Now since the power of governing a society is relative to all which tends to destroy it, it is evident that the subjective power will always be in direct proportion to the offences committed against the society. If the offences increase, the power will increase, as will also the laws which are the expression of it. So before any one had dared to touch the offerings of the faithful, the power of securing them did not manifest itself, it was not known to the faithful, although it existed in the Pope. The first usurpation of the sacred patrimony of the Church made that power subjectively exist, and the repeated exercise of it begot the law against usurpers which is nothing but a permanent power. Wherefore although St. Peter did not promulgate laws against the usurpers of the goods of the Church, whereas his successors had promulgated many, yet it does not follow that he did not have the power, and that his successors usurped it. So then if we find the Papal power amplified and Papal laws increased, it is because the offences against the society of Church were multiplied and hence to this cause, and not to ambition should be ascribed the great subjectivity of the Papal power.

The small number of laws in a human society is a sign of great vitality, just as a large number betokens little vitality or in other words the many offences committed against it. In fact accordingly as disorder increased in civil society through barbarity and consequently in the discipline of the Church, so the subjective power of the Pope increased, the laws increased, and so did the need increase of compiling them in a collection, so as to render permanent by material proofs that power, which was rendered morally such by the laws. .

In this principle we find living and as it were palpitating with truth, the reasons for all those changes in discipline which had scandalized the Jansenists. The need of power, the pressing necessity, and the great increase of evils induced the Pope to exercise it suddenly and peremptorily. A dictatorship in republics was engendered by the existence and greatness of the evils that threatened them.

In the time of Boniface the offences against the Church, although combated by the Papal power for many centuries, had taken the form of right, which was that of Princes. Therefore the natural force of evil doubled itself by the power of this form. And when it seemed that in the new-born civilization these offences should diminish in number and strength, they multiplied and increased through the very benefits of civilization. Hence the Papal power, whose strength it seemed should have declined, was also reinvigorated, and far from the old canons losing their force, they reappeared more threatening by the addition of new ones. Therefore just as civilization gave to the offences committed against the Church the form of a lay right, so Boniface gave to all the Papal power the form of his own right, and this form was expressed by the Sixth Book of the Decretals.

Thus reasoning we find ourselves brought to a consequence, which we laid down as a principle in the first pages of this history, namely that Boniface was the man of a passive revolution, that is to say the personification of the civil Papacy in himself, his own ruin occurred with that of the civil Papacy. Therefore if this Pontiff is to be presented to posterity in all the fullness of his personality, he should not be dissociated from the sixth book of the Decretals, which is the strongest expression of him and of the Papacy.

All the Canons collected up to the time of Innocent III, and comprised in the Decree of the monk Gratian, and in the two collections of Decretals of Bernard Circa and John Vallense, although the doctors in the universities made use of them yet they had not as yet the force of laws by the authoritative decree of the Popes. But since Innocent III administered the Papacy in the strength of its power, in order to establish it firmly he was led to put his seal on his collection of the Decretals, which he increased by the aid of Peter, Deacon of Benevento, compiling a third collection which contained those canons which emanated from him. The canons of the Fourth Lateran Council, and the subsequent decrees of Innocent are contained in the fourth collection of an unknown author. The decree of Honorius III had from this Pope approval and force of laws. Finally this particular Papal approval was extended by Gregory IX to all the Decretals from the time of Gregory the Great to his own times, to the Apostolic Canons, to the Canons of the Councils from that of Antioch down to the 4th Lateran Council. All these were combined by Pennafort, and were divided into five books. They were solemnly published and given as laws to be followed in the tribunals and schools.

The last epistles of Gregory IX, the canons of the two Councils of Lyons, and the constitutions of the Popes who succeeded Gregory, and those published by Boniface in the first four years of his Pontificate, were already most important and sufficient for a new collection. The canons of the 1st Council of Lyons, promulgated during long struggles of the Church with Frederick II, and the constitutions of Boniface, published in times of violence had a certain vital energy; they were not to remain outside of the body of ecclesiastical right, nay they were even demanded by the same right as its sovereign form. And this was truly remarkable, that this demand for the insertion of these laws did not come from the clergy nor from the Papal authority, but from the assembly of the doctors of Bologna.

The University of Bologna dispatched to Boniface James of Castello, chaplain of the church of that city to beseech him to make an addition to the body of Canon Law composed of five books; to separate the false from the true Decretals published since Gregory IX, and to sanction it with his authority in the law court. James being kindly received by the Pope, was standing in his presence; but as he was very short of stature, Boniface, thinking that he was in a kneeling posture, gave him a sign to rise. But Cardinal Matthew of Acquasparta who was beside him undeceived the Pope by a joke which hurt the feelings of the honorable messenger, saying: "He is a new Zaccheus." [1]

Boniface set about immediately to put in effect the desire of the famous University. He selected three persons most learned in law, William of Mandagout, Archbishop of Ambrun, Berengarius Fredoli, Bishop of Beziers, and Richard Petroni of Siena. To these he entrusted that compilation,[2] which in 1298 was published under the name of the Sixth Book of the Decretals. Boniface addressed it to the University of Bologna, with that letter which is found in the beginning of the Sixth Book. The compilers as a reward were afterwards raised to the Cardinalate.

These men in the compilation of the work had as a companion Dino of Mugello, a celebrated juris-consult of his time. Born in Florence in that part of the city which was named Mugello by James Rossoni, he applied himself to the study of law in Bologna. In that city he was pro-

[1] Tirabaschi "History of Literature. Book 2nd, pages 239 and 138.
[2] Preface to Book VI of Decretals.

fessor, as well in Pistoja. Such renown for learning did he acquire, that during his lifetime the Veronese established by law that in passing sentence, wherever the laws and the municipal statutes, the Roman Laws, and the commentaries of Accorso did not touch upon the matter or held contrary opinion, all should consult and follow the opinion of Dino. In October, 1297, being summoned to Rome by Boniface for the compilation of the Sixth of the Decretals, he repaired thither, where he taught school. The services which he rendered the Pontificate during that time stirred up in his breast the desire for the dignity of Cardinal, with which he believed the Pontiff should reward him. And so much did his not dishonorable ambition confirm him in this opinion, that having bade farewell to his wife, Bice, he obliged her to devote herself to God in the Convent of St. Columbanus in Bologna, and he became a cleric. Unfortunate expectations! The only honor he gained was that of having put his hand to the Sixth of the Decretals, and perhaps the repentance of marital sequestration. Some will have it that he died of grief. So Dino after instructing so many others in the laws, did not know how to instruct himself. He had not learned that greediness for dignities is a sign of intemperance in the truly wise, who possess the highest of dignities, that of intelligence, which neither princes can accord nor tyranny can steal.

Although Boniface had in a fatherly manner replied to the edict published by Philip the Fair in anger, caused by the constitution "Clericis," yet there was such freedom and authority of decisions in the response that the mind of that king should have been aroused to additional anger. However, there was a mutual continence of the anger which agitated the Papal and royal breasts. The ruined but threatening Colonnas restrained Boniface and a great federation of unfriendly princes curbed Philip. Hence in the course of our history we shall find that the Pope is still a friend and supporter of the king, and the latter if not, is at least not an open enemy.

Philip and Edward were still at war, when Guy, Count of Flanders, came to prolong and increase it. He could not rest peaceful because his daughter Philippa betrothed to the son of Edward, was held a prisoner by Philip. He assembled a large parliament at Grammont, at which were present the ambassador of England, those of Adolph king of the Romans, of the Duke of Brabant, and of almost all of the princes of the Low Countries, and Lorraine. He complained of the imprisonment of his daughter; and all proffered aid against Philip; but before breaking off relations with the latter, they decided to send to him a solemn embassy, to demand the liberation of the innocent princess. It is sent but it returned with a refusal.[3] Then Guy made an alliance with Edward, each one binding himself not to make peace without the consent of the other; the other daughter Isabella was betrothed to the young English prince instead of Philippa, and her dowry was to remain in the hands of the Fleming to carry on the war against Philip the Fair, together with a hundred thousand livre which had been promised by Edward.[4] The Counts of Savoy and of Granson entered into the league, and they were sent to rouse to arms all the lords of Brittany, although John duke of that country had been detached by Edward.[5] They succeeded in their design, for with thirty thousand livre of the English king they induced the Counts of Auxerre, of Montbelliard, the lords of Arlay, of Neuchatel, of Montfaucon, and of Faucigny.[6] The Count of Savoy, Amadeus V, was induced to join the league, by the promise as wife of Jane the niece of Edward.[7] On the other hand Adolph, King of the Romans, rose in arms against France, by whom he was joined by the Duke of Brabant, the Count of Hainaut and of Gueldria, the Bishops of Liege, and Utrecht, and the Archbishop of Cologne.[8] A formidable league, which would have put Philip in the direst straits, if the confederates had not been in separate places, and if the gold of France, more plentiful than that of England, had not dissuaded the Germans from taking up arms against him. And now was the opportunity for Boniface to show himself, if such he was, the enemy of Philip, either by aiding the allies, or by giving the meaning to the Constitution "Clericis" the meaning which the royal ministers attributed to it, namely to deprive him of all subsidy of money to be drawn from

---

[3] Ondegherst. Annals of Flanders c. 132, 1. [4] Rymer, Tom. II, page 737, 742. [5] Idem page 733 [6] Idem Tom. II, page 778.
[7] Idem Tom. II, page 759. [8] Idem Tom. II, pages 752, 763, 768.

the sacred patrimony. But let us proceed and we shall find that Boniface wheedled this unruly prince.

The ardor with which these princes entered into the league, exceeded that with which they came to the war. The hosts of Edward, of Adolph, of the Bishops of the Empire, and of the Count of Gueldria delayed to advance. Guy was the only one who confronted Philip, who on June 2nd, the feast of Pentecost, having assembled the flower of the army at Compiegne, at the head of it entered Flanders and laid siege to the city of Lille.[9] Having sustained defeat at Furnes and Comines the Flemish were compelled to open the gates of Lille, of Furnes, of Castel, and of Berg St. Vinox.[10] Edward arrived only to share in the discomfiture of the Flemish. But before he advanced with his army, assembled at London on the 1st of August, some of the nobles of the kingdom came to him saying how imprudent it was for him to go to war, as he was now an enemy of the Church, and excommunicated by the Archbishop of Canterbury whom he had cruelly persecuted; and that he should be reconciled with him before leaving the kingdom. Sooner than have an enemy in his own household, Edward in full parliament was reconciled with Robert of Winchelsey, Archbishop of Canterbury, in the presence of a large concourse of people. Moreover he intrusted to his care his son Edward and the entire kingdom. He ratified the peace by promising to restore all that was unjustly taken. He asked pardon of the barons for his bad conduct of affairs; and he desired all to pray for him; but according to accounts, all did not pray well for him.[11] He departed for Flanders with a small following and joined Guy; but in a short time through the dissatisfaction of the Flemish, and the misfortune that attended them, they both found themselves beaten back to Ghent, and all the principal cities of the country were captured. The two princes despairing of better terms,

---

[9] John Villani. Book 8, c. 19 . . . . . . William Nangii Chronicles 1297.

[10] Villani. Book 8, c. 20 . . . . . . Nangii Chronicles 1297.

[11] Knyghton. English Events. Book 3, chap 9, page 2510.—"Et orabant quidam publice alii autem sic; alli vero occulte, pauci vero bene"—Walsingham, "Flores Historiae," year 1297.—Matthew of Westminster, yr. 1297.

seeing that the remarkable successes of Philip had discouraged the lesser nobles who had entered the league, asked for an armistice. Philip granted it, both because of the approach of winter, and because his mind was more inclined to diplomacy than to wage war.[12] In October of 1297 William d'Autun, a Dominican Friar and Archbishop of Dublin, who enjoyed the confidence of both Edward and Philip, induced them to prolong the truce.[13] The Papal legates Nicholas Boccasino, general of the Dominicans, and John Minio of Murro, general of the Franciscans[14] arrived, and Charles of Naples himself sent by Boniface to obtain peace:[15] and through their means an armistice for two years was signed in the monastery of St. Martin of Tournai.[16]

A great debt of gratitude was owed by Philip to Boniface, who admirably assisted him during this war which lasted about three months. If in the Constitution "Clericis Laicos" there had been hidden a spirit hostile to the king, and if the interpretation of the malicious courtiers was true, it is certain that Philip would not have received subsidies from the churches, of which he was in extreme need to carry on a rather difficult war. On the contrary when the Pope was asked by the French prelates how they would act towards the king in regard to granting money and men, seeing the kingdom so much threatened, and yet themselves held in check by the Constitution, in the following words he gave a satisfactory answer to their inquiry:[17] " Although we have published this Constitution
" as a preserver of ecclesiastical liberty, yet it was not
" our intention to deprive of subsidies the king, and the
" other lay princes, when in distress, and especially when
" in fear of an unjust invasion from without, and a revo-
" lution from within, with evident danger to prelates,
" Churches, and clerics. We desire simply that this be
" done with our permission, and be the free and sponta-
" neous gift of the clergy for the common defence. And
" just as at other times both by messengers and letters we
" signified to the King and the other princes of the realm,

[12] Rymer, Tom. 78, page 95.   [13] Chronicles Nic. Trivet. 1297.
[14] Spondani year 1298.   [15] Villani. Book 8, v. 20.
[16] Nangis, year 1297. apud Achery Spic tome 3, page 52.
[17] Reg. Vatican. An. 3, page 26, Raynaldus 44.

"that if (which God forbid) the kingdom were in immi-
"nent danger, far from prohibiting subsidies, not only
"would we allow him to be provided with money from the
"sacred patrimony of his kingdom, but what is more we
"would proffer him, as far as our honor and that of the
"Church would permit, the goods, the substance, the
"power of Holy Church, and even our own person, for the
"preservation of his rights and for his relief in dire
"necessity." These kind and amiable words which came
from his heart, Boniface wrote on the 19th of February,
as previously on the 7th of the same month the request
was kind which he sent to Philip, to revoke the edict which
prohibited money to be sent to Rome, and the clergy found
outside of the realm from receiving the revenue of their
benefices.[18] And his actions bear testimony to the sincerity of his words. We find in the Vatican Register of the
letters of Boniface various letters which make mention of
the money given to Philip. He granted him a half of the
alms that had been collected for an expedition to the Holy
Land,[19] a half of the money that was owed by certain
debtors to Hugh, Bishop of Toledo;[20] and finally during
the war, he allowed him to collect for himself the revenue
for the first year of all the vacant benefices in the Kingdom.[21] And in order to prove that the Papal constitutions
sanctioned in favor of the immunities of the clergy, were
not destructive of civil order and safety, he gave him full
power to make himself sure of the person of those of the
clergy whom he suspected during the war.[22] Moreover he
wrote to the Archbishop and chapter of the city of Lyons,
to be on their guard and protect the city, lest it might fall
into the hands of enemies whilst the king was engaged
in war.[23] This indeed was not a sign of that venomous
rancor, that Boniface had been accused of bearing towards
Philip; nor was it a sign that he wished to make him a
vassal, as those most humble courtiers proclaimed, whose
minds were clouded by the famous Constitution. And besides whilst Philip was engaged in the war Boniface released him from whatever censure he may have incurred
by the edict published in opposition to the Constitution,
through the Archbishop of Auxerre[24] and through his

[18] Raynaldus 46. [19] Epistle 54. an 3. [20] Epistle 55 — [21] Epistle 60 —
[22] Epistle 50.— [23] Epistle 63.— [24] Vat. Register, Epistle 4, year 3.

confessor; so he proceeded to interrupt in his favor, in a manner the most advantageous, that Constitution, so shamefully and malignantly distorted by the king's courtiers.[25] And in order that it might not appear, that by any peculiar circumstance he was induced to give these interpretations, he ordered them afterwards to be inserted in the Sixth of the Decretals.[26]

Boniface was no less benevolent to Edward, who a loser in the Flemish War, had great need of powerful mediators, so as to reconcile him with Philip. Adolph could give him no further thought; the Scotch were in a ferment, and were threatening to break out into open war, being aroused by Wallace, a Scottish chieftain, who abhorred the subjection to England. The losses sustained in Flanders were many and heavy; he asked for a truce, and obtained it. This was secured through the influence of Boniface. For we have already seen how Philip flushed by success, interrupted the progress of the war, through the kind offices of Charles II whom the Pope had sent to him; and on Christmas Day, Edward being still in Flanders, Papal messengers came to exhort him, as they had likewise done with Philip, to change that truce into a treaty of peace. For that purpose he should send to the Roman See envoys, who would submit the reasons of their quarrel to Boniface, who not as a judge and Pope, but as a good mediator of peace would define the rights of both parties, and each one would promise to abide by the decision. The messenger had not much difficulty in persuading Edward, who on account of the embarrassed state of his affairs, anxiously longed for some such an arrangement.[27] The proposition was also agreeable to Philip; and the English and French envoys repaired to Rome.[28] See the confidence which these two princes, jealous of their sovereignty, placed in the intelligence and the honesty of heart of Boniface. Is it any wonder then that those Pontiffs of Italian nationality should have dominated over all the princes of Christendom with the arms of justice?

The favors which Boniface had lavished on Philip, whilst the heavy weight of war was pressing down on him,

---

[25] Vat. Register, Epistle 5, Raynaldus 49. Epistle 47, Rayn.
[26] Book 3 de Immun. Eccl. chapter "Clericis."   [27] Walsingham.
[28] Chronicles of Nicholas Trivetti, year 1298—Achery, tom. 3, p. 222.

and also the care with which he brought to a successful end the canonization of his grandfather, Louis, was a splendid proof to that Prince of the predilection of Boniface for the Royal House of France. At the same time in the heart of Edward all hope vanished of a rupture between Philip and the Pope, regarding the affair of the Constitution, which would have been to his advantage in the war. For which reason although he wished to profit by that armistice in order to reunite the league and renew the war, yet he suddenly courted the desire of peace. This also made him exceedingly desirous of deserting Adolph, because other things at home, and the furious uprising in Scotland claimed his attention. Also Philip desired peace, both because he was victorious and not a lover of war, and because the people were no longer enthusiastic, and were assuming a threatening attitude owing to the many exactions. To such well-disposed minds Boniface presented himself as a peace-maker. Edward who was in dire straits first chose him as arbiter of the reasons of his quarrel with Philip.[29] He dispatched six ambassadors to Rome giving them full power by letters he wrote at Ghent the 18th of February of 1298.[30] And to show that he was sincere in his desire for peace, he departed from Flanders, and in March he arrived in the harbor of Sandwich.[31]

Philip also satisfied with the arbiter chosen, and like Edward bound himself to abide by the decision of Boniface under the severe penalty of paying a hundred thousand silver marks. Yet ever fearing that his principality might lose some of its rights, he preferred that the Pope in judging should preside not in his character as Pope, but

---

[29] These courts of peaceful arbitration were of frequent occurrence. By agreement between the two contending princes the settlement of their differences was often intrusted to a bishop, a strong proof of the reverence and confidence which they had for the hierarchy. We find that in 1283 Edward of England, as Duke of Gascony, being at law with the bishop and chapter of Bazas, regarding jurisdiction over the territory of that city, both by agreement confided the settlement of the lawsuit to the judgment of the Bishop of Aine.—" Ista est littera omologacionis et consensus Episcopi et capituli Vasatensium, super quibusdam articulis pertinentibus ad compositionem factam inter Dominum Regem Angliae et ecclesiam Vasatensem." Unedicted document on the History of France. Letters of Kings V, I [30] Walsingham—Trivet. Chronicles 1298—Rymer, tom 2, p. 825.   [31] Idem.

as a private person, that is to say, as Benedict Gaetani. The agreement with this clause added was drawn up in Rome on the 14th of June 1298, and the rights of two great princes tired of war were weighed in the mind of Boniface.[32]

Anxieties at home and the noise of arms which resounded in the Papal court itself, did not divert the truly great mind of Boniface from the consideration of foreign affairs. On the 27th of June, precisely when hostilities with the Colonnas were beginning, in a public consistory Boniface presided as judge in the great contest of Philip and Edward, whose eagerness for war had subsided during the two years armistice. There were thirteen cardinals present, and a countless number of people had assembled to hear the solemn decision. The minds of all were curious to see how Boniface, called to judge as Benedict Gaetani, although he was Pope, and presided as Pope, would render judgment regarding the rights of these two most powerful princes. No one doubted his wisdom, nor his uncompromising judgment; but they suspected that on account of the unusual solemnity of the office and his well-known attachment to things Roman he might be unjust to both, or that a hidden enmity against France might induce him to act too severely towards Philip. Boniface was not a saint, but jealous as he was of the authority of the Papal Chair, he was equally most zealous for the authority of justice. Before a final decision could be reached Boniface would be obliged to quiet the envoys of England who were objecting, that they could not arrive at an agreement with the French King, without violating the faith of their master with Adolph, King of the Romans, and Guy, Count of Flanders, to whom he had sworn not to make peace without their concurrence. However Boniface knew how to surmount even this obstacle, and he decided: "The armistice agreed upon between Edward "and Philip should be prolonged in order to change it into "peace; they should confirm it, and render it durable by "ties of blood: Philip should give in marriage his daugh-"ter, a child who was upwards of seven years, to Edward "the eldest son of the English king, and the latter should "marry the sister of Philip. To each one was to be re-

[32] Idem.

"turned that which belonged to him before the breaking
"out of the war;—Acquitaine was to be returned to the
"control of Edward, but he was even to remain a vassal
"of France; Philip was to have dominion over it. The
"lands occupied by both parties during the war were
"to be surrendered into the custody of the Pope, until
"they could come to some agreement concerning the same.
"And during this time neither one should be considered
"gainer or loser in their respective rights. That which
"they agreed upon should be sacred and inviolable, that
"about which there might be doubts or dissensions was
"always to be submitted to the decision of the Pope." [33]

Having thus decided this difficult affair, Boniface quickly sent the treaty to Edward and Philip, exhorting them by fervent letters, to ratify it, and telling them that they were mutually bound to stand by it, and that he would not have become judge in the affair if they had not requested it. He ordered, that into the custody of Arnold Bishop of Toulouse, Philip should surrender the lands he had seized in Acquitaine, and which belonged to Edward prior to the war, and Edward should give up the lands he had taken from Philip during the war.[34] He absolved Guy of Flanders from the oath which bound him to give his daughter in marriage to Edward, eldest son of the King of England;[35] and dispensed the latter from the degree of relationship which existed between him and Isabella of France.[36] So it seemed there were no longer any impediments to the longed for peace.

The decision given by Boniface as a private person was differently received by the princes who had requested it. If one of the two ought not to complain, that one was assuredly Philip. The Pope on July 3rd had sent a Bull to Philip, in which he promised that nothing would be added to the given decision without his consent declared by letters or special messengers.[37] Moreover on the 10th of the same month he sent another letter to Edward, requesting him not to undertake an expedition of war against the Scotch. These two documents were favorable to Philip; they even exhibit a special kind leaning of Boni-

[33] See Document A at end of Book.
[34] Vatican registers, epistles 233, 236, 237.   [35] Epist. Book 4. 415
[36] Epist. 234—Raynaldus no. 7.   [37] Preuve du diff. de Bonif. page 41.

face towards him. Philip accepted the truce ordered by the Pope, but ever excited by jealousy of state, which his faithful courtiers took occasion to keep alive in his mind, protesting importunately, he said to the papal legates: "that the temporal government of his kingdom belonged "to him, and to no other; in that respect he had no supe- "rior; and that he would never submit to any man who "should pretend to interfere in the civil administra- tion."[38] We believe that Philip was impelled to make this outcry by the fear of being obliged to liberate the daughter of Guy of Flanders, and to restore the estates of the same.[39] But there was no mention of this in the Papal decision. However he accepted the armistice and the decision of Boniface, and the lands taken from Ed- ward were intrusted to the Papal Legate Arnold, Bishop of Toulouse. Edward accepted the decision most kindly and most peacefully. Hardly had he received the letters of Boniface, exhorting him to abide by the decision, and have all confidence in him, than he read them to all the nobles of the kingdom assembled in Westminster.[40] He published an edict to the Gascons, in which having ex- plained all that was effected up to that time, he ordered that all the lands and vassals that he possessed in the French kingdom should be placed in the hands of the Papal legate.[41] The treaty was ratified by the two kings

[38] Tres. des Chart. 16   History of England   Lingard, Tom. II, page 38.

[39] Here we shall call attention to a remark of Hallam which he makes in his History of Europe in the Middle Ages about the decision of Boniface, and the unjust complaints of Philip, and of some French writers: The award of Boniface, which he claims to make both as Pope and as a private individual, is published in Rymer and is very equitable   Nevertheless the French historians agree in charging him with partiality towards Edward, and mention several proofs of it, which do not appear in the Bull itself. Previous to its publication, it was perhaps allowable to follow the common tradition; but Velly, a writer always careless and not always honest, has repeated mere falsehoods from Mezeray and de Baillet, while at the same time he refers to the instrument itself in Rymer, which disproves them. M. Gaillard, one of the most truthful writers that France has ever pro- duced, has pointed out the error of these historians in the Mem. de l'Academie des Inscriptions, and the editors of "l'Art de verifier les Dates have also rectified it." Hallam, page 385.   [40] Westmon. Flor. Hist.

[41] . . . . . . "nous pour honneur et pour reverence du dit pope . . . . . . avons ja mis et assigne en la main et le pouvoir de l'honorable pere R. eveque de Vicence, messager du dit pape, toutes les

through their envoys in June, 1299, at Montrein-sur-mer, by the means of the legate, Bishop of Vicenza.[42]

It clearly appears from the decision of Boniface that peace had not been established by that armistice. The cause of the dissension still remained, namely the division of Acquitaine, and the settlement of the jurisdiction of the two princes, which was to be submitted to a future decision of the Pope.[43]

But the Pope did not wish to reopen the wounds of old sores through fear that the contending parties who submitted themselves to his decision, might escape from his power. He was in hopes that the ties of relationship about to be contracted between them would soften their minds, and render them soon willing for a happy and a lasting agreement. In May, 1299, Edward deputed Amadeus V of Savoy to act as his proxy and that of his son in contracting marriage with Margaret and Isabella, the one the sister and the other the daughter of Philip.[44] In August Jane, Queen of France, in writing promised to Edward her daughter Isabella as wife, as soon as she reached the marriageable age.[45] Robert, Count of Artois, promised the same in the name of Philip.[46] Unfortunate marriages! which contracted for the sake of peace, were nevertheless the cause for a fierce war between the English and French, which lasted for almost a century.

Whilst Edward was at war with Philip, we remarked how the Scotch were striving by arms to recover their lost independence, and how this uprising induced the English Prince to come to some terms with Philip. He had overcome the Scotch in various battles, and had taken their king John Baliol a prisoner. So he believed

terres, vassaux, biens et autres choses que nous tenions au royaume de France, le jour que la dite prononciation fut faite . . . . pour quoi nous vous prions et requerrons . . . . que soyez des l'heure que vous aurez ces lettres recues . . . . . . obeissants et en toutes choses repondants au dit eveque, ou a son mandement, en nom du devant dit pape comme a nous memes." Rymer, Vol. 2 page 832 et seq.

[43] Rymer. Vol. 2, pages 840, 851.

[44] Westm. Flour. Hist.—" Romae per Dominum Papam Bonifacium inter reges Galliae et Angliae pax confirmatur, quae non fuerat totaliter solidata."— [45] See the letter of Edward, the son, to Amadeus regarding this marriage. Unpublished documents, History of France, Vol. I, p. 430.

[46] Idem 76, page 431.   [46] Idem 433.

no one else would oppose him in enjoying a peaceful rule over that courageous nation. But the flight of its armies and the imprisonment of its king do not assure the subjection of an independent people. The foundation of its rights is not in armies nor in a broken scepter, but in the conviction of right, which jealously preserved in the heart, will sooner or later free those who have been faithful. This the Scotch had still preserved in those times, and William Wallace aroused it to generous efforts. Of an humble, but honorable family, he undertook to do that which a king had failed to accomplish, we mean the feeble Baliol.

Scotland groaned, and bore the foreign rule like any other country deprived of its independence. English ministers held the highest public offices, and an Englishman, John Warenne, Count of Surrey, supreme power in the realm, as Viceroy of Scotland. These foreign ministers had laid their hands on the goods of the churches, and for that reason the clergy, more than the laymen, bore with bad grace the English yoke. Edward with all his forces was at Guienne, when Wallace raised the standard of Scotch independence. Having lived in the forest, he had a brave soul, a strength of body, which is necessary for the performance of valorous deeds. At first he had but few followers; success added to their courage and multiplied their numbers; and a fortunate encounter in which William Heslop, Sheriff of Lanarkshire, was slain, gave celebrity to the name of Wallace. They attempted at Scone to surprise the chief judiciary of Ormesby, who lost his treasures, but saved himself by the precipitancy of his flight. On a sudden other chieftains arose in arms in different counties and the people rushed to the standard of independence. The name alone of Wallace guided them. The origin and progress of these numerous parties had been viewed with secret satisfaction by Wistecant, Bishop of Glasgow, and the Grand Master, or Seneschal of Scotland who determined to collect them into one body, and give to their efforts one common direction. Declaring themselves the assertors of Scottish independence, they invited the different leaders to rally round them; and the summons was obeyed by Wallace, Douglas, Sir Alexander Lindsay, Sir Andrew Moray, and Sir Richard Lundy. But dissensions and the fear of Edward separated the weak of heart from the strong. All capitulated save Wallace and Moray, who having nothing to lose persevered in their purpose. This circumstance increased their popularity with the people and the common soldiers. The greater part of the army followed them in their retreat beyond the Firth. On the 10th of September, 1298, they suddenly rushed upon the royal army led by Warenne the marshal of Scotland, routed them and put to the sword five thousand English knights and foot soldiers on the left bank of the Forth. This unexpected disaster broke all the plans of Warenne. Scotland was rid of foreigners. Wallace and Moray crossed the borders, and during a month Northumberland and Cumberland were ravaged by a revengeful soldiery.[47] Wallace reached the height of his power. He called himself "the guardian of the Kingdom, and general of the armies of Scotland," under which title he summoned a parliament to meet at Perth.

Perhaps in this assembly the question of asking aid from the Apostolic See was discussed. It is certain the request was made to Boniface, who openly undertook to defend the independence of Scotland. On July 10th, 1298, he wrote to Edward earnestly exhorting him to live at peace with his neighbors, the Scotch, and to listen no longer to the suggestions of his ambition.[48] To a request conveyed in such general terms it was easy to return an evasive answer. Wallace dispatched envoys to Rome who more powerfully interested Boniface in their favor. They referred their quarrel with the king of England to his decision, because he was the only judge whose jurisdiction extended over both kingdoms: they reminded him that by remaining indifferent, he would suffer Edward to annex to his own throne a realm, which of right belonged to the See of Rome as a fief.

Boniface in welcoming the Scotch envoys had before his mind the rights of the Church, and those of a people struggling for their liberty, which Edward violated. By word and by a document the legates stated their claims, which Boniface sent to Edward. The English historians of this time assert that Boniface was led by the spirit of

[47] Lingard. History of England. Vol. II, pages 181, 182.
[48] Rymer, II, 827.

ambition, more than justice, when he declared Scotland to be a fief of the Church. Yet Edward knew well the contrary to be the truth. For when he desired Nicholas IV in 1290 to confirm the usurped right of the English crown over Scotland, Nicholas replied that he could not do it, because it would be to deprive the Roman See of a realm which was subject to it.[49] Therefore Boniface wrote to Edward from Anagni on June 27th, declaring that the king should know, that Scotland had belonged from the ancient times, and did still belong, in full right to the Roman See. He then proved it was not a fief of the English crown, from the following instances: 1st, When Henry, his father, sought assistance from Alexander, King of Scotland, in his war with Simon de Montfort, Earl of Leicester, he acknowledged by letters patent that it was as a favor, from an independent king, and not as a feudal service. 2nd, When the same Edward, desirous of having Alexander of Scotland present on the occasion of his coronation, he declared by letters patent that the Scottish King came not as a vassal, but through courtesy. 3rd, Alexander's oath of fidelity to Edward concerned, not Scotland, but the lands he possessed in the confines of England, and Edward publicly recognized the oath in this sense. 4th, At the death of King Alexander the custody of Scotland did not fall into the hands of Edward, but of the Scotch nobles chosen by popular vote on account of the tender age of Margaret, niece of Edward and daughter of Alexander. 5th, At the death of Margaret, although the chiefs of the Scottish nation on account of dissensions concerning a successor, had made Edward the arbiter of their quarrel, they did not however constitute him their master. 6th, In the treaty of marriage between the prince of England and Margaret it was declared, that the kingdom of Scotland should remain forever free and independent, and in case of her death be restored in that state to the next heir. Finally as most certain proof of the independence of Scotland and its separation from the English realm was the fact that the Popes always assigned separate legations to those kingdoms. The violent sub-

[49] "Se non posse in regno Scotiae, sedi Apostolicae obnoxio, Ecclesiae Romanae derogare, ejusque fiduciarios Regi Anglo submittere." Year 1290, Vatican Registers, letter 102,—

jection of Scotland manifested itself also in the bad treatment of the clergy, especially the Bishops of Glasgow and Sondor, and other clergy, who having opposed his ambitious projects, were subjected to an ignominious imprisonment; and that crowd of ministers whom he had left in that unhappy kingdom to squeeze out and take away the sacred life substance of the churches. Hence the Pontiff expressed the hope that the king, desisting from an unjust aggression, would set at liberty the bishops, clergy and natives of Scotland, whom he had held in captivity; and if he thought he had any right to the whole or part of that kingdom, would pursue his claim to it within the six months following to the Holy See.[50]

It is true that in the period of time which elapsed between the death of Alexander, and the election of John Baliol to the Scottish throne, Edward had firmly established himself in Scotland, both because she placed herself in his hands to put an end to the contentions of the three pretenders to the crown; and, as he said, because the rights of England over that kingdom went back to ancient times. He had caused the archives of monasteries to be searched, and their chronicles to be consulted, which gave him most favorable answers to his projects.[51] It could not be denied that the Scotch had paid homage to him in the person of John Baliol. But it had been done either by the will of John, who was king by the will of Edward, and for that reason agreeable to him, and not by the people; or because the Scotch through fear of intestine wars had yielded unwillingly; yet it is true that they obtained from Pope Celestine a release from the oath by which John Baliol had bound Scotland to England,[52] and they continued to fight with varied success in order to gain their liberty. Boniface deputed the Archbishop of Canterbury to bear this letter to Edward, under pain of deposition from office if he failed to do so, and to report to him every act and word of the king when he read the Papal document.[53] But the Papal letters did not reach Edward

[50] Lingard's History of England Vol. II, page 185.
[51] Knyghton de Event. Angliae Book 3, col 2470.—Nich. Trivetti. Chronicles year 1292.—Archery ap. tom. 3. page 213.
[52] Knyghton de Event. Angliae, Book 3, col. 2477.
[53] Vatican Register 5. Epistle 465. Raynaldus 99-19.

in time. Only after a year could the Archbishop deliver them, and so they were of no avail to save Scotland and her valiant Wallace. The latter was defeated and his army destroyed by Edward after a bloody battle. He renounced the title of guardian, and hid himself in the forests and lived a roaming life in order not be a witness of the evils of his unhappy country.[54] So Scotland having been inspired with the hope of liberty by Philip the Fair, received no aid whatever from him. The only favor he obtained from Edward was the release of John Baliol, who on July 14th, 1299, was given into the custody of the Papal legate, the Bishop of Vicenza. This unfortunate king retired to his estates of Bailleul in Normandy, France, where he ended his days six years later.[55]

Edward was camping with his army at Caerlaverock when Winchelsey, Archbishop of Canterbury, bearing the Papal letter presented himself on August 26th, 1300. The letter was publicly read in Latin and French in the presence of the King and the barons. It is quite true that the letter was not pleasing to Edward. But peace with France was not yet concluded; Gascony was still sequestered in the hands of the Papal legates; and Scotland conquered but restless under the yoke. Unwilling to offend one whose friendship was so necessary to him, to gain time he replied that in a matter which concerned the crown it was his duty to consult his counsellors: that shortly he would assemble his parliament, and with its advice would return a satisfactory answer to the Pontiff. In fact he assembled a parliament at Lincoln on the 27th of September. All the universities sent their doctors in law; and who brought from monasteries every document in their possession, which could bear upon the question. After some debate a reply was framed, which was signed by one hundred and four earls and barons, in the name of the people of England. In this they show that Scotland never belonged in temporals to the see of Rome; that the indubitable right of sovereignty which England possessed over that realm should not be brought into question; that they were obliged by oath to defend it, and were most ready to defend it so as not to prejudice the rights of the

[54] Lingard. History of England Vol. 2, page 189. [55] Mat. Westm. 431.

crown, the liberties, custom and laws, which they inherited from their fathers.[56]

Edward wrote also his defence, which provoked a reply from the Scotch. Edward made use of a ridiculous invention and traced back his rights to the remote age of Elias and Samuel. The Scots opposed fiction to fiction, and declared that they were sprung from Scota, the daughter of Pharaoh, who landed in Ireland and whose descendants wrested by force of arms the northern half of Britain, and therefore they owe no subjection to the Britons. From fables they both pass on to history; but neither furnished proofs.[57] However, the Scotch remained subject to England, because the only hope of their liberty was gone; for Boniface at that period found himself involved in other affairs, and was engaged in defending his own and not the independence of others.

In the league formed by Edward against Philip the Fair, we have seen that one of its members was Adolph of Nassau, chosen the successor of Rudolph of Hapsburg, to be the King of the Romans. He did nothing against France, but to have declared himself an enemy was sufficient to inspire Philip with the desire of revenge. Adolph had as a rival in the election Albert of Austria, eldest son of Rudolph, who was rejected by the electors, because he was too haughty, and of excessive ambition, although he was possessed of great military courage. Having failed in the strong desire he had of reigning, he hovered about Adolph in order to supplant him. Philip knew this; he offered to aid him to mount the throne in order to revenge himself on Adolph. He sent him money, and promised to recommend him to Boniface. The Archbishop of Mayence, the Dukes of Saxony and Brandenburg embraced his cause, and professed friendship. These three electors having come together again at Mayence in 1298 decided that Adolph was headstrong, under the influence of young and inexperienced advisers, and wanting in mental ability and pecuniary resources; they agreed that he was no longer worthy of the royal crown, which suited better the head of Albert. They acquainted the latter of their will, and entreated him to go and implore the Pope to bestow on him the crown of

---

[56] Chronicles. Nich. Trivetti apud Archery Spicil. tom. 3, col. 224 sq.
[57] Lingard. History of England. Vol. II, page 187.

the king of the Romans. To Albert all this seemed to fall from heaven, and quickly consenting to the request of the electors, he immediately dispatched his ambassador the Count of Hagirloch to Boniface, who not being able to obtain anything from his master, returned joyful with forged Papal letters, which he palmed off as genuine, and which declared that Boniface was in every way favorable to Albert. The legates of Adolph hastened to Rome, and spoke to Boniface of these letters. He assured them that he did not listen to the petition of Albert at all, nor did he send any letters whatever; they should return and report to the king, who in confirmation of the assertion, would be anointed Emperor, if he would come to Rome. But those electors, either because they considered the letters genuine which the Count of Hagirloch had brought from Rome, or because they pretended to believe them as such, repaired to the cathedral of Mayence and announced Albert as king, with slight consent of the Germans; the princes favored Albert, and the people Adolph. Then the rivals began a furious war, and in the battle fought at Glenheim near Worms, Albert, not thinking of anything else but the killing of his rival, threw the whole weight of battle upon him, who, although he fought with incredible valor, yet was killed by the hand of Albert himself on July 2nd. A universal diet at Frankfort confirmed the conqueror as King of the Romans, and he was crowned at Aix-la-Chapelle.

The death of Adolph and the elevation of Albert to the throne with a blood-stained crown could not be approved by Boniface. He did not find any inviolability in the right nor power in the fact that raised Albert to the throne. For the former he declared did not exist, when his approval was asked by the Count of Hagirloch, and the latter was wanting when he would not consent to the violent intrusion of Albert into the government.[58] For the Roman Pontiffs claimed as theirs the right to examine the chosen king of the Romans, to anoint him, to consecrate him, and to declare his fitness for ruling.[59] Nor was this an assumption of rights. The Electors themselves acknowledged it; for they found no other legal argument for

[58] Ptolemy of Lucca. Hist. of Church, Book 24, chap. 37.
[59] Epistle to Mogunt et Trevir. Archiepiscopos. Raynaldus, yr. 1301, no. 2.

substituting Albert in place of Adolph than that of obtaining Papal letters, which would appoint the Hapsburg Prince to the royal dignity. For this reason he rebuffed the ambassadors of Albert who had come to ask him to confirm the election of this prince which he declared to be absolutely null.[60]

In the meantime Albert with that strong disposition of mind, which at first the Electors had feared so much, began to strengthen himself on the throne, by humbling the nobles and depriving the cities of their liberties. And that Philip of France might not undertake to disturb him, he entered into a treaty of peace with him; and in order next to gain favor of Boniface, he spread the rumor that he was willing to engage the Turks in battle.[61] In fact at that time Christian affairs in the East were in the worst possible condition; and if Albert had been truly a king, and had been in earnest in regard to war, Boniface would have most willingly favored his desire. For at the time that Albert having triumphed over his rival ascended the throne, Boniface had received messengers and letters from Scombal, King of Armenia, and from the Patriarch of that nation, appealing to him for aid against the Turks. Boniface replied to them kindly,[62] exhorting them to bear a little longer the afflictions they were receiving at the hands of the infidels. For the establishment of peace between Philip and Edward, the more decided attachment of James of Aragon to the Roman See, and the probable conquest of Sicily inspired him with the hope of seeing again the West in arms for the holy undertaking. But the times of the Crusades were past; and we do not doubt that Boniface was of this opinion. Many had thought that continual recommendation to the notice of Princes the expedition to the Holy Land, had been a cunning device of the Popes, to open for the passions of princes and people in a distant land, so that alone and without molestation they could cause to spread more widely in their states the roots of the tree of the Pontifical power. It may be that in certain distressing circumstances, like those occasioned by the House of Suabia, the Popes encouraged a crusade in order

[60] Ptolemy of Lucca History of the Church. Book 24, chap. 37.
[61] Raynaldus, no. 16.
[62] Book IV, epistle 61. Raynaldus, ibidem epistle 271.

to create a diversion but that their efforts in opposing the vile Islamitic generation, in recovering the Holy Sepulchre, the holiest monument in the land of the divine mysteries, was with a view to their own advantage, this we can never believe. Religion in mankind desires and assumes human forms, in which interior worship is more readily developed and enlivened. In the Middle Ages, a time of pure and candid piety, and of a strong and generous temperament, the Holy Land, the Holy Sepulchre was precisely the exterior form best expressing the interior belief, both because it concerned more immediately, so to speak, Christ the object of the worship, and because in conquering it that martial spirit, which in those times was most abundant, was to be exercised. And the Papacy never having been a stranger to this tendency, but, on the contrary, its guide and support, could not resign its office, except when the spirit of the times having changed, the people would have found some other means of expression. From these religious conditions of the people those military orders originated, which were to unite a brave warrior to the austerities of the cloister (a difficult union), and which from the start wonderfully aided the Europeans in their pious efforts in the East. But afterwards these instruments of war, on account of the existence of a long peace began to rust and degenerate; and later when the love of the Holy War ceased, they began by degrees to be dissolved. In the time of Boniface when the thought of recovering the Holy Land had not as yet died out, these Knight Hospitalers and Templars, were honored and favored by the Pope. When the thought of fighting the infidels had grown cold within the kings they forgot the many immunities and privileges which these religious military orders enjoyed. Although the island of Cyprus was a stepping-stone to the East for the Christians, and had much to fear from the Turks, yet Henry its King, fearing more the power of the Templars, sought to restrain and curtail it. He had imposed a tax of two bezants a head on their domestics and slaves, and as the Templars and Hospitalers could not acquire new estates without the permission of the King and of the Pope, he had enacted a law forbidding them to increase their holdings by even a span. The fear was not groundless. James de Molay,

Grand Master of the Templars, with all his fellow knights, began to make loud complaints, which Boniface heeded. He wrote to Henry telling him not to act harshly towards them,[63] to esteem them for their custody of his kingdom, and for the sake of future expeditions to the Holy Land, and to remember the good service they had rendered religion. For this purpose he sent certain friars with a Constitution, that would reconcile him with these powerful Knights.

The appeal which Boniface made for aid to be extended to the king of Armenia against the Turks manifested his dispositions and his moderation towards Philip. We have seen how his decision as Gaetani had excited in the French prince jealousy of state to such a degree as to call forth a remonstrance in defence of his rights. This was a sign that a poison was fermenting in the heart of Philip since the proclamation of the Constitution *"Clericis Laicos."* The Pope perceived it, and remained silent; although it was urgent for him to complain, because Philip did not desist from violating the sacred immunities. Philip abused this silence. However, externally they seemed friendly, and between them there was such a display of kind offices, that the people without knowing the truth, said the two princes were at peace. As to a most Christian king, Boniface wrote to Philip in October, 1298, recommending to him the King of Armenia harassed by the Turks. In the letter there was a confidence in the piety and good will of the King, and the Pope seemed certain that if he would not go himself, at least he would send a French army to that country.[64] On the other hand Philip affected to be a loving son of Holy Church, and as if consumed by zeal for the Lord, he published an edict which declared: " How in order that the Inquisition might " succeed against the wicked heretics, for the glory of God " and the growth of Faith, he commanded the Dukes, the " Counts, Barons, Stewards, Bailiffs, and Provosts, of his " kingdom, if they wished to show themselves truly faith- " ful to us, to obey their bishops and the inquisitors " deputed or to be deputed by the Apostolic See, by bring- " ing before them, whenever requested, all heretics, their

---

[63] Boniface's Letters. Book 5, 46 apud Raynaldus 21, year 1298–Book V. Epistle 180, Raynaldus, year 1299–38. [64] Raynaldus, year 1298, no. 19.

"abettors, believers, and receivers, and to execute forthwith all sentences of the judges of the Church, notwithstanding any appeal or complaint whatsoever the heretics or abettors might make, as all way of appeal to them was closed."[65] These things he sanctioned against the heretics, who were not troublesome to him, but rather an advantage on account of a pious confiscation he made of the goods of heretics. But he did many other things which truly called for an inquiry. He had an insatiable thirst for gold, and that of his ministers still greater. The Count of Artois had been in possession of the city of Cambrai, which belonged to the Bishop, and in the mildest terms Boniface had entreated him to restore it. Philip had appropriated for himself the revenues of the Church of Rheims during a vacancy of that See, and he refused to restore them to the new Archbishop, Robert of Courtenay. The Pope in the strongest terms recalled to his mind how that custody which the secular princes exercised over the vacant benefices was only tolerated by the Church, and ceased as soon as a new incumbent was chosen; his ministers had shamefully seized the sacred revenues which they should only have guarded, and then should have delivered to the newly-elected beneficiary.[66] Philip turned a deaf ear to these remonstrances. Boniface insisted by letters which he sent directly to the Prince and also made use of the good offices of the Count of St. Paul, that he might prevail upon him to act justly. But the French King wished to abuse all those concessions, which the Pope had been obliged to make in the Constitution " *Clericis Laicos,*" in order that he might not complain. His officials under the pretence of taking the necessary subsidies for war out of the revenues of the churches, seized them, and in doing so made no distinction between the limits of Church and of the State.[67] Philip who certainly did not suffer from scruples, when he was draining both people and churches of their gold, fully understood the wicked rule he exercised over the sacred patrimonies, and the justice of the Pope's remonstrance; but not wishing to depart from a road which was so delightful, he thought rather of strengthening himself in order to present a

[65] Ordonne de France, tom. I, page 330.   [66] Raynaldus, 23.
[67] Raynaldus, 25.

bolder front to Boniface when an open rupture would come.

Albert, the new King of Romans, not having succeeded in obtaining from the Pope a confirmation of his elevation to the throne of Germany, certainly did not bear any good will towards Boniface, whom he well knew was not of such a mild disposition as to yield to him; and he saw dimly in the distance the consequences of that clash, when the fact in his hands would engage the right in the hands of Boniface. Therefore he did not rest content and inactive, but set about energetically in his search for some one, in a like condition in opposition to the Pontiff, who in joining his forces with his, could resist Boniface, or at least intimidate him to their own advantage. Hence Philip of France and Albert agreed in their way of thinking; and those rights which could not be settled by the force of arms between Philip and Alphonsus, they decided by friendly treaties and ties of marriage. The two princes met in December of that year at Vancouleurs in Lorraine, and the former friendly relations were restored which once existed between Germany and France, and which were disturbed by the rights which Adolph claimed over the kingdom of Arles. They were willing to come to an agreement the reason for which was not difficult to find. Albert ceded to France the kingdom of Arles, and France surrendered her rights over Lorraine and Alsace. They defined the boundaries of the two kingdoms; and by oath they both bound themselves to defend each other in preserving their respective rights; and in order to seal this alliance by some stronger argument, it was agreed that Rudolph, Duke of Austria, son of Albert should marry Blanche, the sister of Philip.[68] Philip and Albert concluded these holy peaceful relations with their minds intent on Boniface as if to call forth respect from him by that show of strength they presented in that alliance, the one entreating him to make legitimate the crown stolen from the murdered Adolph, and the other claiming the right to pillage the churches and so act as King and Pope at one and the same time. In fact Albert, whilst Blanche was being escorted to Austria for the marriage with his son, so certain was he that these ties of relationship would

---

[68] Spondani, year 1299, tom. I, page 327.

move Boniface, that he sent another message entreating him to confirm him as King of the Romans. But Boniface would not yield to the murderer of Adolph, nor did he allow himself to be intimidated by the Franco-German alliance. Moreover he gave such a peremptory refusal, as to furnish occasion to a certain Ghibelline writer to relate, that having received the messengers of Albert seated on a throne with a crown on his head and a sword at his side, with the ostentation of king he said: " It is I, I, who am Caesar, it is I who am the Emperor." [69] However since Albert did not ask to validate a false right, he was able finally to arrive at the fulfilment of his desires, because rights are engendered by deeds; but Philip never, because injustice can never be sanctified into a right.

But in the meantime affairs in Sicily did not seem to take so favorable turn as to leave the mind of Boniface free to think of Jerusalem. After the defection of Roger of Loria, Frederick far from fearing the great preparation made in Rome against him, dared himself and incited others to resist, no matter what his fate might be. As long as the Sicilians were faithful, he desired to be king and king of Sicily. We cannot understand how Boniface with his penetration, with his knowledge and practical judgment of men, did not see so far into the mind of James of Aragon as to notice that he showed himself most devoted to Rome, and most ready to wage war against his brother, while the papal favors were falling about him, while he was collecting tithes from the churches, and the crown of Sardinia was on his head, but in the depth of his heart he still nourished bitterness against Rome because of her efforts to drive the Aragon family out of Sicily. Gold and Sardinia were things of the present, services to be rendered were those of the future. The selection of James for the conquest of Sicily did not help the undertaking. Of James' dispositions and of the impropriety of the means Boniface afterward was convinced, but too late.

Everything was prepared for the war in such a manner that there seemed to be no uncertainty of the victory. The Aragonese fleet of forty galleys in union with that

[69] Benven. da Im. Cronic.—Comment. on the Divina Commedia.

of Charles King of Naples was large and very well manned. That eminent warrior Roger of Loria commanded it, who to skill in military affairs added a knowledge of the sea and the Sicilian coasts, where the war was to be waged. James therefore set sail with his fleet; he landed on the Roman shores and went to interview Boniface. In the meantime Frederick was not unprepared, being aided wonderfully by the fiery Sicilians He placed on the sea sixty-four galleys, manned by the choicest sailors, experienced in naval battles. He chose as Admiral, a brave Genoese, Andrew Doria. So much did their courage increase in the face of danger that he was impatient of delays, and wished to encounter the enemy. He sailed as far as Naples to meet it. The Sicilian fleet sailed along the Neapolitan coast, and was ploughing the waves with colors displayed, as if defying to battle, hoping thereby to entice Charles to some feat of arms, or to vanquish him before he was joined by James. But James sent word to Frederick saying that he should not try the fortune of a battle outside of his own kingdom and should withdraw.[70] This does not appear to be the message of an enemy, but of a friend, and we believe the Aragonese king endured more fatigue in pretending war than sustaining it. However, Frederick having retired from Naples, James conducted to that city his fleet, which together with the Neapolitan numbered more than eighty galleys. With Charles of Naples and the Cardinal Legate on board, he directed his course towards Sicily in August of 1298. Roger of Loria opened the way for them. He pointed out to them suitable positions, where perhaps still linger the memory of his power and where were his friends and vassals. So the ecclesiastical militia sailing along the east coast of Sicily, the city of Patti and some other fortresses soon capitulated. The name alone of Loria was more effective than arms. The fleet set out for Syracuse and laid siege to it; but the city stubbornly held out. In the meantime the provinces that surrendered either were forced, or by their own will returned to the rule of Frederick, and the pontifical army between disease and the sword was greatly decimated, for Frederick taking refuge in Catania sent his light soldiers in small bands

---

[70] Fazzelli, Book IX, cap. 3.

to harass the enemy often by furious and deadly skirmishes. In these encounters the brave Blasco of Alagone at the head of a band of Catalonians was ambushed, and made prisoner with them; and also John of Loria, nephew of Roger, suffered a defeat and was made a prisoner, on his return from provisioning Patti with a few ships.[71] Avoiding therefore great battles, and thus harassing the hostile army, Frederick obliged James to return without advantage to Naples, but before his departure James asked his brother for some ships which the people of Messina had prepared for John of Loria and promised him peace, but Frederick's reply was to offer battle which James prudently refused.

It was now the month of March in the year 1299, and Boniface saw that little or nothing had been gained; yet he did not lose confidence in James. He imagined perhaps the cause of his return was the threats made on the frontier of his kingdom, for which reason he suddenly left Naples for Spain. So in order to renew the war he allowed him to collect tithes from the churches of Valencia, Catalonia, Aragon and the Balearic Islands.[72] He took him under his protection, and restrained other princes from molesting him during the Sicilian war.[73] And that the soldiers might know that the war was to be waged for the common Mother the Church, he granted them holy indulgences.[74] He afterwards deputed William, Archbishop elect of Salerno to see that confessors were not wanting in the fleet, who would immediately absolve from censures those of the enemy, who would pass over to the party of the Church, and who would oblige them by oath to remain faithful.[75]

The tithes were a good gift but for the present war ready money was necessary. James did not have it and Boniface was slow to give it to a servant whose honesty of purpose he began to suspect. The Aragonese Prince tried to get it from the Neapolitans. Having returned from Spain, he joined his fleet to that of the Neapolitans, and on the 24th of June he set sail steering his course for Sicily with the intention of trying again the fortunes of

[71] Special. Book 4, c. 6, 7.
[72] Ibidem, Epistle 206, 207, Raynaldus 2.
[73] Book 5, Epist. 208. Ray. I.
[74] Ibidem, Epistle 193, Raynaldus 1.
[75] Ib. Ep. 193, Raynaldus 2.

war. The famous Roger of Loria commanded the fleet, and the presence of James, Robert Duke of Calabria, and Philip Prince of Taranto inspired them with courage. Frederick set out with forty galleys from the harbor of Messina with men eager for the fray, and led by most skilful captains and many Sicilian barons. He wished to engage the enemy, to prevent it from reaching the Sicilian coasts, and to vanquish it in open battle. But either because the winds were unfavorable, or the Catalonian pilots were more skilful and their fleet was handled better, the latter arrived at Sicily near the coast of St. Mark, and immediately they formed in line turning their prows towards the Sicilian fleet, which ardently desiring battle, sailed directly to meet it. We shall not relate how furiously the two fleets fought, since Nicholas Speciale had written at length about it;[76] we shall only say that the victory won by James over his brother was entirely of the work of the invincible Roger of Loria, who to the hate he had for Frederick added an incredible thirst for revenge on account of the death of the incautious John of Loria, his nephew, whom the Sicilians had imprisoned, as we related. He planned the battle; he ordered the sudden attack from behind upon the assailants, and inspired the minds of all with his own implacable hate. Eighteen galleys were surrendered to James, and six thousand Sicilians perished in those disastrous waters, among whom were many barons, who by the authority of their name, and the number of their followers, had up to that time confirmed Sicily in its determination of not being subject to the Papal will.[77] Crushed and blood-stained the Sicilians retreated, and with them Frederick, who in that battle mingled with the soldiers with so much bravery, that he seemed a common soldier more than a king. Villani, who lived at that time, declared afterwards that through the artifice of James with his Catalonians, Frederick was allowed to escape, as it was publicly reported.[78]

---

[76] Book IV, Chap. 14.   [77] Speciale. Book IV c 14.

[78] Here are his own words: " It is said with reason, that if King James had willed it, Don Frederick, his brother, would have remained a prisoner after his galley fell under the power of the prince of Aragon, and that the war in Sicily would have ended. But, whether such was the will of James, or such was the will of the Catalonian nation, they allowed him to es-

Such was the result of the naval battle of Cape Orlando, that if James had passed through Sicily, without giving time to the enemy to recover their spirits, it is most certain that the war would have been terminated by the conquest of the island. But, contrary to the expectations of the two sons of Charles, and of Roger of Loria, having exchanged prisoners with Frederick, he allowed Robert of Calabria and Roger to continue the war. It is true that if the power of his brother was broken, he himself did not come out of that terrible battle unscathed, and his fleet was badly injured, but nevertheless he was victorious, and Roger was with him; and then the awful defeat and the loss of those valient barons made the Sicilians more docile, as the desire for revenge had not as yet succeeded to the distress of adversity. He set sail for Salerno where he expected to meet the afflicted Constance his mother, who in those days was the most miserable of mothers, as she perhaps had never taken her eyes off those waves, which might have been reddened by the blood of one of her sons. He then sailed for Naples, and saw Charles who did not accord him the best welcome.[79] Even on him this sudden departure made a bad impression. So James returned to Catalonia in bad repute with the Angevines, and detested by the Sicilians, who however, if he wished, he could have reduced to the direst straits.[80]

Boniface was very displeased over the return of James to Catalonia; on considering that this prince had not arrested Frederick in the battle of Cape Orlando, and had abandoned the affair at the very moment in which he could have gathered the fruits of a signal victory, he clearly perceived that the reasons of his departure were pretended, and that he acted in bad faith.[81] This motive, added to a desire of not interrupting the course of prosperity in Sicily, fixed his attention more strongly on that country; but he had still more at heart not to lose that which he had reconquered, and not to expose to danger the army which remained entirely in the hands of Charles.

cape." Book 8, chap. 29.—Ptolemy of Lucca, also a cotemporary writer affirms the same, Hist. Eccl.

[79] Speciale. Book IV, chap. 15 . . . . "a quo non multum diligenter acceptusest."

[80] Speciale, Book IV, cap. 15.   [81] Mariani, Book IX, chap. 3.

James being at a distance, and probably caring very little for the enterprise which had been intrusted to him, Boniface trembled; for if the fleet would encounter a defeat, it would be difficult to repair it. He restrained Charles and exhorted him not to trust to the chances of fortune. But this prince who had drafted other soldiers could not restrain himself, especially since the good news arrived of the deeds of Robert, his son, and Roger of Loria, who were making many fine conquests in Sicily, and among them of Catania itself. To his son Philip prince of Taranto, impatient and desirous of engaging in some signal enterprise, he intrusted forty galleys and a goodly number of soldiers. The commander was the valiant captain Peter Salvacossa, who had deserted the party of Frederick.[82] From the distance Boniface protested against Philip venturing a battle with that force. He wrote to Charles to restrain him and to prevent him from going, or if having gone to Sicily to recall him. He would also have him remember his oath of fealty to the Roman See, and know that he would be visited with censures in order to restrain him and his son from the foolish enterprise; and that he had intrusted to the Archbishop of Naples the infliction of the censures.[82] The Pope wrote these things on the 2nd of November, and in the beginning of this month the young prince had set sail for Sicily, steering towards the promontory Lilibeo, where he landed with his army. The entreaties and commands of Boniface were, as it were, a certain presentiment of disaster. For a month had hardly passed since his departure from Naples, when, on the plains of Falconaria between Marsala and Trapani, Philip measured his strength with Frederick, by whom he was defeated and made prisoner. Thus was lost the fruit of the victory of Cape Orlando, and those enmities and the war were prolonged without any benefit to either party. Then Boniface saw wither all the hopes he had placed in James which afterwards he sought to revive in Charles of Valois. Had he from the beginning entrusted to this prince the rights of the Church over Sicily, affairs might perhaps have taken a more prosperous turn, and the war might have been waged more honestly by a Frenchman, who was not a brother of Frederick.

[82] Book V, Epistle 591, Raynaldus 4.

Now we can not dismiss the account of the Sicilian war without mentioning a most atrocious fact, which as an instance of the ferocity of those times, also makes known to us the vigilance of Boniface, and his immediate remedy for every disorder that offended the sacred laws of nature. Among the followers of Frederick, there was a certain Montanero Sosa, who not by the art of war, but by perfidy had put to death a handful of Frenchmen and being possessed by the demon of avarice conceived a wicked plan for making money. He set about to boil the dead bodies of the slain, in order to remove the flesh from the bones, which he afterwards sold at a high price to the relatives of the dead, that they might carry them for burial to their own country. And thus, says Fazzelli, he sold the dead whom in life he had betrayed.[83] It is true this custom originated among the Crusaders, who in order not to leave in the land of the infidels the bodies of the men either dear to them, or illustrious by birth, removed the flesh from the bones, that they might bear them away with them, as we read was done with the body of St. Louis of France. This treatment of human bodies even if they were corpses, was a great irreverence shown to the divine handiwork. And yet it was often made use of by those in high position, either to bury their dead relations in grand sepulchres at home or with the pious desire of securing the bones of their relatives who died in far off countries, they disembowelled them, and boiled them in loathsome boilers. Boniface published a Constitution,[84] in which detesting the horrible practise, he threatened with solemn excommunication all those guilty of the barbarous practise of removing the flesh from human bones.

Although, as we have related, Boniface did not lose sight of those foul heretics, the Fraticelli, and quickly brought them to trial, yet they did not stop their evil practises, and in the false garb of sheep they were worse than ravenous wolves. Miserable religious they were, expelled from monasteries and fanatical founders of new orders and reforms. They fixed their abodes in the Abruzzi mountains and in the Marches of Ancona. As we have previously stated, these poisonous shoots had sprung from some poisonous root. Censures had little or no effect

[83] Fazz. ib.   [84] Extrav. Commun. Tit. De sepultura, cap. I.

upon them, because they did not care to know or have any connection with the Pope or Church. Strict observers of the rule of St. Francis, this was of more value in their eyes than the Gospel, or anything else. At the solicitation of Boniface, Friar Matthew of Chieti, Inquisitor, pursued them.[85] That is to say that the pursuit was relentless. They then left the continent, and fled to Sicily; and there surfeited with food, and heated by much wine, they formed a procession of real bacchanals, and to the accompaniment of certain reed trumpets, they sang a hymn which began thus: "*Rejoice, O Harlot Church,*" meaning thereby to slander the Roman Church. And afterwards they broke these instruments and a cup to signify by this the end of the Church. They passed over to Greece, where they spread their bad doctrines; but Boniface preceded them by a letter to the Patriarch of Constantinople. and the Archbishops of Patrasso and Athens, in order that they would suppress them. They took refuge in Achaia. This vile troupe of heretics was certainly not to be treated with indifference nor despised, because the people, deceived by those appearances of rigid poverty, began to consider them as saints and to venerate their relics. Bernard Guido,[86] relates that the inquisitors of heresy were obliged to disinter the ashes of Herman, a heretic of Ferrara, and scatter them to the winds; and demolish an altar which the people had erected to him as a saint. The same was done with the remains of a low-bred English woman who declared herself the Holy Ghost become incarnate for the salvation of her sex.[87] Now if these stupid doctrines could not prevail so much as to deceive cultured minds, they however were among the people as a ridiculous expression of certain theories which sprang up in minds, not altogether uncouth nor uncultured, and which could menace the nobler parts of the Church. In this very year John Oliva died, of whom we have spoken, who in his commentaries on the book of the Apocalypse of St. John, after giving utterance to many extravagances concerning St. Francis, his rule, his strict poverty and so forth, bitterly assailed the Church and Pope, calling the former a New Synagogue, Babylon, a harlot, and already

[85] Reg. Vatic. epi. 170 Ray. 55.   [86] Chron. Rom. Pont.
[87] Annal. Domin. Colmar. year 1301.—

dying; and the latter Antichrist in flesh.[88] Now these doctrines taught by a man considered a saint outwardly, and learned as Oliva was, could be agreeably embraced by those, who, impatient of the jurisdiction of the Church, were restless under the lash of Boniface. This is the reason why Boniface was vigilant, and the inquisitors active.

As we have said, the Fraticelli were a most wicked offspring of the excellent Franciscan Order, and hence Boniface pursued them relentlessly; so it is well to remark that this Order had no greater admirer and protector than this Pontiff. He removed them from the jurisdiction of bishops; he conceded to their rectors full power of judgment over their subjects according to the constitutions of the order without regard to the general prescription of the law; and confirmed all their privileges in a Bull entitled "*Mare Magnum.*"[89] He often employed Franciscans in legations and in the government of churches. Friar Porchetto Spinola was placed by him over the Archiepiscopal see of Genoa; Friar Alamanno of Bagnorea over the Archiepiscopal see of Abora in Sardinia, who also had the privilege of exercising episcopal jurisdiction in Rome as Vicar of the Pope, even while he himself was present; Friar John of Lamois, created Penitentiary of the Pope, and sent on many embassies, was appointed to the see of Rennes, and afterwards translated to that of Lisieux.[90] These favors were granted in return for the great services given the Church by these friars. The character of the Order was such that it corresponded well to that of the times; and many men of rare learning became members of it. And since it was still in its first fervor, the Mendicants, and also the Dominicans were ever most ready for all those works in the performance of which there was needed a perfect abnegation of human nature. Therefore poor, penitent, zealous and diligent in preaching and in the administration of the sacraments, they alone confronted the dangers in the far off missions of the infidel countries.

But the justice of the recompense did not seem clear to

[88] Constit. 66, John XXII, in Extrav. Communiter nonnullos.
[89] Wadding. Annal. Minorum Tom. V, page 340.
[90] Wadding. Idem, years 1298, 1299.

the bishops and pastors. They saw on a par with them certain companions who up to that time were unknown in the exercise of their ministry. The Friars were bearers of Papal ordinances, which rendered them no longer subjects of the bishops but their helpers, and they lessened the ministry of the pastors. The decrees were just, because the diocesan clergy in those times were in need of help and co-laborers, and the Pontiffs of ministers freer and more active in the application of their power; but the bishops complained, because they did not wish to have the Friars Minor on a par with them, but under them. We shall not speak of the dissensions which this state of affairs engendered; but only of the provisions made by Boniface in favor of the Friars. In the year 1299 he published the Bull *"Super Cathedram,"* [91] in which he gave full permission to all the Mendicant Friars to preach in the Church or on the square, provided at the same moment the Bishop did not preach there, or they did not preach in his presence. When invited and with the permission of the pastor they could preach in the parish churches; only the permission of the bishops was to be asked for the friars selected by their superiors to administer the sacrament of penance; if the bishop should refuse, they could do so by concession of the Pope; the friars could bury the dead in their churches, reserving however for the pastors the fourth part of the money they received for the obsequies. Finally he exhorted the bishops and pastors not to molest the friars, but to favor them, and assist them with alms. Little good resulted from these provisions; the quarrels did not end, but rather increased in intensity.

The times were hard and embarrassing, and a Pope who did not wish to close his eyes to the course events were taking needed to be a man of a strong and resolute nature. We have already seen how Boniface, after declaring war against the Colonnas, had sent Cardinal Aquasparta to start a crusade against them, promising the same indulgences that were granted to the crusaders in the Holy Land. The report of the rebellion of the Colonnas, and the help which Boniface stood in need of to repress them agitated the people greatly; and they answered the appeal

[91] Extrav. communiter.

beyond expectations, they rushed to arms, and took the cross. Even the Orsinis the enemies of the Colonnas agitated the undertaking of this war.[92] Florence had sent to the aid of the Pope two hundred cavalry and six hundred infantry under the leadership of Cianco of Montespertoli and Davizo of Galiano; (Villani reports only six hundred in all, arches and spearsmen,) also two hundred cavalry from Orvieto,[93] and other soldiers from Matelica[94] under the banner of the municipality of Florence.[95] If we may believe the chronicles of Paulinus of Piero, even the women were filled with the desire of aiding the Pontiff, and as they were unable and unfit, by reason of their sex, to go to war, they hired soldiers to fight in their stead. In a short time a mighty army was assembled under the chief command of Landolph Colonna, which sufficed and exceeded the expectations of the Pope. So with the blessing of the Pope, and endowed with bountiful indulgences, the crusaders advanced to the attack of Nepī, a strongly fortified town of the Colonnas, which they brought to terms, but with a great loss of soldiers occasioned by the poisonous atmosphere.[96] Soon other castles and towns surrendered to them. The stronghold of Palestrina alone remained, which, because of its difficulty of approach and strong fortifications, was rendered difficult of capture. Moreover the Colonna princes were there, Agapito, Sciarra, and the two Cardinals, who saw within these walls pushed to their last extremity, their own fortune and a people strongly devoted to the Colonnas. And right here Ferrettus of Vicenza,[97] and Pipino,[98] strong Ghibellines, intrude themselves and relate that Boniface, as it were, despairing of capturing Palestrina by force, thought of Guy of Montefeltro, now a friar, who in old age was living in a monastery at Ancona attending to the things of God and his soul. He sent a messenger to him imploring him, a man skilled in war, to come and direct the siege. They declared that he refused to come, because he had a

---

[92] Villani, Book 8, chap. 21.
[93] Manente, History of Orvieto.
[94] Petr. Mem, Proenest. Page 158.
[95] Tosa Cronac. an. 1297, add. ad. S. R. T, tom. 2, p. 53.
[96] Tosa Cronac. an. 1297, add. ad. S R. T, tom. 2, p. 53.
[97] Chronicles of Tuscany year 1297
[98] Chronicles Tom. 1, add. ad S. R. I page 53.

repugnance for such a cruel occupation, but that afterwards he yielded, and having examined the strong city wall, he told the Pope that it could not be taken by force, as it seemed impregnable. So much for these two writers. They were followed by Dante in his verses, and more openly by his commentator Benvenuto of Imola, who declared that Guy had indicated a means for accomplishing the purpose, but would not adopt it because it was sinful; that Boniface answered him and told him to have no fear of sin, as he himself would absolve him from it before it was done; and that the plan was to draw the Colonnas from their stronghold by fair promises, then to break them, to destroy them, violating sacred oaths. Such is the poetical fiction of Dante, and after him Ferrettus of Vicenza and Pipino as historians narrate this story.[99] We beg the reader not to neglect to read this note.

But this account cannot be followed, because they alone narrate it, and do not agree in their recitals, and are only in faithful accord with that which afterward the Colonnas spread of the treachery of Boniface.

It is true that the Papal soldiers labored much and for a long time around Palestrina, with a great shedding of human blood; but finally in September the four Colonnas came out and surrendered the city to the Papal commander, whether on terms or at the discretion of the conqueror the ancient writers do not say. But it is evident from that which followed. For leaving the city in the hands of the Papal general they repaired to Rieti, where the Pope was dwelling, to implore forgiveness from him.[100] Having reached the gates of the city, they dismounted from their horses, and went on foot clothed in garments of mourning and with halters about their necks[101] to throw themselves at the feet of Boniface. The Pope was seated on his throne with a crown on his head, and surrounded by the Cardinals and Prelates of the Curia together with a great multitude of laymen, among whom was Charles, Prince of Taranto. He manifested no harshness, but received them graciously and kindly, to use the

---

[99] 2 B. in relation to this at end of book.
[100] Villani Book 8, cap. 28,—Paolo di Piero, Chronicle S. R. I., tom. 1, p. 53. Add. ad S. R. I.   [101] Pipi. Chron. S. R. I.

words of Piero.[102] In fact they were so humble in word and action that they excited pity; with tears in their eyes they kissed the feet of the offended Pontiff, acknowledging themselves guilty and unworthy of forgiveness. One of them, to move the heart of Boniface, made use of the words of the Gospel: " O, Father, I have sinned against " Heaven and before thee, and I am not worthy to be called " thy son." And afterwards: " Thou hast punished us " for our wickedness." If this is to surrender on terms, we would like to know what it is to surrender unconditionally. Boniface restored them to favor, and absolved them from all censures. But his pardon did not extend so far as to restore them to their former state, nor to leave unpunished the rebellious Palestrina, which had so fiercely resisted the Papal forces. He ordered Theodore Raniero, Bishop of Orvieto, his chamberlain,[103] to raze to its foundation the unfortunate Palestrina, and when levelled to the ground, to pass the plow over it and sprinkle the furrows with salt, in order that nothing living would remain in remembrance of it. The Church of St. Agapitus alone remained standing. A like severe sentence was passed upon the people. All their goods and fortunes as of rebels and schismatics were confiscated. So, deprived of their dwellings, and destitute of everything, they were conducted by the Pope to found and dwell in another city, which was called Papale. This storm also struck Jacopone, who also had been rebellious, and had aided the schism. He was cast into prison, not in Palestrina, as it no longer existed, but in a certain monastery. And there having repented of the consequent schism he shed tears, grieving not so much for the vexations of imprisonment, as the remorse he felt in having incurred the Papal censures. These lamentations clothed in rude verses are found among his poems. Such was the mournful end of most ancient Praeneste, the reason of which whether it was the inordinate pride of its nobles, or the excessive judgment of the Pontiff, we are not sure. However we must not forget to mention that in July of the next year all their possessions were restored to the citizens of the new city Papale, to be enjoyed as fiefs, and be allowed to

---

[102] Loc. Citato ut supra.   [103] Ughell. de Epis. Praen., n. 53.

transmit them to their descendants. And in the course of a few days in a Bull he declared them free, imposing on them the annual payment of twenty-five livres in token of the restoration of their liberty; and he gave them permission to draw up particular statutes, restraining them however by certain laws the better to keep them in subjection.[104] The destruction of their stronghold, Palestrina, and the terrible punishment meted out to John, Lord of Ceccano, Annabeleschi, an enemy of Boniface and their ally, astounded the Colonnas. Whilst the war was going on around Palestrina, John had gone about spreading rumors against the Pope in Campania and the maritime provinces.[105] Having recovered from the humiliations into which they had fallen, they began to fear that the angry Pontiff after the absolution from censures might subject them to as dire a fate as that of Palestrina. So they again arose in rebellion, but being defeated by the Pontiff, they fled to other parts. Stephano went to France, and Sciarra followed him, after having suffered slavery for a time at the hands of corsairs, who captured him in the waters of Marseilles, according to Giovio. Philip the Fair received the fugitive Colonnas in defiance of Boniface. During their residence in France they nurtured that fire of revenge in their breasts which afterwards burst into a flame in Anagni.

Another religious Order arose at that time, and was approved by Pope Boniface; inasmuch as it expresses the character of the age, it may be well to say something of its history. In the twelfth century the body of St. Anthony Abbot was brought to Vienne in Dauphiny by a nobleman of that country named Joselin, to whom the Emperor of Constantinople had given that rich present. An excessive devotion to the saint gave him rather dishonor than reverence. For Joselin, being a soldier, thinking of a place where the sacred relics might rest, did not wish to lose the benefits which the possession of them brought him. Wherever he went to give battle he carried the body of St. Anthony along, that it might serve as his protector. When he died, he left it as an inheritance with other things to a certain Guigo, also given to warlike pur-

[105] Epistle 65, Raynaldus, year 1299 no. 9.
[104] Vide Petrini Mem. Prenest.

suits, and the pious but irreverent translation of the holy body in the midst of battles did not cease. However, Pope Urban II made him deposit the body in a resting-place. It was placed in the Church of La Motte St. Didier, not far from Arles, then a Benedictine priory belonging to the Abbey of Mont Majour. Around this priory Guigo began to build, at the expense of the faithful who contributed bountifully, a church and hospital which was served by laymen called hospitallers. Afterwards it was given to the Benedictines of Mont Majour, and thus arose the priory of St. Anthony.[106]

Now it happened that in 1089 a pestilential distemper broke out, which like a fire inflamed the legs and feet, which swelling and assuming a brown color, mortified and inevitably led to a wretched death.[107] It was called the holy fire, the infernal, and finally St. Anthony's fire, because the recent arrival of the body of St. Anthony having inspired the victims of this plague with the thought of invoking him, it proved a powerful relief. Public prayers and processions were ordered against this scourge. At length it pleased God to grant many miraculous cures of this dreadful distemper to those who implored His mercy through the intercession of St. Anthony, especially before his relics. Those afflicted with the Holy Fire flocked to the Priory of St. Anthony, where the good lay hospitaller received them, converting the building into a hospital, by the leave of the monks of the Priory. Great numbers of pilgrims repaired to the shrine of St. Anthony, and his patronage was implored over the whole kingdom against this disease. But the rich oblations were a cause of dissension between the monks and the hospitallers, and they quarrelled over the possession of them. Boniface attended to this scandal. He dismissed the monks, bidding them to return to the monastery of Mont Majour; but the hospitallers he allowed to remain. He converted the Priory into an Abbey which he bestowed on the hospitaller brothers, and gave them the religious rule of the regular canons of St. Augustine. They had already taken as the mark of their society the letter T, whose meaning is disputed. Some said that it meant the Greek letter Tau, the

---

[106] Translatio St. Antonii ap Bolland. Mense Jannarii, pages 153, 154, 17, tom. II.   [107] Du Cange Glass. Lat. Tom III, Ignis.

mark that the prophet Ezechiel saw on those exempt from the divine scourge,[108] as it were to signify that those consecrated to St. Anthony would be proof against the pestilence. Others say that it was the image of a crutch, emblematic of the malady which the saint miraculously cured.[109] Boniface desired[110] that on their habit the hospitaller Augustinians should wear this sign. St. Anthony was chosen as a protector against all pestilences, and just as in the remotest times the faithful made large offerings to churches and monasteries for the salvation of the soul (*pro redemptione animae*), so also at that time did they give bountifully to this new Order for the relief of the body. For the failure of the public authorities to provide against contagion, the limited knowledge of physicians, and the miserable kind of life led by a half-civilized people, rendered more formidable a malady domestic or foreign, and men, despairing of human aid, more eagerly had recourse to divine remedies. The Order of St. Anthony by this means soon became very rich; but it came to a bad end. On their part the Friars of St. Anthony departed from their primitive piety, and besides many impostors clothed in their habits went about extorting alms with bold promises of spiritual favors, which Dante termed paying money without the coin.[111]

Whilst the mind of the reader is foreboding the approach of the stormy period of the Pontificate of Boniface, it seems to us, that besides giving an exposition of the reasons that justified him in his resistance of the usurpers of the property and liberty of the Church, it is necessary at the same time to give an exposition of facts, which by reason of their more sensible power of conviction, may

[108] "Onmen autem super quem viderities signum Tau, ne occidatis" Ezechiel 9, 4.   [109] See Bollandists.   [110] Bullardium Tom I

[111] "Which now the dotard holds in such esteem,
That every counterfeit, who spreads abroad
The hands of holy promise, finds a throng
Of credulous fools beneath. St. Anthony
Fattens with this his swine, and others worse
Than swine, who diet at his lazy board,
Paying with unstamp'd metal for their fare."
               Dante's Paradiso, Canto XXIX, Wright's translation.
See the commentaries of Chevallier de Cesare on this passage, Acts of the Academy of Pontaniano, vol. II. fasc. II.

gently lead the mind of the reader to the truth. The Greek Church although separated from the Roman has always a place in the history of the Pontiffs, and its appearance there is but the manifestation of either the vice which devours it and sinks it deeper in death, or of the efforts of the Popes to restore it to life by a reunion with it. During the years that Boniface occupied the Papal Chair we do not find among the Greeks any particular event that had relation with the Latins; but we find one permanent and general, namely the contrast of the evil produced by their Church with the good flowing upon all Catholics from the Roman Church. This contrast is a source of knowledge and instruction and is one of the designs of Providence which mingles here below, for our benefit, truth with error. And if there be a life of a Roman Pontiff, in which the historian ought to study the Greek Church to learn facts regarding the Latin Church, that one is unquestionably that of Boniface. For in the impetuous exercise of his power in the face of tyrants, this great Pope shows in strong relief the degradation of the priestly dignity at Constantinople; after those combats maintained in defence of civil and divine justice, he places, so to speak, the drapery of triumph upon the episcopal thrones of the Greek Church.

The history of the usurpers of the rights of the Church always follows that of the protectors. For protection rendering the benefactors too confident, and the Church less jealous of its liberty, it happened that from being protected she becomes enslaved. The favors which Charlemagne and his successors bestowed on the Roman See prepared that way for the subsequent usurpations of the Emperors; and the most cordial welcome given by Charles to the persecuted Pope Leo in France was afterwards changed into bitterness in the disputes over the investitures. The princes entered the house to defend it, and afterwards refused to leave in order that they might rule there. Constantine the Great was the first and most striking example of what we assert. He openly embraced the persecuted religion of Christ, he built churches, he enriched them and took the clergy under the imperial protection, but he intruded himself in the affair of Arius, and that pest which should have been confined to the deserts, was reinstated by him in the bosom of the Church. The usurpation of the Church's power proceeded beyond measure under his successors. The definitions in dogmatic questions given by Constance, Valens, Heraclius, and Zeno would excite laughter, were it not that they caused grief on account of the destruction they brought upon souls. The Patriarchs of Constantinople were men of wonderful learning and courage, (among whom the most conspicuous was John Chrysostom who possessed the genius of a Demosthenes with the heart of a St. Paul,) and they manfully resisted the imperial supremacy. But the resistance did not last long, and the Greek Church, enticed at first to syllogize in the Court, remained there and afterwards became its servant and handmaid. That jealousy towards old Rome, and in the degradation of it the desire they had of acquiring for their Byzantium the name and power of Rome, was the cause of this cowardice of the clergy. Municipal love unnerved their hearts, and blinded their minds. The latter became blinded in viewing the seat of the supreme priesthood of Christ in eternal Rome, and the former became degenerate, by drawing strength from the palace of the Emperors. The fact of the Roman See being so far away contributed to deaden in the sacerdotal breasts the love of unity. There was a time when the voice of the Pontiffs reached as far as the Greeks, and this it was that animated with the spirit of God the great Councils of Nice, Ephesus, Constantinople and Chalcedon. But the noise of the Barbarians bursting into Italy weakened it, and Byzantine pride, stung to the quick by a sacred command from Rome, finally silenced it entirely; and the Greek Church, having left the sanctuary of God, and being stripped of its priestly trappings, entered the palace of Constantine, and put on the palatine livery. Photius and Michael Cerularius engrafted their Church to the imperial trunk, and preferred to be an incrustation and an offshoot of a human and perishable power rather than a branch of the tree of life.

The sad effects of the imperial influence were soon seen. Arianism and Nestorianism heresies, clothed in the imperial purple, owed their origin to the Greeks. We do not mean to say that there were no heresies in the Latin Church, for heresies even entered in the economy of the divine counsels, as St. Paul says, for the manifestation of the good. But these two errors for the reason that they were received and caressed in the palace in their early period of existence and because a Church deprived of the Apostolic force of Rome was powerless to arrest their march, they became most terrible and formidable on account of their magnitude and their duration. At the mere mention of these heresies the Waldenses, the Albigenses and the Fraticelli sink into insignificance. These latter afflicted the Latin Church, but the Arians and Nestorians like pestilences gnawed and ate into the Greek Church, which afterwards, altogether vitiated, breathed its last breath in the arms of the schismatic Photius. The Greek Church remained excluded from the providential benefits which the Roman Church scattered over the entire West. These regions underwent great tribulations, but they were born again to a new life. The Orient went to rot under the foolish pride of its despots, and it encountered that slow death that was prepared for it by vile Islamism. In the West the Latin Church struggled with usurping princes; but, she was represented by the Pontiffs who upheld the clergy in their high ministry, she did not bow the head in submission, nor did she descend from the throne on which God had placed her, but triumphed over error, and took the opportunity to plant the seeds of a new birth in the heart of civil society. We have said that the Church did not bow in submission, but Frederick submitted to Pope Alexander III in Venice, and Henry IV asked pardon of St. Gregory VII at Canossa.

This noble fortitude of the Church, and these subjections of kings, proved that the principle of the Papal supremacy was not dead in the West, although combated by events. Even granting that the Byzantine princes had been always wicked, but yet if the clergy had always strongly resisted them the affairs of the Greek and Latin Churches would have proceeded nobly on the same way to a most holy term, but alas! the pride of the princes and the cowardice of the clergy raised that wall of separation between the Greek and Latin Churches long before the time of Photius. A wonderful lesson. The West with the cross upon its breast arose to arms, and went to meet the East shining as yet with an ancient light, to consult it, and crave a ray to illumine itself, and it is Christian Byzantium which interposed itself an enemy to impede the union fruitful of so much civilization.

Material misfortunes sometimes aroused the Greeks from the sleep of error; but yet this awakening occurred rather among the Emperors who had worldly possessions to lose, than among the clergy who placed all their happiness in preserving themselves free from all allegiance to the Roman See. When Charles of Anjou took up arms against Byzantium, it was not the clergy who became alarmed, no, but the Emperor Michael Paleologus. Through fear of Charles, and with the hope of obtaining Papal aid he suddenly acknowledged his belief in the supremacy of the Pope and in the procession of the Holy Ghost. Any one who reads the history of George Pachymer [112] will find that Paleologus did not conceal the reason of his ill-timed belief, but he openly stated it in those discourses which he delivered before the Patriarch Joseph and the clergy in order to persuade them to follow his opinions. In the efforts of Michael Paleologus to reunite the Greeks with the Latins, in the futility of the same the Greek Church came, as if by divine decree, to reveal to the Latin her internal wretchedness. The reason why the Greeks having first agreed to the union, soon afterwards shrank from it, was because their minds wavered, being tossed about by every wind of doctrine. If in the dogmatizing proceedings of the Emperor he made use of prisons and exile in order to force his commands, it was because liberty was wanting. And if those abhorring a union with Rome displayed obstinacy, it was because they were wanting in unity and for that reason the truth. This is how Nicephorus Gregoras,[113] who lived a little after the times of which we speak, and although he was a Greek, tells mournfully the state of his Church: " In the remotest times the Church abounded in " learned doctors, who on various days and in different " places of Constantinople were wont to expound some " the Psalms of David, others the Epistles of the great " Paul, and others the Gospels of the Saviour. Then all " the priests in turn preached the divine word in the

[112] Historiae Bizantinae Script. Tom. XIII, lib. V.
[113] Hist Byzant. Script., tom. XX, par. 1, pag. 93, V and XI.

"houses, and in different quarters of the city; in the
"courts and in the parish churches. In human life there
"was something of the divine, that is to say, the true
"manner of apprehending religion, and a certain path-
"way to virtue, or rather a certain irrigation from the
"great and heavenly spring, which watered the souls
"of the hearers, and gathered them together, and pre-
"pared them for better things. But in the course of
"time all these things have disappeared. In our days
"every holy custom is lost, being submerged as it were in
"the deep sea. Hence a like contagion infesting the other
"churches, the souls of all Christendom in these days
"find themselves, as it were, in a desert plain without a
"pathway and without water. And to such a degree of
"shamefulness have things arrived, that for a small obo-
"lus one may hear the rattling of most horrible oaths,
"which the hand of the writer dare not record. For the
"salutary light of religion and reason having disappeared,
"all is confusion. Many being fallen into a brutish
"stupidity, there is no one who can arrive at an under-
"standing of what is useful or how piety is distinguished
"from impiety." Such is the sad state to which the
Greek Church had come. This state of affairs was not the
result of human frailty, nor of those vices which always
are plotting against the life of the spouse of Christ, but
came about because the priestly spirit had died in the
clergy; that is to say from the lack of a barrier to these
vices. For the episcopate established by God to govern
his Church, is charged not only to provide it with a life-
giving pasture, but also to protect it from death, which
certainly occurs when it is deprived of its liberty.

For this reason Boniface at the door of the Church
refused an entrance to those who desired to plot against
its life, and if through the imperfections of human nature
anything is to be censured in his holy ministry, yet he
should be commended and honored for having preserved
all Catholicism from those evils which shamefully disgraced the Greek Church.

BOOK V.

SUMMARY.

1300--1303.

How the Papacy had resisted the abuses of force and law by the faith of the people.—This latter having languished, the Pontificate of Boniface becomes difficult.—He sees a new civilization born in Italy at the foot of his throne.—He wishes to sanctify it by faith—He institutes the Jubilee.—He first proclaims it.—Immense number of pilgrims at Rome. —Great offerings—Giotto, and the works confided to him by Boniface. —The singular embassy sent to him from Florence.—The impulse which the Jubilee gave to Italian minds—The Tartars or Mongols send envoys to Boniface, to ask aid against the Turks.—His fruitless efforts to arouse a Crusade.—With the end of the Crusades the Ottoman Empire arose.—Efforts of Boniface against Sicily.—His letter to Charles II.—Disturbances in Florence—The White and Black Guelphs —Unfruitful legation of Cardinal d'Acquasparta—Boniface calls Charles of Valois into Italy.—Dante, Ambassador to Rome.—Civil dissensions in Florence—Dino Compagni—Charles of Valois enters Florence.—Instead of pacifying it, he arouses dissensions.—Boniface wishes to remedy the mischief of the Frenchman, by sending Cardinal d'Acquasparta to Florence, but in vain—The evils of Florence reach their height under Charles of Valois.—The exile of Dante—He becomes a Ghibelline, and creates a new epic poem.—Dante and Boniface. —Charles of Valois instead of waging war, makes an agreement with Frederick of Sicily.—The treaty concluded by him—Rejected at first by Boniface, he afterwards approved it—Moral conditions of Philip the Fair and Boniface at the time of their rupture.—Why Boniface according to the ancient tradition of the Holy See loved France— Quarrels between the Archbishop and the Viscount of Narbonne.— Boniface takes sides with the prelate.—He wishes to recover to the Church the country of Melguevil—He dispatches the bishop of Pamiers as legate to Philip.—Philip fabricates charges against him and imprisons him—Parliament of Senlis.—Its message to Boniface.—His reply to it.—The Bull "Ausculta Fili," and the summoning of a synod at Rome—Insolence of Peter Flotte, and the false letters which he fabricated—James Norman as Papal Legate brings that Bull to France—It is burned by Philip.—Parliament in the Church of Notre-Dame of Paris—The discourse of Philip in the mouth of Flotte.— Faint-heartedness of the French prelates—Letter sent by the Parliament to the Pope and Cardinals.—Consistory in Rome, and the discourse of Cardinal De Murro, and then that of Boniface.—An observation on the indirect power of the Pope over the states of Princes.—Egidio Colonna.—The doctrine of the English and Spanish churches concerning the sacred immunities—Synod held by Boniface.—The Bull "*Unam Sanctam.*"—Another observation on the power of the Pope and the appeals to the Councils.— Efforts of Boniface to maintain peace with Philip—Disturbances in Hungary over the succession to the throne—Boniface protects the Minor Carobert, and sends a Legate to Hungary.—His letters to the Legate—Other letters to Wenceslaus King of Bohemia.—He is reconciled with Albert of Austria, and acknowledges him King of the Romans

IN narrating the events that happened under the Pontificate of Boniface VIII at the beginning of the fourteenth century, we rejoice to say that the Papal throne was occupied by this man, who reviled by many, cannot but be admired by all as the last support of that magnificent civil Pontificate, at a time when, having created a pure and noble civilization in the heart of Italy, misunderstood and calumniated by its own children, it retired weary and sad to repose in the holy and inviolable recesses of religion to which it gave form. When the Papacy, called upon to sit in judgment on the human race, to consider and dispense the rights of kings and people, had given the decision which strongly and sweetly should have brought men together in friendly relations by the bonds of justice; when it had consecrated on the altar of God that liberty which, by freeing human society, permitted man to seek for the good, then the adult generations, in their fair youth, advanced admirably on the way of the beautiful and the good. The Roman Papacy had to encounter many difficulties from the fall of the empire of Augustus up to this time. It was its duty and its wish to preserve and increase the principle of life in human society, by directing it so as not to allow it to relapse into barbarism, which is the principle of death; and for that reason it had triumphantly fought the twofold enemy of that life, namely the despotism of law and the despotism of force. The former was a difficult fight, and the other was superhuman, because the Papacy found itself face to face with a despotism complete in matter and form. That power was wonderful which softened the hearts of the savage tribes which overran Europe; and that power was assuredly divine which built up as a wall the law of God in opposition to the force which called itself law. And for that reason the holy rights of the Church, her immunities and liberty were the formal expression of the law of God, which prescribed a limit to the right of princes; if this limit did not exist, that right would be injurious to God, as being emulous of His power; and would be fatal to men, as being the destroyer of the law, which protects them. We speak not of men; but of that supreme medium, the Papacy, which divine providence made use of in order to make human life less unhappy. Wherefore if at times the heads that wore the Papal mitres seemed to be clouded with worldly thoughts; if the hands that held the scales of justice seemed weak and trembling; and if the eyes of the mind seemed turned towards worldly objects, yet the person as Pontiff always sought the end to which the finger of God pointed, invested with and conducted by his power. We do not mean to say that at the beginning of the year 1300 the external enemy of civil society, barbarism, and the internal, the abuse of public rights, had disappeared or were harmless. On the one hand Islamism in the East threatened from without the civilization of Europe; on the other hand the terrible difficulty of conciliating order and liberty harassed in a bloody manner the democracies, and was already slowly tormenting people ruled by absolute monarchs. The Roman Papacy continued the war against these two enemies, and will continue as long as the religion of Christ will be the benefactor of men, but not with as much force as at first, owing to the want of means, by which it aroused the people and led them on to this double combat, namely, by the ardor of their faith. By means of this Pope Urban II aroused the West to meet and repel the barbarism of the children of Mahomet; and by which Gregory VII kept the imperial power within bounds. After the beginning of the XIVth century, the Church defended civilization against the above mentioned adversaries, not by the spontaneous devotion of the people, but at times by using the interests of the princes and the people, at other times by immediately enlarging her power. Urban aroused the people as a whole by reason of the equality of their faith and devotion to his throne. Pius V incited the individual princes through the inequality of their interests. Gregory VII and Innocent resisted the imperial tyranny by the faith of the people; Pius VII by the immediate power of the Papacy, which is absolute and omnipotent like God himself who established it. It is for that reason that the former of these Pontiffs obtained more abundant results and appeared less merely human than the latter.

Boniface found himself at the head of Christianity precisely at that time when the powerful means of faith was losing its force; his duty by reason of being Pontiff, was to combat with human means the two enemies of the young civilization, to even oppose his own bosom to them; that is why he appeared a man, and his adversaries displayed so much fury and bitterness. However, if he had the ill-fortune of being obliged to make the Pontificate advance in the same way, but by different means, he had, on the other hand, the remarkable good fortune of being destined by Heaven to see and welcome to his arms, so to speak, the holy and true civilization which the Pontificate had conceived from the time of Augustus to this epoch. This was the civilization which the Pontificate had animated and vivified, not by the corrupt spirit of the Cæsars, but by the virginal purity of the Church. He saw, in this well-beloved and charming Italy, a nursery of good plants, in this Italy fructified by the sweat of the Popes, the Latin genius awaken as out of a long sleep, and the fine arts arise about him, as a festal crown; he saw that our soul could represent in the arts of thought and fancy the brilliant forms with which God himself had clothed religion. So whilst he was calling to arms to oppose a barrier to Islamism in the East; and from the height of the Vatican stronghold he was hurling thunderbolts against usurpers, he saw developing around him a band of men, who in the greatness of their genius seemed superhuman; and who within the shadow of the Papal chair, were opening the age, upon the threshold of which they had been placed, to a new light, which was to shine from the summit of the Alps and diffuse itself throughout the world. Dante, Giotto, Blessed Angelico, Marco Polo, Flavius Gioja, and others, all Italians, all crowned and resplendent with the aureola of religion, were the glorious fathers of the civilization of which we are to-day so proud. Dante created a new epic, which is after the manner of neither Homer nor Virgil, inasmuch as it is altogether spiritual in nature and altogether divine. For his all powerful imagination taking wing from the eternal foundations of good and evil, of reward and punishment, arrested its flight only in the infinite region of the immortality of the soul, which is the essential dogma of the true religion; and the sublime poet so confesses this in verse, that the claim will last as long as remains the idea of the true and the beautiful. Giotto and Fra Angelico, and all of their seraphic school, as if no longer conscious of the material envelope of this human mind, infused into the art of painting a ray truly of Paradise, mystic and holy like the virgins and saints they represented. And that knowledge of spiritual beauty they did not receive from the ancient Greeks, nor from the Byzantines, but from the Church alone. Dante and Giotto are crude in external forms, but divine in soul; their poetry and painting without form because of the innocent youthfulness of the fine arts, exhale the odor and life of the maternal milk which they drank at the breast of Mother Church. Those voyages which establish communications and relations among men, which open ways and outlets for human thought, that it may not become stagnant, but may increase the mutual contact in order that there may be an uniform diffusion of goodness in the social moral body, began to be frequent in this age, and religion pointed out the way, and encouraged and animated the first discoverers of new lands, "not by oak nor triple bronze," as Horace says, but by charity. The daring Marco Polo and the missionaries whom the Roman Church sent to distant and almost unknown countries in this century, taught posterity that this base world is altogether a thing of man, which he can traverse and measure by his steps; and their teaching and example begot Columbus, the donor of a new world. Moreover these wonders were wrought in our Italy still harassed by domestic wars. It seemed that irascibility of spirit nourished the flame of genius. A great lesson resulted from this fact, namely, that even from the vices of an active and progressive people some good can come, but never from those of poltroons and idlers.

The fourteenth century dawned; and if the great soul of Boniface rejoiced at the brilliant progress of the generations issuing from infancy, it felt also a deep pain at the sight of the decline among the nations of that faith, which in ages past had been the source of such deep respect for the Papacy. Princely encroachments on the rights of the Church had taught him how weak in their opinion and hence in that of the people, had grown the power of ecclesiastical thunderbolts. He saw daily how princes and people who but lately had laid their complaints before the Holy See as a tribunal recognized by all, remained more and more aloof; he saw the Papal decision replaced by that of the people, who, having escaped their tutor, wanted to act for themselves. The Magna Charta in England, the States-General in France, the Courts of Aragon were proofs that the nations knew how to construct bulwarks, and make use of them to check the powers threatening to degenerate into tyrannies. That the Pope was pleased with and applauded these noble efforts, we cannot doubt; but at the same time it was impossible for Boniface not to foresee that, in case of collision between the two parties, the fight would be long, and the victory of one over the other would result in tyranny or anarchy. Therefore Boniface, although admiring the movement, put no hopes in it and sought to call back the minds of men to the principles of faith, in order that the rude nations after having laid aside the trappings of youth, should yet preserve a respect for Mother Church, and not despise her old and tried wisdom. And so he instituted the "Jubilee," as a last means to unite during a few days the children to their mother, Holy Church, that close to her bosom, they would feel the maternal warmth, and naturally their filial affection would return, and by love for her they would be conducted to peace and justice.

It seems to us that the efforts of certain writers were vain and fruitless, who endeavored to show that the institution of the Jubilee antedated the time of Boniface in the Church, as if he, in instituting it, did something either superstitious or what was not authorized by previous Papal authority. But the granting of centenary indulgences to those visiting the great Basilicas at a certain time, was not an act that exceeded the Papal authority, nor was it superstitious, and for this reason to Boniface all credit and glory must be given for this pious and magnificent institution, which can be said to be the noblest act he performed in the supreme priesthood. He did not invent indulgences, for if the immensity of the merits of Christ, and the power of the Keys in the Pontiffs be true, then are indulgences most true and as old as the Church herself; but the distribution of these merits solemnly administered for the full remission of the temporal punishment at the beginning of each century of those who would visit with faith the mystical rock of the Church of God, was a solemn and most holy thought that was conceived solely in the mind of Boniface. To renew by one's personal presence that charity which runs like a perennial spring of life from the head to the members of the Church; to honor by universal homage the tomb of the Apostles, the chief founders of the Church; to call the nations to the tombs of the martyrs, that the memory of these heroes might invigorate faith; and finally in order that the chief Shepherd of every age amidst the joy of pardon might embrace his flock in the bowels of Christ, this was the wonderful purpose, that God suggested to this Pope in instituting the Jubilee. However Boniface did not wish to rely on his own judgment alone in this matter. He ordered Cardinal Stephaneschi,[1] who has left in prose and verse an account of this Jubilee, to search the old writings, to see if he could find any vestige of those centenary indulgences in past ages, and he found nothing else but the antiquity of the pilgrimages to the tomb of the Apostles (and the pilgrims were called Romei), and the indulgences that were granted the pilgrims. Therefore at a meeting of the Cardinals he presented the new project, to have their advice, and they all applauded the holy and beautiful thought. On the feast of the Chair of St. Peter in the Vatican Basilica filled by a large multitude of the faithful, Boniface ascended the pulpit, which was resplendent with gold, and adorned with festive drapery of silk. He preached the Jubilee to the people, and exhibited to the view of the astonished multitude the writing bearing the Papal seals which pro-

---
[1] James Card de Jubilee c. 1.

BONIFACE VIII PROCLAIMING THE JUBILEE.

claimed the precious pardon. Boniface made known to those of that time and to posterity, that from time immemorial it was a faithful tradition, that all those visiting the Roman Basilica of the Prince of the Apostles gained bountiful forgiveness of their sins and indulgences; and that he by reason of his office, anxious for and attentive to the spiritual salvation of every one, held valid that pardon and those indulgences and confirmed and approved them by Apostolic authority, and strengthened them by the force of that document, in order that the honor paid to the blessed Apostles Peter and Paul would henceforth be increased, the pious visits to their Basilicas would be more frequent, and as a result the faithful would feel consoled by a greater abundance of piety. So trusting in the mercy of God and the merits of the Holy Apostles, with the advice of the Cardinals and from the fullness of his power he was pleased to grant the most bountiful indulgences to all those who, penitent and confessed in that year, and as well in the beginning of every century, would undertake with all reverence to visit those Basilicas. In order to obtain these indulgences the inhabitants of Rome were obliged to continue their pious visits for thirty days while those of the country and the pilgrims were allowed to make them in fifteen days. The treasury of the indulgences was closed only against those in rebellion, chief among whom were Frederick and his Sicilian abettors, and the Colonnas. For, as the monk John Rossi,[3] remarks "they were to be deprived of the " clemency of him, whose majesty they despised." [4]

The religious excitement which the publication of the Papal decree produced throughout Europe was extraordinary. As if the indulgences promised by Boniface to those coming to Rome were to be the last, an immense multitude of the faithful, regardless of sex or age and undeterred by the distance, flocked to the Eternal City so that it was filled to overflowing. Those who were physically unable to come were brought thither. Cardinal Stepaneschi relates the incident of an old Savoyard peasant, a man over one hundred years of age, who did not wish to die without the spiritual consolation of these in-

[3] James Card. de Jubilee c. 3.   [2] Vit. Bonif. cap. XI, page 221.
[4] Vide Doc. D.

dulgences, and made his sons convey him to Rome. Moreover besides the citizens of Rome there were counted two hundred thousand pilgrims continuously throughout the entire year, besides those who were on the way coming or returning. In the beginning the throng of people was so great and so impetuous, that many lost their lives by suffocation. A remedy was thought of, which Stephaneschi [5] says was even insufficient, namely a breach was made in the walls, in order to facilitate the entrance and departure of the immense multitude collected within and without the walls of the city.

But if the throng of visitors was marvellous, no less wonderful was the skill of Boniface in providing that there would be no scarcity of food for both men and beasts. It was nothing short of a miracle as Baronius narrates, that the sanctity of these days was not disturbed by any disorder in that vast multitude, since it could easily happen both from the immense crowd, and the first meeting of so many people differing in language and customs.[6]

If the Pope had been more than generous in spiritual indulgences, the faithful were not behind in their donations to the Basilicas. Ventura, an eye-witness, declares that day and night he had seen clerics with rakes in hand, gathering the money which poured in at the foot of the altar of the Apostle. By the light of that vein of gold the eyes of many historians were so blinded as to believe that Boniface had opened the fountain of indulgences in order to drink copiously at the stream of pious offerings. They accused him of being greedy after money, and capable of confounding heavenly and earthly things in order to obtain it. But Villani, Compagni and other Ghibelline writers, eyewitnesses of these facts, when they saw the clerics collecting the money, they saw as well two hundred thousand human beings besides the animals, in the circuit of Rome, being fed, and having an abundance of food which was provided by the Pontiff. What did he do with

[5] "Nam ut intra et extra moenia compacta multitudo aggarebatur, eo amplius quo magis in dies erat processum. Pluresque multitudine oppressi deinde remedium, etsi haud penitus sufficiens, salubre appositura facta in moenibus alta, quo peregrinantibus compendiosior pateret via inter monumentum Romuli ac vetustum portum." [6] Raynaldus 7.

the offerings which they placed at the foot of the altars but spend it on these people? These offerings did not lose anything by this; being blessed by the virtue of the sacrifice, they returned for the relief of those necessities for which God created gold and silver in the bowels of the earth.[7]

We are of the opinion that of the money collected during the Jubilee which was used by Boniface to increase the patrimony and the pomp of divine worship in the Basilicas,[8] that which he used in embellishing them with paintings by Giotto was the most pleasing and acceptable to God and men. He esteemed highly this singular genius, who as Lanzi well says,[9] was the Raphael of painting in the beginning of its renaissance. Vasari who wrote his life, gives us to understand that Giotto was first called to Rome by Benedict IX to decorate St. Peter's Church.[10] But this is one of the many errors of that biographer. Benedict IX assumed the Pontificate in the eleventh century (1033), which was very far remote from the time of Giotto. And even if we would substitute in the writings of Vasari XI for the IX, we could not admit that Benedict XI had arranged with that artist to execute many paintings. For that Pope occupied the Papal Chair only eight months and seventeen days, and the times were so stormy and troublesome that there was no thought given to painting. It is true that Boniface, who proclaimed the Jubilee, was portrayed by Giotto, and the painting still exists in the Lateran Basilica, which work could not have been ordered except by that Pope.[11] And since this painting was but the relic of the many others which he executed in the vestibule of the Lateran Basilica, it is fair to conclude, that all those works which Vasari says were performed at the solicitation of Benedict XI, should be attributed rather to Pope Boniface.

It is probable that Giotto arrived in Rome during the year of the Jubilee which brought so many there. In this city he was acquainted with Oderic of Gubbio, a famous painter of miniatures, who had been called by the Pope

[7] See note E.
[8] Card. James of St. George. De Jubilaeo Anno, chap IX.
[9] Hist. of Painting. Florentine School first epoch.
[10] D'Agincourt, tom. 4. part II.   [11] D'Agincourt, idem.

to embellish many books of the Palace, as Vasari narrates, and which in his time had been going to ruin. The Jubilee being ended, Boniface wished to preserve the memory of it by means of a painting. He had himself portrayed between two attendants, while a third one read from an unfolded parchment the famous Bull of Institution. All these figures were placed above the pulpit, which was handsomely adorned with drapery, bearing the Gaetani coat of arms. The Pope is depicted clothed in the pontifical robes and wearing the tiara on his head, his head inclined a little towards the reader, and his right hand raised in the act of blessing. Giotto also executed in mosaic in the vestibule of St. Peter's the mystic bark of the Church in a great storm, with the Apostles working to save it. Vasari marvelled at the skill which the painter displayed in assembling those pieces of glass, so as to surpass in effect that which he could have done with the brush, especially in the swelling of the sail which in the lights and shadows was done with surprising cleverness. Lanzi laments the ill-advised restoration of this mosaic, after which nothing remained of the original save the memory. The Pontiff had employed Giotto in other works, namely the histories of the Old and New Testaments, which the artist painted round about St. Peter's. In the time of Vasari some of them had already been restored, or rather destroyed, while others had been removed when the walls were rebuilt. How many sins has Italy committed against those who had raised her to a throne as Queen of the arts!

The example of the Pontiff served as an incentive to others in Rome to make use of the good services of Giotto. Among these must be noted those miniatures of Cardinal Stephaneschi. He engaged this painter to enrich with miniatures his books of the Life of St. George, and to decorate with frescoes the church bearing that saint's name.

From pious things we now pass to public affairs. Florence at the end of the thirteenth century was in a most flourishing condition, and enjoyed domestic peace, which encouraged men of talent in cultivating the fine arts, and at that time she began the erection of those most beautiful monuments, for which after Rome there was no other

Italian city that could equal her in the splendor and elegance of monuments of art, and which entitled her to be called the Italian Athens. It was during that time that there arose that sanctuary of true Italian splendor, Santa Croce, the Church of S. Maria del Fiore, the palace of the Priors, and the fine walls which still surround the city. The people had become tired of domestic turmoils. At first that ardent tribune Giano Bella had aroused the people against the nobles, then the nobles exerted themselves to drive him out of the country, and finally they quieted down, the Guelphs becoming so strong, that the Ghibellines were entirely overwhelmed. This predominance of the Guelphs was derived not only from factional strength but from a certain, as it were, natural tendency which the city possessed of regulating itself according to popular and Guelphish forms. Florence then being altogether Guelph, as soon as the Jubilee was proclaimed, wished to give evidence to Boniface of the love she bore the Roman See. She sent numerous and splendid embassies, which inasmuch as they intended to represent the Guelph Cities close to the Papal See, whose throne is above the royal and imperial thrones, were composed of various personages, each one of which was to represent some ruling potentate of those times. Thus Vermulio Alfano went as an envoy of the Emperor of the West; Simon Rossi, for the Emperor of the East; Musciatto Franzese for the King of France; Ugolin de Cerchi for the King of England; Romero Frighinello for the King of Bohemia; Guicciardo Bastaro for the Khan of Tartary; Mano Miamano for the King of Apulia; Bernard Vayo for the King of Sicily; Beneviente Folco for the Grand Master of the Knights of Rhodes; Lupo Uberti for the republic of Pisa; Sino Diotisalvi for Gerard Verano, lord of Camerino; and Benedict Nerli for the lords of Scala, Verona, and Padua. Pallas Strozzi represented Florence. This embassy truly poetical in conception, lacked nothing to make it appear marvellous in outward splendor. It was accompanied by fully five hundred knights who in the richest of robes, and in the various costumes portrayed the different people and princes they intended to represent. It is surprising that Vallani and Compagni make no mention of this singular embassy, nor would we have touched upon it, were it not that Rossi, a conscientious writer, had corroborated two Florentine writers.[12] We are not certain of the month in which this embassy was sent, whether before or after the unfortunate dissensions between the Cerchi and Donati in Florence, and the Cancellieri in Pistoja. For if it occurred afterwards, we would say that perhaps under the appearance of a solemn manifestation of homage which Florence paid to the Pope, it was the work of the Guelph party which still governed the city, whence Boniface might endeavor to reconcile the parties, as we shall soon see was done through the means of another special embassy.

Among those who hastened to avail themselves of the Papal indulgences were many distinguished bishops and princes, either under the garb of pilgrims, or openly in their official dress.[13] Among these was Charles Martel, eldest son of Charles the Lame of Naples. His mother was Mary, sister of Ladislaus, King of Hungary, and as such up to that time he bore the title of King of Hungary, and contested with Andrew III for the possessions of that kingdom. He was of Papal creation, being aided by Nicholas IV and Celestine V to ascend the throne, and now he set out for Rome because Boniface made the way clear for him to succeed to his paternal throne of Naples, and assured his son Carobert of the Hungarian throne. He saw the Jubilee, but he did not see the fulfilment of his desires. In the following year he met with a premature death in Naples. His brother Robert, greedy for power, was suspected of poisoning him.[14] But so good and honest of heart was Robert that this infamous charge was doubtless unfounded.

The people derived at once some benefit from the Jubilee. It is certain that in this year the minds of people being engaged with the thought of the Papal indulgences, they were restrained from giving vent to any animosity. And Italy especially derived immense benefit from the visit which so many made to the city of most wonderful

---

[12] Peter Calzolari. De Vir. illust. Florentiae—Paul. Minus. De Nobil. Flor. Cap de Flor. eloqu. Claris ap. Rossi, Life of Boniface, chap. XI, pages 121, 122.

[13] Summonte lib. 3 chap. 2.   [14] Trithemius Chron. Hirsaug.

memories. The Latin monuments, though damaged by the barbarians and much more so by the brutal fury of the inhabitants, were not all demolished and upon these was enthroned a thought of civil greatness, which appealing powerfully still to lofty minds, encouraged them to noble deeds The Capitol, the Flavian Amphitheatre, the triumphal arches, the Palace of the Cæsars, the temples in their majesty and beauty of form brought back the mind to the time when Rome, a wearied conqueror of the world, softened the fierce warlike spirit by a cultivation of the fine arts and a love for learning, with which she wished to share that throne, upon which she sat as mistress of the world. Foreigners marvelled, the Italians felt themselves Latins, and that blood which was Roman warming up in them, they aspired to Roman greatness. Florence alone will ever be a living witness of those noble efforts which began through the means of that holy pilgrimage. John Villani had left beautiful stories of Florence, which he wrote as soon as he returned from Rome, where he had gone to gain the indulgences. Rome inspired him: " Find-
" ing myself by that blessed pilgrimage in the holy city of
" Rome; seeing her grand monuments of antiquity; and
" reading the history and the great deeds of the Romans
" told by Virgil and Sallust. . . . . , I have adopted
" their style and form, although their unworthy disciple
" I am incapable of works so beautiful as theirs." [15] But Rome with all her great monuments of paganism would have been only a cold corpse were it not that the moral magnificence of the Christian Pontificate had given life to the material virtue of the Cæsars which had died with them. For this they who felt great ideas rising within them, opened at once the heart to those chaste emotions of religion, after the manner of the Florentines who by civil virtue, by daring deeds, and by words of magnificence had emulated pagan Rome and now in every instance proved themselves children of Catholic Rome. Dante, it seems without doubt, was present at the Jubilee.[16] In that

[15] John Villani, L. 8, chap. 36.
[16] " So, o'er the bridge, the concourse to convey,
" Which flocks, the year of Jubilee, to Rome,
" Means are devised to form a double way,—
" That on the one side, all may keep in front

solemn Papal pardon; in that judgment of Boniface, which refused the spiritual favors to those in contumacious rebellion against the Church; in that meeting of the universal Christian people; in that wonderful display which the Roman Pontificate made of its greatness, we would surmise that Dante conceived and fashioned the sublime idea of the Divina Commedia. Catholic Rome spoke to his heart and there awakened religious inspiration, by which, leaving the wilderness of vice, he was moved to contemplate and sing of Hell, Purgatory and Paradise. Pagan Rome spoke to his mind, and gave him as a guide on his journey the poet Virgil; and that fancy which is the offspring only of Italy, joined together the mind and heart so strongly and lovingly, that Papal Rome also had her Virgil. While Boniface was dispensing spiritual indulgences, and thereby strongly arousing the Italians to great works, he was attentively guarding the Church, both as a congregation of the faithful, and as the sovereign provider for the civil order. As we observed previously, the new and rising civilization was threatened by an external and internal enemy. The first was the power of the Turks, and the latter was the unbridled power of princes, and the rebellion of the people which the rulers could not check. Boniface opposed both. He set about to remedy the evil of the Turks. In Asia along the banks of the river Silinga there dwelt a savage people called Tartars or Mongolians. Spondano narrates many things about their origin,[17] which any one can read in the authors which he cites. It is sufficient for us to know that they were of a most fierce nature, but on the other hand they had not been spoiled by the effeminacy of cities and the sensual indulgences of the Mahometan religion. At first they had not known the great Prophet, and practised a religion of their own; but afterwards they were incorporated into the great family of Islamism. Possessing a lively imagination like every Oriental people, through their ignorance they could be led to the performance of great deeds by a man shrewd and ambitious, who knew how to make use of this pliable people by the lan-

"The castle, to St. Peter's as they throng,—
"All on the other, journey to the Mount."—Dante Infer. XVIII
Wright's Translation [17] Ann. 1202 no. X.

guage of the supernatural. Such a man precisely was Temudhsin Genghis-Khan, a man very brave and of unmeasured ambition, who knew how to subdue the Mongolians and lead them on to brilliant victories. These were continued by their descendants, who threatened Europe in the XIIIth century with new incursions and barbarities. But Heaven would not allow the old wounds made by the ancient Barbarians to be reopened by new savage invasions. For after having devasted Hungary, and intimidated Berlin, they turned back into Asia. By the sword they became masters of Bagdad, Aleppo, Damascus, and even pushed on as far as Palestine. This people, so powerful as to resist the power of the Mohammedans, awakened the attention of the Roman Pontiffs, and they used every means to convert them to the true faith, so as afterwards to get them to do what the Crusaders could not and would not do—conquer the Turks. Up to this time these Barbarians never entered the minds of the Pontiffs, except to be considered and repelled as Turks. In fact Innocent IV wrote a constitution to repress their fury.[18] Alexander IV took care to convoke councils against the Tartars, as for instance in Paris,[19] in Ravenna,[20] in London[21] and elsewhere. Urban IV left nothing untried to arouse a crusade against them. Clement IV was compelled to drive them out of Hungary. But finally the Tartars learned by the experience of the Turks that power which the Pope possessed over Christendom, and the great benefit to them which a friendship with the Christians would be, in overcoming the Turkish power with which they were contending. So a certain Abaka, King of the Oriental Tartars, was the first to send ambassadors to the Roman See, seeking an alliance. Nicholas III accorded them a most joyful welcome, and was assured by them that Abaka offered to unite all his forces with those of the Christians against the Saracens; also that the uncle of King Abaka, by name called Quolibey, Great Khan of all the Tartars, was already a Christian, and he asked that missionaries be sent to convert his subjects to the faith of Christ. Nicho-

---

[18] "Christianae religionis cultum." [19] Nangius Life of St. Louis.
[20] Rossi. History of Ravenna. L. 6.
[21] Matthew of Westminster, year 1261.

las III wrote letters, which Wadding relates,[22] to both Abaka and Quolibey, full of affection and congratulation; and he sent five experienced friars of St. Francis for the conversion of the Tartars.[23] From that time afterwards the Popes never ceased, and especially Nicholas IV, to send often friars to keep alive the faith, which was spread widely among that barbarous people. The Great Khan and the other tribal chiefs sent frequent embassies to retain the Papal benevolence. The Register of the letters of Nicholas IV records many directed to the chiefs of that people.[24] This conversion of the Tartars to the Christian religion would have assisted greatly the affairs of the Holy Land, if the Christian Princes had been mindful of the Holy Sepulchre, and had sent liberators of it, who would have found in the Tartars a most powerful support. And just in the Pontificate of Boniface there was a most striking proof of this. In the course of the year 1300 Cassano, Great Khan of the Tartars, having united his forces with those of the King of Armenia, led this numerous army against the Sultan of Egypt, in order to take from him Palestine. He met him in battle near the city of Emesa, defeated him, and drove him back into Egypt.[25] He wished to advance further, but having received the news that a certain relative of his was invading Persia, he withdrew from his conquest, leaving a portion of his army in Syria, commanding that when the Christians arrived from the West, this region should be left under their sway. He believed firmly in their coming, and had sent ambassadors to the Pontiff and the King of France, in order that they might avail themselves of this favorable opportunity for relieving the Christians in the Levant. It is beyond doubt that Boniface rejoiced over this embassy and the good tidings it brought. The thought of conquering the Holy Land although it was not so popular as in the time of the Council of Clermont, yet was predominant in the minds of the Pontiffs, and especially was

---

[22] Annal Min. tom. V. page 36 and following.

[23] Ab. page 40 and following.

[24] 2 April 1288 "Habet" to Queen Tultani.—13 July, 1299, to Cobla reat Cham. "Gaudeamus":—2 Aug., 1291, "Exultat" cor. See Aython Hist. of the East. chap. 45 —Maria Sanuto lib. 8. part. 13, 8 Chap.

[25] Haython, chap. 41.—Villani, lib. 8, chap. 35.—Ptolemy of Lucca Ann.

it ascendant in the mind of Boniface. He summoned a Council in Rome; he touched upon the question of the Holy Land; he besought its delivery, and dispatched legates to the Christian princes to gather money and men for the holy cause. France had always been the first to heed the cry for the Holy War, and was the special defender of the Christian cause in the East. So Boniface bearing in mind the favorable opportunity which Syria in Christian hands offered, immediately and especially turned to Philip the Fair, asking for the tithes of the churches that were collected in his kingdom for the affairs of the Holy Land, and exhorting him not to be behind St. Louis, who was a martyr to this cause. But Philip held Flanders in his clutches, and having renewed the war, to carry it on he needed money, and so did not care to hear anything about Tartars or Saracens. He refused Boniface the tithes that were collected. And since he foresaw that these injustices would exasperate the redoubtable mind of Boniface, as if to hold him in deference not only did he extend hospitality to the Colonna refugees in his kingdom, but he lavished upon them public favors and courtesies in order to bring disrespect on Boniface and cause him to fear. Thus while Boniface entreated Philip to undertake a crusade against the Turks, Philip was making friends with those who were fugitives because of a Papal crusade against them. Therefore they became puffed up with pride, but we shall soon see how shameful will be their outbreaks. John, Duke of Brittany, was the only one who was truly prompt to the call of Boniface, and showed himself ready not only to aid, but also lead an expedition to the Holy Land. He wished to start in June, and had even implored the usual indulgences, which Boniface granted profusely to the Crusaders.[26] But no one set out. Perhaps the sad news from Syria had then arrived, of how in Cassano's absence the Tartars were driven out by the treachery of a certain Capehick, guardian of the city of Damascus, and the affairs of the Christians returned to their former sad condition.[27] This last chance of liberating the Holy Land from the hands of the infidels which the Christians allowed to pass, was followed by the impossibility of arous-

[26] Lib 6 ep 278. [27] Raynaldus, 33.
[28] Hayton, History of the East. Chap. 43.

ing any more Crusades. The powerful and crafty Osman, son of Erdogrul, another conqueror who had extended his dominion over the mountain districts of Asia Minor and in the valleys of the Taurus, began to make himself formidable by his conquests. The retreat of Cassano, Chief of the Tartars, and the imbecility of the Byzantine Emperor opened to this audacious Turk the way to an empire, which, for largeness of territory and prolonged existence, is unique in history. He made the foundation of it in Bithynia, fixing his seat in the city of Prusa in Mysia at the foot of Mt. Olympus. Such was the foundation of the terrible Ottoman Empire, and like a wave of the sea which from time to time dashes itself against the remains of a once grand edifice in ruins on its banks, so it stifled the expiring breath of the Grecian power as far as to place Mahomet II on the throne of Constantine. Islamism then being predominant in the East, it began to spread its roots even in the West, and pollute those beautiful shores of Europe which look towards Asia. This was the barbarity that threatened all Europe for many centuries, and which the Popes checked by the holy wars. This empire still exists solely because the division of the spoils could never be satisfactorily adjusted by the would-be sharers.

The Turkish Empire arose, and the civil power of the Pontiffs declined, yet slowly, because the shoulders of Boniface were strong enough to support it still. He saw himself surrounded by a fickle people, as were the Italians, and he had a presentiment of the struggle that was to ensue. Of Florence we shall speak later; let us return to the affairs of Sicily. We have seen how she neglected the admonitions of Boniface. Philip, Prince of Taranto, through a juvenile imprudence was defeated, and taken captive in the battle of Falconaria. Now this reverse, which Charles II, so to speak, went in search of, greatly grieved the mind of Boniface, already saddened by the sudden return of James to Aragon, after his victory over Frederick at Cape Orlando. The bad faith of James of Aragon, the weakness of Charles of Anjou, and the constancy of Frederick and the Sicilians would have depressed the minds of other men, but not that of Boniface.

The Papal coffers had been replenished by offerings during the Jubilee, and the Guelph party in Italy offered help in money and men; Boniface at the same time saw his hopes revived in Charles of Valois, whom he made his champion. Thus encouraged he renewed the attempt to expel Frederick from Sicily. Frederick had received powerful assistance from Ghibelline Genoa, and for that reason Boniface by mighty efforts strove to sever their union with the Sicilians. He threatened, he stormed, he implored the aid of James and even of Philip the Fair against them,[28] but Genoa would not yield. Finally whilst two millions of the faithful were joyfully availing themselves of the Papal indulgences in .Rome, these Genoese were the subjects of most severe chastisement, which seemed over severe in the time of such great pardon and indulgence. Boniface hurled the solemn excommunication against Oberto and Corrado Doria, Corrado Spinola, and their relations and retainers, and placed an interdict over the entire territory of Genoa, threatening them with further penalties upon their estates, if by Ascension Day they did not sever their connection with the Sicilians.[29] The Genoese were frightened, and they made a treaty with Charles of Naples. That weakened the force of the opponents, and to increase his own Boniface had since January complained loudly against that ill-advised expedition of Philip, Prince of Taranto, in a letter which he wrote to the Legate Gerard, Bishop of Sabina;[30] and he filled the minds of Charles and Loria with such terror, that they repaired to Rome in person to pacify him. In the liveliest manner he explained to Gerard the hope he had of seeing this affair come to a happy termination, by means of the fleet he expected from James. In fact at the same time he had written to James, that he expected assistance even from Genoa; that the Knights Templars and those of St. John, by promises of particular favors, had been induced to wage war in Sicily; that the Guelph cities would send him a choice and well-provisioned body of cavalry; finally he recommended him to hold himself in readiness and to be full of hope.

But whilst Boniface was encouraging the Legate to war, Charles appeared to be inclined to peace. The imprisonment of his son Philip distressed him, and he was tired of war. Frederick knew this, and he used it to his

[29] Raynaldus, n 12, 13. [30] Raynaldus 1300, n. 10.

advantage. He sent him envoys to draw up an agreement, but both sides feared Boniface. They would rather treat in secret, in order that he might not thwart their negotiations. Charles, like a child under the rod of a rigid pedagogue, made the treaty, and trembled. But Boniface discovered the plot, and he scolded him severely, both because Sicily concerned the Pope more immediately, and because of Charles' poor judgment. The Pope spoke harshly to him: "That he had still present in mind that "which Charles was known to have done in the treaty "concluded with James, at the siege of Gaeta, without "having consulted the Papal legates; that he remembered "also that other treaty, an astonishing monument of "prudence and wisdom, which he made with the same "James for the liberation of his son; long experience had "taught him that when Charles was left in his affairs a "little to himself alone, it led to nothing but disaster. "The unfortunate expedition of his son Philip, was a "clear case in point. Where was his prudence, where his "respect for the Church? To meet in a secret conference "on a galley with the legates of the common enemy Fred-"erick, and not allow one word or deed to be known." And he ended this severe rebuke by displaying to him the fetters of excommunication if he persisted in that evil course of wishing to act alone and in secret.[31] This language addressed to Charles and that used with the Legate reveal the mind of Boniface exasperated by the condition of the affairs of Sicily, and at the same time full of vigor to surmount obstacles. On the 14th of June Loria obtained a signal victory over the Sicilian fleet in the waters of Ponza; but because little fruit was derived from it, and because the Guelph party in Italy was not prosperous, the mind of Boniface was not jubilant, but rather filled with great anxiety and a study of means to meet the situation. We come now to speak of Tuscany, but it is necessary to prepare the mind with some facts, because they are strong means of instruction to posterity.

It is clear the civil Pontificate entirely rested in that party of the people, which was Guelph, and for that reason the Guelph character was that of the Popes. Nay more,

[31] Ib No. 12 . . . . "ex suae fatuitatis impulso in timore periculi pouissee."—

this party never had any other truly natural head than the Pope. The clash of parties far from being harmful, was useful to Rome. Friction quickened life; and either losing or victorious the Guelph party was ever active, and the Popes were in need of this. Therefore an idleness too prolonged, or a superiority too marked over a rival faction was prejudicial, either because there was lacking the stimulus to keep them active, or because inactivity was productive of corruption and schism in the party. When Guelphism had reached that state of division, then it could be surely maintained that the civil Pontificate, feeling itself dissolving and shaken in its foundation, would also have a presentiment of the decline of its power. Boniface was destined to have this presentiment, and Florence was to inspire him with it. This powerful republic experienced all those vicissitudes to which states are subject, no matter what may be the form or the solidity of the government, or the condition of their citizens; for imperfection involves and penetrates everything here below. Power is a divine thing; but its manner and location in human society is not divine. This indetermination of circumstances and the excessive cupidity of men engender rebellions in states. These revolutions at times are necessary, to reveal human infirmity, and disconcert the confidence of legislators in the sanctity of laws, as well as that of princes, in the empire of force. We have said rebellions are necessary, because it is not possible to prevent at times wealth or power from becoming centered in one party in a state and by stagnation causing moral infirmities, much as in the human body physical maladies are caused by derangement of humors. In order to arouse and dissipate this sluggish and pestilential mass, Heaven allows these civil revolts, which like storms are not desirable, yet they are a means which a free Providence employs for the common good. In a monarchy they are of rare occurrence, but more terrible in character; on the contrary more frequent in a republic, but not so terrible. For in the former reverence for him, who holds in his hands the entire power, restrains and retards the fury of the people, but confined for a long time, it breaks out more fiercely. In republics civil liberty and the division of power render the sudden uprisings less difficult because of few obstacles, but also less imposing. Therefore after the audacious but yet honest tribune, Giano della Bella, had been banished from Florence in 1295, the nobles of the city had attained a high degree of power and splendor. Peace reigning and commerce, which thrived with that industrious people, had greatly increased the wealth of the citizens. There were at that time families who by their riches and the number of their adherents could have exercised the influence which at a later period the Medici family acquired. Among these families were the Donati and the Cerchi. The head of the former was Corso, the latter Veri. Their deeds and the origin of their disgraceful feuds are well told by Compagni and Villani. It suffices for us to know well that they displayed towards one another hostile feelings, and through envy at times they took up arms.[32] Now while these two chieftains, Corso and Veri, to the great scandal of the public were warring against each other, there appeared from without another cause of dissension and the fire which was enkindled in Florence assumed frightful proportions. The family of the Cancellieri of Pistoja, by the perpetration of a savage and most cruel deed, became divided into two factions, called the Whites and the Blacks. As was customary the whole city took sides, citizens lost their senses and murdered one another. Florence as the head of the Guelph party hastened to effect a peace; she assumed the sovereignty over Pistoja, and rashly confined the two factions, the Whites and the Blacks, within the confines of the city's walls. This was only adding fuel to the flame that burned between the Cerchi and the Donati. The Blacks united their interests to those of the Donati, and the Whites to those of the Cerchi; and there began in the city a furious war, between these two rival factions. Florence was Guelph, and for that reason this division was a blow at the very heart of Guelphism; and the Ghibelline party profited thereby, because the moderate Guelphs were necessarily obliged to incline towards the Ghibelline party, and thus, as Villani narrates, the Whites, or that of the Cerchi, was the more powerful faction. Hence staunch Guelphs were sent to Pope Boniface beseeching him to take in hand the unfortunate affairs of Florence, and ad-

[32] Raynaldus, year 1300, no. 15.

just them, otherwise there would be nothing left of the Guelphs save the memory, on account of the advantage which the Whites with the Ghibellines possessed. Boniface was deeply grieved at this news. He restrained their animosity, and sought to control their minds, in order to reconcile them. So he sent for Veri, head of the Cerchi and the Whites, and by the promise of every spiritual and temporal favor, he endeavored to persuade this proud soul to make peace with the Donati. But stubborn and whimsical, he replied, that he was not at war with anyone, and he left without complying with the request of the Pope. When Veri had returned to Florence, the two factions, agitated and threatening hitherto, finally came to blows, and a bloody civil war ensued. The Whites were victorious; the Blacks became alarmed and invoked the aid of the Pope.[33]

In June of 1300 Matthew Acquasparta, Friar Minor, Cardinal of Porto, as Legate of Boniface to the Republic arrived unexpectedly in the disturbed city, to pacify it.[34] Their angry feelings were quieted, and their reception of him was hearty and becoming. He effected a peace, and wished to establish it firmly and with justice to all. He asked from the Commune of Florence the authority to arrange affairs, distributing the offices of the city equally between the two parties. But the Whites who possessed the major part, would not for the sake of peace relinquish any. They rejected the wise and temperate advice of the Legate with great anger; they refused to obey, and they stirred up fresh rage. The Legate discouraged and irritated by the brutal obstinacy of the Whites, departed from Florence, justly leaving it under an interdict. When he was gone, the factions flew at each other more fiercely, disgracing their city by the shedding of fraternal blood.[35]

When Cardinal Acquasparta was in the Roman Court making a report of his unsuccessful embassy, Boniface foresaw the grave evils produced by these new factions, which, although they were contained within the walls of Florence, nevertheless had a most injurious effect on the entire Guelph, or Papal party. Recent events in the Papal province of Umbria confirmed this foresight of Boniface. Frederick, Count of Montefrelto, son of Friar

[33] Villani, Book VIII. [34] Raynaldus, 24 Epist. 16, lib. 6. [35] See Doc. G.

Guy; Hubert Malatesta; and Uguccione Faggiula, powerful Ghibellines,[36] ruled in that province. The latter, a famous warrior, exercised there a very great sway, and being head of Gubbio, he had expelled all the Guelphs. Boniface dispatched Napoleon Orsini, Governor of the Duchy of Spoleto, to reinstate them in the city. Orsini succeeded in his design, being aided by the Perugians. He entered the city accompanied by the Guelphs, but the victory was disgraced by rapine and murder. Even the cities of the Romagna were in commotion, but there was no bloodshed. Matthew Acquasparta, who became in October Papal Governor, quelled the riot.[37]

These agitations gave Boniface much to think of, and caused him great apprehension. This was further increased by the clamors which the Blacks made in his court, who were magnifying maliciously the injustice of the Whites, and the reports which they were spreading were more dangerous "*Than the point of the sword,*" as Compagni relates.[38] The Colonna refugees were always causing alarm, and the Blacks were making use of this in order to cause Boniface to be suspicious of the assistance which the rising Ghibelline party would be to them. This made him expedite matters, and execute a project which the Pope had contemplated with regard to Charles of Valois, namely to make him a peacemaker in Tuscany.[39] In that good thought Compagni found hidden a most wicked proposition, the suppression of the Whites. Compagni was a White Guelph. The resolution was taken with the advice of Corso Donati himself and the more powerful agreement of Geri Spini and his associates, bankers of the Pope.[40] It is never good policy to invite a foreigner to meddle in the affairs of one's country. The despair, the impossibility of otherwise obtaining order can alone legitimize this appeal. In factions this despair is always on the side of the vanquished. So the Ghibellines when beaten invoked the aid of the German emperors, and the Guelphs when oppressed turned to the French. As the Pope himself appealed to the latter, this circumstance rendered the invitation of the Guelphs less dangerous than

[36] Chron. Dino Comp L. II. [37] Chron. Caesen. S. R. I. T. 14.
[38] John Villani, Book 8, Chap. 43. [39] Chron S. R. I. T. IX book VII.
[40] Chr S. R. I. T. lib. 11.

that of the Ghibellines. For the Pope was so powerful as to make use of the French prince only as an instrument, and the authority of the priesthood was sufficient to put sense into the head of Charles if he aspired to supreme power. But the Ghibellines, after having invoked the aid of a powerful foreigner, were not able to prevent this charitable assistance from degenerating into an insolent tyranny. Boniface knew this, and no one as much as he had the strength to restrain a foreigner who refused to obey his orders. But either to reassure the great number of Italians who thought that the presence of a second French prince among them would be unbecoming, or in order to induce the French clergy to give him the tithes for this expedition, he wanted to justify by weighty reasons the coming of Charles, and the levy of the tithes. He did this in a letter expressly addressed to the French clergy. In it he said that Sicily was still in revolt against the Church, and the other ecclesiastical towns were in disorder; that Tuscany was so disturbed as to entail all Italy; that the Holy Land was clamoring for aid to liberate it from the hands of the infidels; that Charles was to come as peacemaker into Italy; and afterwards go to liberate the Christians in the East.[41] Then to induce Charles to willingly accept this expedition, besides the grant of those tithes, he dazzled his eyes with the charm of empire, by insinuating that the imperial throne was vacant. Meanwhile affairs grew worse; Corsi, always at the side of the Pope, kept importuning him to let him see the longed-for Charles of Valois. New Papal legates went to hasten the coming of the future peacemaker. The reader need not be curious to know if it was a pleasure for Charles to come to Italy; for what foreign prince ever felt it a pain to enter this beautiful country? He welcomed the legates most cordially, who urged him to make haste. Immediately he sounded the trumpets, ordering the banners to be unfurled, and the knights to assemble, and post-haste he set out for discordant Italy.[42] Charles came with a good number of soldiers, and the news of his near arrival differently affected various parts of Italy. Florence and the court of Boniface were the places where the minds were most agitated. The Blacks at Rome had been successful

[41] John Villani, L. 8, ch. 42.   [42] See Document H.

in securing Charles as peacemaker by plying all their devices, counsel and money. The Whites did not desist from working most sedulously in the Roman Court, and frustrating the designs of their adversaries. The Whites sent an embassy to Boniface, at the head of which was Dante Alighieri. This man, to use the words of that eloquent writer Boccaccio, was then in the zenith of his fame. The heart of this virtuous citizen, whom heaven adorned with the highest intelligence, was grieved at seeing his country so wickedly divided, and he foresaw the misfortunes which always follow in the train of this scourge. By word and deed he strove to soften the anger of the parties and pacify them; but having failed in his purpose, he wanted to sever all connections with public affairs, and bid them an eternal farewell. But the love of his country restrained him; and perhaps also being mindful of his own worth he could not close his heart to the sweetness of glory, which arises from the virtuous administration of public affairs, he concluded to remain, and resolved to follow the party of the Whites.

When Florence was certain of the coming of Charles, the Whites were startled and feared for their liberty. They assembled in council, and decided to send ambassadors to Boniface, that he might stop the coming of the foreigner or retard him, and in any case to inspire him with peaceful dispositions towards them. And in that assembly Dante being unanimously chosen as head of the embassy, he unbecomingly gave utterance to the following: "If I go, who remains? If I remain who will go?" At all times such words sound badly from the mouth of any man, and are detestable in the mouth of a statesman in a time of fierce factions. They were displeasing even to his friends.[43] The embassy strengthened by that of Siena set out; and it was to act quickly, so as to give no time to the intrigues of the Blacks. But a certain Ubaldino Malvolti a Sienese Judge and a member of the embassy, injured the opportunity of the journey. He stopped on the way to demand from the Florentines jurisdiction over a castle which he said belonged to him. This delay for a private gain damaged that of the community, as the

---

[43] History of Pistoja, S. R. I., tom. XI 377 B.

ambassadors did not arrive in time. When the legates arrived in Rome they were admitted into the private chambers of the Pope, who when he had them alone said to them secretly: "Why are you so stubborn? Humble "yourselves before me. I tell you truly that I have no "other object in view but your peace. Return at once two "of you, and they will have my blessing if they obtain "obedience to my will."[44] The secrecy of this conversation showed the fear of causing suspicions among the Blacks who were in the court. We know not what the terrible Dante said. But it is certain that if Boniface could have foreseen those creations that were to be produced by the imagination of that ambassador, exiled afterwards through the stupidity of Charles of Valois, and the hideousness of the Hell into which the poet was to hurl him, we believe that the Whites would have gained their cause. For the thrust of a sword is not so agonizing to the body, as is to a generous soul the anathema of the word which is eternalized by the immortal genius of him who utters it.

The Florentine legates were still in Rome, and in Florence the arrival of Charles was awaited. It pleased none as citizens, it pleased many as partisans. However, just as one trembles when strong and painful remedies are to be applied, so hearts were trembling in unhappy Florence. It seemed the presence of the foreigner softened the angry minds. Men of temperate habits and with love for peace and their country were chosen for the government of the city, among whom was that charming character, Dino Compagni. These men undertook to distribute the offices in common among the factions. The Blacks began to make advances towards the Whites, who held the sovereignty, under the leadership of Compagni. But they could not revive a fraternal peace, as mutual mistrust and suspicion still influenced them, which in factional differences ever stifle the breath of good feeling. In fact while the one was making advances to the other, and in exterior politeness there seemed a hope of peace, in both parties minds were timorous and they dared not trust one another. In these friendly negotiations it must be said that the greater frankness and sincerity were displayed by the

[44] Bocc. Life of Dante.

party of the Whites, who wished to see peace ensue from the spontaneous agreement of the citizens, whereas the Blacks desired it through the ever dangerous ministry of a foreigner. The ambition of the Blacks overcame the holy affection they had for their unhappy country. The first messengers from Charles appeared in Florence. The domestic troubles could have been concealed from them, but the Blacks spoke openly to them, and extolled to the skies Charles who was at hand. Words of servile flattery freely fell from their lips, a sign of drooping spirits and of a hopeless despair. The question whether Charles should be welcomed or not was agitated. The opinion of the Blacks prevailed, and Charles was welcomed by an embassy, and was even furnished with money to increase his resources. Such was the action of the party of the Blacks, but not of that model of civic moderation, Dino Compagni, who, in every way the equal of the most virtuous citizen of either the Grecian or Roman republics, surpassed them all by that nobility of heart which the Christian religion alone can instil. If there is a man to whom all Italy owes a solemn debt of gratitude, that man is Compagni. He wrote only the history of Florence; but the events of Florence are of such a nature, and are narrated by him in such a manner, that they reproduce in outline an image of the whole of Italy in every epoch, and they are a source of salutary instruction. Statues have been erected to actors and dancers, but not a stone has been raised to the memory of the Father of Italian history, Dino Compagni. Seeing that the efforts to make the Frenchman return to his country were hopeless, Compagni would at least have him not find the citizens in riot, but peaceful. For there is nothing more favorable to tyranny, than the intervention of a stranger in the affairs of a city that is rent by factions and especially of a stranger who feigns honorable and peaceful pretexts. He made one last effort, which would not have failed, if in the heat of civil tumult, men had been men. In the church of St. John he assembled a parliament of many and excellent citizens whom he urged in eloquent terms that laying aside all hatred they should oppose to the foreign maker of an uncertain peace, a certain domestic peace, and they should swear on the baptismal font that such would be done. We cannot refrain

from quoting his words: "Dear and valiant citizens, you
" who have all received holy Baptism at this same font,
" reason forces and constrains you to love one another
" because you are brothers, and also because you possess
" the noblest city in the world. Among you there has
" arisen some enmity in the struggle for the offices, which
" my companions and I on oath have promised to distrib-
" ute equally among you. This foreign lord is coming,
" and it is becoming for us to show him honor. Lay aside
" your enmities and make peace with one another, in order
" that he may not find you divided. For the love and
" benefit of your city pardon and forget all offences and
" evil desires, and upon this sacred font where you re-
" ceived holy Baptism, swear to a good and lasting peace,
" in order that the French prince may find the citizens all
" united." Most touching words coming from a very holy
heart. These very few words, by an impressiveness of
form, altogether Italian; by the force of feeling and a certain heavenly unction, surpass the many words so loudly
launched from the height of foreign tribunes. And Oh!
would that they were engraven on Italian minds! For
from these alone they would learn how manliness of spirit
in being a true citizen and a virtuous magistrate is not engendered by the example of Greeks and Romans, but by
religion which before Rome and Greece knew how to place
man in society and educate him in virtue. Then they all
swore; but many violated the oath. At this the good
Compagni's heart was deeply grieved, as if his charitable
expedient had been an added scandal. From him and
Villani it is clear that the Blacks, elated over the arrival
of Charles, were puffed up exceedingly with pride.

While minds were thus agitated in Florence, Charles
appeared before Boniface in Anagni in September of this
year. On seeing Charles honorably received by Boniface
at this time, the reader might be inclined to believe that
Boniface had sanctioned the excesses of the Blacks, so
much deplored by Compagni. But it must be remembered
that their excesses were abhorred by Boniface. He in
truth desired peace, and he well knew that the disorders
of the Blacks far from achieving it only prevented it. The
struggle was Guelph against Guelph, and the Pope as the
head of Guelphism did not care to be the head of two

bodies, but of one; and for this reason he loved to see harmony existing among the Guelphs, not only as Vicar of Christ, but also as a civil potentate. The calling of Charles was the fault of the Whites, who were not inclined to make an equal distribution of the offices, by reason of which the efforts of Cardinal Acquasparta entirely failed. Unarmed and feeble he did not succeed in his honest purpose, so Charles called to attain it by arms. And Boniface, who knew Charles, did not let him come prepared to do evil, because five hundred knights (the number of the forces which Charles led) would be insufficient for that; but only to add strength to the efforts of the Legate. The mind of Boniface will appear clearer in the course of this narrative.

Charles came then to Anagni to kiss the Pope's foot,[45] after having a taste of Italian gold, which the Marquis Azzo d'Este presented to him with great honors as he passed through Modena.[46] Charles II of Naples also came to Anagni, as he placed the greatest hopes in Charles of Valois to recover Sicily. Before going to effect a peace in Tuscany, he wished to wage war in that island, longing to pass over into Greece, to place himself as Emperor on the throne of Byzantium, having married Catherine, daughter. of Philip, titular Emperor of Constantinople, and granddaughter of Baldwin, rightful Emperor. If the French prince regarded Tuscany already pacified, Sicily recovered, Greece conquered, and perhaps even the Holy Land freed from the infidels, it is not surprising. The titles of Vicar of the Empire; Prefect of the Roman Church; the peacemaker of Tuscany; the jurisdiction which the Pope gave him over the Duchy of Spoleto, over the March of Ancona, the province of Emilia, and other territory;[48] the ecclesiastical tithes which he collected plentifully in Italy, in Corsica, in Sardinia, in France, in the principality of Achaia, in the Duchy of Athens,[48] besides the money furnished him by the Blacks, were of a nature to inspire him with lofty opinions of himself; but it will be seen how he deceived the hopes of his adherents and failed in the designs he had himself conceived. Postponing the expedition to Sicily until spring, Charles with his barons set

[45] Dino Compagni.
[47] Chron. Esten S. R. I. T. XV.
[46] Ptolemy of Lucca in Ann. brev.
[48] Raynaldus, year 1301, no. 12.

out for Florence, which they entered on the 1st of November, being welcomed with all honor by the citizens.[49] His first imprudence was to allow himself to be followed by the banished Blacks, who swelled the number of his soldiers to twelve hundred horsemen, and to take up their abode in the house of the Frescobaldi, a family belonging to the party of the Blacks, and to fortify it. This was not a peaceoffering to the opposite party, but a sign of war. Therefore the Whites grew suspicious and the Blacks became elated. The Priors, and among them Compagni, did not desist from that calmness and honesty of counsel which should ever attend magistrates in time of great crises. They formed a parliament of forty citizens, chosen from both parties, to conduct affairs in such calamitous times. But the remedy was useless, because some had lost energy and others had a criminal intent, and because the Blacks wanted the victory to be complete by demanding the dismissal of the Priors and the recall of those banished.[50]

The imprudence of Charles and the excesses of the Blacks came to the knowledge of Boniface, with whom still were the ambassadors of the Whites, among whom was Dante. These men remained round about the Pope to show him effectively by the irresistible argument of facts how harmful Charles was to Florence, and how unjust and arrogant were their opponents the Blacks. Boniface charged two of these ambassadors, Maso Minerbetti and Corazza, to go and speak to the rulers of Florence and such was the power of this communication that the latter obeyed on the spot. They wrote to the Pope to send them Gentile of Montefiore, a Cardinal of Holy Church, to arrange affairs. The obedience which Boniface exacted was to put in execution the distribution of the offices, which had been requested in vain by the Legate, Matthew Acquasparta.[51] From this it is clear that the work of Charles was displeasing to Boniface; neither did he desire the ruin of the Whites, nor approve the excesses of the Blacks. These latter, having had an inkling of the movements of their opponents with the Pope, brutally broke out

---

[49] Raynaldus 15 Ep. Book 7, 196. [50] John Villani, chap. 58, Book 8.
[51] Dino Compagni.

into all kinds of violence. The Priors reported everything to the Pope, and Dante pressed the matter vehemently. This being told to the Blacks, they destroyed all hope of accord. For after they obtained the desired community of the offices, three Priors being chosen from one of the parties, and three from the other, they were not even then satisfied. They wanted the ascendency in order to crush their opponents.

They dared to attempt their object because Charles acted neither as a loyal nor as an honest man. They exhibited publicly the instruments of justice to terrify the evil-doers, but secretly they circulated money to corrupt the ministers of justice itself. Charles was not ignorant of these corrupt practices so hostile to the public safety. He knew their source, because the Blacks made no secret of their boast: "We have a sovereign amongst us. The "Pope is our protector. Our adversaries are equipped "neither for war nor for peace. They have no money, "and the soldiers have not been paid." Their boastings were followed by deeds. On the fourth day of November the Blacks armed themselves; Charles took up arms under the pretext of restraining criminals, and the Florentines being apprehended, he sent his French soldiers as guards over the gates of the sixth district of the city, beyond the Arno. At the head of this guard Charles placed himself and by oath he swore to defend the gate, and hold it at the disposal of seigniory of the town. But his oath was a wicked perjury. He opened the gates to Gherarduccio Buondelmonti with many of those that had been banished, and gave the signal for open lawlessness to the Blacks. He desired the mastery of the city, and he obtained it. He swore to keep it in a peaceful condition and yet he allowed the turbulent Corso Donati to enter, and swore another time that he did not know of his entrance at all, and wanted to hang Donati. But he knew it, and allowed him to do all that he did, on account of which the city was all in a tumult; the Whites betrayed; the Blacks unrestrained for the perpetration of every evil deed; the Priors dismissed from office, and for some days all rule ceased. Meanwhile Charles the peacemaker through an imbecile malice, peacefully beheld men murdered, houses burned, rapine and civil fury. With hypocrisy and perjury he created new Priors, all of the party of the Blacks, and of the worst reputation.

Boniface was absent in body but in thought he was close to this villany which the Peacemaker fostered. Dante still in Rome in a certain way too must have shown by his silence alone how vain was the hope that was centered in Charles of Valois, and yet at the same time he must have recalled those peaceful negotiations of Cardinal Acquasparta, which failed of success through the obstinacy of his own party, the Whites, who were the cause of the coming of Charles. Boniface at once sent Cardinal Acquasparta a second time as legate to Florence more to remedy the evil of Charles than that of the Blacks. For although in the letter in which he appoints the Legate, he styles Charles a man tried, good and skilful in arms, who entered the province of Tuscany with prudence, yet he addressed some words to the Cardinal which say that Charles was in sore need of counsel and prudence in conducting these affairs with moderation and tact.[52]

This was an excellent precaution of the Pontiff, but too late. The people were too exasperated, and the Blacks too puffed up with pride. The Legate, an unarmed peacemaker, and a sincere seeker of peace, effected some sort of an agreement. This, however, was only a particular arrangement which was founded on an alliance between the Cerchi, Ademari, Donati and Paggi. This could not be lasting while there remained in the city that focus of discord, that is to say Charles, around whom all the fury of the Blacks assembled. In fact when Acquasparta undertook to distribute in common the offices, just as he found the Whites intractable in the previous year, so at this time the Blacks were most inexorable, and despairing of a remedy, he ended his legation by placing mad Florence under an interdict. Hardly had he departed than the Blacks more wrathful than before attacked the Whites; and although they did not accomplish with the assistance of Charles a general expulsion of their rivals, yet they continued an abominable system of confiscations and of arbitrary banishments.[53] This interdict was placed over Florence through the incorrigible wickedness of Charles

[52] Dino Compagni.   [53] See Document at end of work.

and the Blacks, so these latter ought to have felt it deeply, if indeed this species of men can suffer qualms of conscience. After the scandals which he occasioned, Charles went to Rome, and we do not know with what effrontery, and why, he presented himself before Boniface. We are certain that he requested money, and Boniface replied: "That he had placed him in a golden fount." These words could not proceed from a tranquil soul, but were the cry of a heart indignant at the infidelity of Charles in fulfilling his mission and at his insatiable avarice. Tyranny in governments engenders conspiracies, formed either by the oppressed or the oppressor. The oppressed form them to put an end to the evil, the oppressors for greater profligacy of rule. The former are real to destroy the oppressor, the latter are imaginary to find a means, with an appearance of justice, to destroy him who could restrain and check the tyranny. Charles and the Blacks in Florence certainly did carry on a very bad government and made the party of the Whites groan. We know not whether the conspiracy to murder Charles, which made so much commotion at that time, was real, that is to say, the work of the oppressed, or imaginary, that is to say, invented by the oppressors, to expel the former with an appearance of justice. It is certain that after certain nightly and sudden judicial meetings held by Charles immediately after he had returned from Rome, a furious storm burst on the heads of the party of the Whites, of which more than six hundred had their goods confiscated, their property burnt, and the punishment of exile inflicted on them, by reason of which "they wandered about the world some here and some there suffering from want." The crime of the exiles was a conspiracy against the peacemaker. Villani tells us that not the Whites but a wicked baron of Languedoc formed the conspiracy, who forged letters bearing their seal, in which he disclosed the conspiracy and carried it to Charles.[54] The threads of these villanies were held by the Blacks. Peter Ferrant, as the Baron was called, had woven them. But it cannot be alleged that Charles was ignorant at all of this dark plot as to become stupefied at the sight of these letters, as a

[54] Villani, L. VIII.

thing unsuspected; on the contrary, it would be much nearer the truth to affirm that he had a full and entire knowledge of the treachery of which the poor Cerchi and all the Whites were the victims. He had Boniface on his side, who called him not only to be a peacemaker in Florence, but also and perhaps more especially, to be a warrior in Sicily. He pressed him to undertake this last expedition, and Charles had to go. But to depart and leave the Whites in their own homes in Florence, seemed to him to be their restoration. He must then act quickly, strike them, and lead them to final destruction. In this he was instigated by the Blacks, who approved it, because it was of vital importance to them. And just as even the wicked love, if not justice itself, at least an appearance of it, they imaged conspiracies or provoked them by dark treachery, which is the more expeditious, and the more honest way apparently, to lead to destruction those whom they fear, and of keeping an opinion of justice for some time on their side. For some time, but not forever, because history is the faithful revealer of wickedness. At this juncture in Florence there thundered forth a voice truly sublime, because it came from the depth of an incorrupt heart. Dino Compagni, than whom a more beautiful character Florence never had, was bewailing the miserable spectacle presented by his country, which after having disclosed her wounds to a stranger, received not the remedies that would heal them, but the points of the sword which opened them. Compagni revealed to posterity the infamy of the wretched citizens who were to blame for these misfortunes. The reader will pardon us if we enrich this narrative with a wealth of Grecian, but yet Christian, eloquence. " O, wicked citizens, procurators of
" the destruction of your city, whither have you led it!
" And you, Amanto di Rota Beccanugi, disloyal citizen,
" wickedly you turned to the Priors and endeavored by
" the threats to get the keys from them: see what your
" malice has brought on us. O Donato Alberti, where is
" your arrogance, you who hid yourself in a vile kitchen
" of Nuto Marignolli! And you, Nuto, provost and senior
" from your quarter of the city, because of animosity of
" the Guelph party you have allowed yourself to be de-
" ceived! O Sir Geri Spini, satiate your soul; eradicate

"the Cerchi, in order that you may live safe from the
"price of your perfidy! O Sir Lapo Saltarelli, menacer
"and oppressor of the rulers, who did not serve you in
"your disputes, where did you arm yourself? In the
"Pulci palace, by remaining in concealment? O Sir
"Berto Frescobaldi, since you showed such friendship
"for the Cerchi, and made yourself a mediator in their
"quarrels, for borrowing from them twelve thousand
"florins, where have you merited from them? How do
"you now appear in the eyes of the public? O Sir Man-
"etto Scali, who desired to be considered so great and
"feared, believing yourself at all times a lord, why did
"you take up arms? Where is your following? Where
"are your barbed horses? You have allowed yourself to
"submit to those who in comparison with you were con-
"sidered as nothing. O you commoners, who longed for
"the offices, and appropriated the honors and occupied
"the palaces of the rulers, where is your defence? It is
"in falsehoods, at one time promising, at another dis-
"sembling; condemning your friends and praising your
"enemies for the sole purpose of self-preservation. There-
"fore weep over us, and over your city." Such were the
sentiments of Compagni within Florence. Dante from
without gave utterance to another kind of eloquence,
that of an exile. Like those Numidians, who while fleeing turned round to shoot their arrows, he discharged at
Charles of Valois a most poisonous dart. He revealed the
plebeian origin of the Capets, and then puts on the lips
of Hugh Capet himself scorching words against his
descendant Charles of Valois.[55] And having taken a farewell look at Florence, rather than weep, in the same manner that Compagni was comforted, he composes his feelings with a smile of bitter sarcasm, whose eloquence has
never been equalled; he flails with the lash of cutting
derision his ungrateful, but infortunate, country.[56]

[55] Leonard Aretino says that he saw these letters a century later in the Florentine archives, and found them assuredly forgeries See Balbo, Life of Dante.

[56] "Hugh Capet was the name I had on earth:
The Philips and the Louis, who bore sway
In France of late, from me derive their birth:
My Sire at Paris plied the butcher's trade."
He strikes Charles of Anjou:

The banishment of the White Guelphs filled all Italy with compassion. There had been other banishments, but this one seemed more cruel because it was effected by a foreign prince, the number was greater, and because virtuous and upright citizens were the sufferers. These men were dispersed, roaming here and there throughout Italy, stripped of all their property, driven from that sweetest of nests their native place, and their wives and children were torn from their bosoms. They cursed Charles the peacemaker, and Boniface who called him, for their ruin. As their misfortunes filled all hearts with pity, Charles and Boniface were condemned to execration. They had been so prescribed and so brutally expelled by the Black Guelphs that they broke the barriers which separated them from the Ghibelline party, and wishing to no longer share the Guelph name with the Blacks they became all Ghibelline. Dante Alighieri was among these, no more a Guelph, but a Ghibelline; upon him Charles of Valois seemed to inflict all his rigor, because the poet had opposed his coming most strenuously of all the Florentines, and had denounced his acts in the Papal court, where he sought a remedy. He was involved not only in the general condemnation by the fact of the conspiracy, but in two other preceding condemnations [57] He departed from

"Charles entered Italy, and for amends,
"A victim of young Conradin made,
"And sent to Heaven Aquinas for amends."

Then he lashes Charles of Valois:
"I see from France, ere many years have flown,
Another Charles Italy's peace invade,
Thereby to make his race more fully known.
Unarmed he goes, save with that lance alone
Which Judas tilted with: and thus he bears
So, that e'en now is Florence overthrown.
Land shall he reap not, but of shame and guilt
The heavier load, as, light the heart he swears,
While blood around him is profusely spilt."

He puts all this in the mouth of Hugh Capet.
                    Purg. Canto XX V. 70. (Wright's Translation).

[57] After having spoken of all Italy, he turns to Florence:
"My Florence! well contented may'st thou be
With this digression—thee it toucheth not;
Thanks to the people who advise thee.
Many have justice in their hearts; but long

Florence leaving behind his wife and children and a small portion of his dowry saved by him during the civil disturbances, and which scantily supported his dear ones. He took away with him none of those things which are wont ordinarily to assist men in misfortune. But the brilliant renown of his virtue and genius preceded him, and opened the courts of Princes, and what is more gave him an entrance into the hearts of those whom Heaven destined to taste the pleasure of pitying the misfortunes of most distinguished mortals. In his worn-out and battered body he bore enclosed a mind similar to that of Homer and Virgil; and in his heart a wrath, and such a wrath as in men of genius enkindles the fever of creation. *When he had eaten bitterly the bread of strangers, when he ascended and descended the stairs of others,* his terrible imagination, being fertilized by grief, conceived and brought forth that grand Epic poem, The Divine Comedy. Aristotle would also have called it an Epic poem, if he had known that those cantos did not contain the unity of one fact or of one people, but the unity of the whole Middle Ages, united by the warmth of its faith and strength of its passions; divided by those noisy jolts of virtue and vice, and by the hostility of the elements, which war against each other, they would strike each other mortally, and from this the edifice of modern civilization would finally arise. Homer sang of Greece, Virgil of Rome, but Dante's song was of the whole world.

Being made most famous by those cantos, not only in

> Delay, through fear, the meditated shot;—
> Thy people have it on the very tongue.
> Many refuse the burdens of the state;—
> Thy people answer with officious haste
> Ere they are asked: 'I bow me to the weight.'
> Then be thou joyful, for good cause hast thou,—
> Thou rich! Thou peaceful! thou with wisdom graced!
> That truth I speak, the facts themselves avow "— .

Then rendering the veil of bitter irony, he concludes:

> "If thou rememberest well, and art not blind,
> Thou'lt see thyself like one distraught with pain,
> Who on her bed of down, no rest can find,
> But, ever turning, seeks relief in vain."
>
> Purg. canto VI V. 127, etc.

the estimation of the Ghibelline party, but of all Italy, he anathematized his enemies, and especially those who had brought about his misfortunes, and all minds centered around him. Those who shared with him the sentence of exile, or factional opinion, coincided with him by revenge, and others by pity. For fully nine times he poured forth his vengeance on Boniface. He begins by plunging him into the dark hole of those guilty of simony. He snarls at him as a traitor; as a wolf; as unmindful of the Holy Land; as an usurper of the See of St. Peter, and we know not what else, in such a manner that like Hector dragged many times around the walls of Troy, so was Boniface in the Poem of Dante cruelly dragged through the Inferno by the angry imagination of Dante. Losing all reverence for the power of the Keys, he enters furiously the Papal Court. He strips the ministers of their mantles, he reveals their human failings and now strikes them with a scourge, then galls them by the poison of a most terrible sarcasm. Then passing blindly from men to things, he irreverently aims a blow at that Pontificate which in his calm moments he had respected, and had loved in the peaceful times when he was a Guelph. The suspicion of the simoniacal intrusion of Boniface into the Papacy proclaimed from such a powerful source, bore a semblance of truth; the severe sentence passed on the Colonnas appeared a manifest injustice; the calling of Charles appeared a horrible betrayal of the Guelph party. So the friends of Pope Celestine, the Colonnas, the exiled White Guelphs, and all the Ghibellines formed but one body closely united, and sworn enemies of Boniface. As if the phalanx was not sufficiently strong, Philip the Fair came to join it and offer it the support of arms and the royal power. All these arose in a threatening attitude, not to judge but to condemn Boniface. Quick and direful vengeance was visited on the *magnanimous sinner,* which he would be obliged to bear for a long time, for the opprobrium which Philip the Fair had cast on him was too grievous, the soul of Dante which guarded this opprobrium was too noble to easily remove it.

Dante, and by this name we express all Ghibelline Italy, strengthened by the party of the White Guelphs, was a man who was all bloody by the outrages of the Blacks;

and as one wounded by the sword does not rush against the steel, but against the arm that brandished it, so he consigned to Hell the Black Guelphs his enemies, and venting his hatred for Charles, he stopped to become more furious against Boniface as the primary cause of his misfortunes. Boniface had called and urged Charles to come. He did not dismiss him when he found him unsuited for making peace, and did not prevent his wicked deeds against the White Guelphs. Such were the faults of Boniface in the eyes of Dante. But judgment could not be passed fairly by one who was banished from his country, despoiled of his possessions, and above all excluded from taking part in public affairs, which were administered by a foreigner and an opposing faction. His grief was too intense, and his wrath too impetuous. This impossibility of judging calmly and dispassionately was shared not only by those who suffered but also by those who sympathized with them. For this reason the cry that was raised against Boniface in Italy was almost universal. And chroniclers could not free themselves from the dominion of an opinion so general and so manifest. That blind vengeance which was frequently practised in Italy during the disturbances between the Guelphs and Ghibellines was exercised by Ghibelline writers against Boniface. And if it is folly to think that with justice and calm minds men animated by factional hatred could commit murder, now in ambush and now in open places, there is less reason to believe that a faction so cruelly hurt, could justly and with a dispassionate spirit have estimated the character of this pontiff. We must recognize in Dante and all the enemies of Boniface this human nature which in the heat of passion loses that calmness and clearness of reason which is so necessary in judging men, and especially those who by reason of the power they exercised are found enclosed in the mysterious reasons of state. These reasons are not apprehended by anyone but in the course of centuries, and for that reason only after a long time men's real characters are laid bare to history. Boniface did not wish to see the Guelphs divided, but united and in peace. He wished to recover Sicily, a fief of the Church, which he could not renounce. The calling of Charles was decided on in desperation of all other means, as we have seen, to accomplish these two ends. While Charles deceived his hopes in Florence, he could not check him, because he had become too powerful by reason of the party of the Blacks, of whom he had been made head. He wished, however, to do so, and his will was manifest in his acquiescing to the propositions of the Whites, in the second legation of Cardinal Acquasparta, and in the interdict which he placed over Florence. Boniface afterwards could not expel him and send him back to France, because he would have ruined the affairs of Sicily, which he was sure could be restored by the power of Charles; and he would have lost all the money collected from the tithes, and from the pious offerings of the faithful with which he had enriched the French prince to carry on the war in Sicily, and afterwards in the Holy Land, The affair of the Holy Land in the beginning of the XIV century, if less grave than in the previous century, was still of importance and seriously engaged the attention of the public. Moreover, precisely at this time the quarrel with Philip the Fair began, and the solution of the difficulty still appeared possible. To embitter Charles was the same as to precipitate matters to that sad state which followed later, and which at that time there was hope of arresting.

Here now is Boniface obliged by these reasons to remain an idle spectator of the wickedness of Charles and the Blacks, and the unjust calamities of the Whites. So inactive was he, that he appeared to the Whites not only abetting but even urging on Charles to their ruin, as Villani thought.[58] But could he rejoice in the dissolution of the Guelph party? Could he be glad of the increase of the Ghibellines? Could he be contented with that portion of the Guelphs, called the Blacks? Could he continue to trust in Charles urging him on to such wickedness, which would make him hateful to all Italy, and an unseemly captain of the Church in Sicily? We do not hesitate to acknowledge that Boniface was the material cause, so to speak, of the injustices of the Blacks, but not the moral cause. For the moral cause was entirely the Whites when they rebelled against Cardinal Acquasparta in his first

[58] Balbo. Life of Dante.

legation, and the Blacks in the second legation. Dante himself sheds a bright light on this fact, when suspending for a moment his personal hatred, when recovering his right reason he turns to Italy and vigorously charges the misfortune under which she groaned to the discord among her own children, which Boniface evidently strongly labored to stifle in the interest both of others and of himself. But the reasons which we have submitted to the reader could not be apprehended by a man who was carried away by the whirlwind of a party so arrogant as the Ghibelline was, and which was cruelly harassed by the opposite party to which the Pontiff belonged. Therefore as later observers of those facts, let us pity in Dante this human nature, which, mortally provoked by anger flies into a passion and rejects all explanations; let us pity these irreverences towards the Vicar of Christ. Such feelings did not proceed from the philosophical wantonness of our epoch, nor from corruption of heart, but from the blind passion of anger, which transformed him into another man. But Dante was always the same, Italian and thoroughly Catholic. In fact afterwards hardly had it been made known to him that Boniface had been insulted by two ruffians, Nogaret and Sciarra Colonna, than the fever which made him delirious, immediately disappeared; there leaped up in his heart a fountain of filial love, which extinguished within him the desire of revenge, and conducted him to the feet of that Boniface, whom he no longer abhorred as simoniacal and criminal, but whom he revered not only as Vicar of Christ, but as Christ himself.[59] And in this action we find in Dante the model of every Italian who is truly Catholic. Now if it be allowed a historian to ascend to the sphere of poetry, we will venture to assert that, if these two noble souls, Boniface and Dante, had met pure and freed from the imperfections of this lower nature, there is no doubt that they would have been united in the kiss of pardon, and the Papal Keys would have been placed as a sign of peace on the volumes of the Divina Commedia. This latter was the fruitful source of Italian civilization. The Keys did not bring forth the civil independence for the attainment of which

---

[59] Villani Book 8, Chap. 48.

Gregory VII and Innocent III exerted themselves. God rendered them barren in civil effects, in order to punish those who would have enjoyed them.[60]

After having spoken of the wrath of poets, we now come to that of princes. But it is necessary that we first dismiss that ineffective peacemaker, Charles of Valois. The spring having set in, the time appointed for the expedition to Sicily, Charles departed from Florence, loaded with infamy, and set out for Naples. After the defeat of the army of the King of Naples at Falconeria, the affairs of war had taken a disadvantageous turn for the Church. Hence Robert, Duke of Calabria, was forced to ask a truce from Frederick, which being obtained strengthened the latter's sovereignty over Sicily. But they were to resume their arms with great ardor; for the new conditions in which Boniface had placed affairs promised great victories. Genoa, very powerful in her navy, was finally detached from Frederick, and joined her forces to those of Charles. In the previous summer a treaty of peace was signed between Naples and this republic, which being eminently commercial in its interests, suffered considerably from its hostile relations with Naples. For the ports of Apulia and Calabria being closed against her, she could not draw away the wheat and other grain with which they abounded, for the sake of trading, and she lost thereby immense profits. So among the conditions introduced into the treaty in favor of Genoa, the principal were the free entry into and departure from the ports of Apulia and Calabria of the Genoese ships, the privilege of exporting the cereals, and the assimilation of that republic to every other friendly and allied State in the amount of custom duties.[61] The aid of the Genoese was a

---

[60] " Entering Alagna, lo the fleur-de-lis,
And in his Vicar Christ a captive led!
I see him mocked a second time,—again
The vinegar and gall produced I see;
And Christ himself twixt robbers slain."
Purgatorio Canto XX, line 86, etc.

[61] " Dictus Dominus Carolus venit Florentiam, et facta est ibi magna commotio, et spoliorum direptio, et domorum combustio in civitate, et in comitatu qualis non fuit a tempore, quo Guelphi et Ghibellini Florentiae fuerunt." Ptolemy de Lucca. Annals.

great help to the war. There was gathered a fleet of fully one hundred large vessels, with the flower of the cavalry and a great number of French barons;[62] the Archbishop elect of Salerno, Papal Legate, was endowed with the faculty of absolving from censures, and of dispensing graces. The army departed for Sicily. Roger of Loria, who commanded, directed their course to the Val of Mazzara. In May they reached the coast of Termini. Having captured the city, they encamped there; for the country was favorable for movements of the cavalry, which formed a considerable part of the army. Then they made an attack on the cities of Polizzi and Corleone; but as it was useless and also injurious, they proceeded afterwards towards the southern coasts, and laid siege to the city of Sciacca. The walls were strong, and stronger still were the defenders, and the besiegers with all their energy fought to conquer it. But it was in mid-July; the heat was scorching like in Africa, to which country this was very near, the sun darted its rays of fire over the marshy ground, and there arose from it putrid exhalations. A frightful mortality decimated the horses, so that in a few days there remained only five hundred of all the large number. The men themselves suffering from the effects of the bad air saw their ranks considerably decreased from day to day. Charles of Valois despaired of success,[63] and felt the necessity of a treaty; disgusted with a war so unfortunately begun, he turned all his thoughts towards empire. Although Robert, Duke of Calabria, was opposed to every sort of treaty, lamenting the loss of Sicily, as well as the treasures and the blood shed so abundantly and so uselessly to wrest it from Frederick, nevertheless he was forced to submit, because the reverses exacted it, and because Charles induced him. They came to a parley with Frederick on the 24th of August in a country house between Caltabellotta and Sciacca. Charles spoke first alone without being heard by Robert of Calabria, who finished by taking part in the conversation. There were present Roger of Loria, a witness for one side, and Palizzia, most ardent admirer of Aragon for the other,

[62] Letter of Boniface. Raynaldus, nos. 16 and 17, year 1307.
[63] John Villani, book 8, chap. 49—Ptolemy of Lucca Annal—St Antoninus 3. par. tit 20, 16.

and many other barons. For five days they were deliberating. The treaty was concluded on the 29th of August and sworn to on the 30th. In the annals of Raynaldus [64] is found the summary of the terms of peace. Frederick was to retain the sovereignty over Sicily with the title of king during his life, and was to marry Eleanor, daughter of Charles; his children were to receive the kingdoms of Cyprus and Sardinia, and failing in these, either they were to retain Sicily as the dowry from their mother, or would be recompensed with one hundred thousand ounces of gold; there was to be a gratuitous and mutual liberation of prisoners, a mutual restoration of the territory seized by Charles in Sicily and by Frederick in Calabria; the goods taken in the beginning of the wars in Sicily were to be returned to the churches; and each prince was to grant pardon to his respective rebels.

From these terms of peace it is clear that, apart from that future and possible restoration of Sicily to be made by the sons of Frederick in the event of not receiving Cyprus and Sardinia, Charles, after his profuse outlay of money, and after a long war, did not derive any benefits; on the contrary he granted to the enemy that which in open war he strove to take from him. Boniface, that is to say the Church, fared worse. He was not summoned, or consulted in drawing up the terms of peace. Charles of Valois treated with Frederick about Sicily as if it were a kingdom subject to the right of conquest, and completely independent of the Papal See, which public opinion at that time recognized as the rightful master of that island. This is the reason why Boniface, pressed by the ambassadors of Frederick to approve the treaty, declared by letter that the conditions of agreement drawn up by Charles could not be approved by him without impugning his own dignity and that of the Apostolic See; the substance of the treaty being maintained, some censure was necessary for the honor and the recognition of the dominion of the Church.[65] From which it appears that Boniface outwardly complained only that the honor of the Church was not upheld, inasmuch as he had not taken part nor even

[64] Nic Special. Book 6, cap. 6, cap. 8, cap. 10.—Villani, Book 8, chap. 50.—Ptolemy of Lucca Amal S. R. I T XI, p. 1305.

[65] Raynaldus, 1302, 2, 3, 4, 6, 7.

was called to take part in the composition of the articles of agreement. Inwardly, however, any one can surmise whether he approved or not that surrender of the rights of the Church in Sicily into the hands of Frederick, and for the same reason if in truth the sum and substance of the treaty was pleasing to him. However he sent an answer immediately, absolving the Sicilians from the long-imposed censures, and dispensed Frederick and Eleanor from the impediment of consanguinity, in order that they might wed, which they did. But we do not wish to pass over in silence a certain observation on the conduct of Boniface in the matter of this treaty drawn up by Valois without his authorization.

We now see Boniface changed into a new man. The reader may remember how, having heard that Charles of Naples, anxious to liberate his son Philip, the Duke of Taranto, from the custody of the Sicilians, made overtures of peace to Frederick without consulting him, Boniface severely reprimanded the king and made him desist from the overtures. Now Charles of Valois concluded a treaty without the knowledge of Boniface, and Boniface says nothing. He asks only the privilege of taking part in its confirmation, not to change the substance of the agreement, but only to save the honor of the Papal See, which had been compromised, because it was not thought of in the management of an affair, which was altogether its own. Who then restrained Boniface? Who made him inactive and patient at this time? It is evident that it was Philip the Fair, with whom he had already a misunderstanding. Foreseeing the effect of this division would be terrible, to avert it he carefully avoided every pretext that could arouse the proud spirit of this prince, or lend a color of justice to his violence. For Charles of Valois was a French prince, and if the Pope punished him and sent him back in shame to his own country as he deserved, this would have aroused and precipitated the anger of Philip the Fair. Now if Boniface for these reasons remained patient in affairs of his own, what fault was it for him to be likewise patient in the affairs of the White Guelphs for the same reasons? And this was why this Charles of Valois, called to establish peace in Florence, and undertake a war in Sicily according to the will of the

Pontiff,[66] was allowed to continue the strife in Tuscany, and to effect a peace detrimental to the Church in Sicily, without Boniface speaking a word. And Boniface was not a man to bear in silence such foreign impertinence. Therefore that slander set upon the memory of Boniface by certain people, who accuse him of causing Dante's woes, appears to us to have no reasonable foundation.

To arrive at the truth, so far as it is possible for man to do so, of events which happened at times far remote from us, and over which human passions had been greatly and for a long while exercised, it seems to us that the historian, to reach a right decision, had two solemn duties to perform, in which if he fail, far from combating and rectifying the error of others, he only confirms them by his own. First of all, documents which others made use of beforehand must be submitted not only to the laws of criticism, but also to the philosophy of history; and afterwards men must be coolly considered not so much in the material as in the moral condition of their lives which are manifested in the circumstances of times and places. Such a study distinguished the chronicler from the historian. The former narrates, the latter in narrating discusses, that is, passes in review the circumstances of which we speak, and by this reflects a sure light on the individual, whom he treats, and not only brings to light the facts, but also their moral reason. The reader may clearly perceive from these words that we are now approaching that famous struggle of Boniface with Philip the Fair. The reader may also be certain that it is with a faltering heart that we approach the subject, both because the mission of the historian in the narration of facts of this nature is a very difficult one, and because the love of truth forces us to differ in opinion from many a worthy writer. Now let us consider the characters of these two personages, Boniface and Philip the Fair, whom the fiery human passions of their times have handed down to us, clothed in mystery. We have already spoken of Philip in the second book of this history. But if the reader will allow, we

---

* Raynaldus 2302, p. 5 et seq . . . . "in principalibus integra remanente substantia, ad emendationem et reformationem ejus, secundum aequam rationabilemque censuram, pro reverentia et honore, ac recognitione debita nobis, et eidem ecclesiae, tuum convertas animum."—

will recall his moral traits, because we come to a fact which the prime cause of his conduct, a conduct which will confirm our assertion. There is no doubt that Philip was a man of unbounded ambition and of unbridled lust for gold. And when we consider the laws enacted by him, and the acts of his reign, we find that wearing the crown meant to him no opposition whatever to his absolute and despotic authority. Feudalism, which rested entirely in the civil aristocracy and clergy, was an obstacle which he resolved to remove, and to this end he fought vigorously and with little opposition, for at that time in France neither with the people nor the feudal lords was there a legal means of resisting a possible derangement of the royal will. The French kings from Charlemagne down to this time were absolute monarchs; but that identification of the monarch with the state was not for a personal but a public benefit. Philip the Fair was the first who united in himself all public authority to the detriment of others, solely for his own use. He was the state, and the state had to bear the weight of the yoke, and not enjoy the favors of him who imposed it. He penetrated the remotest part of French society to imprint there by laws conceived in his brain, undisciplined by anyone, the character of his absolute power, and to wrest power from others. The right to coin money which was invested in other lords in France, by him was reserved alone to the king. This was right and proper, if it had been done for the public good, but wicked and improper if for private and profligate gain, as was the case. Observe how, being king, he was not ashamed of becoming a base counterfeiter of money; in other words guilty of the greatest rascality, the consequence of which is that a people is separated from others, deprived of the benefits of commerce, and condemned to domestic miseries for a solemn betrayal of a public trust. In his encounter with feudalism, he had to face two enemies, the civil and clerical aristocracies. The former was overcome, because not being invested with legal forms as a body, it was consequently wanting in the power given by unity of rights and of chiefs. The latter resisted, because it was acknowledged by public opinion of the time, and was very powerful owing to the unity of its rights and of its head, who was the

Roman Pontiff. The former being overcome, easily passed from subjection to servitude, and strengthened the king. The other resisting irritated the king, but it could not long preserve inviolate its rights, because oppressed by the king and the lords themselves, when the latter, it seems, should have remained united to it by a community of rights in a community of fiefs. The times were past of pure barbarism in which the will of the conqueror imposed itself, inflexible and blood-stained like the point of sword upon which it supported itself. The generations once being civilized, princes hid their sword, and to the eyes of the people, whom they desired no longer to intimidate, but to persuade, if they could, they displayed the book of Law in order to create their power. There was needed for this work not soldiers, nor an armed hand, but jurists and subtleties. And as there are soldiers just defenders of their own goods, and soldiers unjust despoilers of the goods of others, so also there would be honest jurists true interpreters of the law, and jurists without honesty, who violated it under the mantle of justice. Our readers may remember how Frederick Barbarossa, in order to have himself considered another Cæsar Augustus, and as a consequence natural master of Italy, made use of jurists, and especially of that kind of whom we have spoken in the second place. Philip the Fair had a good number of this stamp to legitimize his attacks against the rights of the Church. He could not openly strike the Church, for he would not have had many followers or companions. He hid himself behind the sublety of his jurists, and chiefly Enguerrand de Marigny, William de Plessis, and those two adventurous ruffians Peter Flotte and William de Nogaret. They directed their efforts to destroy the distinction of the different species of the goods of the Church. Some were really offerings of the faithful, and being placed on the altar of God, every law human and divine forbade them to be touched by man, even were he most powerful. Others were donations of Princes, in title of fiefs, and over this the prince could exercise rights, as their supreme master. The exercise of this right Philip wanted to extend without distinction to the goods of the Church of the first kind, and in this he was ably assisted by the jurists who confounded the nature of the patrimonies. In a word Philip desired to do in the matter of the Church's property, what the emperors had done in the affairs of the Investitures. In fact every disagreement arising betwen him and Boniface had its origin in the usurpation of some sacred thing. At one time he issued an edict in opposition to the constitution "Clericis Laicos," preventing the pious offerings from being sent to Rome for the expedition to the Holy Land; again allowing his minister Count Robert of Artois to usurp a part of the city of Cambrai, subject to the Bishop even in temporalities; again delaying to restore to the Archbishop elect of Rheims, Robert of Courtenay, the possessions of the Church, which he held in custody while the see was vacant;[68] seizing the return of a year from all the prebends and ecclesiastical benefices in France, during the war in Flanders. Consulting the register of the letters of this Pontiff one can see that other princes also had from time to time been guilty of the same fault, but none to such a degree as Philip the Fair, who used every effort to sanction by law usurpations of the goods and the rights of the Church.

He with his ministers actually became indignant at the complaints of Boniface, as if menaced by a robber, who wanted to deprive him of his crown, and they raised the cry that Boniface wished to make himself King of France. From this it appears, he considered that to control the churches was only to exercise his right as king, as over any other part of his kingdom. Moreover every way of escape from the error was closed to the unfortunate King by these jurists, who, interested in magnifying his power to satisfy more fully their own covetousness, never tired in their dishonest adulations and in the work of seeing the king triumphant over the Pope. For this reason ever whispering falsehoods into the ears of the King, and misrepresenting the words and actions of Boniface, they injected into him the mania of authority; on account of which poor Philip, like the Saul of Alfieri, enjoyed no rest nor peace and at every turn the terrible Pontiff appeared to him striving to precipitate him from his throne. The old story of the misery of Princes lulled to sleep by flattery!

[67] John Villani, 5 8. c. 49.   [68] Raynaldus 1299, no. 22.

A strong support was given to his nefarious work by Philip, in his convocation of the States General, which if it was not the first time that the citizen class was called to take part in public affairs, at least Philip did it more often than other kings. It makes us smile when we hear of some, who think themselves well versed in political economy, lay open their hearts not to a mere hope, but to an assured civil happiness if they see a prince assemble parliaments; as if from these there should come forth that mysterious means whereby liberty and order are harmonized. Philip of France was greatly extolled by some for his convocation of the States General, but yet he convinces us and he should convince those facile promisers of good, that these assemblies in an absolute monarchy are not productive of good at all, but often of evil. Called upon to deliberate they are either too free, and then the royal power being subservient, lest tyrannies be multiplied there is need of a check, which is however nowhere to be found; or else they are too servile like the parliament of Henry VIII in England, and then far from tempering, they increase a thousandfold the power of the prince, who used them as vile satellites.. And since we speak of France, we find among the French examples of these two kinds, but we do not wish to speak to such recent events. It is not to be doubted that the States General which Philip convoked were composed of servile men. He derived from them two of very great benefit. One was that by his having invited the citizen class to take part in public affairs, thereby gratifying their vanity, and as it were making them participators of the royal power, they were most pliant in the imposition of those taxes and subsidies, which he so ardently desired; and the other advantage was, that being in a state of war either with princes or Popes, the sight of him being surrounded by all the people of the kingdom, increased greatly respect and reverence from without, as if fortified by the moral force of the assistance of the entire people. Such was Philip the Fair; such were the reasons of his actions; and such were the means he adopted. Now we come to Boniface.

Boniface was Supreme Pontiff, and therefore watchful of the rights and the affairs of the Church, in a word, of her liberty, for which he could not be blamed. The times were very dangerous especially for that liberty and as time went on the danger became greater. The day had passed when the mere presence of the Sovereign Pastor was sufficient to arrest the march of an Attila, and when the brutal force of an invading army could be restrained by the force of supernatural faith. As monarchies took refuge behind the bulwark of right, the Pope was obliged to do likewise, for two objects in view; the one to strengthen, or at least to maintain the rights of the Church, such as follow from the constitution purely divine of the Church; and the other was not to allow it to lose the position which the public right had given in the civil institutions of the Middle Ages. The first of these duties created for the Pope the necessity of a contact with secular states by reason of the immediate relation between the spiritual society and the temporal; to accomplish the second, a simple contact with these states would not suffice, but it should penetrate to the inmost depths of the States, in order to appeal to the justice of public right. Now since the monarchies were absolute, the request of the Pope, and consequently the severe measures which the denial of justice provoked, would have to be addressed immediately to the King, and not to the people. An excellent reason why we find the Popes in opposition to kings. If the latter little by little withdrew the concessions made to the Pope by them and the people, diminishing thus the benefit of the public right in favor of the Church, the opposition of the Pope was reasonable; but if in the process the kings happened to strike at that right altogether divine, which is the chief foundation of the Church, any defence raised by the Pope was not only reasonable but rigorously obligatory. So those Popes were reasonable and just, who wished, for example, to preserve the judgment of the civil cases conceded to them by princes and the consent of the people, and which was consecrated by public opinion. But most just and bound by duty were those Popes, who to repair the loss of souls, intruded themselves into states to prevent wars and to punish those princes, who, engaging in unjust wars, became the causes of so many massacres and rapines and injury to the churches. And hence that absolution of the people from the oath of obedience to princes became just and necessary; no one being obliged to swear to defend a wicked act, such being the obedience to a rascally prince, because it would be binding oneself by oath to co-operate in the wicked deeds of another. We speak of those times.

Boniface saw snatched away by the French king not only that which from religious fervor had been conceded by Pepin and Charlemagne, but also that which no king could give or take away, the liberty of the Church, which is a thing entirely divine. Therefore the Pope held out against a downright robbery, and for that reason we are not to wonder at the vigor of the resistance.

And in the quarrel with Philip the Fair if some one finds Boniface excessive in his anger (which we have not found), he must consider the temper of mind of the Pope, and the ingratitude of Philip for all his benefits. That *magnanimous sinner,* (as Benvenuto of Imola, St. Antoninus and even Villani call him), shows us, that within that Pontifical breast there was contained a strong and generous heart. This firmness it seems to us was displayed more brilliantly in his self-control, than in his holy pursuit of justice. For from the years 1296 in which the Constitution "Clericis" was published, until 1300, the year of the legation of the Bishop of Pamiers, the beginning of the quarrel, the Pope had been an example of forbearance. To publish an offensive edict in opposition to a Papal Constitution, which was directed to weaken the enemies of Philip, was an impertinence sufficient to arouse the indignation of an anchoret; and yet Boniface did everything to please Philip, favoring him with a benign interpretation of the Constitution, by which the French kings began to enjoy a new privilege. But favors did not reclaim Philip, they served only to make him more rascally, and yet we find no record of censures hurled against him by Boniface, but instead he repealed those which had already been fulminated in the body of the law. Boniface was not a man to be frightened, and for this reason this control of temper is wonderful in a soul so ardent and vigorous.

We do not know if a personal friendship united Boniface to Philip the Fair. We find that up to this year he did everything to favor him, and refrained from everything that would tend to hurt him. But since we are speaking of persons placed in the highest offices, the discovery of this friendship would be vain, as it may have ceased on the morning of public life. There is no doubt that the Pope loved the King of France. For that movement undertaken to restrain his enemies round about him, at one time exhorting Edward of England, then Adolphus, to lay down their arms, and not disturb the peace of France; that constancy in taking revenge upon Sicily for Charles of Naples, a Frenchman; that confidence placed in Charles of Valois, and the desire to elevate him to the rank of Emperor; and finally that control of temper towards Philip, who was in a fury, were most certain proofs that the Pope wished the French King well. There can be no doubt of this love. It was enshrined for a long time in the counsels of the Papal Court, and it could never be lessened. There are certain benefits in human life, which can never be banished from the mind, such as we may receive in youth, and whatever might be the offence coming to us from a benefactor, our love even grows stronger. Such were the benefits which the Popes had received in the youth of the civil Pontificate from the French kings. Unable to resist the power of the Lombards from without, and the tyranny of the Romans from within they found a liberator in Charlemagne, and he found in them magnificent remunerators. In those times, we speak of the eighth century, to be anointed and to receive a crown from the hands of the Pope, and that cry: *"To Charles most pious Augustus crowned by God, great and peaceful Emperor, long life and victory,"* were truly worth an empire. And from that time on account of this exchange of friendly offices, France was always considered the support of the Papal See, and as a defender to be invoked when serious civil difficulties arose. When the Pontificate was oppressed by the might of the Suabians, it was relieved by the French family of Anjou. In the boundless expansion of the monarchy of Charles V, the Popes never lost sight of France, and this country from time to time they favored, in order to show respect for that lord of such a vast domain. France was always a place of refuge for persecuted Popes. Leo III, and Gelasius II, so brutally treated by the proud Roman patricians, sought an asylum and assistance in France. That solemn Council of Lyons, in which there was such a long deliberation over sacred and civil destinies, was held in France as a place of safety. Therefore it was established in the counsels of the Papal Court, that France would be the defender of the Church in time of danger. The French better than any other people suited this design, for although they did not wed the intellect to a certain maturity of judgment, from which is generated a tenacity of purpose, yet they superabound in liveliness of the heart, from which deeds burst forth rather than proceed, and in that generosity of soul by which on the very-first meeting of obstacles they seem entirely superhuman, and hence most powerful propagators of good and of evil.[68] And so they are found always the first in those actions, in which the heart plays a greater part than cold reason. The Crusade being proclaimed, the French are the first to raise the standard of the Cross and march. Is there a certain country to be enlightened by the preaching of the Gospel, the French are the first to hasten, lavish of their life. Is there a society to be formed in the interest of the faith, or for the relief of distress, they are the first who come forward lavish of their goods. The Catholic religion, which in man likes to dwell in the fervid regions of the heart rather than in the sombre recesses of the brain, will always have need of this race of men. For this reason the faults of the French could never withdraw the Roman Pontificate from that innate trust which it placed in them in its human calamities, and for the disrespect of these sons it always holds in readiness a paternal forgiveness. In fact whilst France, like one shipwrecked, was still tossed about in the tempest of that revolution, by which Pope Pius VII, wrested from the sacred precincts of the Vatican, was by French hands borne across the Alps to exile; France, we say, threw herself prostrate at his feet revering him with immense love, like Magdalen at the feet of Christ; and Pius wept with a holy joy. Pius VI after having endured the philosophic tyranny of Joseph II, was induced to visit Austria. Austria, however, did not revere

[68] See Guizot. "History of Civilization in Europe," page 16.

him, nor do we find that Pius wept with joy; rather he shed tears of grief. The reader will understand from this comparison what we think of France, and how sincere was the love Boniface bore for Philip the Fair, as a successor of Charlemagne. The moral portraits of Boniface and Philip the Fair being traced, there is no doubt that approaching them nearer in order to observe their conduct in the famous quarrel, the truth will be seen more plainly and more easily. And since it is impossible henceforth to find the culpability in the substance of the acts of Boniface, our judgment will be restricted to the examination of the manner of action, that is to say, to see if he did not sin by excess in the defence of justice; this will be clearly shown in the narration upon which we are about to enter, and in which we are about to refresh ourselves after being unnerved, as it were, by the judgment we have passed on such great personages.

Philip up to the year 1302 had been most obstinate in working injury on the Church. Neither the favors, nor the threats of Boniface had been able to dissuade him one iota from his purpose, on the contrary he proceeded from bad to worse. The tithes which he was allowed to collect from the churches for the war in the Holy Land, he greedily seized. He kept the Clerics a long time deprived of their prebends, and imprisoned them. He totally ignored the sacred immunities.

From the year 1298 Philip, exceeding all limits of justices provoked Boniface to the severest exercise of his power. The ministers and courtiers knew the pain the King suffered by reason of the laws which forbade him to steal the property of another and especially that consecrated to God; and therefore between the desire of assuaging the royal ills, and because the same malady had attacked them also, they shamefully pounced upon the possessions of the churches. The kings of France enjoyed the privileges delegated from the Pope, of guarding and holding in custody vacant benefices. Here was a right that had sprung from a privilege. But whither did it tend? From custody Philip passed on to robbery, and he confiscated the possessions he guarded. If a bishop or beneficiary, not by death but by some reason of absence, left the church while living, he on the strength of that right of guardianship seized everything with a free hand. His ministers did the same, and even worse.

Gazon, Bishop of Laon, for some fault or other, being suspended by the Pope from the spiritual and temporal administration of his diocese, set out for Rome, in answer to a summons to appear there. Hardly had he departed than Philip enters, declares the see vacant, makes himself custodian of the same, and as such master of everything he finds. Boniface warned him, but in vain: "Be "most assured that by an interdict of administration, by "suspension and even excommunication of a bishop, the "see is by no means vacant."[69] Philip knew this. John, Cardinal of the title of St. Cecilia, by his last will left some of his property for pious works in France, among which was the foundation of a college for poor clerics in Paris. Philip and his ministers seized these goods, presumably to guard them, but only to steal them. Boniface sent John, Cardinal of Sts. Peter and Marcellinus, and the Archbishop of Narbonne to execute the will of the pious Cardinal, and prevent the goods from being stolen.[70] But he obtained nothing. The Count of Artois, one most intimate in the counsels of Philip, declared that a part of the city of Cambria subject temporarily and spiritually to the Bishop, belonged to him, and without any form of proceedings, took possession of it in 1299. Boniface admonished and besought him at least to inform them by what right he established his claim.[71] He refused. In the same year the Archbishop elect of Rheims, Robert de Courtenay, found that Philip had laid hands on the goods of his church, under the pretext of guarding them. He requested Philip to relinquish his custody over them, but he refused to do so. Boniface admonished him, and wrote to him that as the See of Rheims was no longer vacant, there was no need of a custodian and a trustee for its property.[72] But he spoke, as it were, to the dead. The royal ministers had already settled themselves there, and were being enriched thereby. Then a cry was raised throughout France by all the clergy, that the hand of a Pharaoh was upon them, and they implored the help of

[69] Letter of Boniface to Philip, Raynaldus, 1298, no 24
[70] Raynaldus, *idem* [71] Raynaldus, 1299, no. 22.
[72] Raynaldus, 1299, no. 23. Letter of Boniface to Philip.

the Roman Pontiff. And in such circumstances was he to do nothing else but weep over these violences?

And now we have come finally to the lamentable quarrel with Philip the Fair. Certain controversies had arisen between the Archbishop of Narbonne, Egidius Asceline and the Almaric viscount of this city. The former declared that he held supreme dominion over the city; and for this reason whatever the Count possessed in the city and suburb, he held as a fief of the See of Narbonne; but the latter denied this, and said he was a vassal of the King. In support of this he had obtained letters from Philip, which proved his pretensions, but they violated the agreement made before by his predecessors and the See of Narbonne. At the end of October of 1299 the Archbishop held a Council at Beziers, which was attended by the Bishops of Beziers, Nimes, Maguelone, Elne, Pamiers, Agde, Lodeve, and by the Abbots of Grasse, St. Pons, William of the Desert, and others.[73] The question of the usurpation of the Count was debated, and it was decided to send the King a letter which would set forth the rights of the See of Narbonne; and among these was the oath of homage taken by the father of the Viscount. They complained of the letters which the Viscount had obtained from Philip.[74] The Bishop of Bezier, an Abbot and a Canon were the bearers of the complaints to Philip. If Philip had given letters to the Viscount, by which he removed him from the dominion of the Bishop, it was not hard to imagine in what manner these complaints would be received. Therefore the Archbishop of Narbonne had recourse also to Boniface.

There arose another controversy, or better another usurpation of Philip. The Bishop of the now destroyed city of Maguelone, in Narbonnese France, possessed the county of Maguelone as a fief of the Holy See. During the reign of St. Louis IX, the royal ministers began to invade the jurisdiction of the Bishop and undertook to place this county under the dominion of the King. But Pope Clement IV, being consulted by the King, returned such a well-reasoned reply, sustained by such an array of documents,[75] that the ministers desisted from the unjust

[73] Coll. Max. Concil tom. 11, page 1430. [74] The same.
[75] See Raynaldus, year 1300, no. 30.

invasion. During Philip's reign, the documents of Clement were forgotten, and as a finished case, without proceedings, his ministers deprived the Apostolic See of the county of Maguelone. Boniface was aroused and he wrote Philip a very temperate letter, which we collate among the documents of this work. For from the writings of this Pope one can form a more certain judgment than that which others have given of this famous quarrel.[76] In this letter, after having mentioned Philip's grandfather, King St. Louis IX; after having explained the rights of the Church over the county of Maguelone; after having complained how the churches, elevated to great splendor by his predecessors, were by him and his ministers oppressed, reduced to servitude, and ruined, he concluded in these words: " Tolerating, my son, these abuses in the churches
" of your kingdom, you have good reason to fear that God,
" the Lord of judgment and King of Kings may be aroused
" to vengeance, and that His Vicar will not remain silent
" to the end, lest perhaps he may hear this sentence
" against him: 'A dumb dog is not fit to bark;'—who
" although he waits patiently for a time, in order that the
" way of mercy may not be closed, yet one day he will
" arise for the punishment of the guilty and for the honor
" of the good. May God grant that you may understand,
" and weigh well the suggestions which are offered you
" as from bad angels; and pay no attention to the wicked
" counsellors, false prophets with honeyed lips who make
" you see false and foolish things. . . . Be careful,
" then, lest the counsel of those who have already blinded
" you by flattery, may lead you to a wicked end."

To allow Philip full reign any longer was on the part of the Pope yielding too much to prudence, and neglecting his office of supreme guardian and defender of the rights of the Church. Therefore Boniface thought to restrain Philip by a legation, with the hope that the things explained by letter might be more effectual in the mouth of a Papal legate. He deputed Bernard de Saisset, Bishop of Pamiers, who had been abbot of the monastery of St. Antoninus, lord of Pamiers, which from being an abbatial was raised to an episcopal see, and he was ap-

[76] See Document: Letter of Boniface to Philip about the county of Maguelone.

pointed the first bishop. This appointment of the legate was displeasing to Philip, because on a former occasion he found Bernard most tenacious of his right of dominion over the city, which he wished to usurp.

(1301) Bernard explained to the King the decision of the Pope, but Philip would not abide by it. The Legate threatened him with the usual spiritual penalties, and those which always obtained in those times. The authorities of the time have not handed down to us any account of what passed between the Legate and the King. Some have conjectured that he went too far, even daring to reprove the King for imprisoning Guy of Dampierre, Count of Flanders, and his daughter, intimating that he should liberate them. But there is no foundation for this conjecture.[77] Others said that the Legate was excessive in his threats.[78] But the only witnesses they could quote of the importunities of the Legate, would be Philip and his ministers; now in the proceedings which they afterwards instituted against the Legate, there is found no mention of that crime of lese-majesty. There is no doubt that the flatterers who surrounded Philip, being ever ready to do his will in wrong or right, and seeing him badly disposed to the legation of the Bishop of Pamiers, suddenly brought up so many charges against him, as to make him guilty of high treason. It was necessary to find the crimes. Philip had recourse to his jurists, who were truly omnipotent. They deputed the Archdeacon of Auge and the Vidame[79] of Amiens to collect through the Seneschal's Court of Toulouse secret information concerning the Legate.[80] According to the desire of the jurists, twenty-four witnesses were found, who with one accord swore to seven different charges, namely that he had published how King St. Louis had prophesied, that the kingdom of France would go to ruin under the rule of Philip the Fair, and fall into the hands of a foreigner; that he had conspired with the Count of Fois (the reader will remember

---

[77] Sismondi. History of France. T. VI, page 45.

[78] Spondani, year 1301—Pag 218. Brev. Gest. Pontif. Sec. XIII, Tom. 111, page 335

[79] A *Vidame* in France during the Middle Ages was he who guarded the temporal affairs of a bishop, and who defended them.

[80] History of Languedoc, Book XXVIII, c. 63, p. 99. apud Sismondi.

that the Count was precisely that deadly enemy of Bernard with whom the latter had waged war for a long time on account of his usurpations) against the King, and had plotted with the same to remove the county of Toulouse from obedience to the King, and to prevent the marriage of the royal daughter to the son of Count Philip of Artois, in order to arrange it with the daughter of the King of Aragon; that he had reported that the city of Pamiers was not comprised in the kingdom of France, and consequently was not subject to Philip; that he had declared the King to be a bastard, and a falsifier of the coinage of the realm. As usual in addition he was accused of heresy, blasphemy and simony.[81]

The Legate knew of the inquisition that was going on in his diocese, and in order to escape the storm which was gathering about him, he decided to set out for Rome. But the Vidame of Amiens on the night of the 12th of July having forced himself into the episcopal palace, dragged forth the Legate, to whom he gave notice to appear on the first of the month in the royal presence. He subjected his servants to cruel tortures in order to wrest from them that which was necessary. Saisset presented a pitiable sight broken down by infirmities, enfeebled by old age, dragged by the master bowman to the court, and thrust into a dark prison. Peter Flotte, a man accustomed to this, acted as prosecutor.

Philip was furious on hearing of the felonies that were imputed to the Legate, and on the 24th of May 1301, having ordered the proofs to be collected, he declared the accusations true. It was decided to proceed on the lines of a trial, and in order to give to the proceedings an honorable character by observing the ordinary rules of justice, Philip summoned a council of the nobles of the kingdom at Senlis, with many doctors of laws and clerics. After taking counsel from them he imprisoned the Legate and proceeded against him. He was condemned to be degraded from the episcopate, and left in the power of the Prince. As a prisoner he was consigned to the custody of Egidius, Archbishop of Narbonne.[82] In Raynaldus we find the chief charges against the Legate, which were sent to

[81] Martene Thesaurus Anecdotorum T. 1, page 1319-1336—Continuat. Chron. Nangii 1301, page 54. [82] Hist. du Differ, page 634.

the Pope by Philip, but we do not find an account of the trial, in which these charges were proven to be true. (Instead we read in another author,[83] not a Catholic in belief, but truly a philosopher, who examined the details of this trial, declared that it was an example of downright injustice and violence.) Yet Spondano, Page the Younger, and Fleury agree in accepting with hands joined this sentence of the most pious and most temperate Philip. And these Frenchmen had leisure and eyes to read this trial, just as well as this other writer. Poor History! Those crimes were not committed by the Bishop on the exact day on which he exercised his office as legate to Philip, they were (if true) committed at a time far remote. Why this sudden inquisition at the moment in which Bernard commenced the exercise of a mission which demanded respect, and placed him under the safeguard of all laws? Can one believe that the accusers at that time only learned of these crimes? Should not they have waited either until Bernard had fulfilled his legation, or had been dismissed, in order not to drag to judgment the person of an ambassador, that is to say, the person of the prince himself whom he represented, namely the Pope? But we shall soon see that Philip had sufficient spirit to judge and condemn even the Pontiffs.

Peter Flotte, William de Nogaret and the other two jurists, whom we named before, directed the affairs of the parliament of Senlis, in order to make them proceed with an appearance of justice. It was decided to send a messenger to the Pope to report the resolution passed in the assembly. He was to state humbly that although King Philip had a right to condemn Bernard de Saisset to death as convicted of grave crimes, yet he refrained from doing so, in order to imitate the example of his ancestors, zealous preservers of the rights of the Church, and above all the Roman Church, their mother. The messenger was to beseech the sovereign pontiff to deprive the felon bishop of the dignity of orders and every clerical privilege, in order that he might be punished as an incorrigible criminal. They instructed the messenger in the replies he was to make to all proposals of Boniface, and charged him to

---

[83] Guizot. "History of Civilization in France," 45th lesson, page 588, Brussels edition, 1839.

point out the means of renewing the proceedings against the accused, in case Bernard was not condemned at Rome.

We are not certain if from this messenger Boniface learned of the imprisonment of his legate, his trial and condemnation, or by some other way. However he was very ready to receive with prudent firmness the embassy of Philip defining in that consistory of jurists, and the following is that which by private letters he wished them to know: That by divine and human right he is the guardian of the liberty of clerics; that laymen are powerless over them; that the predecessors of Philip had known and acknowledged the same; that it pained him to learn, how notwithstanding this pious example, he had summoned to trial in his presence his venerable brother the Bishop of Pamiers, and imprisoned him in the custody of the Archbishop of Narbonne, under the pretext of personal security; that he should allow the imprisoned legate to come to Rome; that he should restore all the patrimony he had sequestered; that he should know that he incurred the penalty proclaimed by the Canons against those laying violent hands on clerics; that he wrote all this to the Archbishop of Narbonne.[84] So much privately. The public insult offered the dignity of Bishop and Legate demanded a public reparation and Boniface publicly provided for it with the Bull "*Salvator mundi,*" which he sent to the king in a letter beginning: "*Nuper ex rationabilibus causis.*" In this he revoked all the privileges and favors granted by the Roman See to the King of France, which revocation was to last until the Prelates of France assembled in Council in his presence, deliberated concerning the same.[85] And on the same day the 15th of December he published the famous Bull: "*Ausculta.*"[86] "Listen,
"my son, to the precepts of a father and to the instruc-
"tions of a master, who holds the place of him who is the
"sole Master and Lord; open your heart to the admoni-
"tions of a most loving mother, the Church; dispose your-
"self to return to God from whom either by weakness, or
"by the bad advice of others you have strayed away.
". . . Let not the king flatter himself that he has no
"superior on earth but God, and that he is not subject to

[84] Raynaldus, 28—History of Diff., page 661. [85] Raynaldus, 32.
[86] See Document at end of work.

" the power of the Pope. He who thinks thus is an infidel."
—This preamble is followed by an enumeration of the
Sovereign Pontiff's complaints against the King of France,
whom he charges with bestowing benefices without consulting the Holy See; of admitting no judgment but his
own, either within or without his kingdom, on the unjust
and violent acts committed in his name; of arbitrarily
seizing upon Church property; of appropriating to his own
use the revenues of vacant sees, which abuse was not saved
from odium by the specious name of *regale;* of his debasement of the currency; and of imposing on his subjects intolerable burdens. "We have repeatedly," continues the Pope, " but vainly, warned Philip to return to
" justice. Therefore now we enjoin all the Archbishops,
" bishops, abbots and doctors in France to meet Us in the
" month of November of next year (A. D. 1302), that, by
" the help of their counsel, We may take measures for the
" reform of clerical affairs in the kingdom and the restor-
" ation of order." Boniface finally concludes with a most
pressing exhortation to give assistance to the Holy Land.
This Bull although addressed to Philip, was sent by Boniface to all the Prelates of France,[87] in order that coming
to Rome for the Synod, they should know in what condition the affairs of the King were, in order the better to
deliberate on them. The multiplicity of copies has made
it possible for us to have the original words of this famous
document in spite of the fact that it fared badly in that
base and shameful obliteration, obtained by Philip, of the
Bulls and letters of Boniface from the Vatican Register,
chiefly those which stung him most. For this reason the
copies which were at hand were not uniformly complete,
and we preferred that published by Rossi,[88] because it
seemed to us to be less deficient than that produced by
Raynaldus.[89]

The tone of this Bull was vigorous, but yet it was temperate even in its reproaches. We do not find any censures, any threatened absolution of the French from their
oath of obedience to their King, and no forfeiture of the
throne. Boniface perhaps had no hope of it succeeding in
its intent, because it was hard to believe that one who for
a long time had progressed on a wicked path, would re-

---

[87] Raynaldus, 32.   [88] Life of Boniface, chap 17, p. 167.   [89] No. 51.

trace his steps. But he could not entirely persuade himself, that Philip would arrive at such a degree of iniquity, the like of which was not seen in past ages. Proud he was, but still worse were those false prophets, as Boniface called those counsellors, who with the most refined malice placed themselves between him and the Pope, violated the truth, published falsehoods, and aroused fatal quarrels.

But before we come to speak of the effects produced in France by the Bull "Asculta," it is necessary for us to tarry a moment, and rectify, or better set in right order the facts disarranged through an innocent error by Spondani, and Page the younger. The reader must not forget that when these facts are not viewed in their natural order, an opinion founded on them is always erroneous. They relate,[90] that Peter Flotte, had been sent to Rome by Philip to uphold him, not previous to the publication of the Bull "*Ausculta fili,*" but instead after the legation, which followed, of the Archdeacon of Narbonne, the bearer of the solemn censures incurred by Philip through his disobedience. They, or rather Spondani, a little later contradicts himself, when he declares that Flotte had falsified the Bull "Ausculta Fili," and had even substituted instead a brief letter full of venom from Boniface to Philip, and hence he was found in Rome in 1301, the precise year in which the Bull was written and promulgated. How does he locate Flotte the messenger of Philip, in Rome, after the threatening legation of the Archdeacon of Narbonne, which took place in the following year? Therefore Flotte the falsifier of the Bull was in Rome when it was written, for he could not falsify it, when it had been already promulgated in France. Hence we can say without any hesitation, that that messenger sent to the Pope by Philip and the parliament of Senlis, was none other than Peter Flotte; and to present himself before a Pope and a Pope such as Boniface, after the imprisonment of a legate, there was needed a countenance not less brazen than that of Flotte, called by Natalis Alexander: "*diaboli-*
"*cum, caecutientem corpore, caecum mente, acetosum,*
"*fellitum, haereticum, discordiae Regem inter et Eccle-*
"*siam Romanam inventorem.*" "Diabolical, blind in
"body and mind, full of rancor, a heretic, and a fomenter

[90] Spond. 1301. n. 7—Pagi. Brev. R. R. P. P. Bonif. VIII, n. 55.

of discord between the King and the Roman Church." The reader may judge the Prince from this sort of an ambassador. Now Flotte present in Rome, being sent, as was said to clear Philip of the accusation of violence against the Legate, understood to defend and justify every bad action of his Prince, with an assurance the like of which the most innocent of men would not have shown before a most furious tyrant. Boniface contented himself with only threatening to strike Philip with the sword of spiritual censures, to which the impudent legate retorted with this insulting reply: " Your sword is only verbal, but that of my master is real and well-tempered." By this was presaged even from that time how this controversy of respective rights was to terminate in Anagni by a violent decision of ruffians. Our reader can imagine whether the impertinence of Flotte aroused the indignation of Boniface; not to have resented it, would have been a fault in a Pontiff. Then passing to fraud, Flotte, in order perhaps to forestall the Bull "*Ausculta fili*," forged a certain brief letter most bitter in tone, addressed to Philip, to which he attached the name of Boniface as the author, and which Spondani published, taking it from the Victorine manuscript: " Boniface, servant of the servants of " God, to Philip King of the French: Fear God and keep " His commandments. We wish you to know that you " are subject to us in both temporal and spiritual things; " that the granting of benefices and prebends belongs to " you in no way; that if you have in custody any vacant " ones, you are bound to reserve their revenues for those " who succeed to them; and that, if you have conferred " any benefices, we pronounce such collations to be null " and void. We regard as heretics all who believe otherwise.". Now to lessen the guilt of Philip some think that it was owing to these deceptions of his ministers that he transgressed so far beyond the limits of reverence towards Boniface. But Philip was not stupid; we admit that the dissension was caused to a great extent by infamous ministers, such as Flotte, but that he allowed himself to be controlled and led by them, we shall never concede. Philip knew too well the virile style of Boniface, with which in his letters he admonished him, to be led to attribute to him this sickly note, so devoid of vigor. It was the whelping of a wanton cur compared to those noble roarings that are heard in the Register of the Papal documents. But although the forgery was most evident, yet it was not altogether without some result. These venomous writings, in which Boniface was depicted as a ravisher of crowns, and a disturber of peace, were circulated among the people, who quick to believe and incapable of criticising, decided unfairly and formed that terrible thing, which is called public opinion, from which the writers of the time, a little prejudiced as they were either for party advantage or through private spleen, could not withdraw themselves. Hence the Bull "*Ausculta fili,*" was preceded and followed by the evil rumor that Boniface insane from ambition wished to dethrone Philip and make himself King of France.

James de Normans, Archdeacon of Narbonne, a notary and Papal Legate, a man of approved worth, brought the Bull into France, where Peter Flotte returned, the bearer of the pretended brief, and a spreader of the blackest calumnies on the character of Boniface. De Normans was commissioned to support by word of mouth that which the Bull had expressed. We know not where Henry Spondani[91] had learned that he had a secret order from the Pope to declare the French people absolved from their oath of allegiance to Philip, and that the kingdom devolved to the Roman See, if Philip refused to conform to this Bull. This was perhaps a calumny of Flotte. The Legate then appeared before Philip, and explained to him the contents of the Bull, which are reduced to the following heads: that the Pope is superior to princes; it is clear from that which follows that Boniface spoke of spiritual dominion, since there is no word of temporal affairs, except the hint at the debasement of the public money and the oppression of the poor subjects;[92] that the king cannot without the permission of the Roman See take the revenues of vacant churches, and confer benefices;[93] that

---

[91] Spondani, n. 7.

[92] Atque uti de mutatione monetae, aliisque gravaminibus, et injuriosis processibus, per te, ac tuos magnis ac parvis regni ejusdem incolis irrogatis, ac habilis contra eos, quae processu temporis explicari poterunt, taceamus . . . . . .

[93] Quod in ecclesiasticis dignitatibus . . . . Beneficiis . . . in

he should not take possession of the goods of the churches as fiefs, and for that reason he cannot by right of fief summon clerics before his tribunal;[94] that he should only with moderation make use of his right of "*regalia*" over the revenues of vacant sees.[95] We are not looking now at the modifications which the civil laws made on the rights of the churches in later times; we are speaking of them as they were in the beginning of the XIVth century, as Boniface wished to maintain them and as they were recognized everywhere, even in France.[96] But Philip and his ministers and even Bossuet would not read in the Bull the sentiments of the Pope, but interpreted them according to their own liking. According to them these defences were only an insane effort of Boniface to make the king of France a vassal.[97] So when de Normans had explained his legation and had read the Papal Bull, Philip and his courtiers amazed at the excessive requests of Boniface, showed themselves greatly disturbed. They hastily entered into a consultation in which flattery exerted itself and they decided to convoke a parliament of the nobles of the kingdom, the Abbots, the religious orders and the secular clergy. In the meantime Philip, who could not bear the sight of that Bull, on February 11th, 1302, ordered it to be burned publicly in presence of

curia, vel extra . . . R Pontifex summam, et potiorem obtineat potstatem ad te tamen hujusmodi ecclesiarum dignitatum . . . beneficiorum collatio, non potest quomodo libet pertinere, nec pertinent: nec per tuam collationem, in ipsis, vel eorum aliquo, potest alicui jus acquiri, sine auctoritat et consensu Ap. Sedis.

[94] Prelatos insuper, et alias ecclesiasticas personas . . . etiam super personalibus actionibus, juribus, et immobilibus bonis, quae a te non tenentur in feudam ad tuum judicium protrahis, et coarctas . . . licet in clericos et personas ecclesiasticas nulla sit laicis attributa potestas.

[95] Vacantium etiam regni Ecclesiraum redditus, et proventus, quos tu et tui appellatio Regalia per azusum, tu ac ipsi tui non moderate percipitis sed immoderate consumitio.

[96] Let the reader consult among the Italians, Bianchi, "The Power and Policy of the Church," Book VI, sect. VI, Tom. II; and among the French, Antonine Thomas: "The Power of the Church," chap XIII.

[97] Tom. I, par. 2, lib. 7, cap. 24: Quas si valuissent, vel de regni regimine R Pontifex Romae, rege sive absente sive praesente, decerneret, nempe regnaret Pontifex: ipse rex nudum nomen regis obtineret. Now who would believe that Bossuet from the Bull "Ausculta" could have drawn this consequence?

all the nobility then in Paris, and afterwards the news of the act was proclaimed by a public crier through the streets. It was the Count of Artois who having snatched the Bull from the hands of the Legate, threw it into the fire. History records only two public burnings of Papal Bulls. This one done by a French king, and the other by a friar, namely Martin Luther at Wittenberg. Every one knows the sad consequences which ensued from the sacreligious insolence of the friar; and the reader may imagine what was in the minds of the people and French clergy as a result of this act of Philip.[98] The Legate was banished, and the other Legate the Bishop of Pamiers, was allowed to depart with him. Guards were placed at the frontier, and Philip forbade any of the French clergy to go to Rome, and to send money out of the country. All those summoned to the memorable parliament met in the great church of Notre Dame at Paris on April 10th, 1302. The King presided, and Peter Flotte arising forthwith spoke as follows in his name: " A certain letter from the Pope " has been brought to us by the Archbishop of Narbonne, " which declares that we are subject to him in the tem- " poral administration of this kingdom; and to him and " not to God alone, as has always been believed, do we " owe our crown." Then summing up the complaints of the government against the Sovereign Pontiff, he concludes: " He, the Pope, aims at subjecting the King of " France to the power of the Holy See; but this monarch " protests here before you all that he acknowledges no " superior but God alone; and he calls upon you, as your " friend and sovereign, to lend your earnest co-operation " for the support of the ancient liberties of the nation and " of its church; and you should return an open and quick " reply to these propositions."—The Barons and syndics of the communes having retired to deliberate, soon returned ready to do the King's pleasure, and as his most obedient servants, to give to him not only their fortunes but also their lives, in assisting to resist the covetous Pope. The spiritual lords took a longer time to deliberate. Their necks were bound by an ugly halter they were unable to unloose. Obedience to the King meant rebellion to the Pope; refusal to do the will of the King would start

[98] Hist. du Differ., pp. 68 and 69.

a furious conflagration which would be injurious to the church of France for a long time. They returned to the King not with offerings, but with counsel and admonitions, representing how the Pope did not think of offending the liberty of the kingdom and the dignity of the Prince; and how they should not endanger their necessary union with the Roman See. But Philip and with him all the Barons did not care to listen to more sermons, and they notified those prelates that if they did not at once give a satisfactory answer, the clergy would be proclaimed hostile to the King and to the state. Then the prelates knowing they had to deal with Philip, and with a flock of enslaved barons, allowed it to be drawn from their lips, that either by reason of the fiefs they held, or by reason of loyalty to the King which was obligatory on all even the clerics they were all disposed by counsel and every other aid to defend the King, in person and in dignity, and in the liberty of the realm; but they besought him to allow them to go to Rome, so as not to be wanting in obedience to the Pope, who called them. He answered this request with positive refusal. Such was the liberty of the Gallican church, for the defence of which Philip was willing to offer both his wealth, his life, his sons, his wife and we know not what else.

The Barons reported the decisions of the assembly of Notre Dame to Boniface in a letter, which they addressed to the College of Cardinals. The clergy wrote directly to the Pope. The former wrote in the French language; and Fleury remarks that they did this in order to show even by their words that their sentiments were French. They did nothing but repeat what the King had said in the assembly; they only added that the opinion of the Pope was deplorable, and worthy of the times of Antichrist. They charged the cardinals to leave Philip in peace, that he might be able to fight the infidels in the Holy Land. Thirty-one lords, and the first men of the kingdom signed their names to the letter. The prelates themselves being astonished at the novelty of the doctrine of Boniface on the subjection of the King to the sovereign Pontiff in matters temporal, besought him with tears to dispense them from the obligation of going to Rome, and represented to him that censures would have little or no effect on Philip and his abettors. These letters, which sufficiently manifest the shameful imbecility of the clergy, were brought to the Pope by the three Bishops of Noyon, Constance and Beziers.[99] Philip dispatched the Bishop of Auxerre to obtain from the Pope a postponement of the council.[100] This fact, which even Spondani relates although he quotes falsely the monk continuator of Nangis, published by Achery, clearly shows us that another letter bearing the title of Philip to Boniface, in which that king descends to the vilest abuse against Boniface, was purely the work of Flotte, truly possessed by the devil. Although unfit to appear on the page of history, yet for the information of our readers we produce it.[101] "Philip, by the "grace of God, King of the French, Boniface, who giveth "himself out for sovereign Pontiff, little or no greeting. "Let thy Extreme Fatuity know that we are subject to "no one in things temporal, that the presentation of "churches and prebends that are vacant belongeth to us "by kingly right, and the revenues therefrom are ours; "that the presentations already made and to be made are "valid both now and hereafter, that we will firmly support "the possessors of them, and that we hold as senseless "and demented those who think otherwise." The French messengers, the bearers of these letters, were received in full consistory. The Cardinal of Porto, Friar John Minio of Murro of the Friars Minor, arose and in the presence of the Pope and all the Cardinals addressed them, taking his text from Jeremias: "Lo, I have set "thee this day over the nations and over kingdoms, to "root up and to pull down, and to waste, and to destroy

[99] Jordan, MS. Vat. n. 1960.

[100] Jordan: "Rex quoque episcopum Antisidorensem mittit rogans ut suspenderet usque ad tempus magis postea opportunum" Rayn. 1302, n. 11.

[101] "Philippus Dei gratia Francorum Rex Bonifacio gerenti se pro summo pontifice, salutem modicam seu nullam, Sciat tua maxima fatuitas, in temporalibus nos alicui subesse. Ecclesiarum ac praebendarum vacantium collationem ad nos jure Regio pertinere, fructus earum nos tros facere: collationes a nobis factas, et faciendas fore validas in proeteritum et futurum, et earum possessores contra omnes virliter nos tueri: secus autem credentes fatuos et dementes reputamus. Datum Parisiis, etc." See Page Brev. Rom. Pont. 73, page 559. Also it is related in l'Histoire du Diff.

"and to build, and to plant."—"How truly applicable to
"Peter and his successors are those divinely revealed
"words of the Prophet, that he was placed over all to
"destroy and to build up, just as one deputed for the
"degradation of the wicked and the exaltation of the good.
"There has arisen a quarrel between the Pope and the
"Roman Church on one side, and the King of France and
"his ministers on the other, which in truly slight and
"trivial causes had its origin. But if the causes of the
"irritation were slight, most serious were those which
"moved the Papal mind to resort to remedies. A long
"and serious complaint had been made to the Pontiff in
"relation to the disturbed state of affairs in the French
"kingdom, and of the oppression of the churches. There-
"fore a private letter was written with the consent of the
"Pope and the Cardinals, which was read and reread
"often, pondered and considered in full Consistory, and
"was full of charity and sweetness, and kind admonitions
"to the King. Some went about declaring that in it was
"contained that judgment that the King owes the crown
"he wears to the Church, whereas there was not a sylla-
"ble of this either in that letter, or on the lips of the
"Pope or the Cardinals. The source whence a certain
"other letter came addressed to the King is unknown;
"but let it be known positively that it was the work
"neither of the Pope nor the Cardinals. Philip is an hon-
"est and Catholic Prince, but it is to be feared that he
"is surrounded by evil advisers. Why did the King take
"so much to heart the calling of the French prelates to
"Rome for consultation on most serious matters? It was
"not the summons of strangers, of rivals or of enemies,
"but of friends and servants, certainly most jealous of his
"honor, and of all the kingdom. To be called in fine to
"Rome was not to be called to the extreme limits of the
"earth, nor to dwell there eternally, but return after
"transacting business. Why did Philip show himself so
"badly disposed to the pleasure of the Church in the mat-
"ter of conferring prebends? The right of patronage and
"presentation is admitted, but the bestowal and enjoy-
"ment of them without Papal approval did not belong to
"a layman. Philip claims the right by prescription. But
"this does not exist nor does he prove he possesses it, as

" he asked the Pope for the privilege of that which he
" now said was prescribed. For he who has possession
" of a thing of right, does not ask a privilege. The Pon-
" tiff has the fullness of power, inheriting it from Christ,
" is a truth that is to be witnessed to even by blood; and
" for this reason not only does he become judge in spiri-
" tual things, but also in temporal things whenever there
" enters the question of sin." Boniface himself then followed with a discourse, in which he displayed such sweetness of manner, such cogent reasoning, and such mildness of temper, that it is really a wonder, when we consider whom the legates represented, and the object of their mission. At first he recalled that holy bond by which France truly could be said to have been wedded to the Roman See in the baptism of Clovis, and how on the observance of those espousals, according to St. Remigius, the whole prosperity of the kingdom and the king depended. This fact he had called to the attention of Philip, while he was a legate in France, and this remembrance Philip acknowledged with pleasure and gratitude. A man of perdition, Peter Flotte, with his satellites the Counts of Artois, and of St. Paul, in the worst spirit tried to sever this solemn union, by so urging Philip to the most desperate projects. While the College of Cardinals were considering maturely the Papal letters to Philip, Flotte had forged another, which he presented to the King, in the beginning of which he had inserted that it was the intention of the Pope to make him a Papal vassal. The Pope incensed at these indignities, continued in a spirited manner: " During
" forty years we have studied law, and have learned that
" on earth two powers, the temporal and the spiritual have
" been ordained by God. Who can believe that such fool-
" ishness can have entered into our mind to unite in the
" Pontiff one supreme power? But on the other hand who
" can in matters of sin? And coming to the question of
" the conferring of benefices, we have often declared to
" the messengers of the King that it is our wish, for his
" spiritual good that he do licitly that which he had done
" illicitly, being most ready to gratify his every wish;
" for it is certain that the Canons forbid benefices to be
" conferred by a layman, as if he were invested with spiri-
" tual power. We have conceded to the King the power to

"confer one canonry in each church of the kingdom; and
"to dispose of all the prebends in the church of Paris,
"provided they be conferred on Doctors of Divinity, or
"Law, or any other ecclesiastics distinguished for learn-
"ing. . . . . We desire nothing more than peace and
"friendship with the King, as we have always had an
"affection for France, insomuch that we were considered
"more French than Italian. But if then Philip does not
"retrace his steps, and allow the prelates to come, it is
"our duty not to allow the affair to go unpunished."[102]

The doctrine which the Cardinal of Porto and the Pope expressed in full consistory, was confided to letters which were to be carried to France by the Bishop Legates. The Cardinals replied to the nobles, the Pope to the Bishops.[103] Now if from the Bull "*Ausculta fili*," the King and his followers had apprehended the excessive ambition of Boniface of wanting to rule France in temporal affairs, those discourses and those letters which expressed the contrary, should have removed all suspicion of such from their minds. But Philip and his ministers renewed their assertions and their complaints; very evident proofs that these loud lamentations were only tactics and a pretext with which they covered themselves that they might act according to their own will in the things which concerned the authority purely spiritual of the Pope. Here it is necessary to enlighten the reader on a point without which the subsequent acts of Boniface might appear in contradiction with the language we previously reported, especially when he will have heard him speak, in full consistory and in another Bull, of the dual power in the Pope and the subjection of kings to the latter.

Boniface and the cardinals with him declared that they had nothing to do with the temporal affairs of the French kingdom, but that the King was subject to the Pope in matters of sin. We do not wish to enter into a discussion of that question of the Papal and royal powers, debated between the partisans of the Pope and the satellites of the King, both because the times have changed, and because we do not believe that the palm of martyrdom is held in reserve for historians who defend old truths, even if indeed truth can grow old. But we ought and we will

[102] MS Vittorino. Spondani, fol 82, 84.   [103] Hist. du Diff. p. 65.

explain the terms in order that the reader may know what happened between Boniface and Philip; and that briefly and simply, that it may be understood by all. It was the common and accepted opinion in the time of Boniface and even now-a-days, it is believed that every faithful Christian was subject in spiritual things to the Vicar of Christ. Prince or Plebeian if he desired to be a Catholic, should remain thus subjected. But from this truth, it did not follow that the Prince, or the father of a family should leave to the Pope the affairs of the kingdom or of the home; (nor would the Popes have had the desire or leisure to attend to these); however, it did follow that whenever they departed from the evangelical law they became subject to the decision, the admonitions and the punishments of the Pope, and should bear them patiently. Therefore the recognized Papal authority, and human peccability were the basis of the truth; that the Pope was superior to every one, who wished to be a Catholic. And since the dogma is unchangeable and this world will never be free from this cursed proneness to sin, it necessarily followed that this supremacy should be perpetual and unchangeable. From this it is evident that inasmuch as not all sins, or violations of the evangelical laws, are purely spiritual, but some are concerned with material things, the Pope who is the judge of them, indirectly touched the object of the sinner's disorder. Thus for example, to a robber he did not only say, "you have acted wickedly in "stealing," but he further added, "restore the booty." Thus in short he judged the sin and indirectly the object of the sin. This is the reason why a Prince in those times wanting to be a Catholic, was subjected to the Pope not only in things purely spiritual but also material, when these latter were the object of his sin. So if one place himself in the position, for example as Philip, of falsifying the public money, of shedding the blood of his subjects, and waging an unjust war, he should not resent the voice of the Pope, if he should say at first "you have done "evil, return the good; because you are a counterfeiter "and unjust," and then indirectly: "withdraw from circulation that counterfeit money, restore the property of others; do not shed the blood of your people, which does not belong to you. And this is how the Pontiff exercised over the King and kingdoms not a direct, but also an indirect supremacy. All Catholics in the Middle Ages thought thus, and in the same manner that the species is formed from the individuals, and the genus from the species, so from the unanimous consent of all the individuals was formed a general opinion, which became the public law, by which the Pope not only judged Princes in temporal affairs by reason of sin, but also judged them when requested to do so as a civil magistrate. In those times he who did not wish to acknowledge this judgeship, threw off at one toss also the evangelical yoke. Wherefore he who wished to be a Catholic, and would not accept in this fulness the Papal supremacy, was in open contradiction with himself and was guilty of two sins, one against faith and one against reason. Thus Philip the Fair, who above all wanted to be considered very Christian, was less than a Christian, and less than reasonable, when he refused to submit to the Pope. On the contrary, we cite this fact for greater clearness, Henry VIII of England sinned only against faith and not against reason. For having changed the principles, he had all latitude to change the consequences. He said: "I am the Pope" (that was the principle). "That which is the more pleasing to me to do, will be right," (this was the consequence.) Men have always debated between the admission of a principle and the rejection of the consequences, making always, by a sad vicissitude, a failure of one or the other. Up to the XVIth century the failure had been in the consequences, and principles were betrayed, though admitted; and these anomalies, or injuries to human reason, were infected with heresy, because they had occurred in matters of religion. In the XVIth century when Martin Luther preached reform, reason tired of the struggles, of these contradictions, overturned the principles; the consequences were logical, the heresies were unalloyed, but not guilty of an abuse of reason. In which of these two states do we find ourselves now-a-days? We will not say, because the mission of a historian is to narrate past, not present events. We hope the learned will willingly be indulgent to the simplicity of our reasoning, when they consider that it is not written by a doctor of laws, and that many will not be such who read these pages.

This, however, will suffice to throw a little light on the object of the controversy between Philip and Boniface. But we will not without comment, pass over those prelates of the parliament of Senlis, who were so weak and cowardly as to let themselves be vanquished by Philip. It is necessary for them to appear before us, in order that their conduct with regard to the Pope in this controversy may be shown aright. If the things previously stated are true, as they seem to us to be, it follows that the body of bishops and other clerics in those times should have held themselves as a most solid wall to defend not only the direct authority of the Pope, but also the indirect, as the latter is the legitimate and necessary consequence of the former.[104] And since they form a body so long as they are joined to the head, it is evident, that in giving aid to him who attempts the moral life of the head, is to attempt their own life. "We are most devoted sons of the Roman Pontiff," said they, "and most faithful subjects of "Philip." These were futile words. Filial devotion to the Pope had been destroyed at once by their submission to Philip, not as a Prince, but as an enemy of the Papal supremacy. Their weak virtue did not bind them very strongly to the Pope, and they were wavering between him and Philip. Obliged to decide they preferred to throw themselves into the arms of Philip, rather than on the bosom of their head, because that wavering on their part was already a separation from the Pope. They saw afterwards the need of justifying their action by proclaiming Philip a most patient Prince, Philip who had deprived them of their sacred patrimonies, who would not even allow them to repair to Rome, and who caused them to cry out in desperation; and afterwards they represented Boniface as an ambitious persecutor, who, as they well knew took action only to hold in the path of duty their criminal benefactor.

But this was not decisive, it left them still wavering, as the Prince was not their natural head in the exercise of their priestly power, and so a strange member they

---

[104] By direct power the author means that which Jesus Christ has given to the Church over consciences: and by the indirect power, that which flows from this power purely divine, in its relation with temporal things. (Note of the translator.)

could not receive from him the food of life, but rather an impulse to death. Thus they remained in bad odor with the Pope, and unfriendly with the King. Left in such a manner dismembered, they should then provide for themselves the means to exercise their power. Whence derive the power? Not from the Pope whom they accused of boundless pretensions, but rather from the Prince whom they considered their protector, whilst he drove them to extremes, when he compelled them to desert the Pope. Then it was they sought the royal privileges and purchased them with that liberty, which is the life of the power and which naturally flowed to them from the Pope. Therefore enslaved, they called themselves free; and in that slavery they scattered the seeds of that later liberty, called Gallican. A striking proof that what are called privileges of a particular church to liberate it from the Roman, and to exempt it from the dependence in which the others are in relation to the mother and mistress of churches, are not privileges at all but fatal occasions of severing the salutary bond of unity. One God, one Church, one is the obligation of adhesion to the supernatural truth, before which all are equal. In discussing these things we wish to remark that if Philip a Catholic committed a grave offence against human reason by rejecting the indirect power of the Pope over him as a secular prince, the French clergy transgressed much more grievously by their shameful surrender to court influence. We speak not of the consequences, because all know them and because it is dangerous to touch upon them. In those times there were very many, and even Frenchmen who defended this Roman doctrine, among whom we find Hugh of St. Victor,[105] St. Thomas,[106] St. Bonaventure,[107] and Durandus.[108] Moreover that ardent debater, Friar John of Paris, of the Order of Preachers, in the work "*De Regia potestate et Papali*," in which he defends Philip, gives utterance to a certain opinion, which, if Boniface had expressed it, would have aroused a storm [109] But among all

---

[105] Book 2, part 2, chap. 4.   [106] In fine 2 Senten.
[107] De Eccles. Hierarch. Part. 2, cap. I.   [108] De Origine Jurisd. Quest. 5
[109] "Papa vero, qui est supermum Caput non solum clericorum, sed et generaliter omnium fidelium, ut fideles sunt, tanquam informator fidei et morum, in quo casu omnia bona fidelium sunt communia, et communi-

these special mention should be made of Blessed Egidius Colonna, who educated in the wisdom of St. Thomas of Aquin, was a singular defender of Boniface in his controversy with Philip the Fair. He was born in Rome in 1247, or thereabouts, and being a member of that powerful Colonna family, we may know if he had any love for Boniface. At first he studied the sciences in his own country, then having entered the Augustinian order, he was sent to Paris in 1269 to prosecute his studies. He had as teacher St. Thomas of Aquin, whose doctrine he afterwards defended against William de Mora, a Friar Minor of Oxford. Crevier [110] asserts that Egidius became the most famous doctor of his time in Paris. In fact according to the custom then prevailing, he was called by the splendid surnames of Prince of Theologians,[111] the Most Profound Doctor.[112] He was appointed tutor to Philip the Fair, to whom he dedicated his treatise, "*De Regimine Principum*,"[113] a work different from that attributed to St. Thomas. From the education he received, according to Crevier, Philip derived his love for learning.[114] When after having been anointed as king at Rheims, Philip was entering Paris, Egidius met him and paid homage to him in a eulogistic speech.[115] This made him very dear to the King. But perhaps he was even dearer to Pope Boniface, in whose favor he wrote the treatise "*De Renunciatione Papae*," when owing to the singular renunciation of St. Peter Celestine, many were undecided in relation to the legitimacy of the Papacy of

---

canda, etiam calices Ecclesiarum; habet bona exteriora fidelium dispensare, et exponenda decernere, prout expedit necessitati communi fidei" Chap. 7. And chap. 14, " Si princeps esset haereticus et incorrigibilis, et contemptor ecclesiasticae censurae, posset Papa aliquod facere in populo, ut privaretur ille seculari honore, et deponeretur a populo. Et hoc faceret Papa in crimine Ecclesiastico, cujus cognitio ad ipsum pertinet, excommunicando, scilicet omnes qui ei ut Domino obedirent." See Ordin. de Script. Eccl. 75, page 635.

[110] History of the University of Paris, Tom. 2, page 106.
[111] Cave. Saec. Scholast. Sol. 658.
[112] Labbe, de Script. Eccles. Tom. 1, page 13.
[113] Tiraboschi. Hist of Literature. St. 74, page 114. See Oudin. de Script. Eccl. Seculo XIII, Col 139.
[114] Crevier. History of University of Paris, Tom. 2, page 113.
[115] Gallia Christiana, Tom. 2, page 76.

Boniface. As a reward for this he was created Archbishop of Bourges. A man of austere habits, he was considered a saint, being always styled Blessed; and he was temperate in action in those stormy times. For we find that besides the aforesaid proofs of his love for Philip, he had manifested his benevolence in two synods by conceding to him the ecclesiastical tithes.[116] On the other hand, the terrible quarrel having broken out, he wrote on the royal and papal power, deciding in favor of Boniface against Philip. This opinion was not to be despised inasmuch as he was a man dear to the two rivals, and he was well acquainted with the things he saw. We have said the things he saw, but he never felt them. For by reason of tithes and taxes his income was so reduced, that from being a very rich prelate, he was obliged for the necessities of life to serve as a simple canon in the Order, in order to receive a portion of the daily distributions. The continuator of Nangis asserts that it was the Pope who had so cruelly appropriated the patrimony of the Archbishop of Bourges.[117] Unfriendly to the Popes the writers of the *" Gallia Christiana "* seem to accept this opinion.[118] He died at Avignon in 1316, and was buried in the church of his Augustinians in Paris.[119] The opinions favorable to the doctrine of Boniface, as we have shown, which caused so much commotion in France, were not a scandal to other Catholic churches of Christendom, but were received as sacred. If we call to mind the provincial councils held at that time, we find scarcely any that did not establish some canon affecting the ecclesiastical immunities in the same manner as they were regarded by Boniface. The English Church was a splendid example of what we here assert. We have seen with what reverence the constitution " Clericis " was welcomed; and with what great solemnity and vigor, the illustrious Robert, Archbishop of Canterbury and Primate of England, set about to promulgate it. Now whilst the parliaments in France were acting against the Pope, Robert was ever the more fortifying himself against Edward, taking refuge behind the Papal authority, the only bulwark of liberty for the

---

[116] Gallia Christiana, Tom 2, col. 77.
[117] Spicil. Archery, Tom. 2, page 620. [118] The same place.
[119] See note at end.

churches against the assaults of laymen. He did not repair to the royal court to defend himself against an imaginary Roman supremacy. Guided by the same prudence and by the same views, his predecessors, and particularly the noble Stephen Langton had obtained from King John for the English people the famous Magna Charta, the foundation of their common rights. So that the immunities of the Church were ever the parent of those of the people. Stephen with invincible courage had fought for the liberty of the clergy, and for this reason he also with the same energy directed and led that warlike band of Barons, known as the League of God and of the Holy Church. He triumphed in the sanctuary, and he triumphed on the field; and from the trembling hands of King John the Magna Charta fell into the hands of Stephen. The rights of the English people were established by this; but the first articles of the agreement were an acknowledgment of the inviolability of the rights of the Church. And when this was confirmed in full parliament in the palace at Westminster by Henry III, the king who swore to keep it as a man, a Christian, a knight and a king, more than by the arms of the Barons was he intimidated and frightened by the action of the bishops under the leadership of Langton, who extinguished and threw on the ground the lighted candles they bore to indicate thereby the maledictions they pronounced against the violators of the Charta, calling down upon them the darkness and confusion of Hell. Thus while the people obtained their rights through a victory of the Church, the latter enclosed and strengthened herself within these rights. And the ambitions of Rome only tended to compel the Prince to respect the rights of his subjects and the Church. That edifice of English rights, so venerable and so admirable, rested in the hands of those bishops, who anointed by the God of justice, had for a long time exerted themselves in defending it. We do not find that the shameful imbecility of the French clergy in subjecting themselves to Philip produced any Charta for the people, unless we would acknowledge as a worthy fruit of such a plant, that liberty which is called Gallican.

Not less vigorous was the temperament of the Spanish clergy in those times. They stood firm as a wall against secular tyranny, and with breasts of bronze defended their liberty. We read that precisely in the year 1302 Egidius, Archbishop of Toledo, convened the Synod of Pennafield, in which the bishops clamored loudly for the immunities of the churches, and this was nothing else but an echo of the voice of Boniface. Canon XIII of this Synod is very clear and expressive. It established and commanded that if any one even of royal birth violated the immunities of the churches, the bishops and the dioceses in which it happened, were to notify them to desist, and if they refused, their lands were to be interdicted. And as those bishops were in earnest, they proceeded against persons of high degree with apostolic firmness, mentioning by name Henry, son of the illustrious Ferdinand, King of Castile and Leon, and also a certain Princess Infanta of Portugal, commanding them to restore that which they had wickedly usurped from the churches of Toledo, Segovia, Lagunto, and Concha.[120] In the affairs of the Church of France, that evil which more than any other to be deplored, was a certain cowardly feeling occasioned by the fear of the royal power, that is to say, the most pitiful consequence of the death of liberty and the triumph of

[120] Item ea quae Divini juris saeculari non subjaceant potestati et nonnulli potentes, nescimus quo ducti spiritu, vel odii fomite, vel cupiditatis radice Ecclesias infringere, et earum libertates, et privilegia imminuere moliuntur, eis earum libertates, et onera gravia imponendo, proinde nos, qui ex officii nostri debito, tanquam murum pro domo Israel opponere nos debemus, hujusmodi excessibus, quantum cum Deo possumus, resistere cupientes; statuimus, et ordinamus, ut si Regina fuerit, quae facere acceptaverit (forte attemptaverit vel prandia indebita exegerit, vel filii Regum; Episcopus, in cujus Diocesi atentare vel etiam perpetrari contigerit eis penitus denunciet, ut satisfaciant de commisso: et si requisiti satisfacere noluerint infra mensem, juxta modum, et qualitatem culpae, vel damni dati, cujus aeitimatio Diocesani arbitrio relinquatur, prout viderit expedire, terra eorum, si qua in sua Dioecesi habuerint. Ecclesiastico subjaceat inter dicto . . . . . Verum quia quia Domini Henrici filli illustristrissimi domini Ferdinandi quondam Regis Castellae, et Legionis, qui ab Ecclesia Tolestana Passadicilam, et ab Ecclesia Segobiensi Riacamaldeas indebite detinet occupatas, nec non et Episcopa Seguntino quaedam mobilis postquam fuit de eo provisum Seguntinae Ecclesiae usurpavit, excessus est notorius, statuimus, et ordinamus, ut nominatim requiratur, quor praedicta loca restituat—Seguntino Episcopo satisfaciat de ablatis. Idem penitus statuentes de Infantissa Portugalliae super restitutione poenarum de Viana Conchensi Ecclesiae facienda." Aguir Conc. Hisp.

tyranny. We have said that Boniface wanted to hold the Council in Rome, and he did hold it. Philip feared this more than censures. He knew full well that those prelates, who had been inclined towards him, if for however short a time they would have left France, and breathed the air of Rome, their courage would be revived, and they would acknowledge their unbecoming weakness, and feeling ashamed of themselves, would give a final blow to his projects. Spondani does not believe that Boniface held the Council; but there is no doubt of it, as the anonymous author of the life of Boniface [121] affirms it, and mention of this Council is found in the great collection of Mansi,[122] and it was held on the 30th of October. It seems to be true that not so many Frenchmen attended as this anonymous writer would have us believe. He says that the Council was held in the presence of the prelates of the French kingdom, and of all the French Doctors of Divinity and of Law. Philip had carefully placed safe barriers on all the roads leading to Rome, and all those Doctors could not, nor do we believe would they care to, escape from France at their own peril. It is probable that when the author declared that the Council was held in presence of prelates, he referred to the presence of the French legates in the consistory who listened to the discourses of the Cardinal of Porto and of the Pope. Great was the moderation of Boniface in this Synod. There were no censures, and not even was Philip named in the famous constitution "*Unam Sanctam*," which was the work of this Council. Moreover this same anonymous author of the life of this Pope had wondered, writing figuratively, how amidst so much lightning against the King, there did not follow showers; [123] and measures were not taken even against great prelates of the kingdom, mistaken through love for their own interest, and solicitors only for themselves for the time being.

The constitution which begins "*Unam Sanctam*," emanated from this Council. In this Boniface did nothing

[121] Auctor vitae Bonif. Raynaldus, year 1362, 12.

[122] Collec. Concil. Tom. 25, page 97.

[123] "Ibi corruscationibus multis praeviis contra Regem, nulla pulvia apparuit subsecuta; defeceruntque sibi Praelati magni in regno, quaerentes quae sua sunt, et sibil ipsis ad tempus tantummodo consulentes."—

more than repeat that which he had heretofore said in his Papal documents and in presence of the French legates. But since in that violent command given to the Bishops, in which Philip forbids them to repair to Rome, and for this reason to communicate with the Pontiff, he openly offended his ministry, Boniface more openly treats of the Papal power, and its complete independence. He says, that the Church is one; that it forms one mystical body; that it can have but one head; the head is Christ, through him Peter, and his successors, namely the Popes, and this is of faith. That there are two powers in the Church, the spiritual and the temporal, figured by those two swords, which the Apostles presented to Christ, saying to Him: " Behold, here are two swords," the material sword to be used for the Church, and the spiritual sword by the Church; the second in the hand of the priest, and the first in the hand of the king, but according to the order and direction of the Pope. Hence the material is subject to the spiritual, and the spiritual power teaches and guides the temporal. He concludes by defining, that it is necessary to believe in order to be saved that every creature must be subject to the Pontiff.[124]

We do not believe that ever in the world anything caused such controversy, and aroused such great and lasting commotion, as did these words of Boniface. The courtiers and the theologians of the time of Philip were aroused, and this is not much to be wondered at. But when in after times Natalis Alexander, Fleury and Bossuet, the famous bishop of Meaux, and so many others, so unreasonably have raised a diabolical disturbance in the time of the most Christian Louis XIV, the reader can easily perceive that under the garb of a zeal for the liberty of particular churches, of a desire to restrain Pontifical ambitions, there must be hidden some reason, which evidently did not depend on times or circumstances, but existed absolutely in the minds of the disturbers; and they themselves either did not know the final consequences of their theories, or else they wished to conceal them. We will state briefly what this reason was. It was their repugnance to the absolute monarchy of the Church, and the foolish idea of tempering it either by a consistorial aris-

[124] See document J at end of work.

tocracy, or worse, by royal authority. If we would not wish to penetrate the labyrinth of opinions concerning the dual power, of which Boniface speaks, the task would be wearisome to me and of little service to the reader, and not worth the time which is so precious. But we have come at length to the time of proceeding to a consideration of the causes of the great controversies, and of leaving aside with the greatest respect the two bodies of contending canonists. Natalis Alexander especially summoned around him a host of writers, who were of his opinion, and with the supercilious tone of a pedant demanded their opinion of the dual power, which he believed was fabricated by Boniface. They all replied that it is an impertinence; it never existed, and is an excessiveness of sovereignty on the part of Pope Boniface; and so he triumphs. Even the partisans of the Pope or rather those who, adopting the principles, do not wish to resist the consequences engendered thereby, seem to us to have erred in their manner of defence. They also gather champions who agree with them and they triumph. But it is still undecided which of these two parties gained the victory. Many still continue to clamor, terming Boniface a rascal, and very few consider him honest and just. However whilst the Gallicans, like Natalis Alexander, are consuming time in enumerating how many writers of the University of Paris coincide with them, and whether Boniface had made a right or wrong use of Scriptural passages, we shall treat the reader to a short and simple consideration which touches the very heart of the question, and not of men who are engaged in quarrelling with one another.

In this constitution Boniface had reminded Philip of the doctrine as old as the Catholic Church, namely that the Pope is superior to lay Princes by reason of sin. We have explained the sense and truth of these words. Now in the Constitution "*Unam Sanctam*" he traces this doctrine to the principle from which it is derived, by defining that there are two quite distinct powers on earth, the spiritual and the temporal, and the latter is arranged and directed by the former. If this be not admitted, Boniface decided, there was nothing else to do but bow the head and adopt the Manichaean phantasy of two principles.

No one is ignorant that there is one God, one power, one order. Power and order among men are derived from God, to be multiplied accidentally, but remaining one and absolute by nature. If there is a great number of beings outside of God, these should be reunited by the bond of subordination, as is evident from the natural order of things, which ascend to God by a succession of dependence and empire. A similar law presides over the moral order. Hence tracing all the various powers to their own peculiar sources, we shall find the spiritual and temporal powers supreme moderators of Catholic Christian society. The question arises to which belongs the office of ruling over the other, both not being able to exist independent. The spiritual power is adjusted to an infallible and eternal legislation, and to a head or determined master. Therefore both by the law of which it is the custodian, and through the person who is invested with it, this power comes immediately from God; there being nothing human in it save the infirmity of him who exercises it, as a Pope is not transformed into a God. The temporal power then is established with a view to a temporary and fallible legislation, owing to a diversity of times and of men, and with a view to an undetermined master. Therefore the temporal comes immediately from God, mediately as to its forms. So if it is necessary to a civil Catholic society that there should be a governing power, it is not however necessary that by the immediate will of God this power should be placed in the hands of an aristocracy or of a monarch. This determination comes from men, and hence is changeable like the civil laws, fallible and not perpetual. On the contrary the spiritual power immediately both in its substance and in its form comes from God; as it is not the office of men to determine into whose hands it should be placed. The Bishop of Rome, as the successor of St. Peter, is chosen by God to exercise it. He shall be a perpetual, unchangeable minister of it, just as the law, of which he has been designated custodian and master, is perpetual, unchangeable and infallible. Hence the Pope alone is rightly called the Vicar of Christ, and to no republican form of government or monarchy has this appellation been given. Moreover the Pope applies an infallible law to faith and morals, and he is the head of an infallible society, which is the governing Church. There are two sources of infallibility, faith and morals, that raise the Vicar of Christ so high, as to make him unaccountable to any one on earth in those judgments with a view to which his power has been established.

Therefore just as the infallibility of the Church in the Pope elevates him so high that he has no supérior, so the fallibility of a Prince calls for some other power superior to him, except in case of his immediate deputation received from God. If therefore no things outside of God are perfect equality with one another, and if besides, the Papal and the civil powers are both derived from God, the reason by which one of the two is more nobly derived, will furnish at once a reason for its preeminence. Destroy this preeminence and the civil power will clash with the laws of nature, which as they will not have independence even in power, will be destructive of the society over which they are exercised, and will be rebellious against God who confided his power to the head of His Church. Therefore if the court of appeal be closed to the society ruled by the fallibility of a Prince, and to the faults of the ruling power, the governed will reply with brutal force, which can never be sanctioned by right. Then when the combatants have become wearied of the strife there will arise the necessity of absolute justice, which is not to be found in the bosom of a convulsed society, must be implored from the spiritual power, or else the combatants will become delirious over the sovereignty of the people or the rights of man. These are phantasies which give birth to princes intolerant of restraint, and nurtured by the people under the pressure of a moral and terrible necessity. It is true that the civil power is not derived from the spiritual, but equally strong and equally free both come from God to reign, the latter over the Church, and the former over the people. So that the spiritual power freely unfolds itself, and is not restrained by a superior; and the temporal is directed and regulated by the former, as there can be no subjection without the direction of a superior. The power for example of a father over his children is not destroyed in a republic by the subjection of the parents to the state government. This direction, or order is manifested every time the civil government is in disorder, that is sins. Its fault is always a violation of commutative justice, which imposes on the rulers and the people, an equal command of mutual preservation. One of the contracting parties, which fails in its duty, releases with good reason the other from its obligation. But inasmuch as that right can resolve itself into a fact, there is always need of a judge, to be chosen either by the consent of the parties, or already in the selection of a Religion infallible in her laws, and in those who expound them. And here again we behold, as a consequence of the two powers, the one subordinate to the other, the pre-eminence of the Pope over other civil rulers by reason of sin. And therefore there is not a creature, as Boniface defined, which is not subject to the Pontiff. A king or a president of a republic, who desires to be a Catholic Christian, can never withdraw from this subjection, unless he wishes to subject himself to God in a manner different from that established by Christ, or prefers rather to try the benefits of tyranny or anarchy, which wrestling in the bosom of society increase the miseries of this short journey of life. These theories were not the production of the human brain, but of the Christian religion, as soon as men embraced it not only as individuals, but also as members of a civil society. Therefore those who make Boniface the author of them either do not know, or do not care to know that they were always defined by Popes his predecessors, confirmed by Greek and Latin Fathers, and defended by Doctors, even Frenchmen. In fact that which we have called a "directive" or "administrative" power of the Pope over Princes, was a long time previous considered as such and called such by Gerson, a Frenchman.[125] The application of the Scriptural passages, especially the one of the two swords as a symbol of the two powers, the one subordinate to the other, was not altogether the work of Boniface. It was first discovered by a holy French Doctor, St. Bernard.[126] The application to the Pope of the words spoken by God to Jeremias, was a thing much older than the time of Boniface both in the Greek and Latin Churches.[127] Boniface has been accused

[125] De Potestate Ecclesiae Consid. 12 [126] Book 4 De Consid. ad Eugenium Papam [127] See Bianchi. On the Indirect Power of the Church Book VI, 7, Tom 2.

of a violent distortion of Scriptural passages, and of the fabrication of an unlimited ecclesiastical right, because he had to resist immediately the transgressors of the same. But in this precisely we discover his greatness of soul. For when a man comes to be identified with a theory, in such a manner that war against the theory means war against him who defends it, it must be that the soul of this man is capable of comprehending it, and able to defend it alone. Hence hatreds have survived against Boniface, because the truth he defended has survived. And whenever the hand of the powerful attacks the Church in her rights, it digs up from the tomb the ashes of that magnanimous soul in order to execrate them. Four centuries have elapsed since the death of Boniface, and yet Bossuet rushed against him with the same fury as was displayed against him in the assembly of Senlis.

After the definition of right Boniface proceeded to action. He published sentence of excommunication on the same day November 18th against all, and even crowned heads, who would dare to molest, hinder, or imprison those going to the Roman See or returning. In this Bull he could have struck Philip heavily, by naming him, since he was guilty of this kind of violence, but he held to generalities. For in all those barefaced proceedings of Philip against him, Boniface never dismissed from his mind the hope of being able to lead him by reason to a better course. He desired peace. But he could not endure those public violations of the liberty of the Church, of which he was the supreme guardian and defender. He negotiated with Charles of Valois, that he might use his good influence with his brother, King Philip, to reconcile him with Rome. Charles promised, but as we have seen in Florence, this peacemaker was fit for everything else, except to make peace.[128]

In this Roman Synod where the Bull "*Unam Sanctam*" was published, John Lemoine, Cardinal of the title of Sts. Marcellinus and Peter, a Frenchman, was sent to France as legate in order not to give umbrage to Philip. He was a man of grave character, endowed with many virtues, of tried prudence and also a most courageous man, for considering the fate of the other legates in their dealings

---

[128] Raynaldus, 1302, n. 15.

with the brutal Prince, there was much reason to fear. The Pope had granted him the amplest faculty to release Philip from censures, if he requested such.

But before we come to speak of the outcome of that legation, we must narrate the doings of Boniface elsewhere. For the affairs of France, although most grave, were not so important as to take his attention from other churches and other states of the universal Church.

The kingdom of Hungary at this time was in great disorder owing to factional fights over the uncertainty of its ruler. Ladislaus III, surnamed Cumano, King of Hungary dying childless in 1290, left only his wife Mary, daughter of Charles I of Anjou, King of Naples. The majority of the Hungarian nobles greeted as their king Andrew, the third of that name, called the Venetian, because born in Venice of Thomassina Morosini, and he was crowned in August, 1290. But Mary, the sister of the dead Ladislaus, the wife of Charles II, the Lame of Naples, believed that her son Charles Martel deserved by right of succession the crown, and Popes Nicholas IV and Celestine V, ever ready to promote the interests of the house of Anjou, twice in Naples had crowned Charles Martel, King of Hungary. In the meantime Andrew reigned in fact. In 1295 Charles Martel died prematurely leaving his rights to the crown to his son Charles Robert, shortened into Carobert, who, supported in his claims by the Papal Court, disputed with Andrew the throne of Hungary. The question was, which was of greater weight in the establishment of legitimacy, the selection by the nobles or the succession of heredity? Boniface, endowed as he was with a keen knowledge of human affairs, saw clearly that since this people was only half-civilized, and menaced round about by a most fierce tribe, as the Cuman Tartars were, to leave to them the selection of a king, would have given a lasting occasion for war within, and invasions from without. As Pope he saw a way closed to extend the power of the house of the Angevines of Naples, the recognized defenders of Papal rights. Moreover the kings of Hungary were never elective, but the nearest relative of the dead king inherited the crown. Therefore his ward Carobert had the best right to succeed Ladislaus; nor could a party of nobles by making a selection destroy a law prescribed by a long period of years. Boniface therefore took the part of Carobert according to justice. He set to work with great ardor, negotiating not only in the interests of one man, but of the whole kingdom, and of the Hungarian Church. The former was in great disorder, the result of factional fights, the latter was disturbed in its liberty and oppressed.

On the 13th of May, 1301, Boniface had appointed Nicholas, Cardinal Bishop of Ostia and Velletri as his Legate to settle the affairs in Hungary by establishing Carobert on the throne. He had given him the fullest power to negotiate also as his Legate in Poland, in Croatia, in Dalmatia, and in other regions. It is well to remark here how he expressed to Nicholas the nature and the duties of his mission: "We send you as an Angel of peace:[129] enjoin"ing you that, in that kingdom and in the aforesaid prov"inces, you consult with the clergy and laity, whatever "may be their rank and dignity, on all things which con"cern the divine worship, the honor of the Apostolic See, "the observance of the ecclesiastical canons, the restora"tion of the liberty of the Church, the prosperity of the "kingdom and those provinces, the decorum of divine "worship, the return of peace, spiritual health and bodily "tranquillity." The Legate brought with him from the Pope very important letters to all the Prelates of Hungary exhorting them to receive the Legate as himself in person, to give him whatever he needed and a kind reception. But in July of the same year, 1301, Andrew III had died and the nobles of Hungary having heard of the near arrival of the Papal Legate, feared that they might suffer the loss of their liberty, if they allowed Boniface to choose a king for them. So they appealed at once to Wenceslaus, King of Bohemia, son of Anna, a daughter of Belo IV, King of Hungary, who died in 1271, beseeching him to accept the crown of Hungary. The Bohemian king far advanced in years did not wish to leave his old kingdom, and relinquished to his son Wenceslaus the throne to which he was invited by the Hungarians. Wenceslaus was crowned king by John, Archbishop of Colocza in Alba-Reale, as the see of Strigonia was vacant, upon the Archbishop of which devolved by right that ceremony.

[129] "Tanquam pacis Angelum destinamus." Raynaldus, 1301, n. 4.

As soon as Boniface heard of this sudden coronation, he overtook the Legate with letters, as he was about entering the kingdom. The affairs of France had embittered his mind, and rendered him more jealous of the Papal power; for which reason from the time of the open rupture with Philip he adopted in letters more solemn language to magnify the supreme power of the Church, as we see in this letter which he dispatched to the Legate, Cardinal of Ostia. It began: "The Roman Pontiff estab-"lished by God over kings and kingdoms is the supreme "high-priest in the Church militant; and prince over all "men, being seated on the throne of judgment, he judges "quietly, and with one glance he causes all manner of "evils to disappear." He then reminds him of the care with which the Apostolic See had protected Hungary from the fury of barbarians, and says that not departing from the custom of his predecessors, he designated him Legate to that kingdom so violently disturbed. He condemns the rashness of the Archbishop of Colocza, for having dared to place the crown of Hungary upon the head of Wenceslaus, since Carobert had been already crowned, and he summons him to appear before him within the period of four months, and give a reason for his conduct.

To Wenceslaus the elder, the aged King of Bohemia, he complained by letter, and demanded that he annul at once the things done with such little prudence. He asked by what right of succession or by what title his son had appropriated the kingdom of Hungary; and what reason was there for the temerity of the Archbishop of Colocza to meddle in an affair in which he had no right. That he should not have despised the Apostolic See, the mother and teacher of all, and that in cases of doubt, and affairs of great moment he should have had recourse to her. The kingdom of Hungary was brought almost to nothing by the fury of the Cumans, the Tartars, the Pagans and the schismatics, and this rash act will serve only to open a way to further lacerate her. That if his son had any rights in Hungary, he should expose them before the Holy See, and if proven, they will be preserved whole and intact.[130]

In the meantime having arrived in Hungary, the Cardinal Legate assembled the nobles of the kingdom. He

[130] Raynaldus, year 1301, no. 10.

tried every means to reconcile them, and have them recognize Carobert as king, but all in vain. Then he left that country, and repaired to Vienna, whence he dispatched a messenger to the Pope to acquaint him of the unsuccessful result of his mission. On the other hand Wenceslaus, King of Bohemia, replied to the Papal letter, and declared that his son had been legitimately elected King of Hungary. Boniface did not yield; he insisted and undertook to present the rights of Maria, mother of Carobert, to the Hungarian throne. He invited the King of Bohemia, Maria and her son Carobert to appear before him to discuss the affair. And since in his letter Wenceslaus had taken also the title of King of Poland, in the strongest terms he exhorted him to abandon it, telling him that that was a crime of state, as Poland was a fief of the Roman See. He wrote to this effect in June 1302; and the Cardinal Legate according to his command cited the pretenders to the throne of Hungary.[131]

Maria and Carobert dispatched their procurators to the Papal Court, Wenceslaus deputed three not as exponents but as defenders, against any decision of the rights of their lord. Boniface decided with the advice of the Cardinals, that the throne of Hungary was hereditary and not elective, and to Carobert the crown belonged. He published this decision in a Bull, beginning "*Spectator Omnium,*" given at Anagni on May 30th, 1302, and ordered the Archbishop of Colocza and the Bishop of Zagrabiense to announce it to the Bohemian elected king.[132] This decision was followed by an encyclical to all the Hungarians, commanding them under the pain of censure to yield obedience to Carobert; and a letter to this young man exhorting him to the practise of virtue, written also at Anagni on June 3rd, 1302. The care exercised by Boniface over Hungary brought the desired peace to that kingdom. All acknowledged Carobert as their king; the two Wenceslaus of Bohemia renounced their claims, and Hungary was quieted, and was governed very well by that prince.

The firmness of this Pontiff, as it appears from the narration of the affairs of Hungary, did not always bring disaster. As in defence of the rights of his ward Carobert he

[131] Raynaldus, year 1302, no. 20, 22   [132] Raynaldus, year 1303, no. 17.

showed himself a most tenacious observer of justice, so afterwards in the affairs of Germany he showed that he knew how to moderate himself with prudence in affairs of great difficulty. We have already seen how strenuously he opposed Albert, son of Rudolph of Hapsburg. This prince violated his oath to Adolph, King of the Romans, and having raised a rebellion against him, slew him in the battle of Spires. Up to this year, 1303, Boniface had been inexorable to the entreaties of Albert, who sought his approval wherewith to acquire the Imperial crown. Moreover as we have seen he had aroused the ecclesiastical Electors of Germany to carry on war against the usurper, which they did. He was induced to this rigor, both because justice was wronged by Albert rebelling against and slaying his lord Adolph; and because of the violation of the rights of the Papal See, as it is the right of the Pontiff to examine the person selected as King of the Romans, to consecrate him, to crown him, and if unworthy of the office to reject him. The first reason, as it was a fact that violated, but did not make sacred, a right, would disappear, as soon as the consent of the Electors and the Pontiff made that fact legitimate.

The second, although it was a violation of a right, also would cease, as soon as reparation for the same was made. And both ceased when Albert submitted to the judgment of Boniface, and confessed that he had wickedly acquired the crown of King of the Romans and had ignored the rights of the Roman See. Moreover it must be further added, that an unbending spirit would have prolonged still more the damage of the intestine wars and quarrels in Germany, and would have deprived the Pope of a support in his stormy controversies with Philip the Fair. Therefore Albert sent ambassadors to the Pope to express how willing he was to do his pleasure, seeking not judgment but mercy.[133] They promised in his name fidelity and

---

[133] Raynaldus, year 1303, no. 4 . . . . "tu devoti et prudentis more filii, de solita patris benignitate confidens, super iis non judicium, sed misericordiam humiliter implorasti. Praestitisti quoque nobis et eidem sedi fidelitatis et obedientiae juramentum et nonnulla alia etiam promisisti, et juramento firmasti, quae tam a praedicto patre tuo, quam a praedecessoribus ejus Romanorum Regibus jurata, promissa facta, recognita et concessa fuerunt sicut haec et alia in duabus patentibus lit-

obedience to the Apostolic See; and they promised also
under oath to stand by what his predecessors, the Kings
of the Romans, had conceded to the Popes. From this it
is evident, that it was not through fear of Philip that
Boniface had recognized as just the usurpation of Albert,
and ratified it after having condemned it. The change of
sentiments in this prince who craved pardon for his injustice, and promised obedience to the Holy See, induced
the Pope to change his dispositions. The letters of Albert
to Boniface, found in the annals of Raynaldus, afford
pleasant reading. In these not only does he mention his
obligation to the Roman Pontiffs, but he discussed at
length with a solemn profession (profiteor) how the Imperial crown had been transferred by the Apostolic See
from Greece to Germany in the person of Charlemagne.
Hence the chief duty of the emperors was to defend the
Church; to swear never to take sides against her, but ever
to guard her; and strenuously to uphold her liberty and
her rights. This did Albert of Nuremburg write on August 17th, 1303.[134] And Boniface in reply to that which
the ambassadors had reported, solemnly confirmed his
election as King of the Romans,[135] in a document which
begins: "*Patris aeterni filius,*" and which he concludes
with a beautiful exhortation to be grateful to the Church:
" We advise and beseech you by the Son of God the Father,
" to fix the eyes of your body and mind respectfully on
" God and on the Church, if you desire to rule nobly;
" meditate piously in your soul on the kindness of us and
" of that holy Mother, who, you should not forget, had
" anticipated you; engrave it in the inmost recesses of
" your heart, and there let it remain as a perpetual re-
" minder of favors received."

teris tuo sigillo signatis, quae in ipsius Archivio conservantur Ecclesiae, plenius continuentur." (Letter of Boniface to Albert, King of the Romans). [134] Raynaldus, year 1303, no. 9.

[135] Raynaldus, year 1303, no. 2. See document at end of book.

BOOK VI.

SUMMARY.

1303-1314.

Philip renews the war with the Flemish —The defeat of the French at Courtrai.—Reparation demanded of Philip by the Legate, Cardinal Lemoine.—Philip's reply.—Mission of Nicholas Benefratte to Philip, who imprisons him.—Parliament in the Louvre Palace.—Charges against Boniface —The wretched picture the bishops present us —A consistory in Rome, and punishments proclaimed against Philip and France.—Of appeals to the Council.—Certain ruffians cross the Alps to seize the Pope.—Their number is increased by the soldiers of Charles of Valois, and Sciarra Colonna is at their head.—They lay siege to Anagni, and the inhabitants rebel against the Pope.—They enter the town and invade the Papal palace —How Boniface received them, deserted by every one.—Low insolence of Sciarra Colonna and Nogaret. —The people of Anagni return to their senses —Magnanimity of Boniface.—He goes to Rome —His death —Judgment of his actions —His body is found after three centuries almost incorrupt.—Philip the Fair, after the death' of Boniface —Benedict XI.—His indulgence to the French, he tries to bring Philip to his senses —His prophecy concerning the affair of Anagni.—He wishes to punish the guilty.—He dies of poison —The Conclave, and how it happened that Bertrand de Got, Clement V, became Pope.—Philip the Fair interferes with him, and the Papal See is transferred to France.—Clement is urged by Philip to proceed against the memory of Boniface.—The lamentable position of Clement in the clutches of Philip at Poitiers.—The Templars.—Philip wants to plunder them, he demands their death from Clement —They are burned at the stake.—After the burning of the Templars, there was a demand to burn the bones of Boniface.—Proceedings against Boniface in presence of the Pope —End of the proceedings —Heaven punishes Philip; his last days and his death —A calamity visited on Anagni.—Conclusion.

IT seemed that Heaven wanted to allure the blinded Philip from the precipice by an awful disaster, that filled all France with shame and mourning. When Edward of England and Philip the Fair had agreed to submit to the judgment of the Pope, as a private man, the reason of their dissensions, the English King had included in the treaty of armistice, which followed the Papal decision, Guy of Flanders, his ally. But Boniface in his decision, in order not to give offence to Philip, made no mention of Guy and his Flemings. Being protected by Edward they were guaranteed against annoyance by Philip. But having for some unknown reason come to a misunderstanding with the English who were assisting them in guarding the city of Ghent, it happened that their allies withdrew from Flanders, and thereby they were left exposed to the anger of Philip who longed for the moment to fall upon them. In the beginning of 1300 the truce between England and France expired, under the shadow of which the Flemings reposed; when suddenly there appears in the field the French army moving against them under the leadership of Charles of Valois. In two battles Robert of Bethune, the eldest son of the Count of Flanders, was defeated, and in a short time all Flanders was under the power of the French. There still remained well fortified the city of Ghent and Count Guy within, who had the courage and resources to arrest the progress of the conquerors by a long resistance.[1]

This resistance irritated Charles of Valois, who wished to subdue his enemy without fatigue. He proposed articles of capitulation to Guy, and that he should trust himself to the generosity of the King of France, and to the justice of the court of Paris, of which he was the chief member: he should lay down his arms, and should come unarmed with all his family, and some fifty Flemish nobles and deliver himself into his hands;—besides he should present to Philip in writing his sincere desire of being reconciled to him. Charles in return promised that he would protect him at the court of Philip; and have him restored to the sovereignty of all his provinces, the dignity of first Count, and have him made a Peer of France; and as a guarantee of his promises he staked his own honor and loyalty. Guy then surrendered: and the port of Ghent, and all the other fortresses opened their gates to the French. But Guy and his sons and chief barons went to France to experience in prisons the generosity of Philip, and the inviolate good faith of Charles. This is

[1] Chron. Nangii.

the Charles of Valois who afterwards went to Florence, of whom Dante well said, *" that he fought with the arms of Judas."*

All Europe was stupefied at this infamous treachery, and the suspicion that Philip had put to death the unfortunate daughter of Guy whom he had held imprisoned for a long time, became a certainty. Philip went to view his new conquest, and appointed as governor James of Chatilon, brother of the Count of St. Paul, and he was a very cruel governor of the poor Flemings: he was the Verres of Flanders. But like Sicily, Flanders also had its Vespers. Robert, Count of Artois, hastened with chosen troops to create the storm. Guy of Flanders, the younger, and William, the grand-nephew of Guy the elder, led the Flemish force and encountered the French at Courtrai. Some mysterious hand must have guided them to the bank of a river. They chose their position skilfully behind a narrow canal, which concealed the view of the water from the opposing forces. The attack was begun by the French archers and foot soldiers, but the barons and knights, imagining in their contempt for the popular troops that the victory would be easily gained, and afraid that the foot soldiers should have the honor of it, ordered them to fall back on the flanks, and make way for the cavalry to charge. Almost immediately the whole line of the French cavalry dashed at full gallop, and swept down upon the Flemings. But in their imprudent haste they had not made themselves acquainted with the existence of the canal, and were only made aware of it by falling over into its deep bed. The whole mass of the cavalry was rushing forward with such impetuosity that it was impossible to stop, and as one line rolled over the other, continually pushed forward by those behind, who knew nothing of what had happened in front, the confusion became fearful, and multitudes were crushed or suffocated under the weight of their own horses. The Flemings at this moment, separating into two bodies, crossed the canal at opposite points, and fell upon the flanks of the French, whom they found incapable of defence. The Flemings attacked all indiscriminately, sparing no one. It was not a battle, but a carnage. Among the slain was Robert, Count of Artois, who was pierced with more than thirty wounds; Peter Flotte, the Chancellor, whom the reader knows; the Duke of Brabant and his son; and the son of the Count of Hainault; Raoul de Nesle, the constable of France, and his brother Guy, marshal of the army; the Count of Tancarville; James of St. Paul, governor of Flanders, the cause of the war; together with two hundred other barons, and six thousand cavaliers who perished ingloriously on that day. "This defeat humiliated greatly " the honor, the rank, and the fame of the ancient French " nobility and prowess, as the flower of the world's cavalry " was defeated and humbled by as low a class of people as " were in the world, weavers and fullers. . . . . and as a " result of this victory their pride was raised to such high " degree, that one Fleming foot-soldier with spear in hand " would have met two French cavaliers on horseback." Thus writes Villani.[2] This stroke of divine vengeance should have brought Philip the Fair to his senses, or at least have made him suspect that his attacks upon the Church were displeasing to God. He did not see returning from Courtrai, his cousin and close adviser, the Count of Artois; nor Peter Flotte his chief minister; nor the flower of the French cavalry; and this affair taught him a salutary but a bitter lesson. This was a time in his reign when he employed cunning more than tyranny. Flanders was victorious, Edward was restless, the French people were irritated, and Rome was threatening, yet he knew how to navigate the ship of state on these troubled waters. We shall not speak of the way he did it, as that would cause us to digress, but we shall mention only that malicious cunning with which he manifested his most tender compassion for the distress of the people, not in the reduction of taxes, nor the free course of justice, but in the hypocritical cry raised against the Inquisitors of heresy.[3] We would not declare that these latter walked immaculate before the Lord, but we will say undeniably that these same Inquisitors a short time previous had been piously exhorted by Philip the Fair to deal severely with heretics, because it helped to make him appear zealous in the eyes of Boniface. Now he compassionates his dear and faithful

---

[2] John Villani, L. VIII, c. 56.
[3] Martene Collect. amplis. Tom. V, p. 541 et seq.

subjects tortured by these same Inquisitors. Philip wanted to estrange the people from the clergy.

Cardinal John Lemoine had been received in audience on December 24th. He was sent as Legate to Philip with the power of releasing him from censures, published not against him in particular, but in general against all those who had hindered the French prelates from going to Rome. But before the Legate moved in the matter, Boniface in Rome negotiated with Charles of Valois and the ambassador of Philip, to whom having presented twelve accusations against the King, obtained a promise from them that to each of the charges Philip would give the required satisfaction. The Legate set out for France bearing with him the twelve accusations and the promise of Charles and the ambassador, if this promise at the end of a month's time was not fulfilled, the Pope threatened to resort to spiritual and temporal chastisements.

The Legate presented himself to Philip, and explained under twelve specifications the requests of the Pope, which were the following: 1st. The King should recall his prohibition, direct or indirect, against the French Prelates and Doctors repairing to Rome to attend the Synod convened by the Pope;—2nd, he should admit that the Pontiff has the supreme and chief power to confer any vacant ecclesiastical benefice within or without the Roman Curia; and in the bestowal of the same a layman could not obtain the right without the tacit or expressed consent of the Apostolic See;—3rd, that the Roman Pontiff can send at will Nuncios and Legates to Princes in any empire or kingdom, independently of any petition or consent;—4th, in spite of contrary usage and customs the administration of ecclesiastical goods should only be in the hands of clerics and not laymen, and the supreme administration and dispensation of them rested with the Apostolic See, which with a certain necessary consent can dispose of them, and impose a hundredth part, tithes or any other tax;—5th, that the King and other princes are forbidden to seize ecclesiastical goods and rights except those conceded by right or granted by the Holy See, and to summon before his own tribunal ecclesiastical persons by reason of property or rights, when they are not held in fief;—6th, that the King should restore to the Prelates, and especially to the monasteries, over which he had the right of custody, the use of the spiritual sword, and free jurisdiction, no matter what privileges had been granted to the King and his ministers;—7th, that the King should send to the Pope his procurator with sufficient power, and prepared in his name to do the will of the Pontiff by apologizing for the most grievous insult to the Apostolic See, when he allowed the Papal Bulls to be burned; and he should know that he had determined to recall all the privileges formerly granted by the Apostolic See to the King, to his sons, to his brothers, and to his ministers, that the punishment for such wickedness might serve as an example for posterity; —8th, that the King should not abuse the rights of Regalia, and of custody over vacant sees; but the usual expenses being taken, the remainder of the revenues should be faithfully reserved for future prelates.—9th, that he should made amends for injuries, especially his adulteration of the public money, of which within brief intervals he had thrice been guilty of;—10th, that he should remind the King of other abuses committed by him or by his ministers, and contained in sealed letters of which the legate James de Normans had been the bearer,—11th, that the city and borough of Lyons with all jurisdiction, and pure and mixed government belonged not to the King, but rather the Church of Lyons; and he commands him to repair the injuries and offences given to the Archbishop, the clerics, and their vassals; 12th, and finally if within the space of time agreed to by Charles his brother and his ambassadors he did not begin to correct the above mentioned abuses, and satisfy the Apostolic See, he the Supreme Pontiff, would proceed to spiritual and temporal chastisements.[4] Now any one can see from these articles how rigorously Boniface entrenched himself in the right of the Church recognized by the public civil law of the times; and how he revoked that which his predecessors had granted as a privilege to the French kings in the matter of the bestowal of ecclesiastical benefices.

Philip met these charges with that mantle which the artifices of lawyers and the cunning of courtiers have ever ready to throw over a Prince, when he is intent on plun-

[4] Brov. Ann. Raynaldus, year 1303, n. 34.

der. He replied, as Natalis Alexander says, with incredible modesty: That the war against the Flemings in difficult and troublesome times had hindered the transport of money, arms, and horses outside of his kingdom; and in this he made use of a right which he believed he held in common with other princes.

It should not displease the Pontiff, in case he truly loved the King and the realm, if he had opposed the Prelates leaving France, because they should be near him to assist him by word and deed in his defence of both Church and State in such troublesome times; and yet he had never denied permission to those who lawfully and honestly wished to go to the Roman Curia. He provided that those having gone to Rome contrary to his wishes should have a free passage, and that when they would return to their sees, their benefices should be restored to them out of reverence for the Apostolic See. By right and custom regarding the bestowal of benefices, he conferred them like his predecessors from remote times. He granted a free entry to Papal Nuncios and Legates, so long as they were not suspected by the King, and there were not other just reasons for preventing them. He took possession of the goods of the Church in cases only where they were granted either by custom or by right; he summoned clerics to his tribunals only in those cases in which it had been lawful to his predecessors. He had never prohibited nor would he prohibit the exercise of the spiritual sword by the prelates whenever right and custom justified it. It was true the Papal letters were burned, but not in contempt of the Holy See; it was commonly admitted that, not relating to spiritual but purely material things in the court of the King, this Bull was without value, and consequently had been thrown into the flames as useless so that none might abuse it. He made no innovation regarding the Regalia! he made use of them without abuse like St. Louis and his other predecessors. Acting within his rights, for the needs and urgent defence of the kingdom, he had changed the public money, but he made reparation forthwith on petition of his subjects. Concerning the grievances set forth in the letters given to James de Normans, he was most ready to indemnify the churches, the bishops, the barons and the people for all the damages which his officers might have caused them; he would make a rigorous inquiry into the past, and to prevent others in the future, he had published most salutary ordinances. If the Archbishop of Lyons had suffered in any way, it was his own fault, because he had refused to swear fidelity to the King; still he was about to negotiate with him concerning the disputed rights, in order that everyone may know that content within the limits of his own power, he respects those of the Church. Finally he entreated the Roman Pontiff not to injure the liberty, the privileges, and the royal indults, and not to sever those kind relations which always existed between the French kingdom and the Roman See. Moreover if his replies were not satisfactory to his Holiness, and if there still lay hidden a spark of discord, he would be willing to abide by the decision of the Dukes of Burgundy and Brittany, being accepted by him as arbiters, owing to their honesty and devotion to the Roman See.

A prince who believed that without a scruple he could falsify the public money, and doing so was acting within his rights; and that he could, like a miscreant, throw into the fire without a shadow of sin, the Papal letters, under the pretext that they did not treat of spiritual things, certainly could not understand that princes had no right over the goods of churches, or in the collation of benefices; and finally that what his predecessors had done by virtue of Papal concessions and privileges, could be denied him by the Pope by the withdrawal of these privileges. That Boniface had excellent reasons for withdrawing them, every one will know who perceives, up to this time, Philip pass from violence to the boldest impudence and to a hypocrisy, sufficient to weary the patience of a saint. So for good reason, when Boniface had received the answers of Philip, and after having them well examined and discussed in his presence by distinguished prelates and doctors of divinity and law, he wrote to the Legate:[5] that some of the answers did not agree with the truth; others were so obscured by verbosity as to be worthless, and others expressed such evasion and delay that they held the mind uselessly in suspense. But that in order to manifest the

---

[5] Letter of Rubeus, Life of Boniface VIII, page 201.

purity of his intentions, and that he acted openly, and not in the dark, he proposed to have recourse to the advice of the Dukes of Bretagne and Burgundy, according as his own honor and that of the Apostolic See would permit. He wrote these things from the Lateran Palace April 15th, and ended the letter by threats of spiritual and temporal chastisements, and exhorted the Legate to acquaint him by person and not by letter of the result of the negotiations.

This letter contained threats of particular censures, but not a sentence of excommunication. Now why does Natalis Alexander, place in the hand of Boniface the thunderbolt of excommunication, and have him hurl it against Philip while he was trying to effect an agreement? He was learned in history, and why this location of events, or rather dislocation of them, unless it is from a desire to incriminate the Pope by accusing him of having used unjustly and inopportunely his authority against Philip? These are not the times of canonical disputes, nor the times to sacrifice historical truth for the friendship of Cæsar. Let us proceed more orderly. Boniface did not resort to extreme measures until the 13th of April, that is two months after he had received the royal reply, and forty-nine days after he had written a letter to Charles, the brother of Philip, in which he exhorted him to prevail upon Philip to moderate that reply. With the letters of the Pontiff under one's eyes, it is easy, from the date of their issue, to place his acts in an orderly series. Could not the learned disputant Natalis Alexander have done this, or was he unwilling to do so?

Moreover it is not to be denied that the above mentioned letter to the Legate, and another addressed to the Dukes of Burgundy and Brittany,[6] where there was still question of an agreement, were carried into France by Nicholas Benefratte, Archdeacon of Constance. To this letter was joined a solemn sentence of excommunication against the King, to be published in all the provinces of the kingdom. This envoy was also charged to summon again to his tribunal all those prelates and doctors, who had refused to come to Rome at the time of the first con-

---

[6] History of Diff., page 95.

vocation; and to pronounce a special sentence of deposition and deprivation of every dignity against any bishops who would not appear in his presence at a stated time.[7] But the excommunication and the other punishments were to be resorted to only when all means of agreement and submission failed. So that Benefratte carried two kinds of documents, one gentle in tone in hope of peace, the other severe in despair of a remedy. We shall tell later on how these acts at the same time were given publicity.

The time was finally come when the tightened knot was either to be loosened by reason, or broken by force. Nicholas Benefratte entered France, and as soon as he arrived at Troyes he was set upon by the satellites of the King, who probably were placed there for that purpose. They robbed him of the Papal letters, and then violently cast him into prison.[8] The Legate Lemoine would have liked to protest strongly against this violence, but it was better to remain silent, because Philip was more powerful than he, and was moreover in this matter disposed to make use of his rights, like the rights which the robber feels in the dagger and the wild beast in its claws. Nay more, surrounded as he was by spies, perhaps so as not to pollute the respected majesty of an ambassador with the obscene contact of spies, and convinced by the brutal violence exercised against Benefratte that all hope of harmony was gone, he fled secretly to return to Rome.

After the departure of the Legate and the imprisonment of Benefratte, Philip remained alone with the stolen letters of Boniface, hesitating what to do on the brink of a precipice which he had constructed with his own hands. A perusal of the letters made known to him his condemnation. He could not disguise the fact that the terrible burden of excommunication, with which he had hitherto been only threatened, at last rested heavily on his soul. How

[7] History of Diff., page 98
[8] Natalis Alexander who accused Boniface of being too hasty with excommunication, narrates this infamous imprisonment with the greatest coolness: "Qui (Nicolaus) Pontificis diplomatibus interceptis, Trecis comprehensus in carcerem conjectus est Regia jussione, frustra postulante Legate ut libertate donaretur." We believe in truth that if the article was not ended there, Alexander would have extolled Philip for this. He had the boldness to do so.

this anathema was likely to be to him a source of a most cruel embarrassment before the eyes of a nation oppressed and impoverished by his robberies. The Barons and the Bishops, seizing the opportunity, could at the same time harass him, and take revenge upon him for curtailing their power. There came perhaps to his mind the memory of Henry of Germany who was driven from his throne, and had anathemas hurled against him by Gregory VII. But Philip ruled a people in whom the most exalted love of country swiftly succeeded to the ardent desire of domestic revenge; a people who although rent, oppressed and divided by most furious factions, yet when attacked from without presented a bold and undivided front to repel the foreigner. A malicious report was spread that Boniface in his defence of ecclesiastical liberty intended to injure that of the French kingdom, and subject it as a fief of the Church. Boniface was thus made to appear in the eyes of the French an ambitious Pontiff, who making his spiritual authority subservient to his temporal interests, attacked their country in order to enslave it, and forcibly drive their king from the throne in order to make it his footstool. And even if any idea of fear had existed in Philip's mind, the thought prevailed that when a prince is so well entrenched in injustice, those who could restrain him, sooner than oppose a generous resistance, choose rather to aid him, in order to enjoy in the tranquillity of servitude the shameful honors he thrusts upon them.

Philip did not remain long undecided. He was not wanting in advisers, nor was he devoid of expedients when he was intent on usurpation. He assembled the orders of the kingdom in the palace of the Louvre on the 13th of June. The reader will remember what we have said elsewhere about these assemblies under a king of the character of Philip. The ordinary purpose of this assembly of the States General was to take counsel for the safety of the state, to obtain money, or to submit to their deliberations similar matters. On the present occasion they were not summoned around the throne of Philip for any other purpose but to judge the Pontiff, to wrest from his hands the holy Keys, to gain time by an appeal to Councils and future Popes, and to evade the power of the Church which could not be destroyed, because divine, nor made to yield, because it was exercised by a most vigorous hand. All the acts of this assembly were decided in advance, all that remained was to justify the arbitrary violence by the forms of a false justice. Seated with the Barons in that assembly were the Bishops and Abbots, and they presented a pitiful appearance. They came from the churches which they had surrendered to the custody of a prince, even sold them, either through abject fear, or through courtly blandishments which had softened them. They knew by whom and for what purpose they had been called to that place; they knew that from the rock of the Vatican the Vicar of Christ was observing them. They heard the lamentations of the churches despoiled of that liberty, which had been defended by the sweat and blood of so many priests; but one voice ran through that assembly! "If you do not release unto us Barrabas, you are no friend of Cæsar." —and at these words, deserting the sanctuary, they attached themselves to a throne established, not on a firm rock, but on the changeable and unsteady foundation of human vicissitudes.

William de Plasian a knight, advanced to the centre of that assembly, with his hand perhaps over his heart to check its throbbings; his head bent in horror of the vile accusations he was to beget; and his eyes perhaps suffused with some tears of compassion for Holy Mother Church. He had at his sides as agents, to sustain the accusations, Louis, Count of Evreux, brother of the King; Guy, Count of St. Paul; and John, Count of Dreix. He commenced his harangue by a venomous diatribe against Boniface, in which from torrent of villainous abuse the following accusations against the Pontiff are collected:[9] Boniface was tainted with heresy; he did not believe in the immortality of the soul nor in the life to come, nor in the Real Presence of Jesus Christ in the Eucharist. He practised the diabolical art of sorcery and enchantments; he had publicly preached that the Roman Pontiff can not be guilty of the sin of simony; he was an intruder in the Papal See, being the murderer of Pope Celestine; he indulged in

[9] God be praised; Natalis Alexander when he wrote the IVth article of the IVth dissertation, was in such a state of reason and justice as to find that these accusations were black calumnies "immania accusationum, immo calumniarum capita."

heinous sins; he was a hideous defender rather than a reprover of fornication; he was a jesting violator of fasting and abstinence; he was insatiable of riches acquired by simony, for the advancement of his relations; he condemned ecclesiastical ceremonies and all holy things; he was a calumniator of prelates and the religious orders; he was guilty of blind implacable hatred against the King and the kingdom of France; he was the fomenter of rebellion against the majesty of the King. In confirmation of these charges he cited the forged indictment of William Nogaret against the Pope, and boldly placed his hand on the Book of the Gospels, swearing solemnly to the truth of all the charges. Silence reigned in the hall; even the clergy remained silent. De Plasian continued in a loud voice, that he was moved to these accusations not out of any hatred for Boniface, but by ardent zeal for the Faith, and by devotion to Holy Mother Church; that he appealed to a general council, to the Holy and Apostolic See, and to all those to whom it appertained, saving always the rights and honor of the Holy See. (Surely at this, methinks, the holy man should have crossed his arms on his breast, and bowed his head). Then turning towards the King, he besought him, in his quality as defender of Holy Mother Church, and of the Catholic Faith, and the prelates who should sit as judges in the council, to use their every endeavor to convoke the council. Such was the result of the first two meetings of the States.[10]

In that assembly there were five Archbishops, namely of Nicosia in Cyprus, of Rheims, of Sens, of Narbonne, of Tours; twenty-one bishops; eleven abbots, among them those of Cluny, of Premontre, and of Citeaux. These were horrified at the calumnies of Plasian, and hence they refused to be a party to the accusations; but condescending to the demands of the King and the Barons, they favored the convocation of a council, to make clearer, (as they said) the innocence of the Pope. Their words were accompanied by the ardent and usual formulas of devotion to the Holy See, and they invoked a rigorous observance of the Canons and the statutes of the Fathers. Moreover because they feared the Pope, and they had good reason

[10] Hist. du Diff. 107.

for it, in order to evade just punishment for their mighty and shameful defection, on the 15th of June they presented to the King a document with thirty-two seals attached, in which they promised him aid and favors in case Boniface proceeded against their insolent appeal. The King promised his protection to them and all who would attach themselves to his cause. And behold in the twinkling of an eye the ramparts of the Church levelled to the ground, and Episcopate enfeoffed to the King, the sacrifice of ecclesiastical liberties consummated, the Pontiff enchained by his brethren, and ignominiously betrayed to the tribunal of a Council convoked by Philip the Fair, and in which he proposed to take part.[11]

On the 24th of June an immense crowd of laymen and ecclesiastics flocked to the garden of the royal palace. The King there acknowledged his acts. He ordered the sequestration of the goods of all the prelates and other members of the clergy who were found outside of the kingdom; he published the appeal to a Council; and this was the birthday of the inviolable liberties of the Gallican Church. The royal edict was scattered profusely throughout the kingdom; and all bowed the head to this most Christian King, crying out that they appealed to a future Ecumenical Council to be convened, and to the legitimate Pope that was to be chosen. The Church of Paris appealed, the University of Paris appealed, the Friars Preachers appealed, and we know not how many others, for this most reasonable and most holy purpose of not incurring the resentment of the King.[12] Some religious of Montpellier, sustained and encouraged by Fra Raymond, their provincial, refused to appeal and were banished by Philip. The same fate befell those few others who had the courage to resist the will of the insensate despot. Such were all the Italian bishops, who were in France, and the Abbot of Citeaux, whom he imprisoned. In order that the reader may know what this appeal to a council signified, (the learned will pardon us; we write also for those ignorant of these things), it is necessary for us first to hear what a reprobate Boniface was in the eyes of the French.

[11] Personaliter intendit interesse. Nat. Alexander, Art. IV, n. 1.
[12] Hist. du. Diff. 163. "Ne indignationem Domini nostri Regis incurrere . . . . possitis."—

The news of scandalous conventicles held in France, and an appeal made to a general council and to his successor, was made known to Boniface not by the legates, but probably by some victims who escaped from the hands of Philip. Accused by an infamous calumny of the grossest depravity, he an old man, a more than octogenarian; accused of disbelieving the dogmas which he had so long and so strongly defended, he felt his heart pierced by grief, not so much through danger to his reputation, as through the excesses and irreverence of a people, which still called itself Christian and Catholic. Neither times nor circumstances permitted him to remain silent. Duty obliged him to speak, not so much to defend himself, as to show that his sovereign dignity was not lowered nor crushed by the vile slanders of a mad prince. On the 15th of August in a sermon in full consistory he cleared himself with a solemn oath of all the crimes with which he was charged in France. Then he dispatched various constitutions, one of which, in order to provide against the violence of Philip, declared that the citations to appear before the Apostolic See made to kings and emperors, or any other persons whatever, even if intercepted or not received, would have their full effect, as they would be affixed to the Apostolic Palace, and to the doors of the principal church of the place where the Papal Court then resided. It began with these words: "*Rem non novam aggredimur.*" And by two others he deprived the Doctors of the University of Paris of the faculty of teaching and conferring degrees of the licentiate and doctorship; and he reserved to himself the provision of all the vacant churches in France, until Philip would submit to the Holy See. On the 1st of September he published from Anagni for a perpetual memorial of the thing, the following: "We have "been informed of the acts committed in France on St. "John's day in the garden of the royal palace; we know "the crimes of which we have been accused; we know of "the requested convocation of a Council, and of the ap-"peal to this same council, in order to prevent us from "proceeding against the King, the barons, and the French "prelates. We know of the league entered into between "Philip and the prelates, to relieve them of all subjection "to us; we know the friendly welcome extended to Stephen

"Colonna, our enemy. Reflecting upon these things, it
"will be seen that by men, whose tongue was in mire
"whilst their eyes were fixed on Heaven, we have been
"accused of heresy, our reputation has been blackened
"with as many crimes as their imagination could invent."
"But," continues the distressed Pontiff, "when was it ever
"heard that we were tainted with heresy? Who shall
"say that our family, and all Campania whence we
"sprung, were ever suspected of such? It is certain that
"yesterday and before, as long as we were indulging him
"with favors, we were considered as Catholic by this same
"king, but to-day he covers us with infamy. Whence
"comes this sudden change? Whence this irreverence of
"a son? Let the whole world know that the remedies
"which we wished to prescribe for his correction, for the
"cure of the wounds of his sins, and the bitterness of the
"penance by which we wished to cleanse them, put in his
"hands the arms of fraud, and have cast him into the fire
"of infidelity. Certainly we are greater than a Bishop
"of Milan, and a king of France is less than a Valentinian
"Augustus; yet this humble and Catholic emperor was not
"ashamed to submit, as a sinner, to the bishop of Milan,
"and to accept, the remedies which the charity of the
"holy bishop had offered. But Philip, this new Sen-
"nacherib tossing his head in derision, let him tremble at
"the words addressed to Sennacherib:—' Whom dost thou
"dishonor? Whom dost thou blaspheme? Against whom
"hast thou raised thy proud face and voice? Against the
"Holy One of Israel.'—This holy one of Israel is the
"Vicar of God, the successor of Peter, to whom was said:
"*Thou art Peter and upon this rock I will build my*
"*Church, and the gates of Hell shall not prevail against*
"*it; and whatsoever thou shalt bind upon earth shall be*
"*bound in Heaven.*"—Hence he who will not follow the
"bark of Peter will be lost in the storm, and he who fol-
"lows should submit to the orders of the pilot. Lately
"in his letters he called us most holy Father in Christ;
"now whereas the voice of conscience and the obligation
"of our pastoral office will not allow us to defer correc-
"tion any longer, this well-beloved but vain son, puffed
"up and arrogant, rebels against us, and adds to former,
"new and viler abuse. What! Has the state of the Church

"changed? Has the authority of the Roman Pontiffs "sunk into the mire, that this way will henceforth be "wide open to kings and princes? In a short course of "time it would occur that to escape the chastisements of "the Roman Pontiff to humble his sovereign power, he "would be treated as a heretic, as soon as he raised his "hand to keep them in bounds. Prompt must be the reme- "dies for such contagious errors; promptly must the "sword be drawn to suppress the wicked example, other- "wise kings and princes at each tightening of the rein, "would not refrain from blaspheming the Sovereign Pon- "tiff, and appealing to the convocation of councils with- "out a head. Punishment must be promptly given, if all "hope of repentance is lost, so that God may not demand "their blood from our hands."—These were the last words that were uttered by the mouth of Boniface.[13]

On the 8th of September Boniface published finally the bull of excommunication against Philip, and the first words were the following: "Seated by divine dispensa- "tion on the high throne of Peter, we hold the place of "Him to whom the Father said: Thou art my son, this "day have I begotten thee. Ask of me and I will give thee "as a heritage, and place in thy power the utmost parts "of the earth; thou shalt rule them with a rod of iron, and "shall break them in pieces like a potter's vessel."—And this to admonish kings, and teach the judges of the earth; Then he mentioned the faults of Philip, and excommunicated him, and ordered the Papal Bull to be affixed to the doors of the Church of Anagni.

The reader will observe, that even if Philip and all the crowd of courtiers, clerics and laymen, had erred in nothing but in an appeal to a Council, he deserved to be excommunicated, because in breaking with the Pontiff, he fell into schism and dragged with him into the abyss the entire Church of France. Certain authors, theologians or lawyers, we know not how to call them, have often disputed the question of an appeal from the Pope to a council, and have been divided as to whether the one is superior to the other, from which opinion is derived the other of the legitimacy or illegitimacy of these appeals.

[13] See document Q.

We shall repeat here what we have said elsewhere on another point, namely that we do not wish to swell the ranks of either one of the two parties in dispute; but rather turning aside we prefer to ask human reason, what teachings flow from this truth: that the true Church of Christ has a supreme head, who is the Vicar of Christ himself. The two parties agree on this truth, and how then do they arrive at opposite consequences? The reader will see this in the explanation we propose to give, not as a theologian or a jurist, but only as a reasonable man.

The fallibility of judges in every society concedes the right of appeal to a superior tribunal. But the necessity of not arresting the course of justice, and the fear of destroying the force and dignity of the laws, has placed a necessary limit to successive appeals, and has constituted a judge from whom there is no possible appeal, and whenever done, this appeal is considered an open rebellion against the laws. This supreme judge then should be invested with permanent authority, and always ready to receive the appeals, so that injustice be not allowed to triumph, nor power to languish in a scandalous inaction through the uncertainty of law and the want of a decision. In fact, not to go out of France, if a Frenchman injured in his goods or rights by a sentence of the King would have appealed to a tribunal or judge higher than the King himself, Philip certainly would have imposed silence on this rash appellant by delivering him to the gibbet. For by the fact of appeal he would have questioned the title of the Prince as the sovereign head of the kingdom, and would have robbed him of his power. Now a Catholic, who of his own free will is a Catholic, freely believing that the Church is a human society endowed by God in its ruling body with an infallible authority, although the individuals charged with its direction may be subject to error, if on account of this fallibility this Catholic recognizes that he and his coreligionists have the right of appeal to a superior judge, then likewise he ought to believe that there is in the Church also a supreme judge, before whom this right resolves itself into blind submission. So far the opposing theologians agree. But they commence to separate as soon as they undertake to decide who is this supreme judge. Some hold he is the sovereign Pontiff, while others say it is a future council.[14] But we think that in the opinion of the latter there is a contradiction. He who appeals, submits himself and the judge, with whom he is dissatisfied, to the judge to whom he appeals; therefore before the council, the appellant and the Pontiff are equally amenable, and in this condition the Pontiff will be and will not be at the same time the supreme Pastor of the Church. If, at the first cry of appeal he lowers himself to the condition of party, how can he at the same time raise the voice of pastor and sovereign judge to convoke an assembly of pastors who could not stir if he were silent? Besides a future council to be convoked, (we speak of a general council), is wanting in the quality and principal characteristic of a sovereign judge of appeal, that is to say, it is not invested with an authority permanent and uninterrupted which permits it to reply to the first request of the appellant. A council is a very uncertain tribunal, and events sometimes render it impossible. A plague, a war and other circumstances which would hinder a convocation of bishops, would close for a long time this tribunal to the appellant; and in the meantime the authority of the Church would remain mute and uncertain, the laws would be violated, and crime would go unpunished. If then the opinion of appealing to a council was true, either the bishops would be obliged to remain perpetually in session in order to judge and define, or the faithful be ever fluctuating on points of faith and morals. But Christ established the bishops to rule the particular churches, and not to form permanent councils. He has constituted a judge, who, by the universality of his power, sits at the pinnacle of the Church, and arrests the course of ascending appeals, and he is the Sovereign Pontiff.

If someone, alarmed at the human peccability of this judge and forgetting that he lives among men and not angels, would wish to appeal to a higher tribunal, we would advise him for the love of God and of reason to submit in the same manner that he would submit to a civil prince through fear of the halter or guillotine. Hence, in that which concerns Boniface, Philip did not

[14] This work was written before the Vatican Council, in which the question who is the supreme judge was forever settled.—Translator's note.

appeal to a Council, but he himself judged and condemned the Pontiff. He invoked the Council and the future legitimate Pope, because he judged Boniface whom he already considered a false Pope. Now, this sentence of the illegitimacy of the Papacy of Boniface, from whom did it emanate? If it came from a legitimate tribunal, why appeal to a Council, whence it might emanate? If on the contrary from a illegitimate tribunal, that is to say, from the assembly of the Louvre, it should have judged and condemned Philip, and by no means Boniface, who in the opinion of these same Gallicans, did not cease to be the legitimate Pope, until pronounced so by an unappealable tribunal. Among the defenders of Philip, Bossuet was an appellant. Once there lived in Italy a King called Theodoric, a Goth, and consequently considered a barbarian, an Arian in religion, beset by the followers of the anti-pope Lawrence, who accused Symmachus, the legitimate Pope of heinous crimes, and besought the King to send a bishop to inquire into the affairs of the Pope. The King sent on this mission, Peter bishop of Altina. But Symmachus convoked a synod of all the bishops of Italy, not for the sake of being judged, but of being solemnly vindicated. The Arian king coöperated actively in this convocation, and admonished the bishops that they were assembled precisely because he did not wish to intrude in the affairs of the Church. When they were all assembled before him, they boldly asked him why they were summoned, they who were so infirm and so worn out by years. The Arian replied: "To establish the innocence of Symmachus by your judgment." Strangely surprised, the holy prelates protested that they could not be called together except by the order of that Pope who was accused, and pleaded their incompetence to judge his Apostolic see, which was above them. But reassured by Symmachus, who appeared among them, that it was he who assembled them, they immediately restored the Pontiff to the dignity of which he had been deprived by the Schismatics,[15] and they would not even examine the charges against him, leaving it to himself whether to answer or not the complaints of his enemies. Theodoric, informed of the facts, approved of them

---

[15] Council Rom. apud. Labbe, Tom. 5, concil. coll. 501–502.

fully, and pronounced this sentence which should be engraved on the crown of all the kings of the earth: *"In "ecclesiastical affairs I have no other right but reverence."* [16] These Italians bishops came out of the sanctuary, and not from the royal court; and this prince although a heretic, had however a deep sense of justice and right. We offer this explanation as pertinent to the appeal of the French to a general council.

Philip was aware that he could lodge the cry of an appeal, but could not assemble a general council to receive him as an appellant. The Church is not confined to the frontiers of France. Wherefore if the French bishops were dragged to a council by the royal satellites, notwithstanding the silence and without the order of the pontiff, the remainder of the episcopate could not be summoned; and then Philip would have to be contented with his council in the garden of the Louvre. He wished to seize a right, but he found in his hands the sword, which is the right of force, and he resolved to use it. He entered into a diabolic counsel with Nogaret and Sciarra Colonna, a most profligate wretch, in which a nefarious crime was planned, which we would not have the courage to narrate, were it not that others had done so previously.

A handful of satellites sent by Philip crossed the Alps into Italy. At their head marched Nogaret, Du Plasian and Sciarra Colonna, animated by the same fury of the King, and thirsting for revenge. To hide their purpose they falsely announced that they had come to negotiate a peace between the Pope and Philip. Believing that the money they carried was insufficient, they brought with them royal letters of credit on the Petruccis, Florentine bankers.[17] So true is it that it is in the destiny of our unfortunate country, that the foreign treacheries of which it is the victim, have been bought by gold, and achieved by the treason of her own children. They arrived in Tuscany, and assembled near Siena in the castle of Staggia, the property of Musaccio Franzese, who had come from France, says Villani,[18] to serve as guide for Charles, and by his counsels had powerfully contributed to the ruin of affairs at Florence. Although the authors who be-

[16] "Nec aliquid ad se prater reverentiam de ecclesiasticis negotiis pertinere." . . . . , [17] Rossi, Life of Boniface. [18] Book 8, chap 48.

THE OUTRAGE AT ANAGNI, BONIFACE VIII AND HIS ASSAILANTS.

lieved Musaccio to be French are contradicted by Baillet,[19] we are not allowed to follow their opinion, owing to the clear and precise terms of Villani. In that castle a wicked council was held; and there is not doubt that the death of Boniface was plotted. From the height of that fortress the dastardly satellites of Philip of France, took occasion to plan their crime and prepared the means. Three of their accomplices John Mouchet, Thier d'Hiricon, and James di Gesserin, traversed the cities of the patrimony of St. Peter to sound the dispositions of the people, and prepare their minds in favor of the Kings, whence they would be less amazed at what was about to happen. They called in aid the Ghibellines; they won over the wicked by money, and they quieted the good with the lying pretext of coming as ambassadors of peace. The sons of John of Cessano, imprisoned by Boniface; those of Maffeo of Anagni; Rinaldo of Supino, governor of Ferentino, and other barons of the province of Campania, offered their services to the French. While still dispersed through Tuscany there remained the dishonorable soldiers of Charles of Valois, called into Italy at so great a price, and with promises by Boniface, not having anything better to do they offered their services to Nogaret to cooperate in his horrible sacrilege; and those arms so dearly bought for the defence of the Holy See, now are turned against the pontifical breast of Boniface. A terrible proof that the assistance of a stranger is always fatal to those who seek it in their own home.

Nogaret had at his disposal a good number of soldiers. Sciarra had collected three hundred cavalry, and some companies of infantry, to which were added two hundred more of cavalry, detached from the army of Valois; and the number in all was about eight hundred armed men. The gold of France flowed at Anagni, where the Pontiff was holding his court; and this shameful motive power of so many actions there exercised its fatal influence on hearts. Many of the chief men of the town, some cardinals of the Ghibelline party, the very domestics and servants of the Pope entered into the designs of the conspirators. Unrelenting history should mention among these second-

[19] Hist. de Demelez, page 211.

ers, Richard of Siena, and Napoleon Orsini; she should tie them to the pillory and dishonor them before all ages; loaded with benefits by Boniface they betrayed him with the most barefaced ingratitude. It is easy to explain the mystery and the rapidity with which corruption had crept into the pontifical palace, when we reflect that elective governments greatly arouse ambitions and the love of novelty; that the inflexible severity of Boniface had perhaps restrained some wrongdoers too much; and finally the most holy counsels of religions and honesty, are powerless in factional hatreds.

Thirsting the most for vengeance, and knowing better the locality, Sciarra Colonna with three hundred cavalry and a small company of infantry, was the first to advance, and he secretly reconnoitred the environs of Anagni.[20] Boniface noticed nothing for the reason that he did not believe that the bloody era of Nero, in which the Pontiffs were persecuted by the sword, could possibly return. During the night, the gates of the town were opened and the French entered Anagni, displaying the banner of the lilies of France, and shouting: " Death to Boniface, long live the King of France." The people of Anagni betraying this Pontiff, their countryman, followed them, and repeated their cries. The house of Peter Gaetani, nephew of the Pope was taken and plundered. On the 7th of September at the break of day, the brutal satellites rushed against the doors of the palace, where a venerable old man, protected by the sanctity of his office of supreme Pastor, was quietly sleeping. The noise of the tumult, and the influence of money had left his palace deserted. The Cardinals fled in disguise to save their lives; only two remained, whose courage showed itself greater than this unheard of and terrible misfortune; they were Nicholas Boccassini, Bishop of Ostia, and Peter of Spain, Bishop of Sabina. Thus aroused and startled by the approach of danger, the troubled Pontiff looked around and found himself almost alone. But he remained himself, and that sufficed. He asked a truce from Sciarra, and he obtained only nine hours, during which he strove to prevail upon the inhabitants of Anagni to liberate him, but in vain.

[20] Ferreti, Vic. Hist. Book 3.

Then, he demanded of the proud Colonna what he wanted of him. Thirsting for vengeance, and gratified at the plight of the Pontiff, he replied in writing: "Let my "brother, my uncle, and all the members of our family be "restored to their former rank, and let you renounce the "Papacy." The noble Pontiff refused; then he remained silent, his heart being moved by the thought of the extremities to which the cruel Sciarra would be carried. In fact the French despairing of succeeding in their purpose by intimidation, furiously had recourse to violence.

The doors of the Pontifical palace had been closed, and fortified as it was it resisted the attacks of the assailants. But as it was joined to the Cathedral of Anagni, in order to enter, they opened a way through the Church, which they set on fire. Gaetani, a nephew of Boniface, bore the first shock, but after having fought courageously he and his retainers were obliged to surrender. The rebels advanced, leaving behind the profaned cathedral; the flames which were consuming it, cast a weird light on the bodies, lying dead around, of those who perished in the fray, among whom was the Archbishop elect of Strigonia. The evening of this infernal day arrived; and the darkness of the night favored this horde of robbers who invested the palace. The venerable Pontiff retired to his apartments, and there awaited death. Some tears trickled down his cheeks; but scarcely had he heard the windows and doors of his palace broken, and had seen the light of the conflagration, than feeling ashamed of his tears, he dried them, and said to two ecclesiastics who were beside him: "Now since I have been betrayed like Jesus Christ, and "delivered into the hands of my enemies to be put to "death, I desire and wish to die as Sovereign Pontiff." And after saying this, he put on the pontifical cloak; he placed the tiara on his head, he held the holy keys in his hands, together with the cross which he kissed and pressed to his heart, in order that he might draw from it that power and strength which Christ gave to it to overcome error and injustice. So clothed in the Pontifical robes, and prepared to meet death, he ascended his throne and there sat; the two cardinals shielded him with their robes. There was not found even one Italian! The white locks of the venerable old man; the consciousness of the liberty of the Church, for which he was to die a martyr; the beauty of this great soul, as depicted on his countenance, and in his entire personality; and that mysterious and touching dignity which surrounds the man on the brink of the grave, restrained for an instant the arm of the angry Sciarra, who, after having battered down the door, entered the apartment of the Pope to strike him in that tremendous majesty. The rough and proud Nogaret followed him, and with the insolence of a butcher, said to the Pontiff: "We are come to lead you captive to Lyons, to de-"prive you of the dignity of Pope, in a council to be con-"vened in that city to judge you;" and then he dragged him violently from his throne. Boniface replied to him with incredible courage: "Here is my head, here is my "neck; I, a Catholic, legitimate Pontiff, Vicar of Jesus "Christ, am willing cheerfully to be deposed and con-"demned by the Patarini. I long to die for the Faith of "Jesus Christ, and for the Church." These words were more loud-sounding than a thunderbolt to that ruffian. Boniface was unarmed; but a superhuman strength shone in his eyes and appeared in his words, that strength of God, who never abandons his ministers in time of persecution. Ah! would to God that people were always convinced of this, and never dishonor the venerable dignity of the priesthood, by stooping to the great ones of this earth to beg for that support which is so frail, that an infuriated people shatters it at every toss of the head. Nogaret, startled and ashamed, because the word Patarini recalled the memory of his grandfather who was burned as a heretic, could make no reply.[21] But the brutal Sciarra found words and means worthy of him; he loaded the venerable Pontiff with abuse, and went so far as to strike him in the face with his glove.[22] Despairing of subduing

[21] Baillet. 225.

[22] Violently opposed though he was to Boniface, Dante relented at its contemplation, and indignantly sang of his enemy:

"Entering Alagna; lo the fleur-de-lis,
And in his vicar, Christ a captive led;
I see him mocked a second time;—again
The vinegar and gall produced I see;
And Christ himself twixt living robbers slain."

Wright's translation. Purgatory, canto XX.

the indomitable spirit of the Pope by force, these ruffians left him guarded by soldiers, and they returned to their followers who were sacking the palace. The treasury was plundered; the relics of the saints were scattered and the precious reliquaries stolen; and the archives and privileges of the Roman Church were torn to shreds. For three days this whirlwind ravaged the Papal palace. During all this time Boniface took no food of any kind, either because distress of mind over these misfortunes removed the desire for it, or because his jailers desiring his death, refused to give him any. The inhabitants of Anagni had committed a sacrilegious betrayal. A man, their countryman, the universal father of the faithful, had been not only abandoned by them, but was also perfidiously sold to his enemies, at a time when, sojourning among them, he confided in their care and fidelity. Treason needs no avenger; it is itself its own judge and its own executioner. The third day of the French invasion, the inhabitants of Anagni, aroused by Cardinal Fieschi di Lavagno, were seized with a lively and sudden feeling of repentance and shame, and in view of the crime of which they were guilty, they flew to arms, and rushed against the French, crying out: "Long live the Pope, death to the traitors." Many were slain; all were put to flight; a great part of the treasure was recovered; and the standard of the fleur-de-lis was trailed in the mire.

The tempest having subsided, and those robbers dispersed, the venerable Pontiff presented himself at the head of the stairs leading to the palace worn and exhausted, and with serene countenance spoke words of pardon and of peace. He pardoned all those who had betrayed him, and those who had held him a prisoner, and the Cardinals Richard of Siena, and Napoleon Orsini, and even Rinaldo of Anagni, the chief and leader of the domestic treason, whom the people brought to him, bound in chains with his sons. That soul which had been able to stand like a rock in the midst of daggers, knew how to resist faultlessly the fury of revenge.

When the news of the dastardly crime at Anagni reached Rome, the inhabitants arose in great indignation at the injury done to the Pontiff, and forthwith sent four hundred knights under the leadership of Matthew and James

Orsini. Under the protection of these, he departed, leaving Anagni plunged in grief. The inhabitants besought him not to leave and allow them to have time to efface their infamy by unequivocal marks of repentance. When he arrived in Rome, he was met by a vast concourse of people who came to fête and applaud him, so that the entry and reception partook of the nature of that of a conqueror; and yet the Pontiff was returned from the greatest tribulation, in which he appeared humiliated and vanquished. This teaches us that the ruin of the material force of the Church, far from weakening her, on the contrary strengthens and elevates her power in the hearts of the people. Cardinal Napoleon Orsini followed him; and the Pontiff, in order to show that he had sincerely pardoned him, graciously invited him to his table. But that boorish man, fancying that the Pope may have been enfeebled not merely in body but also in mind by the injuries inflicted on him, had the audacity to say to him with a proud air: "that it was at length time for him to "restore the Colonnas to favor; and grant all that had "been taken by force." It is certain that this language in view of the recent crimes of Sciarra Colonna, was a piece of outrageous insolence. Boniface answered the haughty Orsini by a refusal. He would be willing to pardon, but without compulsion, as his dignity of sovereign demanded. And at that time we believe there happened that which Ferrettus of Vincenza, and the Chronicler of Parmo narrate, that the Orsinis held the Pope in such rigorous seclusion, that it served as a second imprisonment to him.

Boniface perceived, from the audacity of the Cardinal, that the scandals of Anagni had greatly injured his authority; that the anger of Philip not sufficiently appeased, would become worse; and that the Orsinis also would offer their services to this prince. Hence he wrote a letter to Charles II, King of Naples, beseeching him to come to his aid; but the letter was intercepted by Cardinal Orsini. These new injuries on the part of the Cardinal, greatly favored by him, and generously received at Anagni, pierced his heart, and convinced him that he plotted his death. He was so grieved thereby, that he was at the point of death. A horrible fact, according to Ferretus, made memorable the last moments of Pope Boniface, who died, says this historian, in the transports of despair. He narrates that this great Pontiff, having become mad by a dose of poison administered to him, and having sent away his servant John Campano, shut himself up alone in his room, gnawed his staff, dashed his head against the wall, so as to imbrue his gray hairs with blood, and then strangled himself with the bedclothes, calling on Beelzebub. When we consider that Boniface had reached an extreme old age, and was altogether broken by misfortune; that being shut up alone in his room, there were not witnesses to bring to Ferretus those disgusting details; and that the death of this magnanimous Pope is quite differently narrated by eye-witnesses, we do not know for what sort of readers Sismondi believed he was writing, when he spoiled his history with the fables of Ferretus.[23] It is beyond doubt that Boniface died a peaceful death in the Vatican Palace. The testimony of Cardinal Stephaneschi, who was present, and the process afterwards drawn up on the acts of this Pontiff, admit of no doubt.[24] Eight cardinals and other honorable personages surrounded the bed of the dying Pope. In a feeble voice he made to them a profession of faith according to the custom of his predecessors, affirming that he had always lived in the Catholic faith, and in it he wished to die. Then fortified by the Holy Viaticum, on the 7th of October, thirty-five days after his imprisonment at Anagni he surrendered to God that soul wearied after the long combat it endured for the rights of the Church, saddened by the wickedness of man, but unconquered, and unsullied in its grandeur. His body was borne to the tomb, which he while living had prepared in the Vatican Basilica, near to the altar of St. Andrew. His obsequies were Papal. Among the many illustrious personages who were present was seen Charles II of Naples. He had come too late to succor the besieged Pope while living, but opportunely to assist at the honors

[23] History of the Italian Republics.
[24] . . . . . . "Lecto prostratus anhelus
Procubuit, fassusque fidem, curamque professus
Romanae Ecclesiae, Christo tunc redditur almus
Spiritus, et saevi nescit jam judicis iram,
Sed mitem placidamque patris cui credere fas est."

shown after death. In fact when we reflect that Heaven had punished the too great human confidence of the Popes in the French house of Anjou by the ingratitude and secret plots of this family, we understand how necessary it was that a prince of Anjou should bear to the sepulchre Pope Boniface, in whose breast, as in a sanctuary of apostolic stability, the civil Roman Pontificate was buried. So Charles came rather to the funeral honors of that Pontificate, than to those of the Pontiff.[25]

During the life of princes, fear restrains the opinion of people. But when they are laid away in the tomb, the doors of their palaces being open to the people permit them to examine and judge their actions. Now liberty at this time too unrestrained compromises the truth. For we know that sovereigns on their departure from this world leave in the custody of their court a secret or mystery which reveals itself only to the severe and patient investigation of history. Hence this was the cause of so many and unrestrained judgments at the tomb of Boniface. The resistance with which he opposed all manner of injustices, ceasing at his death, opened a way to resentment which furiously assailed his memory and oppressed it. The chroniclers of the time were not historians; their tendencies being in favor of either the Guelph or Ghibelline party, they portrayed the actions of this Pontiff according to their own point of view, and according as public rumor expressed them, everyone knows transforms everything when it is allowed to run unchecked. Nor were there philosophers, strong enough to arrest and grasp with the arms of criticism, the truth which was distorted. Philip the Fair in France, the Colonnas in Italy, the proud Roman patriciate, and all those who had experienced the strong temperament of Boniface in anger, allowed the stone of the sepulchre to be lowered upon the head, and upon this they did not raise a complaint, but a cry of execration and vengeance.

They were ashamed of their acts of violence by the aid of which they shortened the life of this Pontiff, and they found it necessary to dishonor his memory in order to exculpate themselves, and give to their wickedness an ap-

[25] Here there is no question of the spiritual Pontificate, which is perpetual like the Church.

pearance of a just defense. During all his Pontificate Boniface aimed at nothing else but to preserve intact the rights of the Church not only in the sanctuary, but also in the heart of civil society itself, over the temporal destinies of which he could no more cease to preside than the soul over the purely material functions of the body. Hence for this reason he was a most valiant defender of her interior and exterior rights, and every prince who overstepped his bounds to meddle in the affairs of the Church, or beyond his own authority, always found Boniface standing before him as a rock to impede his progress. For this reason he was a zealous preserver of the sacred patrimonies, and of the jurisdiction of the Church; he was an indefatigable peacemaker; vigilant in preventing quarrels, and in ending them by agreements, in which he offered himself as mediator in his quality of pastor and universal father, rather than by war which wastes the goods and the blood of the people. He was an inexorable reformer of princes who founded their perversity on the weakness of their subjects. The proof of our assertion is that some kings, and some cities trusted spontaneously to his judgment the settlement of their differences, and his decisions were always models of justice. No other pope showed such zeal as Boniface for the propagation of the Gospel among barbarous and distant nations; he enriched churches, especially the Vatican and Lateran basilicas; he founded new academies, assigning them revenues; he waged wars to preserve Sicily, at that time a patrimony of the Church. Now to bring all these great affairs to a successful issue there was needed large pecuniary resources. As his life was full and entirely composed of these honorable actions, he was always open to contradictions, and those who would wish to attack him, would have to find in these actions themselves the arms with which to strike him. And hence besides his simoniacal intrusion into the Papacy, his assassination of St. Peter Celestine, his zeal for the rights of the Church was called thirst for empire; his punishment of those whom he wished to despoil was called tyranny; his apostolic firmness was foolish pride; his opposition to the excesses of Philip, a passion for a universal monarchy, and the spirit of prudence which he displayed in gathering riches, gross avarice. But Boniface appears under far different colors from the facts in this book which we have dedicated to him, and the moral portrait which we have traced here is admirably confirmed by some contemporaneous historians and especially by Villani.

Boniface was a man most remarkable in his time for magnanimity; and as the office which he filled was great, he administered it so attentively and so energetically, that he identified himself with it. And as the estimate which he had of this ministry did not allow him to endure words or deeds against it, so possession of it aroused within him every human passion to resist these attacks. For this reason equal to every other Pope in the greatness of his conception of the Roman Pontificate, he surpassed them all by the ardor with which he displayed his power. Knowing that the Pontifical edifice is not supported by material means like the thrones of other princes, he raised from the crowd, for the sake of using them, those whose mental acumen and learning brought them to his notice, and he loaded them with favors and riches to attach them to him. The people were accustomed to distinguish power by the splendor of its forms; he presented himself to them in the glitter of worldly pomp; and as he was superior to kings by reason of his double power direct and indirect so he wished to surpass them in the outward signs of authority. As his views were so were his actions. In the times when he lived princes were ashamed of the unaffected piety of their infancy and their ancient inability to govern the people, so that whereas in former times they laid even their crown on the altar of St. Peter, they withdrew it in these times with great violence, and in withdrawing it they shook the foundations of the Church. It was by reason of this that Boniface appeared angry and proud; that his voice resembled that of a roaring lion; and that his shoulders were as of bronze to sustain the tottering edifice in guard of which he had been placed. Wonderful in his quickness of perception, in comparing and in judging momentous affairs; very clever and prudent in the way of conducting them, he employed, in their order, and with an unbending spirit, the means capable of assuring success. Most courageous against others, he was not weak regarding himself; so that during the impulse of passion and anger, his heart not only remained unmoved but even opened itself to generosity, of which the pardons at Anagni are of proof. Profoundly versed in the science of law both human and divine, he interpreted them with eloquence in his discourses, with elegance in his writings, and he defended them with a courage superior to all. His haughty and disdainful nature, his many and important occupations, the vigilance and hatred of his enemies had humanely rendered him chaste, while religion made him pure. He celebrated mass regularly and with great piety; and the tremendous sanctity of the sacrifice made him shed abundant tears;[26] it preserved him from those stains with which his enemies in accusing him dishonored rather themselves than him. His tall figure corresponded to his grandeur of soul; his limbs were robust and in perfect harmony; and his every movement and pose revealed a man made for the throne. His forehead was high and broad; his cheeks full, and the interior majesty of his soul disclosed itself in the calm severity of his gaze, and his countenance. In a word, from qualities of both mind and body he was what Petrarch judged him to be: "The wonder of the world."[27]

The common people are credulous; the strange and the impossible arouse their eager curiosity. Many perhaps believed on the authority of Ferretus that the proud Pontiff lay in his sepulchre with gnawed wrists and a fractured skull; and perhaps no one could approach that sepulchre without a certain feeling of horror, on thinking that it enclosed so much pride and despair.

Three hundred and two years had elapsed since the death of Boniface, when Paul V captivated by the gigantic project which Pope Julius II had devised, of raising a basilica over the tomb of the Apostles, entered upon the execution of it. We could pardon Julius for destroying an ancient and venerable church through love of the great; he had engaged Bramante and Michelangelo to make his thought magnificent. But Paul would ever be held inexcusable if he had taken the initiative, because Bernini and Borromini were not the men to reproduce, by the power of genius, that mysterious beauty which ever sits

[26] Justinian. in Chron. Riccar. Ab. S. Just in Reg S. Ben. See Document 2 R.   [27] De otio Religiosorum.

as queen over the rugged works of our ancestors. But the impetuous de la Rovere had already demolished a great part of the ancient Basilica to build that striking cupola, the sight of which would serve to frighten the barbarians whom he wished to drive out of Italy; and so Paul V was forced to complete the destruction of the ancient part so that the new would not be left unfinished. Wherefore in the first year of his Pontificate on the 26th of September, Paul after having obtained in a consistory the advice of the Cardinals and skilled architects, resolved to demolish that which remained of the ancient basilica. We do not know whether a certain remorse of conscience for that irreverent violence to ancient walls determined the architects to say that there existed a deviation of five palms between the top and the base of the walls, that the timbers had rotted, and that the roof and the entire edifice were threatened with ruin; or whether the danger was real and certain. However, it is a fact that on the 28th of the same month Cardinal Pallotta, archpriest of St. Peter's ordered all the altars in the great nave of the Basilica to be removed. These works of removal, always detrimental, brought the workmen to the chapel of the Gaetani family. The altar was surmounted by a Gothic tabernacle of exquisite design which Boniface had ordered made: (*cuspidum operis Germanici*); the forms were sharp and severe, and the top was in shape like an arrow. The chapel itself had been built by Boniface VIII after the design of the architect Arnolpho, who left his name inscribed in it. A remarkable picture in mosaic by Charles Conti contributed to its ornamentation, in which was seen, in those holy forms and styles now a long time lost, the blessed Virgin, at one side of whom was St. Peter, presenting Boniface to her,[28] and at the other St. Paul with St. Boniface. The entire work was roughly carried away and afterwards lost. The tomb was placed on the wall in such a way as to be always visible to the priest who celebrated. It was of marble of the most unpretending kind, such as it is still seen in the Vatican Basilica. This mausoleum having been built during the life of Boniface, we consider it right to observe that in it there is found no indication of

[28] The Pontiff was probably kneeling, and of smaller proportions, according to the custom of the times.

TOMB OF BONIFACE VIII IN THE CRYPT OF ST. PETER'S.

an immoderate love of display. It is a simple sarcophagus on which reposes the statue of the Pontiff in a sleeping attitude, and clothed in the priestly vestments; the head is covered by the tiara, and the hands are joined in the form of a cross and rest on the lower part of the stomach. Two cushions slightly elevate his head; a coverlet placed under the prostrate figure and displaying the coat of arms of the Gaetani family, falls in natural and graceful folds over the face of the monument. Who would not have imagined to find on that sepulchre signs and emblems indicating the boundless ambition and pride of him whose remains lay within? As soon as the despoilers reached the tomb, they stopped, as they wished the Gaetani family to be present at the opening. The three Gaetani brothers, Anthony, Archbishop of Capua, Boniface, Bishop of Cessano, and Peter, duke of Sermoneta, were present with all the canons of the Basilica and other prelates. The cover having been raised a wooden coffin was found within which contained the bones of the Pontiff, and this was opened on October 26th, the anniversary of his death. All present were struck with wonder at seeing how well preserved the corpse was, and how lifelike and sound the flesh looked. The head was not denuded of skin, the upper and lower membranes of the eyelids and the membranes of ears were intact; the cheeks were full; and with the exception of two teeth lost during life all the other teeth were firmly set in the gums; the nose and the lips alone showed marks of decay. The countenance was severe. His body was seven palms and three quarters in length; his hands were long and so beautiful, "as to fill with admiration all who saw them," the nails on them had grown; and from the nerves and the color of the veins, one would believe them full of life, and that blood still circulated through them. All the vestments were entire and well preserved. The border of the alb, representing different subjects taken from Holy Writ, was composed of a rich and wonderful embroidery in silk and gold. Such was the state of the body of Boniface. We have entered upon these details, not because we considered marvellous the perfect preservation of the corpse of Boniface; for that could happen either by the body not being decomposed and the humors vitiated by a long illness, and by a perfect exclusion from the tomb of the air, the principal cause of putrefaction. But we wished to show by the integrity of the skull and the fingers, by the calm pose of the entire corpse, how very calm also had been the departure of the soul which once vivified it.

Men ordinarily are gracious to tombs; their hatred ends there and is appeased, and vengeance is disarmed; because those who rest there become something sacred. But such were not the hatred and vengeance of Philip the Fair. He had been struck by a spiritual sword, not of a Gaetani, but of a Sovereign Pontiff, who although dead, had left as a heritage to his successors, the duty of punishing, as an example to others, the French prince, a violator of the sacred rights of the Church, and a brutal persecutor of her head. The thundering voice of Boniface was silent. but the scandal of Anagni cried for vengeance, and Philip wished to stifle that cry. So after having cast upon the agents of his fury the culpability, from which they were to be purified by some spiritual penance, he intended to present himself before the new Pope and the council, not as guilty and deserving of condemnation, but as a man injured in his honor and in his rights, to whom a just reparation was due. Not only did he hope to succeed in his purpose, but he believed it certain upon the arrival of the messengers coming in all haste to apprise him of the death of Boniface. This information filled him with joy, and for the time to come unopposed, he promised himself a most brilliant future. But if the rumor then current is not false, a certain Bishop of Morienne met in the Alps the messenger bringing the news of the taking of Boniface and by a sudden and divine inspiration broke forth into cries; "Alas! Philip will rejoice greatly over this infor-"mation, but his joy will be followed by a great cause for "sorrow. Ah! that judgment will fall on his head and "that of his children." If the Bishop whether humanly or supernaturally spoke the truth in those words, the course of this history will prove.[29]

The nine days of mourning having passed, the Cardinals assembled for the election of a new Pope. Still terrified by the misfortune of Boniface, they felt their spirits were too feeble to hold the reins of government which Boniface

[29] John Villani, Book 8, c. 64.

had managed with so much vigor; their hearts palpitated between the apostolic resolution of continuing the work of the magnanimous deceased, and the arguments of prudence, which counselled peaceful concessions. By firmness one courted martyrdom; by concessions a not distant invasion,. and the enslavement of the entire Catholic priesthood would ensue. If, through the imperfections and weakness of humanity, ambitions for the tiara were aroused in that assembly, they should have been curbed by the thought that he who would be chosen to direct the bark of Peter, should descend ignominiously from the heights of the pontifical dignity where Boniface had courageously held it, that is to say, either make criminal arrangements with Philip, or suffer the violence of some other Nogaret. After one day of conclave, all the suffrages united on Cardinal Nicholas Boccasini, Bishop of Ostia, a religious of the order of St. Dominic, who was of humble extraction, of pure morals, and of a sweet disposition. We shall not speak at length of his pontificate, nor of the one that followed, but we shall narrate only those facts which have a bearing on the affairs of Boniface. And here we are forced to remark to the reader that we enter upon an epoch far different from the ancient times, and from those which have been subject of our narration. The tragedy of Boniface put an end to that glorious era of the Papacy. Therefore such kings as Henry, Frederick Barbarossa, Manfred and Philip the Fair will not be seen again; princes restrained by the severity of command, but managed by arrangements which contain a certain equality of power. The Papacy, surrounded and defended by the moral power of the priesthood, which at first had solemnly opposed the laws, now negotiates by treaties, which prudence dictates. It did not fear martyrdom but the inefficacy of the spiritual arms despised by the people, as if Christ in placing them in the hands of his Vicars, had not thought to temper them so as not to render them useless in the lasting defence of the Church. However, in view of the prosperous situation in which the policies of government have placed the rights and the liberty of the Church, one can easily judge whether prudence has succeeded better than force.

One of the first acts of Benedict was to raise his voice

against those who pillaged the treasury of Boniface, and to threaten them with censures. He entrusted his chaplain, Bernard Riardi, with the difficult mission of recovering it. The bells were tolled, the candles were lighted, anathemas were hurled; but not one of the plunderers restored the booty.[30] The cause of the scandals continued; Nogaret still hovered around the environs of Anagni, his heart full of anger, because of the disgraceful expulsion of the French from that town. As soon as he heard of the death of Boniface, he sought Rinaldo of Supino, in the town of Ferentino, to renew his courage for new crimes, offering him men, money and royal favors. He remembered the events of Anagni, and he resolved at any cost on revenge.[31] In the meantime another messenger of Philip, Peter of Peredo, a prior, being sent into Italy to arouse the people against Boniface and fill Rome with the usual complaints against him, had arrived in the city a day before the death of the Pope. Hardly was Benedict seated on the Pontifical throne, than Peredo began to complain, in his presence and before the Cardinals, of the injury which the dead Pope had done to the Church. He related to the new Pope all that had passed in the States general; he renewed the appeals to the council and to the Pope; he entreated him to convoke a council at Lyons, or in any other place not dangerous to the French; and he concluded by execrating the memory of Boniface. The envoy did not have credential letters; and for this reason Benedict replied that he could not deliberate on the affairs in consistory, and he also made Nogaret leave Italy, with the promise of pacifying and reconciling France with the Roman Church.

Nogaret returned to France opportunely to aid Philip by his counsel, of which he was in great need. It was not prudent to wait until Benedict notified the King, according to custom, of his elevation to the Pontificate through the medium of a Nuncio. For in case this Nuncio did not come, Philip being excommunicated, Benedict would thus show clearly that he confirmed the Bulls of Boniface. It was of no value to await the coming of any Legate bearing arrangements, because it could not be foreseen with

[30] Raynaldus, no. 37.   [31] Process. p. 174 apud Baillet, p. 233.

what instructions he would be charged by Benedict; and supposing that Philip did not accept them, he would be forced to prolong the hostility against the new Pope also, from whom he expected benign concessions. Therefore, with the advice of Nogaret he anticipated Benedict by sending to him three ambassadors, Berardo, lord of Mercueil, William Plasian, lord of Vezenobre, and Peter of Bellepercho, a canon of Chartres, and a most renowned lawyer. They had the most extensive power to conclude a peace with the Pope, and a procuration from Philip to receive absolution from the censures imposed on the King, and the kingdom of France. Nogaret was to accompany them, but he could not take part in the affair of the censures, because he had been personally struck by the anathema of Boniface. But, either being afraid of the relatives of Boniface, and of the impression which the sight of him would produce on the Pontiff, or because his presence was useful to the prince, he remained in France, where he occupied himself in preparing the particulars of the suit that was to be instituted against the memory of Boniface.[32] The ambassadors departed; the French people followed them with these acclamations: "The "liberty of their country consisted in acknowledging in "the temporal matters no one superior to the king, ex-"cept God. Boniface should be declared a heretic, for "having maintained the contrary; this should be sup-"mitted to a council or the new Pope; and that his con-"demnation would justify France in the eyes of poster-"ity." In the meanwhile the French understood how advantageous it was to them that Philip had no one but God above him, when they saw what respect he had for their liberty. Benedict found himself navigating in difficult waters. He had been one of the Cardinals faithful to Boniface; the memory of that terrible night at Anagni ever present in his mind, reminded him that it would cost Philip and his ministers very little to renew the horrible acts of violence of which he had been a witness. Guided either by these fears or by prudence, he resolved to come to a peaceful settlement with Philip. But in order that by this he would not be considered as wanting in courage,

---

[32] Process. p. 174 apud. Baillet, page 239.

and his indulgence would not have the appearance of constraint, he sent to Philip the absolution from the excommunication, before the arrival of the ambassadors, and before any previous request of this prince. An act, which the fear of something worse counselled, assumed thus the appearance of generosity. On April 2nd he published two documents, one for the perpetual memorial of the thing, and the other addressed to Philip, by which he removed the censures against Philip and the church in France, and "this to avoid scandal, because it is neces-" sary to relax a little of the rigor in the interest of the " multitude. He revoked all the other acts of his predecessor against Philip, he accorded new privileges; but always excluded formally from the general favor William de Nogaret, whose absolution " we reserve to ourselves, and to the Apostolic See." Benedict also wished, in order to soften Philip, to modify the constitution "Clericis laicos," by tempering the penalties. It condemned solemnly, not only those who without permission of the Holy See, exacted subsidies from the clergy, but also those who, on request, consented to these exactions, and to the collection of tithes, and other taxes. Benedict released these latter from all penalty.

The ambassadors not having arrived as yet at Rome, these absolutions and pardons were received in the name of the King, but without deputation by William Chastenay and Hugh de Celles, two of the numerous agents whom Philip kept in Italy in order to press the affair of the council, to which he wished to appeal. Seeing that everything was progressing wonderfully well, they took with them a notary of Rome; and six days after the publication of the Bull of pardon, they went to see different Cardinals successively, in order to prevail upon them to enter into the views of the King regarding a Council. Five of the ten there declared that they were in favor of calling a council, whereas the other five would abide by the decision of the Pope. But Benedict would not hear of a Council and appeals. He had sacrificed even too much for peace.[33]

The royal envoys arrived bearing a letter from Philip

[33] Baillet, 242, 243

to the Pope. It was full of congratulations on his elevation to the Papacy; of hopes; of abuse against his predecessor; then followed excessive and hypocritical praise of Benedict. He called him a man of brilliant qualities, a mirror of virtue, a model of sanctity, a man after his own heart, who did not seek his own glory, but only that of God, the interests of the Church, and the prosperity of Christianity in the Holy Land. He recommended himself and the whole Gallican church to his Holiness. We have said that these praises were hypocritical; because if the hopes failed in their intent, Benedict would be another Boniface to him. Hypocrisy is always the most poisonous and most dangerous weapon of usurpers.[34] Benedict replied in most polite terms, striving to bring back by gentleness this prince, against whom all rigorous measures had failed. Passing over in silence Boniface and the excommunication emanating from him, he said: " Judge " of our tenderness in releasing you from all censures be- " fore you came or sent to ask it;[35] we have welcomed " with joy and benevolence your envoys and your letters. " And far from repenting of our indulgence, we feel it a " duty as Vicar of that good Shepherd, who having left " in the desert the ninety-nine sheep, goes to seek the one " hundredth, and after having found it places it joyfully " on his shoulders, in order to return it to the fold." And he concludes by recalling the example of Joas, King of Juda, who reigned gloriously and practised virtue as long as he followed the counsels of the high-priest Joad, but when he departed from them he fell into disgrace and was finally assassinated by his own servants. " Listen to your father," said he, " in order that God may strengthen your " kingdom and render it glorious." But Boniface had used similar language before he had recourse to rigor; it caused a violent death to this Pontiff and we shall see what kind of death it procured for Benedict. Any one can notice that, in all these acts, the prudent Pontiff, in pardoning the King of France, did not condemn Boniface. On the contrary the pardon granted to Philip the Fair and to France, supposes their revolt against the Apostolic

[34] Raynaldus, 1304, 8.

[35] " Tibi absenti et non petenti."—Pagi Brev. Pont. Rom. Tom. III, p. 553.

See, and the justice of the chastisements by which they had been punished. He called Philip an illustrious, a noble, a distinguished, but always a lost and a stray sheep.[36]

The Colonnas did not lose time; they exerted themselves greatly, in order to turn to their advantage such indulgent dispositions. The good Pontiff, who was clemency itself, released them from the enormous weight of excommunications, suspensions, and interdicts which they had deserved;[37] allowed them to return home, extending his indulgence so far as to restore them to their family privileges, and their civil rights. But he refused to restore to the two Cardinals the hat and the ecclesiastical benefices; and forbade the rebuilding of the fortifications of Palestrina. By these restrictions he acknowledged the Colonnas to have been truly seditious, and men dangerous to the state and Church.[38] With these favors the Colonnas showed themselves apparently satisfied yet the two deposed Cardinals did not cease their agitations. They addressed to Philip, their friend, a memorial, in which they entreated him to continue his former protection to them, to unite his efforts to theirs, in order to finish the proceedings against Boniface. " The cause of a Cardinal," they remarked, " could be tried only in an Ecumenical " Council. Leaving to the Pope the power to dispose and " banish a cardinal, is to expose to ruin the government " of the Church. The cardinals are a salutary counter- " pose to the Papal power. They form the counsel of the " Pope, they sit in judgment with him, and are members " of the same body. It is a destruction of the kingdom of " Jesus Christ to deprive the cardinals of the right and " liberty of opposition to the Pope, in cases where it is " necessary to defend truth and justice against him, and " where he would overstep the limits of his ministry. " They had been neither denounced, nor cited, nor con- " victed of any crime which merited such chastisement. " They hoped that his Majesty by his favors would obtain " in entirety for them, from Benedict, the justice which " this Pontiff had already begun to render them." [39]

[36] Namquid tantam ovem, tu es, sic Nobilem, praecepuam, et praeclaram relinquemus Pagi Brev Pont. Rom. Tom. III, p 553
[37] Preuves du Diff., page 227.   [38] Baillet, 248.   [39] Baillet, 249.

Up to the end of May, Benedict followed the inspirations of his kind and indulgent heart; but then a secret voice sounded in his heart and urged him to resume a little of that courage becoming to a Pontiff; because justice has some duties which clemency must not forget. The pardons granted were so many revocations of penalties sanctioned by Boniface when alive. But there were enormous crimes to be punished, which, from the depth of the tomb of that Pontiff cried for and deserved vengeance. We speak of those who had committed, or favored the incredible crime of Anagni. Silence and impunity would have been considered a sort of approbation.

So this excellent Pope then determined finally to act, and on June 7th [40] he wrote and published a Bull in which there was betokened the grandeur and majesty of a prophet; after having recalled the tragic event of Anagni, and named all the leading conspirators, among whom were Nogaret and Sciarra, he burst forth and allowed to escape, in his grief, some fiery words: " And these crimes
" were committed publicly and under our very eyes. . . .
" crimes of lese-majesty, of rebellion, of sacrilege, of
" felony, of theft, of rapine, the mere thought of which
" excites horror. Who would be so cruel as not to shed
" tears; so spiteful as not to be moved to compassion?
" What judge would be so negligent as not to be eager to
" proceed; or so merciful or clement as not to become
" severe? Security has been violated, immunity offended.
" One's own country has not been a protection; the do-
" mestic fireside has not been a refuge; a Sovereign Pon-
" tiff has been outraged; and with her spouse a captive,
" the Church herself has been a captive. Where hence-
" forth find a safe place? What sanctuary will be re-
" spected, after the violation of that of the Roman Pon-
" tiff? O, inexpiable crime! O, unfortunate Anagni!
" May the rain and dew fall on thee no more, but descend-
" ing on other mountains pass to the side of thee. Be-
" cause the hero has fallen; that which was invested with
" strength has been overcome under thy eyes, and thou
" couldst have prevented it. O, most wretched malefac-
" tors! In your actions you would not imitate the ex-

---

[40] Rayn., 1304. 13.

"ample of holy David, who not only refused to lay a hand "on the anointed of the Lord, although his enemy, perse- "cutor, and rival, but even ordered to be struck down by "the sword the one who had dared to do so. For it is "written: "Touch not my anointed." Inexpressible "grief! lamentable action! pernicious example! inexpi- "able fault! Intone, O Church, the mournful chant of "lamentations; let tears course down thy cheeks; and as "aiders in thy vengeance let thy sons come from afar, "and thy daughters rush to thy side."

He ended the Bull by heaping on the heads of the malefactors, and all their aiders and abettors, by favor or advice, all the censures described in the holy canons, and cited them to appear before him in the short space of twenty-two days.[41] There is a reason to believe that after so many indulgences, the malefactors considered themselves safe. But Benedict thought of them, and if he was slow in punishing them until this time, it was because he was hindered by just reasons.[42]

Philip was not mentioned but he was comprised among the abettors, counsellors, and supporters of the crime; he was included indirectly among the named chiefs; because there was no man in the world who did not believe that the treachery of Anagni was entirely his work. Spondano with the ingenuity of a child thinks that the King neither knew nor approved of those wicked crimes. But it would be useless to contradict him. The simple reflection that Nogaret and Sciarra Colona would not have dared to commit such an enormous crime without the power and the wealth of the King, is a complete refutation of this charitable and ingenuous assertion. Dante assigns the rôle of Pilate to Philip the Fair in that tragedy.[43] This rôle did not satisfy him, for the reason that proudly trampling under foot the holiest laws, he

---

[41] See Document 2 S.   [42] "Puniendum prosequi ex justis causis."
[43] "See the modern Pilate, whom avails
No cruelty to sate, and who, unbidden,
Into the temple sets his greedy sails.
O thou, my Lord! when shall I joyfully,
Behold the vengeance, which profoundly hidden
Makes sweet thy anger in thy mystery?"
          Purgatory, canto XX. Wright's translation.

forced himself into the sanctuary of the Church, and there held sway. Did the publication of that Bull, which was received with joy by the multitude, cause these thoughts to arise in his mind? Let the reader not ask us, considering that this pious and clement Pope on July 7th (one month only after the publication of the Bull) passed out of this world by poison which was administered to him. Philip was not near, but the Colonnas, Napoleon Orsini, and his other most faithful ministers were very close at hand. Some contemporary writers accuse them of poisoning the Pope.[44] Ferretus of Vincenza goes right to the point and flatly accuses Philip the Fair.[45]

Pardons, and Popes precipitated into their sepulchres did not satisfy the fury of Philip. These were only triumphs over men materially weaker than he; he wished to triumph over right, that is to say, he wished to give to his actions an appearance of justice, by proving that Boniface had been an illegitimate Pope, a heretic, a monster of iniquity, while he himself was guiltless of any fault, and a victim of his wickedness. Now it is here precisely that one distinguishes the common brigand from the tyrant. The former by force deprives you of your money and your life; he violates justice, but he does not profane it by changing its nature. The tyrant robs you of both life and possessions, he crushes you under foot down to the grave, and drags along justice in order to sanctify his wickedness. Benedict having been poisoned, Philip had recourse to other measures in order to succeed in his design. Tired of acts of violence, and perhaps despairing of their efficacy, because dead Popes have successors he tried corruption. We now come to another profanation of the Apostolic See.

If there was ever a time, in which, considering only men, and not Heaven which governs the things of this world, it was practically impossible to elect a Pontiff on account of dissensions among the electors, it was precisely this time. The obstacles to a prompt and peaceful election do not come only from that weakness of human nature, which is not cured by the sanctity of the office, but rather (a sad thing to say) from fear within, and tyranny without. The

[44] John Villani. L. 8. c. 80.—Dino Comp. Lib 3.—Fran. Pipino, Lib. 4. c. 49.   [45] S. R. I. Tom. 9, page 1013.

one prolonged the widowhood of the Church; the other prepared chains, which the diabolic inventive genius of the Cæsars of pagan Rome had not found. A Pope persecuted by Nero, and hidden in the Catacombs, at the most was at the summit of his moral majesty and power. A Pope imprisoned by a most Christian king, and sweetly dragged within his kingdom, was and will always be the most shameful despoliation of power and dignity. Therefore the stake and the gallows rather than perfidious caresses. Philip knew it well, and he aspired to this degradation of the Pontificate by favors.

The cardinal electors were divided into two parties, the one favorable to the French, and the other to the Italians. Matthew Orsini and Francis Gaetani, nephew of Pope Boniface, were the chiefs of the latter, while Napoleon Orsini and de Prato, who as relative and friend of the Colonnas desired their restoration, were the heads of the latter. Scandalous dissensions: they assembled, they adjourned, they met again without doing anything; the people were indignant; the Church sorrowed; Philip was negotiating. Tired of these skirmishes, De Prato and Gaetani one day met in secret, and agreed that the Italian party should choose at their pleasure, three French prelates, from whom the French party would make their selection within the period of forty days, and the other would abide by the choice. The combination conciliated all interests; because if the French faction had the advantage of obtaining a Pope of that nation, the Italian faction had the privilege of proposing three prelates devoted to the memory of Boniface, and enemies of Philip the Fair. Gaetani and his adherents chose three archbishops who owed their promotion to Boniface, and whom Philip had ostensibly persecuted; Cardinal di Prato, with his followers, chose from among the three, as Pontiff, Bertrand de Got, a native of Bordeaux, and the Archbishop of that see. De Prato speedily acquainted Philip of the choice, the archbishop being as yet ignorant of the fact, in order that the King might negotiate, and take possession of him. Philip was shrewd and he knew that the Pope elect was ambitious and greedy for honors. He made an appointment with him in a forest, near the Abbey of St John d'Angely. In the first place he requested him to be reconciled to Charles of Valois, against whom he entertained an old aversion; then showing him the letter of de Prato, he said, that the Papal Keys were in his hands, and if he wished to obtain them he would have to promise: 1st, to reconcile him fully to the Church; 2nd, to absolve him and his partisans from the censure of excommunication; 3rd, to condemn the memory of Boniface; 4th, to restore the two Colonnas to the dignity of cardinal. 5th, to grant him the tithes of all the French churches for five years; the 6th favor was to remain a secret until the king deemed the time opportune for its disclosure. And many conjectured, not incorrectly that it was the removal of the Papal See to Avignon. Dazzled by the glitter of the tiara, the Archbishop opened his mouth only to swear on the holy Eucharist that he would observe faithfully all that Philip wished him to promise to do. After having given to the King as a guarantee his brother and two nephews as hostages, the prelate departed; some messengers sent by Philip, went quickly to inform de Prato of the conclusion of the shameful compact.[46] Faithful to their promise, and ignorant of this secret interview, the Italians cast their votes for the Archbishop, who was solemnly elected sovereign Pontiff. He took the name of Clement V. The Cardinal electors announced to the faithful this election, but they kept silent on the compromise agreed to by the chiefs of the two factions, and the artifices of the French party.[47] The Italians perceived the ruse, as soon as the new Pope ordered them to come to him in Lyons, where he wished to be crowned. They manifested loudly their surprise, and chagrin, but they were already in the trap, from which they would not escape, so that turning to Cardinal de Prato, Matthew Orsini, dean of the sacred College, said to him: "You succeeded in leading us into "the trap; the Roman Court had crossed the mountains; "it will not be seen soon again in Italy; I know something "of the temperament of the Gascons." Clement was a Gascon.[48]

While the Cardinals were striving in Perugia to elect a Pope, Philip and Nogaret were not losing time in France. The latter, notwithstanding his harangues and

[46] John Villani L. 8. c. 80.   [47] Raynaldus, 1305, 1306.
[48] Villani, ibidem, c. 81.

blustering, was severely tormented by the censures imposed on him. Those of Benedict especially weighed very heavily on him, and he saw clearly that, as time calmed the resentment against Boniface, he would end by showing a disgraceful rôle with his calumnies and his robbery of Anagni. So in order to free himself from the excommunications, and rehabilitate himself in the public favor, he issued manifestoes, in which he justified his acts. He addressed five of them to the officials of the Church of Paris; and all could be reduced to the following: " He
" should not be surprised to see him ask absolution from
" censures; sent to negotiate with the Roman See, he
" asked only for greater security. The decrees of Boni-
" face were not binding before God or men. He did not
" retract one single word of his grievances against this
" Pontiff; he was ever ready to accuse him of heresy, of
" schism, of idolatry, and this for the instruction of prel-
" ates and too indulgent kings, through love for his coun-
" try, so horribly maltreated by that Pope. Sent to Rome,
" by his majesty to urge the convocation of a council, to
" which all France appealed, he had employed success-
" fully all means of avoiding extreme measures, which the
" obstinacy of the Pontiff had voluntarily provoked. He
" had nothing to reproach himself with in the events of
" Anagni with regard to a Pope, who by his contumacy
" was acknowledged guilty of heresy, and all other crimes
" imputed to him. While there prudence and humanity
" had been the rule of his conduct; he had forbidden the
" pillage of the Papal palace and treasury; but the fury of
" the soldiers exceeded the command of the chief, and if
" Boniface had escaped alive from their hands, he owed
" it to him, Nogaret, alone. Restored to liberty, that
" Pontiff had pardoned all those who had maltreated him,
" and he found himself named among those pardoned.
" After the death of that Pontiff he had interrupted his
" proceedings against him only through deference for
" Pope Benedict, but he renewed them now more vigor-
" ously than ever; he was well prepared to justify him-
" self, and prove the truth of his accusation, either in a
" full Council, or even before the convocation of this coun-
" cil, before the Holy See, provided there would be suffi-
" cient protection against the resentment of the relatives

"and partisans of Boniface." He complained in the other documents, of the injustice of Benedict, who had excommunicated him; and he asked, as a measure of precaution, for absolution from the censures, in order that he might proceed more freely against the memory of Boniface, not through hatred, but for the glory of God, the good of the Church, and the preservation of the public right.[49]

Nogaret was depressed and agitated. But the elevation of the Archbishop of Bordeaux to the sovereign Pontificate raised his hopes, and those of Philip. These hopes were manifested at the feasts of Lyons. Clement desired to be crowned in this city and not at Rome. He invited to this grand ceremony the King of France, and the King of England, of whom he was a subject, being a Gascon, who could not come, as he was detained in his kingdom by the affairs of Scotland. When Cardinal Matthew Rossi Orsini, who as we remarked was the first to foresee the long exile of the Roman Pontiffs, had placed the crown on his head, Clement set out triumphantly with a cavalcade for his palace. Philip the Fair for a part of the time appeared on foot in the procession holding the bridle of the horse on which the Pontiff was mounted; the two brothers of the King, Charles of Valois, and Louis of Evreux, and John, Duke of Brittany performed the same office successively for the Pope. Speaking of Avignon, we do not know whether it was in triumph or to prison that Philip led Clement. The feast was marred by a sad accident. An old wall which lined the way of the procession, fell under the weight of the numerous spectators with which it was laden, at the very moment the Pope was passing; Clement was not injured, but only thrown to the ground, and his crown, fallen from his head, rolled in the mire. Twelve persons within the compass of it were mortally wounded, and died a few days afterwards; among the number was the Duke of Brittany; the Duke of Valois was badly injured. The Italian cardinals considered this lamentable accident a bad omen. The festivities were followed by the fulfilment of the promises made by Bertrand de Got. In December the two Colonnas were reinstated in the dignity of cardinal, became

---

* Preuves, pp. 237, 239, 252, 269, 274.

again electors and elegible to the Papacy themselves; ten other cardinals were created, all Frenchmen; the sentence of Boniface against Philip and his ministers was revoked, and tithes were granted for five years. The Pope as yet was not pressed to condemn the memory of Boniface, and in the meanwhile Philip and Clement parted very well pleased. Philip went home, Clement could not, and he went to Bordeaux. Either the secret favor which Philip has asked from him was not to leave France, or Clement, fearing the anger of the Gaetani, did not want to go to Rome.

Clement found himself in a difficult and an embarrassing position. He was a Frenchman, and a French prince, if he had not placed him in the Pontifical chair, at least aided him to arrive there; therefore, although the voice of duty of his high office spoke strongly to him interiorly, it was stifled by the love of country, and a feeling of gratitude towards Philip. Benedict also would have granted him the tithes, and would have given him absolution from censures, and we have seen how that good Pontiff in all the indulgences he lavished on Philip, avoided, with wonderful cleverness, all that which would appear as a revocation of the acts of Boniface. Past and present reasons impelled Clement to revoke the Papal constitution of Boniface, and it came to that. The most vexatious to Philip were the constitution "*Clericis laicos,*" and the one which began by the words: *Unam sanctam;* they were nightmares which made sleep impossible to Philip. Clement published two decretals the 1st of February;[50] one of them abrogated the first of these Bulls, as a cause of dissension, and condemned all the subsequent acts of Boniface in defence of it, recalling however the faithful to the observance of the regulations of the councils, especially of the Council of the Lateran relative to the taxes which laymen levied on ecclesiastical property. The other decretal did not revoke but rather renewed the constitution *Unum sanctum.* Here are the words: "The entire and " sincere affection of our dear son Philip, illustrious King " of France, towards us and towards the Roman Church; " the brilliant deserts of his ancestors; the pure and sin-

[50] Ber. Guido. Chron. R. Pontif.

"cere devotion of his subjects, merit for him and his king-
"dom signal favors. We wish accordingly, and intend
"that the dispositions of the Bull *Unam Sanctum* of Pope
"Boniface VIII, our predecessor of happy memory, bear
"to them no prejudice whatever; that they do not subject
"them more strictly than before to the Roman Church;
"but that everything remains, regarding the Church, the
"King, the kingdom and its inhabitants, in the state in
"which it was previously." [51]

Now supposing that the constitution *Unum Sanctum* was here revoked, there is no denying the fact, that the revocation regarded only France, and it effected the letter rather than the spirit. In fact in speaking before of this Bull, we remarked that Boniface had not put forth any thing new. Hence recalling to Philip (as in the abrogation of the Bull *clericis*) the old rules, Clement did nothing but bind this prince tacitly to the very constitutions which he believed were abolished. But Philip was pleased by appearances; hence notwithstanding the praises given him for his merits, his devotion, and his ardent love for the Roman See, he could not bear the epithet happy applied to the memory of Boniface VIII. It disturbed his own happiness, and turned into bitterness the sweet and paternal concessions; he wanted his name cancelled from the Papal writings and from the hearts of all faithful Christians. He vigorously importuned the Pope to condemn Boniface, as he had sworn to do. Pressed by the ambassadors of the King, Clement was in torture. To use the keys given to St. Peter to open the gates of Heaven, for the opening of a tomb wherein a Vicar of Christ reposed, to revive his memory; to drag it before the bar of a tribunal instituted to protect justice; and to immolate him with infamy by weapons furnished by a brutal prince —such were the series of enormities which a sovereign Pontiff was called upon to sanction. Clement felt his position as Pontiff, and full of horror, he tried to temporize; but that expedient has ever been ruinous to the weak against a violent enemy. For it is always necessary to reply to force by force and not by weakness. Philip cut short these evasions and delays, by inviting him to an

[51] Raynaldus, 1306.

interview at Poitiers in the spring of 1307. Strongly importuned by Philip the Pope had to obey. He went to Poitiers, and the King repaired thither with a splendid court; Charles of Valois, and his sons accompanied him. Robert Count of Flanders; Charles II of Sicily, and the ambassadors of Edward I,[52] by their presence added eclat to this assembly. Hayton, an envoy from the King of Armenia, was also present, through the report circulated by Philip that the affairs of the Holy Land would be treated in that meeting. But the sole affair was the condemnation of Boniface. By his own presence and that of so many princes Philip wanted to wrest from Clement the fulfilment of his sworn promise. The Pope trembled, and the Cardinals were no more tranquil. The latter advised the Pope to flee in disguise from Poitiers; but Philip intercepted him, and forced him to remain.[53]

The assaults of the King were terrible, and horrible were his demands. He demanded that the proceedings against the memory of Boniface, which he considered had already been begun, be brought to an end; and the truth of the crimes alleged by Nogaret having been established, the body of that Pope should be dragged from the tomb, and be publicly consigned to the flames. Philip insisted, and he reminded the Pope of his oath in the forest of St. John d'Angely. In these straightened circumstances the soul of Clement was perplexed, and he tried to influence Philip, now by magnifying the difficulty of such a procedure which could not be had without the advice of the Cardinals, now by lessening the enormity of the faults imputed to his predecessor, and persuading the King to exercise moderation in this affair, by checking the impetuosity of the accusers, and not close the way to justification.[54] But Philip was deaf to every entreaty, and angered by the obstacles he pursued his project with greater ardor. Clement believed himelf lost. Cardinal de Prato came to his assistance, and suggested an expedient. Although French in spirit, yet as a Cardinal and a creature of Boniface he could not bear to allow that prince to proceed unchecked not only against the memory

[52] Villani, L 8, c. 91.
[53] Vita Clem. Joan. S. Vic. apud. Baluz. Tom. 3, p. 452.
[54] Raynaldus, 1307, no. 10.

of a Pontiff, but directly against the Apostolic See. With great cleverness he advised Clement to represent to the King the inconvenience of proceeding directly to a trial, in a consistory composed of cardinals, who, for the most part fond of Boniface, would not fail to oppose and defeat his design; the advantage there would be of entrusting the affair to a council which he could convoke at Vienne in Dauphiny, in which the sentence, being of greater weight and more authoritative, would thus afford greater satisfaction to the King. The Cardinal further added that Vienne being a neutral city, the French would not predominate in the assembly, in which it would be easy to save the memory of the detested Pontiff.[55] Clement hastened to represent these things to Philip in the sweetest possible manner, and if he did not succeed in subduing that proud and fiery nature, he calmed it a little, and gained time, which is almost a salvation to pusillanimous men.

The announcement of a Council quieted Philip; which idea since the assembly of the Louvre, was a dream of his and inspired him with the hope of a more splendid triumph, and thus moderated the fury of his impetuous revenge. This was rather a truce than a peace. The more Clement tried to clear him and his ministers from the infamy of their evil deeds, so much the more this obstinate prince clamored and strived to have the corpse of Boniface exhumed.[56] Courage began to leave Clement; he saw by experience that in a foreign country a Roman Pontiff was always a slave; that to the cry of alarm no one would reply in France; and that the will of a king who had no regard for the Papal dignity, imposed it on him as a yoke to bind him in an injustice. In times of old on the contrary when the voice of a Pope was freely heard from the Vatican hill, the voice of the entire Church always responded with aid, and before he could reach him to disturb him on his throne, a prince had first to trample upon dust consecrated by the blood of martyrs, and from which there arose as fire a secret power of memories, which was more destructive than a sceptre. He had exhausted the treasury of Pontifical favors; the assembly

[55] Villani, L. 8, c. 92. [56] Raynaldus, 1307, no. 10.

of Poitiers had been a triumph to Philip. Charles of Valois whose character we have seen from the affairs of Sicily and Tuscany, appeared in that assembly as the Emperor of Byzantium chosen by Clement.[57] The latter had previously granted him the tithes of all the churches of France for two years, and indulgences to all those who would accompany him in the war against the Greeks. Now although Charles of Valois, being contented with the sacred money thought very little of Byzantium, yet Clement, for the sake of his dear son Philip, to whom at any cost he wanted to be agreeable, spoke strongly to the faithful to arouse them to a Crusade apparently against the Turks who threatened Andronico, but in reality to dislodge Andronico and place Valois on the throne.[58] The remark that Clement wanted to be agreeable to Philip, relieves us of the necessity of declaring that neither the Pope nor the faithful had the Turks in view. Philip wanted to place his son, Louis le-Hutin (the quarreller) on the throne of Navarre, and Clement gave him a helping hand,[59] and the young prince took possession at Pampeluna.[60] Philip requested Clement to confirm Carobert, son of his cousin Charles II of Sicily, in his possession of the crown of Hungary, and this he did, by striking with anathema Otho of Bavaria, his rival.[61] Philip asked that the debt of 360,000 ounces of gold which his cousin owed to the Holy See be remitted, and Clement remitted a third, intending the remainder for the expense of the Crusade of Charles of Valois.[62] Philip triumphed, but Clement deceived himself if he believed that he was satisfied. There was one glory lacking in his triumph, and that was that the Pope should descend into the tomb, and search for the ghost of Boniface in order to condemn it. This Saul of the XIVth century wished to change by force a Roman Pontiff into a pythoness.

We have seen that the primary cause of the quarrel between Philip and Boniface had been the rapacity of the King and his demands on the property of the churches. This lust for gold was not satisfied, but increased from day to day, both because of his cupidity, and because the

[57] Raynaldus, 1306, no 2.
[58] Raynaldus, 1307. 6.
[59] Raynaldus, 1307. 14.
[60] Conti Nangii, p. 60.
[61] Raynaldus, 1307, 15-21.
[62] Raynaldus, 1307. 23

long and obstinate wars in Flanders had exhausted the sources of the public revenues. Philip in his search for money had recourse to quick expedients; and he had no scruples regarding the means he adopted; to wish with him was the same as to have. The counterfeiting [63] of the public money was a holy measure justified by necessity; the spoliation of the churches was a venerable exercise of the royal rights; and when the monies were weary of these repeated falsifications, (for Philip had committed them often), and when the churches either could not or would not gratify his wishes, he pounced upon whoever had money to extort it from them, always covering his royal dignity with the mantle of justice. In 1291 on the same day he robbed all the Italian merchants residing in France; he accused them of usury. In 1306 he treated the Jews in the same manner.[64] And since in those times to render an action commendable and justifiable in the eyes of the people, there was need of the intervention of religion, many times this wretch dragged the clergy in his train and exacted their coöperation in his robberies. A strong proof of this is that which we have narrated of his insolence to Clement in his endeavor to have the bones of Boniface burned. If he had lived after the reformation of Martin Luther, and the revolt of Henry VIII, it is not to be doubted that in order to extirpate the scandals of the monks and the clergy, he would have piously confiscated their property, having already proved that Bulls and canons of Councils are small obstacles in the way of a king who is resolutely intent on his purpose. But the times were not ripe for actions of this nature. He operated in detail, and always on societies. For just as they could more easily bear calumnies than individuals, so it was likewise more easy to bestow on the blow that struck them a semblance of justice and morality. After having robbed the Italians and the Jews, he cast his eyes on a society, remarkable for its immense wealth, and which, by reason of the faults of some of its members, could without doubt present the aforesaid appearance of justice and morality to his attacks, to be sanctioned always by a judgment of the Church. We here refer to the famous

[63] Sismondi Hist. of France, chap XXI, Tom. 6, page 87. Brussels 1839.
[64] Sismondi. Hist. of France, chap. XXII, page 122.

Templars. The reader will bear with us while we narrate briefly the story of this holy militia, whose ruin was allied to that with which Philip threatened the memory of Boniface.

The pious pilgrimages in former times to the holy places in Palestine originated, as it appears, by Helena, mother of Constantine in the fourth century, were the first causes of the Crusades, and of the Military Orders. No one can read without emotion the recital of the dangers to which the pilgrims were exposed on the way, and the affronts they had to bear from the avarice of the infidels, the guardians of the Holy Places.[65] The afflictions of these devoted people touched the heart of all Christendom; and just as some took up arms for the conquest of the Holy Land, so some societies were armed in defence of those who desired to visit it. These societies were the Military Orders, deputed either for the care of sick pilgrims, or for the protection of pilgrims against the Turks during the journey. The Templars were chosen for this noble purpose Their Order was founded by five knights who took part in the first Crusade, and all the names of whom are lost with the exception of two, Hugh de Payens, and Ganfred of St. Aldemar.[66] They bound themselves, in the presence of the Patriarch of Jerusalem and of other bishops, for the remission of their sins, to hold and guard against robbers the roads on which the devout pilgrims would travel, and to observe perpetual chastity, obedience and poverty.[67] They were called Templars, from the name of the place, which Baldwin, King of Jerusalem, first assigned them as a residence, which was near the temple of Solomon; for which reason afterwards all their houses in France and England were called Templars.[68] In the year of 1125 Hugh de Payens, with some of his knights, appeared before the council of Troyes, presided over by the Legate of Honorius II, and asked for a rule to

[65] Guil. Ty Hist Bell. sac. lib. I, c. 10. Sed qui in itinere cuncta perdiderant, et vix eum incolumitate membrorum ad loca pervenerant optata, unde tributum solverent, non habebant. Sic enim fiebat, ut ante urbem ex talibus mille vel plures collecti, et expectantes introeundi licentiam, fame et nuditate consumpti deficerent.

[66] Guill. Hist. bell. Sac. L. ib. 12, c. 7.

[67] The same and Matth. Paris—Jac. de Vetri. Hist. Hier, c. 65.

[68] Du Fresne Gloss.

follow. St. Bernard was deputed to write it, who was most enthusiastic in all matters relating to the Holy Land, and recognized in the Templars a most powerful aid sent to the faithful from Heaven.[69] It is pleasant to read how the holy Abbot with a fertility of imagination extols the nobility of the Temple of knights which he even elevates above that of Solomon.[70] They received from this Council a common habit of white color. Later in 1145 Pope Eugenius III made them place on their cloak a cross of red cloth.[71] Thus the whiteness of the habit indicated the innocence and candor of their lives, and the cross of red, martyrdom for which they should be prepared by the defence of the Holy Land, and by the destruction of the enemies of the cross.[72] The field of their escutcheon was colored equally with white and black, to signify kindness towards friends, and severity towards enemies.[73] In principle they were anchorites in military dress, and one does not know which to admire in them the more, the observances of evangelical perfection or their formidable military virtue. They were most obedient and respectful to the Patriarch of Jerusalem;[74] they practised poverty to such a high degree that their founders Hugh and Ganfred had but one horse between them; so that in memory of this poverty and singular humility, they had engraved on their seal the figure of two knights seated on the one same horse.[75] The integrity of their morals was such that they observed in word and laughter the most austere reserve.[76] Valiant in war, closely and prudently united to their chief, they were always the first to advance in the line of battle, they were the last to retreat and in retreating they never turned their heads to the enemy; nor without obeying the orders of their chiefs. In a word they were the wonder and delight of all Christians. Such is the statement of James de Vitry.[77] William

[69] Exort. ad milit, c. 1.
[70] The same C. 8 . . . . . . "Pro candelabris, thuribulis, atque urceolis, domus undique frenis, sellis ac lanceis communitur"
[71] " UT inter caeteros essent nobiliores." Wil. Tyri. 1. 12, c. 7.
[72] Jac. de Vitriaco, c. 65.   [73] Idem de Vitriaco.
[74] St Bernard exhort, ad milites, c. 4.   [75] Matth. Paris. Chron.
[76] St Bernard. Exhort. ad milites.
[77] " Nulli molesti erant, sed ab omnibus propter humilitatem et religionem amabantur,"

of Tyr declares that their wealth and numbers were immense in his time, and James de Vitry said that their number had increased indefinitely. This wealth was at first a temptation, and later it became a scandal. Now it is undeniable that the object which these pious knights had in view in the beginning was most holy; and we do not doubt that the head ones who showed the way acted under the holy impulse of faith; but just as the Crusades themselves were soon profaned by the ambitions of the chiefs, and the licentiousness of the multitude, so the knightly orders wandered away from the sublime purpose of their institution. The monastic orders ran the same risks, but the rigor of material discipline, the separation from the world, the individual poverty, the authority of superiors, and the absence of hope of ever acquiring a brilliant reputation, were a harbor which welcomed on its bosom the shipwrecked members; and if all did not feel themselves sufficiently strong to renew their noble and dangerous career, all at least remained hidden, that is to say, the cloisters cast their charitable shadows over the deformities and infirmities of human nature. So although having lost their first fervor, the monastic orders had the means to revive it, and to hide the lukewarm spirits; scandals began with the ending of this discipline. Similar to the monks in the first glow of faith, the Templars, and with them all the sacred militia, differed from the monks through lack of means which would sustain them on the supernatural road on which they walked, and which would aid them to arise from their falls. They were servants of Christ, but clothed in armor, and obliged by duty to fight actively in a country in which the fervor of religion could not always triumph over the unfavorable conditions in which they found themselves placed; we speak of the contact with their enemies and also of the climate. The tumult of camps, the passions of war, the joy of victory, and the sweet thought of booty, could not but oppress the spirit, and cause it to fall from that sublime mysticism in which the solitaries of Thebais had maintained themselves with so much effort, and at the price of the privation of all earthly things. Moreover in this epoch chivalrous exploits called forth more esteem and consideration than any science; and as these were sung in verse, they aroused the warmest and liveliest affections in the hearts of those who had most capacity for poetry; and hence between these hearts and a knight who returned from the Holy Land narrating his combats with the Saracens, there would course such a strong feeling of sympathy against which the strongest coat of mail of a Templar would be a powerless protection. A monk was never exposed to such dangers as these. If then the Templars, by preserving the bonds which held them in subjection to their Grand Master, could persevere in the conditions of a regular militia, they however with difficulty remained monks. William of Tyr[78] declares that in his time they had already departed from their first intent, and Matthew of Paris makes the patriarch of Jerusalem say against these knights these words of the Bible: " I have nourished and " exalted my children and they have despised me."

But even though the Templars had continued in their first discipline, they would always have aroused the jealousy of the prince in whose country they resided. In fact if the Church by only the moral power she exercised over the people, aroused the jealousy and cupidity of kings, the latter should for a stronger reason feel the same sentiments with regard to a society of men, not only respected by the people by reason of the holiness of their institute, and of the red cross they wore on their mantles, but feared by reason of the material force of their weapons, the mighty power of their wealth, and their relations with persons of high degree. A Pope could be imprisoned by open force, but a Grand-Master of the Templars could only be by cunning, and by means of deceitful forms which were called at that time criminal right. Gregory X thought to reform them, and he wanted to unite them to the Knights Hospitalers.[79] Pope Nicholas IV wished to do the same in 1289, and he wrote to the Grand-Masters of the two orders but nothing came of it.[80] The violation of their vow of chastity did not disturb Philip of France, but their poverty being changed to immense wealth, and their obedience into a proud command forcibly aroused him; he had moreover through his own fault, just reasons to fear them. He had succeeded in establishing his do-

[78] Book 12, c. 7.   [79] Magn. Chr. Belg. ap Pistor, Tom. III, p. 260.
[80] Annal Eberhard, apud. Canis, T. I.

minion over the rights of the lay and clerical feudalities, but he was not able, for reasons we have given, to dominate the formidable militia of the Temple, more numerous in France than in any other country, and who, intrenched in their privileges, defied the royal authority. We found bishops and barons in the assemblies of Notre Dame and of the Louvre, but not Templars; we heard everywhere, in the churches and monasteries, the cry of appeal to a council, but in the temples of the holy militia all was silence; and for that reason we must conclude that the Templars viewed these impieties of the King with fierceness and independence, hiding their hatred and contempt within their breasts, and perhaps manifesting it secretly. Philip feared them, but to the fear of their power was united the desire for their wealth. He determined then to destroy with the appearance of a legal trial, and confiscate their possession. He must commence through the Pope.

Clement forced by Philip to a most outrageous and most deadly act against the Roman Pontificate, that is, the condemnation of the dead Boniface, resembled those travellers, who, surrounded by brigands in a dense forest to be assassinated, beseech, and deliver up everything in order to save their lives. We have seen all that he had conceded to Philip to escape from his importunate demands against Boniface. Now, the cunning prince, availing himself of the sad position of Clement, and knowing that compared to the monstrous condemnation of a sovereign Pontiff all concessions would appear trifling, multiplied and enlarged his demands in proportion as the council of Vienne drew near. So, whilst asking, he nurtured in the breast of the unhappy Pope the hope of escaping this supreme difficulty, he took advantage and proceeded towards the object he had in view. So then at the difficult meeting at Poitiers, the King demanded of the Pope the abolition of the sacred militia of the Temple. James de Molay assisted at this princely meeting; he came expressly from Cyprus. This Grand-Master of the Templars had been loaded with caresses by the King and by Clement. The reason for the suppression of the Templars was the horrible unnatural crimes of which the Templars

* John Villani, L. 8, c. 92.

were accused, and which were disclosed by the confessions of the priors of Montfaucon in Toulouse, and a certain Naffodeus of Florence, most execrable members of the Order. Imprisoned by the Grand-Master on account of their crimes, they offered, in order to gain their freedom, to say everything that would please Philip the Fair.[81] Clement had to remain in suspense; for Philip having departed, the Templars appeared before him and entreated him to do justice to their order, and not to proceed against them except according to the usual forms. But whilst the Pope was wavering between Philip and the Grand-Master, the former gained his point in an expeditious way that was characteristic of him. On the 13th of October the knights in all France were suddenly imprisoned and all their possessions were confiscated by the officers of the King, in virtue of secret orders to all the governors of the provinces. If someone asked if the knights had truly been guilty of the faults for which they had been suddenly punished, we would not be able to answer, as the proofs of the truth of the faults were wanting even to contemporaries. The punishment preceded the trial, and the judgment and trial which followed, did not deserve the name; they were but a continuation of the punishment, namely torture. The torments to which the Templars were subjected, to wring from them a monstrous and irrational confession, show that the judges searched eagerly for grounds of conviction, which they did not have, and consequently the crimes were not manifest. We leave it to anyone whomsoever, not devoid of reason and humanity, to judge whether the dislocation of their bones would serve to manifest and prove the guilt of the prisoners. Torture was always the most stupid debasement of the human reasons in those things which closely concerned the preservation of society, that is to say, the administration of justice. When sufferings triumphed, that was nearly always, over the courage of the victim, a confession of the most absurd crimes escaped from his lips; but this was not a confession of guilt, but rather a confession of that natural instinct in man to repel pain, and the destructive causes of life. Whence a confession in the midst of suffering, and a retraction afterwards; and so there arose on the foundation of a very natural contradiction, a judgment contrary to nature and to reason. That the Templars in that epoch were relax in discipline and wicked, we shall always believe, both on the authority of the historians who recount it, and from rational conjectures; but that they were guilty of all the crimes of which they were accused by Philip the Fair, solely because such was the judgment of their torturers, we shall never believe. Dupuy has compiled from original documents the history of the condemnation of the Templars.[82] In reading it one can get a knowledge of the monstrosity of the judgment, but not of the guilt of the accused. We shall have to go elsewhere to be convinced of the truth of the last point. We shall conclude, by saying that in this affair the condemnation was just, the procedure unjust, the punishment too severe.

Philip gave to his brutal procedure a certain ecclesiastical character, by charging his confessor, Friar William Humbert of Paris, Grand Inquisitor, to proceed against the Templars. The intervention of a Friar in these barbarous trials, and the sudden confiscation of the goods of the knights grieved Clement, who was Pontiff, and who remembered that in France the Church enjoyed immunities by virtue of which it was forbidden to despoil, to suppress, and to torture any religious society without the judgment of the Pope. He complained of the independence which Philip assumed regarding the Holy See;[83] but afterwards either because the spontaneous confession of their faults, made in his presence by sixty-two Templars[84] had convinced him; or because he did not wish Philip to deprive him of his jurisdiction; or because he would not withstand Philip's noisy insinuations, he summoned them also, and began an inquiry himself.[85] He would have the chiefs of the sacred militia appear before him, but they were so infirm that they could not ride horseback, by reason of their bones being displaced on the rack.[86] In consequence he deputed three Cardinals to

[82] History of the Condem. of the Templars. Paris 1654, n. 4.
[83] Dupuy. Condemnation of Templars, p 11.   [84] Raynaldus, 1308. 5 —
[85] Bulla Clement. apud. Raynaldum: "Clamosa insinuatione dicti Regis."
[86] Idem num. 6. "Sed quoniam quidam ex eis sic infirmabantur tunc temporis, quod equitare non poterant, nec ad nostram praesentiam quoquomodo adduci."

examine and interrogate them, before whom they confessed under oath, and without a shadow of coercion, to the truth of their faults.[87] By his order, the bishops themselves proceeded against the Templars, and the Archbishops of Treves, Cologne, and Magdeburg were chosen to take charge of their property.

At the sound of so many royal and Papal inquiries, in the face of the indignation which the iniquities of the Templars excited, who could restrain the zeal of the Christian Princes? They all followed the example of the King of France, and took possession of the rich property of the Templars. The spoliation would have been a small affair, but they followed it by executions at the stake. Fifty-six Templars were burned by a slow fire outside of Paris, and died appealing to Jesus Christ and the Holy Virgin for aid, and protesting their innocence with shrieks of despair. Clement was still at Poitiers. The sacrifice being consummated, he retired to Bordeaux, afterwards he went to establish his residence at Avignon.

If Boniface had lived, the Templars would not have been burned. In fact the provincial councils which Clement and Philip had convoked in France, condemned the Templars, those in Germany, Spain and Italy absolved them not finding them guilty, nor were they put to torture.[88]

The abolition of a knightly Order could have been accomplished in an age, in which the intellectual life more mature would have been able to study it under its own religious covering. In the beginning of the XIVth century this was a premature act. Clement did not act as a Pontiff, but as a prelate reduced to slavery by Philip. The funeral piles and the bones of the knights were as yet smoking, but Philip still pursued Clement, because he wanted to see the bones of Boniface also in the flames. The Pope had promised the King to treat the case of Boniface in the approaching Council of Vienne, but this was for Philip too long a delay; he pressed the Pope so hard that he was forced to begin the proceedings. Therefore on September 15th he wrote from Avignon for the certainty of the present, and the memory of posterity, an

[87] Idem. 7. "Libere ac sponte, absque coactione qualibet et timore deposuerunt." [88] Labbe. Concil. Gene. Tom. XI, p. II, p. 1533.

act in which we read these words:[89] "From the time that
"we assumed the Supreme Apostolate, our very dear son
"in Jesus Christ, Philip King of France, urged by his
"zeal, (as we believe and as he has shown) for the ortho-
"dox faith[90] and piety, has entreated us at Lyons and
"Poitiers, to lend ear to Louis of Evreux, Guy Count of
"Saint Paul, John Count of Dreux, and William, who
"declared that Pope Boniface died tainted with heresy,
"and that they have the proof, in order that we may con-
"demn legally the memory of this Pontiff, we find it diffi-
"cult to believe that Boniface was a heretic, born of a
"Catholic family, raised in the Roman Court, sent by
"Popes Martin and Adrian as legate to France and Eng-
"land, honored with the office of advocate and notary of
"the same court, created Cardinal, and finally raised to
"the sovereign Pontificate. Yet as heresy is the most
"detestable of crimes, and the accusation which is made
"against anyone should not rest without an examination,
"especially when the dignity of the accused renders the
"fault most grievous, we have resolved, at the instance
"of the King, and in the interest of the orthodox faith, to
"give a hearing to the aforesaid accusers. We fix the
"coming Lent as the time within which they should ap-
"pear before us, the King and the said lords who know
"so much about the actions of Boniface."

The memory of a Pontiff dragged before the tribunal of another Pontiff, as that of a heretic, was a thing unheard of; for that reason, at this publication of the Pope, all Christendom was seized with a just horror. The Kings of Castile and Aragon dispatched legates to Clement, complaining of the scandal given to the faithful by imputing heresy to a sovereign Pontiff.[91] In Germany, in Belgium and in Italy a cry of execration was raised against the outrages of Philip.[92] It was impossible, however, to break the chains which bound Clement. He named the commissioners to receive the deposition, and commit to public writing that which the witnesses related against Boniface;[93] the witnesses were guaranteed against every

---

[89] Raynaldus, 1309. 2.
[90] "Zelo ut credimus et ipse promebat, fidei orthodoxae et devotionis accensus credensque ecclesiae statuii plurium expedire" [91] Rg 1310–37.
[92] Surita Annal. Book 5, chap. 87.   [93] Albert Mussatus, Book 1, c. 3.

offence or obstacle on the part of their adversaries,[94] after which the scandalous debates began. The accusers and defenders of Boniface appeared before Clement seated in full consistory. Philip, considering himself dishonored if he appeared there as an accuser, (the Pope had summoned the princes also) refused to appear, and obtained from Clement a Bull in which it was declared that the King was not considered a party in this affair, but only a promoter of the glory of God, and the good of the Church.[95] After his example, Louis Count of Evreux, Guy of St. Paul, and John, Count of Dreux, exempted themselves from attending. Only Nogaret, William di Plasian, Peter Galard, Peter di Blanase, appeared as representatives of the king, with the Archbishop of Saint-Brieux, Alain de Lamballe, a clerk of the King. These were the accusers. The defenders were Francis, son of the Count Peter Gaetani; Theobald, son of Vernazzo, a gentleman of Anagni, nephew of Boniface; Gotto of Rimini; Baldred Biseth; Thomas Murror; James of Modena; Blaise of Piperni; Crescentius of Palliano; Nicholas of Veroli; James of Firmineto; Conrad of Spoleto, all doctors in law. The two parties were accompanied by a numerous escort of men-at-arms. They mutually feared each other.[96] The proceedings opened on March 16th. We shall speak briefly of the accusations, and the final sentence, then, of the manner in which the affair ended. For if we would descend to particulars, the torture to which Clement was put, and the cruelties that entered into trials at this epoch, would disgust the reader, without any benefit to the truth of history.[97]

The numerous accusation were reduced to two chiefly: heresy, and enmity to Philip the Fair. The first was clearly expressed in these words: Boniface had been an atheist, and guilty of all the actions, a natural consequence of this monstrous error. The other had been already expressed by the Constitutions published by Boniface against Philip the Fair. Many were the witnesses of the crimes of Boniface; and to consider only those who related that Boniface, in the year of the jubilee, denied

[94] Idem 38.   [95] Baillet. Demeles, 282.   [96] Baillet, 289.
[97] See in Dupuy the original acts of this trial.

publicly, in the presence of the ambassadors of Lucca, of Florence, and of Bologna, the immortality of the soul, the future dissolution of the world, and the divinity of Jesus Christ,[98] clearly show how the gold of the Templars dropped into the hands of these witnesses. If Boniface was jealous of power, and if this power was founded entirely on Religion, no one will ever believe that he would shake this foundation. We do not find in the statement of the facts of Anagni that there was any accusation of madness against Boniface.

The two parties contended before Clement till the winter of the following year 1311. The Pope was wearied, and began to fear the anger of the defenders of Boniface; he entreated the King to free him from this anguish, and to submit to his private judgment the conclusion of this affair; and to ensure success he interposed the good offices of Charles of Valois. Philip still refused to yield; but finally, both by the influence of Valois, his brother, which was very powerful over him, and because the greater part of the noblemen of the kingdom were tired of these scandals and wanted them ended, he yielded to the entreaties of the Pope. Nevertheless it must not be passed over in silence that the despair of obtaining a sentence which would declare the truth of all the faults imputed to Boniface, was also a factor in this determination. The absence of proofs and the disposition of the judges made him forebode the infamy due the calumniators. This presentiment had already entered French minds, in such a manner that Valois demanded the blood of Enguerrand of Marigny, whom he accused of being the cause of the differences that arose between Boniface and the King, and consequently of the disgraceful stain thus cast on the royal name.[99] Both parties became silent; Clement had all the evidence of the trial collected, so as to be preserved in the Vatican Archives, showing thereby that he did not want to desist from that inquiry, in which his dignity would lose not a little by not concluding an affair undertaken with so much solemnity. He afterwards wrote a Bull, the greater part of which is given by Rinaldus, and over which a faithful Catholic can not cast his eyes without

[98] Dupuy, pages 550, 568, 570.
[99] Paulus Emil. in Lud. Hutino apud. Raynaldum, 1311, 30.

shedding tears, on seeing there the usurpation of a prince triumphing over the inviolable power of the Church.[100]

Philip the Fair is represented in this Bull as the greatest defender the Church ever had; and all his acts against Boniface proceeded from sincere, pure and just zeal, and from the fervor of his Catholic faith. He was innocent of all the outrages at Anagni, because Nogaret had said so. He praised the King, beyond all expression, for his royal mildness, his devotion, and his respect, and to discharge his obligations to him, he abrogated all the suspensions of privileges, censures and other Papal constitutions promulgated after November 1st, 1300, by Boniface, and by Benedict XI, which could displease his Majesty. Finally Clement ordered that all these Bulls be stricken from the registry of Papal letters; that no one should retain copies of them, not even the notaries and the judges, under pain of excommunication, and that all copies should be burned. The two constitutions *"Unam Sanctam"* and *"Rem novam"* were modified, with this declaration that they would have the force of law in all Christendom, except in France, in which country things would remain as they were before the publication of these two decretals of Boniface. He reserved to himself, for four months, the examination of the witnesses, or the accusers of Boniface, and his defenders, provided it did not contain anything which concerned the King and all France.

The pages of the registry upon which were inscribed the detested documents were carefully erased, but all of the copies were not destroyed; some of them have come down to us.[101]

Philip being declared innocent, and entirely contented, there remained Nogaret, and with him all those who had contributed to the imprisonment of Boniface, to the capture of his place, and the pillage of his treasures; they were Reginald of Supino, Thomas of Morolo, Robert-Peter of Gennazzano, Stephen Adenolfo, Nicholas Giffred Bussa, Orlando and Peter of Luparia, Sciarra Colonna, John of Landolfo, Godfrey and John of Ceccano, Maximus of Treves, and all the inhabitants of Anagni who had given them assistance. The conscience of Clement had a repug-

---

[100] See Document 2. T.   [101] See Document 2. U.

nance to releasing from censures those men who merited even additional punishments; in fact he excluded them from the pardon.[102] But Philip did not want even these wretched men punished. An accusing witness, their punishment would always remind him of what he himself had merited, and which he escaped only by violence. He encompassed Clement to secure their pardon, and he granted it because of their love for the King of France, and because they had sworn that they had not taken part in the events of Anagni with any bad intentions. Nogaret with hands joined received pardon as a safeguard, as none knew whether he was a good or bad Christian, nor whether or not he had overstepped the orders of Philip in relation to Boniface. However Clement imposed on him certain penances of which he was the only witness, such as to visit the most famous sanctuaries of France, that of St. James of Compostella, and to go and fight in the Holy Land with the first expedition setting out, and stay there for the remainder of his life.[103]

Thus the proceedings at Avignon ended. There was no sentence that declared Boniface to have been heretical and simoniacal; but Philip had succeeded in his design of defaming his memory. The shameful accusations which were prolonged for seven months; the bought testimony sufficed to accredit and sustain the bad reports circulated about that Pontiff, whom the King wished to cover with disgrace in order to shield himself. The slowness of the trial proved clearly how repugnant were these scandals to Clement, but it could not palliate the deadly wound it gave to the Pontifical dignity. From the summit of the high throne on which he was seated, he dominated all the faithful; Vicar of Jesus Christ, sovereign Teacher of justice, he knew full well that among the gems of the tiara there protruded the thorns of the crown of martyrdom. His mission was supernatural, the means to accomplish it supernatural; he should, if he wished to be Pope, arm himself with supernatural courage. His vestments, his body, his liberty, could fall into the power of tyrants, but his soul never could. But alas! he was at Avignon and to fortify himself he had not even the sight of the tomb of

---

[102] Raynaldus, 1300, 50.   [103] Raynaldus, ibidem.

those, who knew how to transport the church of Golgotha to the Capitol by the double virtue of the apostolate and of martyrdom.

These things should have powerfully agitated the soul of Clement; and although the slavery to which Philip had reduced him hindered him from acting differently, nevertheless he nourished within the thought of repairing what was done, as soon as he was a little more free. In the year 1307 he had intimated the convocation of an Ecumenical Council in the Bull *Regnans in Coelis,* written on August 12th,[104] to be held at Vienne in Dauphiny in October, 1309. Philip was anxious for this council in order to present his appeal to it, and the accusations that were examined at Avignon. Clement also desired it, both because the Church needed to be reformed in its members, and because his own conscience needed to be quieted concerning Boniface, by a final judgment, emanating freely and unrestrained from the tribunal of last resort. Having then renewed the convocation of the council, Clement repaired to Vienne in the middle of September, 1311. A large number of Bishops, about 300, answered the call;[105] they were men eminent in learning and virtue. The Pope in a discourse made known the three principal reasons for convening the prelates namely; the judgment of the Templars, affairs in the Holy Land, and the restoration of ecclesiastical discipline. He said nothing about Boniface, probably so as not to give umbrage to Philip, but he kept him in mind. Pagi does not believe that the memory of Boniface[106] was discussed in this council, both because that affair had already been ended in Avignon, and because fully six historians of the life of Boniface say absolutely nothing of the renewed examination. However in spite of their silence, and although we cannot be enlightened by the acts of that Council, which have not come down to us, yet we cannot without reason deny the testimony of Villani,[107] St. Antoninus, Friar Francis Pipino[108] and others. The cause of Boniface was agitated, and the validity of his election by reason of the valid abdication of Celestine V. Cardinals Richard of Siena, Peter of

[104] Raynaldus, 1307. [106] Villani lib. 9, c. 22.
[105] Brev. Rom. Pontiff. [107] Villani ib.
[108] Chron. S. R. I. T. t 9.

Spain, and Francis Gaetani, gloriously refuted the charges of heresy. The latter especially undertook to defend him in matters concerning the Colonnas. There is good reason to believe that the speech of defence of Gaetani published by Paterini [109] from the Vatican Archives, is precisely the same one he delivered in the council of Vienne. In spite of the clamors of Philip, the Bishops, not being in France, decided that Boniface had been a legitimate Pope, and pure in his faith.[110] Public indignation against the anger of a prince trying to tarnish the memory of a magnanimous Pontiff began to appear. We have a splendid proof of it in the action of two Catalonian knights, whose names Villani has preserved for us, Caroccio and William d'Ebule. When the cardinal defenders had fought with the arms of reason, these brave and valiant knights, desirous of defending the memory and innocence of Boniface by a trial of arms, appeared before Philip challenging to a single combat two of the enemies of Boniface. An expression of a noble and a generous devotion! It was as it were the discharge of a holy debt which the knightly spirit paid to the memory of a Pope, who was the last prop of that Roman Pontificate which excited in the generations the life of the heart, the one and only source of the sentiments of loyalty, honor and glory. The courageous defence of the cardinals, the definition of the council, and the bravery of the knights, which savored of the ancient, revealed to Philip and his ministers all the deformity of their hearts which they had so much dishonored by the infamy of calumnies and perjuries. The King and his ministers, says Villani, were confused. But the confusion of the wicked, especially when they are powerful, is never a sign of repentance, but rather the

---

[109] Menn Praenes. Monu. 53.

[110] Villani lib. 29, 22. "It was declared in this council that Pope Boniface had been a Catholic, and innocent of the crime of heresy of which the King of France accused him, and this for many reasons advanced, in presence of the King and his counsel by Cardinal Richard of Siena."

St. Antoninus Page 3, tit. 21, c. 3: "Cum Clemens de delenda memoria Bonifacii ex ecclesia, cum praelatis Concilii tractaret, quia rex illum haereticum fuisse probare intendebat, Concilium nullo modo assentiri voluit, sed contrarium declaravit, scilicet illum fuisse catholicum, et indubitatum pontificem."

indication of a fury which abates its force, and is only to be feared the more.

At last the bones of the wearied Boniface were at rest. If the ignorance and the partisanship of the chroniclers and the historians defiled the stone of his sepulchre by new injuries, still the truth was not to be so subjected by tyrants, that its free and sincere lovers could not gain it. It rejoices us to think that the first one who dared to approach Boniface with a mind free from prejudice, to recount his life, was a Benedictine, John Ross who lived in the XVI century. He an Englishman saw in Boniface a calumniated Pontiff; we Italian, have seen more in Boniface, the magnanimous Italian trampled under foot by that fate, which disturbs this land, where not even the memory of its old grandeurs remains inviolate.

We have spoken of the things done by men on earth, we shall now say a word on what God did in Heaven. Philip was secure on his throne, and the fear of the punishments, which for his crimes against Boniface could have been inflicted on him and his children by the Roman See, was dissipated by the indulgent measures of Clement, who, in the council of Vienne, had forbidden him or any of his descendants to be disturbed, on account of that affair. But the trial of a dead Pontiff, and that of the sacred militia of the Temple, conducted by torture, and ended by the torments of so many men burned at the stake, left in his mind those frightful images, which in a malefactor, though unpunished, take the place of human justice. When James Molay, Grand-Master of the Templars condemned to death by fire, mounted the funeral pile with the aspect of a man who is no longer of this world, but sees and lives in the next, he appealed from the judgment of men to the true and living God who is in Heaven, and summoned to his tribunal Clement and Philip, to reply, at the end of a year and a day, to his accusations. This fact is recounted, not only by Ferretus,[111] but also by Godfrey of Paris, an eyewitness.[112] The constancy with which this man suffered death; his prayer with joined hands; the petition he made that his face be turned towards the Virgin Mary,

---

[111] S. R I. T. IX, col 1017, 1018.
[112] Chron de Godofsoide, Paris, published by M. Buchon, 1827.

from whom Jesus Christ was born,[113] that is to say, towards the church of Notre Dame; and this formidable appeal, considering the age in which these things happened, must have sent a shock of terror into the souls of the spectators, and especially that of Philip.[114] Superstition caused the crimes true or false of the Templars to be considered worthy of such cruel punishment; but religion still spoke in the venerable virtue of Molay, in his profession of a sacred knight, and in his words which disclosed a pure soul. If then to 'those feelings of a disturbed heart of the King there was joined a secret remorse of conscience, one can easily conjecture that the spectres of the unhappy Templars must have haunted the palace of Philip. Heaven seemed to answer the appeal of Molay. He had expired on March 11th, 1314, in the midst of flames with the chief knights of the sacred militia. Forty days afterwards Pope Clement passed out of this life to the next. At this sad news Philip must have thought of the Grand-Master, and must have felt the ground giving way under him. In the meanwhile the people impoverished by taxes, and by the falsification of the money, which still continued, became riotous; and nobles for the same reasons were excited and besides by reason of their diminished power; from without the Flemings were emboldened by a truce very disgraceful to France; in fine a cry of malediction and horror was raised against him for the blood which superstition and cruelty had caused to flow in torrents throughout the kingdom.[115] The mind of the unfortunate prince was obscured. But the chastisement was but beginning; the infamy of his own family yet awaited him. True or false as it might have been, the adulteries of the wives of his three sons were revealed to him. The defilement of the princely beds filled him with an incredible rage, the last of his life. Public and solemn judgments displayed to the face of the world the ignominy of his race; and a great multitude of victims were cruelly

---

[113] (Idem) . . . . . . "et je vous prie
     Que devers la Vierge Marie
     Dont notre Seignor Christ fust nez
     Mon visage vous me tornez."
[114] Contin. William Nangi., p. 67.
[115] Sismondi. Hist of France, T. 6, 176, 177.

EPISCOPAL CHAIR IN THE CATHEDRAL OF ANAGNI.

immolated by fire and sword to his rage and to the disgrace of his children. The fear of the dead, the suspicions of the living, the infamy of his children broke his spirit; struck by that anathema which God plants secretly in certain hearts, and which he afterwards conceals by the purple, his soul in pain and restless, reacted on his body, and silently consumed it. Philip fell ill in the month of November, eight months after the appeal of the Grand-Master. Neither wound, nor fever consumed him; in appearance he seemed healthy; something was gnawing at his vitals with deadly effect; everybody was astounded, and knew not what to say. Philip died of that death of the spirit, caused by certain mysterious chastisements rarely dealt out by Heaven![116]

Although the Ponitfical acts which were displeasing to Philip, had been erased and burned, that malediction pronounced by the holy Pope Benedict against Anagni, struck with terrible force that unfortunate town, guilty of so great a treason. Leander of Bologna[117] passing there in 1616 found it all in ruins, and in such squalor as to strike the heart with pity. Amid this great scene of desolation, the remains of the palace where Boniface had dwelt, and in which he had been in imprisoned by the treason of the inhabitants of Anagni, still were standing as accusing witnesses of the crimes they had seen, and as guardians, so to speak, of these ruins. The traveller interrogated some of the oldest inhabitants of Anagni as to the cause of this devastation, and they told him that, from the time of the captivity of Boniface, they had had nothing but misfortunes to deplore. Plagues, famine, the exile of her citizens had diminished the number of inhabitants; the walls had fallen by fire and sword during civil wars. The country had been plunged into this abyss of evils by her own children. And continuing they said that, dismayed by the lasting calamities, and almost giving up hope, the

---

[116] "Philippus rex Franciae diuturna detentus infirmitate, cujus causa medicis erat incognita, non solum ipsis et aliis multis multi stuporis materiam et admirationis inducit: praesertim cum infirmitatis aut mortis periculum nec pulsus ostenderet nec urina. Tandem apud fontem Blundi, unde et oriundus se deferri praecepit." Contin. Chron. Nangii ap. Achery, Tom. III, p 69.

[117] See Ciacconio for the year 1294, Col. 302.

few remaining citizens had met in counsel to discover the cause of this continual misfortune; and they all agreed that it was the wickedness of their forefathers towards Pope Boniface VIII. And so they concluded to entreat Pope Clement VII to send them a bishop to absolve them again, and in the meantime the people would pray and implore divine mercy. So whilst in France there was placed on the head of Philip a stone, upon which there could not be recorded what kind of a death had brought him to the tomb, a cloud of mysterious and long-enduring calamities gathered over unhappy Anagni.

Our story is now at length drawing to a close, and it is time to return at the end, to that which was said in the beginning. We have said, the reader will remember, that the Pontificate of Boniface VIII was a generating fact so personified by this Pope, that after his fall the principle defended by him could no longer offer resistance to the contrary principle, but rather had to confess itself conquered, and to yield little by little to the victor. We come to the sad demonstration of what has been affirmed; and seated on that sepulchre which still resounds with that divine sentence, *"every creature is subject to the Roman Pontiff,"* let us raise the mind to the consideration of the consequences which proceeded only too rapidly from the failure of the efforts of Boniface and the victory of his enemies. Because the present generation is taught by the past, it will be permitted to hope, if not for us, at least for posterity, a future equipment of civil happiness founded on a just conciliation of contrary principles which dispute the mastery of the world. This conciliation is not in the sword of the conqueror, nor hidden in the mutable wisdom of human legislators, but is a thing of God the secret of which rests in the bosom of the Vicar, where God himself deposited it.

Some Pontiffs have been persecuted, and tortured for the faith, the fury of the people or the tyranny of Christian Kings have made others suffer the tribulation and sorrows of exile; not one had been judged and condemned. The first one to be put to this sad ordeal was Boniface. The first and the second in persecution and in blood obtained the palm of martyrdom, and were raised up to Heaven from the throne on which they sat. Boniface did not find even compassion in his ignominy; he descended from his throne, and with him the Pontificate, or rather he was dragged from it and led into the Sanhedrin of lawyers and sophists, to force him like Jesus Christ to tell what truth is. All classes of believers in the Gospel once reverently stopped at the doors of the Church, and they did not dare to ask how far their limits extended, what was the book of their rights, nor of what temper was the sceptre he carried in hand. But Boniface dead, they did not merely enter into the sanctuary of God, they rather invaded it, and they pounced upon the Church to show her that the limits of her inheritance were no longer the limits of the earth, but precisely those that men marked out accordingly to their will around her; that her code of laws were obsolete, powerless, and had no light or value except from the will of men; in fine this sceptre by whose touch human societies had been constituted and the throne of a hundred kings had been raised and cast down, was only spiritual, purely spiritual. We come now to show how this limitation of the liberty or rather the life of the Church came about.

Heaven wished to punish the sacrilege of Anagni, and to teach posterity by the severity and bitterness of the chastisements. Although the principal actors in this frightful drama, Philip and his satellites, were French, yet Sciarra Colonna, and the traitors of the Campagna who had taken part in it, were Italian, and Anagni was an Italian city. For this reason then Philip having been punished in his family, which became extinct, Italy must, as the particular seat of the Pontificate, submit to a more rigorous chastisement, and be punished wherein it had sinned. To the astonishment of the whole world the chair of St. Peter was seen transferred from Rome to Avignon, a town in Provence. This removal was rendered necessary not by an incursion of barbarians, nor by the ravages of plagues or wars, but it was the work of an invisible hand, which disconcerts the mind by an occurrence the causes and the meaning of which it does not perceive. The terror excited by the violent acts of Philip and those of the Orsini family, acts which hastened the death of a generous Pope, the expectation of the future prevented the Romans from perceiving all the evils that were engendered by the prolonged exile of Clement V in France, due to Philip the Fair. The Pontifical palace was silent and deserted; the Basilica of the Apostles was bereft of its Pontiff; and that virtue, which rose from their sepulchres, and from the sacred sand of the amphitheatre, returned to disappear through bereavement, not finding the heart to which it had been united for thirteen centuries. Rome was like a conquered city for the Roman patriciate, who, not feeling any longer the weight of the hand of Boniface on their heads, became possessed of excessive pride, without ever ennobling it by a thought of honest ambition. The clergy were many, but poor; the people employed by the patricians in dishonorable work, showed all the evils of want of government. Cardinal Napoleon Orsini, in 1314 after the death of Clement V, wrote some letters to Philip the Fair, which describe to us sufficiently the conditions of Rome.[118] He and his Italian colleagues pursued at Carpentras with hostile cries, and threatened with daggers in the hands of Gascons who shouted: *"Death to the Italian Cardinals, Moriantur Cardinales Italici,"* [119] experienced what it was to create a Pope in a foreign country. Hence in these letters he breaks forth into lamentations at the sight of Rome and Italy reduced to such a deplorable condition. Two things are to be remarked in these letters: the avowal that the see of St. Peter, nay of Christ himself, had gone to wreck; [120] and the particular grief which Orsini seemed to feel at the sight of so much misery, as if he was the cause of it.[121] The Cardinal saw with tears in his eyes, the calamities which had fallen on the Church, because his own firmness had not equalled that of Boniface, and he recognized perhaps the fault he had committed in cooperating to shorten the days of that Pontiff. Nevertheless the evils which he deplored were only a prelude to sadder ones that were to come. Public worship lost its splendor; the clergy were corrupt and simoniacal; the churches were falling into ruin; the

---

[118] Baluz. Collect. Aucto. Vet. Tom. II, p. 289.

[119] Idem. Epist. Encycl. Cardinal. Italo. de incendio urbis Carpentoratensis post obitum Clements V. Pape.

[120] "Sedes B. Petri, immo domini nostri. J. Christi disrupta est." Idem.

[121] "O quot dolores sustinuimus ista videntes, et maxine ego. . . . .

bonds of all discipline were broken, although the bishops of Orvieto, delegated by the absent Popes to take their place in the spiritual things of the Church, appeared still to hold these bonds in their hands. And in order that not even the memory of civil grandeur might remain, the monuments of old Rome were wretchedly demolished and lost. The fury of the citizens made of them a rampart for the combatants, and avarice an object of traffic. Let the reader glance at the letters of Francis Petrarch, that truly Latin personage, and he will find there the sad history of these calamities.

Italy could not have been in a worse state at the period when deprived of the Roman Pontiff. If Heaven perhaps had not destined this country for a future civil and religious resurrection, this then was truly the time in which it could have been ruined forever, and have allowed the proud throne of some Emperor of the Romans establish itself on the ruins of her liberty. The Italian cities had arrived at that stage, in which the republican forms of government were changing into principalities. They were not constituted into republics after the anterior designs of some clever legislator who had known how to regulate the opposing parties in the state, in such a manner as to prevent them from transforming themselves into anarchy, or a tyrannical monarchy; but necessity determined their choice. The republics, in fact, were formed amid barbarism and the devastation of the country, inasmuch as there did not exist among them, on account of the general poverty, great riches, which incorporated into the hands of a few, or one alone, could have been able to make the civil-organization degenerate into a aristocracy, or monarchy (as riches are the first foundation of power). Venice alone, enriched by her commerce with distant countries, was able to establish hirself solidly, and give to her government the character of a powerful aristocracy. So a certain equality of rights among the citizens directed the political organization of the Italian cities, but as soon as the inequality of wealth arose, the jealous love of liberty advised the entrusting of the government of these cities for a year, to a foreign governor; an advice which revealed the absence of a domestic virtue sufficient to prevent the inconveniences which they thought to remedy by means of a transient, and very short, it is true, but a foreign government.

The Popes noticed full well the decadence and the brevity of the life of the republics, and before entering upon the work of their civil reorganization, they thought of averting the present dangers to which the violent German domination exposed them. Alexander III interposed between the Lombards and Barbarossa, arresting him in the conquest of Lombardy, aiding those there to live in the republican league until the Popes would be able to establish themselves as the peaceful arbiters of the future destinies of these republics. But the vices of the democracy increased with the inability to remedy them, and the need of a foreign conciliator increasing also, by reason of their domestic quarrels, the cities had recourse, no longer to governors, but to princes who had in their hands more power, such as Charles of Anjou, and the Emperor of Germany. The imperial vicars, and those of the Angevine prince, represented the principality and not the protectorate in the Italian republics; so that the immediate and first effect of this was the aggrandizement of the aristocracy in the democratic cities. And inasmuch as the house of Anjou of Naples and the Emperors fought with equal strength on Italian territory, it fell to the lot of the Popes, and the young Italian aristocracy, the mission of receiving within their arms the dying republics; the one powerful by reason of its moral, and the other by reason of its material strength. The former tended to a certain magistracy of preservation, the latter to an absolute principality, which would rob the common country of her independence, by excluding the Papal supremacy. Popes Nicholas III and Nicholas IV were fully cognizant of this mission, the accomplishment of which should have been the work of Boniface VIII, as the succession to the throne of Germany was uncertain and Charles II of Naples was narrow-minded, and short-sighted.

But the aforesaid Popes created for themselves, by the disastrous elevation of their own families, obstacles to the execution of this plan. The Colonnas and the Orsini, by their seditious movements, annoyed and kept the Popes busy at home; and far from leaving them free in their laborious struggle with kings for the liberty of the Church, tied their hands and furnished their enemies additional weapons. The whole Pontificate of Boniface was a proof of that which we assert. Moreover, the encounter of a king such as Philip the Fair, with a Pope such as Gaetani contributed also to interrupt quickly the course of this tutelary mission. It was inevitable that the increasing right of princes should one day clash with the immutable right of the Church. But if the encounter had been so delayed as to allow the Popes time to make themselves the Sovereign arbiters and protectors of all Italy and to establish this arbitration and this protectorate by the force of public right, we do not doubt that the Italian country and the Church would have succeeded in the conquest of a common individuality, and the Alps and the sea would have been bulwarks of Italian and ecclesiastical liberty. A prompt and decisive war between men of the character of Boniface and Philip the Fair was necessary; Boniface was defeated, and with him fell mortally wounded the hope of this double independence.

If the defeat was stranger, the effects of it were no less so. For many years Rome was bereft of the Pope, and Italy of the Pontificate. The last acts of Boniface with regard to Florence were followed by sad consequences. The Ghibelline party increased by the persecution; it incarnated in itself the thought of those who, despairing of all other means, turned to the German emperors. Considering only the present, and competely blind to the future, the exiles, together with the more steady and calm spirits made of these emperors their cherished dream; the former, through partisan passion, and with a hope of personal benefit, and the latter through a desire of civil order. For this reason there was revived in Italy, the imperial principle once overthrown in Rudolph, by the power of Charles of Anjou, and which was confronted by the nascent Italian aristocracy already very powerful, although in its infancy; the one or the other had to settle the destinies of Italy; the first by transforming our country into a German province; the latter, by dividing it into many principalities. The imperial idea threatened it with a certain loss of all civil independence; with the aristocracy the same loss was easy, but yet easy to be regained.

The imperial idea, whose character is unity, was ere

long personified by Henry VII of Luxemburg; the aristocracy by the Visconti of Milan, by the Estes of Modena, by the princes of Savoy, and by the Marquises of Montferrato. These representatives of the aristocracy were many, and consequently were jealous of one another; they rose upon the ruins of the republics and were consequently badly established in their dominions. Wherefore emulous of power and desirous of retaining it, instead of combining like the old republics, they were divided and strove to strengthen themselves separately. Unfortunately the love of their family, and not that of country, was uppermost in their thoughts. For this reason being obliged to have recourse to some one more powerful, they allied themselves as vassals to the German emperor, in order to retain on their heads that crown, which if leagued together, they could have retained more honestly, and with greater advantage to their common country.

But this confederation was impossible. For they lacked altogether unity of a centre around which to assemble; they lacked a judge who could define the justice of their rights; they lacked the Supreme Priest, who could have blessed them, like in the time of the Lombard league, in a word they lacked the Pope. However, Italy at that time received, from the House of Anjou of Naples, an unexpected benefit. Robert, a man infinitely superior to his father Charles II, both in courage and in shrewdness, reigned in Naples. Placed at the head of the Guelph party, acknowledged by many of the Italian cities, if not as master, at least as their protector; invited like his grandfather Charles I to constitute the Italian principality for his own benefit; nay even better treated than his grandfather by fortune, since the Pope was no longer at Rome, to hinder, like Nicholas IV the realization of this ambitious design, Robert succeeded in checking Henry VII, who moreover died suddenly; but he did not succeed in grasping the reins of that principality. He drove off an enemy, Henry of Luxemburg, but he could not bring the Italians, his friends, to submit to his sovereignty. The new Italian princes were not heads of factions, but of a state; whence they considered Robert a rival, and a rival so much the more dangerous as he was powerful who could, with the aid of the Guelph party, crush their infant sovereignties. And hence at the first movement of Luxemburg, the princes all became Ghibellines. Amadeus V, and Philip prince of Achaia, lords of Savoy, voluntarily opened the way into Italy. They had been Guelphs, and were even the mainstay of that party; now not only did they allow the German Emperor to freely pass, but also assisted him by their good offices at the court of Avignon to have his election as emperor confirmed, and also furnish him arms. Luxemburg had with him Germans, Burgundians, and French, who could restore the times of the infancy of Frederick II; in front marched the revived Ghibellines. Brescia arrested the course of Henry; it destroyed three fourths of his army, and gave time to Robert and the Guelphs of Florence to oppose efficaciously the invasion of the German Emperor. A signal benefit for which the present and the future generations of this peninsula can never be too grateful to that king and that republic.

At the time of Henry's death, the aristocracy had already accomplished the transformation of the republics into principalities. The Guelphs became stronger and stronger; but they did not possess their former life, for they were only an instrument of the ambitions of Robert. Henry being dead, this prince had himself declared by Clement the vicar of the empire in Italy, and renewed the undertaking of the conquest of the Italian principality. But in place of the unstable democracies of old, he encountered round about him firm sovereignties, the most powerful of which was that of the Visconti in Milan, who could find no reason for allowing Robert to do that which they should and ought to do to prevent them from becoming vassals of the House of Anjou. The Ghibellines and the Visconti presented a bold front to the daring Angevine, and the former under the leadership of Uguccione of Fagginola defeated the army of Robert at Montecatini; and the latter hemmed in this prince so closely in Genoa, that although the city was not surrendered, yet they gave a mortal blow to his material power and to his reputation. This siege, which by contemporaries has been likened to that of Troy, put an end to the hopes of that of Robert, and to the fears of the new Italian princes; and then began the parcelling of Italy into a number of small sovereignties, or seignories, rivals of one another, enemies of concord, blind to the interest of the common country, seeing only their distinctive individuality, hence powerful for intestine feuds, powerless to repulse the attacks of strangers, and bartering their own independence and that of all Italy for the princely interests of the families who governed and personified them.

When Gregory XI returned to Rome from Avignon, the old Roman Pontificate did not return with him. This Pontificate, after being seen in opposition with foreign princes, now was also in strife with the Italian princes; and the Italian people, who under other forms of governments, had been, from the time of Alexander III, the chief source of its temporal power, were unable to assist it, because their own individuality had been absorbed by that of the princes. So then as Italy had to mourn the loss of the Pontificate, the Pontificate was saddened at the loss of the devotion of Italy to its See; but her impotence seemed to make her forget her civil mission. Moreover the Popes who then ruled Christendom, acting exclusively in their capacity as princes, determined, after the example of other sovereigns, to elevate their relations and create principalities for them. They also, yielded to hopes and fears which were neither patriotic nor Italian, but purely individual, allowed themselves to be drawn towards the great foreign potentates, and contributed to the greater division of their country, a division like the one with which Charles V and Francis I threatened it. Thus Italy seemed the prey of foreigners, the prey consecrated and sanctified by the Popes, who consoled themselves with the beautiful domains of the Medicis and the Farneses. A powerful voice made itself heard, that of Julius II, and called for the expulsion of the barbarians from Italy. But the sound of this voice was not reechoed in the courts of the princes, who were equally barbarians with foreigners; and it was not heard by the people, because it came from the breast of a prince, and not from a Pontiff. Men of the time in which these things happened and posterity have cursed the work of the Popes, and wished to make the Roman Pontificate responsible and persecute it; but in this they were deceived. The Pontificate stood no longer in the low regions in which the political destinies of Italy, conducted by human wisdom, moved, but in the sublime regions in which divine providence accomplished the mystery of the catholicity of its Church. Like Jesus Christ its author, whom the Jews threatened to stone, believing that He aspired to royalty, the civil Pontificate had hidden itself, and it went out from that temple in which a double unity assembled the people; unity of faith which still assemble them and will ever assemble them; and that unity of filial confidence with which they intrust to the Pontificate the direction of their civil destinies. The proceedings of Philip the Fair against Boniface drove it from the States, and rendered it invisible; it no longer existed in the temple of civil justice.

We have said that Jesus Christ was the author of the civil Pontificate. Now as He is also the author of the eternal Pontificate which governs visibly the Church militant, it followed that believers having been removed, as citizens of the state, from the civil empire of the Roman Church, were miserably confused as the faithful afterwards; and they began to be wanting in charity, which is the bond of hearts; in faith which is that of the soul, and afterwards in the civil order, which is the social bond. For the civil Pontificate is only a necessary consequence of the eternal Pontificate. For forty years, that is from 1378 to 1418 the Church was torn by the most formidable of schisms; which drew its strength from the doubt and the uncertainty of the true Vicar of Christ; and while the minds were struggling in the search of the true Pontiff, Wyclif, supported by his satellite John Huss, was laying the foundation of all modern heresy, with which the ancient ones had nothing in common but error; but the reason of the error was altogether his own, and up to that time was unknown. From Simon Magus up to the XV century, the heresies, although they were distinguished by the different aberrations of human intellects which conceived them, yet they all possessed one only substantial individuality, namely the denial and rejection of the infallible judgment of the Church in her definitions. But from Wyclif down to our days heresy is distinguished from all preceding heresies by a certain substantial individuality, which consists in the substitution of reason, not of humanity but of man taken separately, for the infallible authority of revelation. The ancient heresies would only destroy; modern heresy raised on the ruins of revelation, a throne to reason defining. This Wycliff was a terrible man, and a real giant of error. We shall not speak in detail of his heresy condemned by the Fathers of the Council of Constance, but rather of that which, according to us, constitutes its own individuality, and that of the later heresies. The prolific germ of so much and ruin is in the "Trialogue" the principal book of Wycliff. In that work he introduces as disputing, Truth, the symbol of the good, Error, the symbol of the bad Theology, and Science, which is a figure of Wyclif himself.[122] Here is the throne erected to individual reason, and the first to sit upon it is Wycliff, a place which he bequeathed later to Luther. He defines; and the judgment could not be anything else but the negation of truth, atheism.[123] Now, this man who, as infallible judge, made himself depository of the truth, did not view it, did not call it atheism, but he preached it implicitly, and gave it, included in the immediate consequences of his principles, as the foundation of the reformed Church in Germany.

The kings had freed themselves from all civil allegiance to the Roman Pontificate; they considered themselves free and independent of that which they called the fetters of the Roman court; they were alone on their thrones and they acknowledged no one superior to them but Almighty God. Human reason defied by Wycliff did not make them fear; on the contrary whilst they were displaying grief, like the Emperor Sigismund at Constance, over the harm which it did to Catholic dogma, they perceived with interior joy that this individual reason had secured an infallibility which could at once guarantee them against the important supervision of the Supreme Priesthood, and the impertinent inquiry of the people. They learned later and too late that the people also had an individual reason. This is why Luther, who concealed under the hypocritical authority of the Bible, the only and infallible authority of his own reason, found favor in the courts of Germany, because he generously made use of this reason towards the Princes; who up to that time held within the limits of

---

[122] Book IV.   [123] Bossuet, History of Variations. Book II.

Catholic morality now saw this heresiarch open to them, and also sanctify all the wicked paths, which it pleased them to pursue. The heresy of Luther first infected the princes, and afterwards the people. It infected especially the former, because they had much to gain by the exclusion of the Papacy.

The Reformation accomplished two sad results, the one mortal, which was the separation of a large number of princes with their subjects from the Roman Church; and the other contagious, which was to chill more and more the devotion of all the other princes to the Papal See. The latter continued to adore Jesus Christ in the Eucharist; to believe in free will and Purgatory; they continued to say and show themselves, in all that did not offend their pride, loving children in Christ of the Pope; but, acting as not very affectionate children, they expelled him from their states, and they repelled the Church, forcing her to confine herself to the invisible sanctuary of her dogmas. They did not proclaim, like Luther that the Church was invisible; but they deprived her of her visibility, scarcely allowing her the sensible forms of her exterior worship. The Church is visible not only in the explicit confession of her dogmas, in the use of her sacraments, but also in that which is the essence of her visibility, subjection to the Pontiff, the Vicar of Jesus Christ. He presides over every Catholic man in the complement of his individuality, that is to say, in his reason. Now as the social life is the life of man, precisely because he is rational, the Vicar of Jesus Christ cannot rule every man with out touching, with his authority, civil society in which there exists the complement of man. The princes expelled the Pope from this society, they confined him in the Church; and while they called themselves Catholic, and most Christian, political atheism dishonored the administration of their States. From political to religious atheism was only a step, and the follies of Henry VIII could be multiplied in other courts. He had been scandalized by the errors of Luther, he had won the beautiful title of Defender of the Faith, having defended it even by his writings, against the German novelties; and yet without attacking at first any dogma, only because he found the Papal authority firm as a wall against his beastly passions, he severed from the Church, England that choice portion of Christendom, not with the sword of the syllogism, but with the axe of the executioner. This separation was not preceded by any new doctrines nor by any disputes, but only by the deep roaring of a heart, stung by the Pontificate in the wound which a criminal lust had inflicted. The Christian kings were surprised and scandalized by the brutal wantonness of the English King, and by his furious schism. They attached themselves more closely to the Roman See; but they no longer believed rightly in its supremacy, and hence prepared the way for new and dangerous schisms.

Subjection to the Roman Pontiff, as Vicar of Jesus Christ, not only in all that affects faith and morals, but also in that which affects indirectly civil society, is for Catholics a dogma like those of the Trinity and the Eucharist. And as this dogma is proposed to our belief by an absolute revealing principle, not liable to a human contingency, so the belief ought to be also absolute, invariable and one. Now to say that some believe in a greater, and others in a lesser supremacy in the Roman Pontiff, is absurd, just as it would be absurd to speak of greater or less affirmation of the dogma of the Trinity. Dogma is one like God; it is so rigorously concentrated in unity, that it allows no room for a diversity of opinions. Hence unless they wish to renounce the Catholic principle, or while admitting the principle illogically deny the consequence,—the faithful should always be subject to the Popes as they once were to Gregory VII, exception being made of political influence, which the modern public right no longer accords the sovereign Pontiff. Therefore the Papal condescensions at the price of which a deceitful peace was bought, should sooner or later engender open war against the essence of the dogma of the Pontifical supremacy. The germ of these hostilities is always in the character of the times and of the men. Now when the first of these concessions was made, the times were already mature, and they awaited the men, with the aid of whom they would be able to produce their venomous ???

The Council of Constance and the Reformation of Luther matured the times, and Louis XIV was the man that the times looked for. Thanks to the removal of the

Holy See to Avignon by the intrigue of Philip the Fair, the Church had fallen into such a deplorable condition, that, during forty years, no Pope had won the universal suffrage for the supreme power with which he was vested. The people and the kings were divided, not on the legitimacy of the right of Papal supremacy, but on the legitimacy of the fact, that is to say, on the person in which this supremacy resided. It was in the midst of such great diversity of opinions in a thing in which the life of Catholic unity entirely rested, that the Council of Constance was convoked. Its legitimacy depended on that of the Pope who convoked it. Now as John XXIII, Gregory XII and Benedict XIII, all called themselves Pontiffs, this fact kept the minds of the Fathers undecided, and wavering and in this frame of mind they took their seats in the Council of Constance. They had to decide the legitimacy of the three Pontiffs, and as all three had followers throughout Christendom, here was the example of a Pope judged by a Council. Their judgment referred to the fact, and not to the right; it concerned the three men who called themselves Popes, and not the legitimate successors of St. Peter; therefore they assembled, although divided in opinion, to decide that all the faithful, even those vested with Papal authority, should submit to their decrees.[124] That which was decided by reason of the circumstances of the times, and affecting the three pretenders to the Papacy, was regarded and received by some as a decision universal, absolute, and affecting all the legitimate successors of St. Peter. For such it did not suffice as an argument to the contrary, that the very Fathers of the Council of Constance, in their condemnation of the heresies of Wycliff, proclaimed the independence of the Papal supremacy; and that Martin V, in a consistory held March 10th, 1418, decided and declared in a Bull, that there could be no appeal from a Pope to a Council. Gerson wrote against the Papal decision founded as it was on the tradition of fourteen centuries, and on reason; and in France especially, where the tradition of the acts of Philip the Fair was preserved, the opinion of Gerson was

---

[124] Coll. Concill. Conc. Const. sess, 4, Vide Schelestrate de Concil. Constant Dissert, 2, c. 2

received, and believed infallibly on account of the decision of the Council of Constance.

This decree of the Council of Constance eased the conscience of French kings as often as the Papal authority appeared to them importunate and excessive. Luther taught them to do things with a certain order. As this heresiarch had admitted a thousand times in his writings, the supremacy of the Roman Church, and had denied it afterwards, in order to escape the reproach of contradiction, he established the distinction between the Roman Church and the Roman Court. A precious distinction for the Gallicans, and one to which they adhered with great eagerness. For as the Council of Constance removed them from the immediate authority of the Pope, who could err and be summoned, as a party, before the council, so the distinction of Luther increased their independence as long as no voice came from Heaven to tell them when the voice of the Pontiff emanated from the Church, and when from the Court. Such was the maturity of the times, we now come to that of the men.

France, although tainted with the heresy of Calvin, remained attached to the Papal See. But unhappily Jansenism, assuming much of the reformations of Luther and Calvin, especially what touched Papal supremacy, was a peaceful vehicle of those poisonous consequences, which we have mentioned, and on account of which all France, while remaining Catholic, did not remain over tolerant of the infallible authority of the Roman Pontificate. The clergy from the time of Philip the Fair had been always looked upon with bias by the body of civil magistrates, who, believing in power, did not want an intermediary power between their own and that of the King. So, the jealousy of the jurists and the despotism of the Prince combined to fight against the liberty of the clergy and the Papal authority in France. Arrived at the zenith of power, feared by all Europe, surrounded by the highest intelligences of his age, deified by the poets, and by a court, which in the worship of the prince partook somewhat of idolatry, Louis XIV, was called the Great. Facts corresponded to the title, so was it easy for Louis to conceive in himself a greatness which unfortunately overpowered his reason. He could not broaden his mind sufficiently to see by whom he was surrounded, that is the people; nor who was placed above him, that is God, reigning visibly over him by his Vicar; and concentrating it all in himself, he found in himself only the principle and morality of all his actions. He appeared Catholic, because he assisted at Mass, communicated and fasted; and to confirm the appearances, he revoked the edict of Nantes, persecuted the Huguenots, and spent much money to convert them. But Louis, exalted by the courtiers, in the expansion of his power, was to encounter God and men. The encounter with men was reserved for the unfortunate Louis XVI, that with God was experienced by himself, He quarrelled with Pope Innocent XI for the same reasons that Philip the Fair disagreed with Boniface VIII; namely, on account of the immunity of the sacred patrimonies to which Louis opposed the rights of the Regalia, supported in his pretensions by his pride, and by Colbert, who did not find sufficient wealth in the public treasury for the royal conquests, for the conversion of the Huguenots, and also for certain other domestic expenses of Louis. The discussion of a particular right opened the way to that of the general right of the Church. The magistrates were the flower of the royal forces in this combat; behind theme were grouped the Jansenists, who furnished them with arms, but hidden, because Louis detested them for their rigor. (Louis was great in everything, even in the weaknesses of human nature); the ecclesiastics formed the rearguard. We shall relate briefly how the clergy came to be found in the ranks of the defenders of the royal power. Louis distributed according to his will some very rich prebends, and chose the pastors from among the noblest families that surrounded his throne; so that the higher clergy formed one brilliant mass with the civil aristocracy. Thus the riches, the favors of the Prince, and the feeling which the French call *enthusiasm,* and which so readily took possession of a French soul in presence of the greatness of Louis, and a certain pride in seeing the French Church distinguished from the others, by that which they believed to be privileges, and a particular liberty; in fine a leaning towards the Jansenistic theories, had, though with not a few exceptions, rendered the clergy most docile to Louis. During the ten years that he lived at court in educating the Dauphin, Bossuet, witness of all that transpired there, and which we will not mention, Bossuet whom La Bruyere has called a Father of the Church, did not utter a *non licet,* in order to shield at least his disciple from the scandals of his father.

In the beginning of the year 1681, all the clergy of France assembled at Paris under the presidency of the Archbishop of that city. Bossuet, then Bishop of Meaux, preached before that assembly; he attempted to prove the supremacy given by Jesus Christ to St. Peter over the Church, and proved from the faults of that Apostle, the necessity for the sovereign Pontiffs to link to their great powers an equally great humility and condescension. This doctrine clearly indicated the purpose for which they were assembled. The French prelates convoked by the King, proceeded to the compilation of the famous four articles, and decided: 1st, that the Pope invested with sovereign power over spiritual things, concerning eternal salvation, has no power whatever over temporal things; hence he cannot depose kings, or absolve their subjects from their oath of fidelity; 2nd, that the power of the successors of St. Peter can not disparage the decrees of the fourth and fifth session of the Council of Constance relative to the authority of general councils; 3rd, that this power is restricted and limited by the canons, and by the rules and usages adopted by the various churches, and especially by that of France; 4th, finally although it belongs to the Pope to decide all controversies relative to faith, and these decisions are binding on all the churches, yet these decisions can be reformed so long as they have not been sanctioned by the consent of the Universal Church. Here then is the Pontiff despoiled by these Catholics of that sovereign authority given to him by Jesus Christ; here are the faithful abandoned to themselves in the affairs of eternal salvation, and continually in the expectation of general councils; here was Catholic dogma conciliated with the invisibility, or better the nullity of the sovereign Pontifical power; here as a consequence was the work accomplished, not of Lutherans but of Catholics, that was begun from the time of Gregory VII, and conducted in such a prosperous manner after the death of Boniface VIII. The Apostolic Church groaned, but the grief she then felt at the recent loss of a beloved daughter, England, counselled prudence and consideration. Louis the Great was always considered a Catholic notwithstanding the increase and abuse of his rights of Regalia. France was considered Catholic notwithstanding the liberties of her Church. Many of her prelates deplored the evils of the wicked epoch, and especially that most amiable Fenelon, who beheld his beloved France in danger of following the example of unfortunate England.[125]

Because the Popes refrained from hurling anathemas against France, many thought that this was caused by fear or by a feeling of impotence. But no, their moderation was the work of God. He wanted to bring back to the truth, this illustrious clergy, which had merited so well of the Church, by a way which the compilers of the four articles had undoubtedly not foreseen. Louis taught the parliaments, by his wars against the Church, the use of that individual reason, which Wyclif and the Reformation had, as we mentioned before, proclaimed an infallible queen, deciding the truth between the just and the unjust. He, with the cooperation of the clergy, banished from the kingdom the detested supremacy of the Pope and the Church, and taught minds a liberty of thought which did not admit the belief in the existence of an absolute and unchangeable order; and each one decided between truth and error. In a word in the joy of his triumph he invited the proud philosophy of the XVIII Century, to behold from the height of his throne, his conquests over the Church; and whilst Massillon, sighing over the bier of the King, exclaimed that God alone was great, that XVIII century philosophy ridiculed both Louis and God.

God could have allowed that poison to escape, which the four articles had stored up in the body of the French nation, by the sharp and penetrating sword of anathema, but he would not. He willed that France should be punished by her own hands, and that the punishment would

[125] " Quae quidem infelicissima rerum spiritualium conditio, quod praesagit pro futuris temporibus, si minus principes regnent, nisi apertam gallicanae defectionem a Sede apostolica? Quod in Anglia contigit, hoc, idem apud nos eventurum valde metuo." Fenelon de Summi Pontif anctoritate, cap. 40.

be profitable to all Europe. The philosophers born in the shadow of the Reformation, grown up and taught in the shadow of the free Gallican Church, were the instruments of divine vengeance. They demolished, with the same stroke, both the throne and the altar. Heaven plunged France in the fire of a great tribulation, purified her, and in the ashes of that conflagration sowed the seeds of an universal generation. This terrible revolution was a design which God selected from the treasures of his anger; but a design wonderfully prolific of good, because God is the sovereign good. The puny minds of men thought that all good morals would be entirely lost; yet from that time the pagan lasciviousness of the court of Louis the Great no longer defiled royal courts and corrupted the people. Religion and worship were mourned as dead, and yet religion and worship lived and will live. The keys of St. Peter were thought to have been broken forever, and the Roman Church reduced to slavery by the crimes of France; and yet from that moment the clergy of St. Remy, and St. Hilary were ashamed of their liberties, as of chains of disgrace; forgetting the four articles, they atoned for their faults by the blood of an astounding martyrdom; the Spouse Jesus Christ, through the French priesthood, resumed her vestment of purple, and presented herself to her spouse delightfully adorned as in the noble days of pagan persecutions. An immense good resulted from an immense evil. The Church and the Reformation of Luther tried their strength in this subversion of human and divine things. The Reformation petrified, has seen the Bible in its hands perused by Strauss; and the Church ever young, standing above the ruins heaped up about her, chants the hymn of victory: "*Selutem ex inimicis nostris.*"

The French Revolution was the encounter of individual reasons, that of the people against that of the kings. Both of them were inimical to the infallible reason of God, which speaks and judges through the Pontificate; and therefore in their quarrels, both are indirectly beneficial to that same infallible reason. Long has been the war which the latter has sustained since God placed her among men; her enemies succeeded one another because they were weary and powerless. No one succeeded her, because she is eternal and immutable like the mind of God. Since this struggle goes on still, between her enemies, and there is seen no possibility or hope of a peaceful settlement between them, should we not foresee the return of that civil Pontificate, which like a father may pardon the ingratitude of his children, and be reconciled with them in the kiss of love?

We do not know if this poor history has succeeded in removing from Boniface, the Italian, that infamy with which both his countrymen and foreigners wished to darken his name. But if, thanks to it, his memory appears to some readers in a more favorable light, let them frame a wish with us; it will find no doubt on the Papal Chair, a heart to welcome it;—Let the ashes of the brave and courageous Gaetani appear in the light of the immense basilica of St. Peter. The obscure crypts of the Vatican where they rest would seem the refuge of a disgraceful greatness. Let them appear in the light, in order that the lineaments of his funeral statue be, before the whole world, a monument of Italian firmness. Let them appear in the light, in order that the civil Pontificate on its return, may find a throne not unworthy of its mission, the tomb of the magnanimous Boniface. We feel it coming, it is returning. May certain readers pardon the presentiment we have of so great a return If it be an error on our part, it is a fault not of the mind but of the heart, and faults of the heart are always pardoned.

FINIS.

NOTES AND DOCUMENTS.

DOCUMENT (A).

BRIEF OF POPE ALEXANDER IV IN FAVOR OF BENEDICT GAETANI.

(Extract from the archives of the Church of Todi.)

Alexander Episcopus Servus Servorum Die Dilectis Filiis Priori et Capitulo Ecclesiae Tudertinae salutem et Apostolicam benedictionem. Volentes Dilecto Filio Benedicto Cajetani Canonico Anagnino gratiam facere specialem recipiendi eum in Ecclesia vestra, in qua praebendarum collatio ad vos pertinere dicitur, in Canonicum et fratrem, et providendi ei de praebenda, si vacet ibidem ad praesens, vel quamprimum ad id obtulerit se facultas, non obstante statuto ipsius Ecclesiae de certo Canonicorum numero, et illo quo ordinatur quod nullum recipiatis nisi sit in Sacris Ordinibus constitutus, etiamsi statuta hujusmodi sint juramento confirmata Sedis Apostolicae, sive quacumque firmitate vallata, ... per alia scripta nostra quibus nolumus ante praesentem. . . . . seu si vobis ab eadem Sede indultum existat quod ad receptionem vel provisionem alicujus minime teneamini per literas praedictas . . . . . quae de indulto hujusmodi plenam et expressam non fecrit mentionem secundum. . . . . indulgentia dictae Sedis, de qua circa tenorem oporteat in nostris literis plenam et expressam mentionem facere, per quam effectus anni gratiae impediri valeat vel differdi, libera auctoritate concedimus ante praesentem facultatem statutis . . . . . per receptionem ipsius . . . . nihilominus roboratis. Datum Anagni VI. Idus Junii Pontificatus nostri Anno VI.

DOCUMENT (B).

DECREE OF THE CANONS OF TODI IN FAVOR OF BENEDICT GAETANI.

In Nomine Domini Amen. Anno ejusdem Nativitate 1260 Indictione III, tempore D. Alexandri PP. IV die 14 exsedentis mensis Augustis in Choro Ecclesiae coram DD. Goffrido Archidiacono Tudertino D. Bartolo Juris Civilis professore, D. Jacobo Cajetani et Maccabrino Canc. S. Joannis de Platea, D. Justinus Prior, D. Bonaefidanza Archipresbyter S. Terentiana, D. Ugolinus Bonifazi, D. Bonavera, D. Ugolinus Lucii, et D. Uffredutius Canonici Ecclesiae Tudertinae volentes vener, patri D. Pietro Episcopo Tudertino gratiam facere specialem ac sibi, placere Benedictum Nepotem ipsius D. Episcopi, Priorem S. Illuminatae communiter concorditer ac liberaliter recipiunt in ipsa Ecclesia in eorum canonicum ac fratrem, et per pacis osculum ac etiam per pannos Altaris de ipso Canonicatu et juribus canonicatus eundem corporaliter investierunt, a Summo Pontifice eisdem super receptione hujusmodi tributa licentia occasione juramenti quo tenebantur de nn recipiendo aliquem nisi esset in Sacris Ordinibus constitutus, et supra aliis quae in ipsis Literis Apostolicis continentur.

NOTE (C)

NOTE RELATIVE TO THE DUEL BETWEEN PETER OF ARAGON AND CHARLES OF ANJOU AGAINST THE INSINUATIONS OF POTTER.

Whilst narrating the embassy confided to Gaetani with the intention of restraining Charles from fighting a duel with Peter of Aragon, there was brought to our notice a book by Potter, an erudite historian, but of notoriously bad faith, who seems to have undertaken the task, not of expounding the truth, but of making history accessory to his own hatred against the Church and the sovereign Pontiffs. The base and dishonorable passion, whose tendency is to build and obscure reason, which it inebriates with a sweet revenge, failed of its intent. For when he arrives at the end of his chapters, inebriated by revenge which he relished and resting with an air of triumph on the thousand quotations from authors devoid of sound judgment, he inspires us with only one feeling for him, that of pity. Describing that duel he declares, "according to writers of the times," (there were no others but Villani[1]), that the ambassadors of Peter swore in the presence of Pope Martin, for their master, to observe the conditions of the duel, and he condemns the annalist Oderic Rinaldi, who declares on the contrary that Pope Martin forbade the duel under pain of excommunication. Finally in order to lead the simple minded into the snare, he gives us to understand that Rinaldi wrote four years after the event, and for that reason he cannot be an authority; and besides his account, said he, is contrary to the Bull of Martin published against Peter of Aragon, precisely because he failed to arrive at the place fixed for the combat. Now to decide with an assurance so magisterial, Potter should learn some facts he did not know.

Without doubt the authority of Villani is not to be despised in that which concerns the events which happened in his time; but on the other hand we are not to believe blindly the testimony of a

[1] Lib. 7, c. 85, 86.

man when proofs contradict him. Authentic documents are always an authority superior to that of any author whatsoever, because they are facts, and facts are undeniable. Now the letter of Martin IV to Charles, which we have already mentioned, is such as to warrant us not to believe the account of Villani. The oath of agreement to the duel taken in the presence of the Pope, and the confirmation of it by the same cannot be reconciled with "*duellum . . . . reprobamus, irritamus ac penitus vacuamus;* the very duel the Pope declares that "*non sit omnino ab Ecclesia tolerandum;*" nor can it be reconciled with the sudden mission entrusted to Gaetani, to prevent the two princes from fighting a duel. Inasmuch as Potter and the others have not succeeded in proving the falsity of the Pope's letter and the mission of Gaetani, it will be impossible for us to accept the statement of Villani without contradicting sound reason. Rinaldi then is not to be judged as a writer who narrates of four hundred years after the event, but rather after he had examined the letter of Pope Martin, and the authors he quotes. We may add that the contemporary writers say absolutely nothing about the oath taken in the presence of the Pope, and approved by him, William Nangis, a Frenchman, who lived in that age, mentions the challenge, but has nothing to say of the Papal approbation; there is no mention of it by Matthew of Westminster, by the English Friar Trivett in his chronicle,[2] by Ptolemy of Lucca,[3] Ferrettus of Vicenza,[4] by Nicholas Speciale, Bartholomew of Neocastro, by Fazello, Sicilians and enemies of Martin IV, these last three would have unmercifully assailed him, if they had known that he approved of the duel.

Potter perhaps would not yield to these reasons; but he should acknowledg the letter of Pope Martin, unless he wishes to call it spurious. And although he should succeed in proving it false, would he succeed in suppressing the stubborn testimony of other documents? We entreat Potter especially to open Vol. 35 of Burmann, and let him stop at page 61 of the collection of Sicilians matters, and he will read this title: "*Acta de pugna Burdegalensi indicta inter* "*Petrum Aragoniae et Carolum Siciliae reges.*" These acts begin with a letter of Martin IV to Charles of Sicily which agrees exactly, as regards the sense, with that published by Rinaldi, and contains the express disapproval of the duel. This letter was not taken from the Papal archives, but from a MS. of the Colbertian Library in Paris. Let Potter read it, and let him tell us if Martin IV could forbid more energetically the disgraceful duel, and if he should swear so blindly by the testimony of one writer, such as Villani was, who mentions the Papal approval of the duel; and finally let him tell us from this example, whether the infallibility of the historian consists in a multitude of quotations, or in the rigor of his judgment as critic.

[2] Ad annum 1282-1283—
[3] Hist. Eccl. Book XXIV, c. 7, 8, S. R. I. T, p. 1188.
[4] Hist. Eccl. Book L. S. R. I. T., p. 953. [5] Thesaurus antiquitat, etc.

If Potter is still unconvenienced, let him consult the letters of Peter of Aragon and Charles of Anjou, inserted also in Burmann in the chapter we have mentioned, which treat extensively of that duel; and he will not find a syllable mentioning the Pope being present and approving the personal encounter between the two princes

When Peter of Aragon and Charles of Anjou agreed to the conditions of the duel, they were not in the same city. The former was at Messina, and the latter at Reggio in Calabria, and so they challenged by letters. The one of Peter ends thus: "*Datum Messanae tertio "Kalendas Januarii anno ab Incarnatione Domini millesimo ducen- "tesimo octuagesimo secundo, regnorum nostrorum Aragoniae anno "septimo, Siciliae vero primo.*" That of Charles: "*Datum Regii "penultima die mensis Decembris, undecima indictione, anno Domini "millesimo decentesimo tertie, regnorum Jerusalem anno sexto, Sicil- "iae vero decimo octavo.*" And the oath was taken neither by Charles nor by the ambassadors of Peter, but instead by forty knights deputed by both parties. "*Nos autem praefati quadraginta "milites, videlicet, etc., ad preces et requisitionem dicti regis Petri*" . . . . (and in the other of Charles) "*Bona et spontanea "voluntate nostra promittimus et juramus tactis Evangeliis sacro- "sanctis nos legaliter ac bona fide proposse factuos et curaturos quod "ipse rex Petrus*" (and in the other, "Carolus") "*praedicta omnia "per eum promissa et jurata firmiter adimplebit et inviolabiliter "observabit.*" It is evident the oath was not made in presence of the Pontiff.

Villani relating how Peter failed to fight the duel, says: "Pope "Martin having learned that king Peter had failed to keep his en- "gagement, deprived him of and expelled him from his kingdom as "excommunicated, a perjurer, a rebel and an unjust retainer of the "goods of the Church; and he excommunicated all who would obey "him or call him king." Potter concludes from these words that Pope Martin hurled the Bull of excommunication against Peter in order to punish him for having failed to fight the duel he so much desired. Nothing could be more false. The Bull against Peter was fulminated, according to the statement of Rinaldi, in the month of March, and the duel was to have taken place in June.

Now these are the pure lies upon which Potter established his theory that the Roman Church approved of the duel. In fact in a note written at the end of the second chapter of the book 5th, and to which he sweetly leads the reader, after having convinced him of the approbation given by the Pope to the duel, he with the greatest authority advances this proposition: "The single combats were made "part of the judgments of God; and they were not only tolerated "and approved, but even counselled, preached and prescribed by the "Church. . ."

Let the reader not wonder; for the facts related by Potter in confirmation of his statement are not the result of great erudition. If we be not mistaken, they were found by him all arranged in a certain work called: "*The Code of Humanity,*" under the word "*Duel*". But what are these facts? For example, that in the year 983 the Emperor Otho II, assisted by the great prelates of the Empire, published laws regarding duelling, and commanded that the authenticity of titles should be proved by a single combat; that in the beginning of the XI century the monks of St. Denis asked and obtained from King Robert the power to defend their property by judicial duels; that in the year 1020 the Archbishops of Ravenna, Milan and Treves approved of the laws of the emperor Henry regarding duelling: that a certain cleric of the diocese of Saintes had fought a duel with William, a monk of Vendome. We tarry here to tell the reader, that the last fact found in the letters of Godfrey, abbot of Vendome, and Cardinal, was immediately condemned by this same Godfrey. Potter himself relates this condemnation: "Godfrey condemns this doubly, at first as being, said he, contrary to ecclesiastical law, and secondly to the decrees of the Holy See." Potter should have omitted this condemnation which completely reverses his statement of the duel, "*approved, counselled, preached and prescribed by the Church*" The fact that two clerics had fought a duel; that a certain number of bishops, taken separately, had approved of duelling; that certain churches and abbeys had recourse to this means of defending their rights, do not suffice to prove that the Roman Church sanctioned and prescribed this cruel and brutal custom Among numerous other citations at the end of the chapter mentioned, Potter quoted also from Du Cange; but we doubt if he read the article; "*Duellum et Monomachia,*" of this writer. He would have found there that duelling as a proof of right had sprung from barbarism, and it was not sanctified as a law by any Pope, or by any council, but by princes still barbarous. And since in the civil court there had been no other way than duelling to guarantee his interests and prove his right of possession, it is no wonder that persons even consecrated to God should use the duel employing to fight in their stead, substitutes whom they called "*Vicedomini.*" If then, in a time of universal barbarism, the clergy had profaned their holy calling by the ferocity of duelling, one cannot conclude from these particular or even general facts that the Church sanctioned and prescribed duels. How many other detestible habits had crept in among the clergy, concubinage, for example, and simony? Yet who will venture to say that this wickedness was sanctioned by the Church?

Potter in his supplementary note speaks also of the prohibition of the Church against these single combats, but we do not know how he succeeds in finding the first example of this prohibition only at the late date of the Fourth council of the Lateran, held in 1215. At that time he seems to have had before his eyes the article, "Duel", of the "*Code of Humanity,*" and in it he could have read that duels had been condemned in the Council of Valencia in 855. Why not relate a prohibition so old?

And to go back to times even more remote, it will be sufficient to read the canon of this council. This is the beginning: "*Et quia ex*

"*hujusmodi juramentorum, immo perjuriorum, contentione etiam
"usque ad armorum certamina solet prorumpi, et crudelissimo spec-
"taculo effunditur cruor belli in pace, statuimus, 'juxta antiquum
"Ecclesiae obvservationis morem,' ut quicumque tam inigua et
"Christianae paci tam inimica pugna alterum occiderit, seu vul-
"neribus debilem redidderit, velut homicida nequissimus et latro
"cruentus ab Ecclesiae et omnium fidelium coetu separatus, ad
"agendam legitimam poenitentiam modis omnibus compellatur."*
Potter then should admit in the first place that the Roman Church never preached, counselled, and prescribed duelling; that on the contrary she has always expelled from her communion duellists as criminal homicides and sanguinary robbers; secondly, that this sentence was not promulgated so late as the Lateran Council, but from the IX century in the Council of Valencia; and finally that the ancient custom acknowledged in the IX century "*Antiquum ecclesiasticae observationis morem,*" means that the Church always abominated and condemned duellists.

From all these we draw a painful consequence for Potter, which is that he has erred through bad faith or through ignorance The first fault is unpardonable; the other can be pardoned provided he is willing to know it, and promises resolutely never again to undertake to write the facts of history without knowing them. Let Potter know that we address these words to him not only as a Catholic, but as an Italian. For as his Roman Church, defamed by him, is the special support and glory of Italy, in reviling her, he stabs to the heart our innocent and beloved country.

NOTE (D).

NOTE RELATIVE TO THE MASTER OF THE COURT (DOMINUS CURIAE) A TITLE GIVEN TO BENEDICT GAETANI BY PTOLEMY OF LUCCA.

Friar Ptolemy of Lucca relates, in his Annals that the first Cardinals to hasten to Aquila, were James Colonna, Peter Orsini, and Hugh Sequin; and he adds that they became masters of the court: "Interim "autem Dominus Jacobus de Colonna, et Dominus Petrus (no other "but Orsini was called by that name) et Dominus Ugo de Bellioneo "Aquilam vadunt, factique sunt domini curiae." He continues: "Quod alii cardinales videntes. Aquilam properant. Tunc venit "Aquilam Dominus Benedictus Cajetani, qui postea Bonifacius se-"quens, de quo credebatur, quod non gratiose videretur ibidem, eo "quod regem Carolum Perusiis plurimum exasperasset, qui statim "suis ministeriis et astutiis factus est Dominus curiae et amicus "regis." There were then according to Ptolemy, four masters of the court, Colonna, Orsini, the Frenchman, and Gaetani, who arrived too late to dominate, because the former three had already

*S. R. I. tom. XI, p. 1300.

taken the place. But then many do not dominate, or at least it is
necessary that these many should agree. Now the reader will remember, that in the conclave at Perugia, Colonna and Orsini were
the heads of the opposing parties; Villani says it clearly: "And
"after the death of Nicholas IV, the Papal chair remained vacant
"for eighteen months, by reason of the division among the Cardi-
"nals, one party of which, wanting a Pope to the liking of King
"Charles, had for its chief Matthew Rosso Orsini; and the other
"party opposed to this, had as head James Colonna." Now how
could they agree in dominating under a Pope acceptable to Orsini,
since he wanted a Pope friendly to Charles, and not agreeable to
Colonna? Colonna then could not be numbered among the masters
of the Court, nor could Gaetani for the same reason. The latter's
ironical interrogation addressed to Cardinal Latino in the conclave
at Perugia in regard to the visions of Peter Morrone; his slow and
all but forced departure for Aquila, evidently prove that he was not
well satisfied with the election of Celestine. As the enmity was still
strong between him and Charles the Lame, who will believe that
suddenly by those "*ministeriis et astutiis*" he had become such a
friend of the King as to make him yield the mastership of the
court (Curia). Charles was the true "*Dominus Curiae,*" and not
Gaetani. The account of Stefaneschi appears to us to be more worthy
of credence. Two cardinals said he, came first to Aquila: . . . . .
. . . . . geminos ex ordine Fratrum. Nom missos gravitate patrum,
sed sponte ruentes." They were Hugh, the Frenchman, and Matthew
Orsini . . . . Ugonem. Scilicet Alvernum ac Ursino stipite
natum." Let us notice the expression: "non missos sed sponte
ruentes." This indicates the discord that existed between these two
cardinals and the others who remained, and especially Gaetani, the
last one to arrive These two men took charge of affairs, since the
first being made bishop of Ostia, is clearly declared by Stephaneschi
to have entered into the secret of Charles with regard to the promotion of new cardinals, as also doubtless the other two Roman cardinals, who were Matthew and Napoleon Orsini, partisans of Charles
the Lame. But Colonna for the reasons given was not among these.
Stephaneschi says nothing at all of the influence of Gaetani at
court, nor of his reconciliation with King Charles. We can conclude
then from the testimony of Stephaneschi and Ptolemy of Lucca,
that the Papal court was divided into two parties, the one led by Hugh
Sequin and Peter Orsini, the first to arrive in Acquila, and the
other by Benedict Gaetani. Thus is explained and reconciled, the
numerous masters of the court that existed according to the testimony of Ptolemy of Lucca. As regards that "*factus amicus regis*"
of his, it is only a conjecture founded on the belief the chronicler
of Lucca had, that Boniface owed his election to Charles. He had
to reconcile these two personages in order to justify himself in saying
that the one favored the ambitious projects of the other. But, besides the reasons we have shown, subsequent facts belie this reconciliation.

If there was an affair to be conducted by the master of the court (Curia), it was assuredly the creation so important of new cardinals. Now the reader may see how, Stephaneschi afterwards Cardinal of St. George, relates what happened:

"Venerat ecce dies, ignota ad culmina tollens
"Qua Caelestinus proceres augere senatus
"Flagitat, et votum complet: nam his repetitos
"Sex creat, et Gallos septem, paucosque Latinos;
"Quinque tamen: Binos Fratres sub lego morantes
"Instituit propria, nullum quem subdita sedi
"Immediata parit tellus, ex ordine Patrum
"Murro dedit Quae causa fuit, quae forma creandi
"Hos proceres, si nosse cupis, depromere gratum est.
"Fertur, ut annuimus, Carolum scripsisse futuros
"Pene omnes proceres; Regique placere volentem
"Hos Gallos statuisse viros splendere Galeris
"Murronem, reliquosque Duces celasse rubentes
"Hoc; tribus exceptis, quos jussit operta tenere;
"Scilicet Alverno, qui longe proescius horum
"Extiterat cum Rege patre, ducibusque duobus[7]
"Romanis Alios proceres non certus habebat
"Rumor adusque diem Veneris, quae proxima cursu
"Sabbata praecessit. Tunc omnes advocat una
"Pastor; et ut structus fuerat, suadente ministro[8]
"Astuto, processit Herus, dans nomina scriptis
"Certa sibi procerum, votumque requirit in illis
"Consiliumque Patrum semotum. Gaudet ab inde
"Se fecisse duos Rex, mire turbidus autem
"Redditur Alvernus,[9] dum sperat ad ardua certum
"Assumi, hec scripta legi, proh! nomina cernit, etc."

If the sudden and unexpected election of those to the dignity of the Cardinalate should have provoked the other cardinals, what must have been the indignation of Benedict Gaetani, when he learned that the leader of that cabal was king Charles, whom he had expelled in disdain from the conclave in Perugia. On the other hand the more Gaetani had of knowledge and skill in affairs, the more he must have felt piqued at being cast aside in this affair, as a man of mediocrity, one who could be beguiled with the others. We lay stress upon all this, in order to place the mind of the reader on guard against the pretended compact, which, according to Villani, was made between Gaetani and Charles after the abdication of Celestine.

[7] Matthew Rosso and James Colonna.   [8] Bartholemew of Capua.
[9] Nam iste Hugo fecerat inscribi unum amicum suum inter alios qui futuri erant Cardinales: et subito, cum facta esset publicatio aliorum cardinalium, non audivit suum nominari: de quo fuit dictus Hugo valde stupefactus

NOTE (E).

CONCERNING THE ABDICATION OF POPE ST. PETER CELESTINE.

If in the course of our narration we have not spoken of that blaring trumpet, nor those other ingenious impositions employed by Cardinal Gaetani to intimidate St. Peter Celestine and make him abdicate, it was out of respect for the dignity of history; but as certain readers might suppose there was no other reason, we propose to return to these calumnies. This is the version of Ferrettus of Vicenza:[10] The Cardinals were informed of the resolution of Celestine: "Quod prudens et astutus Benedictus Cajetanus mente con-
"cipiens, et ad id decus animum suum audacter extollens, illi se
"familiarem et gratum solito magis exhibuit, et, ut, perhibent, in
"obsequis studiosum. Atque interea, dum saepe sibi laudatum vitae
"solitariae otium intelligeret, rite judicasse credebat, ipsumque magis
"ceremoniis et templorum ministerio, quam rei susceptae vocitabat
"aptissimum: cujus persuasione major subibat impetus resignandi.
"*Ferunt* etiam et hunc virum dolosum, quatenus adhoc illum flag-
"rantius incitaret, dum somno incitatus noctu Deum contemplare-
"tur, per foramen, quod arte fabricaverat, voce tenui saepe dixisse,
"se coeli nuntium advenisse illi, ut illecebris falsi nundi relictis,
"soli Deo servire disponeret. Quamobrem idem Papa degener ac
"trepidus, et in proposito consepto persistens, coram fratrum suorum
"aspectu claves sacros sponte projecit, et Chlamydem sacram exuens,
"honori summo renunciavit" Thus wrote Ferrettus Thirty-two years after the events he narrates,[11] and far from the place where they happened. Now let us see how it is related by historians closer to the times and place, some of whom were eye-witnesses.

There exists in the secret archives of the Vatican,[12] a manuscript entitled: A treatise on his entire life (St. Peter Celestine's) by a man who was greatly attached to him. In this is described the interview between Gaetani and the Saint: "Coepit (Celestinus) cogitare de
"onere quod portabat, et quomodo posset illud abjicere absque peri-
"culo et discrimine suae animae. Ad hos suos cogitatus advocavit
"unum sagacissimum atque probatissimum cardinalem Benedictum,
"qui ut hoc audivit, gavisus est nimium et respondit et dicens,
"quod posset papatui libere renunciare, et dedit idem exemplum
"aliquorum pontificum qualiter olim renunciaverant. Hoc illo au-
"dito quod posset papatui libere renunciare, ita in hoc firmavit cor
"suum, quod nullus illum ab illo potuit removere." This observation that the advice of Gaetani confirmed the Saint in his resolution to abdicate is false, because it is contrary to facts. If the advice of Gaetani had exercised such an influence over Celestine he would

---

[10] S. R I. Tom. IX, p. 966.
[11] See Muratori, introduction to the history of Ferrettus S. R. I. T. IX, p. 939.
[12] Armar VII, c. 1, n. 1.

not have asked the advice of other cardinals, as he is reported to have done by Stephaneschi:

> . . . . Vocat inde alium, quo certius esset,
> Consilium
> Attamen absconsi pandet secreta cubilis
> Nonnullis procerum, quorum consulta reposcit
> His super.

Gaetani then was but a simple counsellor called like the others to give his opinion Peter d'Ailly of Compiegne, a strong enemy of Boniface, relates the fact of the abdication as follows: "Ibi ergo "assidue cogitare cœpit qualiter hujusmodi pontificali honore, velut "importabili onere deposito, abjectaque temporali sollicitudine, ad "antiquam solitudinem repeteret. Cumque peritorum consilio id "jure ac sine animae suae discrimine fieri posse comperisset, ita in "hoc cor suum animumque firmavit, ut ab illo proposito nullus hunc "dimovere potuerit"[13] Here Gaetani is not even named, so much was his way of giving it similar to that of the others. The author of the History of Florence[14] states that: Gaetani presents himself "to the Holy Father, perceiving that he had a wish of resigning the papacy." Gaetani then did not suggest this desire to Celestine, but he learned it from him. And the reason why this desire entered the mind of Celestine, the annalist of Milan clearly states:[15] "Qui videns suam insufficientiam papatui renunciavit." It was from a feeling of his own unfitness. Peter della Voragine in the Chronicle of Genoa affirms the same:[16] "Quocirca ipse videns "suam inexperientiam, salubri ductus consilio, Constitutionem fecit, "quod si aliquis Papa insufficiens inveniretur, posset papatum libere "resignare. Quo facto, cum papatum per sex menses vel circa re-"tinuisset, in festo S Luciae libere resignavit" Not one word about Gaetani. Therefore if this constant feeling of his own unfitness for the Papacy, which made itself more manifest by the sad turn of affairs; if the fear of the loss of his soul urged him to resign, Gaetani should not be held responsible for this determination. The verses addressed to the Saint by Jacopone, whilst he was sighing ardently to return to his hermitage, precipitated the execution of his project. By these verses he wished to intimidate Celestine. The complaint which Jacopone poured into the ears of the Saint was very unbecoming; this unhappy man felt only too well the weight of prebenders, barterers and other such, of whom the friar speaks, and against whom the Pope did not know how to defend himself. In fact his anguish was clearly expressed in those words which came from his heart in the cell that had been erected in the castle at Naples. Let the reader not think that we or Stephaneschi have forged these

---

[13] Apud. Surium, Tom. 3, die 19 Maii.
[15] Annal. Mediol, S. R. I. T. 16, p. 683.
[14] S. R. I. T. XVI t 683.
[16] S. R. I. T. 9, p. 54.

words. The Saint really uttered them, and repeated them himself to this very author, who affirms them in the following verses:

> . . . . Et meditans sibimet lacrymabilis inquit
> (Ut nos viva patris docuit vox).

In the presence of the testimony of numerous writers of incontestable authority; in the face of the true reasons which moved Peter Celestine to abdicate, it seems to us that the account of Ferrettus, so greedily taken up by many, cannot be considered as an expression of the truth. The reader will remark that the recital of Ferreto rests on the words "*ut perhibent; ferunt,*" on the rumors then current. Now we ask what value they would have as testimony at the time when a false opinion was formed by the defamatory libel of the Colonnas and the proceedings begun by Philip the Fair against the memory of Boniface. The Colonnas, and especially James, the Cardinal, who was at Naples and assisted at the abdication of Celestine, would they have been ignorant of the artifices of Gaetani? And if they had knwn them, would their charity towards the implacable Boniface have allowed them to pass them over in silence, when they believed strongly that he was a false Pope?

DOCUMENT (F).

PROFESSION OF FAITH OF BENEDICT GAETANI BEFORE HIS ELEVATION TO THE PAPACY.

In Nomine Sanctae, et Individuae Trinitatis, Anno Dominicae Incarnationis 1294. Indictione viij. Ego Benedictus Gaietanus Presbyter Cardinalis, et electus, ut fiam per Dei gratiam hujus sanctae Sedis Apostolicae humilis Minister, profiteor tibi, B. Petre Apostolorum Princeps, cui Claves Regni Cœlestis ad ligandum, atque solvendum in Coelo, atque in Terra Creator, atque Redemptor omnium Dominus Jesus tradidit, inquiens: "Quaecumque ligaveris super terram, erunt ligata et in Coelis, et quaecumque solveris super terram erunt soluta et in Coelis," sancteque tuae Ecclesiae, quam hodie tuo præsidio regendam suscipio, quod quandiu in hac misera vita constitutus fuero, ipsam non deseram, non abnegabo, non abdicabo aliquatenus, neque ex quacumque causa, cuiusque metus, vel periculi occasione dimittam, vel me segregabo ab ea; sed verae Fidei rectitudinem, quam Christo auctore tradente, per te, et beatissimum Coapostolum Paulum, perque successores vestros usque ad exiguitatem meam perlatam in tua sancta Ecclesia reperi, totis conatibus meis, usque ad animam, et sanguinem custodiam, tam de sanctae, et individuae Trinitatis Mysterio, quae unus est Deus, quam dispensatione, quae secundum carnem est. Unigeniti Filii Domini Nostri Jesu Christi, et de ceteris Ecclesiae Dei dogmatibus sicut in universalibus Conciliis, et Constitutionibus Apostolicorum Pontificum, probatissimorumque Ecclesiae Doctorum scriptis sunt commendata, id est quaecumque ad rectitudinem vestrae rectae Orthodoxae Fidei a te traditionem recipiunt, conservare. Sancta quoque octo universalia Concilia, idest Nicenum, Constantinopolitanum, Ephesinum, Primum Calcedonense, Quintum, et Sextum item Constantinopolitanum, ad unum apicem immutilata servare, et pari honore, et veneratione digna habere, et quae praedicaverunt, et statuerunt, omnimode sequi, et praedicare, et quaecumque condemnaverunt, condemnare ore, et corde. Diligentius autem, et vivacius Apostolicorum Nostrorum Pontificum, quaecumque Synodaliter constituerunt, et probata sunt, confirmare, et indeminuta servare, et sicut ab iis satuta sunt, in sui vigoris sublimitate custodire. quaeque, vel quandiu vixero, omnia Decreta Canonum Praedecessorum quos condemnaverunt, et abdicaverunt, simili condemnare sententia, vel abdicare: disciplinam, vel Ritum Ecclesiae sicut inveni a sanctis Praedecessoribus meis traditam, et servatam reperi, non diminuere, vel mutare, aut aliquam novitatem admittere, sed ferventer, ut eorum hic vere discipulus, et sequipedem totius mentis meae conatibus, quae tradita canonice comperio, servare, ac venerari. Si quae vero emerserint contra Canonicam disciplinam filiorum meorum S. R. E. Cardinalium, cum quorum consilio, consensu, directione, et memoratione ministerium meum geram, et peragam, consilio emendare, aut patienter, excepta fidei, aut Christianae Religionis gravi offensione, tua, ac beatissimi Coapostoli tui Pauli patrocinante intercessione tolerare, sacrosque Canones, et canonica instituta Pontificum, ut divina, et coelestia mandata, Deo auxiliante, custodire, utpote Deo, et tibi sciens redditurum me de omnibus, quae profiteor, et quandiu vixero, egero, vel oblitus fuero, districtam in divino judicio rationem; cujus sanctissimae Sedi diurna dignatione, te patrocinante, praesideo, et vicem tuis intercessionibus adimpleo. Eris autem in illa terribili die propitius haec conanti, et diligenter servare curanti. Adjutorium quoque ut praebeas obsecro in hac corruptibili vita constituto, irreprehensibilis ante conspectum Judicis omnium Domini Nostri Jesu Christi, dum terribiliter de commissis advenerit judicare, ut faciat me dextrae partis participem, et inter fideles Discipulos, et Successores consortem. Hanc autem Professionem per Nortarium, et Scriniarium S. R E. me jubente scriptam, propria manu subscripsi, et tibi, beate Apostole Petre, Apostolorum Principi pura mente et devota conscientia super sanctum Corpus, et Altare tuum sinceriter offero.

DOCUMENT (G).

ENCYCLICAL OF BONIFACE WITH REGARD TO HIS PONTIFICATE.

Bonifacius, etc venerabilibus fratribus archiepiscopo Senonensi et eius suffraganeis salutem, etc.

Gloriosus et mirabilis in operibus suis Deus, qui cum sit in misericordia copiosus, in hujus orbis orbita plena malis, conferta dissidiis, innumeras miserationes exercet; Ecclesiam suam, quam ipse summus opifex rerum instituit, ac supra fidei firmam petram alta, et solida fabrica stabilivit, opportunis favoribus prosequi non desistit. Assistit enim illi miserator et propitiator assiduus, non obdormiens, nec dormitans in suarum opportunitatum eventibus pervigil custos eius. Ipse siquidem sibi est in turbatione pacatio, in tribulatione solamen, in necessitate succursus. Tuncque maxime in adjutorium ejus sua pietas larga diffunditur, cum adversus illam mundi nubila tempore calligante levantur, quae inter molestias et afflictiones intrepida, colligens in vexatione vigorem, in ipsa malorum instantia convalescit. Nam divino semper munita praesidio, nec comminationum strepitu deterretur, nec adversitatum superatur incursu; sed in terroribus tutior, et constantior in adversis, pressa praevalet, passa triumphat. Haec est arca, quae per confluentias et multiplicationes aquarum elevatur in altum, et subactis culminibus montium, libera et secura profundas importuosi diluvii calcat undas. Haec est utique navis, quae, vento contrario irruente, strepentis maris furibundis motibus agitatur: firma tamen et solida fragoribus non dissipatur aequoreis, nec marini furoris rapiditate sorbetur; sed elatas procellas obruens, ac spumosa et tumida freta sternens, triumphanter exequitur suae navigationis incessum, quae ad vitalem Crucis salvificae arborem rectae intentionis alis totaliter elevatis, in coelum semper intenta procellosum intrepide mundi pelagus peragrat, eo quod secum habet seduli gubernatoris auxilium marium praeceptoris Unde regente illo et dirigente salubriter, ac Spiritu sancto flante, adversitatum quarumlibet nebulis dissipatis, victorosa peregrinationis liberum agit iter ad patriae coelestis portum supernis nutibus feliciter perducenda: cumque sic adversis innumeris prematur, et turbetur Ecclesia, illa in intimis ipsam acerbius sauciat, duriusque ferit adversitas, cum pastore utili et provido viduatur Sed licet saepius Ecclesia eadem, pastoris regimine destituta, longe viduitatis lamenta pertraxerit, expectando gemebunda diutius consolationem plenariam successoris; in hujusmodi tamen moeroris nubilo dignanter illi clementia divinae pietatis illuxit, doloribus et necessitatibus suis opportune subveniens per substitutionem optatam et delectabilem novi sponsi, ac eam de amissione prioris interdum inutilis per promotionem mulcebrem accommodi successoris instaurans.

Sane vacante Romana Ecclesia per liberam et spontaneam dilecti filii fratris Petri de Murrone, olim Romani Pontificis, cessionem coram venerabilibus fratribus episcopis, et dilectis filiis nostris presbyteris et diaconis Cardinalibus, de quorum numero tunc eramus, ex certis rationabilibus et legitimis causis factam ab ipso in festo beatae Luciae virginis proximo praeterito, et a Cardinalibus proedictis admissam; cum illam posse sic legitime fieri, et primorum gesta Pontificum, et constitutio declararent apertius, et ad eam etiam faciendam expressus accesserit Cardinalium praedictorum assensus; Cardinales ipsi, considerantes attentius quam sit onusta dispendiis, quam gravia malorum incommoda secum trahat urolixa ecclesiae memoratae vacatio; et propterea votis ardentibus cupientes per efficacia et accelerata remedia hujusmodi periculis obviare, die jovis X. Kalen. januarii post festum subsequentem praedictum, missarum solemniis ad honorem Sancti Spiritus celebratis, hymnoque solito cum devotione cantato, se in quodam conclavi apud Castrum novum civitati Neapolitanae contiguum, ubi tunc idem frater Petrus cum sua residebat familia, incluserunt, ut per mutui commoditatem colloquii ecclesiae praedictae provisio, superna cooperante virtute, celerius proveniret Die vero veneris immediate sequente praefati Cardinales, mentis oculis erectis ad Dominum, pia desideria benignius prosequentem, in electionis negotio ferventibus studiis, ut praedicta vitarentur incommoda, procedentes; et tandem, cum divina clementia ecclesiae praelibatae compatiens, eam nollet ulterioris vacationis periculis subjacere; ad personam nostram, licet immeritam, intentum animum dirigentes, quamquam inter eos quamplures magis idonei, et digniores etiam haberentur, nos tunc tituli S. Martini presbyterum Cardinalem in summum Pontificem canonice elegerunt, gravis oneris sarcinam nostris debilibus humeris imponendo Nos autem profunda, et sedula meditatione pensantes difficultatem officii pastoralis, continui laboris angustias, et praecellentiam apostolicae dignitatis, quae sicut honoris titulis altioris attollit, magnitudine ponderis deprimit gravioris; attendentes insuper nostrae multiplicis imperfectionis instantiam, expavimus et haesitavimus vehementer, nimioque concussum extitit stupore cor nostrum. Nam cum ad tolerandas particulares vigilias vix nobis possibilitas nostra sufficiat, ad universalis speculae solicitudinem vocamur, et intolerabile apostolici ministerii jugum instanter debilitatis nostrae cervici, jugiter supportandum, ac meritorum non suffulti praesidio, ad suscipiendas apostolorum principis Petri claves, et gerendum super omnes ligandi et solvendi pontificium angebamur. Verumtamen ne divinae providentiae opus impedire forsitan videremur, aut nolle nostrae voluntatis arbitrium suo beneplacito conformare; ac etiam ne corda electorum concordia per nostrae dissensionis objectum ad discordiam verteremus, voluntatibus tandem acquievimus eorumden, ad subeundum jugum hujusmodi nostros impotentes humeros submittendo: non quod de aliqua nostrae probitatis virtute fiduciam habeamus, sed quia in ejus speramus clementia, qui confidentes in se non deserit; sed eis propitius opportunis auxiliis semper adest, quique de sublimi polorum solio Ecclesiam sponsam suam intuetur misericorditer et tuetur, suaeque illam exaltare non desinit copiosis beneficiis pietatis.

Vestris igitur et aliorum suffragiis propter imperfectum nostrum propensius indigentes, universitatem vestram affectuose rogamus, hortamur attentius, et requirimus confidenter, quatenus assidua nos apud aeterni Regis clementiam intercessione juvetis, humilitatem nostram sibi devotis supplicationibus commendando, ut super nos gratiae suae dona multiplicet, et rorem uberem solitae benignitatis effundat, ut actus nostros ad ipsum devotissime dirigentes, Ecclesiam suam, quam nobis committi voluit, salubriter regere, as de universo ipsius grege, nostrae vigilantiæ credito, curam gerere debitam, sicut expedit, valeamus. Nos vero stabiliter in animo gerimus vobis et vestris ecclesiis benignis adesse praesidiis, ac vestrum et earum profectum condignis favoribus promovere. Dat. Laterani IX. kal. febr. pont. nostri anno 1.

DOCUMENT (H).

LETTER OF BONIFACE TO PHILIP THE FAIR.

Celsitudinem regiam rogamus et hortamur attente, ac obsecramus in Domino Jesu Christo, quatenus diligenti meditatione considerans, quod judicium diligit Regis honor, metas justitiae curiosus observes, illamque sincere diligere studeas, aequitatem non deserens, clementiam non omittens; ut subjectus tibi populus copiosus in pacis pulchritudine sedeat, et in requie opulenta quiescat. Ecclesiam insuper matrem tuam et ipsius praelatos, nostri utique Salvatoris ministros, caeterasque personas ecclesiasticas ejus obsequiis dedicatas; quin potius in illis Regem coelorum et dominum, per quem regnas et regeris, incessanter et solerter honorans, ipsos regii favoris ope confoveas, et in plenitudine libertatum, aliorumque suorum jurium efficaciter protegere studeas et tueri, sicque in iis, tamquam filius benedictionis et gratiae te geras et dirigas, quod clarae memoriae progenitores tuos, qui erga praefatam Ecclesiam summae devotionis et reverentiae titulis, dum viverent, claruerunt, non solum imitari solicite, sed etiam evidenter excedere dignoscaris ad laudem et gloriam Dei Patris, et celebre magnumque tui honoris et nominis incrementum. De nobis autem utpote patre benevolo et sincero, qui te in minori etiam officio constituti affectuose dileximus, et diligere non cessamus, spem certam, et fiduciam firmam gerens in tuis, et ejusdem regni negotiis, et opportunitatibus quae occurrent, ad nos recurrere non postponas. Nam in iis super quibus ex parte regia fuerimus requisiti, libenter, quantum cum Deo poterimus, votis regiis annuemus, tam et ejusdem regni prosperitatem omnimodam, non solum studiis conservare solicitis, sed etiam plenis augumentare favoribus intendentes Datum ut supra.

NOTE AND DOCUMENT (I).

IMPRISONMENT AND DEATH OF ST. PETER CELESTINE.

Stephaneschi, an eyewitness, relates the imprisonment of Celestine thus: " . . . . Ut littoribus Vestiae civitatis maris Adriatici
" inventum (*Celestinum*) fore comperit (*quatenus orbis sui eccles-*
"*iaeque discrimina vitaret*) solemnioribus a se Siciliaque Carolo
" Secundo Rege transmissis nuntiis, *consentientem* Anagniam meare
" fecit; *blande* suscipit, laudemque exhibuit acquitescenti Praesulis
" monitis Castro Fumonis Campaniae provinciae morari. Ubi assue-
" tam, sicuit prius, vitam agens Eremiticam, nolens laxioribus, *quibus*

"*poterat,* uti, anno millesimo ducentesimo monagesimo sexto snacte "religiose defunctus ......"

Ptolemy of Lucca, a contemporary writer and an eyewitness, says, "........ in custodia ponitur ac tenetur *pro cavendo scandalo* "*Romanae Ecclesiae,* quia apud aliquos dubitabatur, an cedere "potuisset, *et sic poterat schisma in Ecclesia generari.* Tentus "igitur in custodia, non quidem libere, honeste tamen"[17] The account of John Villani also a contemporary is almost the same: "He was kept in the castle of Fumone in a pleasant captivity."[18] He says nothing at all about harsh treatment or the famous nail. George Stella, an enemy of Boniface, in his annals writes: "Ipsum (Coelestinum) jubens custodire *ad evitanda scandala.*"[19] Now with this array of testimony of the writers of the times, can any reliance be placed in the words of authors writing long after the times in which the evens happened? The cruelties practised by Boniface on St. Peter Celestine were related at great length and in a most pitiable tone by Peter d'Ailly, who was born fifty years after the death of Celestine, and who was a Frenchman. Now would he know anything clear and truthful on this question, in the country of Nogaret and Philip the Fair? The reader will find an admirable proof of the innocence of Boniface, and the confirmation of that which we have said on the abdication, captivity and death of Celestine, in some chapters of the life of the Saint, as yet unpublished, but which exists in the Vatican library.

It is a very beautiful book, in manuscript, in quarto of double columned pages, and from its style of characters is judged to be a work of the XV century. The preface and the narration evidently prove that the author was a disciple of St. Peter Celestine The life is divided into three parts: "*Ad honorem S. Trinitatis, cui vita* "*Petri placuit, et confusionem hostis triplicis, quem idem Petrus* "*triumphando vicit.*" Then he continues: "*Primam vero partem* "*ipsius libelli* idem pater sanctus (Coelestinus) propria manu scripis "ad aedificationem proximi et Christi laudem, cujus gloriae militavit" These are the chapters that relate to the above facts. The reader will decide whether confidence can be placed in a disciple of the Saint and whether it can be presumed that the wickedness of Boniface would have been palliated by a man, who undoubtedly deplored the retirement of the founder of his order from the Papacy

HIS RENUNCIATION OF THE PAPACY.

CAP. XVII.

"Erat ei temporalis vita fastidio: deformis et squalida videbatur "species terrenorum: et ad solam pulchritudinem Jesu Christi con- "templandam pariter et habendam, toto mentis rapiebatur excessu.

[17] Hist. Eccl, cap. 34.   [18] Cap. V.
[19] Annal. Geno. S. R. I, p. 1026.

"At vero beatus hic vir mirae simplicitatis, et in spectantibus ad
"regimen Ecclesiae inexpertus, utpote qui a teneris annis usque ad
"senium elongatum a mundo cor suum mundanis rebus non accom-
"odaverat sed divinis, prudenter reflectens suae considerationis intime
"oculum ad seipsum, cogitavit oneri papatus et honori cedere; ne ob
"praedicta posset ex regimine suo quodcumque universali Ecclesiae
"periculum provenire; et ut................ vacare posset secus
"pedes Jesu contemplans ocio cum Maria. Ad suos ergo cogitatus
"quendam Cardinalem nomine Benedictum, litterali scientia valde
"redimitum convocavit; cui tantum secreta sui cordis sub sigillo
"poenitentiae revelavit. Cumque respondisset dictus dominus
"Cardinalis quod libere renunciare posset, dans ei exempla aliorum
"pontificum qui renunciaverant, ita cor ejus in hoc confirmatum
"est, quod nunquam ab ipso proposito per dictum alicujus amoveri
"potuisset. Unde cum isto Cardinali omnia praedicta occulte ac
"solicite tractans et ordinans, fecit sibi renuciationem scribi et
"doceri. Qui tandem ad talia preparatus, consistorium ingrediebatur;
"et sedens in throno pontificali summum silentium, ne sibi con-
"tradicerent, omnibus imponebat. Et accepta charta, legem statuit
"decretalem ut quilibet papa possit papatui libere renunciare. Hoc
"autem ipse prior volebat observare. Deposito namque ornato
"pontificali, pronus in terra sedens cessit papatus oneri et honori.
"Videntes autem Cardinales quae numquam antea viderant, in fletum
"et suspiria singuli prorumpebant. Cujus enim vel cor arrogans vel
"durum istius humilitas ad humilitatis et mansuetudinis non flectat
"exemplum? Consideravit namque difficile esse sine cordis elatione
"aliis praesse, et terrenas occupationes absque peccati fomite
"ministrare. Maluit autem in Domo Domini abjectus esse, quam
"in diversoriis hujus saeculi gloriosus habitare. Nec poterat ipsum
"totus mundus erigere quem se ipse dejecerat solus. Porro sicut ejus
"electio ex divina providentia noscitur evenisse, non minus credendum
"est de illius humillima renunciatione.

HIS RETURN TO HIS CELL ON MT. MORRONE.

CAP. XVIII.

"Hac itaque renunciatione peracta, Petrus non post multos dies
"ad cellam ejus, ad quam ante renunciationem redire protestatus
"fuerat, regressus est occulte. Statim autem ut illam ingressus est,
"prostravit se coram altari, gratias Deo referens eo quod ipsum
"taliter reduxisset. Qui projectis vestibus delicatis, induit se
"vilioribus illis quibus ante papatum vestitus fuerat, sperans de
"cetero illic pacifice remanere. Quod audientes cives Sulmontini
"occurrerunt ei omnes, et illum videntes, nimio repleti sunt gaudio;
"gratias Deo referentes eo quod ipsum revidere meruissent. Et illum
"ad cellam perduxerunt.

THE SEARCH AFTER HIM.

CAP. XIX.

"Bonifacius qui post ipsum ad summum pontificatum provectus "est, cum audisset Petrum ad cellam ejus reversum, statim "Camerarium suum misit, praecipiens ei ut ubicumque illum in- "veniret, licet invitum, ad se reduceret abseque mora." Why this command of Boniface to bring back, even by force, St. Peter Celestine? We have already given the reason, founding our opinion on the testimony of contemporary writers and of eyewitnesses who related the facts It was through fear of a schism, possible not certainly through the ambition of the Saint, for he had none, but through the admiratin for his piety and the renown of his miracles: " Cum ergo ille abiens appropinquaret ad cellam Petri, intimatum est "hoc viro Dei. Qui timens abscondit se in quadam latebra illius "cellae, ut ab ipso minime posset inveniri." There are but two possible hypotheses of the causes of the fear which induced Celestine to hide himself. It arose either from the rumor that was spread of the imprisonment that Boniface had in store for him, or from the opinion that the unexpected arrival of the messenger had for an object to make him reascend the Papal throne. As for the imprisonment he could not dread it, since Boniface decided on enclosing him in the castle of Fumone only after he saw that it was dangerous to himself and to the Church to keep the Saint secluded in the Papal palace, which fact is related by the anonymous writer. The Saint then hid himself through fear of losing, by his new elevation, the blessed solitude, which he preferred to all honors: "Cum autem dictus "Camerarius cellam esset ingressus, et nec alibi Petrum invenisset, "anxiatus est in eo spiritus ejus et perturbatus, quia mandatum "Domini sui ad effectum perducere non posset; et furore replatus "quemdam fratrem simplicem in cella Petri repertum secum "abducens, carceri compeditum mancipavit. Qui sic in carcerem cum "compedibus retrusus defunctus est." Boniface is not responsible for the rage of the Chamberlain, nor for the shameful imprisonment of the innocent monk. The best princes can have the worst executors of their orders, and when a moral inability prevents them from anticipating and stopping the wickedness of the latter, they should not be held accountable. Boniface had ordered the Saint to be conducted to him even against his will; his apprehensions render this unquestionable; but all that was done beyond this was the work of the Chamberlain. Is it rare to see the zeal of a too officious agent overstep its bounds, and transform itself into severity? Moreover we are reluctant to believe that a simple imprisonment was of a nature as to cause so suddenly the death of the monk which the author, we have cited, relates; unless the Chamberlain in his "fury of the wolf," (the words of the author) had added blows and cruelties:

"O magna crudelitas! In sanctum Patrem lupus desaevire non
"valens, desaevit in filios, ut hunc fratrem carcerando, irae suae
"furonem de beati Patri amissione placeret. Et quid forte fecerat
"frater ille ut tali poena plecteretur? Numquid Sancti Petri amissio
"causa fuit? Verum non est ambigendum quod poena illa sine causa
"meritorum irrogata in meritorum augmentum conversa fuerit. De
"Petro autem celebris inquisitio facta est in diversis mundi partibus."

HIS FLIGHT ACROSS THE SEA.

CAP. XX.

"Sanctus igitur iste cum per spacium duorum mensium in ejus
"cella latitasset, fugam iniit de nocte uno cum socio versus quandam
"sylvam in partibus Apuliae, per dies quatuor a Murrone distantem,
"ut ibi solitarius ab hominibus ignotus permaneret. Sed audi mirum.
"Quanto magis per viam occultare se studuit, eo amplius cunctis
"fiebat plebibus notus. Retulit namque frater ille qui cum ipso
"ambulabat. Dum sero quodam hospitium quererent in castello
"quodam, pueri in vicis et plateis solito serotino tempore ludentes,
"viso Petro, portinus exclamaverunt: Ecce frater Petrus de Murrone.
"Tandem ad memoratam sylvam veniens ingressus est cum socio in
"cellam duorum fratum. Qui cum in eum respicerent, quem nunquam
"antea viderant, optime cognoverunt dicentes: Vere tu es frater
"Petrus de Murrone; et repleti gaudio glorificaverunt Deum. Erat
"autem tunc temporis Quadragesima major. Petrus ergo in quadam
"cella illius nemoris se includens, sanctum Pascha jejuniis artis et
"orationibus assiduis expectabat. At veniente dominica in ramis
"Palmarum, quidam abbas Monasterii, quod de Corata nuncupatur,
"Ordinis S. Benedicti, ibat cum septem sociis per sylvam huc atque
"illuc, ipsum quanto devotius tanto velocius inquirendo. Videns ergo
"tentabat. Idcirco fratrem suum quendam ad priorem monasterii
"sanctus ille se abscondi minime posse, ad partes ultramarinas pergere
"sancti Joannis in plano praecipiendo misit, ut hoc factum cum
"naucleris, mora postposita, clam pertractaret Quod et factum est.
"Parata igitur nave, ... pater sanctus ad praefatum
"coenobium ad requisitionem dominicam venit. Qui cum illic spatio
"unius mensis moram latenter traxisset, navigandi congruum tempus
"praestolando, abiit ad mare navigaturus. Et ecce subito maris
"procella valida insurgente, ac si aperte mare patefaceret se illum
"recipere nolle, coactus est ibi moram trahere sex diebus. Post haec
"flante prospero vento navem ascendit Petrus cum sociis ejus; et
"data nave flatibus navigare coeperunt. Et iterum tempestate non
"exigua imminente, vix illo die miliaria quindecim facientes, ejecti
"sunt ad littus maris non multum distans a civitate quae Vestia
"nuncupatur. Qui in eodem loco novem mensibus manserunt,
"ventum prosperum expectantes. Sic revera divinae placuit disposi-

" tioni, ut patria tam preciosum talentum sibi creditum non amitteret,
" sed potium divinitus inde lucrum multiplex reportaret.

HIS CAPTURE AND CONFINEMENT IN THE CASTLE OF FUMONE.

CAP. XXI.

" His itaque moram ibi dacientibus, intellexit Captaneus praedictas
" civitalis per quorundam relationem, virum Dei tali adesse loco;
" abiens cum populi comitiva duxit illum ad civitatem praedictam; et
" tenuit, donec rem gestam Bonifacius, cum omni dilatione post-
" posita, missis exercitibus, fecit praedictum Dei famulum ad se
" Anagniam, ubi tunc moram traxerat, accersiri, et in quodam
" domicilio juxta ipsius cameram clam includi. Quantas quippe
" miraculorum virtutes almis ejus meritis, dum per viam duceretur,
" ostenderit Deus in conspectu populi, nequaqam poterit explicari
" sermonibus. Saltem tamen aliqua ipsorum quae Patriarcha
" Hierosolimitanus, Prior sanctae Militiae Dominus Ludovicus, et
" Dominus Stendardus, ipsum deducentes oculata fide vederant et
" scribi fecerant, in tertia hujus libelli particula declarabo. Multi
" autem tam de Cardinalibus quam de aliis in Curia existentibus
" ipsum videre desiderabant; sed prohibente Bonifacio, ad illum
" ingredi non valebant. Tanta namque plebis devotio in eum dictitur
" viguisse, ut ipso vivente, Bonifacius verus pastor Ecclesiae a multis
" minime crederetur esse Dum per viam duceretur ad Papam,
" sequebatur eum multitudo gentium clamans et suadens ut omnino
" sibi resumeret Pontificatum. Quibus ille constanti respondit animo:
" Absit hoc a me, ut talem in Ecclesia Dei faciam dissensionnem: non
" enim renui causa resumendi papatus honorem; sed illam quam tunc
" habui, eamdem nunc, si faciendum esset, habeo voluntatem " If
we look back to the end of XIII century, it will be impossible for us
not to understand what great danger would be to the Church not only
that a multitude of people clamoring and advising Celestine to resume
the Pontificate " *Multitudo gentium clamans and suadens ut omnino
" sibi resumeret Pontificatum,*" but also many of the Cardinals, and
members of the Curia: "*multi de Cardinalibus et de aliis in curia,
" existentibus.*" There was not question of suspicions, or jealousies of
state, but rather of clear and most dangerous facts, which Boniface
had to provide against, if he did not want to see the Church disturbed
and torn by schism. Boniface confined the Saint in an apartment
close to his own in order to save him from the indiscreet and dangerous
devotion of the people. But as a great number of the cardinals and
members of the Papal court would not refrain from approaching the
Saint to urge him to resume the Pontificate, and as the devotion of
the people went so far as to declare and publish that Boniface was
not the legitimate pastor, he was obliged to put Celestine in more
strict confinement, and he shut him up in the castle of Fumone.
Aware of his own unfitness, convinced of the validity of his resigna-

tion, and as a consequence of the legitimacy of the pontificate of Boniface, the Saint repudiated the scandalous exhortations of his partisans, not only because they offended his modesty, but also because they were wicked. He submitted with pleasure, as we have seen, to the Pope, who wished to keep him in the castle of Fumone. "Post-
"quam autem praefatus Bonifaciis Papa ipsum fere duobus mensibus
"apud se tenuisset, fecit eum ad castrum Fumonis nocte transportari;
"et in turri ejus taliter includi, ut nullus omnino, praeter custodes ad
"hoc positos, cum viro Dei loqui potuisset, aut etiam illum intueria.
"Petrus itaque sic inclusus gratias egit Deo dicens: Christe noscens
"occulta cordium, mei nosti tu desiderium. Pro te pati set mihi
"gaudium, mori lucrum; haec vita taedium. Ex ejus quippe fratribus
"duo ad ipsius petitionem dabantur ei quorum adjutorio dicere
"possit officium Dei. Sed fratres illi arctationem turris et careris
"sufferre non valentes infirmabantur saepius, et extractis illis, alii in
"eorum cambium sani debantur. Tanta enim erat illius turris arctatio quod ubi pedes ipse tenebat dum missam diceret, ibi cervicem
"captis reclinabat dum dormiret." And why this so narrow prison? Was the tower so small that it could hold only one man? Certainly not, because there was room in it for the guards and two brothers: "custodes positos, fratibus . . . . duo." We must then say that either Boniface locked the Saint in a corner of the castle to smother him, or that the Saint himself with his own free will chose this narrow space through love of penance. If Boniface wanted to suffocate Celestine, he would have employed more expeditious means, which the gloom of the fortress would conceal; moreover, the very advanced years of Celestine, his greatly emaciated body, would suffice to allay suspicion, in explaining his death. If then we may be obliged to admit these details of the biography of the saint, we should reasonably believe that he who sighed ardently for the dark grotto and the mortified life of Mt. Morrone, had chosen this narrow abode. The above mentioned passage of Stephaneschi clearly proves this: *"Ubi
"assuetam, sicut prius, vitam agens eremiticam, nolens laxiribus,
"quibus poterat uti."* Now if the Saint wanted to fast, to sleep on the ground, to scourge himself, could Boniface be blamed for that? Our anonymous monk finds us equally a little incredulous with regard to that strange succession of religious, his confreres, who assisted the Saint in the horrible fortress, and who were obliged to leave half dead from time to time, on account of the intolerable life they were forced to lead. What? young and full of life when they entered, and in a dying condition on leaving And the holy old man of seventy-five years, worn out by austerities, principal object of the anger of Boniface, remained a healthy witness of these successive replacements of young and vigorous men? No, it is incredible. "Verum
"quia fratribus erat nimin difficile sic manere, semper illos admonens
"confortabatur ut patienter sufferrent Jesu Christi pro amore.
"Et sic . . . ."

HIS DEATH AND MIRACLES THEREAT.

CAP. XXII.

"Opportunum tempus advenit in quo sudores et labores ejus "reponerentur in requie coelesti; et quotidiani agones illius, quod "in palestra monochatus mitis belligerator exegerat, dignis debebant "a Domino compensationibus praemiari. Missa namque per ipsum "devotissima celebrata in die Dominica Sanctae Pentecostes, "coeperunt membra ejus debilia languore ingravescere: Et praelibans "animo menteque degustans dulcedinem spiritualium gaudiorum, "mortis futurae praescius sibi faciebat extremam unctionem con- "ferri. In dextro siquidem latere ipsius quodam apostema "pullulaverat, quod ipsum graviter affligere non cessabat." It is seen that St. Peter Celestine died from an abscess, not from hunger, nor blows, nor suffocation. Now where is the famous nail by which he was killed? This ferocious Boniface, was he obliged to make use of this singular means of assassinating a man, because poison, a rope and other means were not at hand? The above mentioned writers, even Peter d'Ailly himself, say nothing of a nail. The Colonnas and Philip the Fair are silent on this point. Who then had found it? Perhaps the hole that was seen in the withered head of the Saint, and the impression of the cruel character of Boniface, well capable of such cruelty, gave color to the suppositions: "Aspirabat ad aeterna "solatia qui temporalium fuerat contemptor. Infirmus jacebat in sola "tabula qui mundanas oderat honores: et ad messem perennis gaudii "capiendam sanctus ille medullitus aestuabat. Per totam autem illam "hebdomadam usque ad sabbatum ab oratione ferenti spiritum non "relaxabat. Trahabatur ad odorem coelestium unguentorum; et "quantum poterat armis coelestibus muniebat finem suum. Succensa "quippe fuerant ejus praecordia Jesu Christi dulcedine pariter et "amore et capiens jam dissolvi et esse cum eo, ad sabbatum, in quo "ab omni labore quiesceret, plenis desideriis ferebatur. Die ergo "sabbati hora vespertina, aegritudine corporis invalescente, inter "verba orationis, ejus anima de merore ad gaudium, de labore ad "requiem meruit transire sempiternan. . . . ."

DOCUMENT (K).

LETTER OF BONIFACE TO THE SICILIANS, URGING THEM TO RETURN TO SUBMISSION TO THE CHURCH.

Bonifacius, etc , universis hominibus Panormi, aliisque per insulam Siciliae constitutis, spiritum consilii sanioris.

Inter caetera tractatus ab Aragonum rege completa juxta ipsius tractatus seriem insulam Siciliae, quae Romanae Ecclesiae juris et proprietatis existit, cum omnibus juribus et pertinentis suis praefatus Rex per suas patentes literas nobis et Ecclesiae praefatae restituit, et ad cautelam nostram et ejusdem Ecclesiae cira hoc se nobis fortius et firmius obligavit Et cum fuerit in ipso tractatu, et sit cordi nostro cura praecipua de reparatione status vestri, et securitate plenaria, more consulti Patrisfamilias, et superioris domini, ad quem spectat praecipue de vobis, sicut de subjectis Ecclesiae, providere ex nostrae praeeminentia potestatis, quam habemus sicut superior, obsolefacta corrigere, et liberare confractos ab angustiis, ut quiescant, nec minus ex posse nobis ab eodem Rege Siciliae tradito; disposuimus firmiter librato judicio tenere vos in manibus nostris, et ejusdem Ecclesiae, et vestro statui animarum, et corporum securitati, et tranquillitati pacifice, efficaciter, et utiliter providere.

Verum cum populus de facili corruat, ubi deficit gubernator, pro vestra gubernatione utili et humano regimine Cardinalem unum vobis gratum et placitum ad dictam insulam, annuente divina providentia, disponimus destinare: propter quod quis de fratribus nostris per hoc sit vobis acceptus, nobis describite: curabimus enim de ipso vestris effectibus complacere. Et procul dubio redeuntibus vobis ad devotionem sanctae matris Ecclesiae sic in vos, qui longe demeriti fuistis ab olim, ubera maternae dilectionis effundet, ac si prope gratae devotionis impendiis fuissetis; peccatorum enim laudanda conversio in coelis etiam justificatione justorum gratius et jucundius acceptatur, etc. Dat Romae apud S. Petrum IV non. januarii anno 1.

ANOTHER LETTER TO FREDERICK OF ARAGON TO PREVAIL UPON HIM TO LEAVE SICILY.

Friderico nato quondam Petri olim Regis Aragonum spiritum concilii sanioris.

De sinu patris in te spargenda semina prodeunt, fructum germinatura multiplicem commodi, honoris et gloriæ, si devotus illa susceperis, et ad susceptionem ipsorum velut agrum purgatum spinis et tribulis paraveris mentem tuam. Nosti quidem, ut credimus, et latendi locum non invenit tantæ veritatis essentia, quod post apostolatus apicem assumptum a nobis, licet immeritis, inter cæteros nostri cordis aflectus, fuit ille profundus, et fervens, quod clarissimum in Christo filium nostrum Jacobum Aragonum regem illustrem germanum tuum, tunc in devio positum, et te in umbra mortis sedentes et tenebris, nostra provisio revocaret a lapsu, et paterna charitas cum præsidio favoris et gratiæ ad sanctæ matris Ecclesiæ, unde immensus error vos traxerat, reduceret unitatem.

Et ut hujusmodi noster affectus votivum consequeretur effectum, monitis exhortationibusque paternis te ad præsentiam nostram perduximus, mutuoque tractavimus, ut charissima in Christo filia nostra Catharina Imperatrix Constantinopolitana cum certis subsidiis faciendis per nos, tibi matrimonialiter jungeretur, ad Imperatricem ipsam venerabilem fratrem nostrum G. Aniciensem Episcopum, et dilectum filium religiosum virum 1. abbatem S. Germani de Pratis, speciales nuncios nostros, destinare curantes, inducturos eamdem ad complementum matrimonii memorati. Quæ per eos proximo redeuntes ad nos super hoc responsum nobis exhibuit, quod cum tu terram non habeas, et ipsa patrimonii sui sit possessione privata, incongruum sibi videretur et indecens, quod tantae nobilitatis homines carerent domicilio proprio et opportunis aliis, qualitate habita personarum: sed si fieret tibi in terra provisio, unde tu et ipsa saltem usque ad recuperationem terrae suae convenientem vitam possetis habere, circa perfectionem praefati tractatus libenter se nostris inductionibus et beneplacitis coaptaret. Nos vero nostrum salubre propositum prosequentes, et quod coeptum est jam forti et fundato principio, finem prosperum et Deo placitum cupientes habere, cum ipsius pacis Auctore, cujus vices portamus in terris, perfecta sint opera Ecclesiae, ac nobis onus adjicimus ut cum effectu perfecti operis te ad gregem dominicum revocemus; sicque ortum ex bello Siculo rancorem et scandalum in omnibus suis partibus succidamus ex toto, quod ex eorum reliquiis nullum supersit residuum, et laeta pax et tranquillitas in locum adveniat odiorum. Ecce quidem ad dictam Imperatricem certos, et speciales nuncios nostros instanter transmittimus, ut cum praefati sui voti concordia per omnes, quos possumus, tramites ejus affectum expeditum et liberum perfectioni dicti matrimonii coaptemus.

Considera igitur, fili, considera paternae pietatis affectum, et proventurum tibi ex ipsius monitione profectum, et paternis profecto monitis acquiescens. Non enim patris charitas continere se potest quin praecipitem filium, sicut fama, immo infamia volitat, a manifesta ruina retrahat, in qua, ut dicitur, post cessionem et abdicationem occupationis et detentionis illicitae praedicti germani tuni, laudabilite ad gremium redeuntis Ecclesiae, assumendo falsum titulum occupationis, injuste, rationis metas exiliens, prosilire proponis, et a Creatoris tui gratia, graviter ipsum offendendo, decidens praeceps cadis. Cohibe igitur motus tuos, expecta patris salubre consilium, et obventurum·ex eo tibi prae foribus fructuosae ac honorificae reparationis effectum: nec ulla te maligna suggestio retrahat, vel avertat astutia, quin nostris monitis aures intentas adhibeas, et realiter filialis accomodes promptitudinis intellectum. Proculdubio quidem, si semina nostra sicut verus cultor exceperis, fructus tibi uberes gratae prosperitatis adducent. Sed si ut adversus negligendo saltem suscipere illa contempseris, sicut errantem et perditum expositum te videmus periculis, ut in te tanquam praeteritarum culparum excessum successorem vibrans gladium ultionis divina sententia spiritualibus et temporalibus jaculis tarditatem poenae compenset judicii gravitate. Et ecce quod venerabilem fratrem nostrum G. episcopum Urgellensem et dilectum filium religiosum virum fratrem Bonifacium de Calamandrana generalem praeceptorem sancti Joannis Jerosolymitani in partibus cismarinis ad te propter ea providimus destinandos, quos praemissis devotio tua humane recipiat, patienter audiat, et relata per ipsos ad terminos votivae executionis adducat. Dat. Romae apud S. Petrum IV. non. Januarii anno 1.

DOCUMENT (L).

LETTER OF BONIFACE TO THE PROVINCIAL OF THE FRIARS MINOR WITH REGARD TO THE CONVERSION OF GUY OF MONTEFELTRO.

Dilecto filio fratri N. Ordinis Minorum Provinciæ Marchiæ anconitanæ ministro.

Filius nobilis vir Guido Comos Montis-Feltri itam per seipsum, quam per fide dignas personas, aperiens votum suum nobis pluries intimare curavit, quod ipse reversus ad cor, desiderat et proponit pro diluendis peccatis suis, quibus Deum, et Romanam Ecclesiam matrem suam offendit, sub Religionis habitu finire in Dei servitio dies suos, maxime cum conjugis suæ prout dicitur, volentis votume emittere perpetuæ castitatis, ad hoc accedate assensus. Nos itaque devotionem suam, quæ prudenter spiritum consilii velle videtur admittere, in Domino commendantes, ut votum suum hujusmodi libentius prosequatur, volumus ut de bonis mobilibus quæ nunc habet, suam possit remunerare familiam, et de immobilibus conjugis suæ tantum supra sortem suarum dotium assignare, quod centum libras Ravennatum, quod vixerit, habeat annuatim; prius inter ipsum et eamdem conjugem, ut moris est, ea solemnitate qua decet, post votum castitatis emissum, divortio celebrato, prædicta vero mobilia quæ remunerationi familiæ suæ supererunt in quacumque materia, vel forma, in aliquo loco securo, et apud fideles personas interim deponi volumus, et servari; donec tam de mobilibus, quam de immobilibus, quæ in præsentiarum possidet, aliud duxerimus ordinandum. Volumus etiam, præfatam conjugen suam propter annosa insuspicabilis ætatis seæ tempora, posse in statu, in quo nunc est, si ad Religionem induci non valeat, licite permanere. Quocirca discretioni tuæ præsentium tenore committimus et mandamus, quatenus ad eumdem nobilem te personaliter, si in hujusmodi proposito, sicut credimus, perseverans religionem velit intrare, recipias et facias in manibus, et per manus tuas omnia, quæ circa emissionem votorum, et celebrationem divortii prædictorum conjugum, receptionem ipsius Guidonis ad Religionem, prædictorum dispositionem, ipsorum mobilium requirentur, et alia quæ circa id videris facienda, nobis per tuas litteras rescripturus, quod factum et ordinatum fuerit in præmissis. Cæterum licet sibi nostra præsentia constituto dixerimus, quod sive in Fratrum Militantium sive in Minorum Ordinem vellet intrare, opportunam sibi viam et auxilium præberemus, et in utroque ipsorum salutarem et devotum Domino posse impendere famulatum; de Minorum tamen sibi potius, quam Militantium Ordinum per te nolumus suaderi quidquam; quia, quamvis Minorum Regula dignoscatur asperior, personarum tamen conditioni, qualitati mentis et ætati, plenius melius in omnibus et per omnia integra libertas condescendit, Datum Anagniæ X. Kal. Augusti, Pontificatus anno 11.

DOCUMENT (M).

CONSTITUTION ON THE ECCLESIASTICAL IMMUNITIES.

Clericis Laicos infestos oppido tradit antiquitas, quod et præsentium experimenta temporum manifeste declarant, dum suis finibus non contenti nituntur in vetitum, ad illicita frena relaxant, nec prudenter attendunt, quam sit eis in Clericos Ecclesiasticasve personas et bona, interdicta potestas: Ecclesiarum Prælatis, Ecclesiis, Ecclesiasticisque personis Regularibus et Secularibus imponunt onera gravia, ipsosque talliant, et eis collectas imponunt, ab ipsis suorum proventuum vel bonorum dimidiam, decimam, seu vicesimam, vel quamvis aliam portionem aut quotam exigunt et extorquent, eosque moliuntur multifarie subjicere servituti, suæque submittere ditioni. et (quod dolenter referimus) nonnulli Ecclesiarum Prælati, Ecclesiasticæquæ personæ trepidantes ubi trepidandum non est, transitoriam pacem quærentes, plus timentes Majestatem temporalem offendere, quam æternam, talium abusibus non tam temerarie, quam improvide acquiescunt, Sedis Apostolicæ auctoritate seu licentia non obtenta.

Nos igitur talibus iniquis actibus obviare volentes, de Fratrum nostrorum consilio, Apostolica auctoritate statuimus, quod quicumque Prælati, Ecclesiasticæque personæ, Religiosæ vel Seculares, quorumcunque Ordinum, conditionis seu status, collectas vel tallias, decimam, vicesimam, seu centesimam suorum et Ecclesiarum proventuum vel bonorum Laicis solverint vel promiserint, vel se soluturos consenserint, aut quamvis aliam quantitatem, portionem aut quotam ipsorum proventuum vel bonorum æstimationis vel valoris ipsorum sub adjutorii, mutui, subventionis, subsidii vel doni nomine, seu quovis alio titulo, modo, vel quæsito colore, absque auctoritate Sedis ejusdem: necnon Imperatores, Reges, seu Principes, Duces, Comites, vel Barones, Potestates, Capitanei, vel Rectores, quocunque nomine censeantur, civitatum, castrorum, seu quorumcunque locorum constitutorum ubilibet: et quivis alii, cujuscunque praeeminentiae, conditionis et status, qui talia imposuerunt, exegerint, vel receperint, aut apud aedes sacras depositas Ecclesiarum, vel ecclesiasticarum personarum ubilibet, arrestaverint, saisiverint, seu occupare præsumpserint, vel arrestari, saisiri aut occupari mandaverint; aut occupata saisita seu arrestata receperint; nec non omnes qui scienter dederint in prædictis auxilium, consilium, vel favorem publice vel occulte, eo ipso sententiam excommunicationis incurrant. Universitates quoque quæ in his culpabiles fuerint, Ecclesiastico supponimus interdicto: Pralatis et personis Ecclesiasticis supra dictis, in virtute obedientiæ, et sub depositionis pœna, districte mandantes, ut talibus absque expressa licentia dicte Sedis nullatenus acquiescant: quodque prætextu cujuscunque obligationis permissionis, et confessionis factarum hactenus, vel faciendarum in antea, priusquam hujusmodi constitutio; prohibitio, seu præceptum ad notitiam ipsorum pervenerit; nihil solvant, nec supradicti Seculares quoquo modo recipiant. Et sis olverint, vel 'prædicti receperint, in excommunicationis sententiam incidant ipso facto. A supradictis autem excommunicationum et interdicti sententiis nullus absolvi valeat, præterquam in mortis articulo, absque Sedis Apostolicæ auctoritate et licentia speciali; cum nostræ intentionis existat tam orrendum Secularium potestatum abusum nullatenus sub dissimulatione transire.

Non obstantibus quibuscunque tenoribus, formis, seu modis, aut verborum conceptione concessis Imperatoribus, Regibus, et aliis supradictis, quæ contra præmissa in nullo volumus alicui vel aliquibus suffragari.

DOCUMENT (N).

LETTER OF BONIFACE TO PHILLIP THE FAIR.

Regi Francorum Illustri

Ineffabilis amoris dulcedine sponso suo, qui Christus est, Sancta Mater Ecclesia copulata, dotes et gratias ab ipso suscepit amplissimas, ubertate fæcundas, et specialiter inter eas benificium libertatis. Voluit enim peramabilem sponsam ejus libere fidelibus populis præesse dominio, ut velut in filios haberet more matris in singulos potestatem, ac eam cuncti cum filiali reverentia tamquam universalem matrem et dominam honorarent. Quis itaque ilam offendere vel provocare injuriis non pavescet? Quis ausum credulitatis assumet, sponsum in sponsæ contumelia non offendi? Quis Ecclesiasticæ libertatis infractor contra Deum et Dominum cujusvis defensionis clypeo protegetur, ut supernæ virtutis malleo comminui, et redigi nequeat in pulverem et favillam? Non avertas, o fili, a voce patris auditum, quoniam ad te paternus sermo de dulcedine pectoris cum amaricatione dirigitur, quam audita novi casus emersio introduxit. Tua enim interesse conspicimus, attenta mente suscipere quæ scribuntur. Ad nostrum siquidem nuper, non sine grandi admiratione quinimo turbatione, pervenit auditum, quod tu consilio deceptibili ductus, ut credimus, et maligno, et constitutionem talem iis diebus, ut asseritur, edidisti, cujus et si patenter verba non exprimant, suadentium tamen eam fieri (utinam non edentis fuisse videtur intentio) impingere in Ecclesiasticam libertatem, ipsamque in regno tuo, ubi vigere solet ab olim quoad Ecclesias et Ecclesiasticarum personarum bona (ut de nobis et fratribus nostris sub silentio taceamus ad præsens) voluisse subvertere, non sine gravi tua nota, magnoque discrimine, ac tuorum gravamine subjectorum, et aliorum etiam qui solent in regno prædicto hactenus conversari.

Cum igitur intersit veri patris consilium pro filiis capere, bonique pastoris errantes oves a devio revocare, diligentis amici suadere salubria, et in summo militantis Ecclesiæ justitiæ solio præsidentis, non solum omne malum, sed et mali speciem in subditis dissipare; nos qui Pastoris pastorum, et Jesu Christi Filii summi Patris æterni, licet immeriti, ejus favente clementia, gerimus vices in terris, et in excelso solio, summi apostolatus videlicet, præsidemus; teque præcipua sinceritate prosequimur et prosecuti sumus ab olim, dum nos minor status haberet; horum circa te officia pio affectu, et efficaci studio providimus exequenda, pro te filio prædilecto salubre capiendo consilium, teque ab invio revocando, in quod consilii te deviasse creditur impulsio fraudolentis, ac dissipando omne malum et mali speciem, quod consulentium malignorum temerarius ausus induxit; præsertim si ad hoc constitutionis præmissæ referatur intentio, ad quod lata creditur, secundum eorum intentum, qui eam fieri dolose ac improvide suaserunt.

Non debuit, filii, anima tanti Regis in tale venire consilium, non decuit excellentiæ tuæ prudentiam abire in consilio talium impiorum, qui ut flagitant, et te ut demergaris impingunt: sed saltem postquam super hoc tuos oculos paterno lumine aperimus, stare non debes in via talium peccatorum; sed attentius præcavere te convenit, ne impulsu pravorum actuum tui solii cathedra pestilentiæ dici possit. Nec licuit, nec etiam expedivit, quod ad tuam considerationem pateret ingressus, tua et dicti regni moderni temporis qualitate pensata, tam insolitæ quam indebitæ novitati, per quam de regno non oriundis eodem conversandi in ipso, mercimonia licita, et actus non prohibitos cum libertate solita exercendi via præcluditur, et aditus denegatur in multorum et etiam subditorum tuorum non leve dispendium et gravamen.

Ipsi quidem subditi adeo sunt diversis oneribus aggravati, quod eorum ad te solita subjectio multum putatur refriguisse devotio; et quanto amplius aggravantur, tanto potius in posterum refrigescet: nec parum amisisse censetur, qui corda perdit subjectorum Habet interdum usus sæcularium principum, vel abusus, hostibus de suis terris subtrahere commoda, et ut ad inimicorum terras subjecti non transeant, nec suarum terrarum bona portentur ad illos; sed sic generalem proferre sententiam, ut tulisti, non solum reprobatur in subditos, sed etiam in exteros cujuslibet nationis. Non videtur oculatæ fuisse prudentiæ, qui præteritorum non meminit, præsentia non respicit, nec habet ad futura respectum: et si, quod absit, fuerit condentis intentio, ut ad nos et fratres nostros, ecclesiarum prælatos ecclesiasticasve personas, et ipsas ecclesias, ac nostra et ipsorum bona non solum in regno tuo, sed constitutorum ubilibet extendatur, hoc non solum fuisset improvidum, sed insanum, velle ad illa temerarias manus extendere in quibus tibi sæcularibusque principibus nulla est attributa potestas; quin potius ex hoc, contra libertatem eamdem temere veniendo, in excommunicationis sententian promulgati canonis incidisses.

Vide, fili, ad quod præmissi tui consiliarii te duxerint, ut sacramentorum ecclesiasticorum percepitione ac participatione privatus ad tam periculosi status ignominiam devenires Vitavit hoc progenitorum tuorum sancta devotio ad ecclesiastica sacramenta, et promptitudo reverentiæ ad Apostolicam sedem, et a te his temporibus maxime vitanda fuissent dum circa tua, et ipsius regni tui honores et commoda procuranda, et evitanda dispendia sic attente, sic laboriose, sic sollicite vigilamus: ad quod enim venerabiles fratres nostros Bernardum Albanensem et Simonem Prænestinum Episcopos, nobilia utique Romanæ membra ecclesiæ, ad te ac tuum ac Angliæ regem et regna transmisimus: ad quod etiam Senensem, et Papiensem episcopos, ac bonæ memoriæ Regin. Archiepisco pum ad Alemanniæ regem duximus destinandos; multiplicatis nihilominus aliis nuntiis, ad diversas partes propterea destinatis. Nonne pro tua et regni tui procuranda salute, ac adversitate vitanda noctes insomnes duximus et subdivimus intollerabiles quasi labores, postquam ad apostolatus apicem cœlestis dispositio nos vocavit? Nonne quotidianis tractatibus et sollicitudinibus pro tuis agendis insistimus sinen intermissione laborum? Certe non condignum pro iis, nobis offers retributionis effectum, non Ecclesiæ matri tuæ pro grandibus tibi, et progenitoribus tuis impensis muneribus gratiarum, et grata animi vicissitudine correspondes, si prædictæ constitutioni credita ingeratur intentio: quinimmo nobis et ipsi mala pro bonis, et amara pro dulcibus reddidisses . . . . ut a te provocaremur injuriis, et provocati colluctaremur ad in invicem in querelis, ac si etiam Dei et Ecclesiæ adversantia non curares; non considerans provide circumposita regno tuo regiones et regna, voluntatem et statum præsidentium in eisdem, neque tuorum conceptus forsitan subditorum constitutorum in diversis partibus regni tui.

Leva in circuitu oculos tuos, et vide: cogita et repensa Romanorum, Angliæ, Hispaniarum regna, quæ quasi undiquet te circumdant, eorumque potentias, ac strenuitatem, et multitudinem incolarum, et patenter agnosces, quod non fuit tempus acceptabile, non dies salutis, diebus istis nos et ipsam ecclesiam talibus punctionibus tangere, talibus perturbare puncturis: nec revocare debuisses in dubium, quod nostri et ecclesiæ adjutorii et favoris sola subtractio in tantum debilitaret te ac tuos, quod, ut cætera tua perinde omittamus incommoda, persecutiones adversas ferre non posses. At ubi nos tibi et eamdem ecclesiam adversarios efficeres principales, adeo nostra et ejusdem ecclesiæ, ac aliorum prædictorum provocationis gravior tibi sarcina redderetur, quod ad ejus pondus tui efficerentur humeri impotentes. Absit quod insolentia consiliariorum tuorum ad tantum exterminii præcipitium te deducat. Absit tuis sensibus quævis incalescat durities ad talia prorumpendi. Absit quod gratus olim filius tam graviter matri reddatur exosus, et quod suis demeritis solita dulcedinis ubere subtrahere sibi ex necessitate cogatur, et quibusvis periculosis eventibus exponere vel relinquere non adjutum. Præpara in judicio, fili charissime, mentem tuam, et discerne ac judica quid Apostolicæ sedi conceptus considerationis advenerit, dum diebus istis circa discussionem et examinationem miraculorum, quæ ad invocationem claræ memoriæ Ludovici avitui facta dicuntur, cum nostris fratribus vacaremus, talia nobis xenia præsentasti, talia præmisisti dona, quibus Dominum ad iram provocas, et indignationem non solum nostram, sed et ipsius ecclesiæ promereris? Cur degenerat tuæ clementia juventutis a felicibus actibus progenitorum tuorum, quibus dictam sedem fide pura, et devotione sincera summis ab antiquo studiis coluerint, se ipsius beneplacitis coaptando? Succede virtutibus quæsumus, qui succedis et regno, nullam immixturus maculam excellentis tui luminis claritati.

Quod si forsan ad iniquæ suggestionis instantiam assumpseris causam edendæ constitutionis, quam nuper pro ecclesiastica edidimus libertate, talis profecto tam suggestorum quam suggesti motus nullus fulgitur auxilio rationis: constitutio enim nostra, si ad rivalem sensum, postposito congruo, non trahatur, id, si bene perpenditur, statuit, quod alias per sanctiones canonicas est statutum, licet pœnas contra trans gressores adjecerit, nonnullis excommunicatis, quasi vitio peccare desinentibus potius formidine pœnæ, quam amore virtutis. Non enim præcise statuimus, pro defensione ac necessitatibus tuis vel regni tui ab eisdem prælatis, ecclesiasticisve personis pecuniarium subsidium non præstari: sed adjecimus id non fieri sine nostra licentia speciali, adductis in considerationem nostram exactionibus intolerabilibus ecclesiis et personis ecclesiasticis, religiosis et secularibus, dicti regni ab officialibus tuis auctoritate tua impositis atque factis; de futuris potius verisimiliter formidantes, cum expractoritis certitudo præsumi valeat de futuris: sed te non novimus ad tales exactiones auctoritate fulcitum, cujus auctoritatis abusum in te ac quolibet principe seculari divina et humana jura, quinimo judicia detestantur cum tibi sit et eis talis penitus auctoritas interdicta, quod tibi pro tua, et successorum tuorum salute ad perpetuam rei memoriam præsentibus nuntiamus; nullique suggerenti contrarium fidem adhibeas, quinimo nec præstes auditum.

Objicias, si quando per te vel progenitores tuos pro necesitatibus dicti regni ad eamdem sedem habitus sit recursus, et inanis pertransierit petitio aures ejus, quin fueritis efficaciter exauditi. Ubi regni nempe gravis, quod absit, prædicti necessitas immineret, nedum ab ipsius prælatis, et personis ecclesiasticis tibi vel ipsi sedes eadem concederet, ac faceret subveniri; verum etiam, si exigeret casus, ad calices, cruces, aliaque propria vasa sacra manus extenderet, priusquam tantum et tale regnum, tam ipsi se charum, immo charissimum et ab antiquo devotum exponeret minoris curæ defectui, quo minus ab ea efficacis defensionis præsidia sortiretur.

Nunc autem, amantissime fili, considera quis Rex, quisve princeps regnum tuum non impugnatus a te, vel non offensus impugnat. Nonne Rex Romanorum fuisse occupatas a te tuisque prædecessoribus, seu occupatas teneri civitates et terras seu limites ad Imperium pertinentes cum instantia conqueritur, et specialiter Burgundiæ comitatum, quod notum est fore feudum descendens ab Imperio, et recognoscendum ab ipso? Nonne charissimus in Christo filius noster Rex Angliæ illustris de nonnullis terris Guasconiæ asserit illud idem? Numquid super iis dicti Reges denegant stare juri? Numquid Apostolicæ sedis, quæ Christicolis omnibus præeminet, judicium vel ordinationem recusant? Dumque in eos super iis ipsi peccare te asserunt, de hoc judicium ad sedem eamdem non-est dubium pertinere. Profecto qui contra dictos Reges assumptionis, et prosecutionis malum dederunt consulendo vel inducendo consilium, dant periculosiorem progressum: nec est habenda fiducia super hoc verisimiliter boni finis, cum ea, quæ mala sunt inchoata principio, ut frequentius vix bono exitu peragantur. Pone in recta statera animarum pericula, corporum cædes, expensarum voragines, damna rerum, quæ occasione assumptionis et tuorum processum evenerint, rationis sequens judicium, et non impetum voluntatis, a malorum consiliariorum insidiis elongatus, et tunc manifeste cognosces, te fuisse deceptum, nec expedivisse te talia assumpsisse.

Quid ergo tibi accideret, si, quod absit, sedem ipsam offenderes graviter, eamque hostium tuorum constitueres adjutricem, quin potius contra te faceres principalem? Cum nos et fratres nostri, si Deus ex alto concesserit, parati simus non solum persecutiones, damna rerum, et exilia sustinere: sed et corporalem ipsam mortem subire pro ecclesiastica libertate. Sunt et alii, sicut ad nostram notitiam est deductum, qui maligne surrepunt, dicentes: Jam non poterunt prælati et personæ ecclesiasticæ regni tui servire de feudis, vel subventianes facere, in quibus feudorum ratione tenentur: jam non poterunt unum sciphum, unum equum dare liberaliter Regi suo. Non fertur ad tales et consimiles interpretationes subdolas dictæ nostræ constitutionis intentio: tam falsidicos interpretes non admittit, sicut hæc plenius aliquibus tuis nunciis et familiaribus vivæ vocis oraculo sæpius duximus exponenda.

Quantumlibet autem per subdolos impulsus versatus sis, ut caderes ob prædicta, et ea nos turbaverint, et ad indignationem non sine ratione moverint, nos tamen paterni amoris soliti, ac eadem ecclesia te sui uteri filium oblivisci non possumus, quin, suspenso rigore, te in benedictionibus præveniendo dulcedinis, et via mansuetudinis prosequendo, experiamur primitus quam reverenter, quam efficaciter monita paterna suscipies, et medicamenta curantis illius periti medici Samaritani vicarii, qui super vulnera hominis cujusdam de Jerusalem descendentis in Jericho, qui inciderat in latrones, et fuerat spoliatus, ac relictus plagis impositis semivivus: misericordia motus oleum et vinum apposuit.

Igitur tali exemplo a fomentis olei benignius inchoantes, ecce venerabilem fratrem nostrum Vivariensem episcopum, virum quidem probatæ religionis, scientiæ eminentis, circumspectionis maturæ, ex conversatione diutina nobis et fratribus nostris notum et charum, ac tui honoris et commodi zelatorem, qui et de regno et terra tua trahxit originem, ad te providimus destinandum, ut præmissa solerter et clare celsitudini regiæ oraculo vivæ vocis exponat, et exprimat, ut præmittitur, mentem nostram, quem super his et de contingentibus plene duximus informandum. Serenitatem itaque regiam monemus, rogamus, et hortamur attente, per apostolica tibi scripta mandantes, quatenus non ad animum revoces, sed gratanter accipiens, quod et instanter reducere nitimur ad salutem, paterna medicamina suscipias reverenter, nostrisque tibi et tuo regno salubribus monitis acquiescens, errata sic corrigens per te ipsum, nec permittens in antea per falsa contagia te seduci; ita quod a Deo præmium exinde consequaris, nostram et dictæ ecclesiæ benevolentiam tibi conserves et gratiam, et apud homines bonam famam; nec operteat nos adalia et minus usitata remedia, perseveranter instante, ac pulsante, nec non cogente, justitia, extendere manus nostras, quamvis hoc inviti, et involutarii faceremus. Dat. Anagniæ VII. kal. octobris anno. II.

DOCUMENT (O).

DIVISION OF THE FIEFS AMONG THE COLONNAS.

(*From the archives of Constable Colonna, in Patrini Mon.* 19).

In nomine Domini. Anno Dominicae Incarnationis 1252. Indictione X. Mense Februarii die 7. Nos *Petrus* de Colupna natus qm. D. *Oddonis* de Columna, *Landulphus,* et *Oddo* nati ipsius Petri pro nobis, et pro *Petro, Leone,* et *Fortisbrachia* filiis mei Petri, et ipsorum nomine pro quibus promittimus nos facturos, et curaturos, quod ipsi omni tempore omnia, et singula, quae in hoc contractu dicentur rata, et firma habebunt, et contra ea non venient, facient, adimplebunt, ratificabunt expresse propriis nostris voluntatibus in praesentia religiosi viri *Fratris Joannis de Columna Ordinis Praedicatorum* Prioris totius Romanae Provinciae in ipso Ordine, et ipsius arbitrio, seu arbitratu in praesentia DD. Judicum, scilicet Consolini qm. Petri Judicis, Bartholomaei Petri Judicis, Petri Oddonis de Insula, Angeli Com. Baroncii Petri Consulum, Petri Nicoli Albigellae, et Pauli Petri Pauli Rubei, et Notariorum Joannis Nicolai, Jacobi, et Rodulphi damus, et concedimus, renunciamus, et refutamus, cedimus, et mandamus tibi Domino *Oddoni de Columna* nato·qm. *D. Jordani* de Colupna consobrino mei Petri tuisque heredibus, et successoribus perpetuo etc. totam partem nostram, quam habemus, habere, seu vendicare possemus in *Civitate Penestre, Monte, et Rocca ipsius, et* in ejus Territorio, seu Tenimento, et Castris *Zagaroli, Colupnae, Capranicae,* et medietatis castri *Prati Porcorum,* et in Roccis, et Territoriis, seu Tenimentis ipsorum, et Munitionibus Augustae, et Montis Acceptorii. Quae pars contingens me ipsius Petrum in praedictis Civitate, Castris, et Territoriis, seu Tenimentis ipsorum, et Munitionibus, est medietas ipsorum pluris, vel minoris cum medietatibus vassallorum tam militum, quam peditum, et jurisdictionum in ipsos vassallos, et edificiorum novorum, et antiquorum, terrarum cultarum, et non cultarum, sylvarum, pratorum, pantanorum, vinearum, ortorum, canapinarum, et omnium aliorum jurium, utilitatum, et pertinentium ipsorum Civitatis, et Castrorum, Roccarum, et Munitionum. Quae pars nostra unita est pro indiviso, cum medietate, seu residuis, partibus tui Domini Oddonis, et ad te D. Oddonem pertinentibus in praedictis Civitate, Castris, Roccis, et ipsorum Territoriis, et Munitionibus. Item damus, cedmus, mandamus, concedimus, renuntiamus, et refutamus tibi dicto D. Oddoni omnia jura, et rationis generaliter, quae mihi dicto Petro, et praedictis filiis meis, vel alicui ipsorum competunt, competere possunt, aut poterunt quocumque modo, et quocumque jure in predictis civitate, Castris, et Roccis, territoriis, et Munitionibus praedictis tam in ipsa parte per nos nunc data, et concessa tibi D. Oddoni, quam in aliis residuis partibus ad te, dictum D. Oddonem spectantibus, et in totis ipsis civitate, castris, roccis, et ipsorum territoriis, et munitionibus praedictis, et in omnibus, et singulis praedictis occasione arbitrii, seu arbitratuum latorum dudum inter nos per *D. Petrum Praefectum Urbis,* et occasione quarumcumque sententiarum, consiliorum, investimentorum factorum pro nobis, vel aliquo nostrum contra te D. Oddonem in praedictis civitate, castris, roccis, et ipsorum territoriis, et munitionibus, et generaliter quibuscumque aliis occasionibus, et modis ipsa jura nobis, vel alicui nostrum competunt, competere possunt in praedictis omnibus, et singulis, vel ex successione Parentum meorum Petri, scilicet patris, et avi, vel quocumque alio modo, ita quod penes nos, vel aliquem nostrum nihil juris in praedictis aliquo tempore, quoquo modo reservatur, imo in te D. Oddonem ipsa jura per praesentia penitus, et in solidum trasferantur. Item damus, cedimus, concedimus, et mandamus tibi jam dicto D. Oddoni pro nobis, et dictis filiis mei Petri omnia jura, et actiones, quae nobis, vel alicui nostrum competunt, competere possunt, aut poterunt praenominatis occasionibus, et quibuscumque aliis in castris Sancti Viti, Montis Manni, Castri Novi, et Pisciani, et ipsorum territoriis contra possessores, et detentores ipsorum. Item damus, et concedimus, renunciamus, et refutamus tibi jam dicto D. Oddoni omnia jura, et actiones, quae nobis, vel alicui nostrum competunt, competere possunt, aut poterunt contra te, et in bonis tuis occasione fructuum, proventuum, et reddituum perceptorum, seu qui percepi potuerunt per te dictum D. Oddonem de praedictis civitate, castris, et eorum territoriis a te mihi datis, et concessis, ut in instrumentis meis plene poterit contineri, et constituimus te dictum D. Oddonem procuratorem in rem tuam in praedictis omnibus juribus, et actionibus, ut succedas in locum, et privilegium nostrum, ut cujuslibet nostri, et proprio nomine agas pro praedictis juribus, petas, excipias, et defendas, et facias, quae tibi perpetuo placuerit; nulla nobis, et alicui nostrum in praedictis omnibus, et singulis, aliquo tempore reservatione factor Tenutam quoque et possessionem, quam confitemur te D. Oddonem habere de praedictis civitate Penestra, Rocca et Monte, et Territorio ipsius vassallis, et vassallorum juribus, et de castris Zagarolo, Colupna, et Capranica Roccis et Territoriis ipsorum, vassallis, juribus, vassalorum, et de Munitionibus praedictis integram, pacificam, et tranquillam, et vacuam, seu vacantem, tibi per omnia confirmamus, et corroboramus, ut quemadmodum tenes nunc praedicta in solidum, ita semper perpetuo teneas, et possideas. Civitatis praedicta cum Rocca, et Monte cum Territorio ipsius posita est in distructu Urbis in contrata, quae dicitur *Romangna* Fines hii sunt, est Tenimentum Cavae, et Roccae Cavae, est tenimentum Vallismontonis, et Tenimentum Lariani, et Tenimentum Aligidi, et Tenimentum Zagaroli, et Tenimentum Gallicani, et Sancti Joannis Camporacii, et Tenimentum Poli, et Tenimentum Montis Manni. Castra autem praedicta Zagaroli, et Capranicae posita sunt in Dioecesi dictae civitatis cum ipsorum territoriis. Fines ad Castrum Zagaroli, et ejus territorii sunt ii. Ab uno latere est Tenimentum Penestrae, Tenimentum Gallicani, Tenimentum Colupnae, et Tenimentum S. Cesarei. Fines Capranicae, et ejus Territorii sunt hii, videlicet Tenimentum *Castelli Novi*, et Montis Manni, et Genazzani, Sancti Viti, et Penestrae Reliquum autem castrum Columnae positum est in Dioecesi Tusculana, cujus fines hii sunt, scilicet Tenimentum Zagaroli S Cesarei, Roccae Pejurae, Montis de Compatris, Montis porcii, et Pratri porae, Passarani, et Castilionis. Munitiones autem praedictae positae sunt in Urbe. Fines ad Augustam ab uno Flumen, ab alio via, qua itur a Sancto Blaso, et exit in viam, qua itur usque Urbem, et est via, qua itur ad Flumen a S. Marina. Fines ad Montem Acceptorium hii sunt Domus Romanucciarum, et Synibaldorum, ab alio Domus Macellariorum, et Domus Cesarlinorum, ab alio sunt Domus Zarlonum, et Teoderinorum. Praedictam autem dationem, et concessionem, et omnia, et singula, quae supradicta sunt tibi domino Oddoni facimus ex causa transactionis inter nos praesentialiter, et placabiliter initae de multis litibus, et controversiis, et discordiis, quaestionibus guerris, et offensis hinc inde invicem inter nos habitis, et ventilatis occasione dictorum civitatis, Castrorum, Roccarum, et Munitionum dividendo ipsa inter nos; et pro eo quod tu dominus Oddo similiter causa transactionis dedisti, et concessisti mihi dicto Petro *Castra Gallicani, Sancti Joannis, et Sancti Cesarei* cum suis Tenimentis, ut in istrumentis meis plene continetur; nec non ex arbitrio, seu arbitratu inter nos latis per dictum religiosum virum *Fratrem Joannem de Columna* occasione dictarum quaestionum et offensarum, in quo dicta Civitas, Castra, Roccae, Territoria, Munitiones omnes tibi sunt adjudicatae, ut seriatim in dicto arbitrio, et alias plene continetur. Praeterea promittimus tibi domino Oddoni, quod praedictam partem nostram Civitatis, et Castrorum, et Roccarum, et Munitionum, et eorum territorii, et tenimentorum, et praedictarum Munitionum, et jura nobis, et alicui nostrum competentia, et quae in futurum competere poterunt nulli alii personae, vel loco, seu Collegia dedimus, concessimus, vel alienavimus, nec contractum, seu quasi contractum fecimus nos, nec Pater mei, Petri; et si contrarium apparuerit, et tu dominus Oddo in damnum incurreris, et expensas feceris propterea, seu occasione praedicta, vel quia praedicti Petrus, Leo, et Fortisbrachia filii mei Petri non ratificaverint omnia, et singula, quae dicta sunt, vel contra ea quoquo modo venerint, omnia ipsa, damna, et expensas tibi domino Oddoni quilibet nostrum in solidum redere, et solvere, et reficere promittimus. Aliter autem de evictione praedictorum datorum, et concessorum tibi, per nos teneri tibi volumus, nisi de facto nostro, vel *D. Oddonis Patris mei Petri,* et tu ipse D. Oddo sic actum, pactum, et conventum inter nos esse, et fuisse vis, et confiteris. Pro quibus omnibus, et singulis observandis, et firmiter, et plenarie adimplendis omnia bona nostra mobilia, et immobilia, praesentia, et futura tibi D. Oddoni obligamus, quae quantum ad praedicta pertinent tuo nomine possidere constituimus, dantes tibi potestatem liberam ipsa bona tibi obligata auctoritate propria intrare, tenere, et possidere, vendere, obligare, et facere quod tibi perpetuo placet donec praedictis omnibus, et singulis tibi fuerit per nos, et quemlibet nostrum plenariae satisfactum. Haec omnia, et singula, quae superius dicta sunt nos dictus Petrus de Columna, Landulphus, et Oddo filii ipsius Petri pronobis, et pro Petro, Leone, et Fortisbrachia filiis mei Petri pro nobis, et nostris, et praedictorum haeredibus, et successoribus in perpetuum tibi D. Oddoni pro te, filiis, et haeredibus tuis, et successoribus in perpetuum facere, attendere, observare, et implere promittimus sub poena trium millium marcharum argenti; qua poena soluta, vel non, praedicta semper firma durent: praestitoque a nobis corporali juramento de praedictis omnibus firmiter observandis, et adimplendis tibi D. Oddoni, ut superius dictum est. Quam scribere rogavimus Joannem Nicoli Sacri Romani Imperii Judicem, et Scribam in mense, et Indictione X. suprascripta.

 Fr. Yldibrandus de ord. Praedicatorum Testis
 Fr. Paparonus de ord. Praedicatorum Testis
 Stephanus Pappa Clericus S. Laurentii in Lucina Testis
 Praesbyter Petrus Sublasii ejusdem Ecc. Praesbyter Testis
 Dominus Jacobus Guidonis Clericus ejusdem Ecc. Testis
 Dominus Conradus Malabranca Testis
 Dominus Leonardus Clericus ejusdem Ecc. Testis
 Joannes Brenna Testis
 Jacobus Petri Sinibaldi Testis
 Stephanus Cintii Sinibaldi Testis
 Tebaldinus Testis

Joannes Nicoli Sacri Romani Imperii Judex, et scriba rogatus scripsi, publicavi, complevi, et absolvi.

 Loco Sigilli.

DOCUMENT (P).

ACT APPOINTING CARDINAL JAMES COLONNA, ABSOLUTE ADMINISTRATOR OF THE PROPERTY OF THE COLONNAS.

(From the Barberini archives, in Petrini Mon. 21).

In nomine etc. Anno Domini 1292 Sede vacante, die lunae 28 Aprilis in presentia mei Joannis etc. Parlatoris etc. Nobiles viri DD. Joannes, Oddo, Matthejus, et Laudulphus de Columna fratres filii quondam D. Jordani de Columna etc. commiserunt pro se, et heredibus etc. D. Jacobo S. Mariae in Via lata Diacono Cardinali fratri eorum praesenti etc. gubernationem, curam, regimen, administrationem, tenuatam, et possessionem infrascriptarum terrarum, locorum, et rerum suarum, et ipsius D. Cardinalis, vassallorum, et hominum ipsarum terrarum etc. ita quod ea possit per se, et per alium etc. exercere etc. et fructus, redditus, et proventus praedictorum petere, sibi placueri etc., voluerunt etiam, et potestatem dederunt ipsi D. Carpercipere etc. ac inter eos, et ipsum D. Cardinalem distribuere sicut dinali quod etc. possit sua auctoritate etc. terras, res, loca ipsa, et Roccas etc. intrare, accipere, custodire etc., hoc pact etc. quod ipse D. Cardinalis, et sui heredes, et successores nullo modo teneantur ad redditionem rationis dictae administrationis etc., et quidquid ipsum D. Cardinalem occasione dictae administrationis, et divisionis debere contigerit etc. eisdem nobilibus etc., nunc ipsi Nobiles per pactum expressum remiserunt.

Res autem, et terrae, et loca sunt haec: *Civitas Penestrina,* Mons *Penestrinus,* Castrum *Capranicae Penestrinensis dioecesis,* Castrum *Zagaroli* ejusdem dioecesis, Castrum *Columnae* Tusculanae dioecesis, et medietas Castri, seu villae *Petraporti* Tusculanae dioecesis etc., nec non tenimenti *Algidi,* et omnia, et singula jura, quae ipsi habent etc. in ipso teni mento Algidi, et *Castello Algidi* Acta sunt praedicta Romae in Domibus S. Laurentii in Lucina etc.

Ego Joannes dictus Parlator de Secia apostolicae Sedis auctoritate Judex, et notarius etc.

DOCUMENT (Q).

PROCEEDINGS AGAINST THE COLONNAS.

Bonifacius, etc. ad perpetuam rei memoriam.

Praeteritorum temporum nefandis Columensium actibus, et praesentium pravis operibus recidivis, ac futuris, de quibus veresimiliter formidabatur, in considerationem prudenter adductis, venit patenter in lucem, quod Columnensium domus exasperans, amara domesticis, molesta vicinis, Romanorum reipublicae impugnatrix, sanctae Ecclesiae Romanae rebellis, Urbis et patriae pertubatrix, consortis impatiens, ingrata beneficiis, subesse nolens, humilitatis ignara, plena furoribus, Deum non metuens, nec volens homines revereri, habens de Urbis et orbis turbatione pruritum, studuit charissimum in Christo filium nostrum Jacobum Aragoniae Regem illustrem, tunc hostem ecclesiae ac rebellem, Siculisque perfidis praesidentem de facto, in nostrum et charissimi in Christo filii nostri Siciliae Regis illustris grave praeiudicium, et gravamen Christianitatis et Terrae sanctae succursus grande dispendium in rebellione, tenere, tam sibi quam nobili juveni Friderico nato quondam Petri olim Regis Aragoniae, in crimine criminoso favendo. Ut illud notissimum omittamus, qualiter quondam Joannes de Columna tit. S. Praxedis praesbyter Cardinalis, et Oddo de Columna nepos ipsius, pater Jacobi S Mariae in Via lata, et avus Petri de Columna S. Eustachii diaconorum Cardinalium, tempore felicis recordationis Gregorii Papae IX. praedecessoris nostri fuerunt dure et graviter ipsam ecclesiam persecuti, cum damnatae memoriae Friderico olim Romanorum Imperatori, supradictae ecclesiae publico persecutore et hoste, tempore, quo quondam Mattheus Rubeus de domo filiorum Ursi sororius dicti Oddonis senatus in Urbe regimen exercebat ad honorem et obsequium ecclesiae memoratae: a cujus Matthaei domo dictus Cardinalis et Oddo et eorum posteri multa beneficia receperunt: praesertim a sanctae memoriae Nicolao III. praedecessore nostro, qui dictum Jacobum juvenem satis et inscium, perniciosum tamen postmodum, hypocrisim tunc temporis periculose gerentem, ad Cardinalatus provexit honorem: quod utinam non fecisset, quia nec sedi Apostolicae, nec Christianitati, nec dicti praedecessoris Nicolai domui talis promotio expedivit, quam dicti Jacobus et Petrus ac sui, velut ingratitudinis filii, et beneficiorum immemores, multipliciter impugnarunt. Terras etiam subiectas ecclesiae sibique rebelles in rebellione fovebant in hoc, dantes eisdem auxilium et favorem.

Novissimis vero temporibus dicti juvenis Friderici, latenter discurrentibus nunciis per Urbem et loca vicina, ut immissis scandalis ea possent ipsius subjicere ditioni, licet id procurarent homines dictae domus Columnensis, et ad hoc eis ministrarent auxilia et favores; mansuetudinis tamen Apostolicae sedis benigna sinceritas, quae libentius emendat in subditis peccata, quam puniat, nec exerit ferrum praecisionis in morbos, quos sanare potest mulcebris lenitas medicinae; eos studuit nunc paterna lenitatis dulcedine alloqui, nunc verbis charitativae correctionis inducere, ut a talibus abstinerent, ipsorumque elatam pertinaciam, immo effraenem superbiam, non semel sed pluries in fulgore terrifico comminationis increpavit, tendens ante ipsos arcum justitiae in rigore, quo sagitta perpetuae dejectionis, solita non converti retrorsum, emittitur, ut formidabilis vindictae significationis clementer exhibita stupori eorum sensum timoris incuteret, et fugam ad misericordiam per compendium poenitentiae suaderet. Sed nec sic profecimus apud eos: traxit enim illos in desperationis laqueum moles praeponderans peccatorum, ut nec rationibus nec correctionibus, monitionibus, sive minis reduci potuerint ad salutem: quin potius velut aspis surda suarum aurium obstruxerunt auditum, eligentes quasi pro gloria confusionis opprobrium, et irreparabilis ruinae periculum pro tutela.

Periculis vero obviare volentes, dictis Jacobo et Petro Cardinalibus districte mandavimus, ut terras, quas Stephanus ipsius Jacobi nepos, et frater Petri praefati tenere vulgariter dicebatur, videlicet civitatem Perusin. castra Columna et Zagaroli, procurarent custodienda ad nostrum beneplacitum assignari, ne per ea Urbis et patriae possent quies et tranquillitas impediri, et ut ex eis posset praestari auxilium dicto Friderico hosti ecclesiae memoratae; utque ipse hostis, et valitores, seu adjutores ipsius non receptarentur in eis assignationem quorum non revocabatur in dubium ab ipsorum Jacobi et Petri voluntate pendere, quae conficto seu quaesito colore teneri per dictum Stephanum dicebantur, ne dilecto filio Matthaeo praeposito ecclesiae de sancto Audumaro Morinensis dioecesis, et nobilibus viris Oddoni et Landulpho fratibus dicti I. filii saepedicti Oddonis assignretur paterna et hereditaria portio, quae in dictis civitate et castris com-

petebat eisdem, quam propter duritiem et crudelitatem dictorum
Jacobi et Joannis defuncti Petri et fratrum suorum nequiverunt
habere, licet quadraginta anni et amplius sint elapsi, quod obiit dictus
Oddo; quamvis etiam nos pietate moti, pro bono pacis inter eos
interposuerimus solicite partes nostras, ut unusquisque de civitate
et castris suam portionem haereditariam obtineret, oblationibus
magnis factis nepotibus dicti Jacobi in avantagium, ut hujusmodi
concordia proveniret; considerantes fore indignum, ut quibus de una
substantia competit aequa successio, alii abundanter affluant, alii
paupertatis incommodis ingemiscant, quos tamen rationibus, precibus,
sive minis nequivimus emollire. Ipsi vero Jacobus et Petrus Cardinales, a nostra praesentia recedentes non facta hujusmodi assignatione, quae ab eorum beneplacito dependebat, nunquam ad nos
postea redierunt.

Nos igitur attendentes ipsorum Columnensium adeo incaluisse
duritiem, adeo fore nequitiam induratam, quod non rationibus dirigi,
non blandimentis allici, non fomentis reduci, nec minis etiam in-
clinari potuerunt ab bonum, ex quo blandimenta non potuerant, nec
fomenta valebant; deliberavimus apponere manus ad fortia, et ferro
abscindere vulnera, quae, medicamenta non senserunt lenitiva: ac
praemissis et aliis, quae nobis et fratribus nostris rationabiliter occurrerunt, provida deliberatione discussis, providimus non solum
contra filios dicti Joannis, qui peccabant apertius, verum etiam
contra Jacobum et Petrum praefatos, ex quorum adipe praedicta
iniquitas et superbia procedunt, juste procedere, qui consentiebant
ipsis peccantibus, praestando fomentum, favorem, praesidium, et tuta-
men; quia culpa non caret, et delicti efficitur particeps, qui non pro-
hibet delinquentem, dum potest: et negligere, cum quis potest, per-
tubare perversos, nihil aliud est quam favere; nec caret scrupulo
societatis occultae, qui manifesto facinori desinit obviare.

Cumque dictorum Jacobi et Petri Cardinalatus et status dictae
ecclesiae, ejusque fidelibus esset in scandalum, eorumque potestas non
in aedificationem, sed in destructionem; ipsique obessent, quibus
prodesse debebant, nec nostram relevarunt, per suam particularem,
solicitudinem, qua vocati sumus a Deo in plenitudinem potestatis,
immo potius impugnarent; quantumlibet venerabilibus fratribus
nostris episcopis, et dilectis filiis presbyteris etdiaconibus S. R. E.
Cardinalibus, quantum cum Deo possumus, deferamus, ipsorumque
collegium honoremus, eorumdem Jacobi et Petri elegimus domare
superbiam in robore virtutis Altissimi, arrogantiam et praesump-
tionem elatam conterere, eos tamquam oves morbidas a dominico
ovili abjicere, ipsosque, ut culpa supplicium timeat, et virtus proem-
ium retributionis expectect, a loco quantumcumque sublimi perpetuo
amovere, tam ex eorum culpis et demeritis ac suorum, quam ex
causis rationabilibus, quae nos movent; praesertim explorati divini
et humani iuris existat, unum pro altero interdum ex causa puniri.

Eorum ergo absentiam Dei replente praesentia, ad honorem Dei
omnipotentis, B. Mariae semper Virginis, beatorum Apostolorum
Petri et Pauli, et Romanae Ecclesiae saepedictae praefatos Iacobum

S. Mariae in Via lata et Petrum S. Eustachij diaconos Cardinales de ipsorum fratrum nostrorum consilio a Cardinalatibus ipsis sanctae Romanae ecclesiae et praedictarum ecclesiarum deponimus etc.

Excomunicamus insuper praedictos Jacobum et Petrum, et etiam omnes illos, qui de caetero scienter et deliberate pro Cardinalibus ipsos vel aliquem eorum habuerint; et assensum praestiterint, quod pro Cardinalibus habeantur, et quod eos vel ipsorum aliquem in electione Romani Pontificis ad aliquem actum ut Cardinales admiserint, vel vocis eorum suffragium, aut alicuius ex eis. Omnes etiam et singulos cuiuscumque eminentiae fuerint, dignitatis, ordinis, conditionis, aut status, etiam si fuerint S. R. E. Cardinales, qui ipsis Jacobo et Petro, vel eorum alteri postquam, quod absit, in haeresim, vel in schisma, et rebellionem ceciderint, in haeresi, vel schismate, aut rebellione stantibus scienter et deliberate praestiterint auxilium, consilium, vel favorem, publice vel occulte, omni statu ecclesiastico, Praelatura, et honore privamus; omnes civitates, castra, terras, et loca, quae ipsos vel aliquem eorum in haeresim, schisma, vel rebellionem lapsos scienter susceperint, tenuerint, ecclesiastico supponimus interdicto, etc. Actum Romae apud S. Petrum in publico consistorio nostro VI. id. maji Pontificatus nostri anno III.

DOCUMENT (R).

THE COLONNA LIBEL AGAINST BONIFACE.

Universis praesens instrumentum publicum inspecturis, cujuscumque praecellentiae, dignitatis, status, vel conditionis existant, ecclesiasticae vel mundanae, miseratione divina Jacobus S. Mariae in Via lata, et Petrus S. Eustachii diaconi Cardinales salutem, etc. Respondemus ad ultimum verbum inter alia in mandato nobis facto propositum, si tamen mandatum dici debeat quod volebatis scire, utrum essetis Papa, quod vos non credimus legitimum Papam esse, sacroque coetui dominorum Cardinalium denuntiamus, suamque provisionem et remedium super hoc exposcimus, cum hoc expediat universali ecclesiae et fidei fundamento, ut loco domini nostri Jesu Christi et in ejus vices non nisi verus et legitimus vero et legitime pastor praesit, curamque gregis sibi commissi legitime gerat: ne, si (quod absit) non verus pastor insurgeret, seu etiam remaneret, non levem jacturam sed fundamenti talis subversionem reciperet sancta catholica et universalis ecclesia, ecclesiasticis sacramentis indigne (proh dolor!) prophanatis, dum per eum indigne, indebite, et illegitime ministrarentur, qui potestatem et auctoritatem ministrandi legitimam non habere: non enim sacramenta dare possunt, qui ea dandi potestatem non habent; nec ministros creare, qui non sunt. Frequenter namque audivimus a plurimis non levis auctoritatis viris ecclesiastici et saecularis status, et dignitatis dubitari verosimiliter, an renunciatio facta per sanctae memoriae dominum Coelestinum Papam V. tenuerit et legitime et canonice facta fuerit:

cum verosimiliter contrarium videtur ex eo, quod Papatus a solo Deo est: et quae a Deo vel ab alio superiori committuntur, a nullo possunt inferiori removeri. Et sic papalis potestas, quae a solo Deo committitur, a nullo inferiori removeri posse videtur.

Item ex eo, quia nullus potest auctoritatem et potestatem aliquam spiritualem auferre, quam conferre non potest. Sed auctoritatem papalem nullus conferre potest nisi Deus: ergo neque eam auferre. Sed si teneret renunciatio, auferretur papalis potestas. Ergo renunciatio non videtur fieri posse.

Item etiam decretalis. *Inter corporalia*, expresse innuit, quod depositio Episcoporum, translatio eorum, et absolutio per cessionem soli Papae est reservata, nec etiam ipsi conceditur, nisi in quantum Papa quodammodo Deus est, id est Dei vicarius, ut patet ex textu. Ergo remotio Papae, quia Papatus omnes dignitates excellit, per superiorem Papa voluit ipse Deus tantummodo fieri, id est per semetipsum nulla enim ratio capit, quod Deus voluerit inferiores dignitates per ipsum Deum tantum aut per harum superiorem dignitatum tolli posse, nec per ipsum superiorem nisi in quantum ipse superior, scilicet Papa est Dei Vicarius; et tamen voluerit ipsum Papatum, quae est summa dignitas, proprie Christi est, nedum per inferiorem Deo, sed etiam per inferiorem seipsa dignitate tolli posse: et sic solus Deus videtur tollere posse Papatum, et nullus alter, sicut multipliciter videtur colligi ex textu praedictae decretalis.

Item ex eo, quod summa virtus creata per nullam virtutem creatam videtur posse tolli. Sed Papatus est summa potestas in creatura. Ergo per nullam virtutem creatam tolli posse videtur.

Iterum ex eo, quod nec Papa, nec tota creaturarum universitas potest facere, quod aliquis Pontifex non sit Pontifex. Ergo multo magis non videtur posse facere, quod summus Pontifex non sit summus Pontifex. Nam minus est tollere simpliciter Pontificem, quam summum Pontificem. Ergo cum simpliciter Pontificem nullus possit tollere nisi Deus, nec summum Pontificem videtur aliquis posse tollere nisi Deus quod fieret, si renuntiare posset ita, quod valeret.

Item ex eo, quod Papa non est Papa nisi per legem divinam, et non per legem alicujus creaturae, nec omnium creaturarum simul. Ergo nullo modo videtur, quod Papa possit eximi, quin sit Papa: nec enim ex quo consensit et subjecit se legi sponsae potest esse non Papa per aliquam creaturam neque per omnes simul, ut videtur.

Item ex eo, quod nullus potest tollere votum alicujus seu ab ipso absolvere nisi ille, qui est supra votum. Sed papatus est quoddam votum maximum super omnia vota; nam vovet Papa de facto ipsi Deo, quod curam habebit universaliter gregis sui totius, scilicet universalis secclesiae; et quod de ipsis reddet rationem. Ergo ab isto voto solus eum Deus absolvere posse videtur. Ergo de Papa nullus videtur posse fieri non Papa, nisi omnino a solo Deo aliqua ratione: nullus enim alicui obligatus potest ab obligatione seipsum absolvere, qua tenetur obnoxious, maxime superiore obligatus. Sed Papa nullum habet superiorem nisi Deum, et per Papatum se Deo obligavit. Ergo a nullo posse videtur absolvi nisi a Deo.

Item ex eo, quod nullus videtur se ipsum absolvere posse. Sed si valeret renuntiatio, videtur quod seipsum posset absolvere.

Item ex eo, quod papalis obligato non videtur posse tolli nisi per majorem potestatem, quam papalis sit. Sed nulla potentia creata est major quam papalis. Ergo fieri non potest per Papam nec per aliquid aliud nisi per Deum ut qui semel est Papa, non sit semper Papa, dum vivit, ut videtur. Item ex eo quod nulla dignitas ecclesiastica post legitimam confirmationem potest tolli nisi per ejus superiorem. Sed Papa solus Deus est major. Ergo a solo Deo tolli posse videtur.

Item ex eo, quod Apostolus vult et probat sacerdotium Christi esse aeternum; et ad vivere in aeternum in sacerdotio, sequitur ipsum esse sacerdotem in aeternum. Ergo nullo modo potest esse vita summi Pontificis et summi sacerdotis sine summo sacerdotio. Ergo renuntiare non potest, ut videtur. Et nimis extraneum et a ratione remotum apparet, quod summus Pontifex, qui est verus successor et vicarius Jesu Christi, qui est sacerdos in aeternum possit absolvi ab alio quam ab ipso Deo; et quod quandiu vixerit non maneat summus Pontifex: et quod aliquo modo possit esse vita summi sacerdotis sine summo sacerdotio, ut videtur.

Item ex eo, quod si diceretur, quod vita summi sacerdotis esset sine summo sacerdotio, argumentum Apostoli, ubi dicit; Secundum legem Mosaicam plures facti sunt sacerdotes; penitus nullum videretur esse, sed falsitatem contineret; nam posset argui contra ipsum, quia Christus sempiternum habet sacerdotium. Respondet Apostolus: Eo quod manet in aeternum; dico tibi, beate Apostole, non est verum, quia potest in vita sua renuntiare, et non erit sacerdos amplius. Ex hac positione quod Papa renuntiare posset totius Scripturae sacrae et verbi Apostoli falsitas sequi videretur: et ex multis aliis rationabilibus et evidentibus causis hoc ipsum videtur verisimile et iustissime in dubitationem deduci.

Item ex eo, quod in renuntiatione ipsius multae fraudes et doli, conditiones et intendimenta et machinamenta, et tales et talia intervenisse multipliciter offerentur, quod esto, quod posset fieri renunciatio, de quo merito dubitatur, ipsam vitiarent et redderent illegitimam, inefficacem, et nullam.

Item ex eo, quod esto quod renunciatio tenuisset (quod nullo modo asseritur, neque creditur) plura postea intervenerunt quae electionem postmodum subsecutam nullam et inefficacem reddiderunt omnino: ex quo vos, qui principaliter tangimini, merito dubitatis, et in quaestionem deducitis dicendo, vos velle scire, utrum sitis Papa, prout in mandato per vos facto, si mandatum dici debet, per magistrum Joannem de Penestre clericum camerae continebatur expresse, demodo nos, qui ex vera fide asserimus et illuminata conscientia firmiter credimus, vos non Papam, tuta conscientia silere non possumus, quin in tanto negotio, quod sic universalem medullitus tangit ecclesiam, veritas declaretur. Propter quod petimus instanter et humiliter generale Concilium congregari, ut in eodem de his omnibus veritas declaretur, omnisque error abscedat. Et si quidem universale

Concilium, auditis et pensatis supradictis et aliis negotium contingentibus, declaraverit renunciationem legitime et canonice processisse, et electionem legitime et canonice postea subsecutam; eidem declarationi, cui stare et parere nos offerimus, a nobis et ab aliis humiliter deferatur et pareatur omnino. Si vero vel renuntiationem non legitime nec canonice processisse, vel electionem minus legitime et canonice subsecutam, dicti concilii declaratione aut deliberatione claruerit, cedat error, et de vero sponso provideatur legitime et canonice universali ecclesiae sponsae Christi, etc. Sub anno Domini MCCXCVII indictione X. die veneris, X. mensis maji.

DOCUMENT (S).

SENTENCE OF BONIFACE AGAINST THE COLONNAS.

Bonifacius, et ad perpetuam rei memoriam

Lapis abscissus de monte sine manibus, ab aedificantibus reprobatus, et factus in caput anguli, duos et diversos parietes copulans, pastores a Judaea, et magos ab oriente producens, in se reconcilians ima summis, et ordinans in sancta Romana apostolica et catholica ecclesia charitatem, ipsam sponsam suam statuit esse unam, sicut scriptum est: Una est columba mea electa mea, perfecta mea: una est matris suae, electa genitricis suae; per inconsutilem tunicam Domini designatam, desuper contextam per totum. Hanc diviserunt milites, sed sortiti sunt eam. Hanc impugnaverunt haeretici et schismatici, ac blasphemi a juventute sua: sed non praevaluerunt adversus eam divina virtute protectam, et ut castrorum acies ordinatam Sed nondum haereticis, schismaticis, ac blasphemis adeo est finis impositus, quin velut viperei filii, natique degeneres in senectute positum, ejus sabbatum perturbare, et unitatem scindere moliantur. De quorum numero fore noscuntur Jacobus de Columna et Petrus nepos eius, quondam dictae ecclesiae Cardinales, quos, eorum culpis et demeritis exigentibus ac suorum, pridem VI. idus maii Pontificatus nostri anno III. ex rationabilibus causis moti, de fratrum nostrorum concilio Cardinalatu privavimus perpetuo, et deposuimus ab eisdem, variis processibus et sententiis, comminationes et poenas continentibus, contra ipsos habitis; nec non et contra natos quondam Joannis de Columna fratris dicti Jacobi et patris Petri praefati, ac contro omnes, qui per masculinam et foemininam lineam descenderunt hactenus, et descendunt ab ipso Joanne.

Ipsi namque Jacobus et Petrus intraverunt ecclesiam sub pelle ovina, operibus tamen et fructibus se exhibuerunt quasi lupos rapaces; et graves, non parcentes gregi dominico, et in reprobum sensum dati, et oculis excaecati malitia, ita ut lumen coeli non viderent, nec videant; descendentes in malorum profundum, et contemnentes, exurrexerunt loqui perversa: et acuentes ut gladium linguas suas, in blasphema verba, et schismatica proruperunt, aperte monstrantes quod licet ex nobis prodierint, tamen non erant ex nobis: nam si ex nobis fuissent, utique permansissent nobiscum. Quibus verbis redactis in scriptis, ipsa scripta in diversarum ecclesiarum Urbis ostiis affigi, et super Basilicae principis Apostolorum de Urbe altari poni fecerunt: quae quidem scripta eorum ab olim praecogitatam et praeconceptam nequitiam patenter indicant, ipsosque Jacobum atque Petrum blasphemos atque schismaticos fore manifeste declarant, sanctae Dei ecclesiae Romanae catholicae et apostolicae molientes scindere unitatem, et Columnam Dei viventis pene adnutationem deducere, ac sagenam summi Piscatoris procellis intumescentibus ad naufragii profunda submergere, si, quod absit, eis facultas adesset. In hujusmodi namque scriptis, quae universis eadem inspecturis cujuscumque praeeminentiae, dignitatis, status, vel conditionis existant, ecclesiasticae vel mundanae, a Jacobo et Petro praedictis mittuntur sub modo scribendi, quo ante depositionem suam uti solebant, et sub sigillis, quibus antea utebantur; inter caetera continentur, nos divina providentia ad summi apostolatus apicem secundum scita canonum, licet immeritos, evocatos, et non solum ab omnibus fratribus nostris et ab ipsis praevia electione canonica, immo ab Ecclesia universali receptos in Papam, consecratos, eis assistentibus, secundum approbatum morem Romanae ecclesiae, et etiam coronatos, Papam non esse; haec et alia confingentes, quae non solum sunt blasphemosa et schismatica, sed insana, prout eorum scripta indicant manifeste.

Post depositionem etiam et privationem processus et sententias supradictos, Cardinales se nominant, et Cardinalitia portant insignia, annulis et rubeis capellis utentes, et Cardinalitos actus exercent, sicut antequam per nos de fratrum nostrorum consilio essent depositi faciebant et hactenus utebantur: ut illud taceamus ad praesens, quod fere per triennium obedientiam nobis et reverentiam exhibuerunt ut Papae, participantes una nobiscum, reverentiam exhibuerunt ut Papae, participantes una nobiscum reverendum dominici Corporis et Sanguinis sacramentum, ac ministrantes nobis in missarum solemniis et divinis, prout ab antiquo solent Cardinales saepedictae Romanae ecclesiae Romanis Pontificibus ministrare; in ecclesiarum provisionibus et diffinitionibus per nos factis consilia sua dantes, et se in concessis a nobis privilegiis subscribentes, alia faciebant nobiscum et recipiebant nobiscum et recipiebant a nobis, quae cum homine et ab homine cujus non habuissent ingressum canonicum, nec fieri nec recipi debuissent. Nec possent supradicta metu proponere se fecisse, qui nos in scrutinio, more memorate ecclesiae Cardinalium, elegerent et nominaverant eligendum in Papam quando de nobis, timendum non erat: et post electionem, receptionem, consecrationem, et coronationem praemissas factas de nobis, in castro tunc ipsorum, quod Zagarolum dicitur, et quod perdictum Jacobum tunc temporis tenebatur, cum pluribus ex fratribus nostris hopitati fuerimus confidenter, et ipsi ac sui tunc ibidem exhibuerunt nobis papalem reverentiam et honorem, ubi nulla aderat eis causa timoris.

Nos igitur super his et aliis, quae hujusmodi negotium contingunt, vel contingere possunt, habita cum dictis fratribus nostris deliberatione matura, omnes processus, omnesque sententias, comminationes, et poenas; et specialiter dictam sententiam depositionis et privationis Cardinalituum, et cuncta alia quae in nostris super hoc confectis literis continentur, de eorumdem fratrum nostrorum consilio rata habentes et grata; confirmamus, ratificamus, et approbamus, et etiam innovamus; et propter adauctam eorum contumaciam, schisma, atque blasphemiam, de dictorum fratrum consilio ipsos Jacobum et Petrum sententiando pronuntiamus esse schismaticos, et blasphemos, et excommunicationis sententia innodamus; ipsosque, in hujusmodi blasphemia et schismate perdurantes, tamquam haereticos puniendos; et tam dictam depositionis et privationis cardinalatuum sententiam, quam omnia, quae contra ipsos et alios fecimus, et pronuntiavimus, de novo facimus, sententiamus, atque proferimus, et robur habere decernimus perpetuae firmitatis. Omnibus insuper canonicatibus praebendi, dignitatibus, personatibus, officiis, et beneficiis cum cura vel sine cura; pensionibus, ecclesiasticis reditibus seu proventibus, quae praedicti Jacobus et Petrus, et unusquisque eorum habebant, tenebant, et possidebant in quibuscumque seu a quibuscumque ecclesiis, monasteriis hospitalibus religiosis et saecularibus vel specialibus personis, cujuscumque eminentiae, conditonis, ordinis, dignitatis, et status, ecclesiastici vel mundani; ipsos omnino privamus, ipsaque collationi sedis Apostolicae reservamus; decernentes irritum, et inane, si secus a quoquam super iis scienter vel ignoranter contigerit attentari.

Eosdem quoque Jacobum et Petrum, quondam Cardinales; Joannem dictum de sancto Vito, et Oddonem filios quondam Joannis de Columna fratris dicti Jacobi, et patris Petri praefati omnibus iuribus, et bonis mobilibus et immobilibus ecclesiasticis; et tam ipsos quam Agapitum, Stephanum, et Jacobum dictum Sciarram, filios Joannis de Columna praedicti, et alios filios ejusdem Joannis, si qui alii sunt filii eorumdem vel alicuius eorum, omnibus iuribus, et bonis, et rebus mobilibus et immobilibus, hereditariis seu quomodolibet acquisitis, quibuscumque ratione, causa, vel titulo ad eos vel ipsorum aliquem seu aliquos pervenerint, seu obvenerint, obvenire vel pervenire possent; nec non communitatibus, baroniis, comitatibus, civitatibus, sive castris, ubicumque illa habeant, teneant, vel obtineant, vel quomodolibet ad ipsos pertineant, privamus omnino illaque omnia et singula publicamus, et etiam confiscamus; ita quod ad ipsos vel eorum aliquem, heredes ipsorum vel alicuius eorum nullo umquam tempore revertantur, eosque ac unumquemque ipsorum active et passive intestabiles reddimus; ita quod eis et eorum unicuique ex testamento, vel quavis ultima voluntate, seu ab intestato nullus succedere possit, nec ipsi, aut eorum aliquis ex testamento seu ultima voluntate, vel ab intestato succedere, aut aliquod capere possint; nihilque eis, et eorum alicui ratione legati, institutionis, aut substitutionis, seu quovis titulo valeat quomodolibet obvenire: eosque pronuntiamus infames, et legitimis actibus prorsus indignos; statuentes quod nulli eorum portae alicuius pateant dignitatis ecclesiasticae vel mundanae, et si secus fieret, nullum robur habere, ipsisque civilitatem et incolatum et habitatione Urbis, circumpositae regionis, et quorumvis civitatum, castrorum, terrarum atque locorum dictate ecclesiae subiectorum prorsus interdicimus: eosque omnes et singulos ab Urbe, eiusque territorio et districtu, et ab omnibus civitatibus, castris, terris seu locis subiectis eidem Romanae ecclesiae forbannimus: ipsosque Agapitum, Stephanum, Jacobum dictum Scirram, Joannem de Sancto Vito, et Oddonem excommunicationis sententia innodamus; statuentes firmiter, et mandantes, ut nullus dictos Jacobum et Petrum, et praefatos Agapitum, Stephanum, Jacobum dictum Sciarram, Jonnanem, et Oddonem fratres, eos vel eorum aliquem aut aliquos recipiat vel receptat; nullusque eis aut ipsorum alicui, vel aliquibus praestet auxilium, consilium vel favorem; eos, qui secus fecerint, excommunicationis sententia innodantes. Praecipimus etiam sub excommunicationis sententia, quam contrarium facientes incurrere volumus ipso facto, ut nullus ab ipsis Jacobo et Petro, et praedictis fratribus, vel eorum altero, in schismate vel rebellione huiusmodi existentibus, nuntium vel literas recipiat, aut mittat ad eos vel ad alterum eorumdem.

Reddimus quoque praedictos Jacobum et Petrum, Agapitum, Stephanum, et Jacobum dictum Sciarram, Joannem de S. Vito et Oddonem, et alios si qui sunt filii dicti Joannis de Columna, et filios eorumdem inhabiles ad honorem seu regimen, vel officium publicum, ecclesiasticum vel mundanum, quaelibet et quocumque nomine censeantur, per se, vel alium, aut alios quomodolibet exercenda; ita quod nec ad illa vocari, eligi, vel assumi valeant, vel ad aliquod eorumdem; nec ipsi, vel aliquis eorum, seu aliqui ea valeant exercere; et si secus factum fuerit, illud decernimus irritum et inane. Si qui vero ex eis, vel ipsorum aliquis, vel quivis per eas, vel pro eis, vel ipsorum aliquem, vel aliquos in protestatariae, capitaniae, consulatus regimine, vel quovis officio publico hactenus, ubicumque positi, electi, assumpti fuerint, vel recepti; praesertim quorumcumque provinciae, civitatum, castrorum, terrarum, atque locorum memoratae ecclesiae subiectorum; illos ab eis penitus amovemus, executionibus ipsis penitus interdictis, eosque praecipimus nullatenus reassumi; et si secus factum fuerit, illud decernimus nullius existere firmitatis.

Civitatis vero, castra, seu loca, quae scienter dictos Jacobum et Petrum, et praedictos fratres receperint, receptaverint, sive tenuerint, autin quibus publice moram contraxerint, quandiu ipsi vel alter eorum inibi morabuntur, ecclesiastico supponimus interdicto: et personas ipsorum Jacobi, et Petri, et fratrum capiendas exponimus quibuscumque fidelibus, detinendas et custodiendas diligenter, quousque per dictem sedem aliud fuerit ordinatum, etc. Actum Romae in Basilica supradicta, (nimirum S. Petri) in die Ascensionis Domini, pontificatus nostri anno III.

DOCUMENT (T).

BRIEF OF BONIFACE ENTRUSTING THE DIRECTION OF THE WAR AGAINST THE COLONNAS, TO LANDOLPH COLONNA.

Bonifacius etc. Dilecto filio nobili viro Landulpho de Columna civi romano salutem, et apostolicam benedictionem. Ut depressio, et confusio Columnen, Schismaticorum, et Ecclesiae Romanae Rebellium eo celerius, et facilius executioni mandetur, quoad id plurium proborum virorum fuerit ministerium deputatum. Nos de tuae nobilitatis industria plenarie confidentes, volumus, et praesentium tibi auctoritate committimus, ut una cum nobili viro... Capitaneo militum *Talliae Tusciae* adversus scismaticos, et rebelles praedictos, et adjutores, et fautores eorum ad captiones castrorum, terrarum, locorum, et bonorum, ac etiam personarum ipsorum, destructionem quoque, et devastationem domorum, vinearum, et arborum eorumdem, et alias in omnibus, et per omnia, quae in hac parte, ad honorem, et exaltationem Ecclesiae Romanae videris expedire, procedeas viriliter, et potenter, et nomine nostro, et ejusdem Ecclesiae, Castra, terras, loca, et Personas ipsorum, quae capi contigerit, custodias et conserves, seu custodiri, et conservari facias, et procures ad nostrum beneplacitum disponenda.

Dat. apud Urbem Veterem secundo nonas Septembris Pontificatus nostri anno tertio.

DOCUMENT (U).

REPLY OF BONIFACE TO THE ROMAN PEOPLE.

Bonifacius etc. dilectis filiis nobili viro Pandulpho de Sabello Senatori, et Populo Urbis salutem, et apostolicam benedictionem. Romanum Populum peculiares, et praedilectos filios praecipua caritate constringimus, et specialiori prosequimur prerogativa favoris Sane dilectos filios Ambasciatores vestros ex parte vestra solemniter in quantitate non modica nuper ad nostram praesentiam accedentes paterna benignitate recepimus, et quae tam verbo, quam scriptura nobis exponere voluerunt attendimus diligente, ipsi namcue coram nobis, et Fratribus nostris tam oretemus, quam in scriptis ex parte vestra proponere curaverunt, quod iidem Ambasciatores de mandato tuo, Senator, et ex deliberatione Consilii generalis, et specialis, et quamplurium aliorum proborum virorum in ipso congregatorum, et parlamenti more solito publice congregati ad Colupnenses tam clericos, quam laicos scismaticos, nostros et Ecclesiae Romanae rebelles, et hostes nuperrime accesserunt, et ex parte vestra, Senator et Popule, praedictis suaserunt Clericis et induxerunt eosdem, et praefatis Laicis mandarunt, quod ad pedes nostros reverenter venirent nostra, et ipsius Rumanae Ecclesiae absolute, ac libere mandata facturi; ad quae praefati scismatici, et rebelles ipsis ambasciatoribus responderunt, quod ipsi parati erant; et offerebant se venturos ad pedes nostros, ac nostra, et praefatae Ecclesiae mandata facturos; qua responsione a praedictis Columpnensibus Ambasciatores ipsi audita, redeuntes ad Urbem ipsaque relata a te Senatore, sicut ex dicti consilii, et nostra popule ut asserebant ordinatione concesserat (*sic*) suscepere mandatum quod iidem Ambasciatores ad praesentiam nostram accederent, ac nobis ex parte vestra, Senator et Popule, supplicarent, ut intuitu Dei, et consideratione vestra dignaremur praefatos Columpnenses, ut praemittitur venientes benigne recipere, ac misericorditer pertractare. Nos igitur illius vices gerentes qui mortem non fecit, nec delectatur in perditionem vivorum, et filios abeuntes in devium regionis dissimilitudinis (*sic*) humiliter revertentes, suaque recognoscentes peccata ad poenitentiam libenter admittit, praefatis scismaticis, hostibus, atque rebellibus si suas recognoscentes culpas, et scelera humili spiritu, et contrito ad nostra, et prefatae Ecclesiae mandata pure, absolute, absque intendimento aliquo, alte, basse, ac ad pedes nostros reverenter, et personaliter absque morae dispendio venire curaverint, et tam Personas suas, quam Civitatem, Arces, et Castra, quae detinent, detinentur pro eis, in manibus, et posse nostris, ac eorum, quibus mandabimus, posuerint cum effectu, gremium non claudemus quin eos taliter redeuntes, sic misericorditer et benigne tractemus, quod sit gratum Deo, honorabile nobis, et ipsi Ecclesiae, et ex nostris, et ipsius Ecclesiae actibus exemplum laudabile posteris relinquamus. Nec volumus vos latere, quod per verda dilationis deduci nolentes, non intendimus abstinere, quin interim contra eos, ac sequaces, et fautores ipsorum, et terras quae pro ipsis tenentur, temporaliter, et spiritualiter procedatur. Caeterum gratanter audivimus, et quod nobis per ambasciatores supplicastis eosdem ut ad Urbem, moraturi in ea, in istanti hiemali tempore, veniremus: super quo tenere nos volumus, quod alia caetera loca preter illud ubi nostri sedes apostolatus existit minus gratanter incolimus; nam sicut jam vera presagia manifestant nedum vivi, sed etiam post praesentis vitae decursum cupimus in urbe ipsa quiescere, constructa jam in basilica Principis Apostolorum de Urbe specali cappella ubi nostram elegimus sepulturam; sed adhuc de veniendo, vel non veniendo ad praesens ambasciatoribus ipsis responsum certum non dedimus, sed ex causa in suspenso tenemus, ut videre possimus qualiter praedicta procedant, et d .... am quam ad nos gessistis, et geritis effectivis valeamus operibus experiri.

Datum apud Urbem Veterem tertio Kalen Octobris pontificatus nostri anno tertio.

DOCUMENT (V).

TWO SERMONS OF BONIFACE VIII, DELIVERED AT ORVIETO, IN PRESENCE OF THE CARDINALS, ON THE OCCASION OF THE CANONIZATION OF LOUIS IX, KING OF FRANCE.

"Reddite quae sunt Caesaris Caesari, et quae sunt Dei Deo" Mat. XXII. c. Notandum quod reddit Deus, et reddit homo. Deus reddit bonis bona, malis supplicia, utrisque iusta. De malis in Psalmo dicitur: "Reddet retributionem superbus," De bonis etiam in Psalmo: "Redde mihi laetitiam salutaris tui;" id est, gloriam aeternam, quae est laetitia sempiterna. De utrisque dicit Apostolus II. Cor. 5. "Omnes nos manifestari oportet ante tribunal Christi, ut recipiat unusquisque propria corporis prout gessit, sive bonum, sive malum"

Item reddit homo Deo, reddit proximo. Primo debet reddere Deo, illa quae vovit. Unde in Psalmo: "Vovete et reddite Domino Deo vestro, etc" Hoc intelligitur tam de voto tacito, quam expresso. De voto tacito, sicut de illis, quae in baptismo, licet tacite, promittuntur. De expresso dicitur Lucae XVI. "Redde rationem villicationis tuae." Hoc specialiter dicitur de illis, qui ex voto seu promisso expresso obligati sunt Deo specialiter servire. Secundo reddit homo proximo caritatem et concordiam. Unde Apostolus Rom. XIII. "Nemini cuiquam debeatis, nisi ut invicem diligatis." Istud vero debitum est, quod quantumcunque, et quotienscumque redditum, semper nihilominus hominem detinet debitorem.

Ista vero verba primo proposita accipi possunt in persona summi Pontificis, et totius Ecclesiae miliantis, ut dicatur eis pro santae memoriae Rege Ludovico, "Reddite quae sunt Caesaris Caesari, etc." Ut per Caesarem intelligamus istum sanctum Regem, cui honor merito debetur Unde concluditur Rom. XIII. "Reddite ergo omnibus debita; cui tributum, tributum; cui vectigal, vectigal; cui timorem, timorem; cui honorem, honorem." Et ita debemus reddere unicuique quod suum est, tam Deo quam homini, et maxime illi sancto Regi de quo agitur. Reddendo enim honorem homini, redditur etiam Deo, qui est laudabilis in Sanctis suis. Unde in Psalmo, "Mirabilis Deus in Sanctis suis etc." Item ibidem, "Laudate Dominum in sanctis ejus etc." Accedamus ergo ad propositum negotium venerandum, honorandum, et desiderandum, quod jam per XXIIII. annos vel amplius stetit in fornace examinis Curiae Romanae, sue sedis Apostolicae Unde notandum, quod multi vestrum viderunt, et nos etiam vidimus sanctum illum Regem Ludovicum, cuis vita inclyta cunctas illustrabat Ecclesias. Et sicut nos in parte vidimus, et per probata audivimus, e scimus, vita eius non fuit salum vita hominis sed super hominem; non fuit interrupta; sed ab infantia continuata, de bono in melius semper procedens, semper augmentata. Secundum id quod dicitur im Psalmo. "Ibunt sancti de virtute in virtutem, videbitur Deus Deorum in Sion." Ipse enim sic procedens, jam de regno terreno Franciae ascendit ad regnum aeternum gloriae, ut possit dicere illud Psalmi: "Ego enim constitutus sum Rex ab eo super Sion montem sanctum ejus, etc." Et quia dicitur in Proverb. "Justorum semita quasi lux splendens procedit, et crescit usque in perfectum diem:" Idcirco non est passus Dominus, ut lucerna isto poneretur sub modio; sed super candelabrum, ut luceret his qui in domo Dei sunt. Unde voluit Dominus manifestare hominibus qualis iste Sanctus erat, et est coram eo; et hoc tam per testimonium Dei, quam hominum.

Testimonium enim hominum requiritur ibi sicut testimonium veritatis, quantum ad certitudinem vitae suae sanctae, quam in hoc mundo gessit. Vita vero ejus sancta omnibus fuit manifesta, faciem ejus aspicientibus, quae plena erat gratiarum, sicut dicitur Hester XV. Quantum vero ad opera, fuit manifesta specialiter in eleemosynis pauperum, in fabicationibus hospitalium, in aedificiis Ecclesiarum et caeteris misericordiae operibus, quae omnia enumerare longum esset. Nec fuerunt ista momentanea seu parvo tempore durantia, sed usque ad mortem continua. Item quantae fuerit justitiae, apparuit evidenter non solum per exempla, imo etiam per tactum. Sedebat enim quasi continue in terra super lectum, ut audiret causas, maxime pauperum et orphanorum, et eis faciebat exhiberi justitiae complementum. Unicuique etiam reddebat quod suum est. Unde potest dici de ipso, quod dicitur Eccles. XVI. "Opera justitiae ejus quis enunciabit?" quasi dicat, enumerari non possent. Et ideo in pace et quiete magna tenuit regnum suum. Concordes enim sunt pax et justitia. Et ideo sicut sedit in justitia, ita regnum ejus quievit in pace. Unde verificatum est de ipso quod dicitur Proverb. XX. "Misericordia et veritas custodiunt Regem, et roborabitur clementia thronus ejus." Voluit insuper Dominus manifestare sibi, quod erat vas electionis ad portandum verbum suum coram gentibus, et Regibus, et filiis Israel. Et ideo ostendit illi, quanta oportebat eum pro nomine suo pati: quia licet tot divitiis, deliciis, et honoribus abundaret, relinquens omnia, corpus suum et vitam suam exposuit pro Christo, mare transfretando, et contra inimicos Crucis Christi et fidei Catholicae decertando, usque ad captionem et incarcerationem proprii corporis, uxoris, et fratrum suorum.

Quantam vero animi constantiam, et quale exemplum justitiae et bonitatis ostenderit in adversitate praedicta, hoc sciunt illi fide digni, qui ab illis, qui interfuerunt, veritatem diligenter inquisierunt. Nam cum captus esset a Soldano, et fratres sui, et certa summa pecuniae deberant redimi; volebat Soldanus quod illa pactio seu processio pecuniae tali pacto firmaretur, ut si dictus Soldanus a promisso recederet, legem suam et Deos suos abnegaret. Ipse vero Rex e converso, si pactum non teneret, fidem Christi negaret. Pius vero Rex et Catholicus haec audiens, exhorruit, et monitus a fratribus suis ut hoc faceret, dicentibus quod hoc satis licite poterat promittere, postquam non intendebat a pacto seu conventione recedere, respondit eis sic: Dominus faciet id quod voluerit tam de me, quam de vobis. Vos ut fratres diligo, me etiam ut me diligo. Sed hoc avertat Deus, quod tale verbum de ore Regis Franciae unquam exeat, quicquid inde debeat accidere. Soldanus vero videns ejus magnam constantiam tam in gestibus quam in responsis, credidit verbo suo simplici, et ipsum ac fratres suos, ac etiam omnes reliquos, quos tenebat, dimisit. Miracula etiam tempore captionis suae plurima acciderunt, inter quae unum fuit praecipuum, et relatione dignum. Quidam enim Religiosus, qui eum secutus fuerat, et cum eo captus, dum staret secum in una camera secreta, coepit Rex devotus multum conqueri et condolere propeter hoc, quod Breviarium non habebat, ubi posset dicere Horas suas Canonicas. Respondit frater ille, eum consolando: Non est curandum in tali articulo: sed dicamus nihilominus "Pater noster," et alia quae poterimus. Sed cum multum affligeretur super isto, invenit iuxta se subito Breviarium suum proprium, divinitus, ut credimus, sibi et per miraculum est apportatum.

Item postquam a carcere fuit liberatus, non vixit, nec indutus fuit sicut prius: licet vita et conversatio eius prius fuisset satis honesta. Vestes enim, quas postea habuit non erant Regiae, sed Religiosae: non erant militis, sed viri simplicis. Vitam etiam eius, qualiter in aedificationibus Ecclesiarum, et visitationibus infirmorum, caecorum, et leprosorum continuaverit, nullus enarrare sufficit.

Inter caetera vero, hoc exemplum notabile recitatum fuit nobis a fide dignis, dum essemus in Francia; quod apud Abbatiam Regalismontis erat quidam Monachus lepra abominabiliter infectus, in tantum quod propter foetorem et abominationem ulcerum, vix inveniebatur, qui ad eum accedere vellet: sed quae necessaria erant a longe eidem projiciebantur seu dabantur. Rex vero pius audiens hoc de illo, pluries visitavit eum, et eidem humiliter ministravit; saniem ulcerum ejus studiose detergendo, et eidem cibum et potum propriis manibus ministrando. Talia namque et consimilia consuevit facere in dominus Dei et Leprosariis, et specialiter in domo Dei Paris, quod multi et multotiens viderunt. Unde in talibus apparet, quantae compassionis et pietatis fuerit iste Rex factus.

Item quantarum eleemosynarum fuerit ipse sanctus homo, apparet per illos, qui statuta dandi eleemosynas suas noverunt. Inter alia namque statuit, quod quotienscumque de novo intrabat Paris. nouae eleemosynae darentur Religiosis, et specialiter Mendicantibus, et ideo frequentius exibat, ut saepius eleemonsinae hujusmodi redderentur

Praetera non suffecit ei dare sua, sed volens plus reddere Deo, reliquit mundum, uxorem, et regnum, exposuit filios suos, et reliquit siepsum, iterum in Terram sanctam peregrinando. Poterat dicere Domino cum beato Petro et reliquis Apostolis, id quod dixit Petrus Matt. XX. "Ecce reliquimus omnia, et secuti sumus te." Et in tanta perfectione, qua secutus fuerat, vitam finivit sanctissime. Nam secundum quod testificatum est ab assistentibus, iste non fuit finis hominis humanitati, sed quodam modo iam sanctificati servi. Quod apparuit in verbis, et monitionibus Sanctis quas in lecto mortis dicebat: et in signis, quae tunc temporis evidenter in ipso apparuerunt. Quam vero salubria exempla et monita reliquit posteris, indicant maxime documenta sancta, quae pius Rex ante mortem filio suo primogenito, et filiae suae Reginae Navarrae scripsit, et quasi pro testamento eis reliquit. Cum etiam signis evidentibus appropinquaret ad finem, de nullo erat sollicitus, nisi de iis, quae ad solum Deum proprie pertinebant, et ad exaltationem fidei Christianae. Unde in fine dixit: Amodo nullus loquatur mecum. Et sic stans per magnum spacium, quasi nullus permissus est loqui sibi, nisi, Sacerdos sive Confessor proprius. Et sic ad extreman horam veniens, spiritum reddidit Creatori.

Istum vero sanctum Regem merito vocavimus Caesarem, qui possessor Principatus, seu possidens Principes interpretatur. Ipse enim Principatum, seu Principem huius mundi possedit: tres inimicos humanae naturae, mundum, carnem, et diabolum prosternendo. Vicit enim mundum, quia stants in mundo mundum prostravit et calcavit, contemnendo, et Deo subdidit; terrena, quae mundi sunt, in eleemosynis distribuendo. Diabolum etiam calcavit, seipsum sicut superius dictum est, summe et perfectissime humiliando; et signo crucis, quod assumpsit, et tamdiu portavit, ipsum prosternendo. Carnem nihilominus vicit et domavit, eam spiritui subjiciendo. Maxime quia sicut constat ex testimonio plurimorum, este numquam carnem suam divisit in plures, nec cum aliqua peccatum commisit. Ita quod ipsemet, excepta uxore propria, virgo ab aliis permansit.

Videns ergo Deus istum talem et tantum virium sic bene ingressum, sic melius progressum, sic sanctissime de mundo egressum; voluit quod non staret amplius lucerna sub modio, sed per grandia et multa miracula voluit eum manifestare, et quasi super candelabrum ponere. Nam sicut invenimus, vidimus, et nosmetipsi die propria examinavimus per plures inquisitiones a nobis, et a nostris fratribus, ac etiam pluribus summis Pontificibus approbatas: sexaginta tria miracula, inter caetera, quae Dominus evidenter ostendit, certitudinaliter facta cognovimus.

Quia, sicut alias dictum est, actus iste, scilicet ascribere in catalogo Sanctorum per canonizationem Romani Pontificis, singularis excellentiae reputatur in Ecclesia militante, et ad solum Romanum Pontificem pertineat hoc agere: idcirco summam gravitatem in facto tam singulari Sedes Apostolica voluit observare. Quamvis et vita sua fuisset ita manifesta, et multa miracula visa, sicut superius dictum est, preces etiam Regiae, Baronum, et etiam Praelatorum pluries accessissent: nihilominus cum inquisitionibus privatis pluribus iam factis, adhuc voluit inquisitiones solemnes per non parum tempus facere. Duravit istud negocium iam per XXIV. annos, vel amplius. Et licet Dominus Nicolaus III. ante dixisset, quod ita nota erat sibi vita istius sancti, quod si vidisset duo vel tra miracula, eum canonizasset; sed morte praeventus non potuit hoc perducere ad effectum. Ex abundanti tamen fuit adhuc commissum negocium inquisitionis viris venerabilibus et discretis, Archiepiscopo scilicet Rothomagensi, et Episcopo Antisiodorensi, et magistro Rolando de Palma Episcopo Spoletano. Et isti de sexaginta tribus miraculis testes receperunt, examinaverunt, rubricaverunt: et iam sexdecim annis transactis ad Curiam remiserunt. Insuper per illos sexdecim annos continue aliqui ex parte Regis Franciae, necnon Praelatorum, et principum, et specialiter Frater Joannes de Samessio, continue institerunt.

Tandem prodicto negotio, tempore domini Martini commissum est negotium tribus Cardinalibus ad examinandum, qui viderunt, examinaverunt, et pro magna parte rubricaverunt. Sed cum ante mortem domini Martini non fuisset facta relatio negotii, pervenit tandem ad tempora Domini Honorii. Et tunc lecta sunt plura miracula, et coram fratribus nostris Cardinalibus diligenter discussa. Sed dum ventilaretur negotium, superveniente morte Domini Honorii, negotium siluit.

Tempore vero domini Nicolai IV. commissum est negotium tribus aliis Cardinalibus, domino scilicet Hostensi, domino Portuensi, et nobis in statu Cardinalatus adhuc existentibus: quia mortui erant illi Cardinales, quibus negotium prius fuerat commissum. Postea etiam mortuo domino Hostiensi, subrogatus fuit sibi dominus Sabinensis. Et ita per tot, et totiens examinatum est, rubricatum, et discussum negotium; quod de hoc facta sit copia scripturarum, Nos et de manu propria scripsimus, et diligenter examinavimus multa miracula fuisse sufficienter probata.

Temporibus autem nostris non sunt mutati examinatores, sed tamen iterum lecta sunt plura miracula, examinata, et rubricata, non solum per illos predictos examinatores, sed etiam plures alios Cardinales. Et voluimus, ut quilibet sigillatim daret consilium suum in scriptis, ne odio, vel amore, seu etiam timore aliquo aliquis taceret.

Ex istis ergo, et pluribus aliis potest evidenter concludi, quod servata fuit maturitas et plus quam maturitas in praedictis. Et ideo de tam manifesto viro, et sic in sanctitate vitae et miraculorum probato, secure possumus asserere, quod non debet amplius fama sanctitatis eius sub modio latere, sed debemus ei dicere: Amice, ascende superius, ut sit tibi gloria in Ecclesia militante coram simul discumbentibus. Et ideo quasi ex ore Dei dicta sunt nobis et Ecclesiae militanti verba proposita in principio, "Reddite quae sunt Caesaris Caesari, etc." ut in hoc reddatur Deo quod suum est qui laudatur in Sanctis suis. Reddatur Caesari isti quod suum est, scilicet honor, et gloria debita, Sanctis reddatur, et matri nostrae Ecclesiae triumphanti quod suum est, silicet debitum laudis: et hoc in isto sancto, qui connumerari debet merito cum aliis sanctis, quia civis effectus est patriae caelestis. Et sic cum matre nostra debemus conlaetari, et istum tanquam sanctum honorare: ut sic per consequens exemplis vitae eius in Ecclesia militanti recitatis, fides Catholica roboretur, Reges et principes ad bonum animentur, et omnes universaliter in bonis suis operibus et exemplis aedificentur, et ad majora bona provocentur, quod nobis praestare dignetur, qui vivit et regnat, etc. amen.

"Rex pacificus magnificatus est," quia eodem Spiritu Sancto, quo locuti sunt et illuminati patres veteris Testamenti, Patriarchae videlicet et Prophetae, locuti sunt etiam sancti novi Testamenti. Propter quod dicit Apostolus I. Cor. XII. "Divisiones gratiarum sunt, idem autem spiritus, dividens singulis prout vult." Unde militans Ecclesia eodem spiritu loquens, quasi exultando assumit verbum propositum, quo ad sententiam de tertio libro Reg. X. et de secundo Paralip. IX. et tamen mutat verba, quae licet ad literam dicta sunt de Rege Salomone in veteri Testamento; tamen quia de exaltatione Ecclesiae loquitur, propter magnificationem et exaltationem sanctissimi Regis Ludovici, possumus eodem spiritu de ipso verba proposita exponere, in quibus sanctus Rex Ludovicus intribus commendatur, primo de excellenti statu, quia Rex; secundo a donis et virtutibus, quia pacificus; tertio apraemiis et renumerationibus, quia magnificatus in Ecclesiae, scilicet militanti.

De primo notandum, quod qui bene regit seipsum et subditos, suos, ipse vere Rex est. Sed qui nescit regere se et subditos, audacter dicendum est, quod falsus Rex est. iste vero Rex fuit in veritate, quia seipsum et subditos vere, inste, et sancte-regebat. Seipsum enim rexit, quia carnem subjecit spiritui, et omnes motus sensualitatis rationi. Item subditos bene regebat, quia in omni justitia et aequitate ipsos custodiebat. Rexit etiam Ecclesias, quia jura Ecclesiastica, et libertates Ecclesiae illaesas conservabat. Sed qui de facto bene non regunt, vere Reges non sunt.

Secundo, commendatur a donis et virtutibus, cum dicitur pacificus, id est pacem faciens. Per istud enim donum, et per istam virtutem intelliguntur caetera dona et virtutes. Fuit autem pacificus in se, et quoad omnes non solum subditos, sed extraneos. In se fuit pacificus. Habuit enim pacem temporis, pacem pectoris, et idcirco tandem consecutus est pacem aeternitatis. Qualiter vero pacifice tenuit regnum suum, hoc sciunt omnes, qui sunt illius temporis. Ista vero pax non est sine justitia. Sequitur enim justitiam. Et quia iste justus fuit quoad se, quoad Deum, et quoad proximum, ideo pacem habuit.

Ex istis sequitur tertium, quod magnificatus est, id est magnus factus non solum in praesenti Ecclesia, sed etiam in patria. Notandum vero, quod vulgariter loquendo aliquis dicitum magnus quadruplici ratione, secundum quadruplicem dimensionem: videlicet primo quia longus, secundo quia latus, tertio quia profundus, quarto quia altus, sive elatus. Ista habuit sanctus Rex spiritualiter. Fuit enim longus per perseverantiam et longanimitatem in bono. Ab infantia enim coepit bene vivere, et usque in finem perseveravit. Unde potest exponi de ipso, quod dicitur de Isaac Genes. XXVI. "Benedixit ei Dominus, et locupletatus est: et ibat proficiens atque succrescens, donec vehementer magnus effectus est." Iste spiritualiter loquendo fuit Isaac, qui risus interpretatur, quem peperit Sara iam vetula, per quam potest significari Ecclesia istius temporis in senio novissimorum temporum constituta, quæ nobis peperit istum Isaac, qui nobis merito debet esse materia risus et gaudij. Sequitur, "ibat proficiens, etc." ut possit dicere cum Apostolo, II, ad Tim. IV. "Bonum certamen certavi, cursum consummavi: in reliquo reposita est mihi corona justitiæ, etc."

Secundo dicitur magnus, quia latus, sive amplus; et hoc per charitatem. Unde Eccl. XLVI. "Fortis in bello Jesus Nave," et seq:

qui fuit magnus secundum verbum suum, maximus in salutem electorum Dei. Non enim est memoria apud homines, ut credimus, quod inventus fuit isti similis nostris temporibus, qui tantum zelaret pro salute aliorum. Quod bene apparuit, quando ipse et fratres sui capti fuerunt a Saracenis. Non enim sustinuit liberatinem suam, nec fratrum suorum, donec omnes alii quotquot fuerunt capti, prius fuerint liberati.

Tertio dicitur magnus, quia profundus, hoc per humilitatem. Quanto enim magis profunde se humiliat homo, tanto major apud Deum reputator, secundum id quod dicitur Luc. XIV. "Omnis qui se exaltat humiliabitur, et qui se humiliat exaltabitur." Et quia iste profundissime se humiliavit, ideo apud Dominum merito magnus extitit. Unde potes exponi de ipso quod dicitur I. Reg. II. de Samuele, "Magnificatus est Samuel apud Dominum." Ipse vero humiliavit se intus et extra, in lingua, in corde, in veste, in orationibus. Et hoc possumus secure asserere, quod facies sua benigna et plena gratiarum docebat eum esse supra hominem. Intelligitur vero congrue per Samuelem, quod interpretatur, Obediens Deo. Obedivit enim Deo usque ad mortem.

Quarto dicitur magnus, quia altus, sive elevatus fuit per intentionem rectam ad Deum, omnia quæ agebat Deo attribuendo, et ei gratias agendo; secundum quod dicitur in Psalmo: "Non nobis Domine, non nobis; sed nomini tuo da gloriam." Unde de ista magnitudine loquitur Judith XVI. loquens Deo, "qui timent te, magni erunt apud te per omnia."

Apparet igitur qualiter isti sancto competunt verba primo proposita "Rex pacificus magnificatus est." Et quia sic quadrupliciter fuit magnus in terris, sicut dictum est, idcirco omnino tenere debemus, quod etiam sit magnificatus in cœlis. Hoc enim pertinet ad divinam justitiam, quod qui bonus et justus fuit in vita, magnificetur et exaltetur in gloria. Quod apparet de isto per multa et magna miracula: quæ Dominus per ipsum ostendit. Et ideo merito ipsum glorificatum et magnificatum credimus in cœlis, et ideo eum catalogo Sanctorum ascribimus, præcipientes omnibus fidelibus Christianis, quod ipsum tanquam sanctum, et per plura miracula notificatum veneretur, et eius patrocinia corde devoto sibi postulet suffragari. Quod nobis præstare dignetur qui vivet et regnat, etc. amen.

DOCUMENT (2A).

ARBITRAL DECISION OF BONIFACE IN THE PROCEEDINGS PENDING BETWEEN EDWARD OF ENGLAND AND PHILIP THE FAIR.

In nomine Domini Amen. Anno Domini MCCXCVIII. indictione XI. pontificatus domini Bonifacii papae VIII. anno IV. die XXVII. mensis junii, sanctissimus pater et dominus, dominus Bonifacius divina providentia Papa VIII. arbitrium, laudum, diffinitionem, arbitralem sententiam, amicabilem compositionem, mandatum, ordi-

nationem, et alia infrascripta recitavit, legi fecit, dedit, et protulit in hunc modum: Dudum inter charissimos filios nostros Philippum Francorum ex parte una, et Eduardum Angliae Reges illustres ex altera, suggerente inimico humani generis pacis aemulo, super diversis articulis materia discordiae ac dissensionis exorta, tandem iidem Reges per speciales nuntios et procuratores ipsorum, ad hoc ab eis mandatum habentes, in nos Bonifacium, divina providentia papam VIII. tanquam in privatam personam, et dominum Benedictum Gaytanum tamquam in arbitrum et arbitratorem, laudatorem diffinitorem, arbitralem sententiatorem, amicabilem compositorem, praeceptorem, arbitratorem, et dispositorem, et procuratorem super reformanda pace et concordia inter ipsos Reges, ac super iis, quae ad pacem pertinent; et super omnibus, et singulis discordiis, guerris, litibus controveriis, causis, quaestionibus, damnis et injuriis, petitionibus et actionibus, realibus et personalibus atque mixtis, quae fuerant, et erant seu vertebantur, et esse vel verti possent inter ipsos Reges occasione quacumque; de alto et basso absolute et libere compromittere curaverunt ....
....

Pronuntiamus hac vice, ut inter eosdem Reges fiat et sit perpetua et stabilis pax; et quod treguae vel sufferentiae voluntariae dudum indictae, initae ac firmatae inter eos, eo modo et forma, ac omnibus, et illis personis et terris, et sub illis poenis, conditionibus, et temporibus sub quibus indictae, initae, ac firmatae fuerent inviolabiliter observentur. Ad hujusmodi autem pacem confirmandam, roborandam atque servandam infra tempus, et quod duxerimus moderandum, praefatus Rex Angliae Margaretam sororem praedicti Regis Franciae recipere ac ducere cum dotalitio quindecim millium librarum Turonensium, assignando per ipsum regem Angliae in locis compentibus, de quibus inter partes fuerit concordatum, vel (ubi partes ipsae non concordarent per nos arbitratum fuerit, in uxorem: et idem Rex Franciae eamdem sororem suam eidem Regi Angliae in uxorem dare, et tradere cum dispensatione Sedis Apostolicae teneatur: quodque Isabella filia praelibati Regis Francia, quae infra annum septennem dicitur constituta suo tempore Eduardo praedicti Regis angliae filio, qui jam XIII. aetatis suae annum exegit, cum simili dispensatione matrimonialiter cum dotalitio decem octo millium librarum Turonensium, similiter assignando per eundem Regem Angliae pro dicto filio suo in competentibus locis, de quibus concordaverint ipsae partes, de quibus nos duxerimus arbitrandum, si super hoc inter eos non provenit concordia, copulentur, idque firmetur atque valletur ex nunc modis inferius annotatis; ....
....
Item dicimus, laudamus, arbitramur, seu etiam diffinimus, quod de omnibus bonis mobilibus vel se moventibus, ablatis vel alias male subtractis et de omnibus damnis datis hinc inde ante tempus motae vel ortate guerrae praesentis; primo de omnibus, quae extant et consumpta non sunt praesertim in terra, quod Rex Angliae omnia, quae de praedictis extant et consumptu non sunt, praesertim de navibus,

et aliis quibuscumque bonis per Anglicos, et Vascones, et eorum complices ante guarram occupatis in mari vel in terra, quod Rex Angliae omnia, quae de praedictis extant bona fide sine lite et absque figura judicii, omni fraude cessante, ad requisitionem Regis Franciae vel nuntii sui statim faciat ad plenum restitui: et Rex Franciae similiter, si qua talia ante dictam guarram capta vel ablata apud ipsum, vel in sua potestate extantia reperta fuerint, similiter ad plenum restitui faciat a praefato Rege Angliae vel ejus nuntio requisitus. De ablatis vero non extantibus, sed deperditis, et consumptis, laudamus, arbitramur, seu etiam diffinimus, quod Rex Angliae ad requisitionem Regis Franciae vel nuntii ejus satisfieri faciat; et ad hoc faciendum etiam teneatur sine lite ac figura judicii, bona fide, et omni fraude cessante: et Rex Franciae similiter, si qua per gentes suas ablata, deperdita, seu consumpta inventa fuerint, ad requisitionem Regis Angliae vel nuntii sui faciat satisfieri, taxatione nobis circa praedictorum aestimationem contra utramque partem; ubi per concordiam partium negotium super praedictis sopitum non esset, plenarie reservata.

Item dicimus, laudamus, arbitramur, seu etiam diffinimus, quod idem Rex Angliae de omnibus terris, vassallis, et bonis, quae ipse nunc habet, et tenet in regno Franciae, seu tenebat ante motam guarram praesentem, habeat illam quantitatem et illam partem terrarum, vassallorum, et bonorum eorumdem quam sibi ex virtute compromissorum praedictorum laudaverimus, et mandaverimus assignari, vel inter Reges ipsos fuerit concordatum, et sub illis fidelitate, homagio, modis, et conditionibus habeat, sub quibus ipse ac pater suus habuisse hactenus, et tenuisse noscuntur, modis, et temperamentis per nos adhibendis in abusu, si quis ex parte gentis Regis Franciae hactenus commissus inventus fuerit in exercitio resorti; modis etiam et temperamentis, per nos adhibendis in abusu partis alterius, si quis videlicet ex parte Regis Angliae vel suorum hactenus commissus contra jus resorti fuerit inventus, ne talia in posterum committantur, conditionibus etiam, modis, et securitatibus per nos imponendis et adhibendis in terris, vassallis, bonis, et aliis, quae per nostram pronuntiationem, seu concordiam partium praefatus Rex Angliae vel successores ejus contra Regem Franciae vel successores ipsius valeant rebellare.

Dicimus etiam, laudamus, et arbitramur, seu etiam diffinimus, quod ex nunc omnes terrae, vassalii, et bona praedicta, et alia tam quae tenet Rex Franciae de iis, quae tenebat Rex Angliae ante guerram presentem; quam quae tenet Rex Angliae in regno Franciae, bona fide, ac sine omni fraude, absolute ac libere in manibus et posse nostris ponantur, et assignantur, tenenda nomine Regis Franciae, quae ex parte sua et nomine Regis Angliae, quae ex parte ejusdem nobis fuerint assignata; ita tamen, quod per hoc in possessione vel proprietate nil novi juris accrescat alterutri partium, vel antiqui decrescat: super quorum assignatione, si qua fuerit exorta dubitatio vel ambiguitas inter partes, illam nostrae declarationi et arbitrio reservamus Quod si forsan dicti Reges de ipsis terris, et bonis ad invicem concordaverint, volumus, laudamus, et arbitramur, ex nunc id, in quo concordaverint, perpetuo et inviolabiliter observari, alioquin nos ex compromissi praedicti virtute apponemus ad id illud remedium, quod Dominus ministrabit, et ex tradita nobis potestate licebit. Si vero casu aliquo contingente hoc facere non possemus, volumus, dicimus, et arbitramur, quod utrique parti pristina jura sua salva remaneant et illaesa, etc. Acta, lata, et pronuntiata fuerunt arbitrium, laudum, arbitralis sententia, mandatum, diffinitio, ordinatio, dispositio, et omnia supradicta per eundem dominum Papam, ut superius enarrantur, anno, indictione, mense, ac die praedictis, Romae apud S. Petrum in palatio papali, in consistorio publico, facto in sala majori, praesente ibi gentium multitudine copiosa; et presentibus reverendis patribus dominis, Dei gratia, Gerardo Sabinensi, fratre Mattheo Portuensi et S. Ruffinae, et Joanne Tusculano episcopis; Joanne tit. et.

DOCUMENT (2B).

THE EVIL COUNSEL OF GUY OF MONTEFELTRO.

There has not been a single historian who, having occasion to speak of Boniface VIII, has failed to remark that this Pontiff, following the counsel of Guy of Montefeltro, by solemn perjury enticed the Colonnas out of fortified Palestrina, and vented his anger on them.

There is no doubt that the first one to relate the evil advice of Guy was Dante, and every one else only quoted him, in so much that the truth of the fact does not rest on the testimony of an eyewitness, of a contemporary writer, nor of an earnest analist, but on that of a poet, such as Dante, who wrote verses to satisfy his rancor   Here are the words which he put in the mouth of Guy, buried in Hell:

> "A soldier once,—I next around me tied
> St. Francis' cord, in hope to expiate crime;
> And truly had those hopes been verified,
> But that the mighty Priest (whom evil take)
> Allured me to my sins a second time;
> And how, and why, I will disclosure make.
> While yet a form of flesh and bone was mine,
> My mother's gift, my deeds resembled less
> Those of the lion than the fox;—so fine
> The artifice with which I played my game,
> So exquisite my cunning and address,
> The world's fair limits sounded with my fame.
> But when I saw that time of life begin,
> When every man, the port approaching, ought
> To coil the ropes, and take the canvas in;—
> What first had pleased me, irksome seemed to grow;
> And to repentance and confession brought,

> I had been blest,—alas, now plunged in woe!
> The haughty prince of Modern Pharisees,
> Who near the Lateran his warfare waged,
> And not 'gainst Moors or Jewish enemies
> (For all were Christians whom his vengeful hand
> Opposed; and now at Acre had engaged,
> Or e're had trafficked in Sultan's land,)
> Regarded not his own exalted state
> And holy office, nor my sacred cord,
> Which should the form it girds attenuate,
> But, as of old, to cure his leprosy,
> Sylvester was by Constantine implored;
> So in commanding tone he called on me
> To mitigate the fever of his pride:
> He asked my counsel, but I answered not,
> Deeming his words to drunkenness allied.
> Again he said to me; "Be not afraid—
> I do absolve thee;—tell me by what plot
> May Palestrina in the dust be laid.
> Heaven, as thou knowest, I have the power at will
> To lock or unlock; hence the keys are twain,
> What erst by predecessor prized so ill."
> "Then had his cogent arguments full sway,
> For silence could procure me little gain;
> And I: 'O, Father, since you wash away
> The sin I am about to perpetrate,—
> Large by your promise—your performance slack,
> Thus will you triumph in your high estate.'"

Now to summarize the words of Dante. Guy of Montefeltro (for he means no other man) famous more for his cunning than for his bravery, became a religious towards the end of his life. The prince of modern Pharisees, Boniface VIII, made him unfaithful to his pious resolution to lead a holy life. This Pontiff was at war with the Colonnas, who lived in the Lateran quarter of the city of Rome, and he could not conquer them, because they were entrenched in Palestrina, a strongly fortified town. He consulted Friar Guy on the means to accomplish his end. The religious remained deaf to the entreaty, because he considered it unreasonable, and that of an intoxicated man. But Boniface pressed him, granting him in advance absolution from every evil expedient, that he could advise for the destruction of Palestrina. Guy then assured in advance of the pardon of his sin gave utterance to his famous counsel, which was to promise everything and to fulfil nothing. All clear Boniface of this double iniquity, believing that it is sufficient to remark the Dante was a poet, and wrote according to the dictates of his imagination; and that besides he was a Ghibelline and hence an implacable enemy of Boniface. But this one remark which is easy for anyone to make, cannot persuade everybody that Boniface was innocent. For even as a poet and Ghibelline Dante could relate some truths. Let us however examine the fact historically and morally.

Boniface proclaimed the crusade against the Colonnas the 14th of December, 1297, as is evident from his Brief in the register of his letters [21]: "*Dantum Romae apud St. Petrum decimo nono kalendas Januarii, anno tertio.*" Consequently the crusaders could not move against Palestrina sooner than the year 1298. After having seized, in a few days, all the fiefs of the Colonnas, they reached the walls of Palestrina, which they considered impregnable, by reason of the stout resistance of Agapitus Sciarra, and the two Cardinals James and Peter Colónna. Francis Pepino,[22] and Ferrettus of Vicenza,[23] relate that Boniface sent for Guy of Montefeltro, a professed religious of the Order of St. Francis in the monastery at Ancona, and entrusted to him the leadership of the army; but Guy after a complete examination of the fortifications of Palestrina, declared them impregnable. Then adhering closely to the account of Dante, using his very words, they relate that Guy being consulted, gave the Pope the wicked advice in question.

The reader will notice, that before the surrender of Palestrina, we must admit necessarily three periods of time; the one commencing from the publication of the crusade, that is, from the middle of December, 1297, and ending with the assembling of the troops, and their movement against the Colonnas; in fact it is impossible to assemble an army in a day; the second from the movement of the troops to the seizure of all the fiefs of the Colonnas; the third in fine, from these conquests up to the time the capture of Palestrina by force was despaired of. So from January, 1298, to September of the same year, when the city surrendered, the troops were assembled, the fiefs of the Colonnas were conquered, and Palestrina was besieged without result. Guy was not summoned until the war against the Colonnas had already commenced, as Dante relates:

> "The prince of modern Pharisees
> Who near the Lateran his warfare waged."
> That is, against the Colonnas who lived in that quarter.
> " He asked my counsel."—

Ferrettus of Vicenza affirms the same; after having said that the Colonnas were intrenched in Palestrina, he adds: " Turbatus autem
" Bonifacius, quod in contemptu apostlicae Sedis arma sumpsisset,
" illico adversus rebelles suos bellum indixit; assumptisque viris et
" armis circiter oppidum hoc (Palestrina) ubi hostes sui repugna-
" bant, longae obsidionis castra disposuit, multorumque cruoris

[21] Reg. Vat. MS. Anno III, Vaticano Epist. 700.
[22] Chron. Cap. 21, S. R. I., tom. 9, page 741.—
[23] S. R. I., tom. 9, page 970, lit. c.

"utrinque dimicando cominus haustum est. Donec Apostolicus
"segnem moram increpans, quod expugnati hostes diu non succum-
"berent eos dolis et astu, non viribus superare jam statuit. Tunc
"Guidonem de Monteferetro . . . . sedulus advocat."

Guy was then called by Boniface, when this Pontiff despairing of capturing Palestrina by force, desisted from assaults, changing the siege into a blockade, as we perceive from the words: "Longae obsi-"dionis castra disposuit." Guy, according to Ferrettus conferred with the Pope, who was at Rieti, as we learn from the dates of the letters of the latter; and he set out for Palestrina to examine affairs in company with the Pontifical captain. He studied the walls and the moats of the city and found them impregnable. He told this to the Pope, and then upon request gave him the treacherous counsel. Let us fix our attention on this counsel.

Guy did not advise a military stratagem which would require a long time to execute, but simply to promise much and fulfil nothing, that is to say, to entice the Colonnas out of the citadel by fair promises, and afterwards not keep them. The execution of this plan demanded only an exchange of couriers. There was no necessity of long comings and goings; for the treachery being already in the heart of the Pope, these promises were of such a nature as to lead the rebels easily and quickly into the trap. The time is fixed by Ferrettus himself: "Deinde illis, qui hostes, fuerant, (to the Colonnas) trium "dierum spatium benigne constituents, ut intra illud coram suo prin-"cipe devenirent." Now Palestrina surrendered in September, 1298,[24] and consequently the counsel of Guy and the capture of the town can be considered as happening in the same month. Let us now see where Guy was in this September.

Guy became a religious in 1296, at Ancona. Jacobilli, in his work on The Saints and Blessed of Umbria, says in speaking of Guy of Montefeltro: "As he was in the world a celebrated and renowned "warrior, so he was in religion a true knight of Jesus Christ; his "life was holy, and a great example to posterity. He received the "holy habit of the Friars Minor from the hands of the Provincial of "the Marches, in the city of Ancona, on August 17th, 1296. He lived "in continual prayer, humility and edification; afterwards he was "transferred to the city of Assisi in order to gain the indulgence of "the Portiuncula . . . Being stationed in the convent of St. Francis, "at Assisi, he there died a holy death in the Lord, September 23rd, 1298[25] Wading in his annals of the Friars Minor, produces the testimony of Jerome Rossi, who, in his history of Ravenna, writes of the year 1298 "Tertio kalendas octobris Guido Montis Feltrii "Comes, Franciscano jam abitu, ut supra memoravimus, inductus, "Anconae migravit ex hac vita." According to Rossi, Guy died, not on the 23rd, but on the 29th of September, but always in September of that year.[26]

[24] See Patrini, Memorie Prenestine for year 1298.
[25] Riposati Della Zecca di Gubbio, e de Duchi de Urbino T. I., p. 86.
[26] Lombardi in his commentary on the Inferno says of Guy: "A man

It seems then that Guy, who was said to have been summoned from Assisi, where he happened to be on August 2nd, for the indulgence of the Portiuncula, and who died in September, the month in which Palestrina was surrendered, must have been dying at the very time he was declared to be conferring with the Pope, afterwards to be on a tour of inspection of the fortifications of Palestrina, and then to have given his detestable counsel; unless one wishes to believe (which could happen) that he died suddenly afterwards. But if he did not die suddenly during the time he was on his military inspection, and when he had given this evil counsel, Guy must have been ill, and preparing himself for death like the good Christian all declare him; and as a consequence we must admit also that he was unable for these military expeditions, and incapable of giving any counsel. Moreover, immediately before his death he was in Assisi, where he died, and where his body reposed until his son Frederick had it transferred to the Church of St. Donatus, afterwards called St. Bernardine, outside of Urbino. The reader will see then that Guy in the month of September was dying at Assisi, and not at all admitting the Papal army into Palestrina by treason.

We know that the reader, trusting in conjectures, can find that the entire month of September was long enough for Guy to have acted towards Palestrina as he was said to have done, and then have fallen ill of the disease which carried him off. Hence we intended up to this only to cast a doubt on the account of Dante, and afterwards by clear proofs change the doubt into a certainty. We now come to these proofs.

It is certain that the Colonnas surrendered Palestrina into the hands of Boniface; it is certain that this town was not taken by storm. If faith is to be placed in Dante, it surrendered on conditions violated later by the Pope, after the advice of Guy. Now if we see, as clear as day, that the surrender of Palestrina was made to the discretion of the victor, and not under conditions, will it still be possible to believe in anterior promises of conditions, in their violation, and in fine in the wicked counsel of the poor Friar Guy?

During the time the Colonnas were proudly resisting Boniface, they showed themselves nevertheless accessible to a project of peace and reconciliation with him, provided they were not deprived of their fortress, to which the Pope was far from consenting. We have seen

brave in war, and of a mind very penetrating for poetical times; in his old age, wishing to do penance for his sins, he assumed the Franciscan habit, died in the holy convent of Assisi and was buried in this patriarchal Basilica." The commentator supports his opinion by a passage from a book of the Convent of Assisi. "Guy of Montefeltro, count of Urbino and prince . . . . . . entered piously and humbly in the order; he effaced his faults by tears and by fasts, and (notwithstanding the poetical license permitted the sarcastic Dante), he died a very holy death in the sacred house of Assisi where he was buried. Marianus and Jacobi, who lived in his time, denied all that Dante relates."—

how, from the month of September of the preceding year, 1297, the Senator interposed, after a deliberation of the municipality of Rome, as a peacemaker between the Colonnas and the Pope, exhorting the former to make an absolute submission: "Suaserunt .... in-"duxerunt .... et mandarunt, quod ad pedes nostros reverenter "venirent, nostra et ipsius Romanae Ecclesiae absolute ac libere "mandata facturi: ad quae praefati schismatici et rebelles ipsis am-"bascoatoribus desponderunt, quod ipsi parati erant; et offerebant "ae venturos ad pedes nostros ac nostra et praefatae Ecclesiae man-"data facturos." This is what Boniface wrote to Pandolpho Savelli and the Roman people from Orvieto, the 29th of September, 1297. It is evident then that the surrender of the Colonnas to the Pope, which happened a year later, and which was fully and simply at the discretion of the Pope, was not sudden nor the result of perfidious promises of Boniface. It was already a year since Senator Savelli interposed to prevail upon the Colonnas to trust to the clemency of the Pope; and the Pope in the year 1297, was disposed to receive them: "Intuitu Dei et consideratione vestri .... praefactos Columnenses "venientes benigne recipere ac misericorditer pertractare" But as the Pope demanded besides their submission, the surrender also of the towns, fortresses and castles they possessed: "*tam personas suas,* "*quam civitates, arces et castra quae detinent, vel detientur pro eis,* "*in manibus, et posse nostris, ac eorum, quibus mandabimus, posuer-* "*int cum effectu, gremium non claudemus, quin eos* . . . . " The Colonnas refused to consent, and they continued to wage war for a year. When they had lost their fiefs, their last intrenchment, we find that town fallen at last into the power of the Pope, and destroyed after a desperate resistance. How did the Colonnas leave? Were they taken out by force, did they surrender on conditions, or at the discretion of the victor? There are but these three ways of becoming master of a fortress, and only the second of these can coincide with the treason counselled by Guy. Let us see then if the Colonnas surrendered on conditions. Now, this is how their coming over to Boniface is described in a passage of the Chronicles of Orvieto; presented by Cardinal Garambi to Peter Anthony Petrini,[27] and quoted by him in his "*Memoirs of Palestrina.*" "Dominus Jacobus, D. Petrus, "Agabitus, et Sciarra de Columna, et rebelles huic summo Pontifici "venerunt facturi et parituri mandatis Domini Papae cum multa "reverentia et humilitate magna, qui recepti fuerunt a Romana "Curia cum laetitia multa. Et statim post Camerarius D. Papae "possessionem et tenutam habuit arcis Penestrinae, et aliarum terra-"rum nobilium praedictorum." Paulinus de Piero relates the same fact, in his Chronicle for the year 1298, as follows: "At this time, "and in the month of September, Pope Boniface being with his court "at Rieti .... Messer James and Messer Peter, sons of Messer "John Colonna, with all the other Colonnas, came to crave mercy "from the Pope, who pardoned them kindly and graciously, and

[27] Mon 25, pag. 422.

"granted them absolution from excommunication; then Palestrina
"surrendered, but less than a year from that time they severed their
"bonds of obedience and the Pope excommunicated them again."
The Chronicles of Orvieto and Paulinus of Piero speak then only of
surrender at discretion. The first one expressed this clearly:
"*Venerunt facturi et parituri mandatis Domini Papae cum multa
"reverentia et humilitate magna.*" The terms of the second are no
less formal: "They came craving mercy." But why, the reader
may ask, place faith in these two Chronicles in preference to Ferrettus
of Vicenza? We answer, because their narration is confirmed by
other proofs. When the cause of Boniface was pleaded before
Clement V. in France, the Colonnas, ranged among the number of the
accusers, having declared that they had not been humiliated before
Boniface by a confession of their faults, that it to say, that they had
not surrendered at discretion, and as a consequence Boniface had
treacherously destroyed Palestrina, Cardinal Francis Gaetani, nephew
of Boniface, replied thus to these lies: "Falsum est, quia dum D.
"Bonifacius PP. VIII. Reate moraretur, in consistorio publico in
"praesentia Dominorum Cardinalium, ac omnium Praelatorum, qui
"tunc erant praesentes in Curia, necnon Domini Principis Tarentini,
"qui nunc praesens hic extat, quique posset de praedictis verum
"testimonium perhibere, ac etiam aliorum, clericorum et laicorum
"praesente ibidem mutitudine copiosa, dicti Column. tunc humilia-
"tionis spiritum praetendentes, non insidendo equis sed pedes (sic)
"a portis civitatis Reatin, usque ad conspectum praefati Summi Pon-
"tificis, tunc in trono sedentis et coronam gestantis in capite, quam
"nullus nisi solus verus et legitimus PP. gestavit unquam, nec
"gestare debet, personaliter accesserunt; et tandem ad pedes ejus
"humiliter provoluti ipsum Dominum Bonif. per devota pedum
"oscula, ac per verborum expressionem, ex quibus contriti cordis et
"humiliati spiritus indicia praeferebant, verum Catholicum ac
"legitimum Papam publice recognoverunt, et professi sunt; et
"denique suos excessus et culpas longe lateque per orbem notorios
"tunc ibidem sponte recognoscentes, et confitentes expresse se dignos
"poena non gratia, misericordiam sibi fieri non judicium humiliter
"postularunt. Altero quidem ipsorum Dominorum Colomn. illud
"verbum èvangelicum proponente, quod scribitur de filio patris-
"familias profugo: "Peccavi, Pater, in coelum et corum te, jam non
"sum dignus vocari filius tuus."—Reliquo vero impsorum verbum
"propheticum subjungente, quod scribitur;—" affixisti nos propter
"nostra scelera."—Videant ergo qui veritatem diligunt, si ex talium
"prolatione verborum, suos fatebantur vel diffitebantur excessus.
"Quanta ergo fides eisdem Dominos Columnensibus super aliis ad-
"hiberi, quando super praedictis, quae tot et tantis fuere notoria,
"immo per orbem jam ubisque vulgata, eos nogare non pudet, sic
"publicam et notoriam veritatem ex ipsorum manifesta calumnia
"satis colligitur evidenter."

There can be no doubt of the truth of what Cardinal Gaetani
affirms. He speaks of things which happened not in secret, nor in

past ages, but in sight of all, and only a few years previous, and the witnesses of these events, such as the Prince of Tarentum, to whom Gaetano appeals, could confirm them. Now was the surrendering on conditions this: appearing before the Pontiff, prostrate at his feet, and suing for mercy? Was this a case of men presenting themselves before a victorious Pontiff and still relying on the conditions of any treaty? Was it not rather the spectacle of men at bay, despairing of every means of defence, and trusting to the clemency of the Pope? If this is surrendering on conditions, what shall we call surrendering at discretion? And if the Colonnas surrendered at discretion, what then becomes of the perfidious counsel of Guy?

The same reply of Cardinal Gaetani to the accusations of the Colonnas, make known to us clearly, the kind of treason with which they reproached Boniface. They accused him not only of having expelled them from Paletrina, but also of having destroyed that town, after promising them, in case they surrendered, to leave it in their custody, being satisfied if they raised the Papal standard over the walls —" De his quae dicunt per . . . . numcios papales fuisse trac-
"tata, et de eo quod dicunt de ponendis vexillis D. Bonifacii in
"civitate Penestrae et aliis castris, remanente custodia ipsis
"Columnensibus . . . ." Gaetano denied these assertions and proved his denial. " Quomodo enim verisimile, nondum verum est, quod
"praedicti Column. qui post professionem propriorum excessum et
"culparum, et post recognitionem aberrationis suae, solius miseri-
"cordiae beneficium postulabant, et qui confessi erant se justae puni-
"tionis sententiam exceptisse pro pactis aliquibus institissent." In fact the Colonnas, to prove the possibility of treason on the part of Boniface, denied their humiliations at Rieti, their appeals for mercy and pardon not coinciding with the conditions of treaty whose existence they wanted to prove.

And here let us remark the precautions of Ferrettus. He admits the treason; he admits consequently a prior conditional treaty concluded between the belligerents; and he admits the fact of their intention of coming over to Boniface; but he does not make them arrive in his presence, because he would have been compelled to put in their mouths either words of pity and mercy, or a request for the observance of conditions. But who could believe that the Colonnas would have gone themselves to demand the fulfilment of the conditions of the surrender, and place themselves in the hands of a Pope whom they were far from considering as a saint? If they asked for mercy and pardon, then there would not have been either any conditions or treachery. To evade the difficulty Ferrettus says, that on their way to meet Boniface they were warned by one who knew, *secreti conscius* or perhaps by divine inspiration, *divina inspiratione,* that they would be treacherously murdered, and as a consequence they fled. Then according to Ferretto, the treason of Boniface consisted in finding means of putting the Colonnas to death after having driven them from Palestrina. But the Colonnas themselves declared in the presence of Clement that they did not have to leave Palestrina, but

merely raise the Papal standard over the walls. Their journey to
Rieti, to ask for mercy, they formally denied; and if they had left
Palestrina to implore pardon, Boniface would certainly not have
allowed them to escape. It was difficult to make them come forth;
if they once left it was easy to surround them by the vast body of
soldiers which Boniface had amassed. According to Ferretto, the
Colonnas went out full of confidence in Boniface, afterwards they
fled on the advice that was given them. In that first moment of
abandonment of the promises of the Pope, they could have been
imprisoned, and imprisoned immediately by the soldiers that still invested Palestrina. They fled, and whither did they go? If the promise
of pardon was as yet not granted, we cannot believe that the Colonnas
would leave Palestrina deprived of her garrison. If their kindred
were still there, why did they not return and confine themselves
within? If they could not, they should have renewed the hostilities
in the environs of Palestrina. Now we do not see that such a thing
happened. And moreover, what were the conditions of surrender?
According to the Colonnas on the part of Pope he was to grant
pardon; on their part they were to raise the standard of the Pope on
the walls. And what benefit was this to Boniface after such expense, after such an armament, and after a year of obstinate warfare?
If any conditions existed, they should have been equally beneficial
to both parties. But such were not those which were invented by the
Colonnas.

But here the reader can stop us and say that, even supposing a
surrender at discretion, there could have been treachery on the part
of Boniface, because this kind of submission, among civilized nations,
always calls for clemency on the part of the victor. This is all very
well; but what was the act of Boniface that we can call treason
towards the Colonnas? Perhaps, the occupation of Palestrina, and
the subsequent destruction of it? No, assuredly. For if the Pope
had the obligation of being clement, he had also the obligation of defending himself. To leave Palestrina in the power of the Colonnas
after a year of war, would have been an act of stupidity and not of
clemency. He showed clemency by welcoming them kindly, by pardoning them graciously, as di Pietro says, and by absolving them
from excommunication; and he provided for his own defence and that
of the State by taking from them Palestrina and destroying it. If
he had put to death, or imprisoned the Colonnas, after their surrender, there could be found in this a lack of due clemency, and
hence treason; but not so in his disarming them, and depriving them
of the means of doing harm. The other punishments inflicted on the
Colonnas were after their second rebellion, one year after their surrender.[28] The Colonnas most assuredly were rebels, and there is an
enormous difference between the submission of an honest enemy and
that of a rebel, whenever there are no conditions agreed and sworn to
by both parties. The Colonnas had been pardoned, absolved frm ex-

[28] See Petrini for the year 1300.

communication, left free, and hence they should have blessed the clemency of the Pope, like any honest enemy who surrenders himself to the mercy of the victor.

After all then, the Colonnas did not surrender under condition; and for this reason there could be no violation of a treaty with regard to them. Although they surrendered at the discretion of the Pope, the latter by the destruction of Palestrina, may be accused of excessive harshness to the people of Palestrina, yet he cannot be accused of treachery to the Colonnas. Therefore there was no perfidious counsel given by Guy of Montefeltro to Boniface.

But it is incumbent on us here to reply to the question of how could Dante have imagined the entire account of the things which passed between Guy and Boniface, without some foundation of reality of the facts; inasmuch as there is always some element of truth in even the strangest fables of the poets. The question is reasonable, and we cannot reply to it with the same certainty and with such strong proofs as those by which we believe have cleared both Guy and Boniface of rascality. For it is not a question here of proving a truth, but of showing how an error gained an entrance into the mind of a sublime poet. We may be pardoned then a conjecture. The war against the Colonnas, their surrender, and the destruction of Palestrina were three manifest events known to every one, and which no one doubted. The reason and the manner of the surrender could be known to all at the time the event happened, but obscure to those in far distant times, and from this reason springs the liberty to suspect the treacherous Boniface. Those near at hand could see with their own eyes that a town so far distant from the sea as Palestrina was, could not possibly be reprovisioned except by land, and that being entirely surrounded by crusaders, would be obliged to surrender through famine or through a lack of arms. Those at a distance could be ignorant of these circumstances, and doubt the reason of the surrender and the manner in which it was effected. The Colonnas revolted again, and spread the rumor that they had been betrayed by Boniface. The misery of these fugitives, the hatred of the Ghibellines against Boniface gave credence to it, and the proceedings begun in France against Boniface confirmed it Dante, a sworn enemy of this Pope, accepts this evil rumor, and from this gives full scope to the wildest fancy in the Divine Comedy. It is not incredible that some counsel was asked of Guy by Boniface in the matter of conducting the siege, provided however the former was alive and not dying at the time of the storming of Palestrina This circumstance could transpire and be known by Dante. When the rumor of the treachery had spread, it was easy to surmise that the astute Montefeltro had suggested it to the Pope Dante asserts that the thing really happened, but he asserts it not as a historian who strives to deceive, but as a poet who wishes to lash in a bloody manner, not Guy but Boniface. In fact he had praised Guy in his work, "*il Convite,*" (the Banquet), saying: " The knight Lancelot and our illustrious Latin " Guy of Montefeltro would not enter, with sails spread, into the "harbor of eternity. These noble men lowered their sails of worldly "operations by becoming religious in their old age, and by renouncing "all worldly affection and works." Now how afterwards did he cast him so shamefully into Hell in the Divine Comedy? It will be said that *il Convite* was written before the deeds of Palestrina. But is this certain? Do all agree in admitting this? Balbo and other writers before him declare, for good reasons, that this work was written when he was in exile.

Was it then possible that Guy, of such noble sentiments, Guy, a religious, changed so quickly, and made himself the counsellor of a vile treason, especially when his advanced age allowed him nothing further to hope for in this world? Was he so stupid as to believe that a crime could be forgiven before it was committed? And if these odious interviews did take place between Guy and Boniface, were they in public or in secret? If they were in public, both were crazy; if in secret neither one would have revealed it, because both would be defamed And besides, what then was this perfidious and cunning counsel, for which it was necessary to disturb and torment a poor Friar?—"To promise much and fulfil nothing."—This sort of behavior is very well known to even the least cunning of rogues, and if Boniface was such a man as to receive and adopt this line of action, he was also capable of discovering it without the aid of Guy. The assault of Dante is surprising from a poetical but not from a historian point of view. And Alighieri could not strike Boniface with a more subtle weapon than that which he made from the reports of the treahcery of which the Colonnas were the victims, and the evil advice asked from that most clever captain, Guy of Montefeltro.

DOCUMENT (2C).

BULL INSTITUTING THE JUBILEE.

Bonifacius Episcopus, etc.

Antiquorum habet fide relatio, quod accedentibus ad honorabilem Basilicam Principis Apostolorum de Urbe, concessae sunt magnae remissiones, et indulgentiae peccatorum.

Nos igitur qui juxta officii nostri debitum salutem appetimus et procuramus libentius singulorum, hujusmodi remissiones et indulgentias omnes et singulas, ratas et gratas habentes, ipsas auctoritate Apostolica confirmamus, et approbamus, et etiam innovamus, et presentis scripti patrocinio communimus.

Ut autem Beatissimi Petrus et Paulus Apostoli, eo amplius honorentur, quo eorum Basilicae de Urbe devotius fuerint a fidelibus frequentatae, et fideles ipsi spiritualium largitione munerum, ex hujusmodi frequentatione magis senserint se refertos. Nos de omnipotentis Dei misericordia, et eorumdem Apostolorum ejus meritis et auctoritate confisi, de fratrum nostrorum consilio, et Apostolicae plenitudine potestatis, omnibus in praesentis anno millesimo trecentesimo, a festo Nativitatis Domini nostri Jesu Christi praeterito proxime inchoato, et in quolibet anno centesimo secuturo, ad Basilicas ipsas accedentibus reverenter; vere poenitentibus et confœssis, vel qui vere poenitebunt, et confitebuntur, in hujusmodi praesenti, et quolibet centesimo secuturo annis, non solum plenam et largiorem, imo plenissimam omnium suorum concedemus et concedimus veniam peccatorum.

Statuentes, ut qui voluerint hujusmodi indulgentiae a nobis concessae fieri participes, si fuerint Romani, ad minus triginta diebus, seu interpolatis, et saltem semel in die, si vero peregrini fuerint aut forenses, simili modo diebus quindecim, ad Basilicas easdem accedant. Unuquisque tamen plus merebitur, et indulgentiam efficacius consequetur, qui Basilicas ipsas amplius et devotius frequentabit. Nulli ergo, etc.

Datum Romae apud S. Petrum, 8 Kal. Martii, Pont. nostri Anno VI.

DOCUMENT (2D).

EXCLUSION OF THE SICILIANS AND THE COLONNAS FROM THE INDULGENCES OF THE JUBILEE.

Bonifacius Episcpus servus servorum Dei ad perpetuam rei memoriam. Nuper per alias nostras literas omnes remissiones et indulgentias peccatorum concessas accedentibus ad honorabilem Basilicam Principis Apostolorum de Urbe ratificandas et approbandas duximus, et etiam innovandas, ut tamen beatissimi Petrus et Paulus Apostoli, eo amplius honorentur, quo ipsorum Basilicae de Urbe devotius forent, et fidelius frequentatae: et fideles ipsi spiritualium largitione munerum, et hujusmodi frequentatione, magis se sentirent refectos. Nos de omnipotentis Dei misericordia, eorundem Apostolorum ejus meritis et auctoritate confisi, de fratrum nostrorum consilio, et Apostolicae plenitudine potestatis, omnibus in praesenti millesimo tresentesimo, a festo nativitatis Domini nostri Jesu Christi praeterito, proxime inchoato, et in quolibet alio centesimo sequuturo anno, ad Basilicas ipsas accedentibus reverenter, vere poenitentibus et confessis: vel qui vere poenitebunt et confitebuntur, in hujusmodi praesenti, et quolibet centesimo sequuturo annis, non solum plenam et largiorem, imo plenissimam omnium suorum concessimus veniam peccatorum, prout in istis aliis nostris literis continetur. Verum quia multi indulgentiarum gratia se reddunt indignos, declaramus expresse, et dicimus manifeste, quod illos falsos et impios Christianos, qui portaverint, vel portabunt merces, seu res prohibitas Saracenis vel ad terras eorum reportaverunt, vel reportabunt ab eis, nec non Frederiem natura quondam Petri, olium Regis Aragonum: Ac Siculos nobis et Ecclesiae Romanae hostes, et Apostalicae sedis rebelles: et qui receptabunt Columnenses eosdem, et generaliter omnes et singulos publicos hostes et rebelles praesentes, et futuros Ecclesiae memoratae, et impugnatores ipsius: et qui dabunt scientes supradictis, eorum alicui, vel aliquibus auxilium, consilium, vel favorem, publice, vel occulte dum in sua malitia perstiterint, ad dictae Sedis mandata sua malitia redire curaverint, indulgentiarum hujusmodi cum non sint capaces, nolumus esse participes, ipsosque poenitus excludimus ab eisdem. Nulli ergo hominum omnino liceat hanc paginam nostrae declarationis voluntatis et exclusionis infrigere, ei ausu temerario contraire. Si quis autem hoc attentare praesumpserit, indignationem omnipotentis Dei et beatorum Petri et Pauli Apostolorum ejus, se noverit incursurum. Datum Romae apud sanctum Petrum Kal. Martij Pontificatus nostri anno sexto.

DOCUMENT (2E).

THE OFFERINGS OF THE JUBILEE.

ALL the chroniclers of this epoch speak of the vast crowds of the faithful who flocked to Rome from all parts to gain the indulgences of the Jubilee; and they all speak in the highest terms of the admirable foresight of the Pontiff, by which such a vast number of people were well provided with food and lodgment. Paulinus di Piero, who Manni [29] surmises was present at the Jubilee says: " The City of " Rome supported and provided with lodgings this innumerable mul- " titude of people, and with everything else they needed for a year." Villani more diffuse, expresses it thus: " A great part of the Chris- " tians living at that time made the same pilgrimage, women as well " as men from distant and different countries, both near and far; " and the most wonderful thing that was ever seen was that, during " the entire year, Rome supported constantly, besides the Roman " people 200,000 pilgrims, without counting those who were on the " way coming and returning; and that all were abundantly provided " with food, horses as well as human beings. I can bear testimony " because I was present and saw all this. The offerings made by the " pilgrims increased considerably the treasury of the Church, and " the Romans all became rich from the sale of their wares." William Ventura, author of the chronicle of Asti adds some particular details concerning the pious offerings: " Mirandum est quod passim ibant " viri et mulieres, qui anno illo Romae fuerunt, qui ego fui ibi, et " per dies XV. steti. De pane, vino, carnibus, piscibus, et avena " bonum mercatum ibi erat. foenum carissimum ibi fuit; hospicia " carissima; taliter quod lectus meus, et equi mei super foeno et " avena constabat mihi tornesium unum grossum. Exiens de Roma " in Vigilia Nativitatis Christi, vide turbam magnam quam dinu- " merare nemo poterat; et fama erat inter Romanos, quod ibi fuerant " plus quam viginti centum millia virorum et mulierum Pluries

---

[29] Preface to the Chronicle S. R. I., Tom. II of the continuation.

"ego vidi ibi tam vires quam mulieres conculcatos sub pedibus "aliorum; et etiam egomet in eodem periculo plures vices evasi. "Papa innumerabilem pecuniam ab eisdem recepit, quia die ac nocte "clerici stabant ad altare Sancti Pauli tenentes in eorum manibus "rastellos rastellantes pecuniam infinitam." These three eyewitnesses narrate three remarkable circumstances which signalized the unusual event of the Jubilee; the immense multitude of the faithful that flocked to Rome to gain the indulgences; the abundance of provisions; and finally the vast gifts of money given by the pilgrims. The first is a splendid proof of the liveliness of faith which still reigned in the heart of those generations, and of the opinion which they had of Pope Boniface; although his reputation had received some injury by the imprisonment and death of St Peter Celestine, and by the abusive libels of the Colonnas, still it was not so much sullied as to prevent his voice of sovereign Pontiff from having a powerful effect on the minds of the faithful. The Jubilee was a new affair, its institution was not one of the ordinary acts of the Pontifical office which the faithful were accustomed to judge more in the public than in the private person of the Pontiff. The novelty of the publication of these indulgences, the call to Rome of such a multitude; the lively impulse given, so skilfully and so aptly, to piety and in consequence to the pious offerings by exterior pomp of worship, should, in calling attention to the private individuality of Boniface, inspire them at least with doubts of the honesty of his purpose, and the holiness of his object. To his call all responded; and they were not only those of humble life, but the most brilliant intellects of the time who went to gain the indulgences accordingly by Boniface. If this Pontiff had been truly a man like Tiberius and Mahomet, people would have answered his invitation with a smile, indicating that they were on their guard so as not to fall into a snare. Whence we must conclude that the calumnies uttered against the acts of Boniface obtained a certain consistency only from the scandalous proceedings undertaken against this Pontiff by Philip the Fair.

The second circumstance remarked by the chroniclers on the occasion of the Jubilee, namely, the wise provisional measures effected by Boniface, by which so great a multitude did not want for the necessaries of life, reveals to us not only the lofty mind of this Pope, but also his generosity, so great were the expenses that he was obliged to bear in order that a great abundance might continue to exist for the entire year. In fact the high price of things having begun to be felt, as Stephaneschi says,[30] it was prescribed that all the wheat of the neighboring country should be carried to Rome, and that the pilgrims arriving should bring with them a certain quantity of bread. This last measure concerned only the people of the neighborhood and not those who came from afar. The great multitude which during the entire year visited Rome and which reached, according to Ventura,

---

[30] De Jubil, anno, cap. V. Max Biblioth. Patrum, Lyons, Tom. XXV.

the number of two millions (not incredible), were nourished by that which was collected from the Campagna of Rome, and what was transported from the kingdom of Naples. Nothing came from Sicily, because that island was at that time at war with the Church. Now this wonderful abundance of provisions could be brought to the city only because of large franchises granted to foreign traders; the certainty of selling their wares in Rome not being sufficient to attract them, the Pontiff had them come by buying himself their cereals at a price much higher than at what he gave the same to the hungry crowd. We remark that Ventura complains of the scarcity of fodder and lodgings, for which he had to pay dearly during his stay in Rome. Those who know the statistics of Rome at this epoch, and the conditions of the habitable part of this city with its population, can judge of the truth of the words of the chronicler of Asti, when they remember that, according to Villani, 200,000 pilgrims resided daily in the city. But this scarcity of fodder makes us conjecture that the fields which to-day around Rome are uncultivated and produce only grass, were in XIIIth century carefully cultivated and very fertile in grain. Ventura complains of the scarcity of hay, but not of wheat. Stephaneschi [31] himself speaks of the abundant harvest gathered that year. If these details are true, they would induce us to believe that the inhabitants of Rome and the Campagna were at that time more numerous than in our day. Moreover, the abundance of wheat and the dearness of fodder assures us of a greater population. For the human race increases by toil; and the benefited land, responds to lavish care bestowed on it by the purity of the air which preserves life, and makes it cheerful and prolific.

Finally we must say a word on the immense sums of money received by the Pope, during the Jubilee year, because the aforesaid writers speak of this as one thing which could have made the Pope a veritable Croesus. Ventura especially distinguishes himself by his malice; after having regaled the eyes of the readers with the heaps of money raked in by the two clerics, he adds: " Unde sciant Chris-"tiani venturi, quod praedictus Bonifacius et ejus cardinales in "aeternum praedictam indulgentiam omni anno centesimo venturo "firmaverunt et decretum fecerunt." That Ventura had seen these two clerics day and night raking up countless money offered by the pilgrims at the feet of the altar of the Apostle St. Paul; that Villani, de Piero, and all those who were witnesses at Rome, of this concourse of faithful, had heard of these treasures, we do not doubt. But Stephaneschi engages us to moderate the report of these riches by throwing light upon the fact of the offerings. We regret very much that the ignorance of the scribe, or the errors of the manuscript, did not allow the editors of Lyons to publish the treatise composed by this author on the Jubilee, in a manner more favorable to the understanding of the text. Here are his words: " Et nequicquam intactum "oblivioni deseratur temporalis Basilica emolumenti, aliquod devo-

---

[31] De Jubil, anno, cap. V. Max Biblioth, Patrum, Lyons, Tom. XXV.

"tionis signum accreverit Namque quae celeberrima toto terrarum
"orbe altaria singulis jamdudum annis ex peregrinantium oblatis
"Apostolorum principis florinorum auri XXX. m. IIII. c. V. flori-
"norum .... auferebant millia triginta principis circiter annum,
"et viginta millia doctoris hoc centesimo retulere, non ex amgnis
"auri vel argenti donis, sed ex usualis monetae provinciae cujusque
"minutiis, licet non omnium oblationes pressura vel paupertate
"praepediente injectae sint, devote oblata, devote dispensantur castris
"casalibus, praediis, ex ea pecunia, ipso summo pontifice jubente ad
"jus et proprietatem Basilicarum comparandis, ac deinde ex ipsorum
"reditibus divinis, Apostolorumque augendis cultibus officiisque ....
"Erubescant itaque eo vehemtius nostri temporis reges, quod se a
"modicis personarum laboribus numerunque donis superatos norunt,
"qui nequaquam primitias gentium reges Magos imitari, non in-
"fantem, sed ad dexteram Dei patris sedentem Jesum, in ejus Apos-
"tolos visere, sibique offerre munera venire. Heu! illis ecclesiarum
"exigere decimas ut paulatim Deo ab attavis concessa nanciscantur
"sat est, sicque parentum, de quibus gloriantur gesta dum ab eis
deviant, ignominia sunt . . . ."

Not wishing then to omit the temporal advantages which the
basilicas would receive from the Jubilee, Stephaneschi assures us
that the offerings made at the altars of Sts. Peter and Paul amounted
each year to about 30,405 florins, and that in the Jubilee year, if this
meaning is given to the words "*hoc centesimo*," there was given at the
altar of St Peter 30,000 and at that of St. Paul 20,000, so that adding
to the annual 30,000 florins the 50,000 received during the Jubilee we
arrive at a total of 80,000.[32] Stephaneschi remarks that poverty
prevented some from offering anything, (*pressura vel paupertate
praepediente*), and that these thousands of florins were not of gold or
silver, but the small coins in use in each province: "Non ex magnis
"auri vel argenti donis, sed ex usualis monetae provinciae cujusque
minutiis." In reducing then these florins into small coins, one easily
understands how Ventura saw this heap of money at the foot of the
altar, and the two clerics who were engaged night and day in collecting this mass of small coins.

The Pope used all this money to increase the revenue of the
Basilicas and for the splendor of divine worship. The parcimony
of the kings who were not ashamed to allow themselves to be out-
done in generosity and piety by the common people, shows us that
the invitation of the Pope to the indulgences, being entertained by
the masses found no echo in the royal courts; an evident sign that
the venerable and mystical authority of the Pontificate had already
begun to lose its life in the heart of those who were making against
it a tactical war, but one destructive beyond measure.

[32] This sum changed into English money amounts to about £40,000.

DOCUMENT (2F).

LETTER OF BONIFACE TO CHARLES II REPROVING HIM FOR HIS IMPUDENCE.

Carolo Regi Siciliae illustri.

Actus tuos praeteritos recensentes, et recolentes tractatus, quos in tuis agendis interdum hactenus tenuisti, de iis, quos tenes, vel tenebis in antea, merito formidamus. Nec sine ratione timemus: non enim excidit a nostra memoria qualiter, dum essemus in minori officio constituti nos et venerabilis frater noster Gerardus episcopus Sabinensis in adjutorium tuum missi, quando tempore felicis recordationis Nicolai Papae IV. praedecessoris nostri obsidebatur Cajeta, tibique vicinis nobis irrequisitis et insciis, tractasti cum charissimo in Christo filio nostro Jacobo, nunc Rege Aragonum, et perfecisti tractatum; contemptis in hoc non solum nobis et dicto episcopo sed et Romana Ecclesia matre tua.

Non sumus obliti quam providos, quam discretos et utiles habuisti et firmasti tractatus cum praefato Jacobo: tunc hoste praedictae Ecclesiae atque tuo, pro tua et tuorum liberatione natorum. Ex quibus, et aliis quae memoriter retinemus, experientia longa didicimus, quod te proprio in arduis innitente tibi male successit, et hoc processus habiti circa missionem dilecti filii Philippi Tarantini principis nati tui, in Siciliam nuper missi, manifeste declarant. Et utinam ex erroribus habitis in praemissis tu solus detrimenta sentires, et nos et Ecclesia supradicta, et Christianitas non sentiremus ex talibus nocumenta. Quae prudentia, fili, fuit; quam reverentiam ad nos, et dictam ecclesiam habuisti, si, prout accepimus, nuper in quodam galione Frederici nostri hostis ac tui nuntios recepisti, ipsosque remiseris, quid petierint quidve responderis ad nostram notitiam non perducto?

Volentes igitur futuris ex tua praeceptiatione et subitatione periculis obviare, celsitudinem tuam monemus et hortamur attente, per apostolica scripta tibi sub debito fidelitatis, quo nobis et Ecclesiae Romanae teneris, et excommunicationis poenas quam, si secus feceris, te incurrere volumus ipso facto, districte praecipiendo mandantes, quatenus cum Frederico praedicto, vel ejus nuntiis nullum tratatum habitum, vel habendum firmare, aut executioni mandare praesumas absque nostro speciali consensu, per nostras bullatas literas apparente. Nos enim quicquid secus feceris ex nunc omnino cassamus, et cassum et irritum decernimus et inane.

Caeterum pro certo tenere te volumus, quod si te aliter, quam hactenus feceris, nostris beneplacitis, non coaptes; et si salubria mandata nostra contemnas, quantumcumque pro tuis relevandis oneribus, et periculis evitandis innumerabiles quasi effuderimus pecuniae quantitates, exquiremus vias et modos, per quos, quamvis cum danno tuo pax nobis cum praefato hoste proveniat, ne diutius Terra Sancta in manibus hostium fidei teneatur. Dat, Later. v. id. januarii anno v.

DOCUMENT (2G).

LETTER OF BONIFACE TO CARDINAL ACQUASPARTA CHARGING HIM TO PACIFY FLORENCE.

Considerantes attentius, et infra claustra pectoris meditatione solicita revolventes, quod nefanda hostis antiqui nequitia, qui semper quaerit ut noceat, semper in circuitu ambulat ut offendat, in plerisque locis Lombardiae, Tusciae, et Romandiolae provinciarum; Aquilejensis, et Gradensis patriarchatuum, Ravennatis, Mediolanensis, Januensis, et Pisani archiepiscopatuum, Marchiae Tervisinae, Venetiarum, Bononiensis, et Ferrariensis civitatum, earumque dioecesum et territoriorum, locisque vicinis eisdem, discordiarum zizaniam seruit, ingessit lites, commovit scandala, odia suscitavit; grandi utique desiderio ducimur, curisque multimodis excitamur, ut malis hujusmodi, molestis quamplurimum votis nostris, efficacibus et opportunis remediis obvietur; et ecclesiasticis, religiosis, saecularibusque personis, in partibus locisque degentibus memoratis, Apostolicae sedis benigna visitatione praeventis, deformata inibi providam reformationem recipiant, prava et noxia procul penitus profligentur.

Attendentes igitur quod gratiarum dator Altissimus personam tuam scientiae magnitudine, providentiae dono, discretionis virtute, industriae munere, circumspectionis gratia, et aliarum virtutum titulis decoravit, humeros tuos fortitudinis robore muniendo, ut onera grandia facilius supportares; plenam quoque, immo plenissimam de tuis laudabilibus meritis fiduciam obtinentes, licet apud sedem Apostolicam ex tui maturitate consilii tua non modicum opportuna praesentia dignoscatur, nosque illa careamus inviti; te tamen ob honorem et exaltationem Ecclesiae, ac reformationem, et directionem necessarias, ac desideratam quietem partium praedictarum, de fratrum nostrorum consilio illuc tamquam pacis angelum duximus destinandum; fraternitati tuae in provinciis, patriarchatibus, archiepiscopatibus nec non civitatibus memoratis, earumque dioecesibus, districtibus, ac territoriis, et locis, ac partibus supradictis plenae legationis officium committentes, ut evellas et destruas, dissipes et disperdas, aedifices et plantes, ac facias auctoritate nostra quaecumque ad honorem Dei, prosperum statum partium earumdem, ac reformationem pacis fidelium videris expedire, etc. Datum Anagniae x. kal. junii anno vi.

DOCUMENT (2H).

LETTER TO THE FRENCH CLERGY RELATIVE TO THE APPEAL OF CHARLES OF VALOIS.

. . . . Ecce quidem fratres et filii, non latet in abditis, sed per diversos orbis angulos innotescit, qualiter jam fere viginti annorum spatio quondam Petrus olim Rex Aragonum, subdolus nequitiae perpetrator; et subsequenter diversis temporibus nati ejus, sibi succedentes in vitio contra nos et eandem ecclesiam, et charissimum in Christo filium nostrum Carolum Siciliae, Regem illustrem insulam Siciliae occuparunt ac tenuerunt, et adhuc etiam pro majori parte detinent nequiter occupatam. Quarum occupationis et detentionis occasione et causa contigit olim perditio Terrae sanctae; sed nec ei potuit opportunum ministrari subsidium de partibus cismarinis. Et quamvis inopinatis auxiliis, ac insperatis operibus, illucescente illi gratia Salvatoris, sit ipsi Terrae Sanctae via recuperationis, reparationis, inhabitationis, et munitionis civitatum et locorum dudum ibidem deperditorum, aperta; tamen ob induratam antiquatae jam rebellionis nequitiam praedictorum Siculorum et Frederici nati praedicti quondam Petri olim Regis Aragonum, sub cujus devio in tenebris et umbra mortis obdormiunt, et propter alia scandala quae insurgunt, praefata mater ecclesia in adhibendis opportunis eidem terrae subsidiis impeditur. Status insuper Tusciae impetitur admodum fluctibus scandalorum: civitates, loca, et incolae ipsi matri ecclesiae subjecta rebellant, nequitiae venena fundentia et laborantia ingratitudinis vitio contra eam: et nisi eorum insolentiae compescantur, invalescent plurimum ribelliones ipsorum, et periculose succrescent.

Et ideo non solum de prope, sed etiam de longe sub spe divinae potentiae ad obviandum tot fluctibus totque malis, et periculis resistendum, et ad rebellantium superbiam edomandam auxilium, juvamen, et fortitudinem invocare compulsi, dilectum filium nobilem virum Carolum comitem Andegavensem, clarae memoriae Philippi Regis Francorum natum virum utique nobilitatis et generis excellentia praefulgentem, potentia praeditum, exercitatum in armis, et ecclesiae praefatae devotum, per quem speramus et credimus, honores et commoda ipsius ecclesiae in hac parte posse viriliter, potenter, et feliciter promoveri, et satisfieri utiliter votis nostris; advocare providimus in opportunum auxilium et juvamen ipsius ecclesiae matris suae, ordinato jam, ut decuit, cum eodem, ut usque ad festum purificationis B. Virginis proximo futurum iter arripiat cum magna et honorabili armatorum, militum et equitum comitiva venturus continuatis dietis, et intraturus personaliter in Italiam, ac mansurus in ipsius Italiae provinciis sive locis, de quibus Apostolica sedes duxerit ordinandum: ut ad vindictam malefactorum, laudem vero bonorum adventus et mora ejus Domino auxiliante persistant et tranquillato statu Siciliae, aliisque Italiae rebellibus subjugatis, ac ad nostra, et dictae sedis mandata redactis, de opportuno ipsius Terrae Sanctae succursu possit utilius et efficacius provideri, et universalis occidentalis ecclesiae sabbatum procuretur, etc. Dat. Laterani 11. kal. decembris anno vi.

DOCUMENT (21).

LETTER TO CARDINAL ACQUASPARTA, LEGATE TO RESTRAIN CHARLES OF VALOIS.

Venerabili fratri Portuensi episcopo.

Cum nobilis provincia Tusciae multis foret confossa doloribus, guerrarum consitata dissidiis, civilibus bellis licentiae laxatis habenis, ac deformata ruinis, decuit nos ad animarum, corporum, et rerum vitanda pericula in ipsa prosequi vias pacificas, et ad unitatem reducere discordantes, ne se mutuo lacerarent, impeterent, ac molestarent injuste: ut tam nobilis tantaque provincia in tabernaculis fiduciae requiesceret, et in pacis dulcedine habitaret; et per hoc in ea purgaretur haeretica pravitas, cohiberetur praedonum audacia, honoraretur sancta Romana ecclesia, et fidelium devotio nutriretur. Ad nos namque relatio fide digna perduxerat, quod nonnulli de dicta provincia cum malitiae suae consciis atque consortibus habentes de ipsius turbatione pruritum malignitatis suae, in favorem nostrorum et Apostolicae sedis rebellium suos illicitos conatus moliebantur extendere, ut non cuiquam sua confirmaretur justitia, non cuiquam status suis debitus meritis servaretur. Unde cum fratribus nostris habita deliberatione matura, attendentes quod Romanum vacat imperium, cujus ad nos, praesertim hoc tempore pacifica conservatio dignoscitur pertinere; dilectum filium nobilem virum Carolum natum clarae memoriae Philippi Regis Francorum, comitem Andegavensem; de cujus strenuitate, armorum experientia, et bonitate confidimus; conservatorem pacis in ea parte ipsius Tusciae, quae praedicto Imperio subjacet, de fratrum eorumdem consilio duximus deputandum. Qui provinciam ipsam potenter et prudenter ingressus, hujusmodi commissum sibi paciariatus, seu conservandae pacis officium, divina sibi assistente virtute, coepit laudabiliter exercere: ita quod devoti et fideles ecclesiae saepedictae de ipsa provincia habere poterunt, dante Domino, bonum statum, eruntque prava in directa, et viae asperae planabuntur. Verum, ut haec salubrius et efficacius impleantur cum quiete ac pace, te de cujus legalitate, bonitate, circumspectione, et experientia matura confidimus, ad partes easdem providimus destinare, in eadem provincia nostra tibi auctoritate concessa; per cujus dictus comes favorem protectus, directus consilio, et maturitate adjutus, commissum sibi officium, juxta beneplacitum divinum et nostrum, cum moderatione ac mensura tranquillius et utilius possit debitae executioni mandare.

Quocirca fraternitatem tuam rogamus, monemus, et hortamur attente, per apostolica tibi scripta amandantes, quatenus celeriter te accingens, et ad partes illas personaliter festinus accedas et ad ea, quae comiti memorato commissimus, efficaciter promovenda et laudabiliter consumanda in provincia saepedicta per te et alios, de quibus expedire videris, ipsum solerter inducas, et tam tu quam ipse vestra studia convertatis ad seminandum in ea semen charitatis, et pacis;

ut sedatis guerrarum et dissensionum turbinibus, qui nimis invaluerunt ibidem, provincia ipsa tot impulsibus agitata quasi post noctis tenebras floridum diei lumen aspiciat; post glaciei frigus hyemis aurea sibi tempora et serena succedant, in quibus afflicti non solum temporalem laetitiam, sed aeternam auctore Domino consequantur, contradictores et rebelles auctoritate nostra per te, vel per alium, seu alios per spirituales poenas, appellatione postposita, compescendo, etc. Datum Laterani vi. non. decembris anno vii.

DOCUMENT (2K).

LETTER OF BONIFACE TO PHILIP THE FAIR REGARDING THE ARCHBISHOPRIC OF NARBONNE AND THE COUNTY OF MAGUELONNE.

Recordare, Rex inclyte, progenitorum tuorum actus strenuos, meritaque praeclara intuere, ac respice quod Deus regnantium honor et gloria beatum Ludovicum avum tuum Regibus dedit in speculum, et populis in exemplum, quae ipsius nepos, quasi charissimus filius imiteris; prudenter attendens, quod tantam habebat conscientiae puritatem, quod non solum scienter, sed nec ignoranter dispendium aliis volebat inferre, causam quam ignorabat adinstar sancti Job diligentius investigans. Unde cum super comitatu Mergoglii Magalonensis diocesis nonulla auribus instillarentur ipsius, in tantum ut ad quem pertineret comitatus hujusmodi haesitaret; nolens ex abrupto procedere, vel incerto felicis recordationis Clementis Papae IV. praedecessoris nostri, quem super hoc putabat habere notitiam, requisivit consilium, tam humiliter quam prudenter, sicut ex tenore literarum praedecessoris ejusdem, quem praesentibus tibi mittimus interclusum, colligere poteris evidenter. Post cujus praedecessoris Clementis responsum Magalonensis ecclesia a regalium exactionibus conquievit, quae ab olim tenuit et tenet in feudum ab Apostolica sede comitatum eumdem, prout constat ex vetustissimis documentis, et ex iis, quae in ejusdem sedis conservantur archivio, ac ex praedecessorum nostrorum Romanorum Pontificum literis, quae de dicto comitatu faciunt mentionem. Quapropter dolemus non immerito, et turbamur, si relatibus facta respondeant, quod sicut accepimus, officiales tui venerabilem fratrem nostrum Gerardum episcopum, et dilectum filium capitulum Magalonense super comitatu praedicto, et hominibus comitatus, immo nos et Apostolican sedem gravant, impetunt, et molestant.

Cum igitur Deus per suam misericordiam, non sine multimodis nostris et sedis ejusdem praesidiis, adeo dilataverit funiculos et limites regni tui juriumque tuorum, ut nec tibi expediat ad occupanda bona aliorum et jura; praesertim nostra et praedictae sedis, ac Magalonensis ecclesiae memoratae, super comitatu praefato, qui tenetur a nobis et sede praedicta, manus occupatrices extendere; circumspectionem regiam tenore praesentium hortamur et rogamus attente, tibique paternis affectibus salubriter suademus, ut senescallis, officialibus, et balivis tuis districte praecipias, quod de caetero a dictorum episcopi et capituli ac vassallorum super dicto comitatu molestatione desistant: exhortationes et preces nostras hujusmodi sic efficaciter impleturus, quod a Deo premium consequaris, nobisque et sanctae Romanae Ecclesiae matri tuae, te praecipuum filium repraesentes, quicquid super hoc faciendum duxeris nobis tuis literis responsurus.

Ad haec praemissis adiicitur grandis injuria, et amara querela, qua ad nostrum pervenit auditum, quod nobilis vir Amalricus vicecomes Narbonae, antiquorum progenitorum suorum, qui ecclesiam Narbonensem et alias eidem subjectas, quantum et quamdiu potuerunt, multipliciter impugnarunt, vestigiis inhaerens pestiferis; jurisdictionem et omnia, quae dicta Narbonensis ecclesia teneat vel habeat in civitate ac burbo Narbonae et pertinentiis eorumdem, et quae indubitanter tenebat, ac tenere debebat in feudum ab eadem ecclesia Narbonensi; quaeve parentes sui a centum fere annis citra continue archiepiscopis, qui pro tempore ipsi ecclesiae praefuerunt, et pater istius vicecomitis eodem praesente, sciente, et intelligente Narbonensi archiepiscopo, qui nunc praeest, cum sacramento fidelitatis et homagio, praesente quoque multitudine hominum, clericorum et laicorum, nobilium et ignobilium copiosa, ante majus altare in ipsa ecclesia Narbonensi, ut moris erat praedecessorum eorumdem, publice recognoverant a dictis archiepiscopo et ecclesia Narbonensi, se tenere in feudum, ut indubitatis constat Regum Franciae praedecessorum tuorum privilegiis, vicecomitum Narbonensium literis eorumdem vicecomitum sigillis signatis, et aliis etiam luce clarioribus documentis, et haec ipse idem vicecomes procuratorio nomine patris sui, dum vivebat, in tua curia fuit manifeste confessus; a paucis citra temporibus maligno ductus spiritu, in magnum contemptum, praejudicium et injuriam non solum praefatae Narbonensis ecclesiae, verum etiam aliarum ecclesiarum totius provinciae Narbonensis, a te recognovit in feudum: et in damnationis suae cumulum, et evidentius saepedictate Narbonensis ecclesiae nocumentum, non solum ea a te, ut praedicitur, recognovit; sed ut Gallicano utamur vocabulo, advocavit, immo etiam ea a dicto archiepiscopo, et ecclesia Narbonensi deavocavit expresse. Fili charissime, talia mentem nostram amaricant, et perturbant, et ut ad apponenda remedia convertamur, excitant et instigant: nec possumus, nec debemus tam grandia detri menta ac exheredationem quandam Narbonensis ecclesiae supradictae sub dissimulatione transire: nec talia pati debuerat dignitatis Regiae rectitudo, et prudentia circumspecta. Ab olim ecclesia, Regum lactata mamillis, excrevit in potestatem, dignitatem, libertatem, celsitudinem, et gloriam seculorum: nunc, proh dolor! a regibus eorumque officialıbus premitur, ancillatur, spernitur, et multipliciter expugnatur.

Haec, fili, tolerando in ecclesiis regni tui, habes merito formidare, quod ulcisetur haec Deus judicii dominus, et Rex regum, ejusque vicarius finaliter non tacebit, ne forsitan audiat: Canis mutus latrare non valens; qui etsi patienter ad tempus expectet, ut locus misericordiae non claudatur, tandem exurget ad vindictam malefactorum, laudem vero bonorum. Utinam saperes et intelligeres, et novissima provideres, ac plene discuteres immissiones, quae quasi per malos angelos tibi fiunt et susurronibus, ac pravis consilariis facilem non praeberes auditum; et solerter cognosceres, quod quasi mali prophetae, loquentes placentia, vident tibi falsa et stulta, assumptiones falsas et ejectiones; nec attendunt, quod inter naturam et gloriam est media gratia, sine qua a prima ad tertiam non transitur. Caveas igitur diligenter, ne ad stultum finem consilia talium, qui adulatione decipiunt te, deducant.

Nos nihilominus, ne tantum dispendium memoratae Narbonensis Ecclesiae transeat impunitum, neve aliis praebeatur exemplum tam nefanda similia attentandi; contra Almaricum ipsum et alios, quos negotium istud contingit, ex officio nostro et de apostolicae plenitudine potestatis deliberavimus procedere summarie, de plano sine strepitu et figura judicii, prout justitia exiget, et videbimus expedire; ipsumque Almaricum mandamus sub certa forma ad nostram praesentiam evocari. Caeterum excellentiam regiam volumus non latere, quod ex quo stimulamur in tantum, nec blandimenta proficiunt, nec corriguntur errata; literas nostras, quas super talibus et similibus tibi dirigimus, jam ordinavimus regestrari ad perpetuam rei memoriam. Quis autem ex eis et aliis, necnon ex illis, quae nuperrime per solemnes nuntios tibi significanda decrevimus, subsequetur, effectus, novit ille, qui secretorum est cognitor, et praescius futurorum. Dat. Anagniae xv. kal. augusti anno vi.

DOCUMENT (2L).

LETTER TO PHILIP THE FAIR, ANNEXED TO THE BULL AUSCULTA.

Carissimo in Christo filio Philippo Regi Franciae illustri.

Nuper ex rationabilibus causis moti, praesertim ad relevanda gravamina, et quasi importabilia onera ecclesiarum, praelatorum, et ecclesiasticarum personarum, regularium et saecularium, regni tui, literas infrascripti tenoris fieri fecimus, et bulla nostra bullari, quarum tenorem ad tuam providimus notitiam praesentibus deducendum. Tenor autem talis est, Bonifacius, etc. ad perpetuam rei memoriam. Salvator mundi etc. ut in proxima superiori usque in finem . . . . Tu igitur sicut filius praedilectus in iis, quae rationabiliter et pro utilitate publica fecimus, non turberis: sed ea aequanimiter toleres; prudenter attendens, quia ut praemittitur, terminum assignamus, quo privilegia, indulgentiae, gratiae, et concessiones praedictae, nostro conspectui praesententur, et ad nostram et dictae sedis notitiam deducantur, ut consideratis ipsis et visis provideri possit, si dicta suspensio fuerit in aliquo vel aliquibus moderanda. Datum Laterani non. decembris anno vii.

Bonifacius, etc. charissimo in Christo filio Philippo Regi Franciae illustri.

Ausculta, fili charissime, praecepta patris, et ad doctrinam mag-

istri, qui gerit illius vices in terris, qui solus est magister et dominus, aurem tui cordis inclina; viscerosae sanctae matris ecclesiae admonitionem libenter excipe, et cura efficaciter adimplere. . . . . .
Ad te igitur sermo noster dirigitur, tibi paternus amor exprimitur, et dulcia matris ubera exponuntur. Campum siquidem militiae humanae mortalitatis ingressus, renatus sacri fonte baptismatis, renuntians diabolo et pompis ejus, non quasi hospes et advena, sed jam domesticus fidei et civis sanctorum effectus, ovile dominicum intravisti, colluctaturus non solum contra carnem et sanguinem, sed etiam contra aereas potestates, mundique rectores praesentium tenebrarum. Sic veri Noe es arcam ingressus, extra quam nemo salvatur, catholicam scilicet Ecclesiam, unam columbam immaculatam, unici Christi sponsam, in qua Christi vicarius Petrique successor primatum noscitur obtinere: qui sibi collatis clavibus regni coelorum, judex a Deo vivorum, et mortuorum constituitur agnoscitur; ad quem, sedentem in judicii solio, dissipare pertinet suo intuitu omne malum. Hujus profecto sponsae quae de coelo descendit a Deo parata sicut sponsa ornata viro suo, Romanus Pontifex caput existit: nec habet plura capita monstruose, cum sit sine macula, sine ruga, nec habens aliquod inhonestum. . . . .

Ad haec, ne Terrae sanctae negotium, quod nostris et tuis et aliorum fidelium debet charius insidere praecordiis, nos putes oblivioni dedisse memorare, fili, et discito, quod progenitores tui Christianissimi principes, quorum debes laudanda vestigia solerti studio, et claris operibus imitari, exposuerunt olim personas et bona in subsidium dictae terrae. Sed Saracenorum invalescente perfidia Christianorum ac. . . . . Tua et aliorum Regum et principum devotione solita tepescente, terra eadem tuis utique temporibus, heu! deperdita noscitur et prostrata. Quis itaque canticum Domini cantat in ea? Quis assurgit in ejus subsidium et recuperationis opportunae juvamen adversus impios Saracenos, malignantes et operantes iniquitatem, ac debacchantes in illa? Ad ejus quippe succursum arma bellica periisse videntur, et abjecti sunt clypei fortium; qui contra hostes fidei dimicare solebant: enses et gladii evaginati in domesticos fidei, et saeviunt in effusionem sanguinis Christiani: et nisi a populo Dei domesticae insolentiae succidantur, et pax ei proveniat salutaris terra illi, foedata actibus malignorum, a periculo desolationis et miseriae per ejusdem populi ministerium non resurget.

Si haec et similia iis benevola mente revolvas, invenies quod obscuratum est aurum, et est color optimus immutatus. An non ignominia et confusio magna tibi et aliis Regibus et principibus Christianis adesse dignoscitur, quod versa est ad alienos hereditas Jesu Christi, et sepulcrum ejus ad extraneos devolutum? Qualem ergo retributionis gratiam merebuntur apud Dominum Reges et principes, et coeteri Christiani, in quibus terra quaerit respirare praedicta; sed non est qui sustentet eam ex omnibus filiis, quos genuit ipse Deus, nec est qui supponat manum ex omnibus quos nutrivit? Clamat enim ad Dei filios civitas Jerusalem, et suas exponit angustias, et in remedium doloris ejus filiorum Dei implorat affectus. Si ergo filius Dei es, dolores ejus excipias, tristare et dole cum ipso, si diligis bonum ejus. Tartari quidem, pagani, et alii infideles eidem terrae succurrunt, et ei non subveniunt in ea Christi sanguine pretioso redempti; nec est qui consoletur eam ex omnibus charis ejus. Hoc a dissidiis privatis obvenit, dum utilitas publica cupiditatis ardore consumitur, nonnullis quae sunt sua quaerentibus, non quae Christi, quorum peccata Deus ultionum dominus non solum in ipsis vindicat, sed etiam in progenies eorumdem.

Tremenda sunt itaque Dei judicia et timenda, ante quae non parentes justitiam damnabuntur: justus autem de angustia liberabitur, et cadet impius in laqueum, quem tetendit. Tu vero, fili, communiens in tribus temporibus vitam tuam, ordinando praesentia, et commemorando praeterita, et providendo futura, sic te praepares in praemissis . . . . ut in praesenti divinam gratiam, et in futuro salvationis et retributionis aeternae gloriam merearis. Datum Laterani non. decembris ann. vii.

DOCUMENT (2M).

ON THE WORKS OF EGIDIUS COLONNA.

The work "*de Regia Potestate et Papali,*" was published in Paris in 1506, in one volume quarto; Goldasto[33] was vaunted wrongfully as having first edited it. That *de Regimine Principum* was also translated into Italian by Deusdedit Florentino; this translation on parchment manuscript exists in the Magliabecchi library.[34] At the end of it we read: "Here ends the book of the government of kings "and princes, which friar Egidius of Rome, of the order of St. Aug-"ustine, composed This book has been translated, with the assistance of God, from the Latin into French by Messer Ari de Granci, "by the order of the noble King of France, and I have translated "it from the French into the Tuscan, neither adding nor suppressing "one word. Blessed be Jesus Christ. Done and completed this 16th "day of June in the year of our Lord MCCLXXXVIII." There is also another copy, but without the name of the translator in the Riccardi library.[35]

Cave has prepared a most exact catalogue of the works of Friar Egidius. The latter having studied closely the physics of Aristotle on which he has also commented, wrote a book entitled "*De forma-"tione corporis humani.*" Since the occasion is given us, we will remark here that Friar Egidius is also the author of another work mentioned in the learned preface to the life of Ambrose Traversari written by the Abbe Mehus.[36] It is a commentary on the verses of

[33] Monarchiae, Tom. II, page 107.   [34] Class XXX, cod. I in folio.
[35] N. IV, Num. XXII. See the life of Ambrose Traversari, Tom. I, page 159.   [36] Page 124.

Guido Cavalcante. What was the subject of this poem of Cavalcante? Philip Villani in his lives of the illustrious men of Florence, a precious manuscript in the Medici-laurenti library, discoursing on Guido Cavalcante, informs us that, Egidius Colonna, a Roman, an eminent philosopher, commented on his song. " This Guido," says he, "having written a very long and a most profound disserta-
"tion on the nature, the motions, the affections, and the passions of
"popular love, by which through natural instinct we are led to love
"the female sex, he composed an elegant and a delightful song in
"which he introduces like a philosopher the most ingenious and
"novel thoughts. Struck by the perfection of this treatise, by the
"the grace of its conception, Dino de Garbo, whom I mentioned be-
"fore, Egidius Colonna, a Roman, an eminent philosopher, and
"Hugh de Corno, inferior to none of them, deigned to comment on
"it."

DOCUMENT (2N).

LETTER TO THE CLERGY OF FRANCE, ANNEXED TO THE BULL "UNAM SANCTAM."

Verba delirantis filiae, quantumcumque desideriis maternis infesta, quantavis enormitate foedata, nequeunt puritatem inficere piae matris, et affectum in filiationis odium provocare maternum: cum in ipsa miseratione amor inveniatur maternalis, qui licet de miseratione doleat, naturae legibus compatiendo filiis, in ipsa miseria consolatur. Sane conturbata sunt universa ecclesiae pia praecordia in auditu verborum, quae sub fictae consolationis pallio, recitando quodammodo composita sunt, ut credimus, nomine praedilectae filiae ecclesiae Gallicanae in matris immaculatae opprobrium grande malum, quasi ab amico causam quaereret recedendi. Sed legitur quod frustra rete jacitur ante oculos pennatorum Ecce collectis ex parlamento, Parisiis convacto, mendicais suffragiis, ne ad vocationem sedis Apostolicae venirent, eorum verborum compositores necessario concludere voluerunt, damna rerum, et minas corporum praecipue praetendendo. Scimus equidem multorum relatione fidelium, nec latet Apostolicae sedis notitiam, quae et quanta fuerint in eadem concione narrata, et maxime, quae Belial Petrus Flôte semividens, et mente totaliter excaecatus, et quidam alii praedicaverint, sanguinem sitientes. Christiani, qui charissimum Philippum Francorum Regem illustrem trahere nituntur in devium, proh dolor! propinquum, cum tantae Christianitatis sublimitas erroneo ducatu submergitur, cui ducatus a coecis miserabiliter ad mentis interitum, nisi ex alto succurrat divina pietas, propinquatur, quod amare luget mater Ecclesia, circa salutem ejus quaerens remedium; et meditatione solicita contra tantae majestatis naufragium querit portum.

Verum vos, fratres et filii, si professionis vestrae debitum circumspectis considerationibus attendatis, cujus venenosae fictionis suggesto incontemptum tantae matris obedientiae filialis nervum videmini contundere, ac debitum pervertere statum ordinis clericalis: videmini siquidem secundum dicta eorum spem ponere in terrenis, si timore terrenorum contemnitis coelestia, vel seponitis propter timorem judicum, Christi jugum. Multa praeterea superba, iniqua, et schismatica in eadem fideli concione narrata fuerunt per oratores ejusmodi, per quae velle videbantur distrahere unitatem Ecclesiae, inconsutilem tunicam Domini nostri . . . In vestram verumtamen excusationem advertimus, qualiter detractatores praefati, ut coeptum venenum aspidum festinanter evomerent, in corde et corde loquentes aliqui vix inter se moras loquendi gerebant: verum praecipiti in momento temporis responderunt manna dulcedinis, et venenum aspidis infundentes in Ecclesiae matris opprobrium, et status proprii detrimentum: quia si verba eorum justo librentur examine, eos esse praelatos non indicant, sed indignos quibuslibet praelaturis; nec digni sunt regere, verum non immerito corrigendi. Restat ut colligamus ex verbis, quae gesta fuerunt absque nostra scientia machinationibus venenosis, ut et vos fictis coloribus ab unione universalis Ecclesiae abducerent nequiter, vosque contra nos, quos iniquitatis eorum volebant habere complices, provocarent. Sed in vanum laborant, et deficient iniquo scrutantes scrutinio sequaces tantae superbiae exequendo, disponentes ab Aquilone sedem erigere contra Vicarium Jesu Christi. Sed quoniam, ut primus Lucifer, cui non fuit huc usque secundus, cum sequacibus suis cecidit, corruet, quantacumque fulciatur potentia, et secundus. Nonne diu nituntur principia ponere, qui dicunt temporalia spiritualibus non subesse? Hic jam dictis finem imponimus, fraternitatem vestram in Domino exhortantes; utspretis temporalibus, et contemptis minis judicum, nobiscum ascendatis ad cor altum: et exaltabitur Deus, qui dissipat consilia principum, et reprobat cogitationes populorum; pro firmo scientes, quod obedientes gratiose videbimus, et contumaces pro qualitate criminis puniemus.

Ad perpetuam rei memoriam.

Unam sanctam Ecclesiam catholicam, et ipsam apostolicam, urgente fide, credere cogimur et tenere, nosque hanc firmiter credimus, et simpliciter confitemur; extra quam nec salus est, nec remissio peccatorum, sponso in canticis proclamante: Una est columba mea, perfecta mea: una est matris suae electa genitricis suae; quae unum corpus mysticum repraesentat, cujus corporis caput Christus, Christi vero Deus: in qua unus dominus, una fides, unum baptisma. Una nempe fuit diluvii tempore arca Noe, unam Ecclesiam praefigurans, quae in uno cubito consummata, unum Noe videlicet gubernatorem habuit, et rectorem, extra quam omnia subsistentia super terram legimus fuisse deleta. Hanc autem veneramur, et unicam, dicente Domino in propheta: Erue a framea Deus animam meam, et de manu canis unicam meam. Pro anima enim, id est pro seipso capite simul oravit et corpore: quod corpus, unicam scilicet Ecclesiam nominavit propter sponsi fidei sacramentorum, et charitatis Ecclesiae unitatem. Haec est tunica illa Domini inconsutilis, quae scissa non fuit; sed forte provenit. Igitur Ecclesiae, unius, et unicae unum corpus, unum caput, non duo capita quasi monstrum, Christus scilicet et Christi vicarius Petrus, Petrique successor, dicente Domino ipsi Petro; Pasce oves meas. Meas, inquit, generaliter non singulariter has vel illas, per quod commisisse sibi intelligitur nuiversas. Sive igitur Graeci, sive alii se dicant Petro ejusque successoribus non esse commissos, fateantur necesse est, se de ovibus Christi non esse, dicente Domino in Joanne, unum ovile, unum et unicum esse Pastorem.

In hac ejusque potestate duos esse gladios, spiritualem videlicet et temporalem evangelicis dictis instruimur. Nam dicentibus Apostolis: Ecce gladii duo hic; in Ecclesia scilicet, cum Apostoli loquerentur, non respondit Dominus nimis esse, sed satis. Certe in potestate Petri temporalem gladium esse negat, male verbum attendit Domini proferentis: Converte gladium tuum in vaginam Uterque ergo in potestate Ecclesiae, spiritualis scilicet gladius, et materialis: sed is quidem pro Ecclesia, ille vero ab Ecclesia, exercendus: ille Sacerdotis, is manu Regum et militum; sed ad nutum et patientiam Sacerdotis. Oportet autem gladium esse sub gladio, et temporalem auctoritatem spirituali subjici potestati: nam cum dicat Apostolus: Non est potestas nisi a Deo quae autem a Deo sunt, ordinata sunt; non ordinata essent, nisi gladius esset sub gladio, et tamquam inferior reduceretur per alium in suprema: nam secundum beatum Dionysium lex divitatis est infima per media in suprema reduci. Non ergo secundum ordinem universi omnia aeque ac immediate, sed infima per media, inferiora per superiora ad ordinem reducuntur; spiritualem autem et dignitate et nobilitate terrenam quamlibet praecellere potestatem, opportet, tanto clarius nos fateri, quanto spiritualia temporalia antecellunt: quod etiam ex decimarum datione, et benedictione, et sanctificatione, ex ipsius potestatis acceptione, ex ipsarum rerum gubernatione claris oculis intuemur; nam veritate testante, spiritualis potestas terrenem potestatem instituere habet et judicare, si bona non fuerit: sic de Ecclesia et ecclesiastica potestate verificatur vaticinium Jeremiae: Ecce constitui te hodie super gentes, et regna, etc. quae sequuntur.

Ergo si deviat terrena potestas, judicabitur a potestate spirituali: sed si deviat spiritualis minor a suo superiori: si vero suprema a solo Deo, non ab homine poterit judicari, testante Apostolo: "Spiritualis "homo judicat omnia; ipse autem a nemine judicatur." Est autem haec auctoritas, etsi data sit homini, et exerceatur per hominem, non humana, sed potius divina potestas, ore divino Peato data, sibique suisque successoribus in ipso Christo, quem confessus fuit, petra firmata; dicente Domino ipsi Petro: "Quodcumque ligaveris, etc." Quicumque igitur huic potestati a Deo sic ordinatae resistit, Dei ordinationi resistit, nisi duo, sicut Manichaeus, fingat esse principia, quod falsum et haereticum esse judicamus: quia testante Moyse, non in principiis, sed in principio coelum Deus creavit et terram. Porro subesse Romano Pontifici omni humanae creaturae declaramus, dicimus, et diffinimus omnino esse de necessitate salutis. Dat. Laterani XIV. Kal. decembris anno VIII.

DOCUMENT (20).

AN OBSERVATION ON THE CONSTITUTION "UNAM SANCTAM," AND ON THE BOOK OF DANTE, DE MONARCHIA.

We venture an observation on the famous constitution Unam Sanctam. It seems that this Bull had for its opponents only the jurists, and the Gallican defenders of the Regalia, such as John of Paris in the time of Philip the Fair, a Natalis Alexander and a Bossuet nearer our time. Still if our conjectures have any foundation, a poet, a very great poet, Dante Alighieri, was also among this number. We will touch but lightly on the question, leaving to others, if agreeable, the labor of examining it deeply.

It is certain that hardly had this constitution been published, than it created a great stir; and for this reason there was not one who did not know it. In this constitution Boniface, adhering to the ancient doctrines of the universal Church, defines that this Church is one, that its head is one and is endowed with a double power, symbolized by the two swords of St. Peter, which aroused so much fear in Philip the Fair. We have already spoken of this temporal power indirectly exercised by the Pope over kings by reason of sin. The principle of the Guelph party is entirely centered in this doctrine. Dante, an exile and transformed into a Ghibelline, took his exile much to heart; and as he placed all his hope of return to Florence in the Emperor Henry of Luxemburg, no one desired more than he the reestablishment of the Empire in Italy. He was a Ghibelline, because he was an exile; and so the love for his far away country, the hatred for those who governed it, and closed its gates against him, nourished in him the desire of seeing Henry of Luxemburg become *the new hope of a better period for* Italy.[37] His letter to the Emperor clearly proves that Dante, formerly a Guelph, became a Ghibelline, not heartily and by conviction, but because he was an exile, and was such on account of Boniface. The spirit of Dante, proud and opposed to slavery, even in the hospitable court of the Scaligers who sheltered him, was not so weak *as to kiss the ground before the feet of Luxemburg,* nor to call the German the successor of Caesar and Augustus. The love of country and the hatred for his enemies, enslaved the imagination of the Italian Homer in his *Divine Comedy,* and his reason in his book on the Monarchy.

Having returned from Paris into Italy, enticed by the hopes with which Henry of Luxemburg inspired him he wrote three books "*De Monarchia.*" We shall not speak either of the possibility or the jus-

---

[37] Letter of Dante to Emperor Henry of Luxemburg. To the most glorious and happy victor, and illustrious Lord, Messer Henry, by divine providence king of the Romans, and ever prosperous, his very devoted, Dante Alighieri, a Florentine, unjustly banished, and in general all the Tuscans who want peace, kiss the earth before your feet.

tice of the project of an universal monarchy conceived by Dante; we will content ourselves by calling the attention of the reader to the third book of this treatise. Dante tries to show that the temporal power, centered by him entirely in the Empire and in that of Henry of Luxemburg, depends immediately on God, and not mediately on any other divine power on earth. If one will take the pains to peruse this book, of a rough and almost barbarously scholastic nature, and contrast it with the constitution *Unam Sanctam,* he can without doubt easily and reasonably surmise that Dante had really this Bull in view when he wrote his three books of the Monarchy. In the beginning of the third book he alludes to the Pope in the following: "Cujus quidem veritas, quia sine rubore aliquorum emergere nequit, "forsitan alicujus indignationis causa in me erit." Afterwards he enumerates the different classes of those who do not agree with him in his opinion of the nature of the Monarchy: "Officium Monarchae "sive imperii dependet a Deo immediate." He arraigns Boniface, not expressly but in a transparent manner: "Sunt et tertii quos Decretalistas vocant, Theologiae et Philosophae cujuslibet inscii et "expertes, suis Decretalibus (quas profecte venerandas existimo) "tota intentione innixi, de illarum praevalentia credo sperantes, im-"perio derogant." His intention is more clearly revealed in the refutation he makes of the application of the text: "*Ecce duo gladii hic,* to the double power of the Pope. The defenders of the Regalia have found that all the venom of the theories of Boniface regarding his Papal power over kings, was hidden in the figurative sense attributed by this Pontiff to the two famous swords of St Peter. It is curious to read how Dante interprets the passage: "*Ecc duo gladii* "*hic,*" and the other: "*Quodcumque ligaveris;*" to see how that lofty soul had been depressed by exile, and was unfortunate in its efforts to recover the power of its reason: .... "Under the shadow of the "holy wings."

NOTE (2P).

A LETTER TO ALBERT, KING OF THE ROMANS.

Alberto Regi Romanorum illustri ad perpetuam rei memoriam.

Patris aeterni Filius Dominus Jesus Christus, cujus licet immeriti vices in terris gerimus, misericordiae benignitatem exercens, ut in ejus beneplacita feramus jugum apostolicae servitutis, viam nos humilitatis edocuit, nosque suorum doctrinis mandatorum instruxit, ut ipsius vestigia, qui patiens et humilis est acque misericors, quantum patitur humana fragilitas imitemur. Nos itaque ipsius exemplo dirigi cupientes, quos ad nos fiducia devota reducit, libenter brachiis paternae benignitatis amplectimur, illisque sinum mansuetudinis et misericordiae non negamus, dum eis, praesertim devotionis et humilitatis instantia suffragatur ....

Ad gloriam igitur omnipotentis Dei Patris, et Filii, et Spiritus

sancti, et beatae ac gloriosae semperque virginis Mariae, beatorum quoque apostolorum Petri, et Pauli; et ad honorem et exaltationem sanctae, Romanae ecclesiae ac Imperii praedictorum, et prsperum statum mundi; de fratrum nostrorum consilio, praesente quoque praelatorum et aliorum copiosa multitudine curialium, auctoritate apostolica, et de apostolicae plenitudine potestatis, te in specialem filium nostrum recipimus et ecclesiae memorate, ac in Regem Romanorum assuminus, in Imperatorem, auctore Domino, promovendum; volentes et statuentes, ut de caetero talis filius Rexque Romanorum existas, in Imperatorem, ut praemittitur, promovendus; et quod pro tali ab aliis habearis, tibique sicut Romanorum Regi electo legitime, et Aquisgrani coronato obedire debere ab omnibus, et singulis sacro Romano subjectis Imperio, sicut pareri solet et debet praedecessoribus tuis Romanorum Regibus, legitime intrantibus, et a praefata sede hactenus approbatis: supplentes omnem defectum, si quis aut ratione formae, aut ratione tuae vel tuorum electorum personarum, seu ex quavis alia ratione vel causa, sive quocumque modo in hujusmodi tua electione, coronatione, ac administratione fuisse noscatur. Omnia insuper et singula, per te vel alios de mandato tuo facta et habita in administratione praedicta, quae alias justa et licita extitissent, ita valere decernimus et tenere, sicut si administratio ipsa tibi competisse legitime nosceretur...
....

DOCUMENT (2Q).

CONSTITUTION OF BONIFACE REGARDING HIS CONFLICT WITH PHILIP THE FAIR.

Ad perpetuam rei memoriam. Rem non novam aggredimur, neque viam insolitam ambulamus, sed anterioris juris calcatam vestigiis praesentis constitutionis indubitato roboramus suffragio, et inconcusso munimine stabilimus. . . .

Praemissis igitur in debitam considerationem deductis. . . . declaramus de fratrum nostrorum consilio, et nihilominus hoc edicto perpetuo valituro firmamus et statuimus, ut citationes auctoritate. apostolica de quibuscumque personis, undecunque et ubicumque sint, cujuscumque status, dignitatis, vel praeeminentiae, ecclesiasticae vel mundanae, etiam si imperiali aut regali fulgeant dignitate; praesertim si impediant, vel faciant per se vel alies quoquomodo ne citationes ipsae ad eos perveniant, ex quacumque causa faciendo ut citandorum, domicilia sive loca tute vel libere adiri non possint; cum, prout scriptum est, existimare debeamus an eo ire liceat ubi est citatio facienda; provide ad instar edictorum praefatorum propositorum in albo praetoris etiam extra solemnes dies, in quibus Romani Pontifices suos facere consueverunt generales processus publice id nobis specialiter et ex certa scientia jubentibus, factae in audientia literarum nostrarum, aut in aula nostri palatii postmodum affigendae januis majoris ecclesiae loci, in quo Romana communis omnium Christiani populi nationum residebit curia, ut cunctis possint patere, et ita deferri citatis sic valeant, ac arctent citatos post terminum lapsum, quem considerata locorum distantia volumus citationibus ipsis compentem apponi, sicut si ipsos personaliter apprehendissent; non obstantibus aliquibus privilegis, indulgentiis, et literis apostolicis, generalibus aut speciliabus quibuscumque personis pontificali, imperali, regali, vel alia ecclesiastica seu mundana dignitate praeditis, aliisque inferioribus, seu ecclesiis, monasteriis, locis, collegiis et universitatibus in quacumque verborum forma concesssi, per quae talium citationum effectus possit quomodolibet impediri, etiam si de ipsis et eorum totis tenoribus de verbo ad verbum aut de propriis nominibus personarum, et infra, oporteat in nostris literis fieri mentionem. Nulli ergo, etc. Dat. Anagniae XVIII. Kal. septembris anno IX.

NOTE (2R).

THE PIETY OF BONIFACE.

God alone can judge interior piety, because he alone can search the hearts and reins. In judging, men have no other criterion but that of works, which though fallible always suffices on earth to distinguish good men from bad. We have said that it is fallible because hypocrisy hides itself cleverly and so carefully that it is often impossible (not always, however), to discover its shameful nakedness. We have found a proof of the piety of Pope Boniface, in a manuscript in the library of the Dukes of Urbino, numbered 1675, entitled: "*Life, "habits, manners of Pope Boniface VIII., events of his Pontificate,*" and which we have mentioned elsewhere. In this work, after a great amount of abuse against this Pope, we read these words: . . . . "And "nevertheless, all these iniquities had not increased, because showing "much devotion and humility in the churches, and devotion to the "Holy Virgin, he never failed to repair to the church of the Lateran, "and the church named after the Crucifix, where he remained to pray "two full hours daily." Two prayers composed by this Pontiff, the one in honor of Jesus crucified, and the other to the glory of our Lady of Sorrows, very short prayers, but full of tender and sincere piety, admirably confirm the words of this anonymous author. The former being known in Latin, we will produce it from the translation made in XIII. century, probably by Boniface himself. In perusing the manuscript 4839 in the vatican Library, which dates from the XIII. century, and which belonged to Viero dei Vieri, we found on page 94 the following words: "This prayer written here below was composed "by Pope Boniface VIII., and he who recites it each day for thirty "days, who fasts one day devoutly, who repents and confesses his "sins, will receive pardon from all his sins on the part of the said Pope."

"O Lord God, who for our Redemption, was pleased to be "reproved by the Jews, to be betrayed by the kiss of Judas, to be "bound with cords, to be led as to a sacrifice, innocent and faultless "conducted into the presence of Annas, Caipas, Pilate and Herod, "to be accused by false witnesses, to be pierced by sharp nails, to be "scourged, to be loaded with opprobrium, crowned with thorns, to "be struck with the hands, to be raised on the Cross between two "thieves, to be given gall and vinegar to drink, to be pierced by a "lance; O Lord God, by these most holy sufferings, to which I have "recourse, thy unworthy servant, and by the holy Cross, deliver me "from all danger, assist me in my necessities whilst I live in this "world; and at my death deliver me from the pains of hell, and "deign to lead me a poor sinner to that place where thou didst lead "the crucified thief, and where thou livest and reignest with the "Father and the Holy Ghost, true God forever and ever. Amen"

The other prayer to the Blessed Virgin is in verse. It was found by Jerome Amati in an old codex in the Vatican library, and published by Perticari in his treatise on *The defence of Dante*, in chapter XXVI. In this codex it is stated that these verses, which we here produce, were recited, in the XVth century, in the Basilica of St. Paul outside the walls; whereby Perticari proves that the Pope favored the development of our infant language by consecrating it to the service of the Church. In this manuscript we read: "Holy Pope Boniface "VIII. composed the following prayer, and granted to those who will recite it, deliverance from a sudden death." "The Virgin stood "beneath the Cross, she beheld Jesus, the true light, suffer; mother of "the King of the whole universe, she beheld His head which was "bowed, and all his body which was tortured for the redemption "of this wicked world. She beheld her Son who looked upon her and "said: O afflicted woman, full of bitterness and unhappiness, behold "thy son, and He pointed out John to her. She beheld vinegar mixed "with gall given to the sweet Jesus Christ to drink, and a big lance "pierce His heart. She beheld her Son having suffered everything "say with the scriptures: It is consummated. A flood of tears suf- "fused her eyes. The Virgin Mother weeps for the Redeemer of "Heaven and earth. The grief of thy heart was intense, Virgin "Mother, beholding thy dear Son expire. This suffering was so ex- "treme that it surpassed a thousand times the suffering of all the "martyrs, martyred for thee. Mother of Mercy, humble and com- "passionate, the only hope of my soul, grant me victory over the "enemy." These verses which Perticari calls poor verses, and which we find were not so paltry, are an abridgment of that most tender elegy, the *Stabat Mater*. The reader can judge humanly speaking, from these two prayers, whether the heart of Boniface was, as it was accused, a filthy pool, or whether, on the contrary, it was tempered by sweet and holy affections, which revealed a man nourished by the things of God.

DOCUMENT (2S).

BULL OF BENEDICT XI AGAINST THE PERSECUTORS OF BONIFACE.

Benedictus, etc. ad perpetuam rei memoriam.

Flagitiosum scelus, et scelestum flagitium, qud quidam sceratissimi viri, summum audentes nefas, in personam bonae memoriae Bonifacii Papae VIII. praedecessoris nostri, non sine gravi perfidia commiserunt, puniendum prosequi ex justis causis hucusque distulimus: sed ulterius sustinere non possumus, quin exurgamus, immo Deus in nobis exurgat, ut dissipentur inimici ejus, et ab ipsius facie fugiant, qui oderunt eum: dissipentur dicimus, si vere poenitent, sicut ad praedicationem Jonae, Ninive conversa est: alias ut Jerico subvertantur Olim siquidem, dum idem Bonifacius Anagniae propriae originis loco cum sua curia resideret, ipsum nonnulli perditionis filii, primogeniti sathanae, et iniquitatis alumni, omni pudore postposito, et reverentia retrojecta, praelatum subditi, parentem liberi, et vassalli dominum Guillelmus scilicet de Nogareto, Renaldus de Supino, etc. et alii factionis ministri armati hostiliter et injuriose coeperunt, manus in eum injecerunt impias, protervas erexerunt cervices, ac blasphemiarum voces funestas ignominiose jactarunt. Eodem etiam facto et opera per ejusdem factionis complices et alios thesaurus Romanae ecclesiae ablatus violenter extitit, et nequiter asportatus.

Haec palam, haec publice, haec notorie, et in nostris etiam oculis patrata fuerunt In his laesae majestatis, perduellionis, sacrilegii, legis Juliae de vi publica, Corneliae de sicariis, privati carceris, et rapinae, furti, et tot alia, quot ex hujusmodi facto facinora secuta sunt, crimina, et felloniae etiam delictum commissa notamus: in iis stupidi facti sumus. Quis crudelis hic a lacrymis temperet? Quis odiosus compassionem non habeat? Quis deses, aut remissus judex ad procedendum non surgat? Quis pius sive misericors non efficiatur severus? Hic violata securitas, hic immunitas temerata. Propria patria tutela non fuit, nec domus refugium: summum Pontificium dehonestatum est; et, suo capto sponso, Ecclesia quodammodo captivitata. Quis locus reperietur amodo tutus? Quae sancta, Romano violato Pontifice, poterunt invenire? O piaculare flagitium, o inauditum facinus, O Anagnia misera, quae talia in te fieri passa es! Ros et pluvia super te non cadant, in alios descendant montes, te autem transeant, quia te vidente, et prohibere valente, fortis cecidit, et accinctus robore superatus est. O infelicissimi patratores, non imitati quem nos imitari volumus David sanctum, qui in Christum Domini, etiam inimicum, persecutorem et aemulum suum, quia dictum erat: Noli tangere christos meos; manum extendere nouit, et in extendentem irrui gladio juste fecit. Infandus dolor, lamentabile factum, perniciosum exemplum, inexpiabile malum, et confusio manifesta! Sume lamentum Ecclesia, ora tua fletibus rigent, et in adjutorium debitae ultionis filii tui de longe veniant, et filiae de latere surgant.

Verum quia scriptum est: Feci judicium et justitiam; et Honor Regis judicium diligit; nos in praedictis sic judicium, quod ad honorem nostrum pertinet, facere cupimus, quod a justitia minime divertamus Actum Perusivii. id. junii pontificatus nostri anno 1.

NOTE (2T).

THE INFAMOUS ERASURES MADE IN THE REGISTER OF THE LETTERS OF BONIFACE.

Thanks to the obliging kindness of the illustrious prefect of the secret archives of the Vatican, Monsignor Morini, to whom we shall be ever grateful, we had every facility to consult the magnificent register manuscript containing the letters of Boniface VIII. It was with no little anxiety of mind that we read, in the second register, for the seventh year of the Pontificate, on page 140, the protest of the Notary Apostolic, against the erasure of all the writings of this Pontiff which offended Philip, and which this prince had tyrannically demanded. These are the words: " Ego Oddo de sermineto, Pub.
" Apostolica auctoritate notarius ac litterarum apostolicarum re-
" gistrator de expresso mandato reverendissimorum Patrum D.
" Berengarii Episcopi Tusculani, ac D. Arnaldi, tituli S. Priscae,
" Presb. Cardinalis S. R. E. Vice-Cancellarii facto mihi per eos ex
" parte SS. Patris Domini nostri D. Clementis Divina providentia
" PP. V. qui hoc eis pluries mandaverat, ut dicebant, feci, seu in
" praesentia mea et magistrorum Andreae de Setia et Emmanuelis
" de Parma fieri feci rasuras vacuas quae sunt in quarto, quinto et
" sexto foliis proxime praecedentibus, quarum primum immediate
" praecedit quaedam littera, quae incipit; *De statu terrarum,* et se-
" quitur alia quae incipit: *Nuper ex rationalibus.* Secunda vero
" rasura facta in litera, quae incipit *Ausculta*: incipit immediate
" post verba *efficaciter adimplere* et infra: et finit ante verba illa *Ad*
" *te igitur.* Tertia autem rasura in eadem litera facta, incipit im-
" mediate post verba *nec habens aliquod inhonestum* et infra. Et
" finit ante verba illa *Ad haec ne Terrae sanctae negotium.* Ibidem
" in quarta linea subsequenti facta una alia rasura unius tantummodo
" dictionis. Ultima quoque rasura incipit proxime post illa *ut in*
" *praesenti divinam gratiam.* Ideoque praedicta de eodem mandato
" in rei gestae testomonium scripsi sub solito signo meo. Viennae in
" hospitio Domini Cardinalis Vice-Cancellarii supradict, vivae vocis
" oraculo."

Et ego Andreas Taccanius de Setia, public. imperiali auctoritate notarius ae Literarum Apostol. Regestrator, praedicta omnia per eundem modum ut praedictus Magister Oddo de eodem mandato feci, seu fieri feci. Ideoque de mandato praedicto hic in rei gestae testimonium in domo praedicti D. Vice-Cancellarii me subscripsi sub solito signo meo.

These pages erased by the violent order of Philip the Fair were sad to behold We gazed on them for a long time and thinking of these words: "Ex parte Domini nostri D Clementis PP. V.," we deplored more the weakness of this Pontiff than the wickedness of the King.

UCSB LIBRARY
X-79394

CPSIA information can be obtained
at www.ICGtesting.com
Printed in the USA
LVHW081746030622
720460LV00010B/638